CW01053381

AN INTRODUCTIC

TO THE

LAW OF RESTITUTION

AN INTRODUCTION
TO THE
LAW OF RESTITUTION

PETER BIRKS

CLARENDON PRESS · OXFORD

Oxford University Press, Walton Street, Oxford OX2 6DP
Oxford New York Toronto
Delhi Bombay Calcutta Madras Karachi
Petaling Jaya Singapore Hong Kong Tokyo
Nairobi Dar es Salaam Cape Town
Melbourne Auckland
and associated companies in
Berlin Ibadan

Oxford is a trade mark of Oxford University Press

Published in the United States
by Oxford University Press, New York

British Library Cataloguing in Publication Data
Birks, Peter
An introduction to the law of restitution.
1. Restitution—Great Britain
I. Title
344.207'77   KD1605
ISBN 0-19-876074-4
ISBN 0-19-825645-0 (Pbk)

Library of Congress Cataloging in Publication Data
Birks, Peter.
An introduction to the law of restitution.
Includes index.
1. Restitution—Great Britain.
2. Unjust enrichment—Great Britain.   I. Title.
KD1924.B57   1985   346.41'029   84-20639   344.10629
ISBN 0-19-876074-4 (Oxford University Press)
ISBN 0-19-825645-0 (Pbk)

Printed in Great Britain by
Courier International Ltd,
Tiptree, Essex

For Jack
Deine Treu' erhielt mein Leben

PREFACE TO THE PAPERBACK EDITION

This is not a new edition, but I am grateful for the opportunity to include updating endnotes and to make some corrections. For the future, the aim is first to produce a larger and more fully documented textbook, after which this *Introduction* will perhaps be able to fall back in its second edition to a more introductory length and level.

The bibliography has been revised and updated. The most important of the new entries is without question the third edition of *Goff and Jones*, extraordinarily generous in its reception of this book. Also extremely useful for its firm judgment and clear exposition of a difficult subject is A. S. Burrows's excellent *Remedies for Torts and Breach of Contract*, especially chapter 6, 'Restitutionary Remedies'.

The endnotes, which are identified by asterisked markers in the text, do not pretend to call attention to every recent event in the law of restitution; their aim is to bring in new material which develops, or in some cases confounds, the book's structural themes. Some items deserve a mention in advance. It is, for instance, particularly fitting to the year which marks the tercentenary of the Glorious Revolution and the Bill of Rights that we should seem to be on the brink of a leading case on the question whether the subject has a right to restitution of money unlawfully demanded by public authorities (see Endnote 22). The question whether English law is well enough equipped to deal with profitable wrongdoing has been pushed into greater prominence by, *inter alia*, the *Spycatcher* affair (see Endnotes 23 and 25). And an important development in relation to those who receive misapplied trust funds has for the moment turned the law away from the direction pointed to in the text. It has been decided, though at the cost of un-noticed contradictions, that the personal liability of such recipients to make restitution in the first measure (value received) must depend on proof of a high degree of fault (see Endnote 32). Cutting across individual topics, another notable recent theme has been the contribution of the High Court of Australia to the case-law of this subject (see Endnotes 2, 6, 14, 25, 28).

I am grateful once again to Jack Beatson, Fellow of Merton College, and to Andrew Burrows, Fellow of Lady Margaret Hall, both of whom saved me from some errors of omission and commission. As the endnotes reveal, both disagree quite strongly with parts of what is said, especially about 'free acceptance'.

Southampton,
9 August, 1988
P.B.H.B.

CONTENTS

TABLE OF CASES

TABLE OF STATUTES

INTRODUCTION

1. THE UNCERTAIN ANATOMY OF RESTITUTION

IT ought to be possible to take any legal subject and to cut away its detail so as to reveal the skeleton of principle which holds it together. If there is a subject for which that task seems impossible, the probability is that it is so disorganised that it should properly be described as unintelligible. When the elementary structure of principle is once exposed, it ought to be kept under constant critical review. If it is not, its apparent intelligibility may be an illusion projected by some ancient error. In this essential work of critical simplification, not all subjects need the same balance between criticism and description. One may have a long-accepted outline and may need nothing so much as to have it challenged and brought into question. Another may lack any agreed framework and, standing in danger of being unintelligible, may chiefly need description rather than criticism.

Restitution is in the latter condition. The shape of its skeleton has not been established. Its desperate need is for a simple, even an over-simplified, account of how its pieces fit together. There will be time later for criticism and for the complex adjustments and refinements which are an inevitable feature of every mature legal subject. Can the simple account be given? There is a chicken-and-egg problem which makes it difficult. Someone might say that, since a 'skeleton of principle' is no more than a metaphor for the common sense behind a subject's technical detail, a concise account of it can always be given, whatever the state of the literature or the cases in the field. For, necessarily, the common sense comes first, before the professional elaboration even begins. There is a snag in that argument. Common sense can be arranged in different ways. A skeleton of principle is not just the common sense behind a legal topic but rather a particular organisation of its common sense, a version chosen from a number of possibilities. Where is that choice made? Not in the cases, certainly not only in the cases, despite the fact that English law prides itself on being judge-made. The pressures, and consequently the opportunism, of adversarial litigation are such that, left to itself, case-law grows without much regard for principle or for the coherence of one piece of law with another. The agency for describing and defending the anatomy of legal subjects has to be found outside the courts, away from the quarrels of litigants whose only interest is to win. In the law, this is the age of the textbook. Ever since the narrow discipline of the forms of action was given up in the nineteenth century, textbooks have borne the responsibility for restraining the centrifugal tendencies of case-law. If subjects such as contract and tort now seem to have a more or less agreed structure, it is not because settled common sense is by nature anterior to authority, so that all that the cases have to do is to elaborate a Platonic outline. On the contrary, it is because generations of textbooks, from different hands and going through successive editions, have selected and evolved a structure which for the moment seems best fitted to the matter. In the process they have weeded out less well-adapted schemes. This evolutionary process continues. As the books evolve their consensus, so the cases themselves confirm and reflect back the framework selected as best-fitted to the subject. But criticism can still revive the rejected material of earlier schemes. Equitable estoppel mutates the doctrine of consideration. Absolute freedom of contract is modified by the almost forgotten notion that some bargains are unconscionable. In the cases, the potential for change is infinite. Textbooks keep lawyers' minds in shape. Restitution's special problem is that it has a large and long-standing stock of cases but almost no textbooks.

A subject whose case-law has somehow escaped the attention of textbook writers cannot really be said to have any known anatomy. The process of selecting some version of its common sense has not begun. The irony is that, in such a situation, a detailed account of the subject can be given (for the mass of cases can be patiently documented one by one) but a simple one cannot. Of the various ways in which the cases might be related to an intelligible outline of common sense, none has been rejected and none is, therefore, reflected back to the textbook writer from the cases. When it comes to simplifying such a subject, nothing is true. But a mass of cases makes for unintelligible law. Hence, where there are no textbooks, the need for a settled, well-described anatomy is greatest. Yet in the law anatomy is only settled by there being textbooks. And not just one, but generations.

This circle has to be broken. There is to some extent a parallel, and a reason for optimism, the the case of administrative law. Everyone knows that that subject has been transformed in the last twenty-five years. When the first edition of Professor Wade's book was published in 1961 the subject could barely be said to exist, except as a raw mass of cases. He himself decribed it as 'a backward child in the legal family'.[1] Now, when the same book is in its sixth

---

[1] H.W.R. Wade, *Administrative Law*, 1st ed., Oxford, 1961, preface.

edition, few lawyers whould deny that administrative law has a unity and an internal anatomy of its own, made explicit now by many textbooks. In time this change will happen to the Law of Restitution too. Outside these two subjects, it is difficult to think of any other bodies of case-law so long left behind by the avalanche of textbooks which began about the time of the *Judicature Acts, 1873—75*. And restitution is the more remarkable of the backward pair, not only because it now lags further behind but because, while the case-law of administrative law might be said to have been called into existence only by the increasingly assertive role of the modern state, restitution is a central concern of ordinary private law and has been the subject of litigation for as long as the common law has been developing.

2. GOFF AND JONES, DISPERSAL AND RE-UNIFICATION

It is of course not quite true that there is no commentary on this subject. In England there is one great textbook.[2] The first edition of *Goff and Jones* was published in 1966, the second in 1978. The more one uses that book the more one is forced to admire the magnitude of its achievement. In America, where lawyers have undoubtedly been more alive to the subject, textbooks have nevertheless not been written, but there is now an encyclopaedic work in four volumes by Professor Palmer.[3] As the bibliography at the end of this book shows there have also been two recent Canadian additions to the small list of textbooks on the subject. There have been important books on subjects which form part of or intersect with Restitution, notably on the law of quasi-contract, constructive trusts and fiduciary obligations,[4] but it remains a fact that, for the English law of restitution as a whole, *Goff and Jones* has an absolute monopoly. There is, at a time when such books have proliferated, no English collection of cases and materials relevant to restitution. The contrast with the state of affairs in tort and contract hardly needs to be further underlined.

The relationship between this present work and *Goff and Jones* can be shortly stated. The first and most obvious point is that without *Goff and Jones* this would never have been so much as attempted. But, secondly, this book is pre-occupied with the task of finding the simplest structure on which the material in *Goff and Jones* can hang.

---

[2] Sir Robert Goff and Gareth Jones, *The Law of Restitution*, 2nd ed., London, 1978. (This is cited hereafter as *Goff and Jones*.)

[3] George E. Palmer, *The Law of Restitution*, Boston and Toronto, 1978.

[4] See bibliography, below, p. 448: Finn, Keener, Oakley, Shepherd, Stoljar, Waters, Winfield, Woodward.

It is not just a matter of describing that work's chapter headings. The system here proposed is radically different from anything that can be read from its contents pages. If it seems over-simplified, that is all to the good, since the movement from simple to complex is more easily understood and controlled than are attempts to reason with materials and problems whose basic structures have never been exposed or even looked for.

In view of what has been said about the state of the subject's development, it has to be admitted at once that the battle towards simplification is not itself simple. Simplification involves understanding how the subject came to be in its present condition and, which is part of the same story, how difficult terms such as 'quasi-contract' and 'constructive trust' are used and abused. It also involves getting on terms with language and habits of thought derived from the forms of action. Furthermore the search for an analytical scheme for solving restitutionary problems involves a species of argument and presentation which can be painful to lawyers who believe in, and attach importance to, the impersonal rationality of the law. Such people, rightly, prefer to put aside their own opinions as worth nothing, and expect to find the law's own chosen pattern of good sense already in the cases. Here, however, the scheme has sometimes to be forced on to cases which themselves perceived it, if at all, intuitively. According to the thesis of this introduction, the successful evolution of an ultimately acceptable framework cannot begin, and certainly cannot be found in the cases, until versions which may be fragile and idiosyncratic have been thrown into the ring. Until textbooks have taken a grip of the material it is actually anti-rational to be too fastidious.

The first edition of *Chitty on Contracts* appeared in 1826. *Pollock on Contracts* first came out in 1876. Why did Restitution have to wait for *Goff and Jones* in 1966? This question occupies some of the earlier part of this book. The shortest possible answer is that from the end of the eighteenth century Blackstone's enormously influential *Commentaries on the Laws of England*[5] taught everyone that restitutionary obligations in the common law depended on 'implied contract'. This was encouraged by the unintended overtones of the Roman phrase '*quasi ex contractu*'. The effect was to drive these non-contractual obligations into the category of contract. The writers of books on contract then gave this alien matter a short treatment in a final chapter. This does not explain why equitable restitution was also submerged. The short answer to that is that, since equity was conceived to be a series of appendices or glosses

[5] First ed., 1765.
[6] F.W. Maitland, *Equity* (revised by J. Brunyate), Cambridge, 1947, 19 f.

on different parts of the common law,[6] it would have been necessary for the common law of restitution to be openly and independently recognised if it was to attract its equitable supplement. As it was, equitable restitution gravitated elsewhere. Rescission attached to treatments of contract. Many restitutionary obligations were covertly recognised by treating people as trustees who were not trustees, in short by calling them constructive trustees. As a result that part of the law of restitution was expounded in the books on trusts. Other restitutionary matter was dispersed under other heads.

Goff and Jones marked the end of this diaspora. The book's unifying achievement can be seen as the most important English event in a wider movement by which Anglo-American common law has set about rectifying the error of having overlooked the subject for most of the century in which textbooks have re-shaped the law. In America the crucial step was the publication in 1937 of the *Restatement of Restitution*, sub-titled 'Quasi-Contracts and Constructive Trusts'.[7] At the same period, on this side of the Atlantic, Lord Wright did much, both on and off the bench, to show what had gone wrong and what needed to be done;[8] so too Lord Denning.[9] More recently other changes show that this movement has not lost its impetus. The fourth edition of Halsbury has given up the term 'constructive contracts' and has adopted instead, albeit still in the volume on contract, the composite phrase 'quasi-contract and restitution'.[10] The indexing system of the Law Reports has introduced 'restitution' as one of its headings. In the twenty-fifth edition of *Chitty on Contracts* the subject is given a new emphasis and independence.[11] In Canada one new textbook has followed almost on the heels of another.[12] Furthermore, the outlook of the next generation of lawyers and judges is likely to be much affected by the appearance of Restitution in university curricula. Law is now a graduate profession. In this last decade many courses in Restitution have been established in the universities of the common law world, mostly at postgraduate level. Today's postgraduates being tomorrow's teachers and practitioners, it is unlikely that Restitution will ever again be split up and hidden under the fringes of other better-known subjects.

---

[7] American Law Institute, *Restatement of the Law of Restitution*, St. Paul, 1937.

[8] Cf. *Brook's Wharf and Bull Wharf Ltd.* v. *Goodman Bros.* [1937] 1 K.B. 534; *Fibrosa Spolka Akcyjna* v. *Fairbairn Lawson Combe Barbour* [1943] A.C. 32; *Legal Essays and Addresses*, Cambridge, 1939, 1–65.

[9] *Nelson* v. *Larholt* [1948] 1 K.B. 339; 'The Recovery of Money' (1949) 65, L.Q.R., 37.

[10] *Halsbury's Laws of England*, 4th ed., vol. 9, London, 1974, paras. 630–750.

[11] *Chitty on Contracts*, London, 1983, vol. 1, 1063 (J. Beatson)

[12] See bibliography, below, p. 448, Klippert, Fridman and McLeod.

If one is once convinced that the dispersal of Restitution was no more than an intellectual error, a mistake whose causes and effects can be objectively documented, one must equally believe that this movement to repair the damage can only gain momentum. It is right to say that one very influential voice dissents. Professor Atiyah takes the view that energy spent on Restitution would be better employed on more radical re-grouping of the bases of civil liability. According to the plan which he favours the law of restitution would be only one part of a larger field, which he refers to as 'benefit-based liability'.[13]

3. FIVE STRATEGIC POINTS

It is always difficult to say what are the few most important points in any study, since others always press on those which are selected. Nevertheless it is useful to attempt the exercise. Thus, the approach used in this book is based on the following five propositions. The first two relate to the organization of the subject-matter. The next three, though they also bear on the issue of organisation, are more immediately concerned with the method of analysing any given restitutionary problem.

1. The most important division in the subject called 'restitution' is between two different measures in which the plaintiff may recover. The first or normal measure is 'value received'. What the defendant received can be and is determined without reference to whether he still retains it or anything representing it. The second or exceptional measure is 'value surviving'. What the defendant still has left is determined by, often very artificial, rules which go by the name of 'tracing'. The division between these two measures is of much greater importance than the division between personal and proprietary restitutionary rights.

2. The second principal division of the subject distinguishes between the events which give rise to restitution in the two measures. Here the main contrast is between events which do and events which do not amount to wrongs. Within those which do not amount to wrongs, there are some where the reason for restitution is found on the plaintiff's side, some where it is found on the defendant's side and some where it is found on neither side. It is very important that nothing which is not an event (i.e. a set of facts triggering a legal

---

[13] P.S. Atiyah, *The Rise and Fall of Freedom of Contract*, Oxford, 1978, esp. 716 ff.

consequence) should work its way into this second level of classification.

3. No subject can ever be rationally organised or intelligibly applied so long as it is dominated by the language of fiction, of deeming, and of unexplained analogy. Hence terms such as 'quasi-contract' and 'constructive trust' must be rooted out, except to the extent, if any, that they can be shown to do work which is necessary and in which their fictions are openly recognisable and demonstrably harmless.

4. Just as in Contract all lawyers, however much they differ even on large issues, know and share the same pattern of analysis and can therefore run through phases of inquiry without having to explain what they are doing (formation, vitiating factors, breach, remedies) so also Restitution must acquire a stable set of large questions capable of breaking all problems down into instantly recognisable phases. The four questions proposed are these: Was the defendant enriched? if so, Was he enriched at the plaintiff's expense? if so, Was there any factor calling for restitution? if so, Was there any reason why restitution should none the less be withheld? After these four, a fifth question takes the inquiry back to the measures discussed under 1: What measure of restitution should the plaintiff have?

5. No question has been more neglected than the enrichment question in this series of inquiries. Nearly all the law of restitution seems to be about money. This gives the impression that many grounds for restitution (as, for example, total failure of consideration) are peculiar to money. However, there is in reality a perfect theoretical symmetry between claims in respect of money and claims in respect of other subject-matter. The grounds for restitution are the same, whatever the benefit received by the defendant. However, non-money plaintiffs win more rarely because, even when equipped with a good ground for restitution, they often cannot establish that the defendant was enriched as unequivocally as though he had received money.

We can now turn to the substance of the subject. The first business is to establish that we know what is meant by restitution and how exactly the area of law which is given that name relates to other legal categories. The first four chapters are directed to the question: What is restitution? They really form a single discussion, the parts of which are not easy to separate. The first simply defines, as though restitution were the single subject in an otherwise deserted legal universe. The second tries to relate that area to obligations and to property and, in particular, to the events which give rise to those abstract legal phenomena. The third seeks to thin out the language in which restitution is discussed and, in particular, to impose on that language the major division between measures which has been introduced in the first of the five propositions just mentioned. The fourth briefly describes the internal structure of the subject, the pattern on which the grounds for restitution are subsequently discussed.

I

DEFINITION

CHILDREN quickly learn that if they give their toys away they cannot expect to get them back. Anxious about spoiling, parents will not intervene unless there is more to it than a mere change of mind. Between adults the courts maintain the same simple rule. One who parts with value cannot just demand it back, not even if he received nothing in return.[1] The other has an interest in the security of his receipt. If he is to be disturbed there has to be a good reason, one strong enough to be compatible with respect for stability. Suppose that you have paid me £500 and now you want it back, not just because you have changed your mind but because the original payment was made by mistake. Here the impulse to relieve mistakes is something to weigh against the interest in security. In order to get the balance right questions have to be asked about the exact nature of your mistake, but if these are answered in your favour I shall have to repay. So, subject to safeguards, receipt of a mistaken payment is an example of an event which does give rise to restitution. A common case is where an insurance company wrongly believes that the event against which premiums have been paid has happened. Or that a policy which has lapsed had in fact been maintained. Where payment is made under such mistakes, restitution follows.[2] The principal business of any work on this subject is to organise and understand the whole class of events which give rise to that response.

1. REFINING THE WORD 'RESTITUTION'

The last sentence makes clear that the word 'restitution' does not itself denote an event. That is to say, it does not signify a fact or composite set of facts giving rise to legal consequences. In this it differs from 'contract' and from 'tort'. Also from 'trust' if that word is taken to denote the act of reposing trust rather than the relationship so created. 'Restitution' properly belongs in a series of words denoting responses rather then events. 'Compensation, punishment,

---

[1] Even at this point a *caveat* is necessary, for equity's presumptions of resulting trust might seem to contradict this simple starting point, shifting the onus to the recipient to show that the seeming gift was really so: see below, p. 60 f. and 156 f.

[2] *Kelly v. Solari* (1841) 9 M. & W. 54; *Norwich Union Fire Insurance Society v. Wm. H. Price Ltd.* [1934] A.C. 455.

restitution, others' is a properly aligned series. 'Contract, tort, restitution, others' is not. No trained lawyer would ever make an exclusive opposition between 'compensation' and 'tort'. As, for example: 'This action lies in compensation rather than in tort.' The logical nonsense is obvious. There is an imperfect opposition between compensation and tort, just as there is between carnivores and spilled blood. The same kind of danger exists if 'restitution' is substituted for 'compensation' in a similar sentence. 'This action lies in restitution rather than in tort' is a statement which supposes a clear contrast between a response and an event.[3] It could only make sense, and then only fortuitously, if it were true that the event 'tort' never gives rise to the response 'restitution'.[4]

Yet there is a certain temptation into this dangerous form of speech. The source of the trouble is that, like the central example of mistaken payment itself, most of the events which do give rise to restitution are not in fact either contracts or wrongs. So much is this the case that one major benefit of understanding the whole class of restitutionary events is that it provides a map of the relatively unknown land beyond the now familiar contract and tort. There is, therefore, at least some truth in the belief that one mission of the law of restitution is to add a category which does co-ordinate and contrast with contract and tort. Nevertheless, even if there were in practice no intersection at all between restitution and those two heads, it would be foolish in pursuing this aim to risk confusion by mixing vocabulary from different series.

Outside the law 'restitution' is not a common word. Most people use 'restoration'. The meaning is much the same and the two words are often interchangeable. There can be restitution of a thing or person to an earlier condition and restitution of a thing to a person. These two usages shade into one another but it is important to be aware of the difference. Only the second is intended in this book. The existence of the other can lead to confusions. A planning authority might say: 'We think the first condition of our permission for the ground to be excavated should be subsequent restitution of the land to its present arable condition.' A government minister might announce: 'So far as money can do it, we will see that everyone injured in the disaster receives full restitution.' These examples show that when 'restitution' is used in this first sense there is no

---

[3] But see *Strand Electric and Engineering Co. v. Brisford Entertainments* [1952] 2 Q.B. 246, 254f: 'The claim for a hiring charge is therefore not based on the loss to the plaintiff, but on the fact that the defendant has used the goods for his own purposes. It is an action against him because he has had the benefit of the goods. It resembles an action for restitution rather than an action of tort', *per* Denning, L.J.

[4] Contrary to *United Australia Ltd* v. *Barclays Bank Ltd*. [1941] A.C. 1.

suggestion that the person who is to effect the restoration of the status quo has himself received anything which will now have to be given up. The thing or person to receive restitution has merely suffered a loss or damage requiring to be made good. This is the crucial contrast with the second sense. Where restitution is not of someone or something to a prior condition but is rather of something to someone, the implication always is that the person who is to make restitution has received the something. 'The housekeeper who had bullied the old man faced a claim for restitution brought by his personal representatives.' The sentence does not say so, but the inference is that the bullying extracted presents in appeasement. The same implication that a recipient must surrender something received is present even when the person to make restitution is not mentioned. 'Courts will order restitution of mistaken payments.' 'A change of mind is no ground for seeking restitution of a gift.'

The reason why it matters to be alert to and to lay aside the first usage is that 'restitution' in that sense is not distinct from 'compensation'. Suppose that by negligent management a trustee allows the trust property to lose value, exposing himself to an action by the beneficiary to have the loss made good. An equitable claim of that kind has recently been called 'an action for restitution'.[5] But it is not a claim within the scope of this book. If it were we would find it difficult to explain why, for example, the tort of negligence is excluded. The common law claim against a careless motorist also aims to restore the victim to his original position. In the sense which makes no distinction between making good a loss and restoring a gain, it too might be described as restitutionary. But this book is concerned only with the second sense of 'restitution'. That is, with gains to be given up, not with losses to be made good.

Confining our attention to the sense in which restitution is always of something to someone and, therefore, always supposes a previous receipt by the person who is to make the restitution, we can advance a very simple definition. *Restitution is the response which consists in causing one person to give back something to another.* This is based on the ordinary meaning of the word but after cutting away the other usage. This definition is too simple. Some adjustments have to be made. The reason is that the matter which the law of restitution seeks to organise developed long before anyone thought of calling it restitution. Without some refinements the chosen name fails to embrace the intended subject-matter.

There are five of these adjustments. Some are easy and straight-

---

[5] *Bartlett* v. *Barclays Bank Trust Co.* [1980] Ch. 515, 542–3. Cf. in contract, *Bacon* v. *Cooper Metals Ltd.* [1982] 1 All E.R. 397.

forward. Others are not. All are important but their importance may
remain obscure at least until the end of the first three introductory
chapters.

(i) *For 'give back' read 'give up'*   The simple definition speaks of
something to be given back, implying that the person to whom
restitution is to be made is to regain something which he previously
had and which passed from him to the other. That is indeed the
common case. You pay me by mistake, I have to give a like sum back
to you. However, there are many cases intended to fall within the
notion of restitution in which what the defendant has to give up to
the plaintiff has been received not from him but from a third party.
The obvious examples are cases of acquisitive wrongs. If I sell your
car you have a restitutionary claim against me for the price which
I actually receive from the purchaser.[6] If I am your trustee and I
take a bribe or secret commission for placing out trust business I
shall have to give up what I am given by the outsider.[7] There are
other cases which do not arise from any breach of duty. If a third
party gives me £100 to give to you, I come under an obligation
to pay it to you at least from the moment at which I tell you that I
am holding for you.[8]
   To insist on 'giving back' would be to exclude cases of this kind in
which the receipt is not from the plaintiff. 'Giving up' leaves them in.
We can affirm that restitution necessarily supposes a receipt by the
defendant, often but not always from the plaintiff.

(ii) *For 'give up something to another' read 'give up to another
something received at his expense'*   This adjustment is consequential
upon the other. The phrase 'give back something to another' tacitly
explains how the plaintiff gets into the story. He is the person who
has lost something. That is all in 'back'. He had it before and now
he is to have it again. The change from 'give back' to 'give up' leaves
the plaintiff high and dry. 'At his expense' takes over from 'back'.
It explains why the plaintiff makes his claim.[9]

(iii) *After 'give up to another something received at his expense' add
'or its value in money'*   The simple definition supposes specific
restitution of the something received. This rarely happens. Even
where the something is money it is not the very same notes or coins
which the defendant will yield up but others to the same value. Where

[6] *Chesworth* v. *Farrar* [1967] 1 Q.B. 407.
[7] *Williams* v. *Barton* [1927] 2 Ch. 9.
[8] *Shamia* v. *Joory* [1958] 1 Q.B. 448.
[9] For the importance of this phrase and its two meanings, see below, pp. 40 ff. and 22 f.

the receipt is of work, restitution in kind will be impossible. You cannot give back the repair of a car or the burning of rubbish but you can repay in money the value of such services. Goods can sometimes be given up, but again restitution can equally be effected in money.

(iv) *For 'something' read 'wealth' or 'an enrichment'* It is very difficult to say what things count as wealth and what things do not. The use of possessive adjectives is no guide. Your house and your car are items of wealth. Your wife and your children are not, though in some societies a different answer would have been given. Your reputation and your privacy are borderline cases. Some people, not many, make money by selling both. The law of restitution is not concerned with attributes and interests which are not wealth. For example, disputes between parents about the care of children do not belong in this area of the law, not even if the claim takes the form of one adult demanding that the other should give back a child taken from him. Similarly, the old action for restitution of conjugal rights would not have counted.[10]

The reason for this exclusion is to be found partly in the third adjustment, above, and partly in convenience. Restitution is usually effected in money. Claims which cannot be valued in money are necessarily outside the range of such pecuniary restitution. But that only puts them outside the commonest type of claim. Admittedly not much can be said for evicting them from the subject as a whole, except that the necessarily blurred restriction to wealth promotes homogeneity.

We started with this statement: *Restitution is the response which consists in causing one person to give back something to another.* After four adjustments that has become: *Restitution is the response which consists in causing one person to give up to another an enrichment received at his expense or its value in money.*

(v) The fifth refinement does not show in the wording and cannot be conveniently represented by introducing a new set of words. It is a matter of giving a restrictive and technical sense to the phrase 'causing one person to give up to another'. The restriction is best approached through an example. Suppose I lose my bicycle and you find it. Instead of loss and finding we could equally well suppose that I part with it through a transaction nullified by mistake, or that you steal it. On any of these facts the cycle passes physically into your hands but remains mine. Now add that either voluntarily or under

---

[10] Abolished by the *Matrimonial Proceedings and Property Act, 1970,* section 20.

an order of court you give the bicycle back to me. In this story there is no restitution, not at any rate within the intended sense of the title of this book.

Neither in the preservation of my ownership through the catastrophic interruption of possession, nor in the render to me of my own bicycle, does the phenomenon occur which modern lawyers have christened 'restitution'. If this seems surprising and artificial, it is because the choice of a name for this branch of the law has always proved difficult and the one on which we seem now to have settled is not perfectly appropriate. There is an additional danger of confusion too. When not speaking specifically of this branch of the law (now called the law of restitution) the law does acknowledge a looser usage, according to which the render to an owner of a thing which is his own is perfectly well capable of being called restitution.[11]

For the sake of clarity, in relation to this fifth refinement, we must turn from negative exclusions to positive inclusions. What does count as restitution once this difficult adjustment is made?

The crucial moment to look at is the defendant's receipt of the enriching benefit. If at that moment the law passively preserves pre-existing rights, there is no restitution. That is the case of the bicycle already mentioned. By contrast there is restitution if, at the moment of the receipt, the law actively creates new rights. Take the case of a mistaken payment. You pay me £10 by mistake. You put the note into my hand. If the mistake is sufficiently fundamental to prevent the passing of property, the note at that moment in my hand and as yet unmixed with others in my wallet remains yours, even according to the common law.[12] There is no restitution in that; it is just like the bicycle again. But at the same time the law actively, and concurrently, creates a new right in you. Irrespective of the fate of that particular £10 note, you now have a claim against me that I should pay you the sum of £10. That is a new right generated by the receipt in the given circumstances. With the effect of depriving me of value received at your expense. Restitution is that active or creative response at the moment of enrichment.

As we left it, the definition said that restitution happens where the law causes one person to give up to another an enrichment received

---

[11] Cf. the *Theft Act, 1968*, section 28 (Orders for restitution). Under s. 28 (1) (a) the court can order that the stolen goods be restored. This is not restitution in the technical sense. Under s. 28 (1) (b) and (c) the court can order the render of other goods representing the stolen goods or payment of the value of those goods so far as it can be met out of money taken from the accused on his apprehension. Paragraphs (b) and (c) will generally entail restitution in the technical sense since the law has to respond actively, creating new rights and not merely preserving old ones.

[12] *Taylor* v. *Plumer* (1815) 3 M. & S. 562.

at his expense or its value in money. This fifth refinement glosses the meaning of 'causes . . . to give up'. That phrase does not include preserving title or rendering to an owner that which is his own. It does include the creation of new rights at the moment of enrichment, to undo that enrichment.

What is the reason for this artificiality? It lies in the necessity for a line to be drawn between the law of restitution and the law of property. The exact nature of that difficult line and the relationship between the two branches of the law will be considered below.[13] At this point it is only necessary to affirm that there is both a conceptual and a practical necessity for not allowing the two subjects to merge into one. This is vividly demonstrable in the law of real property, originally so called because it formed the subject-matter of 'real' actions, actions in which you could recover the thing itself (the *res*) as opposed to a money judgement.[14] The owner of an estate in land could get back the land itself. That remains true today in the action to recover land, which is the modern successor of the old real actions. Suppose, therefore, that I am in possession of Blackacre in the belief that I hold the fee simple. But I am wrong; owing to some conveyancing disaster I have in fact no estate at all. The fee simple is vested in you. This is just like the case of the bicycle above. The law has preserved your title even though you are out of possession. Now you bring your action and you recover the land.

If we called that restitution what would happen? The whole law of real property would come into the law of restitution on the back of the action. For the action to recover land cannot be explained or understood without an account of the grounds for winning it; and that account would be nothing more nor less than a textbook on the doctrine of estates.

The practical need to stop this happening is, therefore, obvious enough. A subject compounded of property and restitution would be too big. It would have to be broken up in order to be mastered. One place at which it could break would be precisely along the conceptual line between preserving existing rights, so as to prevent enrichment, and creating new ones, so as to reverse it. The convenience of this break coincides with a much stronger conceptual necessity: most restitutionary rights are not property rights at all; they are personal rights (*in personam*), as opposed to proprietary rights (*in rem*). One of the many defects of the category of quasi-

[13] Below, p. 49 ff.

[14] Sir Frederick Pollock and F.W. Maitland, *The History of English Law*, 2nd ed. (repr.), ed. S.F.C. Milsom, Cambridge, 1968, vol. ii, 177 ff, 570 ff. The English use of 'real' in 'real action' or 'real property' is *not* to be identified with the analytical term '*in rem*', as to which see below, p. 28 and pp. 49–50.

contract, which is displaced and taken over by 'restitution', was that it isolated restitutionary rights *in personam* from restitutionary rights *in rem*. If restitutionary rights *in rem* could never be distinguished and separated from other proprietary rights, the only way to stop this isolation from happening again would be to deal with restitutionary rights *in personam* within the indivisible law of property. That conceptual contradiction should be avoided if possible. These matters will be looked at again in the next chapter.

So in the end the reason for this difficult fifth refinement is that without it the law of property and the law of restitution merge into one lump, too large to handle and, worse, analytically impure by reason of drawing into the mass of rights *in rem* those restitutionary rights which, being personal, belong not in the law of property but in the law of obligations.

If there were no such thing as a restitutionary right *in rem* all this would be much easier. The law of restitution would then belong wholly in the law of obligations. The relationship with property would be one of complete separation. And the gloss on 'cause . . . to give up' could be shortly stated: the enrichment must have vested in the defendant, and the giving up must be effected by the imposition upon him of a personal obligation to make over (i.e. transfer the ownership in) the thing or to pay its value.[15] This simpler, crisper and more Roman state of affairs is unattainably out of reach. Because there are such things as restitutionary rights *in rem*.[16]

2. RESTITUTION AND UNJUST ENRICHMENT

It has already been observed that the word 'restitution' cannot stand in the same series as 'contract' and 'tort'. They denote events which trigger legal responses while 'restitution' denotes a response triggered. We have been focusing on one specific example of an event which triggers restitution: receipt of a mistaken payment. The generic conception of all such events is 'unjust enrichment at the expense of another'. The whole phrase is cumbersome and cannot be repeated often without making people seasick. So 'unjust enrichment' is used on its own. For a reason which will be explained later it is crucial not to forget that these two words are an abbreviation. The words 'at the expense of another' are far more important than they seem.

[15] That is, 'give' would have to be understood in the same technical sense as Roman law gave to *'dare'*: 'What is ours cannot be given to us. For we understand that something is given to us when it is so given as to become ours. And what is ours already cannot be made more so' Gaius, *Institutes*, 4.4.

[16] Below, p. 57 ff.

They contain an ambiguity on which a major division of the subject rests.

In the next few pages it will be necessary to refer rather frequently to this phrase 'generic conception'.[17] It only refers to the words which manage to capture at a high level of generality the common quality of a number of apparently different events. It is when a list of events turns out to fit one such description that it is perceived as more than a random miscellany. Its members become species of a genus. Battery, defamation, negligence, intimidation, and so on, are species of the genus 'wrong' or 'tort'. The generic conception of sale, hire, agency, partnership, loan is 'contract'. So here the generic conception of all the events which give rise to restitution—payments by mistake, under compulsion, on bases which fail, benefits freely accepted, obligatory expenditure compulsorily anticipated, and so on (for again the list is incomplete)—is unjust enrichment at the plaintiff's expense: unjust enrichment, for short. It is important that this generic conception should not be thought to have been induced from the members just listed. That would be an impressionistic exercise whose results would depend on the members selected by the observer. And he might not then be able to give a satisfactory account of his principle of selection. In fact this generic conception is deduced from the definition of restitution itself. Its species—that is to say its particular manifestations, as in the list just given—are only recognised and admitted subsequently, and on an objectively fixed basis. The next paragraphs try to explain how this happens.

Restitution and unjust enrichment identify exactly the same area of law. The one term simply quadrates with the other. That is, if one thinks of the area as a square, the name at the top is unjust enrichment, the causative event, and the name at the side is restitution, the response. There are not many areas of law in which such perfect quadration is practicable. Debt includes all obligations to pay or give a fixed sum or quantity, £100 or 100 bushels of wheat. But when we look at the list of *causae debendi*, the events which trigger the single obligation *certum reddere*, we find that they are so various as to defy all attempts to formulate a single generic conception: sale, hire, execution of a deed or promissory note, loan, account stated, waiver of tort, mistaken payment, miscellaneous taxable events and so on. The list is very long and diverse. A generic description is impossible. Again the category 'tort' does not quadrate with 'compensation' because on the one hand a tort sometimes

---

[17] Cf. the language used by Lord Atkin and Lord Devlin to bring together all situations in which there could be said to be a duty of care: *Donoghue* v. *Stevenson* [1932] A.C. 562, 580; *Hedley Byrne & Co. Ltd.* v. *Heller & Partners Ltd.* [1964] A.C. 465, 524.

gives rise to an award measured other than by the plantiff's loss, as where penal damages are given;[18] and on the other hand events other than torts can give rise to claims for compensation, as for example breaches of contract.

The perfect quadration between restitution and unjust enrichment is no more than a fortunate accident. That is, by chance it happens that the particular nature of the response allows a generic conception of the event to be easily formulated. This must be demonstrated, because it is essential that the steps by which unjust enrichment comes on to the scene should be clearly perceived. If the restitutionary response happens when the law causes one person to give up to another an enrichment obtained at that other's expense or its value in money, it follows that, as a matter of observation at the highest level of generality, the event triggering that response must be enrichment at that other's expense. This is a tautology. But there are many enrichments at another's expense which the law does not undo. Most obviously, a birthday present of £100. So there are enrichments which the law does reverse and enrichments which it does not. Some word is needed to express the distinction. In the former cases the obvious inference is that the enrichment which generates the active response ought not to have happened. It is possible, therefore, to add an adjective signifying disapproval. 'Unjust' is the one which has stuck. Hence 'unjust enrichment at the expense of another'.

All this is simple to the point of seeming over-laboured; and yet there has been much resistance in the English courts to the use of the generic conception.[19] This reluctance to deal in the language of unjust enrichment has to be overcome, for it has done and is doing enormous damage to the whole law of restitution, in ways which will be explained immediately below. This problem can be tackled simply enough, in two ways. First, by showing that the rejection of unjust enrichment is based on a needless misunderstanding. Second, by explaining more specifically what work the words of the generic conception could and should be doing.

The judges' unwillingness to use the language of unjust enrichment is based on a fear of uncertainty.[20] They suppose that the

[18] *Broome* v. *Cassell & Co. Ltd.* [1972] A.C. 1027: *Rookes* v. *Barnard* [1963] 1 Q.B. 623.

[19] *Baylis* v. *Bishop of London* [1913] 1 Ch. 127, 140 (Hamilton, L.J.); *Holt* v. *Markham* [1923] 1 K.B. 504, 513 (Scrutton, L.J.); *Orakpo* v. *Manson Investments Ltd.* [1978] A.C. 95, 104 (Lord Diplock); *Re Byfield* [1982] 1 All E.R. 249, 256 (Goulding, J.).

[20] Not unreasonably, since the Court of Appeal's occasional sorties into 'justice' do leave everyone in doubt as to the facts material to the conclusion: cf. *Hussey* v. *Palmer* [1972] 1 W.L.R. 1286, 1289 where Lord Denning, M.R., speaking of constructive trusts almost in the words with which Lord Mansfield spoke of the action for money had and received (see below, p. 34 f.), nevertheless abstained (as Lord Mansfield did not) from specifing the particular facts on which the court would act.

word 'unjust' would invite appeals to abstract conceptions of justice derived from whatever moral and political values might best suit a party's case. There is no wealth which is not unjustly held according to beliefs entertained by at least some members of society. But judges cannot be expected to pass upon such questions. Indeed the wonderful freedom which we call moral pluralism depends to some extent on their not being asked to do so. It should be obvious, therefore, that 'unjust' can never be made to draw on an unknowable justice in the sky. Nor is there any reason to doubt the ability or will of the judges to cut short a barrister unwise enough to advance an upward-looking argument of that kind.

In the phrase 'unjust enrichment' the word 'unjust' might, with a different throw of the dice, have been 'disapproved' or, more neutrally, 'reversible'. Those words might have been better in being more obviously downward-looking to the cases. The essential point is that, whatever adjective was chosen to qualify 'enrichment', its role was only to identify in a general way those factors which, according to the cases themselves, called for an enrichment to be undone. No enrichment can be regarded as unjust, disapproved or reversible unless it happens in circumstances in which the law provides for restitution. The answer to the fear of uncertainty is not to reject the word but to deal firmly with any argument which attempts to detach it from the law.

It might be objected that if 'unjust' is tied strictly to the cases, the generic conception of the restitutionary event as unjust enrichment at the expense of another can have no work to do, that it must be inert and useless. That is not right. Three related evils can be identified in the present state of the law, all of which can be overcome by the habitual and disciplined use of the words of the generic conception.

The first evil is the uncertainty which comes from there being no shared and stable pattern of reasoning. In contract or in tort, whatever differences of detail there may be, everyone knows roughly what analysis must be used to solve a problem or to structure an argument or judgment. The stability in those areas is based ultimately on a common sense grasp of the events which are involved, agreements, careless injuries, defamations and so on. These elementary images, accessible to a child, are starting points from which the evolution of a stable analysis begins. In restitution even this starting point is missing. Failure to adopt and use the words of the generic conception has meant that there has been no description or image to elaborate and analyse. In the result it is almost impossible for two lawyers to converse about the subject, for want of a common framework.

Suppose that a court is proposing to reject some restitutionary claim. It should always subject itself to the discipline of saying that the reason is, (a) that contrary to first impressions the defendant was not enriched, or (b) that he was not enriched at the expense of the plaintiff, or (c) that the enrichment was not unjust, in the sense that it did not happen in circumstances held in authority to call for it to be undone, or (d) that some other consideration barred the claim.

Used in this way the words of the generic conception can provide the shared analytical scheme which the subject lacks. And the old cases which have had no overview, and have used whatever phasing of inquiry has seemed momentarily best, have to be contemplated through the same pattern of questions. The intellectual difficulty and unpredictability of the subject can thus be reduced. Professor Palmer has noticed the irony. Rejecting the language of unjust enrichment the English judges have brought about precisely the uncertainty which they profess to fear.[21] But in fairness to the English judges it has to be said that neither he nor *Goff and Jones* do much to explain how that language can be brought down to earth and made into the instrument of greater certainty. They leave 'unjust' up in the sky, where it cannot do this necessary work.[22]

The second evil is the fragmentation of the subject which comes from not being able to detect important structural similarities between fact situations which are only superficially dissimilar. This means that small groups of cases cohering round a single fact situation tend to develop their own language and technicalities, making the subject seem more heterogeneous than is necessary. Cases on mistaken payments are never cited in relation to, say, compulsory discharge of another's liability; cases on compulsory discharge are not used when considering the problems of intervention to deal with an emergency. This is an immediate consequence of the courts' failure to develop a stable pattern of analysis.

The method described above, based on the text of the generic conception, can quickly re-constitute the whole picture, relating together fragments which seemed to have nothing to do with each other. For example the relationship between mistaken payment and

---

[21] Op. cit. p. 3 above, n. 3, vol. i, p. 6.

[22] *Goff and Jones*, at p. 11: ' "Unjust enrichment" is, simply, the name which is commonly given to the principle of justice which the law recognises and gives effect to in a wide variety of claims of this kind.' And, a little later, 'Unjust enrichment is no more vague than the tortious principle that a man must pay for harm which he negligently causes another, or the contractual principle that *pacta sunt servanda*. The search for principle should not be confused with the definition of concepts.' The difficulty is that in these other areas the open-textured principles are mediated by well-defined concepts whereas, in restitution, unjust enrichment has to do the work both of high-level principle and low-level concept.

compulsory discharge of the defendant's liability can be organised in this way:

1 *Enrichment*. In both cases the defendant is enriched: in the one by the receipt of money; in the other by being relieved of an outlay which he was bound to make.

2 *At the expense of the plaintiff*. In the one case the defendant receives money directly from the plaintiff; in the other he receives his discharge from his creditor who in his turn has been paid off by the plaintiff; and, if the plaintiff who pays the creditor pays less than the defendant would have had to pay, only the sum, less than the whole enrichment, is obtained at the plaintiff's expense.

3 *Unjust*. The cases show that both mistake and compulsion are factors calling for restitution. Both belong in a group of such factors which have in common that they all vitiate the plaintiff's intention to enrich the defendant.

4 *Other considerations*. None is now in question, but on some facts a plaintiff who survives the first three inquiries may nevertheless encounter some obstacle to his claim, either a general limitation imposed as a safeguard against some danger or a particular defence such as estoppel or change of position.

If we knew no more at all we could now bring this information to bear on the problem of an intervention to deal with an emergency. Suppose a field of wheat saved from fire. The questions would be:

1 Could the work done by the intervenor, or the product of that work, be counted as an enrichment of the defendant owner in the same way as a sum of money received or an obligatory expenditure saved?

2 If so, could that enrichment be said on the facts to have happened at the plaintiff's expense by reason of his input of labour or perhaps his outlay to obtain the labour of others?

3 Could the moral force exerted by the perception of danger to another's property be regarded as having an effect on the intervenor's mind equivalent to mistake or legal compulsion so as to qualify by analogy as another factor calling for restitution? It would be an affirmative answer to this question which would attract the adjective 'unjust'.

This is just a mock-up. The aim of this exercise has only been to show, in an elementary way, how the language of unjust enrichment can be made to bridge the gaps between three factually dissimilar stories, something rarely done in the English cases.

The third evil arising from the courts' reluctance to talk of unjust enrichment is their recourse instead to names which are uninformative or misleading. It is impossible to handle any phenomenon so long as it has no name at all. A bad one is better than none. This is why in relation to the restitutionary event the terms chiefly relied upon are 'quasi-contract' and 'constructive trust'. 'Subrogation' too, which is obscure in itself, has sometimes come close to being called 'quasi-assignment' or 'constructive assignment'. 'Quasi-' and 'constructive' have the same sense. Halsbury used to employ 'constructive contract' instead of 'quasi-contract'.[23] The terms 'pseudo-quasi-contract' and 'constructive quasi-trust' have made fittingly shy appearances in the literature.[24]

Among the sillier Oxford stories is that of the Dean's dog. The college's rules forbid the keeping of dogs. The Dean keeps a dog. Reflecting on the action to be taken, the governing body of the college decides that the labrador is a cat and moves to next business. That dog is a constructive cat. Deemed, quasi- or fictitious, it is not what it seems. When the law behaves like this you know it is in trouble, its intellect either genuinely defeated or deliberately indulging in some benevolent dishonesty.

The trouble with language of this kind is twofold. It displaces the truth. And it introduces a lie. These are distinct mischiefs. You lose the benefits of calling the event by its proper name, here unjust enrichment. And you are obliged to suppose instead that it has some affinity with events to which it is wholly unrelated. Unjust enrichment is an event which has nothing whatever to do with making agreements, declaring trusts or assigning assets. Nor with that quality which is common to these three, namely that they are all events which for their efficacy in generating legal consequences depend upon intention. If cuckoos had to be quasi-thrushes or constructive blackbirds we should know less about them.

3. THE PRINCIPLE AGAINST UNJUST ENRICHMENT

We have been thinking of unjust enrichment at the expense of another as the generic conception of the composite event which gives rise to a claim for restitution. But reference is frequently made to 'the principle against unjust enrichment'. There is a Roman root for this. The *Digest* preserves two versions in fragments excerpted from Pomponius. In one he says: 'This is indeed by nature fair, that nobody should be made richer through loss to another (*cum alterius*

[23] Above, p. 5.
[24] Sir P.H. Winfield, *The Law of Quasi-Contracts*, London, 1952, 26, 28; R.H. Maudsley, 'Proprietary Remedies for the Recovery of Money' (1959) 75, *L.Q.R.* 235, 245.

detrimento).' In another, the variation hinting at the ambiguity about to be explored in the next few paragraphs of this discussion, he says: 'It is fair by the law of nature that nobody should be made richer through loss and wrong to another (*cum alterius detrimento et iniuria*).'[25] It must be said at once that the principle rehearsed in these statements did not provide the foundation for, or explain the unity of, the Roman category of quasi-contract, though it was used as the rationale for some prominent members of that category.[26] The transition from event to principle can play some odd tricks. It is important to be aware of them.

The principle restates the conception of the event in a dynamic or normative form. The description, 'unjust enrichment at the expense of another', becomes the prescriptive, 'no-one ought to be unjustly enriched at the expense of another', or (for the form of words is not fixed as though by statute) 'the law does not permit one person to be unjustly enriched at the expense of another'. There are two things to note about this apparently innocuous transformation.

First, the principle threatens to undo the effort taken to make 'unjust' look downwards to the cases. To the extent that it does so it is to be regarded with suspicion. Indeed it may be that the principle can never be other than a moral aspiration. For as soon as steps are taken to bring it down to earth it begins to say nothing other than that the law ought not to be ignored. Thus 'unjustly enriched' (once 'unjustly' is made to look downwards to the cases) must mean: 'enriched in circumstances in which the law says that there should be restitution'. Hence, 'no-one ought to be unjustly enriched at the expense of another', only means 'no-one ought to be enriched at the expense of another in circumstances in which the law says he should make restitution'. In other words, the law should be respected. The other formulation boils down to a similarly unambitious statement: 'There are circumstances in which the law does not permit one person to be enriched at the expense of another.'

The second danger is an aggravation of the first but in a particular area, namely wrongs. It arises from the ambiguity of the words 'at the expense of'. This phrase can mean no more than that value passed to the defendant from the plaintiff. This sense can be rendered by the words 'by subtraction from', and can be illustrated most simply by the case of a payment by the plaintiff to the defendant. Whether reversibly or not, you are enriched 'by subtraction from me' if I pay £100 to you. The other sense is 'by doing wrong

[25] *Digest*, 12.6.14; 50.17.206.
[26] Below, p. 29 ff.

to'. If somebody pays you £100 to beat me up you are enriched 'by doing me wrong' but not 'by subtraction from me'. The quantum of my wealth remains unaffected by the beating.

The principle, both in its upward- and downward-looking form, can and should be divided to cope with this ambiguity. For there are really two quite different 'principles' masquerading as one; and they behave differently as they are restated. 'The law will not permit one person to be unjustly enriched by subtraction from another' then becomes 'there are circumstances in which the law does not permit one person to be enriched by subtraction from another'; and 'the law will not permit one person to be unjustly enriched by doing wrong to another' becomes 'there are circumstances in which the law does not permit one person to be enriched by doing wrong to another'.

There is a dramatic difference in the degree of changed meaning effected as 'unjust' is parapharased. The subtraction principle in its restated form is less ambitious than, but does not contradict, the loftier version. But in the other case the restated principle actually says something quite different. The lofty version implies, incorrectly as a matter of positive law, that the profits of wrongdoing always have to be given up: the law will not permit one person to be unjustly enriched by doing wrong to another. This implication derives from an unfortunate resonance between an upward-looking 'unjust' and the phrase 'by doing wrong to'. The reader infers that all acquisitions by wrongdoing are unjust and, having taken that step, is told by the principle that all such acquisitions are recoverable by the victim, which is false. The down to earth version gets it right: there are some circumstances in which enrichment by wrongdoing has to be given up. That is, the wrong itself is not always in itself a sufficient factor to call for restitution. There is much to be learned from modern civilian systems of the importance of drawing a line between these senses of 'at the expense of', on the one hand direct subtraction and on the other indirect acquisition from some other source by breach of duty to the plaintiff. But it is probably true that the common law is psychologically unable to absorb that information until it has, so to say, first learnt the lesson for itself, from first principles.[27]

When the principle against unjust enrichment is neither divided to reveal the ambiguity of 'at the expense of' nor restated to bring 'unjust' firmly into contact with the cases, this error or overstate-

[27] For a general introduction to the law of restitution in civilian systems, see K. Zweigert and H. Kötz, *Introduction to Comparative Law*, Amsterdam/Oxford, 1977, vol ii, 208–263. Cf. J.P. Dawson, *Unjust Enrichment, A Comparative Analysis*, Chicago, 1951, and 'Indirect Enrichment' (1969) vol. ii, *Festschrift M. Reinstein*, 789.

ment in relation to wrongs does not go away. It is merely hidden. It remains a latent defect whose presence, sensed but not identified, has contributed to the suspicion in which the language of unjust enrichment has been held.

The best policy is to make no use of the so-called principle against unjust enrichment. The neutral, and seemingly less interesting, generic conception has in fact the more important work to do.

4. THREE MODES OF PREVENTING UNJUST ENRICHMENT

Restitution is not the only mechanism against unjust enrichment. If we take prevention as the genus we can distinguish under it three different species: deterrence, anticipation and reversal. Alternatively, it might equally be said that prevention (by deterrence and anticipation) should be contrasted with reversal (by restitution).

Unjust enrichment is deterred most obviously by those parts of the criminal law which punish acquisitive dishonesty. The law of theft and related offences is all about trying to curb the temptation to acquire wealth in modes of which society disapproves. The same can be said of blackmail; and there are many specialised cases, for instance insider-dealing in company securities. In civil law the torts of conversion and deceit can be seen as part of the same picture. So also, in equity, the duties of trustees and other fiduciaries not to line there own pockets. Whether in criminal or in civil law, any duty not to acquire wealth in given circumstances can be seen as machinery to deter unjust enrichment. Deterrence is not used here as a synonym for punishment or as a goal only pursued by punishment. A duty deters in the sense that, like a commandment, it creates a barrier against conduct, here against modes of enrichment.

We have already encountered examples of preventing unjust enrichment by anticipation. The mechanism is the preservation of rights *in rem* through interruptions of possession. You acquire my car through a transaction nullified by fundamental mistake. The preservation of my title is a device which, *quoad* the car (though not the temporary use of it), stops you gaining anything. This passive anticipation of disapproved enrichment is the law's first line of defence. It is usually compressed into the maxim *nemo dat quod non habet*, or the phrase 'the sanctity of ownership'. Wealth is protected precisely because rights *in rem* have this ability to survive. So this is, definitively, what the law of property is all about.

Only the third mechanism counts as restitution, where an active response is made in order to reverse an enrichment which the recipient would otherwise enjoy. This has already been considered

in relation to the fifth refinement of the ordinary sense of
'restitution'. A restitutionary right is one which is newly created by
the defendant's receipt with the effect of undoing his gain.

5. SUMMARY

The word 'restitution' belongs in the same series as 'compensation'
and 'punishment'. The phrase 'unjust enrichment', an abbreviation,
aligns with 'contract' and with 'tort' in the list of causative events.
Restitution and unjust enrichment quadrate, naming the same area
of law from different sides of the square. It is important to recall
that we have noticed that on closer inspection the square 'resti-
tution/unjust enrichment' divides down the middle, because 'unjust
enrichment' is really an abbreviation for two different events. These
are distinguished according to the two senses of the words 'at the
expense of', which are usually omitted and too easily overlooked.
There is 'unjust enrichment by subtraction from the plaintiff', and
'unjust enrichment by doing wrong to the plaintiff'. The picture
can be represented thus.

In *Orakpo* v. *Manson Investments Ltd.*, Lord Diplock said this:
'My Lords, there is no general doctrine of unjust enrichment recognised in English law. What it does is to provide specific remedies
in particular cases of what might be classified as unjust enrichment in
legal system that is based on the civil law.'[28] Nothing said here is

Unjust enrichment

by subtraction	by a wrong

Restitution

---

[28] *Orakpo* v. *Manson Investments Ltd.* [1978] A.C. 95, 104.

meant to contradict that. A 'general doctrine', if it would be intelligible at all, would be unusably vague. Such a 'doctrine' is no more than the 'principle', already laid aside. What is proposed here is a scheme for better ordering the specific instances which Lord Diplock recognises. The generic conception of the event which triggers restitution adds nothing to the existing law and effects no change except what comes from better understanding of what is there already.

II

DIFFERENTIATION

THIS chapter continues the work of the previous one. But this time the focus is on the boundaries between restitution and other more familiar areas of the law. Restitution is always effected by either a right *in personam* or a right *in rem*. The law of rights *in personam* is the law of obligations. The law of rights *in rem* is the law of property. The place of restitution in each will be considered in turn. The exercise can equally be seen as an attempt to assemble together the contribution which each of these conceptual categories makes to the single subject of restitution.

1. RESTITUTION IN THE LAW OF OBLIGATIONS

'Obligations' is not itself a category in every common lawyer's thinking. In the universities there are no courses under that name. As the teaching of Roman law recedes, it comes increasingly as a surprise to be told that the way in which contract and tort are, or were originally, conceived to relate together is as two categories of that larger unity. More exactly, they are two categories which emerge when the larger conceptual entity is divided by reference to causative events. It could be divided differently. For example, you could, albeit inconveniently, distinguish between obligations to pay money, give goods, do work and so on. The inconvenience of such a division by content turns out to be that in any exposition you have to keep explaining how the obligations come into being, and those explanations in terms of causative events do not vary much whatever the content of the obligations. For example, agreement to be bound is a powerful explanation of the genesis of obligations to pay money, to convey property, to do work and to guarantee qualities and other states of affairs. So a system which insisted on dividing its law of obligations by content would have to repeat the contractual explanation in every category. It would be pointlessly uneconomical. Nevertheless unities of content are more easily perceived than unities of cause. Debt, as we have seen,[1] was one such category.

---

[1] Above, p. 17 f. *Quantum meruit* is another: cf. *British Steel Corporation v. Cleveland Bridge and Engineering Co. Ltd.* [1984] 1 All E.R. 505, 509 *per* Robert Goff, J.

From time to time dissatisfaction is expressed about the division between contract and tort.[2] Certainly, even obligation-creating events could be differently divided. For a commitment to that principle of speciation still leaves open the level on which the classification will be made, and the way in which the classifier will describe the entities which he perceives at his chosen level. The test of his success is the survival of his scheme. For the moment contract and tort do survive as the dominant categories of obligation-creating event. To the extent that the law of restitution belongs to the law of obligations, it is therefore to these two categories that it must be related. But not only to these. Beyond contract and tort there is a dimly perceived miscellany of other events, some or all of which are called quasi-contracts. So the four terms in relation to which a position must be taken are: contracts, torts, quasi-contracts and miscellaneous other cases. These will be considered in turn. But since the history and content of restitution is bound up with quasi-contract, that difficult head will be examined first.

(i) *Restitution and Quasi-Contract*

There is in a sense no boundary to be described. For, subject to one doubt, the whole law of quasi-contract belongs inside the law of restitution. These things cannot really be quantified, but the right impression will be given if we say that two thirds or more of the law of restitution is accounted for by quasi-contract. Restitution has taken it over, displaced the name, and added extra matter. The questions which much be answered here are why this take-over was necessary and what kind of matter is added, under the new name, to the category which has been eclipsed. For these to be answered a brief historical account of quasi-contract must be given.

'Quasi-contract' is a noun formed by anglicising the phrase *quasi ex contractu* which itself was coined by Roman jurisprudence. If the texts are taken at face value it was invented by Gaius in the second half of the second century AD; but it may be due to Justinian's commissioners working in the sixth. For, in discharging the task of producing a slimmed-down law library, the commission had the emperor's authority to interpolate changes into the original material.

---

[2] John Austin commended Blackstone for departing from this division. Austin thought Blackstone's method gave room for a more important distinction, between primary and secondary obligations: *Lectures on Jurisprudence*, 3rd ed., London, 1869, 2, 796. More recently, Grant Gilmore, *The Death of Contract*, Columbus Ohio, 1974, esp. 87 ff.; P.S. Atiyah, 'Contracts, Promises and the Laws of Obligations', (1978) 94 *L.Q.R.* 193; cf. his *Rise and Fall of Freedom of Contract*, Oxford, 1979, esp. 1–11, 716–780.

The phrase came into existence in this way. Dividing obligations by reference to the events which brought them into being Gaius affirmed, at his first attempt, that all obligations arose either from contract or from tort.[3] A few lines later he stumbled on the obligation to repay a mistaken payment, which arose from neither.[4] But for the moment he did no more than raise his eyebrows. Later, in another book, he cured the defect of the dichotomy by proposing a third category: other miscellaneous events. This time he affirmed that every obligation arose either from contract or from tort or from various other causes.[5] And either he or someone later interfering with his text then broke down the residual miscellany into two 'quasi' categories.[6]

Justinian's *Institutes* adopt the resulting fourfold division. They say that obligations arise either from contract or *quasi* from contract, or from tort or *quasi* from tort.[7] The common law has found no use for quasi-tort. It has borrowed the term 'quasi-contract' but has not given it the same content as it had in Roman law. Indeed the use of the term by the common law can best be understood by going back to the three term division—contract, tort, and miscellaneous others—which was proposed by Gaius before the *quasi* categories were used to divide the miscellany.

For completeness and not because the content of the Justinianic category has a bearing on the common law story, it should be said that Justinian's quasi-contract was not exclusively a category of restitutionary obligations triggered by unjust enrichment, though it did amongst others include obligations having that content and origin. Its unity was different. It comprised all those obligations which arose from permitted, as opposed to forbidden, acts which were not contracts. Such lawful acts, though they were not contracts, nevertheless gave rise to consequences similar to those produced by one or other figure in the Roman list of contracts. Thus the consequences of receiving a mistaken payment were the same as the consequences of receiving a loan (*mutuum*) and were sanctioned

---

[3] Gaius, *Institutes*, 3.88.

[4] Gaius, *Institutes*, 3.91.

[5] *Digest*, 44.7.1 pr. (Gaius, 2 *Aurea*) *Obligationes aut ex contractu nascuntur aut ex maleficio aut proprio quodam iure ex variis causarum figuris.*

[6] *Digest*, 44.7.5 (Gaius, 3 *Aurea*).

[7] Justinian, *Institutes*, 3.13. 1,2. J. first inserts a division between obligations of the *ius civile* and obligations of the *ius honorarium* (much as we would first distinguish between legal and equitable obligations). He then says: 'The next division puts them into four species: for they arise either *ex contractu* or *quasi ex contractu* or *ex maleficio* or *quasi ex maleficio*.'

by the same action, the *condictio*.[8] Again, one who intervened in the affairs of another without invitation (*negotiorum gestor*), incurred by that lawful act an obligation to conduct his intervention with care. The action which sanctioned that obligation, nothing to do with restitution at all, exactly resembled the action on the contract of mandate. Hence the intervener was in a real sense subjected to a regime 'as though there had been a contract of mandate' even though in fact there had been no agreement between him and the plaintiff. The position of guardians was similar; and, like the *gestor's*, the guardian's principal obligation was not restitutionary. Both had to make good losses brought about by their management of the plaintiff's affairs.[9] But this is a digression. The Justinianic category, as opposed to its name in an adapted form, has never been borrowed by the common law.

However, the Gaian trichotomy does fit the common law facts. We do have the categories of contract and tort. And, equally obviously despite attempts based on fiction to make them exhaustive, those two categories do not cover the whole ground. My obligation to pay income tax sufficiently proves it. So also the obligation to repay a mistaken payment. Manifestly, neither arises from contract or tort. There is no need to multiply examples. It is plain enough that Gaius's division between contract, tort, and miscellaneous other events does tally with the common law facts.

So the critical question is, does our borrowed usage of 'quasi-contract' include all the events in the residual miscellany which comes after contract and tort, or only some of them? A really firm answer would have to come out of a case. But the truth is that no judge has ever found it necessary to review the membership of the miscellany with a view to deciding the exact range of the term 'quasi-contract'. The word does not occur often in the cases and when it does its role is usually to assert that a particular non-tortious claim is capable of surviving despite being non-contractual. In other words the Roman term is used only to assert that there is ground beyond tort and contract; that the miscellaneous residual category

---

[8] Justinian, *Institutes*, 3.27.6; *Digest*, 12.6. The *condictio* was the Roman action of debt. The grounds of that content-based category had to be dispersed when the law went in for classification by events. It was the fact that both loan and mistaken payment gave rise to the same action that brought Gaius, when dealing with loan, into contact with the non-contractual grounds of the *condictio* and, hence, made him aware that the dichotomy between contract and tort failed to exhaust the whole category of obligation-yielding events.

[9] Justinian, *Institutes*, 3.27. 1,2. Both had counter-actions for expenses incurred for the other's benefit. The counter-actions, unlike the direct actions, can be related to unjust enrichment.

does exist. That is how Lord Mansfield used it in *Moses* v. *Macferlan* (1760).[10]

Moses sought to recover back in the King's Bench £6 which he had been condemned to pay Macferlan in the then equivalent of a small claims court. The ground was that Macferlan's action on four promissory notes had been brought in breach of a written promise that Moses would not be made liable on his indorsement of the notes. One objection to Moses's action for restitution was that it was 'impossible to presume any contract to refund money which the defendant recovered by an adverse suit'. To which Lord Mansfield answered: 'If the defendant be under an obligation, from the ties of natural justice, to refund, the law implies a debt and gives this action, founded in the equity of the plaintiff's case, as it were upon a contract (*quasi ex contractu*, as the Roman law expresses it).'[11] This kind of usage, affirming that the plaintiff need not find a contract, does not tell us whether there are any non-tortious and non-contractual claims which are also non-quasi-contractual. The further frontier of quasi-contract is left quite unexamined.

Nevertheless, it is undeniable that there is a consensus amongst modern writers to the effect that quasi-contract does *not* include the entire residual miscellany of events which are neither torts nor contracts. It goes no further than those obligations which arise from unjust enrichment.[12] According to this usage the common law division is between contract, tort, unjust enrichment (= quasi-contract) and miscellaneous other events (a fourth category reduced in size by the excision from it of the third). This conclusion as to the scope of quasi-contract in the common law is more spongy than one would wish. That is the reason for the slight hesitation in saying at the beginning that the whole of quasi-contract lies within restitution. For, if it could be shown to include any but unjust enrichment obligations, then plainly it would extend beyond the territory of restitution. Obligations to pay a tax, or a judgment debt, clearly do not belong in the area of restitution.

Why rename the category? The answer is, partly to add matter excluded from quasi-contract, and partly to break the imaginary link with contract.

Quasi-contract suffers from two inconvenient restrictions of

---

[10] *Moses* v. *Macferlan* (1760) 2 Burr. 1005.

[11] At p. 1012.

[12] Cf. *Goff and Jones*, p. 3f. Sir P.H. Winfield, *The Law of Quasi-Contracts*, London, 1952, 1f: 'So far as current English law is concerned I suggest that genuine quasi-contract may be defined as follows. "Liability, not exclusively referable to any other head of the law, imposed upon a particular person on the ground that non-payment of it would confer on the former an unjust benefit".'

content. First, it has somehow come to be appropriated by the common law, with the result that equitable obligations are excluded even when analytically indistinguishable in point of content and origin. In *Re Diplock*,[13] for example, executors of Caleb Diplock's will had distributed the residuary estate to certain charities in the mistaken belief that they were acting under a valid charitable bequest. The next of kin sought restitution from the charities, and it was held *inter alia* that the beneficiaries were under an equitable obligation to repay. The claim *in personam* correlative to that obligation could not succeed at common law, since there was no mistake of fact. There is no doubt, however, that despite being equitable rather than legal that species of claim is analytically indistinguishable from common law quasi-contractual obligations. The same can be said of personal claims against fiduciaries, who, in acquiring some gain, put themselves in breach of their duty to avoid conflicts of interest.[14] There too the right *in personam* correlates with an obligation restitutionary in content and generated by an unjust enrichment. So good sense requires at least that quasi-contract should be extended to include parallel obligations in equity. By whatever name they are to be known, restitutionary rights *in personam* cannot continue to be driven into separate categories according to their jurisdictional origin.

The second restriction upon quasi-contract is precisely that it is a category of obligations. The division which distinguishes between contract, tort, quasi-contract and other events comes into being as a classification of obligations (or, looking from the other side of a penny, rights *in personam*) according to the events which cause them to arise. Hence a study of quasi-contract naturally confines itself to looking at unjust enrichment as an event triggering rights *in personam*. This inflicts a form of tunnel vision. For, if the event in some of its particular manifestations also generates restitutionary rights *in rem*, any lawyer will obviously want to be able to see them too. Nobody would wish to encourage the inconvenience of dispersing in different books the different species of similar response to a single event.

The displacement of the term 'quasi-contract' is thus intended to have the effect of adding in parallel equitable obligations and, at the same time, of making it possible to reach outside the field of claims *in personam*. The second of these changes means that the event, unjust enrichment, is allowed to prevail over the abstract pheno-

[13] *Re Diplock* [1948] Ch. 465.
[14] E.g. *Boardman* v. *Phipps* [1967] 2 A.C. 46; *Regal (Hastings) Ltd*. v. *Gulliver* [1942] 1 All E.R. 378.

menon of which it initially formed a species, namely obligation. In a limited and unobtrusive way we have allowed the same thing to happen in contract. Treatments of the contract of sale never confine themselves to that event's effect *in personam*. Discussion of the passing of the property and of the principle, *nemo dat quod non habet*, show that the event is contemplated as constitutive not only of rights *in personam* but also of rights *in rem*.[15]

These changes enlarging and adjusting the content of the category might possibly have been made without dispensing with the old name. But 'quasi-contract' was not satisfactory. Most of the case for the honest generic description of the restitution-yielding event was made in the earlier discussion of the work to be done by the words 'unjust enrichment at the expense of another'. None of that needs to be repeated. But something must be said of the strong historical reasons which, from a different angle, increased the urgency of trying to replace 'quasi-contract' by 'restitution'. By the early twentieth century the spurious link with contract had begun to put imaginary obstacles in the way of plaintiffs seekings restitution.

'Quasi-contract' sounds like 'sort of contract'. However hard the impression is combatted, the image is of matter barely tolerated on the fringe of contract. That is where most people find it first, in a single chapter tacked on to a book about contract. One might as aptly find divorce at the end of real property, or income tax in an appendix to administrative law. The Latin is a bit safer: *quasi ex contractu* means 'as though upon a contract', and fairly obviously implies that there is none.[16] But the English noun cannot be turned away from its false overtone. And the misinformation inherent in the word resonates horridly with two historical accidents. It is a quite remarkable coincidence of legal history, to have the same error re-inforced from three angles. The consequence of this history has been that the English law of restitution is only now emancipating ★2 itself from a false dependence on the law of contract. The three distinct historical accidents were, (a) the false overtone in the phrase '*quasi ex contractu*', (b) the overkill of *Slade's Case*, 1602, and (c) Blackstone's recourse to the 'social contract' as a means of

---

[15] Cf. *Sale of Goods Act, 1979*, Part III, sections 16—26.

[16] There is not the least doubt that the Romans themselves did not intend the phrase to suggest 'a sort of contract' but some later civilians mistakenly supposed the contrary, so that the 'implied contract' theory of quasi-contract has its Romanist supporters too: see, for example, Pufendorf's *Law of Nature and Nations* (tr. B. Kennet), 5th ed., London, 1769, 454, n. 7 (notes by Jean Barbeyrac); cf. J. G. Heineccius, *Elementa Iuris Civilis, editio altera*, Amsterdam 1731, 1, 349; 359; 362; R. Eden, *Jurisprudentia Philologica sive Elementa Iuris Civilis*, Oxford, 1744, p. 206. Contrast A. Vinnius, *In Quatuor libros Institutionum Imperialium commentarius, editio secunda*, Amsterdam, 1655, p. 695.

explaining all legal consequences imposed on people by operation of law. The first of these has already been sufficiently considered. The other two must now be briefly reviewed.

In 1602 it was held in *Slade's Case*[17] that the action on a promise (*assumpsit*) could be brought to recover the price due under a sale. By the light of nature there was no reason why it should not be. After all, as Tanfield pointed out in argument, a buyer, though he may say no more than 'Done' or 'I'll have it for £16.00', does impliedly promise to pay.[18] The objection had been that the action of debt would lie for the price. At least in the opinion of the Common Pleas, the action on a promise, being an action on the case, had to be confined to a supplementary role and could not therefore be brought where one of the older nominate actions lay. It was this view, that *assumpsit* was excluded by the availability of debt, which was given up or overborne in *Slade's Case*.

The effect of *Slade's Case* should have been limited to allowing *assumpsit* to be used instead of debt in those cases in which the facts constituting the indebtedness did include an express or tacit promise to pay, those, that is, which did 'import an *assumpsit*'.[19] In outline the form of the action was 'Whereas the defendant promised . . . yet he wickedly broke his promise'. A reasonable man could be forgiven for thinking that it would be impossible for a plaintiff to advance that proposition if the facts which he proposed to adduce under it showed only a debt imposed on the defendant by operation of law, without his consent or even against his will. Nevertheless, during the seventeenth century the courts accepted that a plaintiff could use *assumpsit* to recover any debt.[20] The plaintiff's action would allege the debt facts and would go on to say that the defendant had promised to pay, but he would win by proving only the debt facts. For, once the indebtedness of the defendant had been established, no question could be raised as to whether he had also promised to pay the sum he owed. It did not make any difference whether you said that the allegation of a promise was ignored or that a promise was implied. If you said the promise was implied you would mean

---

[17] *Slade's Case* (1602) 4 Coke Rep. 91. For reports of arguments: J.H. Baker, 'New Light on Slade's Case' 1971 *C.L.J.* 51, 213.

[18] Ibid. 51, 55 f.

[19] The third resolution in *Slade's Case* was that 'every contract excutory imports in itself an *assumpsit*', not that every debt imports such a promise: 4 Coke Rep. 91, 94. If I borrow money from you, I do impliedly promise to repay. If I receive a mistaken payment I make no such promise. Like you, I may believe that the money is due to me, or I may be determined to hang on to it at all events.

[20] *City of London* v. *Goree* (1677) 2 Levinz 174; *Aris* v. *Stukely* (1678) 2 Mod. 260; *Shuttleworth* v. *Garnett* (1688) 3 Mod. 240; *Lamine* v. *Dorrell* (1705) 2 Ld. Ray. 1216.

'implied in law', 'deemed', not that it was genuinely but tacitly made.

This unwarrantable extension of *indebitatus assumpsit* (the action on a promise used in cases of indebtedness) meant that all litigation about even non-promissory debts took place under a form of words which said that the defendant had promised to pay. Which everyone knew that he had not. Quasi-contractual debts (i.e. those generated by unjust enrichment) constitute one category of non-promissory debts. Hence quasi-contractual debts came to be claimed by a form of action alleging a fictitious promise. And that is the first awful accident. The twist in the development of pleading seemed to give substance and even a history to the misleading overtones of 'quasi-contract'. Later it would become difficult to deny the link with contract. Take the obligation to repay a mistaken payment. How in, say, 1920 could it seem distinct from contract? Called quasi-contractual, it had been handled for more than two centuries through the action on a promise.

You can see Lord Mansfield almost courting this danger in *Moses v. Macferlan* in 1760.[21] It was an *indebtitatus assumpsit*. Moses thus said that Macferlan was indebted to him in the sum of £6 and had promised to pay that sum. Macferlan answered, going to the form of the action, that it could hardly be said that he promised (*assumpsit*) to pay a sum which he had only managed to obtain from Moses 'by adverse suit'. Lord Mansfield brushed the objection aside: if the facts were such as to raise a debt the plaintiff did not need to prove the promise. And then follows the brilliant and dangeous attempt to kill two birds with one alien stone, the appeal to the Roman phrase *quasi ex contractu* which seeks both to justify the action's form and to affirm its non-contractual nature. His overt emphasis is on the latter point; but his unspoken purpose is to invoke Roman jurisprudence to dignify the fictitious promise. They too, he implies, understood actions based 'as though upon a promise'. Lord Mansfield no doubt knew what he was doing. And lawyers generally might have kept their grip on the difference between fact and fiction had it not been for the second accident.

The second accident was Blackstone's fondness for the social contract. Wherever the law compelled a man to act in some way without his express consent the justification which Blackstone favoured was that all members of society impliedly agree to act as law, reason and justice dictate.

---

[21] *Moses* v. Macferlan (1760) 2 Burr. 1005, above, p. 32.

And thus it is that every person is bound and hath virtually agreed to pay such particular sums of money as are charged on him by the sentence, or assessed by the interpretation, of the law. For it is part of the original contract, entered into by all mankind who partake the benefits of society, to submit in all points to the municipal constitutions and local ordinances of that state of which each individual is a member.[22]

The duty to make restitution after unjust enrichment is imposed irrespective of consent just as is punishment upon a wrongdoer, though without implying any censure. It was inevitable, therefore, that Blackstone would explain it in terms of implied contract. He would have done so even if there had been no provocation to it in the materials before him. But those fictitious promises which stood in the pleadings as a result of the abuse of *Slade's Case* in the seventeenth century provided not only a historical confirmation of the theory which he favoured but also a ready-made basis for its expression.

A second class of implied contracts are such as do not arise from the express determination of any court or the positive direction of any statute; but from natural reason and the just construction of law. Which class extends to all presumptive undertakings or *assumpsits*; which, though never perhaps actually made, yet constantly arise from this general implication and intendment of the courts of judicature, that every man hath engaged to perform what his duty or justice requires. Thus, . . . 3. A third species of implied *assumpsit* is when one has had and received money of another's without any valuable consideration given on the receiver's part: for the law construes this to be money had and received for the use of the owner only, and implies that the person so receiving promised and undertook to account for it to the true proprietor. And if he unjustly detains it, an action on the case lies against him for the breach of such implied promise and undertaking; and he will be made to repair the owner in damages, equivalent to what he has detained in such violation of his promise. This is a very extensive and beneficial remedy, applicable to almost every case where the defendant has received money which *ex aequo et bono* he ought to refund. It lies for money paid by mistake, or on a consideration which happens to fail, or through imposition, extortion or oppression, or where undue advantage is taken of the plaintiff's situation.[23]

Blackstone was Lord Mansfield's exact contemporary. This passage ends with a sustained quotation from the judgment in *Moses* v. *Macferlan*. But Blackstone gives the implied contract a new emphasis and impetus. Moreover, reading this extract in context one can see that he makes no steady distinction between contracts implied in law (deemed) and contracts implied in fact (genuine but tacit).

[22] *Commentaries on the Laws of England*, 1768, Book 3, p. 158 (facsimile edition, Chicago, 1979).
[23] *Commentaries*, Book 3, p. 161 f.

This meant that he did not prepare his readers to be alert to the difference between real and imaginary facts; and there were many readers. The success of the *Commentaries* had the effect in this field of propelling the imaginary contractual explanation of restitutionary obligations right into the nineteenth century. It thus survived even after the abolition of the forms of action in the middle of the century when the removal of fictions from the pleadings might otherwise have carried it off.

The bad effects can be recognised in the following passage from the speech of Lord Haldane L.C. in *Sinclair* v. *Brougham* in 1914.

Broadly speaking, so far as proceedings *in personam* are concerned the common law of England really recognises (unlike the Roman law) only actions of two classes, those founded on contract and those founded on tort. When it speaks of actions *quasi ex contractu* it refers merely to a class of action in theory based on a contract which is imputed by a fiction of law. The fiction can only be set up with effect if such a contract would be valid if it really existed.[24]

Two aspects of this statement serve to sum up the legacy of the implied contract heresy. First, the category of quasi-contract is asserted to have no independent existence. Darwin would have discovered nothing if he had been so insensitive to observable facts. The obligation to make restitution of benefits received through mistake or oppression or for a consideration which happens to fail are manifestly not generated by contract or by tort. No subject can be considered rationally through such distortions. This matters, less because of the blemish on the law, than because parties win and lose cases undeservedly when lawyers are muddled. Secondly, in the last sentence Lord Haldane begins to bring the fiction to life. When a defendant has been enriched at the expense of a plaintiff the question whether he should make restitution cannot be answered by asking whether a promise to repay would be valid. Looking at a piece of chalk one might as well ask whether it was Wensleydale or Cheddar. In *Sinclair* v. *Brougham* a company had received *ultra vires* payments in the form of deposits by customers of a banking business which it had no power to run. There was no doubt that its promises to repay its customers were void. But that was only the starting point. The question was whether, given the nullity of the contracts, restitution should nevertheless be ordered. So nothing could be less helpful than to begin the analysis with questions about promises.

This account of the historical reasons why English quasi-contract failed to develop independently of contract serves to underline the

[24] *Sinclair* v. *Brougham* [1914] A.C. 398, 415.

need for a new start, with new language and somewhat different content. Nowadays, the most important thing to say about the relationship between restitution and quasi-contract is that the term 'quasi-contract' ought to be given up altogether. It has no work to do. Quasi-contractual obligations are simply those common law obligations which arise from unjust enrichment. They are restitutionary in content, and unjust enrichment is their causative event. To persist in calling them quasi-contractual is to insist on a usage which adds no further information about them but does perpetually threaten to revive their misleading history.

(ii) *Restitution, Torts, and Other Wrongs*

The sub-heading says 'Torts, and Other Wrongs'; this matters. One of the battles which the law of restitution has to fight is against the division between law and equity. Of course, it cannot be got rid of. It is a fact of legal life. But it must not be allowed to obscure important unities, especially unities of fact. People's lives are not divided. Yet the vocabulary with which the two systems respond is often so different as to make it difficult to recognise that they are talking about the same type of event, and perhaps saying much the same thing. This is a general problem which in this particular area is met by treating 'wrongs' as a genus bridging law and equity.

What is a wrong? It is natural to want to define it in terms of moral blame, something done or omitted with malice, dishonesty, negligence, or some other kind of fault. But that path is closed because it would inconveniently exclude torts for which liability can attach without blame, such as conversion, and equitable infringements which can be committed in good faith, as by a trustee who allows himself to get into a position in which, hypothetically, he might be tempted to sacrifice the interests of his trust. To cover these instances of liability without fault the sense in which 'wrong' is used here is 'breach of duty'. An act or omission is a wrong if it triggers legal consequences by reason of being characterised as a breach of legal or equitable duty. This definition does not exclude the wrong of breach of contract (as opposed to the event 'contract' which consists in the act of coming to an agreement). There is no harm in that. Since 'wrong' is a generic term there is no affirmation that breach of contract is a tort, only that torts, breaches of contract and breaches of equitable duty are all species of wrong.

Wrongs normally give rise to compensation. When they do there is a clear division and contrast between them and restitution. The same when, more rarely, they trigger a penal response. This can be represented by another, slightly more complicated, diagram. It is based on the same principle as the earlier one, event on top, responses down the side. The categories 'others' are always added for completeness. They include everything not under immediate examination. So here 'others' at the top includes even 'contract' with which we are not now concerned.

	Wrongs	Unjust enrichments	Other events
Restitution	(×)	√	×
Compensation	√	×	?
Punishment	√	×	?
Other responses	?	×	?

In this diagram a cross affirms that the box has no content, i.e. that the response is never triggered by the event. A question mark is neutral. It means only that the possibility of there being content is not excluded. A tick means that there is content; the event does trigger the response. The parentheses round the cross in wrongs/restitution represent the problem about to be discussed.

In chapter I, when we were discussing the matter in isolation from all other legal categories, we observed the perfect quadration between restitution and unjust enrichment. When there is unjust enrichment then there is restitution, and *vice versa*. That means in turn that unjust enrichment cannot trigger any other response. And it would seem to mean that restitution cannot be triggered by any other event. That is the state of affairs represented in the diagram: only one tick in the vertical unjust enrichment column, and only that same one in the horizontal restitution column.

But the last proposition, that no other event can give rise to restitution, is logically insecure; and in relation to wrongs it turns out to be actually incorrect. The logical insecurity is this: the words 'unjust enrichment at the expense of another' describe generically all the circumstances in which restitution occurs; that description is, therefore, logically capable of embracing facts which constitute other events in a series ostensibly aligned with it; it is, therefore, not impossible that other events named in the series might give rise to restitution. In relation to wrongs this logical possibility does eventuate, but only in one easily defined group of cases.

We noticed that 'at the expense of' has two meanings, the subtraction sense and the wrong sense. Where the victim of an acquisitive wrong seeks restitution in respect of the wrongdoer's gain, and, in order to create a nexus between himself and that gain, has to rely on the wrong sense of 'at the expense of', his cause of action will be the wrong. In other words, although he complains of unjust enrichment at his expense it is only by establishing the wrong that he can make out his case. For example, in *Reading* v. *A.-G.*[25] Sergeant Reading had broken his duty to the Crown by helping smugglers to get their lorries past army roadblocks in Cairo. He had been paid well for it. It was held by the House of Lords that the Crown was entitled to the money which he received by his breach of duty. There was no connexion between the Crown and that money, except that it had been earned by the wrong done. The wealth of the Crown had not been reduced by the amount which the smugglers paid him. It follows that the Crown's right was based on the wrong in the sense that the wrong was an indispensable element in the cause of action. When we take the subject up again later, it will be seen that claims to the proceeds of conversion generally conform to the same analysis.[26]

This is one kind of overlap between wrongs and unjust enrichment. It derives from the fact that unjust enrichment is set at a level of generality above wrongs. There could be other examples of the same phenomenon. That is, there could, as a matter of logic, be causes within the subtraction sense of 'at the expense of' in which the plaintiff would still have to base himself on a wrong in order to establish that the enrichment was 'unjust', i.e. reversible. But as a matter of actual observation there are no such cases. Every example in which a wrong is, as such, the event which triggers restitution is neatly collected by the second sense of 'at the expense of'. The line down the middle of the first diagram[27] turns out to be a major division of the subject.

There are two ways in which this can be handled. One is to recognise that unjust enrichment must be regarded as two events: unjust enrichment by wrongs and unjust enrichment by subtraction. That produces a first variation of the previous diagram.[28]

There are serious objections to that approach. The nature of this kind of exercise, whether aided by diagrams or not, is ultimately to facilitate clear thinking by preparing alignments of properly related, and analytically distinct, terms. That aim is not achieved here because

---

[25] *Reading* v. *A.-G.* [1951] A.C. 507.
[26] Below, p. 138
[27] Above, p. 26.
[28] See top of p. 42, varying the diagram on p. 40

	Wrongs	Unjust enrichments by wrongs	Unjust enrichments by subtraction	Others
Restitution	×	√	√	×
Compensation	√	×	×	?
Punishment	√	×	×	?
Other responses	√	×	×	?

'Wrongs' and 'Unjust enrichment by wrongs' are arguably not distinct. In other words the step taken to eliminate a hidden overlap has not succeeded in drawing a clear line between the first and second vertical columns. 'Unjust enrichment by wrongs' is nothing other than the category of restitution-yielding wrongs.

The other way of doing it is more economical, which is good, but involves some artificial specialisation of the terminology, which is bad but sometimes inevitable. This approach involves resolving to speak, where a wrong is the event which triggers restitution, only of 'restitution for wrongs', not of 'unjust enrichment by wrongs'. In other words, the event ceases to be independently described for the case in which a wrong triggers restitution, just as it is not independently described according as it triggers punishment or compensation. We feel no need to draw separate columns for 'compensation-wrongs' and for 'penal-wrongs' but say, much more simply, that wrongs (the event) can give rise to compensation and/or punishment (the responses). In the same way we have no need to speak of 'unjust-enrichment-wrongs' or 'restitution-wrongs' as events separate from 'wrongs' generally. Instead, restitution is simply identified as another possible legal response to the species of event identified as 'wrongs'. The corrollary is—and this is where there has to be a specialisation of language—that the words 'unjust enrichment at the expense of another' must be understood to use the phrase 'at the expense of' only in its subtraction sense; and the abbreviation 'unjust enrichment by wrongs' thus becomes 'restitution for wrongs' and, as an independent event, disappears. 'Unjust enrichment' becomes solely the event which, when described in full, is 'unjust enrichment at the expense of (= by subtraction from) another'.

The diagrammatic representation of this second method of handling the problem is as follows.

	Wrongs	Unjust enrichment	Others
Restitution	√	√	×
Compensation	√	×	?
Punishment	√	×	?
Other responses	√	×	?

This diagram shows restitution divided in two and affirms, correctly, that it is triggered by two, and only two, events. There is restitution for wrongs and restitution for unjust enrichment (by subtraction). The perfect quadration between it and the wider unjust enrichment has been renounced. The wider concept needs a label in order to be capable of recall when necessary. Since it turned out to be, literally, ambivalent, that word will in future serve to identify it.

The two-fold division between restitution for wrongs and restitution for unjust enrichment (in now and henceforth its restricted univalent sense) provides the principal division of restitution-yielding events. It also corresponds exactly to the Austinian distinction between remedial (or secondary) rights and primary rights.[29] Where restitutionary rights are triggered by wrongs they are always remedial or secondary. Remedial because they come into being as the sanction or solace for a breach of duty; and secondary because the duty breached supposes the existence of a primary right anterior to the remedial right. In the diagram, restitutionary rights arising not from wrongs but from unjust enrichment are primary, just as the rights born of contract (as opposed to breach of contract) are primary. They do not, like secondary rights, stand in a fixed relation to another pre-existing right. This primary quality is a function of the fact that their constitutive event never amounts to a breach of duty.

The exercise of separating restitution for wrongs from unjust enrichment has the effect of eliminating one kind of overlap which existed between wrongs and the larger, ambivalent unjust enrichment. That kind of overlap can be called dependent description, because it involves cases in which proof of one event is essential to the establishment of another. So here, the cases which have been expelled from column 2 are those in which the characterization of

---

[29] John Austin, *Lectures on Jurisprudence*, 3rd. ed., London, 1869, Lecture XLV, 787 ff. Cf. *Photo Production Ltd.* v. *Securicor Transport Ltd.* (1980) A.C. 827, 848 ff, *per* Lord Diplock.

the facts as an unjust enrichment at the plaintiff's expense depended on their first being characterised as a wrong. The Crown could not show that Reading had been unjustly enriched at its expense except by showing that he had committed a wrong. Hence the unjust enrichment could only by established by dependent description.

There is another kind of overlap which can never be eliminated but occurs only at the level of unanalysed facts. The story as a whole may disclose alternative analyses, both the minimum facts of unjust enrichment and also, from another point of view, those which constitute a tort or other wrong. A simple example is this. You insure a cargo of lemons with me for £25 k. Later, in the mistaken belief that the lemons have been lost, I pay you the £25k. This is a well documented case of a mistake of a kind for which restitution lies.[30] And, so far as anything has yet been said, there is no trace in the story of a wrong. But add now that the cause of my mistake was a fraudulent misrepresentation by you to the effect that the lemons had been lost. The story now adds up to either and both a restitution-yielding mistake and the tort of deceit. The simplicity of this example consists in the fact that the two events, wrong and unjust enrichment, are very clearly distinct. There are less obvious cases, but the principle is always the same.

Full discussion belongs later, in the chapter on restitution for wrongs. This kind of overlap causes no trouble to our diagram, because the two causative events, though fortuitously present in one story, are analytically distinct. The one can be proved and relied upon without the other.

(iii) *Restitution and Contract*

This section is concerned with the relation between the now slimmed-down unjust enrichment and the event which consists in the making, not in the breaking, of a contract. Restitution for breach of contract is part of restitution for wrongs.

It is convenient to begin by making a dogmatic assertion: the facts which constitute an unjust enrichment never include, unless fortuitously,[31] a promise to make restitution. Another way of saying the same thing is that restitutionary rights are always created by the operation of law as opposed to the consent of the party enriched. In this way they resemble rights generated by torts, which are very obviously imposed by law irrespective of the tortfeasor's wishes.

---

[30] *Norwich Union Fire Insurance Soc.* v. *Wm. H. Price Ltd.* (1934) A.C. 455.

[31] For example, on receipt of a mistaken payment, which the law would have compelled me to return anyway, I instantly promise to give it back to you.

The nearest that any particular set of facts amounting to an unjust enrichment ever comes to including reference to the recipient's intent or consent is this: on some such facts it will appear that the recipient wanted the benefit and chose to accept it. But the same can be said of a thief. There is all the difference in the world between wanting something and agreeing to pay for it.[32] So unjust enrichment—and this would have been true even before the ambivalent version of the concept was cut down—is a generic description of an event which in no particular manifestation ever entails the inclusion of a promise or agreement to make restitution. This is as much as to say that there is no question in relation to contract of any overlap in the nature of dependent description.

This proposition can be tested by reference to the facts which have the best chance of contradicting it. Suppose a case in which I am indubitably enriched at your expense, but on facts which are such that, on the law as it stands, you have no claim to restitution. That is, according to the downward-looking version of the critical word, the enrichment is not 'unjust'. Let it be that you paid me under a mistake of law. I then acknowledge that you do nevertheless have a moral claim against me. So I promise to repay. To strengthen the facts and to eliminate problems from the doctrine of consideration, let it be that I put my promise in the form of a deed. These facts now amount to an enforceable promise by me to give up to you an enrichment received at your expense. The question is whether the enrichment has by the addition of the promise become an unjust enrichment, whether in enforcing the promise the law can be said to be effecting restitution. The reason why these two formulations of the same question should be answered negatively is that it is the merest accident that the content of my promise happens to be measured by the amount of my receipt. To quiet my conscience I might have promised anything at all, a picture, a theatre ticket, or a good dinner. It is the price of a clear conscience or a sense of virtue which fixes the measure of my voluntary response to my enrichment, not the enrichment itself. Consequently it is plain that the event to which the law reacts when it enforces the promise is the promise itself and in no sense the enrichment at your expense.

The arbitrary nature of the relationship between the promise and the enrichment at your expense is even more clear when I entertain a doubt about my liability and I promise to repay in consideration of your not suing me. For there the measure of my promissory obligation, if I am stubborn enough to be indifferent to

---

[32] For example *William Lacey (Hounslow) Ltd.* v. *Davis* [1957] 1 W.L.R. 932, discussed below, p. 270 f.

right and wrong, will be merely the value to me of being free from
the threat of litigation. The way in which this bears on the definition
of restitution is this. A restitutionary right is definitively and
necessarily measured by the amount of the enrichment at the plaintiff's expense. A promise which appears to have restitutionary
content will always turn out, on closer inspection, to be measured on
a different principle. The event which creates the obligation is,
therefore, not an unjust enrichment at the promisee's expense but
merely a promise contingently related to an enrichment at his
expense. In short the promisee's right is not created by the law in
response to the enrichment; it is born of a different event, the
promise itself.

This argument shows that there can be no overlaps in the nature of
dependent description, but overlaps in the nature of alternative
analysis do exist. The facts may put me under a restitutionary
liability, and, at the same time, disclose a contract which is not
itself necessary to establish that liability, but has the same content.
You can then choose one analysis or the other as the basis of your
claim. If I ask you to lend me £10 and you hand over the note, I
implicitly promise to repay. The implied promise is certainly not a
fiction. It is inherent in the nature of the transaction, though only the
words 'borrow' and 'lend' may actually have been used. But the facts
of a loan also disclose a free acceptance.[33] The same is true when I
order goods or work without discussing the price. I impliedly
promise to pay reasonably, but I also freely accept the benefit in
question. Free acceptance happens when someone knows that a
benefit is not intended for him as a gift and, having an opportunity
to reject, elects to receive it. It grounds a restitutionary claim against
him for the value of the benefit. In other words, a freely accepted
benefit forms a particular species of the genus unjust enrichment.
A free acceptance will usually support a genuine inference of a
promise to pay. It used to be thought that that inference had to be
drawn before any claim would lie; but that view has been given up.
Now we know the claim will lie even if the contractual inference is
obstructed. In cases in which it is not obstructed clearly the
plaintiff can draw it or not draw it as he pleases.

When, as in the transactions mentioned above, alternative analyses
disclose both a contract and an unjust enrichment in the same facts,
the contract may have a content different from that of the restitutionary obligation. Consequently there has to be a rule to the

---

[33] Below, p. 265 f. It is also true that, if I fail to repay, there will be a total failure of the
consideration for your payment, so that there is thus even a choice between different
grounds for restitution.

effect that, at least unless and until the contract is prematurely discharged by frustration or in reaction to a repudiatory breach, the plaintiff can never put himself in a better position by suing in unjust enrichment rather than in contract.[34] Otherwise the law of restitution would subvert bargains. You repair my windows at a price which, after the bargain has been struck, turns out to be below the going rate. If you could subsequently improve your position by switching to a claim in free acceptance my bargain would be spoiled. And the courts would at a stroke have accepted the task of regulating the whole business of economic exchange.

What has been said here of the relation between unjust enrichment and contract applies equally to the relationship with any promise enforced under the name 'estoppel'. Local difficulties may for a time obscure the fact that contracts, like roses, remain the same under all names.[35] If I induce and assume responsibility for your expectation in relation to a particular matter, then, whatever words I have actually used, the effect is that I have promised you that I will make that expectation good. If the law then says that that promise is legally binding and can be enforced against me, then, whatever words the law actually uses to describe that enforceable promise, there is, according to jurisprudential usage freed from local constraints, a contract. Hence, just as unjust enrichments are never constituted by those promises which we, by our local usage, currently call contracts, so also those enforceable promises called estoppels have nothing to do with unjust enrichment. As with promises by deed or supported by consideration, most of them have content which does not look remotely restitutionary. If I promise you that you will obtain the fee simple in my field if (which I do not ask you to do) you build yourself a house there, the promise bears no relation whatever to any enrichment I might receive at your expense either by your reliance on my promise or in any other way. Suppose you build the house. I am only enriched by the enhancement of the land's value; and only at your expense to the extent of your input. Hence, if I am compelled to give you the fee simple, or even a life interest, it will be explicable only as the fulfilment of your expectations and certainly not as restitution. A promissory estoppel which happened to have a prima facie restitutionary content should be analysed exactly in the same way as

---

[34] *Toussaint* v. *Martinnant* (1787) 2 T.R. 100; *The Olanda* (1917) [1919] 2 K.B. 728; *Thomas* v. *Brown* (1876) 1 Q.B.D. 714; *Re Richmond Gate Property* [1965] 1 W.L.R. 335.

[35] Cf. *Crabb* v. *Arun District Council* [1976] Ch. 179, and P.S. Atiyah, 'When is an Enforceable Agreement Not a Contract?' (1976) 92 *L.Q.R.* 174.

a contract having the same content. So far as the right so generated was rested on the promise the restitutionary content would be fortuitious: the measure might have been any other. On the other hand behind an estoppel, just as behind contracts openly so called, there will sometimes be facts which do allow an alternative analysis in unjust enrichment, tied by necessity to the restitutionary measure.[36]

(iv) Restitution and Other Miscellaneous Events

Not much needs to be said. The general characteristic of these residual events is that they trigger obligations which are not mediated by consent. In that they differ from contract. But nor are they wrongs or unjust enrichments. As has already been explained, when only two nominate categories are identified (contract and wrongs), the miscellany is much larger. The third nominate category (unjust enrichment) is formed by the discovery of another unity within that larger miscellany. It follows from the nature of this operation that there can be no example of unjust enrichment left in the then surviving residue.

Only a rash or very learned man would attempt a full list, and fortunately none is necessary. Judgment debts, statutory fees, customary dues and taxes of various kinds form the bulk of the category. Many of these obligations have no similarity to restitution. The one case which does is the obligation to pay a tax on the receipt of a benefit. Take income tax; the relevant event is an enrichment, and there is an active response in the form of an obligation to give up a certain percentage. Why is this not an example of restitution/ unjust enrichment?

There are two answers. First, although there is an obligation imposed by law on the taxpayer to give up enrichment, yet the giving up is not to a person at whose expense the enrichment was received. Earnings are not received at the expense of (in any sense) the Inland Revenue. Secondly, the measure of the giving is not the amount of the enrichment received but only a part. In the case of a tax at 100 per cent, a similar argument would apply as to promises which are fortuitously measured by enrichment. The coincidence between the amount of the receipt and the amount of the giving up would be an accident of the particular operation of a principle which is not logically tied to that measure. By contrast restitution is always of the whole enrichment, unless some defence operates to reduce that liability; and always to the person at whose expense it was received.

---

[36] Below, p. 290-3.

2. RESTITUTION IN THE LAW OF PROPERTY

We have been looking at restitutionary rights *in personam*. The law of rights *in personam* is one and the same as the law of obligations. The reason is that a right *in personam* in one person correlates with an obligation in another. If you negligently run over my foot, I have a right *in personam* to an award of damages. And you are the *persona* against whom my right is exigible. Looked at from your end of this relationship, the same thing can be affirmed by saying that you are under an obligation to pay me damages. The law of property is about rights *in rem*. Examples of rights *in rem* are ownership, fee simple, life estate, mortgage, floating charge. Each kind of right can be the subject-matter of the other. Suppose I contract to buy your house. I have a right *in personam* against you, and the subject-matter of that right is that you should convey to me your right *in rem*, typically the fee simple. Amongst the things in my ownership, and which I might well decide to transfer to you, is my right *in personam* against my debtor who owes me £20. The contrast between rights *in rem* and *in personam* can equally be expressed as the difference between proprietary rights (or property rights) and personal rights. The Latin has one advantage. In English 'personal' easily slips round to mean 'of a person' whereas *in personam* means 'against a person'. It is worth pausing on this distinction between proprietary and personal rights.

(i) *Proprietary Rights and Personal Rights*

The difference turns on exigibility. It has nothing to do with alienability. Rights *in personam* can be alienable, and rights *in rem* can be inalienable. A right *in personam* is exigible against a person by virtue of a contract, wrong, unjust enrichment or other event. It will probably relate to a *res* but it will be capable of surviving the loss or disappearance of that *res*. For to exact a right *in personam* you have to find the person not the *res*. If you come under an obligation to give me the cow Daisy, or to let me have the use of your theatre, it will be impossible to infer from the nature of my right (as opposed to the law relating to the particular causative event) that Daisy's disappearance or the destruction of the theatre will discharge my claim. After all I can still find you, and it is still not nonsense for me to maintain that you ought to give me Daisy or let me have the use of the theatre.

By contrast a right *in rem* is one whose exigibility is defined by reference to the existence and location of a thing, the *res* to which it relates. A right *in rem* cannot survive the extinction of its *res*. I cannot eat my cake and own it. Slice by slice the ownership diminishes. If you have wrongfully eaten my cake I can say I have a right *in personam* against you that you should pay for a cake which I once owned. But I cannot say in the present tense that there is any cake which I still own. By the same token, I do not own and cannot make you the owner of a cake which I shall bake tomorrow, though I can give you a right *in personam* against me to make you owner when the cake is made. That is, I can contract to transfer the cake if and when it comes into existence.

Next, a right *in rem* cannot be exacted from anyone who has not got the *res*. It is nonsense for me to say, 'That's my cake', unless I can identify the cake in the hands of my addressee. Again this is because a right *in rem* is one defined by reference to the existence and location of the *res*. And from this also follows the great strength of rights *in rem*: they can be exacted against any person who can be shown to have the *res*. That does not mean that they always endure until the *res* is extinguished. They may be created for a limited time. And they may be destroyed by special rules designed to protect recipients, as for example upon a sale in market overt or upon *bona fide* purchase for value without notice. But, apart from such exceptions to the maxim *nemo dat quod non habet*, 'That cake is mine' holds good against any holder of my cake.

(ii) *Non-Restitutionary Rights* in Rem

It is not at all easy to say which rights *in rem* are restitutionary. It helps to begin by approaching the question negatively. Which ones are not? The purpose of this section is not to list every case which does not count but to make out certain features which instantly exclude the given right from the whole class of restitutionary rights.

There is an important preliminary point. The question must be asked at the moment when the right comes into existence. Once it has arisen it may behave in a manner distractingly similar to restitution. We have already taken precautions against this misperception.[37] I send you merchandise when I am labouring under a mistake of identity so fundamental as to prevent your becoming owner.[38] Or I go away on holiday, and squatters move into my house.[39] These are cases where my pre-existing right *in rem* survives. Unjust enrichment is prevented, but not by restitution. This is the mechanism which we called 'anticipation'. Suppose we trace these

---

[37] Above p. 15 f.

[38] *Cundy* v. *Lindsay* (1878) 3 Ap. Cas. 459.

[39] Here I can have a summary order for repossession under R.S.C. Ord. 113. Cf. *University of Essex* v. *Djemal* [1980] 1 W.L.R. 1301.

rights *in rem* back to the moment at which I acquired them. Most probably I paid someone money for them. There was a purchase and sale under which the rights were transferred to me. If so they were rights conceded to me by consent. Such rights are never restitutionary.[40]

The tests are to be applied at the moment of acquisition. Bearing in mind the definition of restitution, the question is whether, when judged at that time, the new right *in rem* can be seen to cause one person, D, to give up to another, P, an enrichment gained at P's expense or by doing wrong to P. Breaking this down, we can say that P's new right *in rem* will never be restitutionary unless it, (a) *reduces* D's wealth, (b) by an amount *equivalent* to a receipt by D, and (c) obtained by him *at P's expense or through a wrong done by him to P.*

There are cases where there is *no reduction* of the wealth of any D. Out in the sea the mackerel belong to no-one. I catch one; it becomes mine. My new right *in rem* reduces nobody's wealth. Again, sometimes there is reduction of the wealth of some D, but that reduction is *not equivalent* to any receipt by D. The book which you gave me on my birthday became mine, and my new right *in rem* thereby reduced your wealth. But that reduction was not referable to any receipt by you. In fact there was no receipt at all by you. By contrast the watch which you sold me for £20 became mine, and the new right *in rem* accruing to me reduced your wealth and was related to a receipt by you of £20. But there was still no equivalence between the reduction and the receipt, unless fortuitously. The £20 is what I agreed to pay, but the watch now vested in me may be worth nothing or £500. Again, sometimes there can be a reduction in wealth of D exactly equivalent to an amount received by him, but the receipt by D is nevertheless *not at the expense* of P to whom the right accrues. I find a hoard of gold coins; treasure trove, they vest in the Crown. The Crown's right carries off my find, reducing my wealth exactly by the measure of my receipt. But my receipt was not at the Crown's expense in either the subtraction or the wrong sense of that phrase.

So there are certainly these negative tests, (a) there was no reduction of D's wealth, (b) there was no equivalence between the reduced wealth of D and any receipt by D, and (c) the receipt reduced by the new right was not received at P's expense or by doing wrong to P.

This section concludes by applying these negative tests to the facts of *Crabb v. Arun District Council.*[41] The council represented to

[40] Above, p. 44-7.
[41] *Crabb* v. *Arun District Council* [1976] Ch. 179.

Crabb that he would be granted an easement to allow him access to a road. He acted on that representation so as to become dependent on having that access-point. Then the council declined to proceed with the conveyance unless Crabb paid £3000. But the Court of Appeal held that, in equity, he had already acquired an easement under the doctrine of proprietary estoppel. Could that right *in rem* be described as restitutionary? It reduced the wealth of D, here the District Council; but there was no equivalence between that reduction and anything received by the District Council, for the District Council had received nothing at all. Since there was no receipt, it necessarily follows that the third test—receipt at the plaintiff's expense—is also against counting this as restitution. This is a case of an expectation created by a promise which is given effect in equity because of the promisee's detrimental reliance. It has nothing whatever to do with restitution/unjust enrichment.[42]

(iii) *Event-Based Classification of Rights* in Rem

Although property and obligations are balanced categories, their internal emphasis is different. We have seen that common lawyers have come to accept a classification of obligations by events. It cannot yet be said that they universally recognise the series 'contract, wrongs, unjust enrichment, others'. But, since the late nineteenth century, at least the first two of these terms have been generally accepted, and in one way or another eyes have been kept away from the *terra incognita* which they leave unexplored.

By contrast proprietary rights have never fallen into a classification by events. The reasons are complex. The primary division has been between personal and real property. Partly because of academic neglect, and partly because of its difficult history, personal property has always remained rather disorganised. Real property is divided chiefly by a classification of the different types of right *in rem*: fee simple, lease, mortgage, easement and so on. Only behind that division, and even then not according to a stable system capable of being matched up with the division of obligations, lies a series of causative events or, more familiarly in this area, of 'modes of acquisition'.

The consequence is that it is not easy to balance the two halves of this chapter by considering in relation to rights *in rem* the same series of events as is used to classify rights *in personam*. There is not even an incomplete or inchoate tradition in favour of this exercise. Yet it is useful to do it. The aim is not to restructure the law of

---

[42] This point is considered in more detail below, pp. 290-3.

property, which would be foolhardy, but only to select out as clearly as possible the class of restitutionary rights *in rem*. In one respect the series of events has to be adjusted in order to make any alignment possible. 'Contract' has to be taken at a higher level of generality as 'consent'. The reason is that without this adjustment rights *in rem* granted by conveyance would have to find a home in the fourth category under 'other events', with the effect of needlessly separating the larger class of all rights willingly conferred. With that adjustment, the results then look like this:

		Consent	Wrongs	Unjust enrichment	Other events
Restitution	*in rem*	✗	√	√	✗
	in personam	✗	√	√	✗
Other responses	*in rem*	√	√	✗	√
	in personam	√	√	✗	√

In this diagram the entire subject of restitution is represented by the box marked with heavy lines. The main division is the line which divides the two events inherent in the ambivalent notion of unjust enrichment which has now been given up. The secondary division of the square is the dotted line which distinguishes between the analytical nature of the rights created in response to the event. The diagram thus asserts that the law does contain examples of restitutionary rights *in rem* and restitutionary rights *in personam*, triggered by wrongs and by unjust enrichment. The squares made by 'consent/restitution' and by 'other events/restitution' still show no content. These empty categories will be considered first.

Consent/Restitution The reason why there is no content in this square has already been described in relation to rights *in personam* born of contract. Occasionally a right conceded by consent may happen to conform to the restitutionary measure. But the coincidence will be without the least legal significance. Exactly the same argument applies to rights *in rem*. I give you my car or my farm; you acquire ownership of these things. Suppose that I am deliberately trying to undo an enrichment which I consider to be unjust. I received the car from you in circumstances which were in some way doubtful, so that your new right *in rem* does carry back an enrichment obtained at your expense. This does look like restitution; but on closer analysis the appearance of restitution is fortuitous. The

measure happens to be restitutionary because I choose that it shall
be, and the law, in recognising your right, is responding to my
intention not to my enrichment. There is no such thing as a restitutionary right generated by consent.

This means that express trusts never create restitutionary beneficial
interests. Suppose I transfer shares to you on trust for myself. My
new equitable interest carries back your enrichment at my expense,
leaving you with the bare legal title. But again the restitutionary
pattern is without meaning, because I could have carved out any
interests at all or none. Equity responds to my intent, not to the
enrichment of the trustee. However, there is an important complication here, in the nature of 'alternative analysis'.[43] Just as a
contract can be laid over an unjust enrichment, as most simply in the
case of a loan, so here it is demonstrable that there is an unjust
enrichment analysis latent beneath an express trust. The proof is
that the trust can take effect even if the express declaration of trust
is excluded for some reason, as for instance because it fails to conform to requirements of formality. This will be considered below in
the discussion of *Hodgson* v. *Marks*.[44]

Other Events/Restitution   The blank in this square is also explained
by the reason given in relation to the corresponding rights *in
personam*. It is a matter of classificatory logic. The third column,
namely 'unjust enrichment/restitution', owes its origin to attempts to
discover another nominate unity in the miscellany beyond consent
and wrongs. It follows that the fourth column is the remnant of the
original residue. 'Unjust enrichment/restitution' was excised from it.
Hence no example of restitution can remain under the fourth head.

Other Events/Other Responses   It is convenient at this point to ask
what kind of event belongs in the lower half of the fourth column,
where 'other events' intersects with 'other (i.e. non-restitutionary)
responses'. The reason for pausing on this square is that it is the
proper home of matter which can rather easily be thought to belong
in unjust enrichment/restitution but which certainly has no place in
that square. When we were considering rights *in personam* we noticed
that very little energy has ever been devoted to examining the line
between the two categories of non-contractual and non-tortious
causative events, and we observed that, in the result, uncertainty
had been allowed to develop as to whether 'quasi-contract' included
all those events or only such of them as were restitution-yielding

---

[43] Above, p. 46.
[44] Below, pp. 58 ff.

unjust enrichments. It was therefore necessary to re-affirm the separate existence of the fourth category of event, triggering non-restitutionary responses. In relation to rights *in rem* the same exercise is necessary. The particular danger in this context is that it can otherwise easily be supposed that constructive trusts (which come into existence when equity raises a beneficial interest *in rem* without reference to the intent of the parties involved) all belong together in one square on this diagram and, in particular, in the square called 'unjust enrichment/restitution'. In fact, however, many examples of these equitable rights *in rem* whose coming into existence has the effect of making a constructive trust actually belong outside that square.

There are both legal and equitable examples of rights *in rem* which belong in 'other events/other responses'. At law the example of treasure trove fits in here. The Crown's right to the treasure is not conceded by the finder's consent. Nor is it created by a wrong committed by the finder. Furthermore we have seen that the right cannot be said to be generated by the third type of event because, when the finder discovers the treasure, the enrichment which the Crown's right carries away from him would not have been obtained by subtraction from the Crown. Hence, the Crown's right is not a response to an unjust enrichment at the plaintiff's expense. That leaves only the fourth category. Rather like the taxable events discussed earlier, the finding of treasure is an event which triggers a legal consequence—here the Crown's right *in rem*—by automatic operation of law but not by reason of a wrong or an unjust enrichment. The event is, therefore, one among 'other events', and the response is non-restitutionary. Another example at law is provided by prescription. When a right *in rem* is acquired by prescription, the previous owner's wealth is reduced but there is 'no equivalence' between that reduction and anything received at the new owner's expense, for the previous owner has received nothing at all from the new owner.

In equity some constructive trusts also belong here. It is very important to remember that the series 'consent, wrongs, unjust enrichment, other events' does not correspond with what might be called the section 53 classification of trusts between 'express, implied, resulting and constructive'.[45] We have already located express trusts under 'consent' in the first column, and we have said that express trusts are never restitutionary. Apart from that, there

[45] For the purpose of laying down requirements as to the use of writing, the *Law of Property Act, 1925*, s. 53 creates a distinction between, on the one hand, express trusts, and, on the other, by s. 53 (2), all resulting, implied or constructive trusts.

is no *a priori* reason why any of the other three kinds of trust should be coterminous with any of the three headings 'wrongs, unjust enrichment, and others'. This makes it immediately possible to see that constructive trusts do not logically or necessarily correspond with and only with 'unjust enrichment'. If legal title is in one person, and equity raises a beneficial interest, as opposed to a security interest such as a charge or lien, in another, there is necessarily a trust. And if that trust is not raised by reference to a settlor's intent, express, implied or presumed, it follows that the trust must be constructive.

That statement of the constructive trust's origin is absolutely neutral as between wrongs, unjust enrichment and others. It might fit under any of the three; and, as for its effect, no hint is given as to whether the beneficial interest is restitutionary or not. It might equally fit under 'wrongs/other responses', or under 'other events/other responses'. An example will make this clear.

Suppose that two people, P and D, live together in a house held in the name of D. The cost of the house was £50 000; P contributed £15 000 to its purchase. Afterwards, when the house had risen to £60 000, P contributed a further £10 000 for structural improvements, which immediately raised the value to £75 000. On these facts P may be adjudged to have acquired a beneficial interest in the house. If he is, there will be a trust. D will hold on trust for P, or for P and himself in shares specified by the court. The trust may be resulting, arising by presumption,[46] or constructive; and (as a quite distinct matter) it may be restitutionary or not restitutionary. Suppose that, in awarding and quantifying P's beneficial right *in rem*, the court, (a) does not exclude from its consideration the contribution of £10 000 by P, and (b) makes no attempt to create an exact equivalence between P's beneficial interest and the contributions made by P which have enriched D at P's expense, preferring to say that the combined operation of the substantial contributions made by P, and the common intentions manifested by P and D together, mean that equity must attribute to P a one-third share. Here the first manner of proceeding, at (a), is enough to make the trust constructive rather than resulting;[47] and the second aspect of the approach, at (b), prevents it being restitutionary, since

---

[46] For the relation between 'resulting' and 'presumption', see below, p. 60 f.

[47] Because the doctrines relating to the formation of resulting trusts are incapable of taking into account contributions made after the acquisition of the asset in question (unless, perhaps, such contributions are made on such a regular basis that they indicate an agreement back at the moment of his acquisition that, as between themselves, the parties shall consider themselves as contributing to the joint project in shares fixed *ab initio* but to be made later): see *Cowcher* v. *Cowcher* [1972] 1 W.L.R. 425.

the one-third beneficial interest arising in P has 'no equivalence' to any enrichment received by D at P's expense. The presence or absence of such equivalence cannot be determined as though it were a mathematically exact phenomenon, because quantification is always difficult and often approximate. But it can only be said to exist if the court at least believes and asserts that the measure of P's interest is controlled in principle by the amount of D's receipt at his expense.[48] Here it is given that the court, following the approach at (b), does not believe itself tied to that principle. Hence it does not conceive itself to be effecting restitution.

Where would this trust fit on the diagram? P's interest in the house is non-restitutionary. It must therefore belong in the *in rem* section of the second row, representing 'other responses'. In which column does it belong? It is evidently not generated by consent. That rules out column 1. And column 3 has no content at this level because 'unjust enrichment' cannot trigger non-restitutionary responses. Hence P's interest can only fit under 'wrongs' or 'others', columns 2 or 4. The example is deliberately not stated so as to reveal the court's exact grounds for recognising P's interest. It would conceivably be that P was the victim of a wrong by D which justified this non-restitutionary response influenced, but not exclusively measured, by P's contributions. That would put him in column 2. More probably, P fell within a special class, as for instance 'economically oppressed quasi-spouses', on behalf of whom public policy required a robust protective response.[49] In that case the proper heading would be 'other events' in column 4; and the detailed description of the event leading to the non-restitutionary response *in rem* would be something like 'contribution to home by dependent living-partner'.

This example serves to show that rights *in rem* arising under a constructive trust (or, more accurately, arising in such a way as to create a constructive trust simply because legal title is in someone else) are capable, in principle, of being non-restitutionary and, therefore, of being generated either by wrongs or by events in the miscellany of column 4. And at this particular point in the discussion what matters is the second part of that proposition: interests of that kind can exemplify the contents of the square made by the intersection of 'other events' and 'non-restitutionary responses'.

Unjust Enrichment/Restitution At this point the business is to

---

[48] In *Hussey* v. *Palmer* [1972] 1 W.L.R. 1286, discussed below, p. 290 f., the proportionate interest in the house which the Court of Appeal was willing to give the plantiff thus could be regarded as restitutionary if the principle controlling the 'proportion' was equivalent to the dependant's enrichment at her expense.

[49] Cf. *Cooke* v. *Head* [1972] 1 W.L.R. 518.

identify examples of property rights which are generated by unjust enrichment and which, therefore, are necessarily and definitively restitutionary. Hitherto the emphasis has been on those which are not. The safest approach is through one specific example. I shall say why the interest of the plaintiff in *Hodgson* v. *Marks*[50] does count as restitutionary within this square. And then I shall try to draw more general conclusions from the analysis of that one case. It is convenient to notice before setting out that in the square below, where 'unjust enrichment' intersects 'other responses', there is no content at all. That is a function of the perfect quadration between restitution and the event which triggers restitution: it is impossible as a matter of logic for there to be any response to unjust enrichment other than restitution.[51]

In *Hodgson* v. *Marks* the plaintiff, Mrs Hodgson, was an old lady without much knowledge or experience of worldly matters. She had fallen under the influence of her lodger, Evans. He induced her to give him her money so that he could manage and invest it for her. Then he made her transfer her house to him. The transfer was supposed to be, and was presented by Evans as being, a stratagem to ensure that Mrs Hodgson's nephew would not be able to get Evans out of the house. It was not intended to deprive Mrs Hodgson of her beneficial interest; Evans gave no consideration for it. Later Evans sold the house behind Mrs Hodgson's back. The defendant, Marks, was the purchaser; and there was a second defendant, the building society from whom Marks had borrowed money by mortgaging the house. Marks had not insisted on vacant possession immediately on completion of the conveyance. So Mrs Hodgson, and her lodger, continued to live in the house even after legal title had passed to him. Some months passed before Mrs Hodgson and Marks discovered each other's claims.

The first question was whether Mrs Hodgson had any interest at all. The second question was whether that interest remained exigible agains the purchaser from Evans and the building society. The second question, which turned on the interpretation of the *Land Registration Act, 1925*, s. 70 (1) (g) is not relevant to this present discussion. It was decided against Mrs Hodgson by Ungoed-Thomas, J., but in her favour by the Court of Appeal. But, both at first instance and on appeal, it was held that she did have an interest in the house. The conveyance to Evans gave him the legal title, but in the given circumstances she became entitled to an equitable fee simple, so that Evans became no more than a trustee for her.

[50] *Hodgson* v. *Marks* [1971] 1 Ch. 892.
[51] Above, p. 17.

Both courts had to overcome a difficult obstacle which lay in the path of this conclusion. For the *Law of Property Act, 1925* s. 53 (1) (b) provides that 'a declaration of trust respecting any land or any interest therein must be manifested and proved by some writing signed by some person who is able to declare such trust or by his will'. In the Court of Appeal this was circumvented by recourse to s. 53 (2) which carries out of the section 'the creation or operation of resulting, implied or constructive trusts'. Russell, L.J., with whom Buckley and Cairns, L.JJ., concurred, said: 'Nevertheless, the evidence is clear that the transfer was not intended to operate as a gift, and, in those circumstances I do not see why there was not a resulting trust of the beneficial interest to the plaintiff, which would not, of course, be affected by section 53 (1).'[52]

Mrs Hodgson's equitable fee simple was restitutionary. It had the effect of causing Evans to give up precisely the increment in his wealth obtained at her expense. So it passes the tests of 'reduction', 'equivalence', and 'expense' introduced earlier.[53] Next, the interest cannot be said to have anticipated rather than reversed the enrichment, because it was not a pre-existing interest preserved through a disaster, but a new one created in response to the receipt by Evans in the given circumstances. For Mrs Hodgson was previously entitled at law and had no equitable interest at all.[54] Lastly the interest cannot be said to have been brought into existence by consent, in which case its conformity to a restitutionary measure would be fortuitous. We know that this is right because the manifestations of intention and consent were expressed in a manner which meant that they had to be ignored. In an express trust the interests can be said to come into existence by virtue of the settlor's intention that they should; but, because of s. 53 (1), this was not an express trust. The same can be said of interests under an implied trust, so long as by that term is meant a trust referable to the tacit intent of the settlor genuinely to be inferred from the facts. But this cannot have been an implied trust in that sense. To maintain the contrary would be in effect to repeal s. 53 (1), as though by asserting that every oral declaration which ought to be in writing according to s. 53 (1) can be treated as an implied declaration within s. 53 (2). If the trust was neither express nor implied, it cannot be argued that the interest acquired by Mrs Hodgson was created consensually and that its measure was, therefore, only fortuitously equivalent to the enrichment received by Evans at her expense.

[52] *Hodgson* v. Marks [1971] 1 Ch. 892, 933.
[53] Above, p. 51.
[54] But see below, p. 70 f.

Even though interests under express and implied trusts can never be restitutionary because, for the reason given,[55] restitutionary rights of all kinds are raised by operation of law and not by consent of parties, the characterisation of Mrs Hodgson's interest as restitutionary does not either tell us or depend on our knowing whether it arose under a resulting or a constructive trust. That is to say it is no less a restitutionary interest whether it is rightly called resulting, as by the Court of Appeal, or constructive. We have already seen, in the discussion of 'other events/other responses', that interests under constructive trusts may or may not be restitutionary. If Mrs Hodgson's interest arose under a constructive trust, then that constructive trust happens to be an example of a restitutionary constructive trust.

It is helpful to dispel the doubt whether the *Hodgson* trust should be regarded as resulting or constructive. It is better considered constructive. There are formidable difficulties in the way of calling it resulting. Since the next part of the discussion needs to discuss resulting trusts, it is desirable to explore these difficulties a little at this point. It is essential first to say something of the meaning of the term 'resulting trust'.

The term 'resulting trust' is capable of bearing two meanings. In the first it identifies a feature which has nothing to do with the trust's origin: the trust is resulting (from the Latin *resalire*, to jump back) if the interest arising under it is carried back to the settlor. This can happen however the trust originates, whether by expressed intention, implied intention, presumed intention, or irrespective of intention (constructive). In trusts created in all these ways the beneficial interest can 'jump back'. So the term 'resulting' in this wide sense cuts across other classifications. It is convenient to identify this usage as 'resulting in pattern'. If the *Hodgson* trust is constructive in origin, then it remains true that it is 'resulting in pattern'. In the second sense 'resulting' has reference to the mode in which the trust originates and has come by long usage to be a synonym for 'presumed'. To speak of trusts as 'resulting in origin' ought by rights to be nonsense, since 'jumping back' is not a fact relevant to the trust's creation but something which happens under a trust which is brought into being by other facts. The explanation of the usage is this. The only trusts which arise by presumed intention do in fact 'jump back'. So the habit established itself of referring to these presumed trusts as jumping-back trusts, and no care was taken to avoid the muddle which might one day arise from the fact that other types of trust could also carry back a beneficial

---

[55] Above, p. 53.

interest to the settlor. It is always necessary nowadays to be careful to indicate whether by 'resulting trust' is meant 'resulting in pattern' or 'resulting in origin (= presumed)'.

But the picture has been made still more complicated by a development which has supervened since the narrower usage became familiar. The presumptions arose on two sets of facts: express trusts which fail to distribute the whole beneficial interest; and apparent gifts, either of the resources to buy the subject-matter in question or directly of the subject-matter itself. The view is now establishing itself that the trust arising on the first of these fact situations (where an express trust fails) does not arise by presumption at all. For it is said that the supposed presumption is in fact irrebuttable and is therefore best recognised openly as a rule of law.[56] 'Automatic' is preferred, since that word conveys the idea that when an express trust fails to dispose of the whole interest the undisposed part is carried back by operation of law, irrespective of the intention of the settlor. This re-christening of one set of presumed trusts should have the effect of expelling that set from the narrower usage of 'resulting', for, if 'automatic' is right, these trusts are resulting only in pattern; but such regroupings happen slowly. In consequence it is, for the moment, necessary to respect two shades of 'resulting in origin': first, 'resulting = presumed', and secondly, 'resulting = traditionally believed to be presumed'. The second is wider by the inclusion of those now believed to be automatic.

The trust in *Hodgson* v. *Marks* was resulting in pattern. What was it by origin? We have already excluded express and implied; and there is no question of an automatic resulting trust. For the facts which give rise to such a trust suppose that there has been a transfer upon trust to a trustee; and the function of such trusts is thus no more than to resolve a doubt as to the proper location of an undisposed time in or part of the beneficial interest. In *Hodgson* v. *Marks* the question was whether Evans was a trustee at all. Was there a trust for Mrs Hodgson? Not, where should the beneficial interest be carried to? That leaves only two categories, either presumed resulting or constructive. It is very difficult to say that it was a presumed resulting trust. The facts were indeed *prima facie* right for such a presumption. There was a transfer without consideration. It was an apparent gift in one of the two species of that genus, not

---

[56] *Re Vandervell's Trusts (No. 2)* [1974] Ch. 269, 289 f., *per* Megarry, J; reversed on appeal on a ground irrelevant to this point [1974] Ch. 308. 'Automaticness' is, however, hard to reconcile with *Re West Sussex Constabulary's Widows Fund* [1971] Ch. 1. Ultimately the question is whether equity recognizes the theoretical possibility of dereliction. Cf. A.H. Hudson, 'Is divesting abandonment possible at Common Law?' (1984) 100 *L.Q.R.* 110.

resources given to enable the apparent donee to make an acquisition, but a direct benefaction. However, statute has cancelled, or has at least thrown into doubt, that presumption in the case in which the direct transfer is of land.[57] Russell, L.J., was careful to say that the Court was 'not concerned with the debatable question whether on a voluntary transfer of land by A to a stranger B there is a presumption of resulting trust'.[58] These words are enough to show that the *Hodgson* trust did not arise by presumption. The only other way in which it could in any sense be described as resulting is as 'resulting in pattern', which would certainly not be enough to carry it out of s. 53 (1), but constructive in origin. That seems the best explanation. There was a constructive, restitutionary trust. The interest was raised by the law, without recourse to any presumption of intention, in order to effect restitution of the enrichment obtained by Evans at Mrs Hodgson's expense.

What was the factor which rendered the enrichment 'unjust' and thus called for restitution? There are two types of event identifiable in this case which do regularly, and independently of each other, lead to restitution. On the transferor's side, vitiated or qualified intent to give is one common restitution-yielding factor. On the transferee's side the same is true of free acceptance, receipt in the knowledge that the transfer is not intended as a gift and with an opportunity to reject. Either factor is capable of explaining Mrs Hodgson's right to restitution though possibly only the former explains why it should be given effect *in rem*. She had a house which was hers; she never intended that it should become his; so the law, or more accurately equity, gave it to her again in the fullest sense. The structure of the facts is identical to mistaken payment. That is, there is enrichment at the plaintiff's expense, and there is an imperfect consent to that subtraction. As Russell, L.J., said, 'the evidence is clear that the transfer was not intended to operate as a gift'.[59] Restitution in response to this type of unjust enrichment prevents the formal requirements of a statute from being used as an instrument of fraud.[60] And that is why the restitutionary doctrines are made exempt from those statutory requirements, whether with the statute's own help, as with s. 53 (2) of the *Law of Property Act, 1925*, or without it, as with secret trusts imposed behind wills.[61]

[57] *Law of Property Act, 1925*, s. 60 (3).
[58] *Hodgson* v. *Marks* [1971] 1 Ch. 892, 933.
[59] *Ibid.*
[60] 'Fraud' here is synonymous with 'unjust enrichment': what happens is that the trust ensures that an enrichment which ought to be reversed is reversed. Cf. *Rochefoucauld* v. *Boustead* [1897] 1 Ch. 196; *Bannister* v. *Bannister* [1948] 2 All E.R. 133. This 'policy' may suffice in itself to account for the restitution, cf. chapter IX, below.
[61] *McCormick* v. *Grogan* (1869) L.R. 4 H.L. 82; *Blackwell* v. *Blackwell* [1929] A.C. 318; *Ottaway* v. *Norman*, [1972] Ch. 698.

This discussion of *Hodgson* v. *Marks* enables us to consider two further cases more quickly. If the *Hodgson* trust was constructive in origin but resulting in pattern and restitutionary in effect, what should be said of trusts which are resulting in origin? Subject to one hesitation, it is clear that they are always restitutionary. If I give you shares or money or books, or if I give you the resources wherewith to buy any property, including land, there will usually be a presumption of resulting trust.[62] The presumption will not arise if you have given me value for the apparent gift or if you are in such a relationship to me that the law expects me to improve your material position.[63] And the presumption will be rebutted by your showing that I did affirmatively intend that there should be no resulting trust.

Where the presumption is not rebutted, so that the *prima facie* trust raised by operation of law becomes final, the interest which jumps back to the donor certainly does appear to effect restitution. What is the hesitation about calling it a restitutionary right? The answer is that it can be argued that the reason why the donor obtains his interest is because he intended to do so. We have seen that rights created by the intention of parties, as opposed to the direct operation of law, sometimes seem to be restitutionary but must never be so characterised, on the ground that their restitutionary content and effect is fortuitous.[64] The argument that the rights under a resulting trust are intent-based is certainly inapplicable to automatic resulting trusts, since the very reason why 'automatic' is used by them is that even flatly contrary intent is supposed not to displace them. But even in relation to those which arise by presumption it seems better to say that an unrebutted presumption does not indicate an intent to have the interest but only the absence of an intent not to have it.[65] In other words there is restitution unless there is a flatly contrary intent on the part of the person entitled. That negative role played by intent is compatible with a characterisation of these interests as restitutionary.

In one way these presumed resulting trusts are difficult to integrate in the picture. The usual rule is that the party claiming restitution must advance his reason why restitution should happen and then prove the necessary facts. But a plaintiff who can take

---

[62] *Re Vinogradoff* 1935 W.N. 68; *Fowkes* v. *Pascoe* (1875) L.R. 10 Ch. App. 343; *Pettitt* v. *Pettitt* [1970] A.C. 777; *Gissing* v. *Gissing* [1971] A.C. 886; *Cowcher* v. *Cowcher* [1972] 1 W.L.R. 425.

[63] *Re Roberts* [1946] 1 Ch. 1; *Warren* v. *Gurney* [1944] 2 All E.R. 472; *Shephard* v. *Cartwright* [1955] A.C. 431; *Tinker* v. *Tinker* [1970] P. 136.

[64] Above, p. 53.

[65] Cf. *Re Gillingham Bus Disaster Fund* [1958] 1 Ch. 300, 310, *per* Harman, J. Aff'd. (on other grounds); [1959] 1 Ch. 62. After *Vandervell* (No. 2), above, n. 56, this case would, however, be categorised as 'automatic'.

advantage of the presumption of resulting trust shifts the onus to the other side. It is as though equity cynically supposes that a transferor who receives no value for his transfer must necessarily be labouring under a mistake or some other defect of judgment. This, however, is a problem relating to the reasons for restitution, not to the description of the rights arising under resulting trusts as either being or not being restitutionary.

The conclusion of this discussion so far is that beneficial interests arising under presumed-resulting, and automatic-resulting, trusts are always restitutionary, and that, in the case of constructive trusts, it is a question to be decided from example to example since the conscience of equity may be stimulated to raise beneficial interests in pursuit of other desirable objects besides restitution. There is no need to deny the much quoted statement of Cardozo, J., to the effect that 'a constructive trust is the formula through which the conscience of equity finds expression'.[66] All that needs to be underlined is that there are many injustices to be righted besides unjust enrichment.

In one respect, however, the discussion has been somewhat oversimplified up to this point. The only situations which have been contemplated are those in which wealth which has passed from P to D is carried back again to P. What if the interest is carried forward? When a fully secret trust is enforced someone who is absolutely entitled under a will or by the rules of intestate succession is turned into a trustee for another person secretly and informally nominated by the deceased.[67] There is, at the very least, a difficulty in explaining this conclusion in terms of an express trust. For the *Wills Act, 1837*, s. 9 requires gifts which are intended to take effect on death to be made by an attested writing. But the trust can be explained, on the same lines as in *Hodgson* v. *Marks*, as raised by the operation of law to prevent the formal requirements of a statute from being used as an instrument of fraud. You receive a legacy of £10 000. You have previously been told that it is really meant for me. You are turned into a trustee for me. Everything happens as in that case, subject to this important difference: my interest now arises in such a way as to deprive you of an enrichment which, directionally, you received not from me but from the testator. Would you, therefore, have been enriched *at my expense*? A negative answer must mean that the interest is not restitutionary.

In fact the direction of the receipt is not conclusive even in relation to the subtraction sense of 'at the expense of'. It is, in other words, possible for you to receive at my expense, even though you

---

[66] *Beatty* v. *Guggenheim Exploration Co.* (1919) 225 N.Y. 380, 386.
[67] See n. 61, above.

take from the hand of a third party. You may intercept something which is on its way to me. There is then an anticipatory or interceptive subtraction from me: my wealth is reduced by what would have come to me had you not interposed yourself.[68] The essential condition for a subtraction of this kind is a finding that the wealth would certainly have accrued to me but for your intervention. A chance or hope that it would is not enough. If there was only a chance, then I cannot say you were enriched at my expense, except by showing that you were in breach of a duty not to compete with me. But in such a case I cannot say that you have been enriched by subtraction from me. To connect myself with your profit I have to rely on your wrong, that is, on your breach of duty to me.

In the case of the secret trust there is no difficulty in holding that the wealth in question would certainly have come to me but for your intervention. For the testator must necessarily have manifested a final and settled intention to that effect. The difficulty is not that no such intent has been manifested, but rather that, because of the *Wills Act*, my right cannot be said to have been created by that manifestation of intent. But the fact of that intent is none the less a part of the picture from which the court recognises the need for an active response to reverse your enrichment at my expense. There is a fine but important distinction between intent conceived as creative of rights, as in an express trust or a contract, and intent conceived as a fact which, along with others, calls for the creation of rights by operation of law. When a secret trust is enforced intent is used only in this latter role. The rights thus created are not, therefore, the creatures of intent and do qualify as restitutionary.

If this discussion is right, the conclusion must be that every express trust contains within it facts which, by alternative analysis, will account for the beneficiaries' interests without relying directly on the settlor's intent in an immediately creative role. We have been looking at cases where a requirement for formality has not been complied with, so that the settlor's expressed intent cannot be called directly in aid. Nevertheless, as we have seen, the analysis in restitution/unjust enrichment survives. Where reliance on expressed intent is not blocked, the two analyses must be concurrent. Like a contract, an express trust is not itself, *qua* express trust, capable of producing restitutionary rights. But, as when contracts fail, so when trust intent is defectively expressed, there is revealed an alternative analysis in autonomous unjust enrichment which for most of the time simply remains dormant.

Another species of restitutionary right *in rem* arises in relation to

---

[68] Below, p. 133 ff.

transactions which, whether at law or in equity, are said to confer on the recipient a voidable title. That is, property passes to him but can be recalled by the transferor so long as he acts before third party rights intervene. If you have obtained my car as the result of mis-representation or undue influence, the car for the moment is yours. But that *res* in your hands is liable to be revested in me. I for my part have a right *in rem* which for a number of reasons is difficult to name and analyse. It could be said that I have a floating, or un-crystallised, ownership which I bring down on the *res* if I act in time. But it is probably better to say that my right is a 'power *in rem*', a power to change the legal status of the *res* owned by you.

This analysis certainly reflects the holding of the Court of Appeal in *Car and Universal Finance Co. Ltd. v. Caldwell.*[69] That was a case in which the defendant's car had been obtained by fraudulent mis-representation made by a third party. The rogue thus obtained a voidable title at common law. Unable to find either the rogue or the car, Caldwell notified both the police and the motoring organisations of his intent to rescind the transaction. The Court of Appeal held that that was enough to avoid the rogue's voidable title and to revest the car in himself. The Court would thus seem to have accepted that the right which Caldwell had was a power and that the question was as to the proper mode in which that power could be exercised and the time within which it had to be done.

However, it is not completely safe to treat that case of a voidable title as a straightforward example, from the plaintiff's point of view, of a power. For that analysis runs into trouble when, as always in equity, the right is dependent on the discretion of the court.[70] For it cannot then be said cleanly and without reservation that the plaintiff holds a power, since he cannot successfully exercise it unless the court concurs. It follows that either the court itself holds the power, in which case he has only a hope or expectation of its being exercised in his favour; or, if he holds the power, some way must be found for expressing the provisional nature of any change in the status of the *res* which he can bring about. These difficulties are concealed by saying that what he has as the victim of, say, innocent misrepresentation or undue influence, is an 'equity to rescind' or a 'mere equity'. For present purposes it will probably do no damage

[69] *Car and Universal Finance Co. Ltd. v. Coaldwell* [1965] 1 Q.B. 525. The practical effect of this decision, though not the theory there relied upon, was reduced by *Newtons of Wembley Ltd. v. Williams* [1965] 1 Q.B. 560, allowing the holder to confer a good title on a third party.

[70] In the case of non-fraudulent misrepresentation, this discretion is reinforced by s. 2 (2) of the *Misrepresentation Act, 1967*, which allows the court to award damages in lieu of rescission even where the plaintiff claims that the transaction has been rescinded.

to say that such equities are in fact powers but are qualified in their exercise by being subject to the discretion of the court. These analytical puzzles need not then delay us. In the present context it is enough that such claimants undoubtedly have 'rights' in a loose sense, which rights are undoubtedly *in rem*, correlating with a liability of a *res* to be recalled. And these rights to recall are certainly restitutionary.

It is important to notice that when someone has a restitutionary right in the nature of the power *in rem*, so that he is entitled to rescind a transaction and revest ownership in himself, the exercise of that power will often give him no actual, physical remedy until he subsequently does something to defend the title thus recalled to himself. If you now own the car which was mine and I then recall that ownership to myself, the car itself does not automatically come back to me. In short the restitution effected by my rescission takes place solely on the metaphysical level, or, as we might say, in the eye of the law. A position is thus re-established exactly as though the law's initial reaction to the event had been passive, so that my title had never passed from me. There, when the transaction is void and no property passes, enrichment is, passively, anticipated: in the eye of the law nothing has to be done to prevent it. But, of course, the *res* itself physically passes out of my possession. In these cases, whether restitution is metaphysically effected or metaphysically anticipated, the plaintiff will usually then turn for his actual remedy to the tort of conversion, which yields either compensatory or restitutionary damages.[71]

Wrongs/Restitution   Wrongs do sometimes generate rights *in rem*. A famous but obsolete example is escheat *propter delictum tenentis*.[72] A feudal lord thus received back the land of his tenant when the latter was found to have committed a felony. Even now some criminal offences entail forfeiture, which is as much as to say that the Crown obtains a right *in rem* by the commission of the wrong.[73] But these rights *in rem*, though triggered by wrongs, are not restitutionary. In the diagram they belong in the square below, where 'wrongs' in the vertical column intersects with 'other responses' in

---

[71] *United Australia Ltd.* v. *Barclays Bank Ltd.* [1941] A.C. 1, see below, p. 316.

[72] Abolished by the *Forfeitures for Treason and Felony Act, 1870* (33 and 34 Vict. c.23). See K.E. Digby, *The History of the Law of Real Property*, 5th ed., Oxford, 1897, 91, 426; S.F.C. Milsom, *Historical Foundations of the Common Law*, 2nd ed., London, 1981, 109, 406.

[73] The most prominent examples arise in connexion with smuggling: see *Customs and Excise Management Act, 1979*, s. 49. Cf. *Allgemeine Gold- und Silberscheideanstalt* v. *Customs and Excise Comrs.* [1980] Q.B. 390. Cf. also *Obscene Publications Act*, s. 3 (3); *Firearms Act, 1968*, s. 52 (1).

the horizontal.[74] A smuggler who forfeits contraband cannot be said to have obtained anything at the expense of the Crown. The forfeiture reduces his wealth, but there is 'no equivalence' between the reduction and any receipt at the other's expense.

It is not at all easy to point to a case in which a wrong unequivocally creates a restitutionary right *in rem*. The effect of such a right would be to cause the wrongdoer to give up to the victim-plaintiff an enrichment gained by committing the wrong against him. It might be thought that examples of powers to rescind for fraud would suffice. But they do not, because the defendant's gain is there obtained by subtraction from the plaintiff, and the fraud *qua* wrong is almost certainly not an essential element in the explanation of the restitutionary consequences which follow. The power to rescind is sufficiently explained on the basis that there is an enrichment of the defendant by subtraction from the plaintiff, under the influence of an induced mistake made by the plaintiff, which induced mistake renders the transfer non-voluntary.[75] Equity operates in the same way even in the absence of fraud. Hence, in order to say that the fraud *qua* wrong (as opposed to *qua* mistake-inducement) is essential to the coming into being of the power to recind, it would be necessary to found the argument not on the law as a whole but on the separate and distinct operation of common law and equity. But this subject will never prosper until the analysis of the grounds for restitution—that is, of the facts which give rise to restitutionary rights, whether legal or equitable—transcends that dualism.

A clear example in this square would be provided by a case in which, (a) the defendant's gain could *only* be said to have been acquired by wrongdoing (so as to exclude any non-wrong analysis), and (b) the response of the law was unequivocally the creation of a new right *in rem* restitutionary in effect. We have seen that *Reading* v. *A.-G.*[76] provides a secure example of (a), such that the only connexion between the plaintiff and the defendant's gain is the defendant's wrong. If it could be shown that the Crown acquired a right *in rem* to Sergeant Reading's bribes, the element (b) would also be present. But it is very doubtful that there was any such right *in rem*. *Lister* v. *Stubbs*,[77] which also concerned a secret commission, appears to hold that gains acquired wrongfully from a third party do not generally become the property of the plaintiff, notwithstanding his having a personal claim against the defendant for them.

[74] Above, p. 53.
[75] Below, p. 167 ff.
[76] *Reading* v. *A.-G.* [1951] A.C. 507, above, p. 41.
[77] *Lister* v. *Stubbs* (1890) 45 Ch.D. 1., below p. 388.

However, the result is different where the gain which the wrong-doer receives from the third party is the product or yield of subject matter already owned by the plaintiff, and wrongly converted by the defendant. For example, if you have in your hands a car which is mine and you exchange that car for a motor-cycle, it seems that, at law, I acquire a right *in rem* in that motor-cycle, which is the gain accruing to you from your conversion.[78] Although the survival of my title in the car, first in your hands and now probably in those of your alienee, is merely passive and non-restitutionary, the creation of a new right in the product of the exchange is not. And the effect of that new right is undoubtedly to deprive you of the gain obtained by your wrong. The motor-cycle is not a subtraction from me. The only connexion between me and it is that you obtained it by converting my car.

A similar result is achieved in equity. When a fiduciary misapplies property entrusted to him, the beneficiary becomes entitled to the product.[79] And it now seems clear that equity will raise a right *in rem* in the product of a misapplication even in the absence of a pre-existing fiduciary relationship between the plaintiff and the person doing the misapplication. The need for this arises because the law never developed sophisticated techniques for identifying the product of wrongful exchanges. Consequently it easily happens that a plaintiff, who would be given a legal right *in rem* in the product of such an exchange, is defeated because, on the common law tests, the product is no longer identifiable. Equity goes much further. So, if the product of a misapplication is invisible at law but remains visible in equity, the plaintiff will be given an equitable proprietary right.

The condition upon which a misapplication gives rise to a proprietary right is always the same: the story of the misapplication or series of misapplications must start from the subject-matter belonging to the plaintiff either in law or equity, and nothing must have happened, except on the score of identifiability, to pass the plaintiff's title to the defendant. If at the beginning of the story the plaintiff was entitled in equity, he will become entitled in equity to the product of misapplications until the means of identification are finally defeated. If at the start he was entitled at law, he will become entitled at law to the exchange-product so long as legal means of identification are not defeated; when they are defeated he will be entitled in equity till equitable means of identification also fail.[80]

---

[78] *Taylor* v. *Plumer* (1815) 3 M. & S. 562, below, p. 359 Cf. *Theft Act, 1968*, s. 28 (1) (b).

[79] *Re Hallett's Estate* (1880) 13 Ch.D. 696 and 705, below, p. 369.

[80] Below, chapter XI.

There is considerable uncertainty as to the exact nature of the rights which the victim of a misapplication obtains when his property is sold or exchanged. Suppose that a thief steals your car, which he exchanges for a diamond, which he exchanges for a cheque, which he pays into his bank account. Owning the car, do you become owner of the diamond, then of the cheque and then, depending on whether any other money was in the account, of all of or a share of the claim against the bank? Or do you own nothing at all, except perhaps the car, until you intervene to put a stop to the chain of substitutions? If the latter, what you have is once again a power *in rem* which you can exercise in relation to the product so far as it remains identifiable from moment to moment. There is authority for both analyses. *Re Diplock* strongly favours the 'descent of ownership' approach.[81] In some contexts, however, that approach leads to awkward conclusions which are obviated if the plaintiff is conceived as having only a power to bring down a claim on such assets in the defendant's hands from day to day as can be said to represent the enrichment originally received.[82] One difficulty with the 'descent of ownership' approach is, as we shall see, that it can lead to an alarming geometric increase in the plaintiff's wealth.[83]

(iv) *Recurrent Difficulties*

The last section has shown that restitutionary rights *in rem* are never created by consent or by events in the miscellaneous fourth category. And it has attempted to give examples of restitutionary rights *in rem* created by unjust enrichment and by wrongs. The discussion has ignored two difficulties.

Anticipation and Reversal   The principle is that passive preservation of existing title is not restitution but that active creation of interests to reverse enrichment is.[84] During this discussion it has been assumed that it is easy to tell which is which. But that is not true. Take for example the presumed resulting trust arising on direct transfer of personalty without consideration. This was taken to be clear example of an active restitutionary response. The only doubt was said to be that some might argue that it owed its genesis to the intent of parties rather than to the operation of law. However, the transferor's interest under the resulting trust might also be said to exemplify anticipation rather than reversal of enrichment. For it could be

---

[81] *Re Diplock* [1948] 1 Ch. 465, 531 f, 537.
[82] *Re J. Leslie Engineers Co. Ltd.* [1976] 1 W.L.R. 292.
[83] Below, p. 92.
[84] Above, p. 15.

argued that before the transfer the transferor had both legal and equitable title, that the legal title passed and the equitable title passively stayed behind. Another way of saying the same thing would be to assert that gratuitous transfer is a situation in which, according to the common law, property does pass but in which, according to equity, it does not. Both forms of words see the transferor as retaining an interest which he had before the event in question. The contrary picture, on which the earlier discussion was based, has the transferor receiving an interest which he never had before, an interest newly created with restitutionary purpose and effect. Before the transfer his ownership was legal, not legal and equitable. After the transfer it was equitable, a new interest created in response to the transferee's receipt.

This second picture, where there is an active reversal, is truer to history. In the days of institutional separation between law and equity, the courts of equity had nothing to say at all about the holding of property till some event occurred which attracted their jurisdiction. The notion of a legal owner as having, even before such an event, concurrent legal and equitable title would have been nonsense. Transfer to a trustee created an equitable interest; it did not split legal and equitable interests previously concurrent in the transferor. Yet it can reasonably be said that history should not be decisive in such a matter and, further, that the boundaries of the law of restitution should not be fixed on the basis of assertions which, once deprived of their historical support, are not more than metaphysical speculations. Someone who prefers the passive analysis of the presumed resulting trust or the automatic resulting trust or of a constructive trust in the *Hodgson* pattern, is not likely to fall into deep error in relation to any practical question. But he will be driven to adopt a narrower view of the content of the law of restitution. For example, if I give shares to you without any consideration and a resulting trust arises in my favour by presumption, someone who favours the passive analysis will say that what has happened is that my legal interest in the shares has passed but that my equitable interest has remained behind. Then, applying the rule that interests *in rem* must be examined at the moment of their creation in order to decide whether they are restitutionary or not, he will ask himself when I acquired that equitable beneficial interest. And his answer will be that I acquired it, with or behind the legal interest which I have now lost, at the moment when I originally bought the shares, either from the company or from a previous shareholder. Then, since a right conceded by consent is never restitutionary, he will conclude that, at that moment, I obtained a non-restitutionary right *in rem*, which was later passively preserved for me despite the abortive transfer to you. Hence, he will see nothing restitutionary in the entire story. Legal ownership has passed from me to you, but your enrichment at my expense has been passively anticipated.

There is no cure for this. We can achieve conceptual certainty in the *McPhail* v. *Doulton*[85] sense by saying that restitutionary rights *in rem* are those which are created directly in response to an enrichment received and which then have the effect of reversing that enrichment in favour of the person at whose expense it was received. But we may never be able to agree as to which ones do and which ones do not qualify for membership of this class. Nor is this a case in which difficulties in applying the test can be resolved by an evidential onus. 'Deemed out till proved in' is no way to solve such a problem. It only works when there are adversaries, one of whom can be given an artificial advantage.

Concept and Convenience The other difficulty is to state the rôle of the kind of discussion conducted in these pages. There is of course a sense in which it does not matter whether a given right *in rem* is or is not restitutionary, since what is important to a plaintiff is that the right is recognised, not how commentators describe it. Moreover no legal subject can engage in unending introspection as to its proper content, especially if its evolution of a pure concept of itself is destined in the end to stumble on evidential uncertainty. At this point something must, therefore, be said to show what benefit the exercise is supposed to yield. The key is a sensible balance between conceptual purity and convenience. The rôle of the former is to eliminate intellectual doubts as to whether a subject has any identity independent of one writer's choices. If there is a test which can in theory be applied to any right *in rem* to say whether it is or is not restitutionary, then we know that the law of restitution does not make merely random borrowings from the law of property. That gain in intellectual stability is not lost merely because the questions which the theoretical test tells us to apply are difficult to answer in any particular case. On the other hand the rôle of the concept which thus secures the subject's objective identity is not to determine once and for all what is to be included in or omitted from any particular treatment of the law of restitution. Convenience must to some extent control those decisions.

Two examples will show how convenience can moderate conceptual purity without sacrificing the sense of this subject's identity. First, it has been maintained here that interests under resulting trusts

[85] *McPhail* v. *Doulton* [1971] A.C. 424.

are restitutionary. But the fact that resulting trusts are fully discussed in works on trusts provides a perfectly satisfactory reason of convenience for not dealing with them in detail in a book on restitution, so long only as the exclusion is clearly attributed to convenience and not to an undisclosed conceptual barrier. Secondly, matter may be included though strictly not restitutionary. *Bowmakers Ltd.* v. *Barnet Instruments Ltd.*[86] does find a place in *Goff and Jones.*[87] It was a case in which the plaintiffs had parted with machine tools to the defendants under an illegal contract of hire purchase. When the defendants stopped paying for the tools and, having sold some, refused to deliver up the rest, the Court of Appeal allowed the plaintiffs to recover damages for conversion notwithstanding the illegality. Clearly this is not an example of restitution. The survival of the plaintiffs' title to the machine tools exemplifies the mechanism against unjust enrichment which we have called 'anticipation' rather than 'reversal'.[88] And, that title having survived, the claim was for the conversion of the plaintiffs' goods. So it was formally an action in tort for compensatory damages, based ultimately on the plaintiffs' pre-existing, and therefore non-restitutionary, right *in rem*. Nevertheless, it would obviously be inconvenient to omit reference to the *Bowmaker* type of claim from any extended discussion of the impact of illegality on restitution. The conceptual identity of this subject, once established, is not threatened by that species of borrowing.

It is fortunate that these recurrent difficulties to some extent cancel each other out. The fact that conceptual certainty defends the subject's theoretical independence, while convenience controls the matter actually expounded under its name, means that the evidential uncertainty encountered in relation to rights *in rem* is not intolerable. Considerations of convenience can determine what is actually done about the doubtful matter. Thus one person will say that interests under resulting trusts are omitted because they do not pass the conceptual test which would allow them in, while another will say that conceptually they are included but on grounds of convenience they are omitted.

3. RESTITUTION IN CONTEXTUAL CATEGORIES

Many of the categories in which law is now learned have no unity of concept or event. Education law, labour law, company law, air law,

---

[86] *Bowmakers Ltd.* v. *Barnet Instruments Ltd.* [1945] K.B. 65.

[87] At 325 ff.

[88] The case treats the title as having survivied but it is probably now necessary to say that it had to be recalled: see below, p. 303.

family law, and so on. There is nothing wrong with categories of that kind. They tell you all the law there is about the particular aspect of life which interests you. It is the function and virtue of these contextual categories that they collect together bits and pieces which are kept apart in other ways of dividing up the law. So, for example, in labour law or company law you expect to come across relevant pieces of contract, tort, crime and so on. And obviously the relationship between contextual categories and the response 'restitution' or the event 'unjust enrichment' will be similar. That is, you will come across bits of restitution here and there in very many contextual categories. Thus, if you study 'The Effects of War' you will come in the end to something on restitution after frustration of contracts; and in company law treatment of the doctrine of *ultra vires* leads into some restitutionary problems of now diminishing practical importance. There is no need to add more examples.

This kind of relationship is easy to grasp. It would hardly need mentioning if it were not for one important fact. If the nature of the different types of category is not borne in mind, the unity of the law of restitution can seem to be cast into doubt by its tendency to crop up in different places. And it still needs defending against such dangers, whereas older the more familiar subjects are safe enough. Only recently Professor Atiyah has used this argument against the unity and independence of unjust enrichment: 'In contract, in tort, in family law, in the law of property, in company law, the same development has been occurring. The various cases show little signs of coming together to cohere into one new body of law, and this may be just as well.'[89] We have already explained the relationship between unjust enrichment and three of these. The other two, family and company law, are contextual categories, almost certain to dip into categories belonging to other series. Bats are none the less one species because they crop up also under insectivore, nocturnal, and mammal.

Unjust enrichment makes no claim to be independent of every conceivable kind of legal category. It does, however, claim an independent place in a series of causative events which includes consent and wrongs. The four headings 'consent, wrongs, unjust enrichment and other events' do constitute an analytically distinct and comprehensive series. It is not necessarily the best and most efficient series that a legal system can aspire to—Austin, for one, would have wanted it rearranged to allow for the distinction between primary and secondary[90]—but it is undoubtedly the series to which history has brought the modern common law.

[89] P.S. Atiyah, *The Rise and Fall of Freedom of Contract*, Oxford, 1979, 768.
[90] Above, p. 29.

III

TECHNIQUES AND MEASURES

MEASURES of recovery are what matter to a plaintiff. How much will he get? Techniques by contrast are inside lawyers' heads. By 'techniques of restitution' I mean to denote all the verbal apparatus which lawyers use to think their way from the events which have happened to the measure of recovery to which the plaintiff is entitled. There is too much of it. Action for money had and received, *quantum meruit, quantum valebat,* rescission, account, tracing, personal claims, proprietary claims. Then to that list must be added those obscure terms which have an unstable reference, hovering between event and technique: quasi-contract, constructive trust, and subrogation. Even with these additions the list could be made longer, but there is no point. History is responsible for this too rich growth. Some contributions come from the forms of action at common law, some from equity and some from analytical jurisprudence. Not only as listed here but also as used in the cases, the vocabulary pays little regard to the difference between species and genus. Nor, at any one level, to the danger of reduplication. The apparatus is various and complex. But it is not clear what you get out of it. When you look for learning about measures of restitution you hardly find anything at all. Yet measures are the starting point from which to reach a simpler and more orderly arrangement. The principle to be borne in mind in this chapter takes its name from the fourteenth-century English philosopher, William of Occam: 'It is vain to do with more what can be done with fewer'; or, 'Entities are not to be multiplied without necessity.' That is Occam's razor.[1]

Whatever species may be discoverable beneath this dichotomy, there are generically only two measures of restitution. What the defendant received,[2] and what the defendant has left. There may be better names, but one can manage conveniently enough with 'value received' and 'value surviving'. The first measure, 'value received',

---

[1] Bertrand Russell, *History of Western Philosophy,* 2nd ed., London, 1961, 462–463.

[2] This measure undoubtedly has sub-forms. Just as there are different rules of remoteness controlling the amount actually recoverable under the head of compensation, so, in relation to restitution, rules of remoteness of gain control the amount recoverable as 'value received'. Hence under that general heading the actual amount recoverable may vary from one cause for restitution to another. E.g. if you use my car to earn hire from tourists the 'value received' might be said to be either the user itself or the sums received from the tourists, the choice being a matter for tests of remoteness: further discussion, below, p. 351 ff.

is much the more common; the other is exceptional—it has a chapter to itself towards the end of this book. The phrases 'what he has left' and 'value surviving' are misleading in one respect. They imply a reduction, but there may be an increase. Things can go up in value, as for instance shares on a rising market, and they can grow, as calves into cows. Once one begins to trace one thing into its product or replacement one encounters much more complex cases in which 'what he has left' turns out to be more than 'what he received'.[3] All the same, an increase is unusual. More often the value surviving is less than the value received.

The crucial difference between the two measures is that a plaintiff who claims the value received is not interested in what happened after the receipt. The defendant may have spent, lost, eaten or destroyed the enrichment. Or he may have invested it with huge success or otherwise caused it to increase. Either way, from the plaintiff's point of view the story after the receipt is irrelevant. But that is not to say that the rest of the story will never have any bearing on a claim in this measure. Some part of it may serve to found a defence.

This can be illustrated uncontroversially from an imaginary example. A given jurisdiction might allow a defence of charitable donation: you would not have to repay a mistaken payment if, and so far as, you had given the money to charity. Suppose then that in that jurisdiction P mistakenly paid D £1000, and D then donated £500 to a charity. P claims his £1000, and D relies on what happened afterwards, his payment to the charity.

Here P's claim is still based on the measure 'value received', albeit subject to reduction by virtue of the specific defence available to D. When D successfully raises his defence of charitable donation, P's claim will be cut down to £500. The important point is that it is not cut down simply because D no longer has the money which he received. He may well no longer have the other £500 either, but he has to repay that whether he has it or not. The reason that P's claim is reduced is simply that his *prima facie* right to recover the full value received by D here encounters a specific defence maintainable by D, not just that he spent it but that he spent it in a particular way. This imaginary example is a special case of the defence of 'change of position' which now occupies an uncertain status in English law. The importance of the example, fictitious though it is, is that it illustrates the proposition that a defence of change of position does not have the effect of changing all claims to restitution

---

[3] E.g., *Re Tilley's Will Trusts* [1967] Ch. 1179.

in the first measure into claims restricted to the second measure, namely what the defendant has left in his hands.

By contrast claims to 'value surviving' are those in which the plaintiff himself identifies and demands that enrichment in the defendant's hands which is the remnant of, or represents, what was originally received. In the imaginary example above, P, finding his claim to the value received (£1000) cut down to £500 by the defence of charitable donation, might, if the rules of his jurisdiction allowed, switch to a claim for value surviving. For example, with the other £500 D might have bought a watercolour, now valued at £750. Claiming the watercolour or its value, P would be saying, by way of defining the measure of his demand, 'That is what you now have of the enrichment originally received at my expense.' A claim measured by surviving value obliges the plaintiff to point to what the defendant still has left. He cannot stop at some favourable mid-point. Suppose that D did buy the watercolour and that it did rise in value to £750 but that he then sold it and spent the profits on a car which is now worth £200. Now that car valued at £200 is all that D has left of his original receipt. Unless on exceptional facts, P's only sensible recourse is therefore his claim to the £1000 received, reduced by the special defence to £500.

1. TECHNIQUES FOR THE FIRST MEASURE OF RESTITUTION

Proprietary claims (rights *in rem*) are ruled out at once. For claims to 'value received' ignore what happened after the receipt. And proprietary claims cannot do so. Their exigibility depends precisely on the identification of a *res* in the hands of the defendant. Proprietary claims are, therefore, by nature tied to the other measure, value surviving. But it must instantly be said that that proposition cannot be turned round. That is, nothing entitles one to say that claims to value surviving must be *in rem*.

It is the category of personal claims (*in personam*) whose nature is to be indifferent, or more accurately to be capable of indifference, to the fate of, or the location of, the wealth to which they relate. That coincides exactly with the first measure of restitution, ignoring what happened after the receipt. So restitution in the measure 'value received' is always by means of rights *in personam*. One might equally say by personal rights, which is synonymous English, or by obligations, which are correlative. The choice in any sentence between 'right' and 'obligation' is a matter of convenience and style, according to the context. It can never make any difference of substance. Once it has been said that the technique by which restitution in the measure 'value received' is effected is invariably the imposition of obligations, the only classification of any importance is one which says that such obligations are either legal or equitable and may differ in content, according as the value which the defendant must pay is either a known and fixed sum or else a sum to be ascertained by a reasonable valuation or by the taking of an account.

To this short classification nothing whatever is added by continuing to use the old language of the forms of action or, more accurately, of the different counts within the action of *assumpsit*, for money had and received, money paid, *quantum meruit* (as much as he deserved) and *quantum valebat* (as much as it was worth). There is only one surviving purpose in mastering those terms. The old cases cannot be understood without them. And it is important that they should be understood. But to go on using their language is merely perverse. If a mistaken payment gives rise to an obligation to repay and the words 'obligation to repay' are capable of being understood by everyone, nothing is gained by substituting for them 'an action for money had and received'. The day is not far off when only specialists in legal history will have a clear idea of the meaning in this context either of the word 'action' or of the phrase 'money had and received'. The rest of us use them as a kind of ancient mumbo jumbo, both excusing and at the same time perpetuating the absence of any clear modern analysis of what we mean. It would be even worse if we found ourselves saying that the recipient of such a payment was liable to account as a constructive receiver: we do not. If we manage to avoid saying that he is liable to an action for money had and received, we only say quite simply that he is under an obligation to repay. Yet it is important to dwell on the contrast, because it contains the clearest possible lesson for another set of mystifying words. In equity we do still speak of defendants as being 'accountable as constructive trustees'.

In the sixteenth century—it is not necessary to go back further[4]— the common law's action of account lay against, amongst others, 'receivers of money to my use (i.e. on my behalf)'. The object of the action was not immediately the payment of money but the taking of an account to determine what sum was due. After some hesitation the law accepted that, if you knew what sum was due from

[4] See S.F.C. Milsom, *Historical Foundations of the Common* Law, 2nd. ed., London, 1981, 275–282; A.W.B. Simpson, *A History of the Common Law of Contract*, Oxford, 1975, 177–185.

your receiver, and did not need to take an account in order to ascertain it, you could go straight to the action of debt.[5] So, if the sum to be paid was known, debt would lie against a receiver of money to my use on the ground that he was liable to account, the facts being such that the actual taking of the account was unnecessary. Typically and naturally the receiver of money to my use was a man appointed to that task by me, like my rent-collector. But circumstances other than appointment by me could turn a man into a receiver of money to my use. Simplest of all was the case in which a third party gave him money for me. Unappointed by me, he would at least know that he received not on his own but on my behalf, to my use, not to his own. But even in his case Fitzherbert thought he was not a real, but a deemed or constructive, receiver. Fitzherbert did not use those words. He merely said that on such facts you could have an account against one as a receiver where he was not your receiver.[6] The thought is the same: the 'receiver who is not a receiver' is a constructive or deemed receiver.

Two further developments happened. First, after *Slade's Case*, (1602),[7] all of debt was poured into *assumpsit*, and with it the count in debt against receivers of money to the plaintiff's use. So *indebitatus assumpsit* (i.e. the action on a promise, brought on debt facts) lay against those who, naturally or constructively, had become receivers of money to my use. That development produced the count 'for money had and received to the plaintiff's use'.[8] Secondly, the circumstances which would make a man a constructive receiver to the plaintiff's use were multiplied so that, whenever the facts were such that the law held that a man ought to give up a payment, he was said, whatever his actual intention, to have received on behalf of the plaintiff. These constructive receivers were not only unappointed but also unaware of receiving other than to their own use. We have seen the result of this extension in the generalisation achieved in *Moses* v. *Macferlan* (1760):

[5] *Core's Case* (1537) Dyer, 20.

[6] *New Natura Brevium, s.v.* 'Accompt' (in 7th ed., 1730, p. 266).

[7] *Slade's Case* (1962) 4 Coke Rep. 91; above, p. 35 f.

[8] The count for money had and received was a set of words (a declaration) containing a winning proposition which the plaintiff advanced and aimed to substantiate by later adducing sufficient facts. In its developed form it went like this (shorn of much superfluous verbiage): 'whereas the defendant was indebted to the plaintiff in £100 of lawful money for so much money by the defendant had and received to the plaintiff's use, and, being so indebted, the defendant, in consideration thereof, afterwards promised (*assumpsit*) to pay the plaintiff whenever he should be thereto requested, yet the defendant, not regarding his promise but fraudulently intending to deceive the plaintiff, hath not paid, to the plaintiff's damage.' For the full version, see *Stephen on Pleading*, 3rd ed., London, 1827, 312.

[The action for money had and received] lies for money paid by mistake; or upon a consideration which happens to fail; or for money got through imposition (express or implied); or extortion; or oppression; or an undue advantage taken of the plaintiff's situation, contrary to the laws made for the protection of persons under those circumstances. In one word, the gist of this kind of action is that the defendant, upon the circumstances of the case, is obliged by the ties of natural justice and equity to refund the money.[9]

In this generalisation the old action of account not only lived on but actually expanded within the confines of *indebitatus assumpsit*. The idea of the constructive receiver, the receiver who was not a receiver, had provided the growth-point.

In all the circumstances rehearsed by Lord Mansfield the defendant was under an obligation to pay, but he was under that obligation because he was liable to account, and he was liable to account because he was, constructively, a receiver of money to the plaintiff's use. Lord Mansfield shows that, in his view, a man became accountable as a constructive receiver in quite specific sets of circumstances, but the link between those different sets of facts was that, at a dangerously high level of abstraction, they all created an obligation to pay based on 'natural justice and equity'.[10] Nowadays, therefore, when we say that a man is liable for money had and received, the words 'had and' should be regarded as mere surplusage. More important are the words which are omitted from the customary abbreviation, 'to the plaintiff's use'. We mean that the defendant has received money to our use (i.e. 'on our behalf', or 'for us'), with the effect of putting himself under an obligation to pay a like sum to us, and we imply that the reason why he must be held to have received not on his own behalf but on ours is that the receipt happened in one of those sets of circumstances in which the common law holds that restitution ought to happen, the *ultimate* explanation of the efficacy of all those sets of circumstances being, not agreement, but justice: it would create a strong sense of grievance if such 'receivers to our use' were allowed to retain the enrichment.

At common law we do not talk of defendants being liable to account as constructive receivers. We can reconstruct the history which that formula condenses. But we recognise that it would be comical, clumsy and misleading to acknowledge the history in every

---

[9] *Moses v. Macferlan* (1760) 2 Burr. 1005, 1012.

[10] These words relate back to Roman law which also was driven to explain the non-contractual grounds of indebtedness by direct reference to what is fair and good: D.12.6 (*De Condictione Indebiti*) 66 (Papinian): 'This *condictio*, brought in *ex bono et aequo*, has the rôle of recalling that which one holds from another without any justifying basis.' Cf. D.12.6. 14 (Pomponius). '*Equity*' is the Latin '*aequitas*', not chancery jurisdiction.

utterance. Yet in equity the natural instinct for simple and honest language has failed to emancipate itself from the old vocabulary. The reason is intelligible even if the language is not. Changing the words puts you in dreadful risk of error. You cannot do it unless you are sure that you can perceive the entities beneath the names, and it is rash to be sure. That is the reason for setting out the story of the constructive receiver. It serves to make plain that 'liability to account as a constructive receiver' would be a senseless substitution for 'obligation to pay'. And from there one can more confidently say the same for the equitable equivalent.

In equity no less than at law the word 'account' should never be used as a synonym for 'pay'. 'Account' refers only to the preliminary and often unnecessary stage of ascertaining an amount due to be paid. Entities multiply, and with them mysteries, if it is not so confined. Then, if a man is under an obligation to pay (whether or not the sum must be ascertained by the taking of an account), nothing of substance can be added by the words 'as a constructive trustee'. Suppose three cases; in the first a company director puts himself in a position in which pursuit of his own interest might lead him to sacrifice the interest of the company. In that position he nevertheless decides to take for himself the opportunity which he sees in view.[11] In the second a bank receives from trustees, and then subsequently pays out, at their order, a sum of money which it knows to be a misapplication of trust funds.[12] In the third executors of a will mistake the law and pay out to a legatee a legacy which turns out to have been void.[13] In each of these three cases there is a question whether the director, the bank or the legatee comes under an equitable obligation to make restitution in the measure of value received, irrespective of the question whether they still retain anything of, or representing, what they received. We are not at the moment concerned with any other measure. Is there such an obligation or not? The words 'as a constructive trustee' cannot help the question or the answer. If you were to conclude that these three recipients were constructive trustees you would thereby have decided that they must repay, but the facts which would underlie your conclusion would be the very same as would allow you to proceed directly to the imposition of the obligation. Just as at law you can go from the fact of mistaken payment straight to the

---

[11] E.g. *Regal (Hastings) Ltd.* v. *Gulliver* [1942] 1 All E.R. 378.
[12] E.g. *Rowlandson* v. *National Westminster Bank* [1978] 1 W.L.R. 798; cf. *Selangor United Rubber Estates Ltd.* v. *Cradock* (No. 3) [1968] 1 W.L.R. 1555.
[13] E.g. *Re Diplock* [1948] 1 Ch. 465.

restitutionary obligation without digressing to constructive receivership, so also in imposing restitutionary obligations in equity it is
unnecessary to affirm the constructive trusteeship. Between the
causative event and the measure of the restitutionary response
'value received', there is room for only one technique: obligation to
pay. An account is ancillary. Constructive trusteeship is surplusage.
Occam's maxim rightly says that entities which are superfluous
should be eliminated.

Sometimes equity makes a different detour between the facts and
the conclusion in favour of restitution. The phrase 'constructive
fiduciary relationship' is not used, but it might well be. What
happens is this. The court lacks sufficient authority for basing the
obligation directly on the facts but has authority for recognising the
obligation in the case of a breach of fiduciary duty. It therefore
characterises the relationship between the parties as fiduciary without regard to the question whether it has any genuine similarity to
the relationship between trustee and beneficiary. It is easier, chiefly
because the word 'fiduciary' is rare and somewhat obscure, to extend
the number of fiduciary relationships than it is to justify the new
obligation in terms of the actual facts on which it is based. It may
be that judges under pressure can see no other way to avoid giving
the impression of judicial legislation. If so, other lawyers must subsequently look behind the disguise. The phenomenon of the denatured
or constructive fiduciary relationship is found in relation to both
measures of restitution.[14]

The conclusion in relation to 'value received' is that there is only
one technique of restitution: the obligation to pay, correlating with
a right *in personam*, a right in the plaintiff that he should be paid.
An 'account' is a preliminary procedure designed to establish what
value was received. An account is only necessary when the amount
to be paid is in doubt, typically because a series of transactions has
to be unpicked. The language of the forms of action, money had and
received, *quantum valebat* and so on, refers only to the sets of words
in which claims based on this type of obligation where formerly
expresssed. In equity the assertion that someone is 'accountable as
a constructive trustee' means, in the absence of a need to take an
account, only that he is under an obligation to pay, and, if there is
a need to discover the sum by taking an account, that he is under an
obligation to pay that sum after the account has been taken.

---

[14] *Sinclair* v. *Brougham* [1914] A.C. 398, is the classic example in relation to the second
measure of restitution, see below, p. 381 f. For the first measure, see *English* v. *Dedham Vale
Properties Ltd.* [1978] 1 W.L.R. 93.

2. TECHNIQUES FOR THE SECOND MEASURE
OF RESTITUTION

The first question is whether any value does survive. Has he got anything left? Obviously there is an exercise of identification which has to be conducted before there can be any question of restitution in this measure. That exercise is not properly a technique of restitution but a necessary preliminary. Rather as on some facts the taking of an account is a procedure ancillary to restitution in the other measure, so identification is ancillary to this one.

The business of identification is not easy. There are choices to be made. A jurisdiction might insist on a strict and literal identifiability. If you received a cake, ate half of it and swapped the other half for a packet of biscuits, the conclusion would then be that you had nothing left. The strict test would be whether you had any cake left, the biscuits would not count. Another jurisdiction might be willing to accept clean substitutions. It would then say that what you had left of the cake was the packet of biscuits, on the ground that you gave the cake and nothing but the cake to get the biscuits. The words 'nothing but' indicate a clean substitution. Nothing else was added into the exchange. Suppose that we now take the story further. It is a packet of water biscuits, the store of water biscuits which you keep in your tin is running low, so you open the new packet and empty it in. Then when there are only five biscuits left you swap those five biscuits and a piece of cheese for half a dozen eggs. There has been a mixture now, followed by an impure substitution. But all the same it is not nonsense to say that some of the value of the cake survives in the half a dozen eggs.

To carry identification as far as this, you cannot work by the light of nature, on the basis of instinct or impression. You have to devise rules, often highly artificial, to cope with mixtures and impure substitutions. For example, there is no natural answer to the question whether the last five water biscuits in the tin came from the new packet which you exchanged for the cake or from the diminishing store in the tin, to which you added the new supply. There is no way of telling one water biscuit from another, and it certainly is not true to assert that older biscuits are necessarily eaten first. Nevertheless, it would be possible to introduce a rule according to which the biscuits would be deemed to be eaten in the order in which they were put into the tin. With the aid of that rule identification would become possible, for, on these facts, the last five biscuits must then have come from the new packet. The extreme artificiality of this exercise quickly becomes an argument for not attempting to prolong the indentifiability of enrichments received. No legal system would do it but for the fact that there is a strong pressure the other way. Money loses its natural indentity very easily, so that if you were not prepared to pursue it through mixtures you would be able to do nothing at all, or very little, by way of restitution in this second measure. And money is the commonest case. So, rather than do nothing at all, English law, especially in equity, has preferred to embrace the artificiality. Identification of surviving enrichment is not done by the light of nature. It is done artificially by rules.

The name given to the complex of rules which constitute the machinery of identification is 'tracing'. Tracing tells you whether your defendant has in his hands anything in which the value of his original enrichment still survives. However, it is not only inconvenient but also incorrect on principle and authority to suppose that it can tell you what restitutionary technique will be applicable, if any, to the wealth into which the surviving value is traced. This is not an easy proposition. It will be considered more fully in the chapter devoted to the second measure of restitution.[15]

Let it be supposed that tracing has been completed and has shown that the defendant does still hold some asset in which the value originally received continues to survive. The asset may be of any type: money, a car, a house, a bank account (i.e. a claim *in personam* against a bank), a share (a bundle of rights *in personam* against a company with a potentiality for becoming, in certain events, rights *in rem* against the company's assets). And there is at least one example of a negative asset: a debt discharged. That is, if you pay me money and I use it to discharge my overdraft or my mortgage, my enrichment survives in my release from these burdens. As the asset may be of various different kinds so also it may represent the original enrichment in varying extents, depending on what mixtures and substitutions have happened. Thus my car or my shares may wholly represent the money which you paid to me, as where I received £10 000 and, even before I had reached the bank with those notes, I used half of them to buy the car and half to buy the shares. Or the asset may represent the original enrichment only as to some fractional proportion, as where I used your notes together with some of my own to buy a house, say £10 000 of yours and £20 000 of mine.

Once the value surviving has been identified, the next question is

---

[15] See below, pp. 358 ff.

whether any restitutionary technique can be used. In this chapter we are not concerned with trying to say on which facts which technique is available. Only with the range of possibilities. What restitutionary techniques are in principle available in respect of 'value surviving'?

All restitutionary proprietary claims (rights *in rem*) are tied to this second measure. This follows from the nature of all rights *in rem*: they can be exacted only in respect of something identified as existing in the defendant's hands. But we will come to proprietary rights in a moment. For it is false to suppose, though it often is supposed, that claims *in personam* (obligations) have no role here. They must have, and the cases just allow one to assert that observably they do have, an important part to play. Few points are more in need of clear demonstration.

(i) *Personal claims and the second measure of restitution*

I pay you £5000, you spend £2000 on high living and use the remaining £3000 to buy a second-hand car, now worth £1500. The first kind of claim to come to mind will be in the first measure, for the £5000 originally received. Leaving that out of consideration, there are three questions. (a) Is it theoretically possible to have a personal claim to the value of the car? (b) What would be the characteristics of such a claim? (c) What is the need for it?

(a) *Is it possible?*

There is no theoretical obstacle. You cannot deduce from the general nature of personal claims that if their subject matter abates they will abate with it. But that does not mean that the law relating to a particular event cannot tie a particular personal claim to the fluctuating value of a particular thing. For example, there would be nothing wrong with a promise on these lines: 'Whatever the market value of these shares shall be on the day of your demand, so much will I pay you.' The personal claim generated by that promise would take its value from the shares and would be extinguished with them. In the same way there is no theoretical objection to a non-promissory personal claim measured by the value of particular subject-matter, here a car.

(b) *What would be the characteristics of such a claim?*

The most important to emphasise is that the car would remain yours. I would have no interest in it, only a claim against you. The now routine correlatives would apply: I would have a right *in personam* that you should give me the value of the car, and you would be under an exactly corresponding obligation.

(c) *What is the need for it?*

There are a number of different reasons why a plaintiff may go for 'value surviving' rather than 'value received'. One of them is that the normal claim measured by value received may be unavailable by reason of some defence or bar. The obstacle to 'value received' may on inspection not apply to 'value surviving'. So the plaintiff may be happy to accept second best, recovering half a loaf rather than no bread. In *Sinclair* v. *Brougham*[16] the claim in the first measure was obstructed by the doctrine of *ultra vires* as it used to operate in relation to companies. *Ultra vires* lenders to the company could not recover in contract, and they could not have restitution in the first measure because that would have given them exactly the same amount and would have stultified the doctrine of *ultra vires*. But the House of Lords held that they could have restitution in the second measure, since to return to them that which the defendant identifiably still retained of the original receipt would not flatly contradict the *ultra vires* rule. Thus, if, in the example of the car, the facts revealed a similar obstacle to my claim in the first measure, I might well be anxious to turn from the £5000 which you received to the value of £1500 which you still hold.

Suppose that the story behind this car worth £1500 is this: the £5000 which I paid you was a loan, but in making the loan I omitted certain statutory formalities and thus rendered the loan invalid, cutting off my claim to the £5000 whether under the contract or under any other alternative analysis.[17] What I want to say now is that, even although recovery of £5000 under any theory would make nonsense of the statute, yet the same may not be true of recovery of £1500, the value which you happen to have left. This is a sensible argument. There is at the lowest a real possibility that the policy behind the impediment to the one claim may not catch the other. It is, to take another example, not at all clear that the absolute nullity of a loan to a minor should allow him to retain even the enrichment which survives in his hands when the lender claims.

Yet if it were true that restitution of surviving enrichment could only be effected by rights *in rem*, this line of argument would always fail for an irrelevant collateral reason. Rights *in rem* give priority over unsecured creditors. In the example of the car my reason for

[16] *Sinclair* v. *Brougham* [1914] A.C. 398, below, p. 396 f.
[17] Cf. the facts of *Orakpo* v. *Manson Investments Ltd.* [1977] 1 W.L.R. 855.

claiming the surviving value has nothing to do with trying to gain such priority. It is not said that you are insolvent. I am merely driven down to the £1500 because I have no claim to the £5000. Yet any court which believes or assumes that I cannot get the £1500 without being accorded a beneficial or a security interest in the car will reject my argument on the ground, irrelevant in this particular case, that, if there were a competition against an insolvent, I who started as an unsecured and invalid lender would end as a secured creditor in a better position than unsecured claimants unaffected by an invalidity. If and only if my claim can be purely *in personam*, giving me no interest in the car itself, will I be able to keep it clear of that danger. If my claim is *in rem* I must lose, lest others in my position win too much.

In brief the need for personal claims to surviving enrichment is this: without them every attempt to obtain restitution in this second measure will be decided as though it were an attempt to obtain a questionable priority over other creditors. This will be so even though neither the facts of the case nor the motives of the plaintiff have anything to do with an insolvency.

After these three, there is of course a fourth question: Do the cases support the existence of a personal right in this measure? In the later chapter on the second measure of restitution I shall argue that they do, though frailly. But even if they did not there is room for a perfectly respectable and non-legislative argument in its support, based partly on the gap which would exist without it and partly on the courts' omission to give direct consideration to it. If necessary one would for the moment have recourse to the etymologist's asterisk, the sign for a form which must exist but has not yet been found.

(ii) *Proprietary Claims and the Second Measure of Restitution*

We have already seen what defines a right *in rem* as restitutionary. All those that qualify operate in this second measure. They give the plaintiff the enrichment which the defendant still holds. The question at this point is: What vocabulary is necessary in order sufficiently to describe restitutionary rights *in rem*? Bearing in mind the need not to multiply entities, you can put the same question in this way: What is the minimum or most economical classification of such rights?

Such restitutionary rights *in rem* may be legal or equitable. They are usually equitable. And they may constitute either ordinary beneficial interests or security interests. For example, if you buy a house with money contributed by me you may, in appropriate circumstances, hold the fee simple for me;[18] and if you stand by and watch me mistakenly building on your land, equity may give me a lien on the land for my expenditure.[19] These are straightforward examples, the one of an equitable beneficial interest, the other of an equitable security interest.

Where the restitutionary right *in rem* is equitable and beneficial it follows *ex hypothesi* that legal title will be in one person, D, and equitable title will be in another, P. That is to say, there will be a trust: D will hold as trustee for P. The word 'trust' there denotes nothing but the division of legal and equitable title. In particular, it does not indicate a reposition of trust or confidence in D by any settlor, S. For if the division of legal and equitable ownership were attributable to an intentional declaration of trust, express or implied, by some S, the equitable beneficial interest could not be described as restitutionary. That follows from the proposition that restitutionary rights are never generated by consent: in and of itself (i.e. without looking for an alternative analysis latent in the same facts) an express or genuinely implied trust does not create restitutionary interests. Therefore, to regroup: where a restitutionary right *in rem* is equitable and beneficial there will be a trust, and that trust analysed from the point of view of its creation will not be express or implied. Its causative event may be an unjust enrichment or a wrong. That follows from the earlier discussion. In the terms of division of trusts in s. 53 of the *Law of Property Act, 1925*, it will always be resulting or constructive.

The last proposition cannot be turned round. Although, subject to the hesitations considered earlier, the interests under resulting trusts are always restitutionary, the interests under constructive trusts are not. There are many cases where equitable interests arise *ipso iure* (thus forming a constructive trust) but cannot be said to effect restitution of an enrichment received by D, made trustee, either at the expense of or by doing wrong to P, now beneficiary. So, if D makes a contract in writing for valuable consideration to convey Blackacre to P, under the doctrine in *Walsh* v. *Lonsdale*[20] D *ipso iure* becomes trustee for P. Yet he has not received Blackacre from P in any sense at all. And if D encourages P to build on his land and the court later says that P has acquired thereby an equitable fee

[18] On resulting trust, see above, p. 60 f.

[19] *Unity Joint-Stock Mutual Banking Association* v. *King* (1858) 25 Beav. 72; Cf. *Dodsworth* v. *Dodsworth* (1973) 228 E.G. 1115.

[20] *Walsh* v. *Lousdale* (1882) 21 Ch.D. 9.

simple or life estate, still the trust is not restitutionary in content.[21] For, though D has received a benefit at P's expense, the quantum of P's interest reflects, not that enrichment, but only his, P's expectations. In short, in raising the interest the law is not effecting restitution, but making D answer for creating, or not dashing, P's hopes.

Can the words 'constructive trust' be dispensed with? They are certainly not very useful. They do not tell you anything about the quantum of the interest (fee simple, life estate or something tailored *ad hoc*) which the court will recognise. They do not tell you anything about the event which raises the interest, except negatively that it is not an express, implied or presumed declaration of trust. Worse than being uninformative, they also confuse. First, because they are not unequivocal in their reference to rights *in rem* rather than to rights *in personam* or to the concurrent availability of both in the same set of facts. Secondly, because they are surrounded by an unintelligible and infinitely damaging dispute as to whether they should be regarded as referring to rights at all or only to remedies or a remedy.[22] Furthermore it is observable that at law when interests arise *ipso iure*, as by adverse possession, prescription, treasure trove, forfeiture, it is not said that they are constructive. That is, no need is felt to suggest that the normal or natural way for it to happen is by the expression of intention.

The conclusion must be that the words 'constructive trust' have no active role. Within the law of restitution it is certainly more useful to ask directly whether restitutionary rights *in rem* arise from this or that wrong or unjust enrichment. 'Constructive trust' is at best an inert description, extending beyond the confines of restitution, of the situation in which an equitable beneficial interest has arisen *ipso iure*, such that the person entitled at law is deprived by equity of some or all of the beneficial interest. In that descriptive function it has one merit lacked by 'quasi-contract' or 'constructive contract'.

---

[21] *Inwards v. Baker* [1965] 2 O.B. 29; *Re Sharpe (a Bankrupt)* [1980] 1 W.L.R. 219; *Pascoe v. Turner* [1979] 1 W.L.R. 431. In this last case the C.A. appears to draw a contrast between a constructive trust and an interest arising under a proprietary estoppel, but this seems difficult since the trust is the division of legal and equitable entitlement, brought into being by the event which consists in encouraging detrimental reliance (the estoppel); one is the effect, the other the cause, and there is no contrast between them except in the angle of perception. In *Pascoe v. Turner* the defendant was ordered to convey the fee simple. Hence it is difficult to say that he had not become a trustee for the plaintiff.

[22] R. Pound, 'The Progress of the Law, 1918—1919, Equity' (1920) 33 *Harv. L.R.* 420 ff; A. J. Oakley, 'Has the Constructive Trust Become a General Equitable Remedy?' (1973) *C.L.P.* 17; D.W.M. Waters, *The Constructive Trust*, London, 1964, *passim.* The best contribution to this debate is the judgment of Goulding, J., in *Chase Manhattan Bank N.A. v. Israel-British Bank (London) Ltd.* [1981] Ch. 105, in which he points out that there is no contrast between substantive right and remedy. *Ubi remedium ibi ius.*

There is at least a trust. Only the declaration of trust is imaginary. By contrast the obligations called quasi-contractual bear absolutely no mark of contract. The term 'quasi-contract' thus has nothing to be said for it and can be given up completely. Thus, after a payment by mistake made by P to D, the restitutionary obligation owed by D to P, imposed by law not raised by consent, has no more claim to be called quasi-contractual than, say, quasi-fiscal or quasi-familial. But if the conclusion is also that D obtains legal title to the fund while P obtains the beneficial interest in the eyes of equity, then the language of English law knows no other word or phrase to describe the relationship between them than to say that D holds on trust for P. Hence 'constructive trust', or something very like it, is still needed to describe the cases in which the separation of legal and equitable interests happens *ipso iure*. But the phrase only describes a conclusion. An event brings an equitable interest into being. The interest once in being, the trust exists.

In contemplating the mode by which restitution is effected it is more useful to focus on the interest which arises so as to bring such a trust into being, rather than on the trust itself. For restitution is actually effected by the recognition of the interest, and the trust comes into being as a secondary consequence of that recognition. So in *Hodgson* v. *Marks*,[23] which was discussed when restitutionary rights *in rem* were first considered, Mrs Hodgson's equitable fee simple effected restitution; and because she was given that equitable beneficial interest it followed that there was a trust.

Keeping the entities to the minimum, we come back to the statement that restitutionary rights *in rem* are either legal or equitable, and either beneficial or by way of security. The case of the car provides a simple illustration. You received £5000, frittered £2000, and bought a car with the rest, now worth £1500. The possibilities are, under this head, that I get a lien on or ownership of the car. So long as the value of the car is less than the amount of my money which you put into getting it, the two species of right *in rem* will be worth the same. But the lien can never be worth more than you put in. So, if it turns out that the car belonged to a celebrity and for that reason it suddenly goes up in value to, say, £6000, the beneficial interest will be more favourable to me.[24]

There are also circumstances in which the lien can be more favourable than the beneficial interest. Suppose that when you bought the car you not only spent £3000 of mine on it but also a further £3000

---

[23] Above, p. 58 ff.
[24] *Re Tilley's Will Trusts* [1967] Ch. 1179.

of your own. It was a much more expensive car. The choice is between a lien for the £3000 traced into the car or a beneficial interest consisting in an undivided half share. If the car rises in value above its price of £6000 the beneficial interest will be worth more, as in the simpler example. But, if it depreciates below £6000, the lien will be more attractive. If it has gone down to £1500 the half share will be worth £750, but the lien will give me the whole £1500.[25] A free choice between the two may be difficult to justify. On the other hand one of the inescapable artificialities of prolonging the identification of surviving enrichment may be a plurality of possible assessments. By the unaided light of nature, it is not possible to say whether the surviving enrichment is the car itself or the fund of £3000 invested in the car; and it is that metaphysical difference which indicates beneficial ownership (the car itself) or a lien (the fund of £3000).

There is a counter-principle of 'Occam's razor' though I am not aware that it has a name. It is that, as you must not have too many entities, so also you cannot do with two few. We have already seen one example. If you insist that there are only two sources of obligation, contract and tort, you develop a contorted and impoverished law of unjust enrichment. The question to be asked now is whether the two by two classification of rights *in rem* which effect restitution in the second measure (legal/equitable; beneficial/security) has to be extended. Does it overlook any major differentiation in what is observably done in relation to surviving enrichment?

Possibly it does, though a final answer would require a very extended argument. And at all events it is certain that you can go a very long way without troubling about it. The further difference which may have to be taken is made no easier for having no established name. It can be expressed as the division between floating and crystallised rights.

The need arises thus. You receive £500 from me with which you buy a cow. Then, day by day, you swap the cow for a pig, the pig for a sheep and the sheep for a goat. It is a simple set of clean substitutions, and the tracing exercise shows that the goat wholly represents the £500. Let it be given that the circumstances are such that, when I have identified the goat as the surviving enrichment, I am entitled to full beneficial ownership of it. Whether legal or equitable makes no material difference. The question is: What did I have yesterday and the day before that, before the tracing was done?

---

[25] Cf. *Re Oatway* [1903] 2 Ch. 356.

Did I, without knowing it, own first a cow, then a pig, and so on down the chain of substitutions? Or did I own none of the animals until, having traced, I began to own the goat? If the latter, what did I have when, in rather loose terms, I had a 'right to trace'?

As between these two views of what happens during the chain of substitutions, the latter must be correct, although there is authority for both and rather stronger authority for the former, which can be referred to as 'descending title'.[26] The maxim *nemo dat quod non habet*, which applies at law subject to specific exceptions and in equity subject to the defence of bona fide purchaser for value without notice, makes such nonsense of descending title that it must be wrong. I could end up, and indeed it would be difficult to explain why I would not end up, owning cow, pig, sheep and goat. Not sequentially, but concurrently. For when you gave the cow in exchange for the pig, how could its recipient acquire or give a good title? and if I acquired title to the pig without losing title to the cow, how, when you acquired the sheep, could I lose my title to the pig?; and so on. It is no answer to rely on exceptions to the sanctity of ownership, for they will only alleviate the absurdity in some circumstances.

The other view, that during the substitutions you own nothing but have only a 'right to trace',[27] avoids these difficulties. It allows the chain of substitutions to go on without any prejudice to third parties and without a geometric increase in my wealth. It is your cow which you change for the pig, and so on until it is suddenly my goat. If this is correct, the question still remains as to what it is I have when I have a 'right to trace'. The analogy which fits is that of the floating charge, which leaves a company's assets free but gives the creditor a security interest in potential.[28] In the same way my ownership remains above, and can be brought down upon, the assets passing through the series of substitutions. Yesterday it could have been fixed on the sheep, today on the goat. So what I had during the period of the substitutions was a floating or uncrystallised ownership. It is probably also right to say that I had a power, though that raises further questions as to whether the power is, strictly speaking, vested in me or in the court. Either way it is true that, during the substitutions, I had an uncrystallised ownership, a formula which leaves open the discussion as to the exact source and nature of the crystallisation.

Two further complications have to be contemplated. First, the

[26] *Re Diplock* [1948] 1 Ch. 465, 531, 537.
[27] *Re J. Leslie Engineers Co. Ltd.* [1976] 1 W.L.R. 292, *per* Oliver, J.
[28] Cf. *Re Bond Worth* [1980] Ch. 228.

nature and quantum of the floating right may remain uncertain until crystallisation. In the animal example it was given for the sake of simplicity that the process would end in beneficial ownership of the goat. But different facts or the operation of either judicial discretion or personal choice could crystallise a lien instead without requiring modification of the account of what happens during the substitutions. Secondly, although we are here working under the heading 'Rights *in rem* and the second measure of restitution', it is momentarily necessary to recur to the earlier assertion that tracing can also end in the recognition of a right *in personam* measured by the value identified as surviving. It might be thought that it would be necessary to contemplate that right too as having an uncrystallised phase; but it is not. For the personal claim, taking its measure from the enrichment as it survives from moment to moment, always leaves the assets free to be dealt with. That follows from its personal nature. So there is no pressure to make it float. The same event which for rights *in rem* is crystallisation, for rights *in personam* does no more than fix their fluctuating content.

Rescission also provides a context in which it seems that restitutionary rights *in rem* have a floating phase even before a series of substitutions is set in train. When you fraudulently induce me to part with my car I can revest the title in myself. Until I do my ownership is potential. The power *in rem* is something which I have now. The ownership which, by exercising that power, I can bring down on the *res* remains uncrystallised.[29]

What we have said is that so far as concerns the proprietary technique, which is appropriate only to this second measure of restitution, the vocabulary of constructive trusts has no active role; and the only important distinctions are betweeen legal and equitable rights *in rem*, between beneficial interests and security interests, and between interests which float until crystallised and interests which are crystallised *ab initio*.

(iii) *Restitution by Subrogation*

I hesitate to give subrogation a heading of its own. I shall say that within the law of restitution it really adds nothing to the number of techniques already identified. It is in the nature of a metaphor which can be done without. The cases in which the word 'subrogation' is chiefly used are those in which the defendant's enrichment is negative, in the sense that it consists in his having been relieved of a

---

[29] Above, p. 66.

burden: a claim maintainable against him has been paid off. Often, but not invariably, it will have been formally extinguished.

In some cases the defendant originally receives money or other value from the plaintiff and then, perhaps after intermediate exchanges (as by buying shares and then selling them again), he himself ultimately uses some or all of it to pay off a claim maintainable against him.[30] In other cases the plaintiff pays the defendant's creditor himself,[31] or through a third person.[32] In the second and third types of case the enrichment is ambivalent between 'value received' and 'value surviving'. It can certainly be considered under the former head. But, in that a discharge is a type of enrichment which endures at least so long as the adverse claim would have been maintainable, it is safe to keep both types of case together under the head of 'value surviving'.

The verb 'to subrogate' is hardly encountered at all outside the law (unless in the related substantival form 'surrogate'). It means 'to substitute', and when we say that P is subrogated to X, what we mean is that P is substituted for X. There is a graphic phrase for it: P stands in X's shoes. The substitution is always envisaged for a limited purpose: P stands in X's shoes for the purpose of taking over claims previously maintainable by X. That purpose attracts the analogy of assignment.[33] P's standing in X's shoes for the purpose of availing himself of X's rights can be regarded as an assignment *ipso iure* of X's rights, by operation of law rather than by the intention and act of the parties. There is yet another way of saying exactly the same thing. X can be described as a trustee of his rights for P; and then, because the trust arises *ipso iure*, it will be called constructive.

If I pay you £5000 and you use £2000 of it to pay off your overdraft, then a conclusion in the form and language of subrogation will be that I am subrogated to the claim which the bank had against you. I stand where the bank stood; and you, who are sitting on a surviving enrichment of £2000, in the form of a burden removed which would

---

[30] E.g. *Jenner* v. *Morris* (1861) 3 De G.F. & J. 45, *Lewis* v. *Alleyne* (1888) 4 T.L.R. 560; *Baroness Wenlock* v. *River Dee Company* (1887) 19 Q.B.D. 155.

[31] E.g. *Ghana Commercial Bank* v. *Chandiram* [1960] A.C. 74; *Nottingham Permanent Benefit Building Society* v. *Thurstan* [1903 A.C. 6.

[32] E.g. *Bannatyne* v. *D & C MacIver* [1906] 1 K.B. 103; *Re Byfield* [1982] 1 All E.R. 249 (when, however, subrogation was refused.)

[33] 'The Court closes its eyes to the true facts of the case, viz. an advance as a loan by the quasi-lender to the company, and a payment by the company to its creditors as out of its own moneys: and assumes on the contrary that the quasi-lender and the creditor of the company met together and that the former advanced to the latter the amount of his claim against the company and took an assignment of that claim for his benefit', *Baroness Wenlock* v. *River Dee Company* (1887) 19 Q.B.D. 155, 165, *per* Fry, L.J.

otherwise still impend, will thus be compelled to give up that enrichment. The metaphorical nature of this description is brought out by the fact that exactly the same conclusion can be expressed without speaking of any substitution. It could be said simply that I acquire a right having characteristics and content identical to that formerly enjoyed by the bank. The difference is between the language of substitution and the language of comparison: 'the bank's right' and 'a right like the bank's'. The notion of a substitution is vivid. But strictly speaking it is unnecessary.

The metaphor can become awkward. Suppose in this example that the bank had taken a mortgage on your house to secure your overdraft, with the result that your payment of £2000 to the bank relieved you of two burdens at once, the personal claim against you and the charge on your house. The language and image of substitution immediately suggests that I must stand in the bank's shoes so as to take over both the right *in rem* and right *in personam*. The less graphic language of comparison correctly leaves it more obviously open whether my position is to be selectively or exactly 'like the bank's'.[34]

There is another similar point. Substitution suggests a difficulty in the case in which the bank's rights have not merely been factually satisfied but technically discharged and extinguished. If I stand in the bank's shoes, will there be anything for me to take over? This is nothing but a red herring. The difficulty is only a function of the image.[35] For the real question is about your surviving enrichment, and you are all the more certainly sitting on an enrichment if the bank is not merely content not to sue but is absolutely barred from doing so by the discharge of its claims. The analogy of assignment and the notion of a trust both provoke the same hesitation. If the bank still has rights against you which remain technically unextinguished, it makes sense to say that it must assign those rights to me or that it holds those rights on constructive trust for me. If, however, the bank's rights have been extinguished, there will be nothing to assign or to hold on trust, and it may seem conceptually impossible to bring them back to life for the purpose of my taking them over. The non-metaphorical approach is not troubled by the question whether extinguished rights can be revived. For it does not

---

[34] *Re Wrexham, Mold and Connah's Quay Railway* [1899] 1 Ch. 440.

[35] In *Re Byfield* [1982] 1 All E.R. 249, Goulding, J., said that to evade difficulties of this kind he would have been willing if necessary to abandon the word 'subrogation' and to speak instead of an unclassifiable right designed to defeat a particular kind of unjust enrichment (at p. 253).

contemplate any right as requiring to be taken over or held on trust. It looks at the bank's position only to get the measure of your surviving enrichment at my expense.

Whether one uses the image of substitution or not, the first question is always whether the enrichment received can indeed be said to survive in the removal of a burden from the defendant. In other words, as always in relation to this measure, identification by the rules of tracing must come first.[36] Among the enrichments discoverable at the end of a chain of substitutions may be assets of any kind, even negative. The search may end in a car, or a share, or a debt discharged. It is when it ends in a debt discharged that the vocabulary changes from lien and beneficial ownership to subrogation. That is, if a car is in view the question is whether the plaintiff has a beneficial interest or a lien; if a debt discharged is in view, the question is whether the plaintiff can be subrogated to the discharged creditor.[37]

Once the plaintiff's money is traced into this negative species of surviving enrichment, does 'subrogation' actually entail recognition of any restitutionary technique which has not yet been mentioned? One who insists on the language of substitution will want to say, taking care to avoid the all or nothing approach, that the plaintiff can take over one or more of the former creditor's claims, either the personal claim or the mortgage or both. The phrase 'take over' serves to avoid saying that the right is his or that he 'owns' the former creditor's claim. The need for that evasion stems from the custom of never talking about ownership of rights *in personam*. If that traditional reluctance is overcome one can see, even without removing the metaphor of substitution, that there is no difference between what happens in the case of the car and what happens in the case of the debt discharged. The question whether the plaintiff is entitled to ownership of, or some other interest in, the car merely becomes whether he is entitled to ownership of, or some other interest in, the former creditor's claims. Hence even on this view, which sees everything in terms of substitution or of one person standing in another's shoes, the word 'subrogation' should not be allowed to suggest the existence of a technique of restitution not included in the previous discussion. There is a different kind of asset involved, not a different mode of effecting restitution.

If the image of substitution is rejected, this conclusion is not

---

[36] *Baroness Wenlock* v. *River Dee Company* (1887) 19 Q.B.D. 155. Cf. *Re Cork and Youghal Railway* (1869) L.R.4 Ch. Ap. 748; *Re Johnson* (1880) 14 Ch.D. 548.
[37] For difficulties in relation to *Re Diplock* on this point, see below , p. 372.

changed but becomes simpler. For there is then no need to insist that negative assets such as discharged debts and mortgages are capable of being treated exactly in the same way as positive assets such as cars and shares. For on this view the plaintiff who has traced the surviving enrichment into a negative asset merely has a restitutionary right the quantum of which is fixed by reference to the ex-creditor's claims. So, in the case in which you used £2000 of an original receipt of £5000 to discharge an overdraft secured by a mortgage, I get a claim *in personam* against you for £2000, which is the value surviving as the result of the removal from you of the burden of your bank's claim. But it is my claim, not the bank's claim taken over by me. Then there is a separate question, which will be looked at in a later chapter,[38] whether I am entitled to a charge to secure my claim in the same way as the bank secured its claim. Whether I am or not, there is no suggestion in any of this of a technique of restitution different from those which are described above: I get a right *in personam* and may also get a right *in rem*.

For the sake of clarity it is necessary to underline one last point. 'Assignment' is an event, it is one of the family of causative events which, like contract or conveyance, are consent-based. Just as a conveyance is the event which makes me 'owner' of your land, so assignment is the event which makes me 'owner' of your claim against your debtor. If subrogation is thought of as 'quasi-assignment' or 'assignment by operation of law' there is a danger that it too will be contemplated as an event. But that is certainly wrong. Even according to the metaphor of substitution, the statement that P is subrogated to X says that P takes a right formerly held by X, but it says nothing about the event which brings that about. It has indeed been suggested in the House of Lords that the facts on which subrogation will be allowed are unknowable. 'It is impossible . . . to formulate any narrower principle than that the doctrine will be applied only when the courts are satisfied that reason and justice demand that it should be.'[39] It follows from this that subrogation is a possibility to be borne in mind on all facts which call for restitution; but, if this discussion has been on the right lines, that means no more than that on all such facts it will be a question whether the enrichment still held by the defendant may not include claims from which the plaintiff or the plaintiff's money has relieved him. In relation to all claims in the second measure of restitution there are two questions which the plaintiff must ask. First: Has the defendant

---

[38] Below, pp. 389 ff.
[39] *Orakpo* v. *Manson Investments Ltd.* [1978] A.C. 95, 110 *per* Lord Salmon.

got anything left which represents what he originally received? Then, if he has: Can I make out a claim *in personam* to the value of that surviving enrichment or a claim *in rem* to the *res* in which that enrichment survives? When the first inquiry shows that the defendant's surviving enrichment consists, wholly or partly, in a negative asset (the burden of a liability removed from him), the second question remains substantially unchanged. The same techniques of restitution apply. However, long usage sanctions recourse to different language when the enrichment survives in that form. The switch to 'subrogation' should not conceal that what is happening is still second-measure restitution by rights *in personam* or *in rem*.

We shall see that many different events give rise to restitution. The use of Occam's razor in this chapter has tried to show that, behind the mass of often outworn verbiage, the number of techniques by which restitution is effected is very small. Plaintiffs who claim in the first measure invariably obtain restitution by a right *in personam*. Plaintiffs who claim in the second measure can found on either a right *in personam* or a right *in rem*. This simple classification can be elaborated by further sub-division, but the greatest care must always be taken not to add to it extra categories which are bogus or obscure.

IV

ORGANISATION

WE ought now to be in calmer waters. The last three chapters have been preparatory. They have been concerned with big questions not easily separated one from another. What is restitution? How does it relate to other areas of law? What are the means by which it is achieved? They have been hard going, and if they justify themselves at all it is because they cut down the need for digressions and re-orientations as we proceed to consider the grounds for restitution. The function of this short chapter is to explain the system upon which those grounds will be handled.

The key to the scheme is the division made in the ambivalent or super-generic conception of the cause for restitution. That produces two main sections, restitution for unjust enrichment (by subtraction) and restitution for wrongs. Of these two the first is much the larger. Within it, the system again breaks into two unequal parts. There is the exposition of 'unjust' and the exposition of 'enrichment by sub-traction'. In the order of treatment these two are inverted. It is always easier, both in analysing an individual problem and in a general consideration, to take out first the questions which go to enrichment at the plaintiff's expense.

The word 'unjust' binds together all the most difficult questions and, in sheer quantity, the greater part of the whole subject. How is its exposition sub-divided? 'Unjust', it will be recalled, does not look up to an abstract notion of justice but down to the cases and statutes. It is merely a general word expressing the common quality of those factors which, when present in conjunction with enrichment, have been held to call for restitution. So there has to be a list of such factors and, if possible, the list should have some order to it. It should not be compiled at random. The old lawyers patiently used nothing but the alphabet, but we are past that. All the same, this exercise of sub-classification is as difficult as it is important, and it is certain that it leaves room for improvement. I use three categories, but the neatness is partly deceptive, because the third is a miscellany: 'others'. It is designed to take the pressure off the other two, which do seem able to map out much of the territory. The three categories of factors rendering an enrichment 'unjust' are, (a) non-voluntary transfer, (b) free acceptance, and (c) others. These headings need to be briefly introduced at this stage.

(a) *Non-Voluntary Transfer*

This is an ugly phrase, but it is difficult to improve on. The idea beneath it is simple enough. Where there is 'a non-voluntary transfer', so that the circumstance calling for restitution is 'a factor negativing voluntariness', the explanation of the response is always reducible in the simplest terms to the statement that the plaintiff did not mean the defendant to have the money in question or the other enrichment, whatever it might be. A non-voluntary transfer is a 'not-wanted transfer'. It may be that the plaintiff did not want the transfer to happen at all, absolutely; or, it may be that he wanted it to happen in some events but not in those which have occurred.

An immediate warning must be given. Its structure is similar to the routine homily on the use of the word 'unjust' itself. The notions of voluntariness and non-voluntariness in parting with wealth are controlled by the cases. You cannot conclude in favour of restitution just by looking at the story of a transfer from P to D and deciding, as though it were only a question of fact, that P did not mean D to have the given item of his wealth. The issue is too difficult, too metaphysical, and there are always complex sub-issues. Hence even if as a matter of impression it looks as though the transfer was not voluntary, you have to go down to the cases to see if it was non-voluntary in the way in which the law counts as calling for restitution. Natural non-voluntariness, the layman's commonsensical version, is only a starting point. Mistakes of law illustrate this. By the light of nature a mistake of law is just as effective as a mistake of fact in negativing the voluntary character of a payment. Take the case of a tax. I pay because I believe the taxable event has happened, or I pay because I believe the event which has happened is taxable. Either way, if my belief is false there is equal sense in saying the transfer was non-voluntary: I did not mean it to happen. But the cases are much more cautious about allowing restitution for mistakes of law. There is a fear that mistakes of law are too common, perhaps also too easily made up after the event, so that there might be too much instability, simply too much restitution, if no distinction were taken between fact and law. The restraint in relation to mistakes of law shows how side-issues of legal policy interact with the central question of non-voluntariness in forming the ground for restitution actually recognised in the cases. It is a clear example, but this goes on all the time, often covertly. The question whether, on given facts, a man intended to make a transfer, is so difficult that, outside a core of cases on which all men would agree, reasonable men can entertain different opinions. How bad must a mistake be or how strong a compulsion before you can conclude that a man's judgement in forming the decision to pay was vitiated? *Coactus volui* (compelled I consented) identifies an old conundrum. As philosophers begin to differ, the law has to try to resolve the uncertainties, and it does so with one eye on secondary questions. None of this means that 'non-voluntariness' is an inert or useless notion. On the contrary it is the basis of much restitution. Only it is always controlled by the cases, and they in their turn often have to balance conflicting ideas.

The category of non-voluntary transfer is itself sub-divided. There are two sub-divisions, according to the nature of the reason why we say that the plaintiff did not mean the transfer to happen. In the one his judgement in forming the intent to transfer was vitiated (using 'vitiated' in the widest sense so as to include 'nullified' and even 'not exercised'). In the other there was no vitiating factor: in making or allowing the transfer he exercised his judgement freely but he qualified his intention by specifying the event in which, or basis on which, he wanted the defendant to have the benefit. Here the reason why we ultimately say the transfer was non-voluntary is that the specified event or basis failed to materialise: in the events which have occurred he did not want the defendant to have the benefit. As where he gave £1000, specifying that it was a marriage gift, and in the event the marriage did not happen; or for a reciprocal perfor-mance by the transferee, and none was forthcoming. In these cases non-voluntariness is explicable not in terms of vitiated intent to give but rather in terms of deliberately qualified intent to give. It is convenient to be able to make the contrast simply through those two ideas. Hence the sub-division of 'non-voluntary transfer' is between 'vitiation' and 'qualification'. Typical vitiations are mistakes, com-pulsions and inequalities; but the detailed organisation down at this level will not be explored at this point.

It is sometimes helpful to be able to turn the category of non-voluntary transfer round, so as to have an idea of what is 'voluntary' and who is 'a volunteer'. The voluntary transfer is the one for which there is no restitution within this category. The 'volunteer' is one who makes or allows such a transfer. His hopes of restitution are rather slim and lie only in the smaller categories of 'free acceptance' and 'others', or else further on in 'wrongs'. But can the matter be expressed more positively?

We say that a transfer was voluntary when the plaintiff was con-tent that the defendant should have the benefit either in all events which might happen or at least in the events which have happened. But this is a formal and abstract statement, and it is important that it should be broken down to reveal some characters from ordinary life. There is the man who specified that he wanted a given return and got it: the buyer who gave £50 for his week's groceries. There is the man who freely formed the intention to have no return at all: the gift-giver on your birthday. Then there is the man who made his gift conditional on an event which subsequently happened: the £1000 was for your marriage to X, and now the two of you are married. These three have all got what they wanted: the groceries, nothing, the marriage. They are, let us say, satisfied customers.

There is another and more interesting type of volunteer within the whole category of those 'content that the defendant should have the benefit in question'. He is interesting because he is not a satisfied customer. He says that he has not got what we wanted; he is dissatisfied; and yet we have to conclude that he was content that the defendant should be enriched. There is an obvious tension between the description of him as 'dissatisfied' and the assertion that he must be counted among volunteers 'content that the defendant should be enriched'. The resolution is that at the time of the transfer he was content that the other should have the benefit in all events but now he is dissatisfied. This can happen in two ways. First there is the man who has simply changed his mind. He did want to give the gift but later he wished he had not, or he did want to buy the new gadget but later regretted wasting his money. But more important (because less obviously disqualified from restitution) than the mind-changer, is the second species of dissatisfied volunteer, the risk-taker. He did not specify any condition or stipulate for any return but he did actually want one; he took a risk. If someone cleans your car in a car park while you are shopping he no doubt hopes to get something from you. If so he takes the risk of your being hard-hearted or your not coming back till he has given up waiting. Again, if you are in a position to lend money or to place business, kindnesses at Christmas, a case of wine or dinner in a restaurant, may have a very obvious drift, expectations which you may later disappoint. Wealthy parents may think that a generous settlement will chivvy a tardy child into marriage and responsibility, and then, seeing their money freely spent, regret that they delicately refrained from imposing a condition. These people in varying degrees lack the gratuitous intent which marks the giver of an out-and-out gift. At the same time they stop short of cutting out the risk of disappointment by clearly qualifying their intent to give. More or less grudgingly they will accept classification with gift-givers. But they are a separate sub-category. They are risk-takers.

The risk-taking volunteer gives occasion for another application of Occam's razor. Where a plaintiff claims restitution of an enrichment which consists in some service rendered, the notion of 'officiousness' is often drawn upon by way of explaining why he should not succeed. The man who cleaned your car while you were shopping would find himself numbered with 'officious intermeddlers'.[1] In a loose sense the word 'officious' merely gives pejorative emphasis to the idea already inherent in 'intermeddler', that he should have minded his own business. But it has a more specific thrust against the suggestion that there might have been some need for the intervention: whatever hint there was of a circumstance calling for him to intervene, he was merely snatching at it. 'Officiousness' is the quality of being over-astute to find a duty to be done. Dirty windscreens can be dangerous, but if the windscreen of your car is dirty other people should still mind their own business. One who thinks he perceives a duty to clean it is merely being officious. In using that word we mean to say either that there was no call at all for him to intervene or else, at the very least, that there was no call sufficiently strong to allow him to say that he did not willingly accept the risk of losing the value of his labour.

The word 'officious', common though it is in this particular context, actually has no work to do which is not capable of being done through 'voluntary' and 'volunteer'. If the intervener takes the risk of losing his labour without return then he is a volunteer and his transfer of value is voluntary. To say that he is 'officious' only reaffirms that he took the risk of diappointment. There is no need to introduce a separate word to convey the idea that any element of duty which he might try to point to is insufficient to vitiate his judgment in deciding to accept that risk. For that idea merely goes without saying unless and until the facts are such that some emergency does compel his intervention. Then he may be able to seek restitution on the ground of moral compulsion. And moral compulsion operates as a ground for restitution because it is a factor which negative voluntariness.[2] There is nothing gained by saying that it also negatives 'officiousness'. Hence the entire analysis can be conducted without recourse to the language of officiousness. The same idea should not be pursued by different words in different contexts.

---

[1] *Restatement of Restitution*, para. 2: 'A person who officiously confers a benefit upon another is not entitled to restitution therefor.' The accompanying comment expounds 'officiously' thus: 'Officiousness means interference in the affairs of others not justified by the circumstances under which the interference takes place.' This account of the word emasculates it of all meaning, making it no more than a general label for all the circumstances in which restitution is excluded. Cf. *Goff and Jones*, 35.

[2] Below, p. 193 ff.

(b) *Free Acceptance*

This is the second of the three main divisions of 'unjust'. Many stories can be analysed in the alternative, either as non-voluntary transfers or as free acceptances. But the two are quite distinct. Very frequently a plaintiff will be able to make out one but not the other.

Free acceptance, which is the same idea as is recognised in equity under the name 'acquiescence', occurs where the defendant receives a benefit in circumstances in which he knows that it is not being offered gratuitously and in which, having an opportunity to reject, he none the less chooses to accept. The crucial difference which distinguishes free acceptance from non-voluntary transfer is that the reason for restitution is now found on the defendant's side. Non-voluntary transfer is constituted by facts whose function is, to tell you how the plaintiff's brain was working. Free acceptance is something done, in a certain state of mind, by the defendant.

This opposed orientation of non-voluntary transfer and free acceptance matters most, and most obviously, to the risk-taking volunteer. He is, *ex hypothesi*, excluded from the first type of claim. But he has some hope in free acceptance. If we go back to that man cleaning your car we can see why. When you finish your shopping and return to find the car clean it is too late for any free acceptance. You have no opportunity to reject. But suppose that on your way to the shops you find you have left your bag behind. So you retrace your steps at once, in time to see the job just beginning. You could go forward and protest immediately. If you hang back until the job is finished and then rush up to complain, you are too late and you must pay. You have accepted the benefit freely. Yet the quality of his intervention remains the same throughout. That is, he is the same risk-taking volunteer. He thought you were away at your shopping and was unaware of your return, which therefore had no impact on his mind.

The example serves to show why free acceptance is a ground for restitution. Once a defendant has failed to use an opportunity to reject a benefit, his position is weak even against a risk-taking volunteer. For when he begins to say that the plaintiff chose to run the risk of disappointment he is immediately trumped by the reply that if he had spoken out there would have been no risk to run. Not all plaintiffs relying on free acceptance will be volunteers. Against those who are not it is unnecessary to talk in terms of running risks. It is enough to say that the freely accepting defendant has himself to blame for what has happened. Without trouble to himself he could have stopped it, or at least by speaking out he could have freed himself from all responsibility.

(c) *Others*

The number of cases in this miscellany is uncertain, but it cannot be large. The category supposes a volunteer plaintiff claiming against a defendant who has not freely accepted. In the nature of things it will be rare to find restitution between such parties. Yet sometimes a social policy which stands right outside the conduct of the parties as expressed in the notions of voluntary transfer and free acceptance will require an enrichment to be made reversible. For example, suppose that a public body in good faith makes a levy upon a multinational company. The authority believes the money due in law; the company takes the opposite view but pays. It turns out that the company's view is correct. Even if the company, well advised and neither mistaken nor susceptible to pressure, must be said to pay voluntarily, and even if the authority's mistake obstructs any free acceptance, there may yet be an argument for restitution. The ground for reversing the enrichment would be the social policy expressed in the Bill of Rights: no taxation without parliament. Or, more generally, the constitutional value of respect for the rule of law.

We have been describing the scheme for considering the factors which turn an enrichment by subtraction from the plaintiff into an 'unjust' enrichment. It involves a three-fold division, between *non-voluntary transfer*, *free acceptance* and *others*, followed by a sub-division of non-voluntary transfer between *vitiation* and *qualification*. This introduction does not carry the description down to the lower levels.

At this point it is necessary to go back up to the principal division between unjust enrichment and restitution for wrongs. Something must be briefly said about the internal organisation of the second member of this pair. Care was earlier taken to explain that a wrong is not in itself a sufficient ground for restitution. If it were, the victim of every wrong which brought a gain to the wrongdoer would have a restitutionary claim. It follows that, even within this category, there is a need to divide between the fact of 'enrichment by a wrong' and the superadded 'grounds for restitution'. It will be recalled that 'restitution for wrongs' is terminology formed in exchange for 'unjust enrichment by wrongs', the word 'unjust' having an unfortunate resonance with 'by wrongs' such as misleadingly suggests that every wrongful enrichment calls for restitution. The exchanged terminology should not conceal the exact balance between, in this category, the 'grounds for restitution' and, in the other, the factors gathered into the threefold division under 'unjust'. In other words,

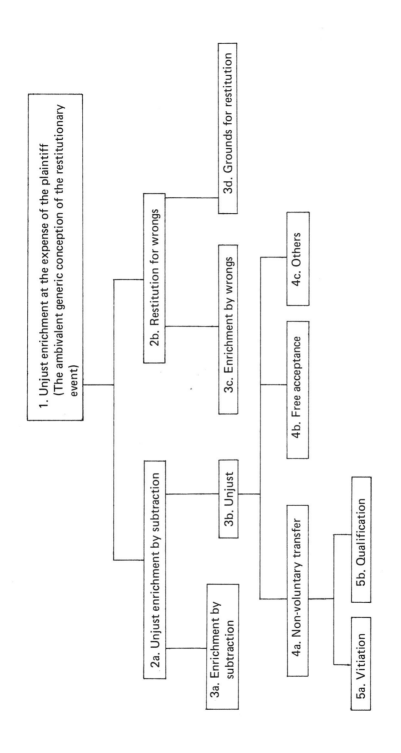

Diagram 1: The map of restitution

A. Restitution in the first measure (value received)

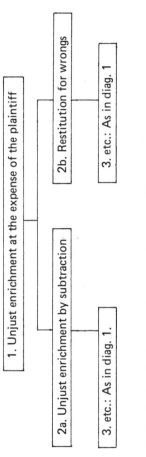

B. Restitution in the second measure (value surviving)

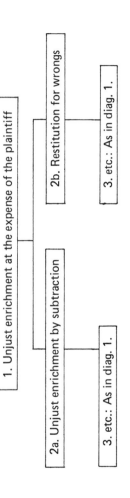

Diagram 2: Reduplication of the map to allow for two measures of restitution

if it were not for the need to scotch the dangerous inference just
mentioned, the word 'unjust' would recur in this category as the peg
on which to hand the factors calling for restitution. At this stage the
scheme offers no further division of these grounds for restitution,
too doubtful for stable classification.

What has now been described in words can be summed up in a
diagram (see diagram 1). The scheme so represented is the nearest
that I have been able to come to a bird's eye view of the whole subject called Restitution. Even so there are two important points at
which the organisation of the rest of this book already departs
from it. First I have found it impossible to integrate the discussion of
both measures of restitution, value received and value surviving, into
the treatment of the causes for restitution. Consequently there is an
assumption running right through the book, until the chapter called
'The Second Measure of Restitution', that only the common or
normal measure, value received, is in question. The formal effect of
this mode of proceeding is to reduplicate the whole scheme. As
though one would print its diagram twice, once for each measure.
And it is worth mentioning that, since the diagram tries to classify
the subject by its causative events, the division by the two measures
of restitution should be horizontal, not vertical (see diagram 2). The
reduplication represented by diagram 2 is, however, no more than a
formality for the purpose of knowing how things relate. There
is of course no question, in practice, of running through the entire
scheme twice. The other departure is the discussion of bars and
defences in the final chapter. In principle the overview is not much
clouded by the postponement of matter of that kind. But in practice
there is a very difficult line to draw between constitutive facts and
defences. Suppose it to be the case that a restitutionary plaintiff
must give up anything he himself may have received from the
defendant. That counter-restitution can be viewed as a pre-condition
of his entitlement and, therefore, as a constitutive element of his
cause of action; or its absence, through his inability or unwillingness
to restore, can be contemplated as a defence. The latter approach is
adopted here. There are other awkward cases. So far as there is a
difficulty about the last chapter, that is it.

V

ENRICHMENT AT THE PLAINTIFF'S EXPENSE

THIS chapter is concerned with two distinct issues. Was the defendant enriched? If so, did it happen at the plaintiff's expense? There is no point in getting to the difficult questions which are collected into 'unjust' until these two preliminary issues have been answered in the plaintiff's favour. They should not be difficult. So far as they do pose problems it is because the courts have not yet organised their approach to restitutionary claims in such a way as to give separate, and explicit, consideration to these questions. In short there is a difficulty not of nature but of authority.

1. ENRICHMENT

(i) *Subjective Devaluation*

The critical distinction is between money and benefits in kind.[1] Where the defendant received money, it will be impossible on all ordinary facts for him to argue that he was not enriched. For money is the very measure of enrichment. By contrast benefits in kind are less unequivocally enriching because they are susceptible to an argument which for convenience can be called 'subjective devaluation'. It is an argument based on the premiss that benefits in kind have value to a particular individual only so far as he chooses to give them value. What matters is his choice. The fact that there is a market in the good which is in question, or in other words that other people habitually choose to have it and thus create a demand for it, is irrelevant to the case of any one particular individual. He claims the right to

---

[1] Cf. *B.P. Exploration Co. (Libya) Ltd.* v. *Hunt (No. 2)* [1979] 1 W.L.R. 783, 799, *per* Robert Goff, J: 'Money has the peculiar character of a universal medium of exchange. By its receipt, the recipient is inevitably benefited; and . . . the loss suffered by the plaintiff is generally equal to the defendant's gain, so that no difficulty arises concerning the amount to be repaid. The same cannot be said of other benefits, such as goods or services. By their nature, services cannot be restored; nor in many cases can goods be restored, for example where they have been consumed or transferred to another. Furthermore the identity and value of the resulting benefit to the recipient may be debatable. From the very nature of things, therefore, the problem of restitution in respect of such benefits is more complex than in cases where the benefit takes the form of a money payment; . . .' Cf. *Goff and Jones*, 15 f.

dissent from that demand. Market value is not his value. Suppose that without his knowledge his car has been serviced or his roof mended. There is a market in car servicing and roof mending. It is easy to find the market value of work of that kind, what the going rate is between reasonable people. But he says that he had decided to go in for do-it-yourself or to take the risk of disaster by doing nothing. Indeed to make his point he does not even have to say that he had actually decided, let alone prove that he had decided, to dissociate himself from the particular demand. For his point is sufficiently made by saying that he has a continuing liberty to choose how to apply his particular store of value and that in the case of this car-servicing or roof-mending he simply had not made his choice.

It is important to notice that subjective devaluation is not defeated merely because as a result of the plaintiff's intervention it happens that the defendant retains some marketable residuum. Many objectively valuable services leave no such residuum. Waste disposal, for instance, or road haulage. Others leave some ephemeral enhancement. A car cleaned or serviced may have a slightly greater value for a short while. Others leave a more durable improvement: a car repaired after a crash or a house extended by the addition of a new kitchen. Yet even in these last cases subjective devaluation is not excluded. Suppose I was away and came back to find that my house had been extended. I did not ask for it to be done. For my own reasons I wanted the house to be just as it was before. You cannot say that I have been enriched when what I have received is something which I did not choose to have. You reply that the house can be sold for £5000 more than it was worth before. But I do not want to sell. It might be that this was where my family had lived for centuries, but I do not have to adduce reasons for that kind. Subjective devaluation is an argument which claims the right to be perverse. It is not your business to make my choices for me.

In the last example I was away when you added a new kitchen to my house. I made no choice at all. Sometimes I will be seen to have made a choice, but still subjective devaluation will be possible. Suppose that you buy me a meal or send me a bottle of wine. I mistakenly believe all along that you are offering me a gift. I choose to do the eating and drinking, but I do not choose to do them at a chosen price. Now I say, perversely, that much as I like good food and wine it is not my habit to spend my money on them. Unless someone else is paying I choose other pleasures.

How does the law respond to this argument from subjective devaluation? Various responses are possible. The argument might be entirely overridden by a direct appeal to the market and the reasonable man. If you burned my rubbish or cleaned my windows the questions would then be whether reasonable men habitually pay for such services and, if so, at what rate. That inquiry would give an objective measure of my enrichment, and we could then proceed to all the other issues relevant to restitution. At the other extreme, the argument might be absolutely deferred to, with the most sensitive respect for the defendant's freedom of choice. The effect would be that restitutionary claims other than for money received would never succeed unless the defendant had chosen to receive the benefit. So the number of restitutionary claims maintainable in respect of benefits in kind would be drastically reduced, especially since in most, though not in all, cases where a benefit is chosen a claim in respect of it will lie in contract. English law has seemed at times willing to adopt this second extreme position. But closer inspection shows that it has intuitively taken a middle way. It does accept the argument from subjective devaluation. But it looks for its limitations and curbs its excesses. However, because the approach has been intuitive it has not been completely consistent. Nevertheless it is true that, by comparison with money received, the law of unjust enrichment relating to other benefits received remains under-developed, and the fundamental reason is that the starting point has always been the courts' willingness to accept that subjective devaluation is a legitimate argument.

This basic orientation is expressed in the wording of the old forms of action. There was a marked difference between claims for money received and claims in respect of other benefits. The operative part of the count for money had and received—that is to say, the part which recited the indebtedness as opposed to the evidently in-operative part which recited the *assumpsit* to pay—said nothing about the defendant's having wanted or chosen to have the money. The allegation was simply that he had received the named sum to the use of the plaintiff.[2] Consequently there was no obstacle to the development of claims which were in every respect independent of the defendant's will. By contrast, if the defendant had received a benefit in kind, there was no form of words for a plaintiff to advance which did not say that the defendant had requested the plaintiff to act. That was equally true whether the plaintiff had conferred the non-money benefit directly on the defendant, in which case his claim would be for *quantum meruit* or *quantum valebat*, or had paid a third party to confer the benefit, in which case the claim for reimbursement would be made by the count for money paid.

---

[2] Above, p. 79.

It is especially important to notice that, in this division between money and non-money benefits, 'money paid' belongs in the latter category. For this phrase is short for money paid to a third party for the sake of the defendant, with the effect that it covers the case in which, by paying the third party, the payor manages to secure for the defendant a benefit which is not the receipt by him of money. For example, if I pay someone to mend your roof, you receive a roof mended. But under the old forms of action my claim would be for 'money paid'. Even in the case in which I pay your creditor to discharge your debt, what you receive is not money but a debt discharged. According to the language of the old pleadings there is thus the strongest possible contrast between the abbreviations 'money received' (or, more commonly, 'money had and received') and 'money paid'. The former indicates that the defendant has received a sum of money and is, therefore, unequivocally enriched. The latter indicates that the defendant has received some non-money benefit from a third party by reason of the fact that the plaintiff paid out money to the third party in order to obtain that benefit for him.

The words of the count for money paid show how, as soon as the claim is for a non-money benefit received, the emphasis swings round to the defendant's freedom of choice. In a slightly abbreviated form, the count went like this: 'Whereas the defendant was indebted to the plaintiff in the sum of £x for so much money by the plaintiff paid, laid out and expended to and for the use of the defendant *at the defendant's special instance and request,* he the defendant, in consideration thereof, afterwards promised to pay.'[3]

★2   The crucial words are 'at the defendant's special instance and request'. The same allegation would have to appear if, rather than paying a third party to confer a benefit on you, I had conferred the benefit directly on you myself, as by doing work for you or sending you goods. I would always have to say that you had asked for the non-money benefit. Hence the development of claims independent of the defendant's will was obstructed. It could only proceed at all if the courts were willing to 'imply' requests where facts of a different kind were strong enough to demand that the plaintiff should have some redress. To a limited extent they were willing. This process provides a clear example of the way in which the law could be judicially developed even while still dominated by the list of plaintiff's propositions which we refer to as the forms of action: advancing a proposition which recited certain facts, A, B, and C,

---

[3] Cf. Stephen on *Pleading*, 2nd ed., London, 1827, 212, giving the fully developed form. For *quantum meruit* and *quantum valebat* forms, see below, p. 269.

the plaintiff would be allowed to substantiate it by proving other facts, say, A, B, and D. C would be said to be implied from D, a form of words which, unless the inference happened to be genuine, concealed the genesis of a fiction.

For the moment we are not concerned with that covert development but with the significance of the original commitment to forms which did recite the defendant's 'special instance and request'. If you received money from me, and there were facts which I believed should entitle me to restitution, there was a form of words—the count for money had and received—under which I would conduct my case without the least reference, pretended or otherwise, to your having asked for the money. Change no facts at all except only the nature of the benefit received. Suppose that instead of money you received a benefit in kind. With only that change I now must say I acted at your request. This is not just an accident. It represents intuitive deference to the argument from subjective devaluation. In relation to benefits in kind the defendant must have chosen to receive them: and why? Because, differently from money which is the universal measure of value, benefits in kind take their value for any particular individual merely from the strength of his desire to have them. That is not the only possible point of view; but it is the point of view taken by a system which allows claims in respect of non-money benefits only when they have been requested.

The same commitment is reflected in the failure of a tactic which might have circumvented it. Suppose that I had conferred some non-money benefit upon you without your request. I might try bringing the action for money had and received against you and then, having recited that you had had and received to my use the sum of, say, £20, attempt to induce the court to allow me to substantiate that proposition by proof of a receipt in kind, of food or wine or work as the case might be. This idea seems never to have got going. The reason is that Lord Mansfield made it clear in *Nightingall* v. *Devisme*[4] that 'money received' meant what it said: the words could not be extended to other things. Consequently, the count for money had and received having proved resistant, such willingness as there was to limit the scope of subjective devaluation had to be expressed under the other counts, by denaturing the allegations of request.

The commitment to a subjective approach to the issue of enrichment is expressed in famous and much-quoted *dicta*. 'Suppose I clean your property without your knowledge, have I then a claim on you for payment? How can you help it? One cleans another's

---

[4] *Nightingall* v. *Devisme* (1770) 5 Burr. 2589; 2 Wm. Bl. 684.

shoes; what can the other do but put them on? Is that evidence of a contract to pay for the cleaning? The benefit of the service could not be rejected without refusing the property itself.' That is Pollock, C.B., in *Taylor v. Laird*.[5] Its premiss is that a choice is necessary, and its immediate point is to affirm that the choice must be free and genuine: you cannot infer a decision to accept the cleaning merely from the later wearing of the shoes. To say otherwise would be to force an owner to renounce the use of his property. Then there is Bowen, L.J., in *Falcke v. Scottish Imperial Insurance Co.*: 'Liabilities are not to be forced upon people behind their backs any more than you can confer a benefit upon a man against his will.'[6] Again, though more bluntly, what is asserted is the individual's right to make his own choices. But, even although these *dicta* do accord with the basic orientation of English law, too much weight should not be attached to them. They come from cases in which the courts were still only at the beginning of the search for a stable analysis of non-contractual claims: issues which ought to be separated could not yet be distinctly seen and the full range of possibilities could not yet be reviewed. The premiss, supposing the necessity of a free choice, had in fact begun to be qualified well before the middle of the nineteenth century.[7]

(ii) *Three Tests of Enrichment*

Given that the possibility of subjective devaluation is not overridden by an appeal to the reasonable man, in what circumstances does English law accept that a benefit in kind does nevertheless constitute an enrichment? There seem to be three sets, (a) free acceptance, (b) incontrovertible benefit (the 'no reasonable man' test), and (c) *3 others.

(a) *Free Acceptance*

This has already been introduced, and later it has a chapter to itself.[8] We have seen that free acceptance constitutes a ground for restitution, going to the word 'unjust'. For when a defendant has passed up an opportunity to reject a benefit knowing that it was not offered gratuitously he has only himself to blame for the resulting situation. But free acceptance also goes to the issue of enrichment. For it defeats the possibility of subjective devaluation. If I have

---

[5] *Taylor v. Laird* [1856] 25 L.J. Ex. 329, 332.
[6] *Falcke v. Scottish Imperial Insurance Co.* (1886) 34 Ch.D. 234, 248.
[7] See, in particular, the discussion of *Exall v. Partridge*, below, p. 117f.
[8] Below, p. 266f.

stood by watching you clean my car, knowing that you did not intend a gift, I cannot easily appeal to my right of free choice. For I made my choice when I had the opportunity to reject. If I did not want the car cleaned, I should have said so. A free acceptance therefore disables recourse to the argument from subjective devaluation.

So free acceptance looks two ways, both to 'unjust' and to 'enrichment'. Among the grounds for restitution it is the only one which has this double rôle. That explains its still dominant role in claims for restitution in respect of benefits in kind. If a plaintiff in such a case based himself for his ground for restitution on a factor negativing voluntariness—typically mistake or compulsion—he might well find himself none the less driven to establish a free acceptance for the purpose of showing that the defendant was enriched; and, where free acceptance must be relied on for that purpose, there will be no need to dwell on the factor negativing voluntariness at all, since because of its bipolarity the free acceptance does both jobs at once.

It would seem to follow from this that there is little practical need to contemplate a 'mixed' claim. That is to say, one in which the ground for restitution, going to 'unjust', would be a factor negativing voluntariness, and the enrichment would be established by free acceptance. However, it is not impossible that, as cases multiply, a divergence may develop between the free acceptance necessary to constitute a ground for restitution and the kind of acceptance sufficient to disable subjective devaluation. If the conditions for a sufficient acceptance in the latter function became less strict than for the other, 'mixed claims' would become a practical reality.[9] Nor is such a divergence unlikely. For the question whether he has only himself to blame might well be said to require fuller knowledge—a more free acceptance—than the question whether he had sufficient scope for choice to disable any attempt at subjective devaluation of the benefit received. The facts of *Boulton* v. *Jones*[10] serve to illustrate this still conjectural possibility.

In that case Jones ordered, obtained, and used pipe hose but escaped having to pay for it. Boulton, who had supplied the goods, found his claim, based in contract, defeated by the fact that Jones' order had been addressed not to himself but to Brocklehurst, the previous owner of Boulton's shop. Boulton seems to have honoured the order on the assumption that it was addressed to the shop rather than to Brocklehurst personally, but the court evidently took the

---

[9] Below, p. 267.
[10] *Boulton* v. *Jones* (1857) 2 H. & N. 564; 27 L.J. Ex. 117.

view that there could be no contract either by his acceptance of an offer not intended for him or by Jones' subsequent acceptance of goods which he supposed to have come from Brocklehurst. There was one other important fact. Jones was in credit with Brocklehurst, so that he would have had to pay for goods supplied by him only by setting their value off against Brocklehurst's debt. For goods supplied by Boulton, Jones would have had to take money from his purse.

If we look for a claim in unjust enrichment on these facts, the first possibility which comes to mind is that Jones freely accepted the goods. He accepted them knowing that they were not offered gratuitously and having an opportunity to reject. But to this it can be reasonably objected that, given the fact of his own mistake, namely his belief that he could set the goods off against his credit with Brocklehurst, his acceptance was insufficiently free for it to be said that he had only himself to blame for not preventing the enrichment. In other words the acceptance was not free enough to make the enrichment 'unjust'. Nevertheless it might equally be maintained that the acceptance was sufficiently free to disable Jones from resorting to subjective devaluation. He could not realistically say on these facts that the goods were of no value to him because they were not chosen by him. Hence it might be said that his acceptance established 'enrichment' but not '*unjust* enrichment'. If so, Boulton's hope of restitution would depend on his finding another factor under that head, and his circumstances suggest that he could probably have relied on mistake. Such a claim would be 'mixed', using non-voluntariness under 'unjust', and a less than completely free acceptance only to establish 'enrichment'.

(b) *Incontrovertible Benefit: The 'No Reasonable Man' Test*

In this category there is no attempt to say that the defendant did somehow make his choice. It is admitted that he did not. So what is said is that on the facts any recourse to subjective devaluation would be so absolutely unreasonable that no reasonable man would try it. Or, put more simply, no reasonable man would say that the defendant was not enriched. There is a great difference between this 'no reasonable man' test and the adoption of a straightforward objective standard of value. The 'no reasonable man' test does no more than moderate the greater absurdities of a subjective approach. Take the case of the car cleaned in its owner's absence. An objective test might come up with a value of £5 on the basis that reasonable men habitually have their cars cleaned for that much money. But the 'no reasonable man' test would come to the opposite conclusion. For some reasonable men do not bother to incur that kind of expenditure; and some of them would say that to them the cleaning of a car was a completely worthless service.

So far as I know there is no case which expressly approaches the issue of enrichment through a 'no reasonable man' test. The phrase is no more than a formulation designed to express the basis of what has been done without much explanation in certain groups of cases. At present it is possible to identify two such groups, but it is important not to suppose that they necessarily exhaust the scope of the test which they seem to illustrate. No doubt there are many different situations in which no reasonable man would deny that the defendant has been enriched by his non-money benefit. The two currently identifiable groups can be called 'anticipation of necessary expenditure', and 'realization in money'. It hardly needs to be added that the commonest example of a benefit which is proved to be an enrichment by the 'no reasonable man' test is the receipt of money itself. But here we are only concerned with non-money benefits. The question is, which non-money benefits can be regarded as so unequivocally enriching as to be equivalent in effect to a receipt of money?

Anticipation of Necessary Expenditure   Where the plaintiff has conferred a benefit on the defendant which was necessary to the defendant in the sense that he would have had to seek it himself, or would have sought it if he had not been deprived of the opportunity (as by absence or disability), no reasonable man would deny that the defendant had been enriched by the amount which he himself would have had to lay out. The necessity making the expenditure incumbent on the defendant may have been legal (he was bound by law to make it) or factual (his circumstances called for it). Recourse to subjective devaluation is impossible in respect of a benefit which the defendant must necessarily have chosen.

In *Exall* v. *Partridge*[11] the plaintiff brought an action for money paid to the use of the defendant. His pleading was that at the defendant's request he had paid money to a third party on the defendant's behalf. But the real facts which he adduced were different. He had paid the defendant's rent, but not because the defendant asked him to do so. The rent being in arrears, the landlord had distrained. He had taken possession of a carriage on the defendant's premises. The carriage belonged to the plaintiff. In order to release the carriage from the distraint the plaintiff had paid off the rent. His claim for restitution succeeded. It was argued that the benefit to the defendant was sufficient in itself to support the

---

[11] *Exall* v. *Partridge* (1799) 8 T.R. 308.

necessary 'implication' of a request. Lord Kenyon, C.J., rejected that. There also had to be, in modern terms, a factor calling for restitution. But that was supplied by the compulsion exerted through the lawful detention of the carriage. At this point we are not concerned with that factor. Why could it so easily be assumed that the defendant was enriched even though he had received no money but only a benefit in kind, namely the discharge of his debt? What is special about that particular non-money benefit? The answer is that one who discharges another's debt anticipates for him an expenditure which he was legally bound to make. It is the easiest kind of case under this head. There is no doubt, therefore, on the issue of the defendant's enrichment.

There are very many cases like *Exall* v. *Partridge.* [12] Very similar, but not quite identical, are the old family of funeral cases in which a plaintiff who had buried, or paid someone else to bury, a body for which the defendant was primarily responsible was able to claim either *quantum meruit* for his work or, through the count for money paid, reimbursement of his outlay. [13] So far as concerns the enrichment issue, these cases formally resemble the others in that the defendant is said to have been under a legal duty to bury the body, which duty was discharged by the plaintiff. So they are again cases illustrating the anticipation of legally necessary expenditure. But they can also be looked at as occupying a position intermediate between legal and factual necessity. For the duty imposed on the defendant, the father or the husband of the deceased, was recognised precisely to provide a basis for dealing with the factual necessity of burying the dead. It is important to emphasise that mention of 'necessity' at this stage had no reference to the reason why the plaintiffs were entitled to restitution (the factor going to 'unjust'); the question for the moment is only why the defendants could be said to be enriched despite the absence of any request or acceptance. The answer is that they were saved an expenditure necessarily incumbent on them.

The defendant may have been under no legal obligation to incur the expenditure anticipated by the plaintiff. Nevertheless there is authority to the effect that a merely factual necessity is sufficient. in *Craven-Ellis* v. *Canons Ltd.* [14] the Court of Appeal took the view that the services of a managing director were necessary to a commercial company. The plaintiff had worked in that capacity for the defendant company in the mistaken belief that he had a valid contract

---

[12] Below, p. 187 f.
[13] Below, p. 197 f.
[14] *Craven-Ellis* v. *Canons Ltd.* [1936] 2 K.B. 403.

for remuneration. His claim for *quantum meruit* was successful. The company could not subjectively devalue the benefit which it had received, because if the plaintiff had not done the work the company would have had to pay someone else to do it.[15]

Craven-Ellis brings out two very important points about this test. First, to rely on a factual necessity of this kind in order to disable the defendant's recourse to subjective devaluation does not entail any comment as to the reason why the plaintiff conferred the benefit. This has to be constantly emphasised because it is easy to slip into the error of supposing that there is an exclusive relationship between this particular test of enrichment and one particular reason for the plaintiff's intervention, namely the moral compulsion arising from an emergency. This incorrect linkage will be avoided if the issues of enrichment and *unjust* enrichment (i.e. the grounds calling for restitution) are kept religiously separate. It is true that, in cases in which the ground for restitution is that species of moral compulsion, the most readily available test of enrichment will generally be the 'no reasonable man' test in its particular *Craven-Ellis* manifestation (i.e. that the expenditure was factually necessary to the defendant). For example, if I respond to your danger by providing medical care for your body, shelter for your horse, storage for your goods, my weapon against subjective devaluation by you is likely to be that these benefits were pressingly necessary for you: if you had not been disabled by unconsciousness, disorientation or physical absence you would have sought them yourself; indeed you would have regarded yourself as bound to seek them. So it is true that emergencies vividly exemplify this test of enrichment, with the effect that claims based on moral compulsion (under 'unjust') will usually employ this approach to the issue of enrichment. But the proposition cannot be turned round. That is, this test of enrichment is *not* tied to the moral compulsion test of 'unjust'. In *Craven-Ellis* itself the plaintiff did not perceive the company to be in danger, a ship with no-one at the helm. He merely supposed, mistakenly, that he had a contract. His reliance on factual necessity was thus directed solely at the issue of enrichment, while his ground for restitution was mistake.

The same phenomenon can be observed in a situation in which food and lodging are supplied to a person whose mental condition deprives him of contractual capacity, as for example in *Re Rhodes*.[16] Provided the supplies come within the notion of necessaries the supplier will have anticipated expenditure which the recipient would

---

[15] *Ibid.*, at p. 412.
[16] *Re Rhodes* (1890) 44 Ch.D. 94.

have had to incur anyhow. But that says nothing of why the supplier intervened; it settles the enrichment issue but nothing else. As for the reason for the intervention it may have been moral compulsion or it may not, as in the case of a tradesman supplying in the normal course of his business. In *Re Rhodes* itself these different questions are not disentangled. We will return to them in the discussion of 'unjust'.

Upton R.D.C. v. *Powell*[17] may provide another example though the plaintiffs' claim was actually, though surprisingly, upheld in contract. The Upton fire brigade went to a fire at the defendant's house. They mistakenly believed his house was in their area, in which case the service would have been gratuitous. The defendant had also not expected to have to pay. He had merely telephoned the police to call for 'the fire brigade'; he had not sought to get help from outside his area. The actual intentions of the parties make it difficult to find any contract. But it could be said that the brigade rendered necessary services which no reasonable man would have rejected. Relying on that test of enrichment, the fire brigade would never the less probably not have been able to rely on moral compulsion as their reason for restitution, since on their own admission what caused them to go to the defendant's house was a mistaken belief that he was within the area of their duty. Yet, even if moral compulsion was excluded, they could, like Craven-Ellis, rely on mistake. Hence a non-contractual explanation of this difficult case can be based on the 'no reasonable man' test of enrichment; and on mistake, as the ground for restitution.

The second important observation emanating from *Craven-Ellis* v. *Canons Ltd.* is that a factual necessity does not have to be absolute. That is to say, a plaintiff can claim to have anticipated inevitable expenditure even though it cannot be said to be 100 per cent certain that the defendant would have incurred the expenditure anyhow or would if he had been able to give his mind to it. A company is not bound by law, or obliged by nature, even to maintain itself in existence, let alone to provide for the active management of its affairs. So when one says that a given expenditure was factually necessary or inevitable for the defendant, one excludes unrealistic *4 or fanciful possibilities of his doing without it.

This raises a question for the future. Since the necessity for the expenditure need not be absolute there is room to choose between either a strict or a liberal interpretation of the test. A strict interpretation would insist on a high degree of inevitability and would be

---

[17] *Upton R.D.C.* v. *Powell* [1942] 1 All E.R. 220.

unwilling to characterise many contrary possibilities as merely fanciful. There is much to be said for not taking too strict a view. For, on the one hand, it is the common experience of modern life that much expenditure is not really freely chosen except within the narrowest limits; or, looking at the matter in another way, we do all value, need, and buy much the same services and commodities. On the other, the phenomenon of subjective devaluation, though not to be callously overriden (because it is, despite the last point, still the outwork of a worthwhile freedom), is not so laudable as to require jealous defence in the nineteenth-century manner. Common law man has lost the rougher edges of his individualism.

The more liberal approach can find guidance in the law which says what constitutes a 'necessary' to a minor or other person under an incapacity. Conservative use of language there preserves the memory of a class system which would better be forgotten. Shorn of those overtones, goods and services are necessary to a minor not only when they serve to support life but also when they maintain him in the circumstances of life in which he happens to find himself.[18] The test of inevitable expenditure should develop on the same lines.

Realization in Money   If the recipient of a benefit which can be turned into money does turn it into money he can no longer resort to subjective devaluation. No reasonable man would say otherwise. For, though he received a benefit which he might or might not have wanted, he has put himself in the position of one who received money. I come back to find that you have built me a new kitchen. I refuse to pay because I did not choose to have it. You say that your input of £3000 has raised the value of the house by £5000. I reply that I have not the least intention of selling. But then I do sell. I take the added value in money, £3000 of it at your expense. If the enrichment issue was the only obstacle to your claim before I sold, you ought now to succeed. The obvious practical difficulties in the event of a long delay before realization are not insuperable.

Have the courts used this test? The evidence that they have mostly comes from a specialised context. Suppose that I mine your coal and sell it or that I repair the bodywork of your car and then realize the full improved value. You now sue me in tort. The law is that you can recover only the pre-improvement value, except in the case in which I was more than a merely technical wrongdoer because I knew that I had no right to deal with the *res* in question. When you recover the pre-improvement value I take the benefit of my input. This con-

---

[18] *Sale of Goods Act, 1979*, s. 3 (2); *Peters* v. *Fleming* (1840) 6 M. & W. 42; *Chapple* v. *Cooper* (1844) 13 M. & W. 252; *Ryder* v. *Wombwell* (1868) L.R. 4 Exch. 32.

clusion is secure. There was some hesitation at first. But a powerful speech of Lord Macnaghten in *Peruvian Guano Co.* v. *Dreyfus Brothers & Co.,*[19] in 1887, set the law on this sensible track. So far as goods are concerned the defendant's allowance for improvements is now statutory, for the *Torts (Interference with Goods) Act, 1977, s. 6 (1),* provides that, when an improver is sued for tortious interference, 'an allowance shall be made for the extent to which, at the time as at which the goods fall to be valued in assessing damages, the value of the goods is attributable to the improvement'.[20]

The relevance of this to the test of 'realized enrichment' comes in the explanation of the contrast between the availability of this allowance to a defendant (a passive claim) and the difficulty in the path of a plaintiff who seeks to obtain the same allowance (an active claim). Take the case in which, while you are away on holiday, I get your car repaired and serviced, not with the intention of selling it, but simply to save you the worry and trouble (but not the expense) of getting it done yourself. On your return you have undisputed possession of the improved car. You do not have to sue for it. Even supposing that I can point to a factor calling for restitution—say, a mistaken belief that you had asked me to get the work done—I will have a difficult task[21] to make out an active claim. For you will take the enrichment issue: you did not want the work done. My only hope, probably vain, will be for a very liberal application of the inevitable expenditure test.

What is the difference between the case in which you sue me in tort and this case in which you retain possession of the improved *res*? The answer must be that, when you have to sue for damages, your claim itself is a form of realisation in money. That is to say, you will recover money, and if you recovered the full improved value you would be in the same position as one who elected to sell an improved *res* still in his possession. The suit for damages turns everything into money and eliminates the possibility of subjective devaluation.

That this is the correct explanation finds support from the more hesitant treatment of the case in which the plaintiff seeks, not damages, but the return *in specie* of the improved *res*.[22] It is tempting

---

[19] *Peruvian Guano Co.* v. *Dreyfus Brothers & Co.* [1892] A.C. 166, 170n. Cf. *Munro* v. *Willmott* [1949] 1 K.B. 295.

[20] The section confines this allowance to those improvers who act in 'the mistaken but honest belief' in their title. Section 6 (2) deals with the case in which an action is taken against a purchaser from the improver and gives the same allowance where this purchaser bought in good faith.

[21] But see *Greenwood* v. *Bennett* [1973] 1 Q.B. 195, 202 *per* Lord Denning, M.R.; *contra*, Cairns, L.J., at p. 203.

[22] Cf. Lord Macnaghten's discussion of the point in *Peruvian Guano* [1892] A.C. 166, 176.

to say that if a defendant improver can take the value of his input against a claim for damages then he must surely have the same allowance against an order for specific return. This may now be the law.[23] But it certainly does not follow automatically. Indeed to allow this passive claim in all cases will require the courts to adopt an entirely new approach to enrichment.[24] For there is no obvious and general reason why *all* improvers should be better placed as defendants. On the contrary, an advantage of that kind ought if possible to be avoided, since it encourages obstinacy in wrongful possession. But there is a rational line between the position of the defendant opposing a claim for damages and all other improvers, whether in possession, looking for a passive claim, or out of possession, looking for an active claim. Only the claim to damages turns the improvement into money. In the other cases, passive or active, the owner of the improved *res* escapes that bar to his argument from subjective devaluation. According to anything said so far the improver must then see whether he can establish that the owner freely accepted his work or, rather unlikely, that the work anticipated necessary expenditure on the owner's part. In other words, passive claims opposed to demands for damages are explicable, so far as concerns the issue of enrichment, by the 'realization' test of enrichment; but active claims against owners in possession, and even passive claims opposed to demands for specific redelivery, require the enrichment issue to be settled by some other test. The issue cannot simply be ignored.

Outside this specialised context where passive claims are made by defendants to actions for damages, there are other traces of the same idea, albeit never reasoned out. In *Stocks* v. *Wilson*,[25] an infant who had received furniture realised its value in money. Lush, J., fastened on that realisation and found the infant liable to repay the amount of money thus received. That was wrong, because, even if the infant had received money to start with, he would not have been liable to repay. Lush, J., never looked into the second measure of restitution. That is, he never asked what happened after the realization, with a view to identifying what, if anything, the infant still had left. So he asked himself: Could you say that the infant had been enriched? He never went on to ask: Does any of that enrichment survive in his hands? Even though it thus attacked the minor's defence too radically, the case remains a valid example of enrichment

---

[23] After *Greenwood* v. *Bennett*, above, n. 21.
[24] See below, p. 124 f.
[25] *Stocks* v. *Wilson* [1913] 2 K.B. 235.

intuitively tested by realization. The case is considered more fully in a later chapter.[26]

In *Greenwood* v. *Bennett*[27] itself, a Jaguar car owned by Bennett was stolen and crashed by the thief, who then sold it as a near-wreck to Harper. Harper repaired it, believing it to be his. He brought it back into good condition and sold it on. The police took possession of it and prosecuted the thief. Then, because there were a number of claimants, they applied to the County Court to be told who should get it. They were ordered to give it to Bennett. Harper, one of the unsuccessful claimants, appealed, claiming *inter alia* that Bennett should pay him some £226 for labour and materials used in the repair. This is, arguably, the case of an improver passively claiming his allowance against a claim for specific return. His claim was successful. How the 'enrichment' issue in the case was settled is something of a mystery. One possible solution will be considered in the next section. At this point it is only necessary to observe that, at the time of the Court of Appeal hearing, Bennett had sold the car at its full improved value and had thus taken in money the value of Harper's input.[28] To what extent if any this fact influenced the court's attitude to the enrichment issue is not knowable. However, that realization in money is a fact capable of explaining why the issue of enrichment seemed to need no attention. Another possibility is that, since Bennett was a dealer in cars, the repair of a car for the purpose of profitable re-sale might have been said to be a commercially necessary expenditure under the other limb of the 'no reasonable man' test.

(c) *Others*

The common characteristic of the previous two heads is that they involve tests which are compatible with the basic acceptance of subjective devaluation. But there are some cases which drop no hints as to how that compatibility might have been perceived, whether intuitively or otherwise. Although one might jiggle them into some corner of the pattern, the safer and more honest course is to admit that they do not fit: in them the court simply took the view that the recipient's benefit was 'obvious'. But that, if it happens, is quite striking. If it were done frequently it would change the whole orientation of the law towards benefits in kind. For to take enrichment simply as a matter of impression, not calling for analysis, would be to apply a rough and ready standard of reasonableness. In other

---

[26] Below, p. 399 f.
[27] *Greenwood* v. *Bennett* [1973] 1 Q.B. 195.
[28] This was stated in argument by Harper's counsel, at p. 198.

words, to adopt an objective approach, exactly the opposite technique from that with which the common law has grown up.

Greenwood v. *Bennett* is such a case. We have just seen how it can be made to fit into the pattern on the basis of the 'no reasonable man' test. But the fact is that the court made no enquiry into the issue of enrichment. One cannot see how they would have approached the question if the car's improved value had not been realized and if Harper's work on the car had been slightly more eccentric, say a conversion of engine and suspension for the special purpose of rally driving. A more obviously controversial improvement of that kind might have alerted them to the need for a firm choice between subjective and objective assessment. As it is, the case seems to exemplify exceptional recourse to an objective standard. But its authority is weak, for want of any analysis of the problem.

In *Greenwood* v. *Bennett* there was some, rather half-hearted, reference to 'equitable principles'.[29] The notion, not spelled out, seems to have been that Bennett, to whom possession of the car had been awarded, could be regarded as having needed the equitable remedy of specific redelivery; in which case the discretion inherent in all equitable remedies would provide the peg on which to hang the order to pay Harper's input. The old case of *Cooper* v. *Phibbs*[30] has a strikingly similar structure. An uncle did work to improve a salmon fishery. His nephew later took a lease of it. It then turned out that it belonged to the nephew all along. When the nephew sought recission, the uncle's trustees were allowed a claim, secured by a lien, for his expenditure on the improvements. But the nephew had not freely accepted the work on his land. Again there is no analysis of the enrichment issue.

In *Boardman* v. *Phipps*[31] the same phenomenon occurs. Boardman, the solicitor to a trust, very successfully, and profitably to both himself and the trust, bought out the majority holding in a company in which the trust had a minority stake. But to do it he had to break his duty as a fiduciary to avoid situations in which his own interest conflicted with the interests of those relying on him. The action was brought by a beneficiary under the trust to make him pay back his profit. Holding him liable to make restitution the House of Lords none the less held that he in his turn must be allowed a liberal allowance for all his work and skill. Again there was no discussion of

---

[29] *Greenwood* v. *Bennett* [1973] 1 Q.B. 195, 198 (arg.), 201, *per* Lord Denning, M.R.; 202, *per* Phillimore, L.J.
[30] *Cooper* v. *Phibbs* (1867) L.R. 2 H.L. 149.
[31] *Boardman* v. *Phipps* [1967] 2 A.C. 46.

the need for free acceptance or some other answer to subjective devaluation.

Cooper v. *Phibbs* and *Boardman* v. *Phipps* (but not *Greenwood* v. *Bennett*) may in this matter share the same explanation. Where a plaintiff seeks restitution he must make counter-restitution. If he begins to insist that some benefit received by him is valueless or cannot be valued as against him because it was not wanted by him, he may defeat his own claim by making counter-restitution impossible. So in such cases it is not so much that the law over-rides his subjective devaluation as that he himself has no interest in resorting to that argument. It may be, therefore, that in the context of counter-restitution the court can make an objective valuation unopposed.[32]

A major inroad into the traditional approach has been made by the *Law Reform (Frustrated Contracts) Act, 1943*. As we shall see,[33] this statute now requires the courts to value non-money benefits which have not been freely accepted, irrespective of any question whether they were necessaries to their recipient. The one great case on the operation of the Act shows what great difficulties attend this exercise. In doing so it reveals one aspect of the rationale behind the traditional deference to a subjective notion of value. Nevertheless, there is no doubt that the law in this field has, to a certain extent, broken the ice, by showing that objective valuation though difficult, is not impossible and, if sensitively done, need not outrage individual freedom of choice.

In a related area the common law has achieved a similar result. Where a party accepts a repudiatory breach by the other and terminates the contract on that account, he is entitled to the reasonable value of any part performance of his own. That is the *Planché* v. *Colburn* claim,[34] an alternative to compensatory damages. Suppose I have built half a house when our contract ends. I can have a *quantum meruit* for the work done. This cannot be explained by free acceptance, since you never had an opportunity to accept or to decline half a house. You thought you were getting the entire building and were content to allow me to work on that basis. Nor can the half-performance be said (unless in some unusual facts) to pass the 'no reasonable man' test. Yet the claim succeeds. How is the enrichment issue settled? It may be that objective valuation is allowable against a party in breach; or perhaps against any wrongdoer. More cautiously it might be said that a party in breach of contract cannot push the argument from subjective devaluation to extremes.

---

[32] Below, p. 419 ff.
[33] Below, p. 249 ff.
[34] *Planché* v. *Colburn* (1831) 8 Bing. 14, below, p. 232.

On these facts there is at least a 'limited acceptance' in the sense that what you have received is part of a project which you certainly did want. It may therefore be that, at least against a party in breach, 'limited acceptance' is sufficient to turn aside any attempt at subjective devaluation.

The common feature of all these examples is that the courts allow themselves to get to valuation of benefits in kind without making sure that subjective devaluation is obstructed by the defendants' free acceptance or by the 'no reasonable man' test. There is one more area in which value is apparently assessed objectively. It concerns living partners, whether formally married or not, who have made non-money contributions to the acquisition or improvement of a home owned at law by the other partner. This is matter which has to be used cautiously, since it is not clear that the courts' response can be said to be based solely on unjust enrichment. There are two divergencies. First, the response is not measured to produce solely restitutionary relief. Secondly, the response is not triggered exclusively by the scale of the benefits conferred by one living-partner on the other, as opposed to the operation of the intentions of the partners at the time of the acquisition or improvement. Nevertheless, this group of cases can be used to show that, where subjective notions of enrichment would militate against a firm policy of protecting an economically disadvantaged group (here non-owning partners, mostly women), the courts can switch without hesitation to objective valuation of such matters as contributions in kind and improvements to homes.

There are three situations. In the first the non-owning partner has contributed to the acquisition of a house. In the second he or she has contributed to the discharge of the mortgage after the acquistion of the house. In the third situation the claiming partner has improved the house after it has been acquired. There was a time, one might equally say before all the post-war social changes, or before Lord Denning presided in the Court of Appeal, when these situations offered the claiming partner little hope, and almost none which could be said to be peculiar to the relationship of formal or informal marriage. Resulting trusts seemed the most promising category. But since they could effect only an initial distribution of equitable title at the moment of acquisition and could not achieve a subsequent redistribution after the purchase they could not securely reach either the second or the third situation.[35] Even in the first situation, the

---

[35] Following *Gissing* v. *Gissing* [1971] A.C. 886, and *Pettitt* v. *Pettitt* [1970] A.C. 777, the proper limits of classical resulting trust doctrines were brilliantly stated by Bagnall, J., in *Cowcher* v. *Cowcher* [1972] 1 W.L.R. 425. His suggestions for systematic development of those doctrines on the basis of 'money consensus' have not been taken up.

contributions which fell to be considered were, in practice, always in money, not in kind.

All this has changed. Resulting trusts can, strictly speaking, still only deal with the first situation; but other doctrines, reinforced by statute,[36] now cover the cases of improvements after the purchase and contributions in discharge of mortgages. Moreover, it has become clear, not only in relation to improvements where the point is self-evident, that contributions need not be in money. A partner who has kept house so as to liberate the other's earning power will be regarded as having made a valuable contribution, and work such as building and decorating can fall to be assessed under the head of contribution or of improvement.[37]

Some examples might be fitted within the notion of free acceptance and some, notably housekeeping work, could be pushed under anticipation of necessary expenditure. But it is perfectly clear that elaborate explanations of that kind would not capture the character of what the courts have been doing. They have not been feeling their way round the obstacle of subjective devaluation. That would have been out of accord with the underlying social policy, which has been to improve the position of the claiming partner without regard to the wishes and choices of the other, often economically dominant, member of the pair. In that spirit, the courts have clearly been willing to look at his or her input of labour and materials and to assess its quantum and value objectively, taking the view of the market or the reasonable man. We have earlier used an example in which I come back to find that you have put a new kitchen on my house. The supposition was that you were a mere stranger. If you are my spouse *vel quasi* there is no room for me to complain about my liberty to choose how my money should be spent.

(iii) *Four More Points*

We have been speaking of tests for enrichment which are either compatible with the basic orientation in favour of a subjective notion of value or which turn aside to an objective approach, asking what a reasonable man would pay on the market for the goods or services in question. We now end with four miscellaneous points all of which

---

[36] *Matrimonial Proceedings and Property Act, 1970*, s. 37, giving the court a discretion to declare that a spouse has acquired an interest or an enhanced interest in a house by reason of having effected a substantial improvement to it.

[37] *Davis* v. *Vale* [1971] 1 W.L.R. 1022; *Cooke* v. *Head* [1972] 1 W.L.R. 518; *Hall* v. *Hall* (1982) 2 F.L.R. 379; *Bernard* v. *Josephs* [1982] Ch. 391.

bear on the issue of enrichment but are not in themselves tests of enrichment.

(a) *Positive and Negative*

A difference is sometimes taken between accretions of wealth and savings of expenditure. Accretions (positive enrichments) are typified by receipt of money or goods. Savings of expenditure (negative enrichments) are exemplified by user over time of somebody else's property, as for instance by driving his car or occupying his land without paying. In *Phillips* v. *Homfray*,[38] the Court of Appeal appeared to suggest that restitutionary claims were concerned only with positive accretions to the defendant's wealth. The particular question in issue was whether a restitutionary claim would lie for trespassory user of the plaintiff's land. One reason why it would not was that such user amounted at most to a negative enrichment.

Phillips v. *Homfray* is a difficult case. Whatever its correct explanation, the distinction between positive and negative enrichments cannot be good. The court seems almost to have embraced the proposition that every restitutionary claim must be in respect of money had and received. If that were right, the enrichment must indeed be positive, since the receipt of money always is so. Yet it is not right, since, if restitution for negative enrichments was impossible, there would be no such claims for debts discharged or for work done. For in both cases the recipient saves outlay: he would have to pay his creditor[39] or he would have had to get the work done.[40] Work which does leave a marketable residuum (something made, built or improved) might be said to be a positive enrichment, but work in the nature of a service (professional advice, medical diagnosis, office cleaning) is indisputably negative. In this it exactly resembles user over time of a chattel or of land. Saving man's dignity, his work is the user or enjoyment obtainable from him over time. It is referred to as his 'time', and he markets his time (time in himself) just as he hires out time in his corporeal property.

The purpose of this section is to affirm that saving of expenditure especially by receipt of enjoyment over time in a person or thing is as well capable of counting as an enrichment as is any other non-money benefit. That is to say, it will so count as long as, on the particular facts, it passes one of the tests of enrichment, whether free acceptance or some other. Negative benefits are not ruled out *in limine*.

[38] *Phillips* v. *Homfray* (1883) 24 Ch.D. 439, discussed below, p. 321 ff.
[39] Cf. *Exall* v. *Partridge*, discussed above, p. 117.
[40] Cf. *Craven-Ellis* v. *Canons Ltd.*, discussed above, p. 118 f.

(b) *Specific Restitution*

There is a difference between cases in which the defendant is asked to give up exactly what he received and cases in which the demand is that he should give up value held in a form different from the actual receipt. Most cases are of the latter kind, and it is in them that the real engine behind the argument from subjective devaluation is to be found. Take the case of work which, from the objective viewpoint of the reasonable man, improves my land. I may be asked to make restitution in money or by giving up a share in or a temporary interest in the land. Either way I am expected to give up something which I undoubtedly do regard as valuable, money or my land, chosen by me. So I can reasonably say: 'If you make me effect restitution on these facts, you will be taking wealth from me for something which is valueless to me because not chosen by me.' The force of my argument comes from the fact that I am being asked to give value for what I find valueless. You want me to effect restitution by giving up something which is indisputably valuable to me (because chosen by me) in place of something which, though you say it has value, has no value to me according to my subjective viewpoint.

It is quite different when I am asked to give up exactly what I received. A claim for specific redelivery is always immune from subjective devaluation. The same is true where restitution is effected, without any actual redelivery, by raising an interest *in rem* for the plaintiff in precisely the *res* received by the defendant at his expense. For example, in *Hodgson* v. *Marks*[41] the fact that Mrs Hodgson's equitable interest came into existence effected restitution in the eye of the law even before any order for conveyance was made or implemented. Similarly, where I exercise a power to rescind, the fact that title is recalled to me in itself effects restitution in the eye of the law, with the consequence that, restitution having been effected, my next practical step may be to defend the interest so reacquired by means which have nothing to do with restitution in the technical sense, as for instance by suing you for the tort of conversion with a view to obtaining compensatory damages. Restitutionary retransfer of title, whether or not accompanied by a retransfer of possession, can never be opposed by the argument from subjective devaluation. The reason is that the defendant, losing only what he received, has all the less reason to complain if in his own view the subject-matter is of no value.

---

[41] Above, p. 58 ff.

(c) *Money Received, Devaluation* Ex Post Facto

We have seen that, because money is the very measure of value, the receipt of money is normally conclusive of enrichment. If necessary this conclusion can be referred to the 'no reasonable man' test. There is, however, one important qualification. Suppose I receive £5000 and then, exulting in my sudden and unwonted material freedom, I do something with some of the money which I would not otherwise have done. I have a new suit made and treat myself to a week at the Salzburg festival. I spend £1500 in this way. And to keep guilt at bay I give £500 to charity. So I have spent £2000 in all. Then it turns out that I face a claim for restitution of the full £5000. It was, say, a payment by mistake. I had no reason to suspect it when I spent the money.

On these facts it is reasonable for me to object that my choice of how to spend the money was so inextricably dependent on my receipt of the money that the claim for restitution, *quoad* the £2000, is in effect to make me pay for benefits in kind rather than in money. The plaintiff's payment led me into vitiated choices. If he gets restitution he will be compelling me to pay for things I did not want. This is an inversion of the test of enrichment called 'realization in money'. There I turn a non-money benefit into cash and thus reveal myself incontrovertibly enriched. But here I turn cash into kind and raise a question whether I do not thereby undo my enrichment. This is important in relation to the defence of change of position.[42]

(d) *Enrichment, Not a Difficult Issue*

This chapter began by asserting that the issue of enrichment was essentially a simple one. It is important to end on that note. If the questions seem less than simple it is because they have not been attended to, not because of genuine intellectual complexity. Where money has been received then, subject to the point just made about changes of position, *cadit quaestio*. With benefits in kind matters are less straightforward. But the elementary structure of the problem should not be forgotten. 'One man's meat is another man's poison.' The law needs to know what its position is in relation to the argument based on that idea. I have called that argument 'subjective devaluation'. Does the law utterly reject it? *Semble* English law does not. If that is right, the problem in relation to non-money benefits comes down to these separate questions. First, what are the natural limits of subjective devaluation? The answer is that nobody can use

---

[42] Below, p. 413.

this argument if he freely accepted the benefit or was incontrovertibly enriched by it to the extent that no reasonable man would say that he was not. Where the argument is naturally excluded the way is open for a judicial valuation of the benefit in question. Secondly, where this argument is in principle available, on what facts, if any, will the court override it? It is here that uncertainty creeps in. At present, examples of objective assessment look miscellaneous, even accidental. A statute or a clear protective policy provide two obvious types of explanation for this more robust approach. Counter-restitution is a context in which subjective devaluation is not in the interests of the party, this time the plaintiff, who might use it. For the rest, the question of other justifications for objective valuation remains open. The crucial lesson for the future is that the issue of enrichment must always receive independent attention.

2. AT THE PLAINTIFF'S EXPENSE

The plaintiff must bring himself within himself within these words. If he cannot he has not even a *prima facie* entitlement to sue. For the defendant may have been enriched, and unjustly, yet unless it happened at the plaintiff's expense it will seem to be no business of his. That is what Goulding, J., meant when he said that the words 'unjust enrichment' fail on their own to identify any plaintiff.[43] We have already noticed that in the ambivalent and super-generic conception of the restitutionary event the phrase has two possible senses; and we have expelled the 'wrong' sense.[44] So at this stage we only have to consider the 'subtraction' sense, according to which the plaintiff's *prima facie* title to sue is simply that he is the person who has lost by the defendant's gain. The word 'subtraction' was chosen only to express this idea and nothing special should be made of its other overtones. In particular it does not imply that the defendant furtively or otherwise took the wealth in question from the plaintiff. It signifies only that the plus to the defendant is a minus to the plaintiff.

When you earn your salary or are given a present, the fact that I, a stranger, did not add my consent is neither here nor there. When you receive something by subtraction from me, the picture changes.

---

[43] 'Unjust enrichment cannot be a complete cause of action in itself, for (short of the law giving an action to a common informer) it does not identify the plaintiff,' *Chase Manhattan N.A.* v. *Israel-British Bank (London) Ltd.* [1980] 2 W.L.R. 202.

[44] Above, pp. 22–27, 40–44.

If I did not consent, the onus moves to you to explain why I should not have it back. This is the immediate importance of the subtraction sense of 'at the expense of'. It opens the way to restitution based on factors negativing voluntariness and free acceptance. The mechanism is this. The *prima facie* title to claim restitution is at first balanced by the social interest in the security of receipts. This means that the would-be plaintiff can make nothing of being the loser by the defendant's gain if he has merely changed his mind after the event. That balance immediately breaks if he can show that he never meant the transfer to be made, or not at least in the events which have happened. If that is so, he has not changed his mind; but he may none the less have accepted a risk of disappointment. Even then, despite being a risk-taking volunteer, he may, by pointing to a free acceptance, be able to show that the defendant chose not to stop the risk from being run.

By comparison with the issues of 'enrichment' and 'unjust', the question covered by the phrase 'at the plaintiff's expense' will almost always be uncontroversial. The plaintiff will have been in possession of the wealth in question and there will have been a simple transfer from him to the defendant, effected either by the plaintiff himself, as where he paid money to the defendant, or by the defendant, as where he crept into the plaintiff's house and took it. But there is one important area of difficulty.

Interceptive Subtraction   Can a plaintiff ever get himself within the subtraction sense of 'at the expense of' if the defendant received his enrichment not from the plaintiff himself but from some third hand? If so, in what circumstances can he do so? These are important issues. They do not only control the question whether he has any *prima facie* title to sue. They also determine whether that title is or is not dependent on proof of a wrong. Suppose that you have sold my car for £3000 to X without my permission or knowledge. You have received the £3000 from X, not from me. If I can get myself within the subtraction sense of 'at the expense of' I will be able to establish a *prima facie* title to sue without relying on your wrong. If not, the only way I can make a connexion between me and that £3000 is by relying on the conversion, so that from the very threshold my claim will be founded on that wrong.

The answer is that it is possible for the subtraction sense of this phrase to reach receipt from a third party, and in principle it is easy to say in what circumstances it can do so. If the wealth in question would certainly have arrived in the plaintiff if it had not been intercepted by the defendant *en route* from the third party, it is true to say that the plaintiff has lost by the defendant's gain. This kind of subtraction has to be distinguished from the normal case as 'interceptive' or 'anticipatory'. Nevertheless the conclusion is not artificial. The certainty that the plaintiff would have obtained the wealth in question does genuinely indicate that he became poorer by the sum in which the defendant was enriched.

There is, however, some difficulty about the circumstances in which you can say that the plaintiff would certainly have received the money if the defendant had not. It is generally not an easy fact to find. There are some cases in which it can be done on the basis that the plaintiff had a claim for it against the third party. The old cases on the profits of an office illustrate that.[45] If you usurp my office and take the money which is due to me you must make restitution to me; and it is clear that, because they are 'my' profits (even though I have never actually received them) I can get myself within the subtraction sense of the phrase and do not have to base myself on your wrongful usurpation. It is the same if you intercept rent due to me from my tenant.[46] You receive from the tenant but in doing so you make me poorer. The conclusion is easy because I had a legal claim for the money against the third party.

Suppose I had no claim. X simply wanted to give me some money; it suited him to send it to you. He told you that the money was for me; you spent it on yourself. The crucial question should be whether X manifested an intent which was final, whether he meant to give up all right to countermand his instruction to you. But the modern common law seems to have decided that that question cannot be answered without the help of an artificial test. It therefore says that I have no claim against you unless and until you have attorned to me; that is, until you have told me you are holding for me.[47] Up to that attornment I have no standing. The matter lies entirely between you and X. After the attornment I can sue. But the attornment itself is nothing but the artificial marker of the moment at which it becomes certain that the sum of money would not have been taken back by X but would, if you had not made off with it, have come

---

[45] *Arris* v. *Stukely* (1677) 2 Mod. 260; *Howard* v. *Wood* (1679) 2 Show. K.B. 21; *Boswell* v. *Milbank* (1772) 1 T.R. 399. It is said by *Goff and Jones*, at p. 446, that such cases can be classified nowadays as examples of 'waiver of tort', but the meaning of that phrase is doubtful (see below, p. 318). It is certain that such plaintiffs can make out a claim in unjust enrichment, without relying on the wrong done by the defendant.

[46] *Asher* v. *Wallis* (1707) 11 Mod. 146; *Lyell* v. *Kennedy* (1889) 14 App. Cas. 437.

[47] *Liversidge* v. *Broadbent* (1859) 4 H. & N. 603; *Griffin* v. *Weatherby* (1868) L.R. 2 Q.B. 753; *Shamia* v. *Joory* [1958] 1 Q.B. 448.

through to me. It cannot be regarded as a contract, because I have given no consideration; nor as an event passing property, because property cannot be passed in a quantity of unspecified money. So my cause of action would seem to be based on your enrichment at my expense—at my expense in the sense that you have committed an interceptive subtraction of wealth which was certainly *en route* to me. That merely *prima facie* title to sue is then completed when I show, just as in the case of interception of profits or rents, that your enrichment happened without my knowledge, i.e. that it was non-voluntary in the sense already introduced in the last chapter.

The approach of equity to the same situation is rather different. It does not look for an attornment by you to me but asks instead whether X's transfer of the money to you was or was not a transfer upon trust. If he expressly said that it was a trust then he will have manifested a final and obligatory intent that the money should come to me; and if (though this is difficult to find) he manifested the same final intent in different words he will, none the less, have created a trust, albeit in the manner of M. Jourdain.[48] Once there is a trust, express or implied, there is no need for my claim to be explained as having arisen, independently of intent, in unjust enrichment on the basis of non-voluntary enrichment by subtraction. In most cases that alternative explanation is eclipsed by the other, simpler and more obvious. But in one case, as we have seen, it does show up, though want of familiarity has made it difficult to name.

If X ought by statute to have declared his trust intention formally and failed to do so, I will not be able to rely on it directly in order to justify my claim against you. Suppose, therefore, that the way in which X gave you money was by will, taking care before he died to tell you that the money left to you was meant for me. Effective on his death, this gift to me should have been attested.[49] Hence I cannot rely on this declaration of trust as in itself creative of any right, not even when the trust would, but for the statute, be finally constituted by the arrival of legal title in yourself. Nevertheless the testator's final intent, although shorn of its immediately right-creating effect, does remain a fact. And it shows that the money was destined for me. You intercepted it. Hence you have enriched yourself at my expense and without my consent, and restitution must follow in

---

[48] 'It is true that . . . a person may create a trust, as Monsieur Jourdain talked prose, without knowing it, but unless an intention to create a trust is clearly to be collected from the language used and from the circumstances of the case, I think that the court ought not to be astute to discover indications of such an intention.' *Re Schebsman* [1944] 1 Ch. 83, 104, *per* Du Parcq, L.J.

[49] *Wills Act, 1837*, s. 9.

my favour.[50] This conclusion would have to be inhibited if it seriously threatened the policy of the *Wills Act*; but it does not. Fully secret trusts are too risky to provoke a stampede away from the sensible habit of formal will-making.[51]

The situation considered in the preceding paragraphs has been that in which a third party, X, transfers to you certain property which you are to pass on to me, and the question has been whether, if you keep it, you can be said to be enriched by interceptive subtraction from me. A weaker version of this situation arises where X manifests an intention to benefit me by giving me certain property but never actually transfers that property either to me directly or to you subject to an instruction to pass it on to me. Suppose that the property, none the less, happens to come to you. Can I ever say, merely on the basis of X's intention that I should have it, that you are enriched by interceptive subtraction from me? The general answer is that I cannot. It is summed up in the maxim that equity will not perfect an imperfect gift. The common sense behind this is that it is virtually impossible ever to conclude that X's intention in my favour remained unchanged. If X is still alive it will be a matter between him and you, whether he wishes, and has sufficient ground, to recall the property from you in order to act on the intention which I say that he manifested in my favour. If he is dead, it must usually remain for ever uncertain whether his intention to benefit me persisted unchanged until he died. Nevertheless, there are some exceptional circumstances in which the contrary conclusion can be reached so that a court can hold that the wealth which you hold was indubitably *en route* to me. First, X may have covenanted with you that he would give you the property for me. In that case, even though he himself never acted on his promise, the arrival of the property in you by another route will allow me to claim it from you.[52] The covenant, though not made with me, shows that the wealth was finally destined to me. Second, although X never himself completed the transfer, he may have done everything which lay on him to do, so that the only reason why the transfer remained in-

---

[50] *McCormick* v. *Grogan* (1869) L.R. 4 H.L. 82; *Blackwell* v. *Blackwell* [1829] A.C. 318; *Ottaway* v. *Norman* [1927] 1 Ch. 698. The test assumes an identity between this unjust enrichment explanation of fully secret trusts and the 'legatee's fraud' explanation which is found in the cases.

[51] This is much less clear of half-secret trusts, a fact which accounts for the restrictive rules which inhibit the symmetry between them and fully secret trusts seemingly established in *Blackwell* v. *Blackwell*, above: see *Re Keen* [1937] Ch. 236; *Re Bateman* [1970] 1 W.L.R. 1463.

[52] *Re Ralli's Will Trusts* [1964] Ch. 288.

complete was that a step which had to be taken by a third party remained undone, as where he completed and posted a share transfer form but the company did not register the change of ownership.[53] Here his completion of his part shows that his intent in my favour was final. Third, it may be demonstrable that X, intending to benefit me, transferred the property in question to you by mistake and, having died, cannot put the matter right himself. Here evidence of the mistake in the execution of the transfer shows that the wealth was finally intended for me.[54]

When a fiduciary breaks his duty to avoid conflicts of interest and in breach of that duty makes a gain for himself it will often be obvious that there was a very small chance, or almost none, that his principal would have obtained that which the fiduciary actually took. Generally, therefore, the principal's claim to the gain received from the third party can only be based on the wrong sense of 'at the expense of': it was obtained by reason of the breach of duty. Sometimes, however, the courts are willing to affirm, or presume, that the principal would certainly have obtained what the fiduciary took. As, for example, where an agent employed to sell land takes a secret commission from the purchaser.[55] Where such a finding can be made there is a claim available without reliance on the breach of duty, on the basis of anticipatory subtraction. *Cook v. Deeks*[56] is an other example. Directors had been negotiating for a railway contract in the name of their company. At the last minute they decided to stand aside from the company and they took the contract themselves. They then tried to use their voting power to whitewash their conduct. The Privy Council held that they could not do so. They were not merely trying to obtain forgiveness for a breach of duty but were giving away a company asset. For when they took the contract the company was, in equity, already entitled to it. The reason is not spelled out. It is obvious that the directors were guilty of breach of duty. It is not obvious how it could be said that this company was already entitled to a contract which in point of fact it did not get. But, looking at the story as a whole, it seems that this was a case in which it was possible to take the view that the company would certainly have obtained the contract if the directors had not intercepted it. Just as in the case of the express trust discussed above, the crucial fact, that the benefit was certainly proceeding to the

---

[53] *Re Rose* [1952] Ch. 499.
[54] *Lister v. Hodgson* (1867) L.R. 4 Eq. 30, 34, *per* Lord Romilly, M.R.
[55] As in *Mahesan* v. *Malaysian Government Housing Society* [1978] 2 W.L.R. 444.
[56] *Cook* v. *Deeks* [1916] A.C. 554.

plaintiff, is submerged in the conclusion that the plaintiff was already entitled to it.

The case in which you sell my car for £3000 provides a counter-example. I cannot in fact connect myself to the £3000 received by you from the purchaser except through your wrong. You have enriched yourself by converting my car, and in that sense at my expense, but not by subtraction from me. It is not certain that I would have received that £3000 if you had not. I might not have sold. I might have sold at another price. This uncertainty is conclusive in itself. But other considerations tend in the same direction. First, although you have received £3000 by your conversion, if we leave that wrong aside it may appear that you were not enriched at all: you yourself paid £4000 for the car, so that you are £1000 down. Secondly, my ownership of the car will probably be preserved in the hands of your purchaser, because *nemo dat quod non habet*. So, although it remains true that you were enriched by your wrong, when the focus is off the wrong and the story is looked at simply in terms of the movement of wealth, which is what 'subtraction' is all about, it turns out that in the eye of the law I have lost nothing except the use of the car over the period during which I have been out of possession. The car was mine and still is. We said earlier that the preservation of existing title prevents unjust enrichment, but by anticipation rather than reversal.

Conclusion   Just as, in the case of enrichment, there is a simple case (money) and a more complex case (benefits in kind), so also with 'at the plaintiff's expense' in the subtraction sense: the simple case is the two-party situation in which value has flowed from plaintiff to defendant; the more difficult case is where the defendant has received from a third hand. It must then be possible for the court to say that the wealth would certainly have accrued to the plaintiff. If it would, then the defendant can be said to have effected an anticipatory or interceptive subtraction.

A major difficulty in the organization of the Restitution is the perceived need to divide the matter between two-party and three-party situations.[57] The notion of interceptive subtraction makes that division virtually unnecessary. One set of three-party situations is covered already by the separation of restitution for wrongs. That

---

[57] Cf. *Goff and Jones*: Part II, 'The Right to Restitution', is divided into three sections: 1. 'Where the Defendant has Acquired a Benefit from or by the Act of the Plaintiff'; 2. 'Where the Defendant has Acquired from a Third Party a Benefit for which he must Account to the Plaintiff'; 3. 'Where the Defendant has Acquired a Benefit through his own Wrongful Act'.

topic cannot but include every case in which the plaintiff claims that the defendant has been enriched by a receipt from a third party obtained by a breach of duty to himself, as for example by wrong-fully selling his property. All other three-party claims will involve interceptive subtractions. Factually different from two-party subtractions, these cases, once recognised, nevertheless fall under the same law so far as grounds for restitution are concerned. They do not need separate treatment. In other words, inasmuch as all restitutionary problems involve an inquiry into 'enrichment' and into 'at the plaintiff's expense' and into 'unjust', these three-party cases require special attention only in that phase of the analysis which is concerned with 'at the plaintiff's expense'. If the inquiry then shows that the defendant obtained the enrichment from the third party by a wrong and not by an interceptive subtraction, all remaining questions arise under the head of 'restitution for wrongs'. If, on the other hand, the inquiry shows that his receipt was an interceptive subtraction from the plaintiff, the next phase of the analysis remains the same as for all ordinary two-party subtractions. Some cases will, of course, offer the plaintiff a choice of routes, in that the inquiry will show that the defendant received both by a wrong to the plaintiff and by an interceptive subtraction from him.[58]

Once it is clear that the defendant has been enriched by sub-traction from the plaintiff the inquiry can move to the main question, whether the facts reveal a ground for characterising the enrichment as 'unjust' and therefore reversible. Chapters VI to IX now consider that question. What circumstances call for the restitution of enrich-ments by subtraction? The subject of restitution for wrongs is separately considered, in Chapter X.

[58] Below, p. 321 f.

VI

NON-VOLUNTARY TRANSFER I: VITIATION

IN a book less concerned with the structure of the law of restitution and more with the molecules which make it up, this long chapter would be much longer still. Indeed it would be chopped up. Its sections would be chapters. Perhaps even its sub-sections. The danger would then be that the unity and coherence of this distinct group of restitution-yielding events might be obscured. In what does that unity consist? Throughout this chapter the plaintiff is saying, by way of establishing a claim to an enrichment received by the defendant by subtraction from him, 'I did not mean you to have it.' But that is not quite precise enough. The plaintiff in the next chapter can say the same. On closer inspection, it is the idea of vitiated judgement which isolates this chapter from the next: 'I did not mean you to have it' is said here in this sense: 'My judgement was not properly exercised (or, was not exercised at all) in the matter of your getting it.'[1]

One step below this level of generality, there are four identifiably different versions of this same bid for restitution, (a) 'I did not know', (b) 'I was mistaken', (c) 'I was compelled', and (d) 'I was unequal'. Of these the least happy is the fourth. Also, general principles of safety in classification suggest that the possibility should at least be admitted that a fifth miscellaneous category might be needed. This breakdown provides the chapter's programme. 'I was mistaken' and 'I was compelled' are readily intelligible. The others will be explained as they are met.

1. IGNORANCE

This has nothing to do with being unlearned or ill-educated. The word is chosen here to denote the factor which calls for restitution when wealth is transferred to a defendant wholly without the knowledge of the plaintiff. He is unaware of the transfer. Unconscious of

---

[1] Robert Goff L.J. has said *obiter* that the reason why a mistaken party has restitution is *not* that his consent was vitiated. *Semble* his view is that the reason for restitution is, by contrast, that the circumstances giving rise to the mistake (fraud in that particular case) merely constitute 'unjust enrichment'. But one is obliged to answer, with respect, that there is no contrast, since the reason why the enrichment becomes unjust (i.e. calls for restitution) is that the transferor's judgement is making the transfer was vitiated: See *Whittaker* v. *Campbell* [1983] 3 All E.R. 582, 584.

it. This is the most extreme case on, or more accurately before, the spectrum of vitiated intention. In cases of mistake or compulsion the plaintiff almost invariably points to a factor which disturbed or confounded the process of thought by which he formed the intention that the transfer of wealth should happen. There is a strong example of compulsion where that is not true. Suppose I tear your purse from your grip, overcoming by force your physical power to prevent me. There you have no intent at all that I should have the purse, but at least you do know that I have obtained it. In a case of 'ignorance' the plaintiff will have been unaware of even the fact of the defendant's receipt.

I cannot often get my hands on your wealth without your knowing, and still less often without committing a wrong against you. Generally it will be theft or one of its specialised off-shoots. Suppose I am your employee and I put my hand in your till,[1a] or I forge a cheque so as to syphon your money into my bank account.[2] In such cases your right to restitution can be made out without your having to characterise my conduct as a crime or civil wrong. I am enriched by subtraction from you, and you, in the strongest possible way, did not mean me to be. You did not know I was taking the money. Restitution for mistake does not involve the proof of any wrong; and total ignorance is *a fortiori* from the most fundamental mistake. Hence a system which believes in restitution for mistake cannot but believe in restitution for ignorance, quite independently of any wrong incidentally committed. In *Neate* v. *Harding*[3] the defendant broke into the plaintiff's mother's home without lawful authority and took away money belonging to the plaintiff. The action for money had and received was held to lie. In *Moffat* v. *Kazana*[4] the defendant found and spent money which the plaintiff had left behind in the loft of a house which he had sold. The plaintiff recovered the sum. There is no need for cases of this kind to be pushed into the category of 'restitution for wrongs'. Non-voluntary transfer sufficiently explains them. Their relation to the phenomenon called 'waiver of tort' will be considered in the chapter on wrongs.[5] Whatever the precise meaning of that term, these plaintiffs need have nothing do with the wrong. They neither found on it nor waive it; they just ignore it.

[1a] *Bristow* v. *Eastman* (1794) 1 Peake 291.

[2] *Banque Belge pour L'Etranger* v. *Hambrouck* [1921] 1 K.B. 321; *United Australia Ltd.* v. *Barclays Bank Ltd.* [1941] A.C. 1.

[3] *Neate* v. *Harding* (1851) 6 Exch. 349.

[4] *Moffat* v. *Kazana* [1968] 3 All E.R. 271.

[5] Below, p. 315.

Sometimes the line between ignorance and mistake is hard to draw. A clerical error or, increasingly common these days, a computer malfunction can bring about an unintended credit, as for instance in the payment of salaries or pensions. Though some such cases may be reducible to a misperception of fact or a wrong view of the law nothing is gained by trying to force all of them into the category of mistake. And there is no pressure to do that if the spectrum of non-voluntariness is seen to begin, not from mistake, but, beyond that, from ignorance.[6]

Ignorance and Interceptive Subtractions   The discussion has so far assumed a simple two-party situation where wealth has passed out of the hands of the plaintiff and into those of the defendant. Can ignorance be a ground for restitution in triangular situations, where the defendant has received from a third party? It depends on whether the plaintiff can bring himself within the subtraction sense of 'at the expense of'.[7]

If you have obtained £100 from X then *prima facie* it is none of my business and it will do me no good to affirm, however truthfully, that I knew nothing of it. To connect myself to that £100 I will normally have to show that you earned it from X by doing wrong to me, as by taking a profit-making opportunity in breach of a fiduciary duty to me, or by accepting a reward for setting my house on fire or beating me up. In short I have to rely on the wrong sense of 'at the expense of'. And the only possible rôle of my knowledge or ignorance would be in determining whether you did in fact commit the wrong which I allege. For if I knew and consented perhaps you will not have committed the wrong which I am trying to prove. But such cases clearly belong in the chapter on wrongs.

There are, however, some triangular situations in which the plaintiff can get within the subtraction sense of 'at the expense of' even though the defendant's receipt was from a third hand. If it was legally or factually certain the wealth would have come to the plaintiff if not taken by the defendant there can be said to have been an interceptive subtraction. For example, if you take rent from my tenant or if you usurp the profits of my office I can have restitution

---

[6] It is a difficult question whether the defence ought to be allowed to argue in such cases that no mistake was made or that any mistake which was made was of an inoperative kind, as for example, a mistake of law. Cf. *Avon C.C.* v. *Howlett* [1983] 1 W.L.R. 605, 613 ff. But 'ignorance' is outside the mischief which inhibits restitution for mistakes of law, as to which see below, p. 164 f.

[7] Above, p. 133 f.

from you.[8] The money was due from the outsider to me and was intercepted by you. It is therefore just the same, except that the wealth never was reduced to my possession, as where you secretly take from my purse or from my till.

The next of kin's claim in *Re Diplock*[9] conforms to the same pattern. By mistake of law the executors of a will made payments to charities who were not entitled to receive them. The next of kin sued the recipients and obtained restitution in the full measure of the amount originally received. As between the executors and the recipients there was a mistake. But the next of kin themselves were not mistaken. So it is more true to say that this was money to which they were entitled from the executors and that it was transferred away from them without their knowledge.

On this analysis of *Re Diplock* there is a triangular situation, the executors being the third hand. But if we say that the next of kin had a right *in rem* in the fund before it was transferred to the charities, we can then view the situation as a simple two-party subtraction, the charities taking, so to say, from the next of kin's till. But either way the factor rendering the enrichment unjust is the ignorance of the next of kin: the fact that they did not know at all that wealth destined for them (or already theirs) had been intercepted by the defendants.

To speak of *Re Diplock* as a 'triangular' fact situation is strictly speaking not right, since it might be objected that, since the plaintiffs recovered money which the charities received from the executors, who in turn received from the deceased, it involved a story in four, not three stages. The simpler case is where a trustee or other fiduciary himself makes off with a fund received for the plaintiff from a third party settlor. Here there really are only three stages in the story. The beneficiary-plaintiff can be regarded as the victim either of an interceptive subtraction or, on the basis of being the owner of the fund in equity, of an ordinary subtraction of wealth already vested in him. Either way the trustee is in the same position as the employee who steals. He commits a wrong; but, because of his entitlement, the victim's ignorance of the enrichment is enough to explain his right to restitution without characterising the facts as a breach of duty.

---

[8] *Asher* v. *Wallis* (1707) 11 Mod. 146; *Lyell* v. *Kennedy* (1889) 14 App. Cas. 437 (receipt of rents); *Arris* v. *Stukely* (1677) 2 Mod. 260; *Howard* v. *Wood* (1679) 2 Show. K.B. 21 (profits of office).

[9] *Re Diplock* [1948] Ch. 465. On the same basis equity will sometimes perfect a gift which a donor has destined for the plaintiff: *Re Ralli's Will Trusts* [1964] 1 Ch. 288; cf. *Thompson* v. *Witmore* (1860) 1 J. & H. 268, 273.

At law, if a third party passes a fund to you to be passed on to me, and even, according to *Shamia* v. *Joory*, [10] if he tells you to hold for me what you owe him (a debt, not a fund transferred for the purpose), I can claim the sum from you once you have attorned to me. [11] That is, once you have told me that you are holding for me. Your attornment to me cannot be analysed as a contract or as a promise made binding by estoppel, since it requires no consideration and no detrimental reliance on my part. It must be regarded not so much as a promise as a part of a factual picture which shows wealth *en route* to me. That is, after the attornment the court is able to conclude as a matter of fact that the wealth would have accrued to me if not detained by you. It breaks the balance of doubt between me and the outsider.

The explanation of this restitutionary figure is thus that the attornment creates a sufficient factual certainty that the money will accrue to the plaintiff unless the defendant pockets it; if the defendant does pocket it, he becomes enriched by subtraction from the plaintiff; and the fact that the subtraction happens without the plaintiff's knowledge is then enough to explain why the enrichment would be unjustly retained.

The last example is from company law. The directors are in a fiduciary relation to their company and therefore have a duty to avoid conflicts of interest. A profit acquired in breach of that duty must be made over to the company. But *semble* the director can be exonerated by the company's general meeting so long as he makes a full disclosure. That is *Regal (Hastings) Ltd.* v. *Gulliver*, [12] which also seems to say that it makes no difference that the meeting is itself controlled by the director's own votes. But there is a case in which the meeting cannot be made to ratify the secret profit. In *Cook* v. *Deeks* [13] directors negotiated a contract for the construction of a railway. They acted throughout in the name of their company. Then, at the last minute, they diverted the contract to a second company made ready by them to intercept it. Then they used their voting power to ratify the diversion. The Privy Council held that they could not. For the contract already belonged in equity to the first company, and the majority could not defraud the minority by stripping the company of its property. The crucial question in this context is: Why was it possible to treat a contract which was still

[10] *Shamia* v. *Joory* [1958] 1 Q.B. 448.
[11] *Israel* v. *Douglas*, (1789) 1 H.Bl. 239; *Liversidge* v. *Broadbent* (1859) 4 H. & N. 603; *Griffin* v. *Weatherby* (1868) L.R. 3 Q.B. 753.
[12] *Regal (Hastings) Ltd.* v. *Gulliver* [1942] 1 All E.R. 378.
[13] *Cook* v. *Deeks* [1916] A.C. 554.

to be signed as already belonging in equity to the company? The other party could have withdrawn. So there was in that sense no contract which could yet belong to the company.

The only explanation which satisfies is that this was a case in which the court was prepared to treat an asset factually about to accrue to the plaintiff just in the same way as one which had already accrued. It is one thing to take an opportunity which might or might not have accrued to the company (a breach of duty within reach of corporate absolution) but an altogether different thing to expropriate the company; and within the notion of expropriation comes not only the diversion of assets already vested but also the interception of those indubitably proceeding to the company though not yet vested.

Viewed in this way *Cook* v. *Deeks* is important, albeit oblique, evidence for two propositions. First, interceptive subtraction can be handled in the same way as the ordinary two party version.[14] Second, the finding that the wealth would certainly have passed from the third party to the plaintiff can be made by direct assessment of the facts. That is, it does not depend on the third party's being liable to the plaintiff to make the transfer, as in *Re Diplock*, or an attornment, as in *Shamia* v. *Joory*. Only the history of the negotiations showed that the contract would have been given to the first company. The crucial finding of fact once made, the ground for restitution is then supplied by the fact that the person entitled did not know of and therefore did not consent to the transfer.

Ignorance and Benefits in Kind Suppose that what you receive is some benefit in kind. Without my knowing, you use my bicycle or eat my cake. The first principle to apply is that the law must remain the same except so far as a different conclusion can be explained by the change in the facts. And the only fact to change here is the nature of what has been received. We know what difference this makes. It is more difficult to establish enrichment when what is received is not money.[15]

There are various ways of dealing with the enrichment issue. We have seen that they divide between establishing a free acceptance and proving objectively, without reference to the defendant's exercise of free choice, that he was incontrovertibly enriched just as though he had received money. Taking either route the plaintiff

---

[14] Cf. the discussion of 'at the expense of', above, p. 138 f.
[15] Above, p. 109.

can, if he chooses, continue to rest on the same ground for restitution, namely ignorance. But in practice if he establishes enrichment by relying on free acceptance he is likely to abandon ignorance altogether. Because free acceptance is bi-valent.[16] It both establishes enrichment by trumping the tactic of subjective devaluation and is in itself a ground for restitution. So switching to free acceptance for one purpose the plaintiff will almost always turn to it for the other.

The clearest examples under this head are cases in which I knowingly[17] use or consume your property without your permission. The wrong can once again be ignored, for my free acceptance can be made out without reference to it. In *Hambly* v. *Trott*[18] Lord Mansfield contemplated *quantum valebat* for user of a horse where I ride him on a journey other than that for which I have borrowed him. For the reasons given such a claim can be regarded as based wholly on free acceptance or as being 'mixed', based on ignorance *quoad* 'unjust' and on the acceptance *quoad* 'enrichment'. The most obvious function of the 'mixed' analysis is to retain in view, for the case in which there is no free acceptance, the possibility of satisfying both these chief requirements by proving other facts.

2. MISTAKE

Mistakes are sometimes induced by misrepresentations made by the defendant. For the rest, their provenance is so various that they may safely, though with some inaccuracy, be called spontaneous. They often do have some external cause. But their genesis is legally irrelevant, and they must, therefore, be contemplated just as though they were literally spontaneous. The phrase 'spontaneous mistake' can thus be used to denote the ground for restitution on which the plaintiff relies when he says that he was mistaken, and does not at the same time seek to make anything of the way in which his mistake came about. Suppose I read a false report that you are soliciting funds for such and such a charity. I send you money and then find

---

[16] Above, p. 114 f.

[17] There can be no free acceptance where I am unaware of the true facts. Cf. *Boulton* v. *Jones* (1857) 2 H. & N. 564; and contrast *Lightly* v. *Clouston* (1808) 1 Taunt. 112.

[18] *Hambly* v. *Trott* (1776) 1 Cowp. 371, 375: 'So, if a man take a horse from another, and bring him back again; an action of trespass will not lie against his executor, though it would against him; but an action for the use and hire of the horse will lie against the executor.'

out the truth. The newspaper caused my mistake. But, *quoad* my claim against you, that is not relevant.

(i) *Spontaneous Mistake*

(a) *Mistakes and Mispredictions*   *5

The first thing is to make a distinction between mistakes and mispredictions. Suppose I look after you because I think you will leave me money when you die;[19] or I do months of work preparing plans for your building in the confident belief that you will give me the contract to clear the site and carry out the development.[20] These are predictions and, when I find myself disappointed, mispredictions. I may call them mistakes, but they are a kind of mistake which does not count. If you stood by without warning me that my hopes were vain, I may be able to make out a claim based on free acceptance, but not on mistake. Nor does this have anything to do with the fact that these are examples of non-money benefits. Suppose I pay you money thinking that you will look after me when I am old or • believing that you will support my point of view in some coming contest. It is just the same. A claim for restitution cannot be founded on a misprediction.[21] Even if after the event the recipient promises to pay, his promise will not be actionable in the absence of a deed or some new consideration. The mispredictor still has to bear the risk he ran.[22]

The reason is that restitution for mistake rests on the fact that the plaintiff's judgement was vitiated in the matter of the transfer of wealth to the defendant. A mistake as to the future, a misprediction, does not show that the plaintiff's judgement was vitiated, only that as things turned out it was incorrectly exercised. A prediction is an exercise of judgement. To act on the basis of a prediction is to accept the risk of disappointment. If you then complain of having been mistaken you are merely asking to be relieved of a risk knowingly run. The reason why a claim based on free acceptance can still work is that the freely accepting defendant is not able to drive the plaintiff back to bear the risk he took. For if he freely accepted, then *ex hypothesi* he has himself to blame for not rejecting the benefit.

The safe course for one who does not want to bear the risk of

[19] *Deglman* v. *Guaranty Trust Co. of Canada* [1954] 3 D.L.R. 785.
[20] *William Lacey (Hounslow) Ltd.* v. *Davis* [1957] 1 W.L.R. 932.
[21] *Re Cleadon Trust Ltd.* [1939] Ch. 286. *Kerrison* v. *Glynn, Mills, Currie & Co.* (1912) 81 L.J.K.B. 465, cannot be explained as a case of mistake since any mistake was as to the future.
[22] *Re McArdle* [1951] 1 Ch. 669.

disappointment which is inherent in predictions is to communicate with the recipient of the benefit in advance of finally committing it to him. He can then qualify his intent to give by imposing conditions, or by making a contract, or sometimes by making a trust. That prepares the ground for restitution on the basis not of mistake but failure of consideration, the subject of the next chapter.

(b) *Fears which inhibit the right to restitution for mistake*

If the plaintiff did make a mistake as to the present or past he can rightly say that in deciding to make the transfer to the defendant his judgment was vitiated; he operated on the wrong data; and, *prima facie*, he has a claim to restitution. For it is perfectly sensible, even if too simple, to start from the proposition that what is given by mistake should be given back. Yet everyone knows that restitution for mistake is not straightforward. Given the simple starting point, what makes it so complex?

The answer is that the simple inclination in favour of the mistaken plaintiff meets not one but several strong counter-arguments which express fears about what would actually happen if restitution for mistake were freely available. The effect of these counter-arguments is to inhibit the *prima facie* cause of action suggested by the proposition that mistakes should be undone. This is the source of the intellectual tension, and the best way of coping with it is to try to name the pressures which militate against allowing restitution on the ground of spontaneous mistake. So far as they have a common focus it is to the found in concern for the interest which the recipient has in the security of his receipt. It is reasonable for the mistaken party to want to be saved from the consequences of his mistake. But it is also reasonable for the recipient to say that he needs stability in his affairs, that he cannot hold himself ever ready to give back what seems to have been fairly and finally acquired.

The first fear is that there would just be too much restitution. People are always making mistakes of one kind or another. If they could have restitution for every mistake nobody would ever be safe from claims. This then has a gloss or amplification: also, a mistake is easily concocted after the event to cover a mere change of mind. So not only are mistakes very common, they are also easily invented. In one area this fear of too much (and perhaps some dishonest) restitution is intensified: nobody nowadays, not even the lawyers, knows what the law is. So if restitution were freely available for mistakes of law nobody would know when he could safely spend his money and the courts would be clogged with claims.

The second fear is focused on those cases in which there is some element of bargaining. Its premiss is that merit in bargaining is precisely the ability to avoid mistakes. So, easy restitution for mistake would interfere with the hopes of advantage and fears of disaster which are inherent in that game and would take away the winner's just reward. This is partly an argument about the winning bargainor's interest in the security of his transaction. But it can also be developed into an argument about society's need, in the interests of maximising wealth, to have an efficient market. Here 'efficient' is a modish word describing a market in which economic forces are unrestrained by notions of fairness which conflict with the maximisation of profit.

The third fear is more technical and internal to the legal system. It is the fear of problems likely to be encountered in trying to reverse transactions which have involved performances in both directions, not only by, but also to, the mistaken plaintiff. This is the problem of counter-restitution: if the mistaken plaintiff were to be freely relieved he would have to give up anything he himself had got, or its value. And could it be done? Would it not be impossible to balance off parties who had proceeded down the path of a complex exchange?

These fears can be differently weighed by different minds. But they are not hysterical. The effect of their collision with the common sense proposition in favour of restitution is drastically to reduce the number and types of mistake for which restitution is actually available. To such an extent is this true that the plaintiff is not on completely safe ground if the mistake on which he relies is not, (a) a mistake of fact, which (b) gave him the impression that he was legally liable to confer the benefit in question on the defendant. There is a famous dictum of Bramwell, B. in *Aiken* v. *Short*:[23] 'In order to entitle a person to recover back money paid under a mistake of fact, the mistake must be as to a fact which, if true, would make the person paying liable to pay the money.' It is wrong to say that the law still goes no further. All the same, these liability mistakes are the base from which to move out cautiously to the more shifting ground.

(c) *Liability mistakes*

These can be of fact or of law. And so far as negativing the voluntary character of a transfer is concerned both have exactly the same effect. But mistakes of law encounter the intensified version of the fear about too much restitution. They will be considered below, in

---

[23] *Aiken* v. *Short* (1856) 1 H. & N. 210, 215.

their own place. That leaves two questions: What precisely is a liability mistake (of fact)? Why has it been found relatively easy to allow restitution for this kind of mistake?

What is a liability mistake? It is best to start from some examples. Suppose I am bound by a contract of insurance to pay you the value of your cargo of lemons in certain events. Let it be that I must pay if they are destroyed by a peril of the sea.[24] If I believe, incorrectly, that the insured event has happened, then I am labouring under a liability mistake. On the facts as I see them I am liable to pay. But more than that, it was certain even before my misperception that, if the fact happened, or the state of affairs came about, I would be liable. From which it follows that, if and as soon as I came to imagine that it had happened, I would automatically suppose myself liable. I know that if I earn income I must pay income tax. Hence, if I believe I have earned I automatically suppose myself liable to pay. A mortgagee knows that if he sells the asset for more than the debt he must pay the surplus to the mortgagor or the next mortgagee, as the case may be.[25] Once he believes he has received a sum surplus to the debt, then necessarily he supposes himself legally bound to pay it over. A bank knows it must honour its customer's instructions so long as he has funds. As soon as the bank supposes it has received an authentic instruction to pay such and such a person it necessarily also forms the view that it is liable to its customer to pay the third party.[26] A liability mistake is one which, when it is made, creates the impression of a state of affairs in which the mistaken party is, without further choices to be made by himself, legally bound. In the false picture which he sees, this kind of mistake appears as the satisfaction of a condition against which his liability is suspended.

The last example in this list is importantly different from the others in that the imagined liability is not to the payee but to a third party. This case has caused hesitations. It has recently been the subject of detailed consideration by Robert Goff, J. in *Barclays Bank Ltd.* v. *W.J. Simms, Son and Cooke (Southern) Ltd.*[27] In that case one of Barclays' customers owed money to the defendant builders. The customer sent the builders a cheque for the sum but, discovering that the builders had gone into receivership, then telephoned Barclays to stop the cheque, an instruction afterwards confirmed in writing. Barclays programmed their computer to stop the cheque but, when it

---

[24] *Norwich Union Fire Insurance Society* v. *William H. Price Ltd.* [1934] A.C. 455.
[25] *Weld-Blundell* v. *Synott* [1940] 2 K.B. 107.
[26] *Colonial Bank* v. *Exchange Bank of Yarmouth, Nova Scotia* (1885) 11 App. Cas. 84.
[27] *Barclays Bank Ltd.* v. *W.J. Simms Son and Cooke (Southern) Ltd.* [1980] 1 Q.B. 677.

was presented, one of their employees overlooked the computerised instruction. Hence, in the incorrect belief that they had a valid mandate from their customer, Barclays paid Simms the sum and now successfully sought restitution. That such a mistake gives rise to restitution is no longer in doubt. But there are two possible analyses. It can be regarded as within the class of liability mistakes. Or it can be taken as a very proof that mistakes outside that class can trigger restitution. Robert Goff, J. took this second line.   *6

Definitely on the other side of the frontier are two cases, one obviously different from a liability mistake, the other deceptively similar to such a mistake. The obvious case is where the mistaken party never entertains any idea that he is liable. I want to give you a gift because I think, incorrectly, that you are the person who saved my life when I fell into the sea. Or, less far removed from commerce, I decide that my best tactic to improve my security as second mortgagee will be to pay off the first mortgagee,[28] but all the time the morgaged asset has never existed or has been destroyed or has belonged to someone other than the mortgagor. Sound as my tactic may be, in this case I have to no security to protect. Here, neither the belief that you saved me, nor the belief that I have a second mortage in a given asset, creates for me a picture in which I am legally liable to pay. Even in the picture as I incorrectly see it, the choice is mine, but I falsely seem to have a good reason for choosing that I will pay. There is room for a distinction between the two. In the former I do have facts in view which constrain me morally.[29] In the other, not.

The subtler case is where I make a mistake which leads me to *incur* a liability. That is, when the mistake is made the mistaken picture does not entail liability; it merely leads to my seeking to enter into a contract. Suppose your horse is struck by lightning during the night; it is dead. I believe that it is still alive. In that belief I offer you £1000 for it, and you accept. There is no liability mistake here. In my picture the horse is alive, but the consequence is that I want to buy it, not (until I do something more) that I am liable to pay for it. We make our contract. It is void, though I do not know it, on account of the thing sold having previously perished.[30] Now I send

---

[28] *Aken* v. *Short* (1856) 1 H. & N. 210: 'Here, if the fact was true, the bankers were at liberty to pay or not, as they pleased. But relying on the belief that the defendant had a valid security, they, having a subsequent legal morgage, chose to pay off the defendant's charge. It is impossible to say that this case falls within the rule. The mistake of fact was, that the Bank thought they could sell the estate for a higher price' p. 215, *per* Bramwell, B.

[29] Cf. *Larner* v. *L.C.C.*, below, p. 154.

[30] *Sale of Goods Act*, 1979, s. 6.

you the money. I do conceive myself to be paying you because legally liable to do so. There is now a liability mistake, but that mistake does not consist in the incorrect belief that the horse lives, for, consequential on the first, there is now a second mistake. First I mistakenly thought the horse alive; in that belief I chose to make an agreement with you. Secondly, I incorrectly thought that that agreement amounted to a valid contract; and in that belief in the existence of a valid contract is a liability mistake.

It is important not to elide the two separate mistakes. For while a mistaken belief in the existence of a valid contract will be a liability mistake, and as such will trigger restitution, the question whether the belief in the existence of the contract was actually false will itself depend on the nature and effect of the other, anterior mistake. The essential inquiry into the nature and effect of that mistake will be confounded unless the point is first clearly taken that it is not itself a liability mistake and cannot draw on any magic that liability mistakes may have. My belief that the horse was alive was not a liability mistake. The fact that it, none the less, avoided the contract not only cannot be explained by the magic of liability mistakes but also shows that liability mistakes do not have an exclusive magic.

Why do liability mistakes easily give rise to restitution?   It will be shown below that, without a doubt, liability mistakes are only one species of the genus giving rise to restitution. Undeniably they are the ones which the courts have found least troublesome. Seeing why that is, we may also see which others can safely yield the same result.

First, within the category of liability mistakes, there is no danger, if restitution is allowed, of interfering in bargaining, because mistakes leading to the formation of contracts are necessarily excluded. This has just been explained. Secondly, in such cases there can rarely be a problem of counter-restitution since generally the transfer will have been made solely to discharge the supposed liability, so that *ex hypothesi* the transferor will have had nothing. Thirdly, though even this right to restitution must necessarily conflict with the interest of the recipient in the security of his receipt, yet the general danger of too much restitution is kept in check, because this right is confined to a single category of case and, perhaps more important, because there is no question of the plaintiff's adducing trivial or collateral errors which might or might not have been critical. For the supposition of liability must always be the fundamental or overwhelming cause for the making of the payment or other transfer. Briefly, restitution for liability mistake is not very threatening because it is closely confined to a particular case of very serious mistake.

Behind all this there is comfort of another kind against the fear of floodgates: Roman jurisprudence was known to have worked with this category. When the Roman action of debt (the *condictio*) was divided and explained according to the causes of indebtedness, 'money and other performances not owed' became a prominent category.[31] In fact 'debt for liability mistakes' is as good a translation as any for the Latin *'condictio indebiti'*.

(d) *Non-Liability Mistakes*

When Bramwell, B., spoke in *Aiken* v. *Short* of the restriction placed by the law on the class of mistake giving rise to restitution, he said that there could be no recovery if a payment was made under the influence of a mistake which, if true, 'would merely make it desirable that he should pay the money'.[32] The line cannot be so clearly drawn. The law does allow restitution in some such cases, though it is true that outside the area of liability mistakes it is necessary to proceed with caution.

What kinds of payments or other transfers are in question? The category of non-obligatory payments, those which on the payor's view of the facts may seem to be desirable to be made though not legally obligatory, includes three types, though all are in a loose sense 'gifts'. There are payments designed to encourage a future reciprocation from the payee. In these cases the probability is that any mistake which the payor later claims to have made will turn out to be a misprediction of the recipient's response, in which case there can be no restitution unless the disappointed payor bound him to make that response.[33] Then there are payments made from generosity, as, for instance, donations to charity or payments made by way of sharing one's good fortune with one's friends. Finally, there are payments made under a sense of duty or moral obligation, as for instance from gratitude or family feeling or religious precept. No clear line exists between the gifts made from generosity and gifts made under a sense of duty. It will often be a matter of the individual donor's own perceptions. Beyond these three examples there are cases which are ambiguous and leave room for argument: P pays D because P thinks he is under a liability to X to do so, although he is on no view of the matter under a liability to D him-

---

[31] Justinian, *Institutes*, 3.27.6; *Digest*, 12.6.
[32] *Aiken* v. *Short* (1856) 1 H. & N. 210, 215.
[33] Otherwise if the plaintiff can make out a free acceptance: see below pp. 277 ff.

self. P pays D knowing that he is under no liability to D but believing
that there is a legal relationship between him and D such that, if he
pays, his payment will satisfy a condition of D's being liable to
himself. For all these cases Bramwell, B.'s rule would exclude the
possibility of restitution, unless in a doubtful case the story could be
nudged into the category of liability mistakes. So the crucial
question is whether restitution can follow without the mistake
having to be characterised in that way.

In *Larner* v. *London County Council*[34] the LCC had adopted a
scheme to help its employees if they enlisted in the services. Their
service pay would be lower, but the LCC would make up the
difference. Larner was overpaid because he failed to notify changes
in the level of his service pay. One question was whether, on the
assumption that the scheme was not legally binding on the LCC, the
overpayment could be recovered. The Court of Appeal held that it
could be. It was enough that the LCC thought that they were bound
in honour to maintain the scheme. The result of the case is much as
though the Court had said that the category of liability mistake
included mistakes as to moral obligations as well as legal. But that
step is in fact a crucial one.

Where the transfer is made without any sense of even moral
obligation restitution is not wholly excluded. In *Ogilvie* v. *Little-
boy*[35] the Court of Appeal emphasised that a change of mind is no
ground for recovering a gift but admitted the possibility that a
mistake might be so serious as to compel a court to intervene. In
Lady Hood of Avalon v. *Mackinnon*[36] Eve, J. set aside a deed of
appointment when a mother showed that in executing it she had
intended to equalise the positions of her two daughters and had
forgotten that she had already made provision for her elder daughter
six years earlier. In *Barclays Bank Ltd.* v. *W.J. Simms Ltd*, Robert
Goff, J., gives four different examples of double payments, the
second made forgetful of the first.[37] It is evident, *obiter*, that he,
would allow restitution in such cases. There are *dicta* in *Morgan* v.
Ashcroft which would allow restitution of a gift mistakenly made to
the wrong person.[38] *Morgan* v. *Ashcroft* was a claim by a bookmaker

---

[34] *Larner* v. *London County Council* [1949] 1 K.B. 683.
[35] *Ogilvie* v. *Litteboy* (1899) 15 T.L.R. 294.
[36] *Lady Hood of Avalon* v. *Mackinnon* [1909] 1 Ch. 476.
[37] *Barclays Bank Ltd.* v. *W.J. Simms Ltd.* [1980] 1 Q.B. 677, 680.
[38] *Morgan* v. *Ashcroft* [1938] 1 K.B. 49, 66, *per* Sir Wilfrid Greene, M.R., 74 *per* Scott,
L.J.; and cf. at p. 73: 'In none of the above cases . . . not even in *Aiken* v. *Short*, was there a
decision of the Court that the action failed simply because the mistake did not induce a
belief in liability', *per* Scott, L.J.

to recover an overpayment to a client, said to be the result of a mistake in keeping the client's account. The client successfully advanced the defence of illegality: the Court could not involve itself in accounts of wagering transactions caught by the *Gaming Acts.* But the case also contains *dicta* hostile to the view that an unintended second transfer of a non-obligatory payment is recoverable. Lord Greene, M.R., in particular, favoured a strict application of Bramwell, B.'s *dictum.*[39] However, his premiss was that every payment not made under the compulsion of legal liability is irredeemably 'voluntary'; and, using 'voluntary' in that sense, he excluded from himself the possibility of asking whether a payment which is non-obligatory may, nevertheless, have been 'non-voluntary' in the sense of being made on the basis of an exercise of judgement vitiated by mistake.

Greenwood v. Bennett[40] provides an example of a kind of non-liability mistake as to the identity of the recipient of a benefit: an improver who believes he is working on his own property intends to benefit himself, though if the property actually belongs to another the benefit is actually proceeding to that other person. In that case the Court of Appeal allowed restitution. Finally, where the terms of a gift failed to achieve the purpose which was intended because the words used were misunderstood, *Butlin v. Butlin*[41] shows that rectification is possible. There the settler believed that he had conferred power on his trustees to act by majority but the relevant clause was found to fall far short of that. Brightman, J., rectified the deed even though the settlement was a gift and the mistake was not shared by the trustees.

These cases show that non-obligatory transfers are not exempt from restitution for mistake. They do not allow very much to be said about the type of mistake required. Three lines of approach can be distinguished.

The first would do no more than enlarge the category of liability mistakes so as to include only those other mistakes which can be characterised as fundamental or overwhelming. This is imprecise, since only the judge can ultimately say what is sufficiently serious to count. The underlying pressure for this restriction is the fear of too much restitution. The weapons against the danger are insistence that only very serious mistakes will do, coupled with discretion con-

---

[39] *Morgan v. Ashcroft* [1938] 1 K.B. 49, 66 f. In *Barclays Bank Ltd. v. W.J. Simms Ltd.*, Goff, J., held that this passage was inconsistent with the judgement of the Court of Appeal in *Larner v. L.C.C.*: see [1980] 1 Q.B. 677, 698 f.

[40] *Greenwood v. Bennett* [1973] 1 Q.B. 195.

[41] *Butlin v. Butlin* [1976] Ch. 251.

ferred on the judges by the uncertainty inherent in the notion of fundamentality.

The second line is represented by Robert Goff, J., in *Barclays Bank Ltd.* v. *W.J. Simms Ltd.* He is careful to stand back from the word 'fundamental'. His question is whether the mistake caused the payment. This approach is intended to enlarge the category of operative mistake. What then of the interest which recipients have in security? The fear of instability is met another way, by enlarging the defence of change of position. The theory in the background is that you can allow more restitution in principle so long as recipients cannot be unsettled after they have changed their position in reliance on the receipt. The insistence on fundamentality is seen as the insensitive protection of the same interest: we recognise your interest in being left in peace by not allowing restitution at all except in rare catastrophic cases. Robert Goff, J.'s strategy is noticeable in one other aspect of the same judgement. He says, *obiter*, that the mistake which gives restitution need not be so grave as to prevent property passing.[42] This assertion has secondary effects on another matter, the use of *quantum valebat* as an instrument of restitution.

The third line often escapes mention. Presumptions of resulting trust in the case of what appear at first sight to be gifts, can, if invoked outside those relations which attract the counter-presumption of advancement, displace the need for an inquiry into the type or weight of any mistake which may have been made. They cynically imply that a gratuitous donor must have been decisively mistaken unless the donee can affirmatively prove the intent to give. As a matter of logic these presumptions should be irrebuttable whenever the donor has in fact been labouring under a mistake. In which case mistaken donors should find it easier to base their claims directly on resulting trusts, rather than on mistake.

Between these three—the mistake which is fundamental, the mistake which is causative, and the mistake which is presumed—a firmer choice will have to be made than is now detectable in the cases. Two matters enter into this choice. First, the fear of insecurity and more particularly the weight to be attached to it and the techniques to be used against it: if the recipient's interest in the security of his receipt is worth defending, should it be done by narrowing the class of operative mistake so as to include only mistakes which are very serious indeed, or by enlarging that class to include less serious mistakes while at the same time developing a sensitive defence of

[42] *Barclays Bank Ltd.* v. *W.J. Simms Ltd.* [1980] 1 Q.B. 677, 689.

change of position? That is one matter for consideration, in principle and on authority.

The other is in the nature of a metaphysical problem, and it is very important in that it is common to all restitutionary causes of action which reduce to 'I did not mean him to have it'. The problem arises because mental processes cannot be weighed and measured. Will-power has no voltage. So, if we ask, in relation to the mental process which goes into a decision to transfer wealth, how much disturbance shall count as an operative, restitution-yielding vitiation (or, more particularly, how much pressure or how serious a mistake), the truth is that there can be no exact answer. There are no precise tests to choose from. This difficulty becomes acute whenever the facts leave room to say that the plaintiff might have made the transfer anyway.

Two different ways of dealing with this problem can be detected in the cases. One is to say that since weighing and balancing is impossible with any precision we will not try to do it at all, in this way: if the vitiating factor operated on the mind of the plaintiff in some degree (albeit along with others and not necessarily more strongly than them), we will then and there say that the plaintiff's judgement was vitiated, and vitiated in such a way as to entitle him to restitution.[43] That is, we will not weigh, we will only ask whether the vitiating factor had *some* part in the mental process, however slight. The choice of this approach entails that it will be plausibly arguable in some cases in which restitution is allowed that the plaintiff would have made the transfer anyway. The other approach is to say that, although exact weighing of different factors is impossible, yet we will make some attempt at it, erring towards safety by saying that the only operative vitiation is the one which is so high and wide (fundamental, overwhelming) that no reasonable man would say that the plaintiff might have made the transfer anyway. This second approach is the more inscrutable in application because, although it seeks to avoid the worst problems of weighing the unweighable by allowing restitution only where the vitiation is very serious indeed, it actually has no rationally explicable techniques for dealing with the case in which a very serious mistake (or other vitiation) is mixed with another thoroughly plausible motivation for the transfer.[44]

Whatever may seem best in principle, authority has, as a matter of

---

[43] *Edgington* v. *Fitzmaurice* (1885) 29 Ch.D. 459, esp. 483.

[44] As where I give to such and such a school because I want to support its educational work *and* because I think it is charitable, whereas in reality it is a profit-making company. Cf. In *Barton* v. *Armstrong* [1976] A.C. 104, the question whether money was paid from fear of threats or for the sake of commercial advantage.

observable history, inclined instinctively to the second of these positions in relation to spontaneous mistake. Both the practical fears about too much restitution and the rational problems of balancing the mistake with other factors have been met by insisting that the mistake must be 'fundamental'.[45] This can be seen, on the one hand, in the exclusion of change of position as a defence, which leaves the recipient's interest in security to be reflected, if at all, in the narrowness of the class of operative mistake; and, on the other, in the temptation to take refuge in the typified fundamentality of liability mistake. It is no accident that the commonly used example of a mistaken gift which can be recovered is the double payment, the second made forgetful of the first. This example involves an extreme case, a mistake of which all men would agree that it decisively vitiated the intention to give. Robert Goff, J. mixes such examples with the computer which 'runs mad and pays one beneficiary the same gift one hundred times',[46] a case which can even be argued to belong under the heading of 'ignorance', where the donor is so far from intending the transfer that he knows nothing whatever of it. Finally, further evidence of the commitment to fundamentality is easily found in relation to mistake in the formation of contract, though this might be said (because of the bargaining issue)[47] to be irrelevant.

On the other side it can be said that a commitment which has been only instinctive can always be opened up for rational re-examination, and that, as *Barclays Bank Ltd.* v. *W.J. Simms* shows, it was anyhow not free from flaws and inconsistencies. That major case now favours a change of emphasis, from fundamental mistake to causative mistake. However, it is not yet clear whether the question, Did the mistake cause the transfer?, is intended to be put with or without a gloss to the effect that it must have been a main or predominating cause. So it cannot be said that the case is unequivocally in favour of the approach which declines to weigh the effect of different causes.

As for the presumptions of resulting trust, which represent a position of extreme agnosticism as to the possibility of calculating the effect of mistake in gifts, it can only be repeated that their impact on this issue has never been assessed. They represent a com-

---

[45] 'It is, however, essential that the mistake relied on should be of such a nature that it can be properly described as a mistake in respect of the underlying assumption of the contract or transaction or as being fundamental or basic', *Norwich Union Fire Insurance Society* v. *Price* [1934] A.C. 455, 463 *per* Lord Wright.

[46] *Barclays Bank Ltd.* v. *W.J. Simms Ltd.* [1980] 1 Q.B. 677, 680.

[47] Below, pp. 159 ff.

pletely different approach. The disorganised nature of the subject has left room for problems to be tackled unawares in different ways. If we avert our eyes from this approach through 'presumed vitiation', we can sum up the present law in these propositions: (i) a plaintiff will be entitled to restitution from a defendant who has been enriched at his expense by virtue of a liability mistake (of fact); (ii) a liability mistake is a species of mistake which is *both* causative *and* (though this is imprecise) fundamental; (iii) where the plaintiff's mistake is *not* a liability mistake, he will be entitled to restitution if the mistake is characterised as *both* causative *and* fundamental; (iv) the insistence on fundamentality, as a quality additional to causality, is a measure against 'floodgates of litigation' and consequent insecurity of receipts; (v) there are signs that a different measure against insecurity is beginning to be preferred, namely the defence of change of position; (vi) recourse to that different technique may shortly mean that the additional requirement of fundamentality will no longer be insisted upon.

(e) *Mistaken Belief in Contractual Liability*

This is a special but common case of liability mistake. It requires brief consideration at this point because of the need to distinguish between the operation of mistake in formation of contract and reliance on mistake as a cause for restitution. Mistake in the formation of contract must be a topic for the books on contract and very little will be said about it here.

Where the contract is void but is believed to be valid, the ground for restitution in respect of wealth passing under the supposed contract is the liability mistake. That is, the false belief in the existence of the contract. This has already been explained. The point is reinforced by the observation that the nullity of the contract may itself be explicable on a ground other than mistake. In *Craven-Ellis* v. *Canons Ltd.*[48] the plaintiff wrongly believed that he had a contract to act as managing director for the company. That mistake was the ground on which he could have restitution in respect of the work he had done. But the reason the contract itself was void was that the directors who purported to act for the company in making it were in effect impostors since they had not taken up their qualification shares. Further Craven-Ellis himself was not within the description of persons whom the company's articles allowed to be appointed. So there was no contract with the company because the transaction was conducted by unauthorised agents and was itself unauthorised.

---

[48] *Craven-Ellis* v. *Canons Ltd.* [1936] 1 K.B. 403.

Similarly, in the old case of *Oom* v. *Bruce*[49] the plaintiff had insured a ship from St Petersburg to London. The contract was void because Russia had already commenced hostilities against England and had in fact seized the ship. Knowing nothing of the war and the consequent illegality the plaintiff paid premiums. He could recover on the ground of mistake, but the contract was void for illegality.

Where the ground for the nullity of the contract is itself mistake, the obvious and elementary proposition is that the mistake in the formation of the contract will not ground restitution unless it does destroy the contract.[50] For it is certain that, even if liability mistakes no longer exhaust the category which does give rise to restitution, there will be no restitution if the plaintiff's alleged mistake actually left intact a liability to make the payment which he now wants back.

Even after *Sybron Corporation* v. *Rochem Ltd.*,[50a] the best illustration is still *Bell* v. *Lever Bros.*[51] Lever installed Bell and Snelling as chairman and vice-chairman of their subsidiary, Niger; Niger prospered. Lever decided to agree terms for the subsidiary to be taken over by its principal competitor. They now needed to get rid of Bell and Snelling. They bought them out, at a cost of £50 000. The take-over went through. Lever then discovered that Bell and Snelling had been guilty of some private speculation which amounted to repudiatory breach of contract. In short, they could have been peremptorily dismissed. Lever sought restitution of their £50 000. Wright, J. and the Court of Appeal upheld their claim; the House of Lords rejected it.

Here there was a very serious mistake. It was not in itself a liability mistake, for it merely allowed Lever to form the view that it was desirable to incur a contractual obligation; and then that obligation survived the error. Hence, the payment was made under a belief in liability which was actually true, not mistaken. That is enough to explain the result. But two further factors need special mention because they provide explanations as to why, independently of the quality of the contract, restitution should have been refused. It is unrealistic to suppose that such considerations do not filter back into the handling of the question whether the contract is or is not void.

★7 First, therefore, restitutionary relief would have destroyed a bargain.

---

[49] *Oom* v. *Bruce* (1810) 12 East 225.

[50] 'Of course, if the money was due under a contract between the payer and the payee, there can be no recovery on this ground unless the contract itself is held void for mistake ... or is rescinded by the plaintiff', *Barclays Bank* v. *W.J. Simms Ltd.* [1980] 1 Q.B. 677, 695, *per* Goff, J.

[50a] *Sybron Corporation* v. *Rochem Ltd.* [1983] 2 All E.R. 707 (C.A.).

[51] *Bell* v. *Lever Bros.* [1932] A.C. 161.

Bell and Snelling had sold their positions, without fraud, for £50 000. Lever had managed to get them out of the way, and to allow recovery after the event would have been to reconsider the matter when the pressures, hopes, and fears of the bargaining process had changed, much as though one would help an overenthusiastic bidder at an auction after he has had a period of leisurely reflection on the wisdom of his disappointing purchase. Secondly, Lever could not restore Bell and Snelling to their original positions. That which they had obtained they could not give back. Counter-restitution is always a requirement for restitution unless the defendant had no right to use the benefit in question as an exchange-value.[52] So the conclusion can be represented as affirming that Bell and Snelling, acting in good faith, did have an interest with which they could lawfully deal.

It is crucial that in *Bell* v. *Lever Bros.* the majority of the House of Lords held that the two employees were not under a duty to remember and to disclose their misdeeds. The contract of employment was not in this respect *uberrimae fidei* (a contract of extreme good faith). In *Sybron Corporation* v. *Rochem Ltd.*[52a] the Court of Appeal distinguished the leading case and held that employees in some positions and under some contracts—and, in particular, in senior management—do have a duty to disclose the once discovered delinquencies of their fellow employees even if not those of themselves. A senior manager had participated in a conspiracy to divert the business of his employing company to other companies. On his application for early retirement terms had been settled within the framework of the employing company's pension scheme. He was paid a lump sum, and he and his wife took the benefit of an annuity under a policy held by the company on trust for them. The Court of Appeal affirmed Walton, J.'s decision allowing the company restitution of the lump sum and declaring the trust of the annuity void. For the manager ought to have disclosed the known frauds of his fellows and, had he done so, the company would have discovered his own participation and would have dismissed him without these severance benefits.

A duty to disclose and thus alert the other to his mistake thus makes a decisive difference. For what reasons? The duty has three consequences: it means that the court is not disturbing the legitimate hopes and fears of bargaining, since breach of duty is not a legitimate instrument of advantage; it eliminates the problem of counter-restitution, since one cannot claim back what one ought never to

---

[52] Below, p. 415 ff. esp. 423 f.
[52a] Cit. n. 50a above. Cf *Swain* v. *West (Butchers) Ltd.* [1936] 3 All E.R. 261.

have withheld; it causes the party in breach to forfeit respect for his interest in the security of his receipts. The problems which restrain restitution are thus not present when the defendant is in breach.

One other feature of *Bell* v. *Lever Bros.* is of general importance in relation to the kind of mistake for which restitution can be obtained. Lever would not have contracted 'but for' their mistake. But that was not enough to destroy the contract. Exactly the same can be said of one who pays for a painting by Constable and then finds he has only a copy.[53] So, in the formation of contract, the test of operative mistake is not 'but for': a 'causative mistake' is not enough. The mistake must be 'fundamental'. Imprecise as that word is, it signifies something very serious as opposed to something merely causative, and it takes its meaning precisely from the contrast between the two words: whatever else it is, a fundamental mistake is something more than a causative mistake. The buyer who mistakenly believes he is buying a horse which yet lives is causatively *and* fundamentally mistaken: his contract is void.[54] Mistakes in the formation of contract are parallel to mistakes which lead to non-obligatory transfers, entry into a contract being a non-obligatory act. It follows that, in the tension between 'fundamental' and 'causative' as tests for restitution-yielding mistake, the evidence from formation of contract favours the former. But logic does not dictate that the tests should be the same. For only in the formation of contract—that is, in deciding whether a mistake did nullify a contract—does the court have to balance against the instinct in favour of relief not merely the fear of too much restitution but, more particularly, also the fear of destroying bargains.

Where the law does conclude for nullity, that in itself is a negative and passive response which, *quoad* the contract itself, is not restitutionary. Also, if there is some subject-matter which physically moves, under the void contract, from one person to another, the preservation of existing rights *in rem* in that matter can be regarded as an anticipation of the danger of disapproved enrichment, but not as restitution.[55] New rights created in relation to the receipt, as for the repayment of money or of the value of goods or work, are by contrast restitutionary. In equity, however, there is a group of cases

---

[53] *Leaf* v. *International Galleries* [1950] 2 K.B. 86, Cf. *Peco Arts Inc.* v. *Hazlitt Gallery Ltd.* [1983] 3 All E.R. 193 (drawing by Ingres). There is no suggestion in either case that a *spontaneously* mistaken disappointment of this kind can entitle the disappointed party to restitution.

[54] *Sale of Goods Act, 1979*, s. 6.

[55] E.g. *Cundy* v. *Lindsay* (1878) 2 App. Cas. 459. See above, pp. 15, 25

for which these statements have to be adjusted. It is said that equity will rescind contracts on terms for spontaneous mistakes which are less fundamental than will effect nullity at law.

In these cases the measure of the relief is not necessarily tied to restitution since the imposition of terms can be used to construct a relationship between the parties which cannot be said to reflect any particular measure of relief other than innominate reasonableness. In *Solle* v. *Butcher*,[56] for example, the plaintiff claimed to recover overpayments of rent on the ground that the rent which had been agreed between him and the defendant exceeded the rate laid down by the Rent Acts. Both parties had misclassified the house, believing that after improvements and reconstruction it had become a new dwelling and thus had escaped its pre-improvement rent. The defendant's contention was that if the rent was recovered the lease should be set aside. The Court of Appeal agreed. But what was ordered went beyond restitution and counter-restitution. The lease was set aside only on the defendant's undertaking to permit the plaintiff, if he wished, to stay on as a licensee until all the proper steps should have been taken under the Rent Acts' procedure so as to allow a new lease to be given at the originally intended rent.

Not only the measure of relief is different. On the assumption that mistakes in equity make transactions voidable, not void, the power to revoke rights conceded under the vitiated contract is itself a restitutionary right. Even if no subject-matter has passed under the voidable contract the power to avoid is restitutionary *quoad* the contractual right itself, albeit in the second measure of restitution. At law if I mistakenly promise you £20, nullity will mean you get no right. Hence a restitutionary question can only arise *vis-à-vis* the £20 paid under the contract. In equity if the contract is voidable the right to revoke your claim against me itself counts as restitutionary even though I have paid nothing.

In addition to these differences of measure and analysis, the equitable cases offer relief for less fundamental mistakes, though in this, as in other respects, these cases have a doubtful pedigree. Not their least weakness is that they appear to assume that *Bell* v. *Lever Bros.* only considered the position at law and, therefore, left room for equity to come to a different conclusion on similar facts, which is untrue. Further, since common law might seem to have occupied all the ground compatible with respect for free bargaining, these cases have tacitly introduced, ostensibly under the heading of mistake, a

---

[56] *Solle* v. *Butcher* [1950] 1 K.B. 671, *Magee* v. *Pennine Insurance Co. Ltd.* [1969] 2 Q.B. 507, *Grist* v. *Bailey* [1967] Ch. 532. Cf. *Taylor* v. *Johnson* (1983) 45 A.L.R. 365.

jurisdiction to adjust disappointing bargains. In *Grist* v. *Bailey*[57] the vendor of a house had wrongly assumed that he could only sell subject to a protected tenancy and had fixed the price correspondingly low. Goff, J. set aside the contract on terms which provided that the purchaser should be allowed to buy at the proper price, free of the tenancy. This can hardly be distinguished from the case in which a man sells a painting for £100 which turns out to be worth £100 000, a routine example of irremediable bad luck. In *Grist* v. *Bailey* itself, the purchaser shared the original mistake. If that is a decisive fact, the party standing to gain by the mistake will take advantage from portraying himself in a sharper light. By contrast, the common law is so arranged that a party minded in retrospect to turn a shared into a one-sided mistake must fall out of the frying pan into the fire of *Smith* v. *Hughes.*[58]

(f) *Mistakes of law*

These have the same effect on your mind as mistakes of fact. Suppose a tax matter. You pay too much. In one story it is because you incorrectly think a taxable asset was sold; a mistake of fact, it was given away. In another it is because you wrongly suppose that gifts of that kind are taxable in the donor; a mistake of law, they are taxable in the donee. In both cases your brain works on wrong data. Whatever the legal effect of the upset, no-one would wish to say that it is naturally greater in one case than in the other.

Nevertheless, there is a tendency to say that payments made by mistake of law are 'voluntary'. This is a dangerous use of a difficult word. 'Voluntary' expresses a good reason for denying restitution in some cases but cannot be pressed into service as a universal shorthand for the conclusion that, for whatever reason, restitution is not to be allowed. It is true that mistakes of law do not in general give rise to restitution. But the reason is the fear of too much restitution. The absoluteness of this bar in practice is often mitigated by the courts' leaning against the conclusion that the mistake in question is a mistake of law. The ease with which this is done shows that the cause of action is *prima facie* established by the mistake, of whichever kind; and no other has to be found. The quality of the mistake puts in issue only a policy-motivated exception.

This was clearly expressed in 1810 by Gibbs, J., though he himself did transfer 'voluntary' into his conclusion. The case was *Brisbane* v.

[57] *Grist* v. *Bailey* [1967] Ch. 532.
[58] *Smith* v. *Hughes* (1871) L.R. 6 Q.B. 597.

Dacres.[59] Had it not been abrogated, an old naval custom would have entitled Admiral Dacres to a payment from Captain Brisbane in respect of the carriage of bullion. The payment was made; then Brisbane discovered the change in the customary rule. He sought to recover from the Admiral's widow; he failed. Gibbs, J. said:

> If we were to hold overwise, I think many inconveniences may arise; there are many doubtful questions of law: when they arise the defendant has an option either to litigate the question, or to submit to the demand, and pay the money. I think that by submitting to the demand he that pays the money gives it to the person to whom he pays it and makes it his, and closes the transaction between them. He who receives it has a right to consider it his without dispute . . . and it would be most mischievous and unjust if he who acquiesced in the right by such a voluntary payment should be at liberty at any time within the Statute of Limitation, to rip up the matter and recover back the money. He who received it is not in the same condition: he has spent it in the confidence that it was his and perhaps has no means of repayment.[60]

There is only one way in which this passage could not equally be applied to mistakes of fact: the greater prevalence of 'doubtful questions of law' with, in consequence, a greater threat to the security of receipts. It is that greater danger, not lesser vitiation of mental processes, which inhibits restitution here. The same point had been made by Lord Ellenborough, C.J., in *Bilbie* v. *Lumley*,[61] itself later approved in *Kelly* v. *Solari*,[62] the leading nineteenth-century case on recovery for mistake of fact.

In 1943, in *Sawyer and Vincent* v. *Window Brace Ltd.*,[63] Croom Johnson, J., said that it was 'beyond argument' that in the absence of exceptional circumstances a payment made under a mistake of law could not be recovered. There the defendant tenants had demanded and threatened to sue for a rebate of rent. They said it was due under s. 13 of the *Landlord and Tenant (War Damage) (Amendment) Act, 1941*. The landlords paid: a later case indicated that they need not have done so, so they tried to recover, and failed. The social inconveniences of any other conclusion are obvious.

But many think the rule too blunt. All that needs to be protected is the sanctity of settlements and compromises. Restitution should be more sensitively inhibited, not in all cases of mistake of law but only in cases where the recipient made an honest claim. *Goff and*

---

[59] *Brisbane* v. *Dacres* (1813) 5 Taunt. 143.
[60] *Ibid.*, p. 152 f.
[61] *Bilbie* v. *Lumley* (1802) 2 East 469.
[62] *Kelly* v. *Solari* (1841) 9 M. & W. 54.
[63] *Sawyer and Vincent* v. *Window Brace Ltd.* [1943] 1 K.B. 32.

Jones say:[64] 'In our view the principle in *Bilbie* v. *Lumley* should only preclude recovery of money which is paid in settlement of an honest claim.' Under this influence a more cautious note has crept into the cases.[65]

It is not clear that this narrower bar would adequately meet the mischief. Not only are there many doubtful questions of law, there are also many decent people and institutions whose habit is to meet their liabilities without waiting to be hounded, and necessarily they meet the liabilities they think they see. Mistakes only come out later. Since the law is often misunderstood and even changes under foot, recipients have a special need for security whether they actively claim (which would put them within the narrower bar) or passively receive (which would not).

If for these reasons the present rule seems preferable, there is, none the less, room for a different strategy against insensitivity. The fear is of a general exploitation of the law's uncertainty. It is possible to allow recovery in particular situations without causing that mischief, provided that the reason and scope of exceptions can be clearly laid down. There are exceptions, and perhaps others can also be developed. Three in particular need to be developed and made more coherent.

First, there are cases in which one person is controlling property of another or in the interests of another, typically as trustee or personal representative. This type of stewardship has to be reliable. When the trustee pays out in mistake of law, the outsider's interest in security competes with the beneficiary's interest in the safety of the fund. One possibility would be to make the trustee the sole insurer of the beneficiary's interests. But the competition has been differently resolved. It would seem that the beneficiary's interests and the social interest in reliable stewardship prevail over those of the outsider payee: the beneficiary can look to the trustee but, the trustee failing, the beneficiary can sue the payee.[66] In this claim the fact that the payment reaches the outsider by reason of a mistake of law rather than of fact is irrelevant.[66a]

Secondly, there are cases in which public authorities claim property to which they are not entitled by law, or give it away without authority.

---

[64] At p. 91.

[65] See, for example, *Avon C.C.* v. *Howlett* [1983] 1 W.L.R. 605, 620, *per* Slade, L.J., noting the *Goff and Jones* position. And cf. *Rogers*. v. *Louth County Council* [1981] 1 R 265 (Irish Supreme Court).

[66] *Re Diplock* [1948] Ch.D. 465.

[66a] Possibly this ground of recovery should be classified as 'ignorance' rather than as 'mistake of law': see above, p. 143.

They are stewards of a different kind, for their citizens generally; and again there is a social interest in the reliability of their stewardship. This matter will be further considered below.[67]

Thirdly, there are cases in which mistake of law occurs in a context of inequality, where responsibility is placed on the recipient to observe a rule of law, which is itself intended as, or which must be supported by, a protection of the plaintiff against exploitation. Whenever there is such an additional and identifiable element, or where there is fraud on the part of the defendant, the identification of the special factor constitutes a barrier against the general insecurity threatened by unrestricted recovery for mistake of law. However, in such cases it is almost always true that the ground for restitution can be said to be not the mistake but the special factor itself.[68]

(g) *Enrichment*

At the end comes the need to recall that the issue of enrichment must be separately addressed. The mistake, if of the operative kind, establishes that the enrichment, if there is one, should be reversed. It goes to the word 'unjust'. But, if not before then afterwards, the issue of enrichment must also be settled. If the receipt is in money, that is an end of it. If it is in kind, then so far as title survives (my bicycle in your hands) enrichment is prevented and has not happened; for the rest (enjoyment over time or labour), the obstacle is subjective devaluation. That can be overcome by showing a free acceptance, in which case the whole claim will be drawn under that head (because free acceptance is bi-valent); or by showing, on facts independent of the recipient's free choice, an incontrovertible benefit. This also is the rarest route. *Craven-Ellis* v. *Canons Ltd.*[69] is one example, a mistaken render of services incontrovertibly beneficial because a company cannot dispense with management. *Upton R.D.C.* v. *Powell*[70] may be another, a vital emergency service rendered not under moral compulsion but by mistake, the fire brigade answering a call outside its area.

(ii) *Induced Mistake*

A plaintiff who cannot get restitution on the basis of spontaneous mistake may yet be able to obtain relief if he can show that his

---

[67] Below, pp. 294–9.
[68] *Kiriri Cotton Co.* v. *Dewani* [1960] A.C. 192, discussed below, p. 209.
[69] *Craven-Ellis* v. *Canons Ltd.* [1963] 2 K.B. 403, above p. 118 f.
[70] *Upton R.D.C.* v. *Powell* [1949] 1 All E.R. 220, above p. 120.

mistake was induced by a misrepresentation made by the defendant.[70a] The misrepresentation may have been fraudulent or negligent or innocent, but that difference of moral quality is for the most part relevant only to working out the nature and scale of the relief which the plaintiff can have, after it has been established that he is entitled to redress of some kind. As between spontaneous mistakes and induced mistakes there are two main areas of difference. The first concerns the type of mistake for which relief can be sought. The second concerns the type of relief.

(a) *The Type of Mistake*

When the mistake is induced, the category of operative mistake expands. In simple terms, relief is available for more, and for more trivial, mistakes. The reasons why this happens have a general importance throughout the topic of vitiated voluntariness. We have already seen how in relation to spontaneous mistake the law has traditionally solved the problems of quantifying the effect of a mistake, and of weighing the competing effects of the mistake and other causes for a transfer, by insisting that the mistake shall be very serious indeed, fundamental. This solution of that problem coincides with the need to ensure that there is not too much restitution to be tolerable in a world which values security. Furthermore, since a spontaneous mistake is an inward affair, the restriction to very serious mistakes also minimises the risk of fabrication *ex post facto*. When the mistake is induced the law's choice goes the other way. No attempt is made to confine the response to mistakes which are overwhelming or fundamental, and it is not thought necessary to say even that the plaintiff would not have acted 'but for' the mistake. It is enough that the mistaken view of the facts played some part in his decision.

In *Edgington* v. *Fitzmaurice*[71] the directors of a company invited subscriptions for debentures. They said the loan had been earmarked for certain purposes, which was untrue. But the plaintiff said that in advancing money he had been much influenced by his own incorrect belief that the debentures would be secured by a charge on the company's property. Bowen, L.J., said,

Did this misstatement contribute to induce the plaintiff to advance his money? Mr. Davey's argument has not convinced me that it did not. He contended

---

[70a] For an examination of the nature of this relief by Robert Goff L.J., *obiter*, see *Whittaker* v. *Campbell, cit*. n. 1 above.

[71] *Edgington* v. *Fitzmaurice* (1885) 29 Ch.D. 459.

that the plaintiff admits that he would not have taken the debentures unless he had thought they would give him a charge on the property, and therefore he was induced to take them by his own mistake, and the misstatement in the circular was not material. But such misstatement was material if it was actively present to his mind when he decided to advance his money. *The real question is, what was the state of the plaintiff's mind, and if his mind was disturbed by the misstatement of the defendants, and such disturbance was in part the cause of what he did, the mere fact of his also making a mistake himself could make no difference.*[72]

Again, in *Smith* v. *Chadwick*, where the Court of Appeal had to consider, *inter alia*, whether an action of deceit could be maintained on the basis of a false statement in a prospectus to the effect that a named member of parliament was a director of the company, Jessel, M.R., said,[73]

Again, on the question of the materiality of the statement, if the court sees on the face of it that it is of such a nature as would induce a person to enter into the contract, or would tend to induce him to do so, or that it would be part of the inducement to enter the contract, the inference is, if he entered into the contract, that he acted on the inducement so held out, and you want no evidence that he did so act.

In short, the plaintiff has to show that the misrepresentation influenced his mind in making the contract or transfer. If the misrepresentation never registered on his mind, or if he put it out of his mind while he made his own independent check, or if he found out the truth before being finally committed, it will have had no influence at all.[74] And the same is true of an innocent representation which was immaterial in the sense that a reasonable man would not have been influenced by it.[75] But once the misrepresented state of affairs is shown to have been a factor influencing his judgement no attempt is made to inquire whether it was *the* factor.

What accounts for this liberal approach? The main factors would seem to be these: first, an induced mistake partly involves facts external to the mistaken party, so that fabrication *ex post* is not a danger; second, since he himself induced the mistake the representor has less claim, even if innocent, to recognition of his interest in the

---

[72] Ibid., p. 483, cf. *Amalgamated Investment* v. *Texas Commerce* [1981] 1 All E.R. 923, 936, per. Robert Goff, J.

[73] *Smith* v. *Chadwick* (1882) 20 Ch.D. 27, 44. The decision of the Court of Appeal was affirmed: *Smith* v. *Chadwick* (1884) 9 App. Cas. 187.

[74] *Attwood* v. *Small* (1838) 6 Cl. & F. 232; *Jennings* v. *Broughton* (1854) 5 D.M. & G. 126; *Ex p. Biggs* (1859) 28 L.J. Ch. 50; *Horsfall* v. *Thomas* (1862) 1 H. & C. 90; *Redgrave* v. *Hurd* (1881) 20 Ch.D. 1.

[75] *Smith* v. *Chadwick* (1882) 20 Ch.D. 27, 45 f., per Jessel, M.R.; *Industrial Properties (Barton Hill) Ltd.* v. *Associated Electrical Industries Ltd.* [1977] 2 W.L.R. 726.

security of his receipts; third, since the relief is given on the basis that transfers are voidable and not void, there are almost no fears to the effect that innocent third parties are likely to be disturbed; fourth, just as he forfeits respect for his interest in security, so also the misrepresentor himself disturbs the risks inherent in bargaining and cannot therefore easily appeal to the sanctity of free bargaining.

This expansion of the category of operative mistake when the mistake is not spontaneous but induced leaves unaffected the restrictive rules against restitution for mispredictions of the future and for mistakes of law. This is subject to two qualifications. First, the courts preserve the policies behind those restrictions by respecting the propositions in the abstract, while in the concrete case they lean very hard against finding that the mistake is as to the future[76] or as to law rather than fact.[77] The false metaphysics[78] involved in these exercises can obscure the good sense behind the policies from which individual plaintiffs are thus saved. The second qualification is that, where a mistake of law is induced by fraud, as where the agent of a life insurance company deliberately told clients that a particular type of policy was lawful when it was not, the fraudulent inducement takes the case out of the restriction so that the representee is entitled to restitution.[79] For dishonesty is not universal, and the reason for not allowing restitution for mistakes of law is only that there would otherwise be general insecurity.

(b) *The Type of Relief*

We are not concerned here with the compensatory damages available for fraudulent[80] and negligent misrepresentations[81] at common law; nor with the statutory right to damages for misrepresentations which are not shown to have been reasonably grounded or, at the court's

---

[76] *Edgington* v. *Fitzmaurice* (1885) 29 Ch. D. 459: representation of future application of money includes representation of present intention so to apply it; *Esso Petroleum* v. *Mardon* [1976] Q.B. 801: representation of future 'through-put' of garage includes representation of present capacity.

[77] *Cooper* v. *Phibbs* (1867) L.R. 2 H.L. 149; *Hirschfeld* v. *London, Brighton & South Coast Railway* (1876) 2 Q.B.D. 1: a mistake as to 'private rights' can be regarded as mistake of fact; *Cherry* v. *Colonial Bank of Australasia* (1869) L.R. 3 P.C. 24: misrepresentation of company's powers includes misrepresentation of factual basis for those powers; *Wanton* v. *Coppard* [1889] 1 Ch. 92: misrepresentation as to effect of legal document construed as misrepresentation of its factual content.

[78] Cf. *Holt* v. *Markham* [1923] 1 K.B. 504; *Solle* v. *Butcher* [1950] 1 K.B. 671.

[79] *West London Commercial Bank Ltd.* v. *Kitson* (1884) 13 Q.B.D. 360, 363, *per* Bowen, L.J.; *Hughes* v. *Liverpool Victoria Legal Friendly Society*, [1916] 2 K.B. 482.

[80] *Doyle* v. *Olby (Ironmongers) Ltd.* [1969] 2 Q.B. 158.

[81] Under *Hedley Byrne & Co. Ltd.* v. *Heller & Partners Ltd.* [1964] A.C. 465.

discretion, in lieu of rescission, for purely innocent misrepresentations.[82] These are not restitutionary claims.

The restitutionary response to induced mistakes is normally by rescission. That is, the transactions are good, and pass a good title, until avoided. Common law recognised rescission for fraud. In other cases the right to rescind is, by origin, equitable. When the respresentee rescinds he cuts away the transaction *ab initio*, and he recovers his money or other property. There are pre-conditions: he must be able to make counter-restitution,[83] and he cannot rescind once third party rights have intervened.[84]

Not only in this context, but wherever relief is by rescission, difficult questions arise in relation to the classification which distinguishes between the two measures of restitution, value received and value surviving. That classification is not normally a merely academic exercise, for it focuses attention on very practical questions as to what a plaintiff with a power to rescind is actually entitled to get. At the same time it has to be admitted that, where the power to rescind is held alongside a right to claim compensatory damages, these questions will rarely rise to the surface.

Where the defendant representor has received money it is certain that the plaintiff can have restitution in the measure 'value received'. That is, it is not a condition of restitution that the plaintiff must identify the money he paid as still held by the defendant.[85] Any other conclusion would render the plaintiff's right nugatory. Hence, the defendant must repay even though he has spent the money. From this it follows that the bar to rescission, which usually supervenes when the subject-matter obtained by the representor is acquired by a third party, does not apply when the subject-matter in question is money. This makes good sense, since the third party who gives value for the money which he receives cannot, in this case, be prejudiced by the rescission of the contract between the plaintiff and the defendant. The reason is that when the money passes into currency then, even if it remains identifiable, the recipient's title to it depends on the fact of his having given value in good faith and not on the title of the person from whom he receives it. So, even where you obtain my money in circumstances in which no title passes at all (because the transaction is void and not merely voidable), if you

---

[82] *Misrepresentation Act, 1967*, s 2 (1) and 2 (2).

[83] See below, p. 421 f.

[84] *Aliter* against a third party who is not a *bona fide* purchaser for value: *Clough* v. *London & North Western Railway* (1871) L.R. 7 Ex. 26; cf. *Goff and Jones*, 134 f.

[85] *Kettlewell* v. *Refuge Assurance Co. Ltd.* [1908] 1 K.B. 545, affd. [1909] A.C. 243.

then pass that money unmixed to a restaurant in exchange for a meal, there is no question of my saying that that money so received by the restaurant in good faith still remains mine. *A fortiori* if the transaction under which you received my money was voidable and not void. Hence, it follows that rescission, making void what was originally voidable, cannot harm the owner of the restaurant. But it is also true on those facts that there is no real need to speak of the plaintiff's rights as being based upon a 'rescission'. Ready and willing to make counter-restitution of any benefit received from the representor, he is only relying on a personal right to be repaid a sum of money with which he parted. The effect of restitution and counter-restitution will be completely to reverse the transaction, but there is no need to call it 'rescission'. It would be different if he were claiming, having identified the sum still in the defendant's hands, that, without the defendant's doing anything at all, he had revested that money in himself. For to achieve that effect he must have cut away (rescinded) the cause (the voidable transaction) from which the defendant's title depended.

Where the subject-matter is not money, rescission effects restitution by altering the legal condition of a *res* held by the defendant. Where the contract induced by the misrepresentation is still executory, the *res* in the defendant's hands is a right *in personam* exigible against the plaintiff. Rescission extinguishes that right. Where the contract is executed, so that, say, a car or a house has passed voidably to the defendant, rescission cuts away the contract and gives back to the plaintiff his right in the car or the house. Thus rescission effects restitution *in rem* and, therefore, necessarily in the second measure: it revests in the plaintiff title to a *res* held by the defendant.

However, the right to rescind is lost when a third party acquires the *res* for value is good faith. It follows from this that no restitutionary right *in rem* can then be maintained in respect of the identifiable exchange-product of a sale or barter of the *res*. This is the case converse to that of the restaurant owner discussed above. Here, if the misrepresentor exchanges the *res* for £100, any attempt to assert a right *in rem* to the £100 must be based upon a rescission of the original contract between misrepresentor and misrepresentee, for the misrepresentor's title remains good until it is avoided. But, since the third party's title to the *res* depends on the misrepresentor's, it is impossible to establish a claim *in rem* to the £100 without at the same time disturbing the third party. Hence, although recission effects restitution *in rem*, and in the measure 'value surviving', the right is limited to the *res* as originally received and does not extend to matter substituted for it.

This conclusion entails nothing for claims *in personam*. Even after the right to rescind has been lost, as by the intervention of third party rights or by consumption of the *res*, there is no reason in principle why the plaintiff should not have a right *in personam* to the value of the benefit received. Such a claim would exactly correspond to the claim for money which has just been described. The only difference is the practical one with which we are now familiar, namely that it is more difficult to prove enrichment where the benefit received is in kind and not in money. Apart from that difficulty of proof, personal claims to value received under voidable transactions should lie without regard to the form in which the value is received (whether in money or in an enriching non-money benefit) and without any need to rescind the voidable transaction in question.

3. COMPULSION

The law of restitution for mistake gets complicated because the simple proposition in favour of relief for all mistakes runs into counter-arguments and then, in coping with them, into philosophical problems about weighing different causes of human action. It is the same with compulsion. 'I was compelled' is as good a starting point as 'I was mistaken'. The party who was mistaken says that his brain operated on the wrong data. The party who was compelled says that his brain could not operate freely for fear of some evil consequence. In this way both come under the umbrella of vitiated voluntariness. But a plaintiff who acted under compulsion once again encounters opposing practicalities.

As social animals we are systematically committed to the use of pressure. At the worst it comes to bombs and bullets; when they have done their work we expect the treaty which follows to be re-spected: *pacta sunt servanda*. Within the community the same exploitation of pressures goes on all the time, though so familiarly as to become almost unobtrusive. The market works in this way. If your need is great, you will have to pay more. In a power strike a man with a large store of candles exploits the need for light. He withholds his candles from those who will not pay ten times their normal price. In politics the same happens. One withholds till another gives some *quid proquo*. The same between men and women, sexually. And all without discredit. It is part of life. It follows that the law of restitution cannot yield unthinkingly to the instinct in favour of relief for compulsion. The task which complicates its reaction is the need to draw a line between pressures which are and pressures which are not normal and acceptable incidents of social life. This is specially true of pressures actually used by a defendant as an instrument of enrichment, since the drawing of the line then depends to a certain extent on society's own fluctuating moral evaluation of itself as competitive and individualistic or as collectivist and restrained.

The subject of compulsion will be considered under five heads: (i) Duress, (ii) Actual Undue Influence, (iii) Legal Compulsion, (iv) Moral Compulsion, (v) Circumstantial Compulsion. Of these the first two naturally go together. They, unlike the other three, concern pressures exerted by the defendant on the plaintiff, and they are only divided by the different vocabulary of law and equity.

(i) *Duress*

This is the common law's word for pressure applied by the defendant to constrain the plaintiff to some action. There is, as we have seen,[86] one case which bears much the same relation to duress as ignorance to mistake. Suppose you tie me up and then, before my eyes, take my money. This is not ignorance, for I know what you are doing. But nor are you coercing me to do something, for I am powerless and do nothing. Suppose that I was not tied up but suffered from total paralysis. On that hypothesis, your taking my money cannot be said to be any less distinct from duress than ignorance is from mistake. Some word such as 'powerlessness' is needed. These extreme cases should never be omitted.

There are two principal questions about restitution for duress. First, how is the line drawn between pressures which do *prima facie* give rise to restitution and pressures which are exempt from restitution? Second, must the pressure be very serious ('overwhelming' or 'fundamental') or is it sufficient that it can be shown to have been a cause, even if not the only cause or dominant cause, of the plaintiff's decision to transfer wealth to the defendant. Clearly the second question can only arise if the pressure has been shown to be of a kind *prima facie* capable of giving rise to restitution.

What pressures are prima facie restitutionary? Pressures can be distinguished according as they are lawful or unlawful when con-

---

[86] Above, p. 141.

sidered independently of the issue of restitution. Thus if I put pressure on you to pay me £1000 by threatening to break my contract with you, I am applying an unlawful pressure. For, according to the law of contract, the breaking of a contract is unlawful. By contrast, suppose that you are in the course of buying my house and, when you have had surveys done and made arrangements for a mortgage, I demand a higher price than I originally asked and threaten to withdraw if you will not pay. So long as the deal between us is still 'subject to contract', the pressure which I put on you is lawful. For withdrawal is, according to the law of contract, made permissible by the deliberate suspension of contractual relations which is achieved by the phrase 'subject to contract'. Nobody has suggested that such conduct, unless fraudulent *ab initio*, is unlawful according to the law of tort. The practice of 'gazumping' relies on the lawfulness of withdrawal and, in particular, on its continued lawfulness long after the time when the purchaser has become irrevocably committed to the transaction.

The inquiry into restitutionary pressures can be subdivided by asking whether unlawful pressures always are, and lawful pressures always are not, *prima facie* restitutionary. Until recently it seemed that even the first of these sub-questions could not be answered without heavy qualification.

The common law traditionally limited its notion of duress to two categories: duress to the person, inflicted by doing or threatening harm or detention either to the plaintiff himself or to members of his family,[87] and duress of goods, inflicted by withholding or threatening to withhold goods belonging to the plaintiff in circumstances in which the withholding would be unlawful.[88] Alongside these two categories there was another which was not referred to regularly as 'duress' but which was not substantially different. This can be called 'refusal to perform a duty'. The cases in this category usually involved duties cast on public officers.[89] Willes, J. summed up the rationale of this third category in *Great Western Railway* v. *Sutton* when he said:[90]

When a man pays more than he is bound to do by law for the performance of a duty which the law says is owed to him for nothing or for less than he has paid,

[87] See *Goff and Jones*, 163 f., citing the early authorities.

[88] *Astley* v. *Reynolds* (1731) 2 Str. 915; *Somes* v. *British Empire Shipping Co.* (1860) 8 H.L.C. 338.

[89] *Dew* v. *Parsons* (1819) 2 B. & Ald. 562; *Morgan* v. *Palmer* (1824) 2 B. & C. 729; *Steele* v. *Williams* (1853) 8 Exch. 625. For the question whether these cases provide a root for a modern doctrine in public law, see below, p. 297 f.

[90] *Great Western Railway* v. *Sutton* (1869) L.R. 4 H.L. 226, 249.

there is compulsion or concussion in respect of which he is entitled to recover the excess by *condictio indebiti* or action for money had and received.

If this *dictum* of Willes, J., had been understood literally, all unlawful pressures would have been seen as giving rise to restitution. For if ever a man applies unlawful pressure to another to back up a demand for payment he must necessarily be demanding payment for a duty owed for nothing, since by law he ought to desist from his unlawful threats without being paid to do so. However, there were two respects in which the generality of the *dictum* seemed to be contradicted. First, even unlawful duress of goods was held to be insufficient to render a contract voidable, with the effect that a promise to pay which had been obtained under such pressure could be enforced even though a payment made directly in response to the same pressure would have been recoverable. That was the rule laid down in *Skeate* v. *Beale*[91] by Lord Denman, C.J., who believed that it was necessary in order to uphold the sanctity of promises. Secondly, it was not clear that threats to break a contractual duty could ever be sufficient to give rise to restitution of a payment so extorted. Here the picture was exactly the opposite to that created by *Skeate* v. *Beale*. There was no doubt that a promise to pay a surcharge for a contractual performance could not be enforced, for want of sufficient consideration.[92] But, to establish that a payment could be recovered, it was necessary to rely on a strong, but only persuasive, line of Australian cases.[93]

However, both these inhibitions of the general proposition that unlawful pressures are always *prima facie* restitutionary have now been removed.[94] *Skeate* v. *Beale* was always doubtful. In every case it must be a matter of chance whether a payment follows directly on duress of goods or whether a promise first intervenes and then payment follows. The law never went to the lengths of consciously holding that the enforceability of the promise so obtained nevertheless left any payment made under such promise recoverable, and the intention no doubt was that, if a promise once intervened, there should be no further question of restitution. But the line between direct payments and payments under promises was so fine that, in

---

[91] *Skeate* v. *Beale* (1841) 11 A. & E. 983.

[92] *Harris* v. *Watson* (1791) Peake 102; *Stilk* v. *Myrick* (1809) 6 Esp. 129, 2 Camp. 317.

[93] Esp. *Nixon* v. *Furphy* (1925) 25 S.R. (N.S.W.) 151; *Sundell* v. *Yannoulatos (Overseas) Ltd.* (1956) 56 S.R.(N.S.W.) 323; *Intercontinental Packers Pty. Ltd.* v. *Harvey* [1969] Qd. 159.

[94] *The Soboen and the Sibotre* [1976] 1 Lloyds Rep. 293; *North Ocean Shipping Co. Ltd.* v. *Hyundai Construction Ltd.* [1979] Q.B. 705; *Pao On* v. *Lau Yiu* [1980] A.C. 614.

at least one case, restitution was allowed without the point being taken that the payment had been first promised and then paid.[95] As for the other gap, it was perhpas never more than a lacuna of authority rather than of principle, as the Australian cases showed. It must be admitted, however, that refusals to fulfil contractual obligations do raise some special problems, as will be seen below.[96]

With these two gaps made good, it seems that every independently unlawful pressure can, so long as it passes whatever tests must be applied in relation to the second question below, amount to restitutionary duress. Nevertheless, it ought to be remembered that that proposition is not a necessary or logical truth. For example, it might have been decided that threats to break a contract should not give rise to restitution. There are arguments which tend in that direction, though they have in fact not carried the day. And just as that species of unlawful pressure could have been exempted from the law of restitution, so good reasons might in theory be found for exempting others.

Can lawful pressures also count? This is a difficult question, because, if the answer is that they can, the only viable basis for discriminating between acceptable and unacceptable pressures is not positive law but social morality. In other words, the judges must say what pressures (though lawful outside the restitutionary context) are improper as contrary to prevailing standards. That makes the judges, not the law or the legislature, the arbiters of social evaluation. On the other hand, if the answer is that lawful pressures are always exempt, those who devise outrageous but technically lawful means of compulsion must always escape restitution until the legislature declares the abuse unlawful. It is tolerably clear that, at least where they can be confident of a general consensus in favour of their evaluation, the courts are willing to apply a standard of impropriety rather than technical unlawfulness.

The evidence for this comes partly form the equitable cases on actual undue influence. These will be considered below.[97] The word 'undue' seems not to mean 'unlawful' but, more generally, 'disapproved' or 'unacceptable'. Beyond this equitable evidence, facts amounting to the crime of blackmail also support this position. It may be objected that such evidence cuts the other way; but that is not so, because the punishment of the crime shows that the courts are prepared to condemn as unacceptable threats which are in them-

---

[95] *Tamvaco* v. *Simpson* (1866) L.R. 1 C.P. 363.
[96] Below, p. 182–3.
[97] Below, p. 184–5.

selves perfectly lawful but which become offensive when they are used to exact payments. Suppose you tell me that you intend to inform the local papers that I have taken bribes or that I am a homosexual. If these things are true, it is lawful for you to reveal them. But when you have no interest to protect,[98] it is not proper for you to threaten even such lawful acts to extract money from me; and such threats, if they succeed, do give rise to restitution.[99] If *per impossibile* the criminal law were to change its mind and cease to punish the blackmailer, the right to restitution would survive. The absence of punishment would not affect the conclusion, backed by a strong consensus in society, that such threats are improper at least in the sense that they must not be used as a means of enrichment.

It is more difficult when the morality is contested. Take again the case of the man who finds himself, during a power strike, with a temporary monopoly of the local supply of candles. He charges £10 each, exploiting the people's need for light. It would be very difficult for a court to characterise this as improper duress, since it involves a disputed evaluation of the role of free market forces. So, in such a case, the court would be likely to look for independent illegality as the only basis for restitution. Legislative control of dominant market positions[1] would provide the touchstone of unlawfulness in such a case. If the monopoly was held by a public authority it might alternatively be possible to find some implied restriction on its power to exploit ordinary market forces.[2] But either way the search would be for signs that the pressure had already been condemned by the law, and no judge would escape criticism if he asserted that restitution would follow such behaviour simply because it represented the unacceptable face of capitalism. Where they can be avoided, the judges do not embrace such disputed value-judgements.

Sometimes they cannot be avoided. In *Universe Tankships Inc. of Monrovia* v. *International Transport Workers' Federation*, the House of Lords had to decide whether a payment obtained by ITF as a

---

[98] *Thorne* v. *Moror Trade Association* [1937] A.C. 797.

[99] *United Australia Ltd* v. *Barclays Bank Ltd.* [1941] A.C. 1, 27 f., *per* Lord Atkin.

[1] Principal parts of this machinery are Articles 85 and 86 of the Treaty of Rome, the *Restrictive Trade Practices Act, 1976*, and the *Competition Act, 1980; Belgische Radio en Televisie and Société Belge des auteurs* v. *S.V. S.A.B.A.M and N.V. Fonior*, Case 127/73 [1974] E.C.R. 51; *Valor International Ltd.* v. *Application de Gaz* [1978] 3 C.M.L.R. 87; *Garden Cottage Foods Ltd.* v. *Milk Marketing Board* [1983] 2 All E.R. 770, esp. 777 (*per* Lord Diplock) and 782 (per Lord Wilberforce).

[2] *Smith* v. *Charlick* (1924) 34 C.L.R. 38 (surcharge demanded by monopolist Wheat Board) might now be decided in favour of the plaintiff on this ground.

[3] *Universe Tankships Inc. of Monrovia* v. *International Transport Workers' Federation* [1982] 2 W.L.R. 803.

condition of releasing the plaintiff-applicants' ship from 'blacking' was recoverable on the ground of duress. The Federation had paralysed the *Universe Sentinel* in Milford Haven by withdrawing all port services, including the tugs necessary to move her out of the harbour. This industrial action, which was assumed to be *prima facie* tortious in that it involved inducing people to break their contracts, compelled the appellants to make agreements to improve the conditions of their crew and also to pay a substantial sum to the ITF's welfare fund. The question in the House of Lords was whether that payment could be recovered. By a majority of three to two it was held that it could. In the opinion of the majority the duress was independently unlawful because it was not within the scope of the immunity conferred on trade unions in respect of torts committed in the course of a trade dispute. Hence, according to the law of tort, the blacking was unlawful. However, the important point in this context is that the majority did not regard the issue of independent unlawfulness as automatically conclusive of the quality of the pressure for the purposes of the law of restitution. It was said that, in order to give rise to restitution, the pressure had to be 'illegitimate' and not 'legitimate'. The lawfulness or otherwise of the ITF action was a powerfully persuasive guide to the legitimacy of the pressure.[4] But it was not conclusive. In other words 'legitimate' was chosen as a term capable of drawing on social morals, not merely on the law. That exactly accords with what has been said above: a pressure which in itself is technically lawful can, none the less, trigger restitution if it is characterised as socially unacceptable or 'illegitimate'.

Does the pressure have to be the dominant cause of the plaintiff's transfer to him? There is no doubt that the pressure brought to bear on the defendant must at least have been one of the reasons for the plaintiff's action. But it is no longer clear whether that is enough. It may be that the pressure must have been the overwhelming or predominant reason.

We have seen that a misrepresentation may not register on the plaintiff's mind or, if it did register, may have been discounted and not in any way relied on.[5] In such cases no restitution is available for induced mistake. Similarly it may be found as a matter of fact that pressure was never perceived or was discounted. In *Slater* v. *Burnley*

---

[4] *Universe Tankships Inc. of Monrovia* v. *International Transport Workers' Federation* [1982] 2 W.L.R. 803, 814 *per* Lord Diplock.
[5] Above, p. 169, n. 74.

Corporation,[6] the plaintiff had overpaid his water rates after a wrong assessment had been served on him but he could not make out any action based on duress because he had never been threatened that, in the event of non-payment, the corporation would exercies its power to cut the water off. In *Twyford* v. *Manchester Corporation.*[7] Twyford, a stonemason, had regularly protested against being asked to pay fees when he wanted to do certain work on graves in the corporation's cemetery. These charges turned out to have been imposed without authority. But his claim to restitution failed because Romer, J., held that there was no evidence that he had perceived any threat that if he did not pay he would be excluded or would suffer any other unpleasant consequence. This is a severe finding of fact; but, the fact once found, there was no question of Twyford's having suffered any compulsion. In *Barton* v. *Armstrong*[8] the appellant had executed a deed after threats had been made to his life in order to induce him to do so. He had also believed that the undertakings in the deed were imperatively necessary for the well-being of his company. In the Privy Council, Lord Wilberforce and Lord Simon of Glaisdale, dissenting on an issue of fact, said that, if it was true, as had been found, that the appellant, despite being in fear, had nevertheless executed the deed for other reasons and wholly for other reasons, there could be no conclusion that he had acted under duress. They admitted that such a finding—'That a man in a state of fear may yet act voluntarily, i.e. totally for other reasons'—was exceptional.[9]

Barton v. *Armstrong* very clearly laid down that the duress does not have to be *the* reason so long as it is *a* reason for the plaintiff's action. The majority only differed from the minority in holding that Barton had been partly motivated by fear, even though he had also excuted the deed because he believed that it was in his company's commercial interest to do so. The majority expressly drew the analogy with misrepresentation, showing that the vitiating factor did not have to be the dominant or overwhelming reason for the action.[10] Though the authority of the Judicial Committee is only persuasive, three considerations support this approach. First, all the reasons which support a similar approach in relation to misrepresentation apply to duress, which is also an external matter and one

---

[6] *Slater* v. *Burnley Corporation* (1888) 59 L.T. 636.
[7] *Twyford* v. *Manchester Corporation* [1946] Ch. 236.
[8] *Barton* v. *Armstrong* [1976] A.C. 104.
[9] *Ibid.*, 123.
[10] *Ibid.*, 119.

which forfeits respect for the defendant's interest in the security of his receipts.[11] Secondly, it is virtually impossible, in practice, to determine whether a given pressure was *the* reason for action in the sense that it coerced the will to such an extent as to make no other action possible. Thirdly, as long ago as the leading case of *Astley* v. *Reynolds*[12] it was already said that there was no need to weigh the quantum of pressure applied.

There the plaintiff had had to pay a sum over and above the legal interest in order to induce the defendant to give up the silver plate which the plaintiff had pawned with him. It was objected, *inter alia*, that the plaintiff could have had another remedy, by trover. Having that remedy, he need not have paid, so that the payment was voluntary. To this the King's Bench replied:

> We think also that this is a payment by compulsion. The plaintiff *might* have such an immediate want of his goods that an action of trover would not do his business. Where the rule *volenti non fit iniuria* is applied, it must be where the party had the freedom of exercising his will, which this man had not. We must take it he paid the money, relying on his legal remedy to get it back again.[13]

Here there is no inquiry into the strength of the particular plaintiff's need for his goods. It is enough that he *might* have had an immediate need of them. It is against that possibility that plaintiffs in this situation are allowed either to pay and sue for restitution or to refuse to pay and sue for conversion.

In *Maskell* v. *Horner*,[14] the plaintiff was a trader outside Spital-fields market who had for a dozen years paid tolls demanded by the owner of the market. He always protested, was threatened with dis-traint of his goods, and paid. When it turned out that the tolls were demanded without right he sought restitution of so many of his payments as were not statute-barred. Reversing Rowlatt, J., the Court of Appeal allowed his claim. The focus of attention was the question whether he had paid to settle the claim or to avert the duress of goods. But on close inspection it appears that the dif-ference between Rowlatt, J., and the Court of Appeal was only that he thought the *sole* reason for the payments was that Maskell had accepted the validity of the claim, albeit in a 'grumbling acquie-scence', whereas they thought the pressure was still *a* factor. In other words, the pressure was not quantified as having displaced all other

---

[11] Above, p. 169–70.
[12] *Astley* v. *Reynolds* (1731) 2 Str. 915.
[13] *Ibid.*, 916. (My italics for 'might'.)
[14] *Maskell* v. *Horner* [1915] 3 K.B. 106.

considerations and having left no room for choice. For Rowlatt, J., Maskell was in the same exceptional position as Barton seemed to occupy in the eyes of the minority in *Barton* v. *Armstrong*: he was someone for whom the pressure was not even *a* cause for paying.

Nevertheless it has been said on a number of recent occasions that there must be 'coercion of the will'.[15] Such statements do not in themselves commit the law to the impossible exercise of quantifying coercion, because it can be said that they still leave the way open to hold that the will is sufficiently coerced if the pressure is but one reason for the action. But that avenue of escape is closed when the statement in question is used to negative duress on facts in which the pressure was as a matter of fact a reason in the defendant's mind for the decision which he took. For example, in *Pao On* v. *Lau Yiu*[16] one question was whether a guarantee given by Lau could be avoided on the ground that it had been given in response to Pao's threat not to perform a contract with a company of which Lau was majority shareholder. The Judicial Committee held that a finding of fact, that there had been 'commercial pressure but no coercion',[17] was enough to make it technically unnecessary to go further into the question. Their Lordships nevertheless did go on to indicate that

There is nothing contrary to principle in recognising economic duress as a factor which may render a contract voidable, provided always that the basis of such recognition is that it must amount to a coercion of the will, which vitiates consent. It must be shown that the payment made or the contract entered into was not a voluntary act.[18]

It is indisputable on the facts that this was intended to mean that the plaintiff must have been controlled and overwhelmed by the pressure.

There is a question whether a special test is needed where the pressure is exerted by refusing to perform or complete a contract. For it is no accident that the test requiring the pressure to be, not *a* cause, but *the* cause of the plaintiff's transfer has reasserted itself in that field.

Suppose that a builder tells his client that unless he receives an extra payment of £10 000 he will stop work and go into bankruptcy. Then, in response, the client pays the surcharge. On these facts the

---

[15] *The Siboen and The Sibotre* [1976] 1 Lloyd's Rep., 293, 336, *per* Kerr, J.; *North Ocean Shipping Co. Ltd.* v. *Hyundai Construction Co. Ltd.* [1979] Q.B. 705, 721.

[16] *Pao On* v. *Lau Yiu* [1980] A.C. 614.

[17] *Ibid.*, 635. It is very remarkable that this is said to be 'in line with' *Barton* v. *Armstrong*.

[18] *Ibid.*, p. 636.

Barton v. *Armstrong* approach would mean that the surcharge would always be recoverable. For the pressure in such a case is invariably *a* reason for paying. If the surcharge is always recoverable the builder with a genuine problem has no hope of saving himself by negotiating an extra payment unless his problem is small enough to be solved by a payment in the nature of a loan. This result serves as a stringent discipline against cutting tenders too close to the bone but may not be the most sensible solution. The unanswered question is whether a negotiation for a surcharge should ever be upheld as a reasonable transaction. If so, there are two ways in which it can be done compatibly with the *Barton* v. *Armstrong* approach.

It could be said that, contrary to the general law of duress, this kind of pressure is only restitutionary when applied in bad faith, being intended to exploit the plaintiff's weakness rather than to solve financial or other problems of the defendant.[19] The question would then be whether the threat was *a* reason for the payment, but there would be a further question whether, if it was, the party refusing to complete the contract was or was not trying in good faith to solve a difficulty in which he found himself. Restitution would follow if he was not. It might be said that this would reduce to recovery for fraud, not for duress. The other alternative is to approach the question by distinguising between a threat and a warning. Here the basic question would be the same as before, though differently worded: Was the fear of non-completion *a* reason for paying the surcharge? But there would be no restitution if the defendant had merely communicated a pressure applied by circumstances to himself rather than threatened the plaintiff with a pressure of his own making.

Either approach would leave room for negotiations to avoid a genuine difficulty. At the moment the cases are taking a third path, namely insisting in this area on a more severe test of the degree of compulsion than is found in *Barton* v. *Armstrong*. Since the effect is to commit them to an impossible and inscrutable inquiry into the metaphysics of the will, they thus secure a concealed discretion to distinguish between reasonable and unreasonable, legitimate and illegitimate applications of this species of independently unlawful pressure. The simplest and most open course would be to restrict the right to restitution to the case in which the defendant sought, *mala fide*, to exploit the weakness of the plaintiff. These difficulties go

---

[19] As in *D. & C. Builders* v. *Rees* [1966] 2 Q.B. 617.

some way to explaining the tardiness with which English law came to recognise the possibility of restitution on the ground of pressure applied by the withholding of contractual rights.

(ii) *Actual Undue Influence*

Undue influence is either actual or relational. Where it is relational it does not properly belong under the heading of compulsion. It is said that a relation of confidence gives rise to a presumption of undue influence, but the proper inference of fact, where the presumption is not rebutted, is not that the defendant applied pressure but that he failed to ensure that the plaintiff was emancipated from dependence or excessive reliance on him. In other words what disables the plaintiff in such cases is that his judgement is not his own but is abdicated to the defendant, the senior party in the relationship. Relational undue influence will be considered under
*8 the heading of inequality.

In the days in which common law duress was thought to be confined to two or three restricted types, it made sense to see equitable undue influence as a supplement. But nowadays actual undue influence and duress seem to be one and the same phenomenon, namely improper or unacceptable pressure. It is, however, more clear that equity is concerned with a moral standard. There is no suggestion that the pressure must be technically unlawful. In *Re Brocklehurst*[20] Bridge, L.J., said, with approval, that a layman 'would assume that the legal concept of undue influence must, by the very label which the law puts on it, import some stigma of impropriety or fault'.[21] Later, summing up his conclusion favourable to the defendant, he said there was nothing for which he could be 'fairly criticised'.[22] That was a case in which the plaintiff sought to establish a relational influence, but the remarks apply also to actual pressure.

In *Re Craig*[23] a forceful housekeeper-companion had received gifts of some £30 000 in the last five years of the life of the vulnerable and dependent old man. From the time when she began to work for him in 1959 till he died in 1964 she received from him money equal to roughly 75 per cent of his entire estate. Ungoed Thomas, J., set

---

[20] *Re Brocklehurst* [1978] 1 Ch. 14.
[21] *Ibid.*, 39.
[22] *Ibid.*, 48.
[23] *Re Craig* [1971] Ch. 95.

the gifts aside. He decided the case primarily on the basis of a presumption derived from the relationship. But he also said that the size of the gifts, and the evidence as to his vulnerability and her bullying habits, entitled him to infer, without the aid of any presumption, that she had obtained the gifts by actual pressure on him. It was not necessary to affirm that she had used methods of applying pressure which were independently unlawful.

Similarly it is not unlawful to inform a father that his son will be prosecuted for an offence of dishonesty. But if you use that kind of statement to make a father cover your loss, you will be employing undue influence. In *Williams* v. *Bayley*[24] the House of Lords set aside a mortgage given by a father in those circumstances. In *Mutual Finance Co. Ltd.* v. *Wetton & Sons Ltd.*[25] a finance company was unable to enforce a guarantee obtained on behalf of a customer who had defaulted on his hire purchase instalments. The customer had first forged a guarantee from the family company from which he had earlier been expelled. The finance company had then sought to get a genuine guarantee, using the veiled threat that the black sheep would be prosecuted for forgery if none were forthcoming. His brother then reluctantly agreed because, as the finance company knew, their father was gravely ill and might not survive the shock of his son's renewed disgrace. Setting aside the guarantee, Porter, J., expressly said that common law duress in the sense of 'unlawful force' could not be shown to have been used, but he had no doubt that the veiled threats amounted to undue influence in equity. It would be difficult nowadays to make that distinction.

(iii) *Legal Compulsion*

This is pressure brought lawfully to bear by one person on another as a means of enforcing his rights. Since it is the business of all legal systems to make sure that such pressure is available and effective, the general rule is that there can be no restitution of anything thus obtained. The reason is not that transfers made under orders of a court, or in response to threats of litigation or in the process of execution of judgement, are actually voluntary. They are no more freely chosen than transfers under duress of goods. The right explanation is that, even although non-voluntary, such transfers are made in response to a type of pressure which is exempted from restitution as a normal and necessary incident of social life.

[24] *Williams* v. *Bailey* (1866) L.R. 1 H.L. 200.
[25] *Mutual Finance Co. Ltd.* v. *Weltton & Sons Ltd.* [1937] 2 K.B. 389.

There are, however, certain cases which are removed from this exemption. For the better protection of some positions the law sometimes recognises that a claimant has either acquired or has himself arranged several avenues of recourse against more than one person. The most familiar example is where a creditor has insisted that his debtor should find a guarantor. He thus gives himself claims against both the debtor and the surety. In such a case a restitutionary claim based on legal compulsion can arise, not against the creditor who applies the pressure but as between the people subject to it. A loose way of saying why this happens is that in giving the creditor two claims the law may allow him to get substantially the wrong man. Thus, as between the principal debtor and his guarantor, the debtor is the one who is primarily liable, and the guarantor's liability is ancillary or secondary. The creditor can go against either. But if the guarantor is compelled to pay, the substance of the matter is that he has discharged the debtor's liability rather than his own. Hence the guarantor is given a restitutionary claim against the principal debtor, to which the latter cannot object that the pressure applied to the guarantor was lawful and necessarily exempt from restitution. The reason is that the guarantor's claim does not seek to reverse the remedial force applied with the approval of the legal system (as would a claim against the creditor) but only to ensure that its effect is passed on to the right person.

The proper analysis of this type of claim is that, first, the defendant (the person primarily liable) is enriched by the receipt of a non-money benefit (the discharge of his liability), which is, however, incontrovertibly beneficial to him on the 'no reasonable man' test. That is to say, he is saved necessary expenditure in that he was bound to discharge his debt with no less a degree of inevitability than, in *Craven-Ellis* v. *Canons Ltd.*, the company was bound, factually rather than legally, to pay for the management of its affairs.[26] Then, secondly, the enrichment is by subtraction from the plaintiff, to the extent that his outlay to the creditor obtained the discharge. Then, thirdly, the plaintiff acted non-voluntarily in that he was under legal compulsion, which is the factor going to 'unjust'. Finally, the policy obstacle which usually obstructs claims based on legal compulsion does not apply to claims in this configuration, as has just been explained.

The secondary liability of the plaintiff may have been personal or proprietary. In *Exall* v. *Partridge*[27] the plaintiff was not under any

---

[26] Above, p. 119.
[27] *Exall* v. *Partridge* (1799) 8 T.R. 308.

personal liability. His carriage, left on the defendants' premises for repair, was caught by their landlord's right to distrain for rent. When the landlord took it into his possession, the plaintiff had to pay the rent in order to recover it. Lord Kenyon, C.J., held that, though even an unequivocal benefit conferred by the plaintiff would not be enough in itself to put the defendants under a restitutionary obligation, the addition of the factor of compulsion tipped the balance in the plaintiff's favour. This result was achieved within the framework of the count for money paid. Consequently the conclusion was expressed by 'implying' a request from the defendants that the plaintiff should pay their rent. There was no such request. The case shows how far the courts would go, within contractual forms, when the call for restitution was clear, albeit unanalysed.[28]

Johnson v. *Royal Mail Steam Packet Co.*[29] also exemplifies a secondary liability which was proprietary. Here the plaintiffs were mortgagees of a ship delivered up to them by the defendants. When the plaintiffs obtained possession, the crew of the ship turned out not to have been paid. Since an unpaid crew has a maritime lien, the plaintiffs had to pay the wages in order to clear their own security. But the wages were primarily due under contracts of employment between the crew and the defendants. In this action the plaintiffs therefore successfully claimed restitution of the £5000 which they had had to pay in the place of the defendants.

The secondary liability is more commonly personal. The case of the guarantor is a clear example. *Moule* v. *Garrett*[30] provides another illustration in connexion with the assignment of leases. The assignor of a lease remains liable on his convenants even though he no longer holds the land. So, if the lessor sues him rather than the assignee, the assignor's liability appears secondary and technical by comparison with the liability of the assignee who has the actual enjoyment to which the claim relates. Consequently the assignor has a right to restitution from the assignee. This might be thought to rest on contract and can indeed do so as between an assignor and his immediate assignee. But the non-contractual nature of the claim is revealed when there are intermediate assignments between the plaintiff who has paid and the defendant who is in possession. In *Moule* v. *Garrett* itself, the plaintiff had had to pay damages for breach of a covenant to repair. The defendant was not an immediate, but a subsequent, assignee, and the breaches of covenant had occurred during his time in possession. The plaintiff's claim was upheld.

[28] cf. p. 117, above and p. 269, below.
[29] *Johnson* v. *Royal Mail Steam Packet Co.* (1867) L.R. 3 C.P. 38.
[30] *Moule* v. *Garrett* (1872) L.R. 7 Ex. 101.

Brook's Wharf and Bull Wharf Ltd. v. *Goodman Bros.*[31] is a more specialised example of the same configuration. The plaintiffs were bonded warehousemen. The defendants were importers of furs. Furs stored in the plaintiffs' warehouse were stolen. The relevant legislation in relation to import duties provided that in such circumstances not only the importers but also the warehousemen should be liable to pay. The plaintiffs paid. Lord Wright, M.R., described their obligations as 'ancillary to and by way of security for the due payment to the customs'.[32] The primary obligation was owed by the importers. The Court of Appeal upheld the plaintiffs claim to restitution.

There has been a question whether the fact that the plaintiff discharged the liability under legal compulsion is enough in itself effectively to negative the voluntary character of his intervention without any inquiry into the way in which he came to incur his secondary liability. The argument has been advanced that the plaintiff cannot be said to have been compelled to pay if he encountered his liability in the pursuit of his own interest or convenience.

In *England* v. *Marsden*,[33] the plaintiff had paid the defendant's rent. The reason was that goods which he himself had seized under a bill of sale, but had not removed, had been distrained by the defendant's landlord. But the claim for restitution in respect of the payment of rent was rejected on the ground that he could have removed the goods but chose instead to leave them on the defendant's premises for his own convenience. However, in *Edmunds* v. *Wallingford*[34] that decision was described in the Court of Appeal as 'very questionable'.

In *Edmunds* itself, goods had been seized in the course of execution of judgement and had been sold to pay Wallingford's debt. The goods belonged to his sons and had been taken from a shop which they ran in his name. When the sons, in turn, went bankrupt their trustee brought this action for restitution on the grounds that they had discharged a liability primarily incumbent on the father. The claim succeeded, even though the sons' goods had been on the premises for their own business purposes. The Court of Appeal appeared to limit *England* v. *Marsden* to the case in which the liability was encountered by the plaintiff against the defendant's will, as

[31] *Brook's Wharf and Bull Wharf Ltd.* v. *Goodman Brothers* [1937] 1 K.B. 534.
[32] *Ibid.*, 543.
[33] *England* v. *Marsden* (1866) L.R. 1 C.P. 429.
[34] *Edmunds* v. *Wallingford* (1885) 14 Q.B.D. 811.

where he left the goods in question on the defendant's premises without consent. Only then could the compulsion inherent in the liability be cancelled out by the circumstances in which it was incurred.

More recently the Court of Appeal considered this question in *Owen* v. *Tate*.[35] The plaintiff had paid the defendant's debt to a bank. He had been compelled to pay as a surety for the defendant, but he was denied restitution. He had intervened without the defendant's knowledge. Hence, though compelled to pay, he had voluntarily sought out his liability and consequently had to be treated as a volunteer. It would have been different if circumstances had created a necessity for him to intervene,[36] but in fact he had merely come to an arrangement with the debtor's bank in order to obtain the release of the lady whose property had been mortgaged, by way of security, for the principal debt. The arrangement was in the nature of a favour done for the original mortgagor, to relieve her from anxiety. The result of this case has been criticised. It will be briefly reconsidered in another place.[37]

Other Paths to Restitution For Debts Discharged   The link between this particular kind of pressure (legal compulsion) and this species of non-money benefit (liabilities discharged) should not be allowed to become so close as to make 'compulsory discharge' an isolated topic detached from the rest of the law of restitution.[38] The scheme of this chapter is based on a series of 'vitiations'—mistake, compulsion and so on; another scheme, much less efficient, could be based on types of benefit received—money received, goods received, services, discharges and so on. 'Compulsory discharge' fits in neither, being compounded from both. Nevertheless, there are forces which do tend to detach this topic, and, in order to resist them, it is necessary to make two observations which, strictly speaking, are digressions from the theme of compulsion.

First, legal compulsion is not the only ground on which someone who has paid another's debt can hope for restitution. Secondly, the grounds available depend to a considerable extent on the question whether the liability has technically been discharged. If English law had adopted the rule that payment, even by a stranger, always

---

[35] *Owen* v. *Tate* [1976] Q.B. 402.
[36] *Ibid.*, 409 and 412, *per* Scarman, L.J.
[37] below, p. 311.
[38] In *Goff and Jones* 'discharge' is handled in its own chapter (ch. 14) in such a way as to suggest that legal compulsion is, naturally, the only possible cause for restitution.

discharged and extinguished the liability, the restitutionary inquiry would have been much simpler. The discharge would invariably have satisfied the issues inherent in 'enrichment at the expense of the payor'. So the only question would have been whether the payor could point to a factor calling for restitution. As it is, the general rule is to the contrary effect: in the absence of compulsion, the payment does not discharge the debt or other liability unless and until the discharge is accepted by the debtor.[39]

This has profound effects on the issue of enrichment and on the availability of claims based on free acceptance. For, clearly, if the defendant's debt is not discharged he cannot be said to have been incontrovertibly enriched; and if the discharge depends on his acceptance then the time during which a free acceptance remains possible is not confined to the act of payment itself. If you watch me paying your creditor and have the necessary knowledge of what I am doing, you freely accept your discharge. But, even if you do not hear till afterwards, the rule that makes your discharge depend on your acceptance prolongs your option to reject.[40] Furthermore, if you do reject, so that the discharge is aborted, I would seem to be able to recover from the creditor, not on the basis of the legal compulsion but for total failure of consideration.[41]

So the full picture, not adequately tested as yet in modern cases, is that, where the debt is not automatically discharged by the fact of payment, the payor should pursue claims based on free acceptance (against the debtor) or total failure of consideration (against the creditor) depending on whether the discharge is accepted or rejected. By contrast, where the liability is discharged at once by the fact of payment, the intervening payor must, on general principles, look for some 'unjust' factor calling for restitution from the enriched debtor. The 'no reasonable man' test of enrichment having been applied and passed, the debtor is in the same position as one who has directly received money. But, in practice, the plaintiff's choice of 'unjust' factor is narrowed by the rule that it is only—or almost only—in cases in which he himself is liable, that he seems to have power to discharge the debt. This is what underlies the seemingly exclusive focus on legal compulsion as the factor calling for restitution of this species of benefit received. Yet it now seems that he may also rely

[39] *Belshaw* v. *Bush* (1851) 11 C. 13. 191; *Walter* v. *James* (1871) L.R. 6Ex. 124; *City Bank of Sydney* v. *McLaughlin* (1909) 9 C.L.R. 615, 633, *per* Isaacs, J.
[40] Below, p. 288.
[41] *Walter* v. *James* (1871) L.R. 6 Ex. 124; *Simpson* v. *Eggington* (1855) 10 Exch. 845 (*arguendo*).

on moral compulsion arising from necessity.[42] If that is so, we would have to infer, circularly, that a payment under necessity does discharge. The curious form of this argument tends to show that the other fundamental rule—namely that, whatever the case for restitution, the debt is always discharged—would provide a much more stable basis from which to begin the inquiry.

Where the liability in question is, not to pay but to do some act, as for instance to repair a bridge,[43] the doing of that act by an intervening third party must irreversibly discharge the liability, notwithstanding the general rule. This should mean that in such a case a factor other than legal compulsion can be invoked. *Gebhardt* v. *Saunders*[44] was decided on the basis of legal compulsion but it exemplifies a situation in which the claim might equally have been rested on mistake. A local authority served a notice under the *Public Health (London) Act, 1891*, ordering the 'owner or occupier' of a home to abate a nuisance from a blocked drain, on pain of a fine. The tenant did the work but discovered in the course of doing it that the nuisance arose from a 'structural' cause and was therefore not his but the owner's responsibility. He was allowed to recover his outlay from the defendant owner. But the reason given was that the notice to abate carried a fine for disobedience. This mode of finding a secondary liability is forced and fragile. Mistake would have been a better basis.[45] Nevertheless it must be said that a plaintiff who tries to base himself on a factor other than compulsion in this type of case now faces an uphill battle.

It is tempting to think that subrogation should also be considered as another path to restitution where debts and other liabilities are discharged. It is certainly not another path in the sense that mistake differs from legal compulsion. That is, it is not another factual basis for restitution. If it is another path in any sense, it is an alternative way of reaching the same principal debtor, not directly but via the ex-creditor's position. But this must be regarded as a dangerous or at best doubtful proposition, since detailed analysis will probably reveal that restitutionary subrogation is only semantically different from the imposition of direct restitutionary obligations as discussed in this section.[46] To say, for example, that *Owen* v. *Tate* might have been brought to a different conclusion by subrogating the volunteer-

---

[42] Note 36, above.
[43] *Macclesfield Corporation* v. *Great Central Railway* [1911] 2 K.B. 528.
[44] *Gebhardt* v. *Saunders* [1892] 2 Q.B. 452.
[45] Similarly in *Andrew* v. *St. Olave's Board of Works* [1898] 1 Q.B. 775.
[46] Above, pp. 93 ff.

surety to the bank's claim against the defendant may mean nothing more than that it was wrong not to find a restitutionary right directly available to the surety against the defendant.[47]

Liabilities of the Same Degree   In the examples considered so far there is a relationship between the plaintiff and the defendant such that the compulsion on the plaintiff arises from a liability definitely secondary to the liability of the defendant. This evaluation of the two liabilities usually derives from the fact that any benefit associated with them has been enjoyed by the defendant: a borrower, and not his guarantor, has the use of borrowed money. Once the two liabilities are seen in this way, the effect is that payment by the plaintiff is in substance referable wholly to the defendant's account. It discharges a liability which, the ancillary liability apart, is entirely his. So he has to restore it all. But it can happen that the payor and another person are liable in exactly the same degree, both primarily or both secondarily. Here payment by one relieves the other. But restitution of the full amount will not be the right answer. For payment by the other would equally relieve the first. The sensible course on these facts is to suppose that the burden is shared between the persons liable in the same degree. Then, if one pays, each of the others can be treated as having been relieved of his own share of the burden. Saved inevitable expenditure to that extent, each then makes restitution of his own enrichment. Here restitution therefore takes the form of contribution rather than reimbursement.

The key to the common law regime, though there have always been differences of detail between one situation and another, has been the notion of a common demand[48] exigible against a plurality of people. Persons liable in the same degree to such a common demand can claim contribution *inter se*, and in general the contribution is based on an equal sharing of the liability. The common cases are multiple sureties, contractors, trustees, and executors. However, in *Merryweather* v. *Nixan*[49] the common law set its face against contribution between joint tortfeasors. That rule was finally corrected by the *Law Reform (Married Women and Tortfeasors) Act, 1935*. Recently, following a report by the Law Commission,[50] a major reform was introduced by the *Civil Liability (Contribution) Act, 1978*. The need for the reform was created chiefly by contra-

---

[47] *Contra, Goff and Jones*, 412 f.
[48] *Whitham* v. *Bullock* [1939] 2 K.B. 81.
[49] *Merryweather* v. *Nixan* (1799) 8 T.R. 186.
[50] *Law of Contract, Report on Contribution*, Law Com. 79 (1977).

dictions and lacunae between the statutory regime for tortfeasors and the non-statutory rules.

The new Act deals only with the phenomenon of contribution in respect of liability for damage. The rules for debts are left untouched. Section 1 (1) says that any person liable in respect of any damage suffered by another person may recover contribution from any other person liable in respect of the same damage (whether jointly with him or otherwise); and s. 6 (1) says that a person is so liable in respect of any damage if the person who suffered it (or anyone representing his estate or dependants) is entitled to recover compensation from him in respect of that damage (whatever the legal basis of his liability, whether tort, breach of contract, breach of trust or otherwise). Thus the contribution is in respect of liability to compensate for damage, irrespective of the nature of the event or conduct from which that liability flows. Under this regime the amount recoverable by way of contribution will not necessarily be an equal share, and it may run even to a complete indemnity. Section 2 (1) gives the court a discretion to award the amount which is found to be just and equitable having regard to the extent of that person's responsibility for the damage in question. Thus the enrichment obtained at the expense of the person who has paid the victim of the damage is to be calculated not in terms of mathematical shares but in terms of the contributor's own responsibility for the damage for which the other has paid.

(iv) *Moral Compulsion*

The officious man is one who is too quick to see a duty to intervene in other people's business.[51] But there are situations in which the duty to intervene is real and is perceived by the intervener as a species of compulsion working on his conscience. When a man sees some danger threatening another person or another's property, he will feel called upon to do what he can to avert the disaster.[52] Suppose in winter your neighbour is away and a pipe bursts in his house, threatening to cause a flood. You will feel bound to arrange for a plumber to mend the pipe or, at least, to get the water turned off. Much depends on the proportion between the danger and the steps needed to avert it. The less trouble required from you, the

---

[51] Above, p. 103.

[52] 'The impulsive desire to save human life when in peril is one of the most beneficial instincts of humanity', *Scaramanga* v. *Stamp* (1880) 5 C.P.D. 295, 304, *per* Cockburn, C.J.

more the compulsion to help; and the moral pressure on you is strongest when great danger can be averted with little trouble.

In this type of situation the enrichment issue is likely to be settled on the 'no reasonable man' test. If the threat of disaster is strong enough to call for the intervention, the defendant will normally have been saved expenditure which no reasonable man would have abstained from. Then there will also be no doubt that the enrichment happened 'at the expense of' the plaintiff.[53] So the question will be whether moral compulsion does count as a factor calling for restitution.

It is difficult to give a firm answer. The reason is that *Falcke* v. *Scottish Imperial Insurance Co.*[54] casts a difficult shadow over this area. It contains *dicta* which are strongly against restitution; but its facts did not raise this question, and the judgments fail to distinguish between the general difficulty obstructing all claims in respect of non-money benefits (enrichment/subjective devaluation) and the particular task of identifying in any one case an operative
*9 factor calling for restitution (rendering the enrichment 'unjust'). Recently, in *China Pacific S.A.* v. *Food Corporation of India*[55] Lord Diplock said: 'It is, of course, true that in English law a mere stranger cannot compel an owner of goods to pay for a benefit bestowed on him against his will . . .'.[56] This echoes a famous dictum of Bowen, L.J. in *Falcke*:[57]

The general principle is, beyond all question, that work or labour done or money expended by one man to preserve or benefit the property of another do not according to English law create any lien upon the property saved or benefited, nor even, if standing alone, create any obligation to repay the expenditure. Liabilities are not to be forced on people behind their backs any more than you can confer a benefit upon a man against his will.

The facts of *Falcke* had nothing to do with moral compulsion. *Goff and Jones* also point out that the case involved a claim to a lien and could decide nothing about a personal claim.[58] A life insurance policy had been mortgaged more than once. The owner of the ultimate equity of redemption paid a premium to stop the policy

---

[53] It is possible to introduce a doubt where the plaintiff does not employ an expert to do what is necessary but does it himself. If he, not being a plumber, does work of that kind it can be said that no value passes from him.

[54] *Falcke* v. *Scottish Imperial Insurance Co.* (1886) 34 Ch.D. 234.

[55] *China Pacific S.A.* v. *Food Corporation of India* [1981] 2 All E.R. 688.

[56] Ibid. 688, 695.

[57] *Falcke* v. *Scottish Imperial Insurance Co.* (1886) 34 Ch. D. 234, 248.

[58] At. 269.

lapsing and claimed a lien entitling him to repayment of that premium even before the mortgagees took a penny. The reason why he had paid seems to have been, not moral compulsion, but a self-oriented desire to preserve the value of his own interest. In the court below he had said that he had, in addition, been labouring under a mistaken belief brought about by the fraud of a third party: he thought that he had bought out one of the mortgagees and had therefore acquired an interest in the policy more substantial than the ultimate equity of redemption. The Court of Appeal proceeded on the basis that that mistake had not been established.

It can thus be seen that *Falcke* is at the most authority to the effect that an intervention to serve the intervener's own interest, in circumstances in which the benefit of the intervention is necessarily shared by another, does not give rise to restitution.[59] The factor on which the intervener himself chiefly relied was a mistake as to his own interest, similar to the mistake made by the improver of the car in *Greenwood* v. *Bennett*.[60]

Statements to the effect that liabilities are not to be forced on people behind their backs or against their will are unhelpful. They suffer from a crucial ambiguity between 'without consent' and the stronger sense of 'against the will', namely 'in the teeth of the defendant's prohibition'.[61] Nor is it clear whether the effect of phrases such as 'The general principle is . . . ' or 'A mere stranger cannot . . . ', is intended to leave room for extensive qualification of assertions which seem on first reading to be emphatic and absolute. It is certain, however, that if these statements are taken at face value they are wrong.

All restitutionary liabilities are technically imposed without the consent of the defendant. Only the implied contract theory of restitution could conceal that analytical fact. Even the obligation to refund a mistaken payment is imposed *in invito* in this sense. Furthermore some restitutionary obligations are manifestly imposed without the defendant's consent even in a more substantial sense, namely in circumstances in which he not only does not consent to the obligation, but also does not know of the events by which he has been enriched. This can be true even where the factor going to 'unjust' is not moral compulsion generated by imminent disaster. For example, if legal compulsion is applied to me to make me discharge

---

[59] See, however, *China Pacific S.A.* v. *Food Corporation of India, The Winson* [1981] All E.R. 688, 696, 698.

[60] *Greenwood* v. *Bennett* [1973] 1 Q.B. 195, above p. 155

[61] Even this need not be conclusive in every case, see n. 83, below.

a liability primarily resting on you, as where I have to pay off your crew in order to release my interest in a ship from the crew's lien,[62] there is nothing to say that you must have known that your liability was being discharged. Indeed, typically, I will settle with your creditor in your absence. Again, if I improve your property in the mistaken belief that it is mine, then, so long as the improvement passes some test of enrichment other than free acceptance (which does require your knowledge), I will have a restitutionary claim even though you knew nothing about it, as in *Greenwood* v. *Bennett* and as in the passive claim now allowed to the improver under the *Torts (Interference with Goods) Act, 1977*.[63] Even in *Craven-Ellis* v. *Canons Ltd.*, in which services were mistakenly rendered by the plaintiff directly to the company, the disqualification of the purported directors meant that the company was unable to make itself aware of the benefit being conferred on it.[64] And this must be so whenever the recipient is mentally incapacitated.[65]

The insensitivity of *Falcke's Case* has meant that the question whether moral compulsion can ever have the same restitutionary effect as legal compulsion or duress has not been squarely faced. In *Macclesfield Corporation* v. *Great Central Railway*[66] the configuration of the facts was very close to that which we have encountered in relation to legal compulsion. The only difference was that the plaintiff corporation was not legally liable and could only claim to have acted under the compulsion arising from the need to avert a danger. The defendant railway was under a legal obligation, imposed by statute, to maintain a bridge in good repair. Judging that the bridge needed to be repaired, the corporation issued a notice to get the work done; but it was not done. The corporation therefore effected the repairs itself and claimed restitution of its outlay. The Court of Appeal rejected the claim. Kennedy, L.J., said

Not being under a statutory obligation to pay for or do this work, this local authority has done the work . . . I do not know the legal principle upon which in those circumstances they can throw the burden on someone else who ought in the first instance to have done the work and who therefore is in a position to say, 'You who seek to recover this payment from me have acted as volunteers.'[67]

So the plaintiff failed because, whatever the nature or degree of

---

[62] E.g. *Johnson* v. *Royal Mail Steam Packet Co.* [1867] L.R. 3 C.P. 38.
[63] Section 6 (1).
[64] *Craven-Ellis* v. *Canon Ltd.* [1963] 2 K.B. 403.
[65] E.g. *Re Rhodes* (1890) 44 Ch. D. 94.
[66] *Macclesfield Corporation* v. *Great Central Railway* [1911] 2 K.B. 528.
[67] *Ibid.*, 541.

compulsion upon it, there was thought to be no doctrine which could help it. Consequently there was no way in which the Court could reach any questions designed to test the effect of this particular example of moral compulsion. Had they been able to reach that stage of the inquiry, the judges might of course have concluded on these facts that the corporation's intervention stemmed not from fear of a danger but from considerations of its own convenience as to the best way of dealing with the recalcitrant railway. We cannot know whether, if the facts had been strong and had unequivocally disclosed a response to imminent danger, the Court would have been persuaded to discover, or more accurately rediscover, the principle upon which the corporation could base its claim.

There are two groups of cases which point to the existence of such a principle. Both groups show that moral compulsion has been given the same effect as legal compulsion and is recognised as a factor calling for restitution, but the groups differ according as the plaintiff's claim has, or has not, been conceived as extending from a pre-exising contractual relationship between the parties.

Cases independent of a pre-existing relationship   It will be recalled that in *Exall* v. *Partridge* the 'special instance and request of the defendant' recited by the plaintiff's form of claim was 'implied' from the fact that the plaintiff had been legally compelled to confer the benefit on the defendant. From the same period come many cases in which the same conclusion was drawn from moral compulsion arising from a person's death. What Garrow, B., called 'the common principles of decency and humanity and the common impulses of our nature',[68] clearly require that a dead person should be buried without delay. Someone who responded to this need was allowed to recover from the person primarily responsible for the deceased or from the deceased's personal representatives.[69] The claim was maintained by the count in *assumpsit* for 'money paid' where the plaintiff was the person who had arranged the funeral, and by the count for *quantum meruit* where he was the undertaker called in but not paid by such a person. Anxiety on the score of officiousness—that is, lest someone might snatch at the opportunity to perform this duty so as to interfere with the family's own arrangements—were met by excluding from the right to restitution anyone who was not a proper

[68] *Rogers* v. *Price* (1829) 3 Y. & J. 28, 34; cf. *ibid.* 36, *per* Hullock, B.
[69] *Jenkins* v. *Tucker* (1788) 1 H.Bl. 90; *Tugwell* v. *Heyman* (1812) 3 Camp. 298; *Rogers* v. *Price*, above; *Green* v. *Salmon* (1838) 8 A. & E. 348; *Ambrose* v. *Kerrison* (1851) 10 C.B. 776; *Bradshaw* v. *Beard* (1862) 12 C.B. (N.S.) 344.

person to respond or who could be shown to have pushed himself forward.[70]

These cases come from a specialised context but reflect a consistent approach to the implication of requests. Lord Kenyon C.J.'s approach in *Exall v. Partridge* was, in modern terms, to identify the enrichment and then to look for a factor calling for restitution. So also in the funeral cases the person primarily liable was saved necessary expenditure, and the factor calling for restitution was moral compulsion. There is a clear contradiction of the routine understanding of *Falcke*. For example, in *Jenkins v. Tucker*[71] the defendant was in Jamaica when his wife died and was buried in England. His obligation to make restitution was imposed on him 'behind his back' in the sense that it arose from events which happened wholly without his knowledge.

It may also now be the law that restitution lies where a debt is paid by an intervening stranger acting in response to some need, as for instance the danger of damage to the defendant's business. There are *dicta* to this effect in *Owen v. Tate* which would gain added strength if it could be made clear that the debt is extinguished in such circumstances.[72] In other respects these *dicta* are in complete harmony with the combined effect of the funeral cases and the cases on compulsory discharge. It has also long been established that, after a bill of exchange had been protested for non-acceptance, someone who intervenes to save the credit of the drawer is entitled to be reimbursed. In *Hawtayne v. Bourne*[73] Parke, B., said that this right could not be generalised. It was a peculiarity of the law of merchants. But the action which he was resisting was not a direct claim for restitution. A loan had been negotiated by an intervener when acute financial trouble threatened the defendant. This was an action by the lender. The question was whether the circumstances invested the intervener with authority to contract for the defendant. In other words, was he an agent of necessity according to the narrower usage[74] of that phrase? It would be difficult nowadays to isolate the acceptor for honour simply because his claim originated in the law merchant.

The third fact situation within this group is the supply of nec-

---

[70] *Jenkins v. Tucker*, above: it was important that the plaintiff was the deceased's father, not a mere stranger who had interposed himself. Cf. *Bradshaw v. Beard*, above, 349, *per* Wilees, J.

[71] *Ibid.*

[72] Above, p. 189.

[73] *Hawtayne v. Bourne* (1841) 7 M. & W. 595.

[74] Below, p. 201.

essaries to people who are mentally incapacitated as the result of illness or injury. Those who render necessary services to people who suffer brain-damage in accidents may find their remedy in actions for compensation brought against the party whose negligence caused the injury.[75] But, as between the supplier and the person incapacitated, no difference can be taken between mental illness and mental injury. *Re Rhodes*[76] shows that such a claim will be upheld. But in that case the plaintiff failed for a reason which must be regarded with caution.

The claim was brought by a nephew who had contributed part of the cost of keeping his aunt in a private asylum. He had not made claims against the aunt during her life, but after she died he sought reimbursement from her estate before her money was distributed to her next of kin. The reason the Court of Appeal rejected his claim was that he had shown no intent to recoup his payments, which therefore seemed to have been given gratuitously.

Two claims ought to be distinguished. There is the claim of a tradesman supplying the mentally ill, without any sense of moral obligation, on a basis which would be contractual but for the want of capacity. To this claim an obvious analogy is the supply of necessaries to a minor, against whom a claim lies without proof of any moral compulsion arising, for example, from the minor's want of food or shelter. It is enough for the minor to go into a shop and order the goods. This claim cannot lie unless there is an intent to charge. But, by contrast, there is the case in which the plaintiff has acted because he felt compelled to intervene in favour of the in-capacitated person. It seems likely that *Re Rhodes* was of this kind. The same forces of 'decency and common humanity' already encountered in relation to the funeral cases probably constrained the nephew to lay out money for his aunt. But in the funeral cases it is not said that the plaintiff must have manifested an intent to charge at the time at which he responded to the moral demand made on him, and, quite generally, the effect of factors vitiating voluntariness is such as to call for restitution without more. That is, without in addition evidence of a non-gratuitous intent. A mistaken payor would never recover if he had to show that he intended to be repaid.

Cases extending contractual relationships During a voyage at sea the master of a ship may encounter perils for which he has no instructions and can get none. The law has long recognised that, in such circumstances, he acquires an authority, by the necessity itself,

---

[75] Eg. *Mehmet* v. *Perry* [1977] 2 All E.R. 529.
[76] *Re Rhodes* (1890) 44 Ch.D. 94.

to take such action as is reasonably necessary to avert or minimise the danger. The same doctrine has been extended to carriage by land, and to other relationships in the nature of bailment, such as contracts for safe-keeping. In *Prager* v. *Blatspiel, Stamp and Heacock Ltd.*[77] the plaintiff, who was furrier to the Roumanian court, ordered and paid for furs to be dressed and prepared in England. At the time of the order the First World War had already broken out. Before the furs could be delivered, Roumania was occupied by the Germans. The defendants decided to sell the furs. After the war the plaintiffs sued for conversion, and the defendants claimed to have acted as agents of necessity. McCardie, J., showed that the doctrine could apply to this kind of situation and might, for example, have entitled the defendants to reimbursement of storage charges and other precautions to preserve the furs. But on the facts there was no compulsion on the defendants to sell—that is, there was no danger, as deterioration, to create a commercial necessity for this sale—and, which is a separate point, the defendants had not been motivated by their honest conception of the best interests of the owners but rather by considerations of their own convenience and advantage.[78]

This case shows not only that the doctrine extends to land-based bailments but also that it serves purposes other than restitution. In particular, if he has been compelled to sell the goods, an agent of necessity has a defence to an action in tort; if he has had to make a contract (as for repair or storage or even to borrow money) the outsider will be in direct contractual relationship with the agent's principal; and, if he expends money on the safety of the goods, he will have a claim for reimbursement.

Our concern is with this third consequence, the agent of necessity's right to reimbursement of his outlay. We have already seen that in *Prager*, McCardie, J., would have allowed recovery of storage charges. He relied for that on *Great Northern Railway* v. *Swaffield*.[79] The railway was to deliver a horse to Sandy station for the defendant. There was nobody to collect it when it arrived. The defendant's servant did not appear till after the railway had incurred a stabling charge of 1s. 6d. He refused to pay the charge and finally left without the horse. Over the following days the defendant took an increasingly intransigent position. The stabling charges rose to £17. The railway then decided to pay the bill and deliver the horse. It then reclaimed the sum paid. The claim was upheld on the analogy of

---

[77] Prager v. *Blatspiel, Stamp and Heacock Ltd.* [1924] 1 K.B. 566.
[78] Cf. *Sachs* v. *Miklos* [1948] 2 K.B. 23; *Munro* v. *Willmott* [1959] 1 K.B. 295.
[79] *Great Northern Railway* v. *Swaffield* (1874) L.R. 9 Ex. 132.

the maritime cases, especially *Gaudet* v. *Brown, Cargo ex Argos*.[80]
The railway had had to take these reasonable steps to see that the
defendant's horse was safely looked after.

Recently, in *China Pacific S.A.* v. *Food Corporation of India,
The Winson*,[81] the House of Lords applied these same cases so as
to allow the plaintiffs, who were professional salvors, to recover the
charges incurred by them in storing the defendants' cargo of wheat
after saving it from the stranded ship in which it was being carried.
But in this case their Lordships took the opportunity to make an
adjustment of terminology. They said that the words 'agency of
necessity' should not be used except to denote the circumstances in
which the facts would allow a contractual relationship to be created
between the agent's principal and the outsider. The phrase should
not be used where the only issue was restitution in respect of such
steps as had been reasonably necessary to preserve the owner's
goods.[82]

This adjustment of language was chiefly due to the desire to
explain the right to reimbursement not as an incident of agency but
as a right correlative to the bailee's duty to take reasonable care of
the goods. It appears to entail a change in the conditions required
to be satisfied in order to support the restitutionary claim, particularly in relation to the issue of communication with the owner. On
the earlier view there could be no compelling emergency till such
communication had become impracticable.[83] But on the *China
Pacific* analysis the only question is whether the steps taken to preserve the goods were reasonable in the circumstances, an inquiry in
which the possibility of communication is only one element.
Despite this shift, it seems right to contemplate the bailee's claim as
resting on the moral compulsion emanating from anticipated danger.
The object is still the preservation of the goods and the duty on him
to take reasonable steps takes its force and content from the danger
to them in the event of his doing nothing.

Integrating the two groups   These two groups of cases—those
between strangers and those extending a pre-existing contractual
relationship—can be perceived as different applications of a single

---

[80] *Gaudet* v. *Brown, Cargo ex Argos* (1873) L.R. 5 P.C. 134.
[81] *China Pacific S.A.* v. *Food Corporation of India, The Winson* [1981] 3 All E.R. 688.
[82] *Ibid.*, 693; 698.
[83] *Sims* v. *Midland Railway* [1913] 1 K.B. 103, 107; *Springer* v. *Great Western Railway*
[1921] 1 K.B. 257. But note that an unreasonable or non-responding principal could be
treated as beyond the possibility of communication: *Great Northern Railway* v. *Swaffield,*
above, *Gokal* v. *Nand Ram* [1939] A.C. 106; cf. *Matheson* v. *Smiley* [1932] D.L.R. 787.

principle. That is to say, a pre-existing relationship appears to be no more than one way, albeit the most common, of satisfying pre-requisites of a restitutionary claim which can be satisfied, more rarely, by facts other than such a relationship. This unity under one principle has been obscured, to the extent that it is at the moment difficult to contemplate a simple fusion between the two. In *Jebara* v. *Ottoman Bank*[84] Scrutton, L.J., took steps to limit the effects and potential of McCardie, J.'s judgment in *Prager* v. *Blatspiel, Stamp and Heacock Ltd.* He made it quite clear that the notion of an agency of necessity could not be applied except where there was a pre-existing relationship on which to build. The consequent iso-lation of the relationship cases will not really be diminished if the phrase 'agency of necessity' is displaced by a new analysis in which the right to reimbursement is seen to be correlative with a duty to keep safe. For the duty element will not easily be found without a pre-existing relationship between the parties. Where a stranger intervenes, the duty upon him is moral, not legal.

Nevertheless the two groups ought to, and in fact do, make sense together. What is the function of the pre-existing relationship? It makes sure of certain points more difficult to establish without it. First, if the defendant committed the *res* to a relationship involving safe-keeping, he cannot possibly say that he would have preferred that they perished. So the pre-existing relationship eliminates the argument from subjective devaluation. Secondly, a plaintiff subject to a legal duty of safe-keeping cannot be said to be the wrong person to respond to that duty. So the relationship serves to eliminate doubt on the score of officiousness. Where an outsider intervenes to save life or property or to avert some other disaster, these issues have to be looked at more closely. But the first group of cases shows that, despite the shadow of *Falcke's Case*, all these requirements of a successful restitutionary claim are capable of being satisfied other than as an extension of an existing contractual relationship between the parties. Outside such relationships the cases on legal compulsion provide a guide or template for considering the effects of moral compulsion. That secure analogy gives such claims an intelligible place in the law of restitution, when they might otherwise seem, as they seemed to Scrutton, L.J.,[85] no more than dangerously uncertain departures from the sound principles of agency or bailment.

---

[84] *Jebara* v. *Ottoman Bank* [1927] 2 K.B. 254.
[85] ibid., p. 270–2.

(v) *Circumstantial Compulsion*

The law is not clear whether facts calculated to make the plaintiff acutely anxious for his own welfare or that of his family or property can ever give rise to restitution from a defendant in no way responsible for the fear in the plaintiff's mind. One American case suggests that on rare facts the answer must be that they can. In *Liebman* v. *Rosenthal*[86] the plaintiff and his family desperately needed to escape from France, in 1941, in order to escape the Nazi persecution of the Jews. He gave diamonds to the defendant on his promise to obtain false papers from the Portuguese consul in Bayonne. The defendant took the diamonds and disappeared. After the war the plaintiff encountered him in New York and claimed their value. The defendant moved to have the claim struck out, which the New York courts refused to do. It is tolerably clear that if the case had gone to trial the plaintiff would have succeeded. There is a good case for saying that even if the defendant had obtained the false papers for him the plaintiff ought to have been allowed to recover at least part of the defendant's profit.[87] The illegality of the project cannot be a defence on such facts since a plaintiff under such abnormal pressure cannot be said to have been *in pari delicto*.[88]

The nearest analogy in English law is the approach of the courts in the case in which a ship in danger promises an extortionate reward to a potential salvor. On these facts the judges do not hesitate to sweep aside the agreed figure and to substitute their own award.[89] It may be that cases such as these, as also *Bigos* v. *Bousted*[90] where a father had been driven to an illegal arrangement by the illness of his daughter, should be considered within the equitable jurisdiction to open up unconscionable bargains on the ground of advantage taken of personal weakness. It is at best doubtful whether interventions motivated by a desire to save one's own property, as opposed to one's person or family, can give rise to restitution if they happen to confer benefits on others.[91]

---

[86] *Liebman* v. *Rosenthal* (1945) 26 App. Div. 1062, 59 N.Y.S. 2d. 148.
[87] Unless and until he had received something he could found on failure of consideration, without having to rely on the pressure of circumstances.
[88] Below, p. 424 ff.
[89] *The Medina* (1876) 1 P.D. 272; 2 P.D. 5; *The Port Caledonia and The Anna* [1903] P. 184.
[90] *Bigos* v. *Bousted* [1951] 1 All E.R. 92.
[91] See n. 59 above.

4. INEQUALITY

This term can be used in a broad sense to include all the cases of compulsion. For there is no clearer case of inequality between two parties. especially if the pressure is being applied to one by the other.[92] But here the word is intended to refer only to inequality arising in the absence of pressure. Even when cut down in that way, it is too imprecise to be useful in legal argument except in a co-ordinating role. Its want of precision derives from a very obvious cause: since in brains, knowledge, happiness, wealth, and power we are all always unequal, the word cannot possibly have its normal range. To speak of restitution for inequality must be shorthand for something rather different. It means that there is restitution in cases of exceptional or abnormal inequality, where, in addition, the difference between the parties can be described in such a way as to leave intact the proposition that there is no question of restitution for ordinary, run of the mill inequalities. This supposes a need to think in terms of categories of exceptional inequality. In *Lloyds Bank Ltd.* v. *Bundy*, which was ultimately decided on the basis of undue influence, Lord Denning, M.R., made a pioneering attempt to forge general principles out of the separate categories,[93] but it is certainly too soon to say that there is more than a loose confederation of separate figures.

Apart from the need to combat uncertainty, there are two other difficulties to be mentioned at the outset. First, it is not possible to say that the courts' response to inequality is invariably restitution, as opposed to an *ad hoc* address to the unfairness perceived to have been brought about. Second, it can be argued that some or all of the examples about to be given should not be considered under the head of 'vitiated voluntariness' but properly belong later, among 'policy-motivated restitutions'. The case for keeping them here is this. An unequal party gets restitution because, for one of a number of reasons, he was abnormally unable to weigh up the pros and cons of the transfer which he made. He was vulnerable because his judgment was impeded and vitiated by a factor from which responsible common law man expects to be free. The contrary view would be that his judgment in these cases is free and unimpeded but that the law nevertheless relieves him in pursuit of some social policy.

There appear to be three main categories. They are differentiated

---

[92] Hence, in *Lloyds Bank* v. *Bundy*, below, Lord Denning, M.R., includes duress among the heads of inequality.

[93] *Lloyds Bank* v. *Bundy* [1975] 1 Q.B. 326, 336 f.

according as the reason for the plaintiff's vulnerability arises from his relationship with the defendant, from the nature of the transaction into which he entered, or from a personal disadvantage. Yet *Goff and Jones* rightly warn that the lines between the categories are thin.[94] It is this fact which makes it not only attractive but also necessary to use the open-textured idea of inequality to co-ordinate them.

(i) *Vulnerable Relationships*   *11

We have already divided the topic of undue influence so as to deal with cases of actual influence in the context of pressure. Cases in which a presumption of undue influence is drawn from a relationship existing between the parties cannot be explained as examples of pressure. If the presumption is not rebutted, the proper inference of fact is not that the defendant bullied or dominated the plaintiff, but that the plaintiff, though adult and in full control of his faculties, could not *vis-à-vis* this defendant be expected to keep his guard up and his judgment clear. What the transferee has to show in order to rebut the presumption is that the transferor was able 'to exercise an independent will'.[95] If he cannot show that, it is logically unsound to say that he must have applied pressure. This remains true even if it is correct to say that a transferee who does not rebut the presumption must necessarily have been guilty of some impropriety or victimisation in failing to ensure that the transferor was freed from the influence of the relationship.[96]

The kind of relationship which gives rise to the presumption is that in which the plaintiff has placed trust and confidence in the other. But those words serve only for an outline. They do not sufficiently distinguish these relationships from others between good friends or businessmen who trust each other. Relationships of this latter kind do not give rise to the presumption. In *Lloyds Bank Ltd.* v. *Bundy*, Sir Eric Sachs described the cases in which the presumption does arise in this way:[97]

Such cases tend to arise where someone relies on the guidance or advice of another, where the other is aware of that reliance and where the person on whom reliance is placed obtains, or may well obtain, a benefit from the trans-

---

[94] At p. 199, n. 4.
[95] *Allcard* v. *Skinner* (1887)36 Ch.D. 145, 171, *per* Cotton, L.J.; cf. *Inche Noriah* v. *Shaik Allie Bin Omar* [1929] A.C. 127, 135, *per* Lord Hailsham.
[96] *Re Brocklehurst*, above, p. 184; yet it is doubtful whether any disgraceful inference was intended to be drawn as to the conduct of the spiritual advisers in *Allcard* v. *Skinner*, above.
[97] *Lloyds Bank Ltd.* v. *Bundy* [1975] 1 Q.B. 326, 341.

action or has some other interest in it being concluded. In addition, there must, of course, be shown to exist a vital element which in this judgment will for convenience be referred to as confidentiality.

This additional factor of confidentiality is what serves to distinguish these relationships from those between friends or colleagues. It connotes an element of dependence, a tendency to the exclusion of views other than those of the confidant, a potential for domination.[98] It is exclusivity which transforms 'trust and confidence' into 'confidentiality'.

In Lloyds Bank Ltd. v. *Bundy* itself, the plaintiff bank was attempting to get possession of a house charged by the defendant in order to secure his son's overdraft. Although one case has now gone further,[98a] it seemed at the time to be borderline case. The inequality between banks and customers does not normally create one of these vulnerable relationships. But here the local branch had built up a personal relationship with Mr Bundy over many years and knew that they were dealing with him in a matter of crucial importance, since the house was his last asset and his son's financial future was at stake; and they knew that he was relying on them for guidance. These facts were sufficient to generate the presumption of undue influence, which the bank could not rebut as they had not seen that he took independent advice. In particular, they had not brought in his solicitor even though they knew his identity. In the result, therefore, the defendant was able to avoid the bank's security and to remain in his house.

Re Craig[99] was a more straightforward case. There a woman had moved into the house of an old man as his housekeeper-companion. She managed all his affairs and achieved an ascendancy over him. Ungoed Thomas, J., was prepared to find actual undue influence but based his decision primarily on an unrebutted presumption. In *Hodgson* v. *Marks*[1] he made the same finding in relation to the lodger, Evans, who had taken over the management of Mrs Hodgson's affairs to the exclusion of everyone else.

Re Brocklehurst[2] falls on the other side of the line. In his old age the eccentric owner of a substantial estate had been befriended by the proprietor of a small local garage. The friendship porspered despite the difference of wealth and background between the two.

---

[98] Cf. *Re Craig* [1971] Ch. 95, 104, *per* Ungoed Thomas, J.
[98a] *National Westminster Bank p.l.c.* v. *Morgan* [1983] 3 All E.R. 85.
[99] Above, n. 99 and p. 184.
[1] *Hodgson* v. *Marks* [1971] Ch. 892, discussed above, p. 58 ff..
[2] *Re Brocklehurst* [1978] 1 Ch. 14.

The garage proprietor received gifts of money and, in the end, a ninety-nine-year lease of the shooting rights over the estate. The lease had the effect of massively reducing the value of the estate, so that after the donor's death his personal representatives sought to have it rescinded; they failed. The Court of Appeal, Lord Denning, M.R., dissenting, held that the relationship would not support the presumption. Whatever the garage proprietor had done he had done in the office of a friend, and the deceased's dependence on him was only that dependence which develops within friendship. The deceased had not give up the management of his own affairs and had not cut himself off from other advisers. Also the initiative for making the gifts came consistently from the deceased, who had indeed given away a great deal of money to many people towards the end of his life.

The picture of a relationship characterised by dependent and exclusive reliance, such as to make the dependent party vulnerable unless he has full and adequate advice or is emancipated from the other's influence in some other way, sometimes has to be built up by evidence. But some familiar relationships generate the presumption without more. Doctor and patient,[3] solicitor and client,[4] parent and child,[5] guardian and ward,[6] trustee and beneficiary,[7] religious or spiritual adviser and advisee,[8] all these are cases in which no evidence is required of anything beyond the general nature of the relationship. Other cases might be described as intermediate, requiring some evidence as to the fabric of the parties' dealings with one another. The relationship between engaged couples might be counted in this category.[9] Throughout this list the precise shade of vulnerability may vary from case to case. Some relationships merely lull the judgement of the dependent party, while others contain the danger of domination. It makes no difference. Either way, his freedom to assess the wisdom of his transfer and to appreciate its risks is qualitatively different from that which even friends have when independently dealing with each other.

There is a transition about to be made between 'vulnerable relationships' and 'easily exploited transactions'. The line between the two is thin. For example, in *National Westminster Bank p.l.c.* v.

[3] *Dent* v. *Bennett* (1838) 4 My. & Cr. 269.
[4] *Wright* v. *Carter* [1903] 1 Ch. 27.
[5] *Lancashire Loans Ltd.* v. *Black* [1934] 1 K.B. 380.
[6] *Hatch* v. *Hatch* (1804) 9 Ves. 292.
[7] *Plowright* v. *Lambert* (1884) 52 L.T. 646.
[8] *Huguenin* v. *Basely* (1807) 14 Ves. 273; *Allcard* v. *Skinner*, above n. 95.
[9] *Zamet* v. *Hyman* [1961] 3 All E.R. 933.

Morgan[9a], a case whose facts resemble but are weaker than *Lloyds Bank Ltd.* v. *Bundy* which has just been discussed, a wife and husband in a considerable state of anxiety mortgaged their matrimonial home to the plaintiff bank to secure a loan with which to refinance their existing debt to a building society. The husband was in chronic financial difficulty, and the building society had begun proceedings for possession. So there was a danger that they would lose their home. The mortage to the bank was arranged in this way. The husband negotiated it with the bank manager. He invited the manager to visit him and his wife at home in the evening to explain the matter to the wife and to obtain her signature. The visit was made. It lasted only twenty minutes, of which only five were devoted to a discussion between the manager and the wife. The husband was present throughout, though he withdrew to another part of the room during the discussion just referred to. On these facts the Court of Appeal held that the wife was entitled to have the mortgage of her interest set aside. The Court took the view that the character of the short interview was sufficient to create the relationship of 'confidentiality' from which a presumption of undue influence arises. There was no evidence that her mind had been emancipated from the undue influence, as by independent advice. Formally the basis of the decision is thus the same as in *Lloyds Bank Ltd.* v. *Bundy*. The striking difference is that, though there had been dealings between wife and bank on earlier occasions, there was no standing or continuing relationship of confidentiality to distinguish their relationship from that which obtains between any customer and any bank. Hence the case may more easily be seen as exemplifying inequality arising from the particular transaction rather than from the relationship generally.

(ii) *Easily Exploited Transactions*

Even normal, self-reliant people sometimes embark on transactions in which they are vulnerable because of the way in which the market behaves in relation to the particular good which they are seeking. Different variables can help to make a particular transaction sensitive. The simplest combination is short supply of a commodity universally in demand, such as housing. In times of shortage those who need are easily exploited. But there are other cases. Sometimes personal happiness is too much at stake for ordinary wisdom to

---

[9a] *Cit.* n. 98a, above.

exercise any restraint. General doctrines are difficult to formulate, though it could be argued that protection against the exploitation of 'consumers' has now attained the status of a legal principle. For the most part the law, with or without statutory help, has been content to identify particular types of transaction in which people are easily exploited.

(a) *A Paradigm Case*

In *Kiriri Cotton Co. Ltd.* v. *Dewani*[10] the respondent, who was the plaintiff, had paid the appellant company 10 000 shillings as 'key money' on taking a lease of a flat in Kampala. The *Uganda Rent Restriction Ordinance*, s. 3 (2), made it an offence in the landlord to demand or receive such a premium. Neither party knew that they were doing anything illegal and there was no evidence that, leaving the statute aside, the amount demanded would have seemed extortionate. Having gone into occupation, Dewani sought to recover his payment. The defence was that there could be no restitution for mistake of law and that the transaction was in any event illegal in circumstances in which both parties were equally implicated, whence it followed that the defendants must keep the money, since *in pari delicto potior est conditio defendentis.*[11]

The Privy Council allowed the restitutionary claim. Delivering the advice, Lord Denning said:

In applying these principles to the present case, the most important thing to observe is that the Rent Restriction Ordinance was intended to protect tenants from being exploited by landlords in days of housing shortage. One of the obvious ways in which a landlord can exploit the housing shortage is by demanding from the tenant 'key-money'. Section 3 (2) of the Rent Restriction Ordinance was enacted so as to protect tenants from exploitation of that kind. This is apparent from the fact that the penalty is imposed only on the landlord or his agent and not the tenant . . . The duty of observing the law is firmly placed by the ordinance on the shoulders of the landlord for the protection of the tenant; and if the law is broken, the landlord must take the primary responsibility. Whether it be a rich tenant who pays a premium as a bribe in order to 'jump the queue', or a poor tenant who is at his wit's end to find accommodation, neither is so much to blame as the landlord who is using his property rights so as to exploit those in need of a roof over their heads.[12]

It cannot be inferred that prohibited charges will always be recoverable. Not long before *Kiriri*, in *Green* v. *Portsmouth Stadium*

---

[10] *Kiriri Cotton Co. Ltd.* v. *Dewani* [1960] A.C. 192.
[11] Below, p. 424 ff.
[12] *Kiriri Cotton Co. Ltd.* v. *Dewani* [1960] A.C. 192, 205.

Ltd.,[13] the Court of Appeal had held that very similar words in the *Betting and Lotteries Act, 1934* could not be understood to give the plaintiff bookmaker a right to recover unlawfully demanded payments for entrance to the defendants' racecourse. The purpose of the legislation in that Act had been to regulate the running of racecourses but not to protect bookmakers from exploitation.[14] The question is always whether the object was to protect people in the plaintiff's position. In *Mistry Armar Singh* v. *Kalubya*,[15] the Privy Council held that that exercise in construction could conclude in the plaintiff's favour even if the statute imposed penalties on him as well as on the defendant.

(b) *Some Non-Statutory Examples*

Equity intervened to prevent women being exploited by people who took money to arrange marriages. Relief was given at first in individual cases of abuse. Later it was settled that restitution should always be available. In *Hermann* v. *Charlesworth*[16] the plaintiff had paid a fee to the defendant marriage broker. She had been given some introductions but was allowed to recover the whole sum which she had paid. The basis of this restitution is not failure of consideration or repentance[17] but the need to relieve people from exploitation of their hopes for happiness.

Where someone is in financial difficulties and needs to reach an arrangement with his creditors, no individual creditor is obliged to join in the composition. But one who stays out in order to win better terms or to prevent any settlement at all must not take a secret payment as an inducement to come back in. For an extra payment to him is a fraud on the others. If the debtor, or someone for him, pays over such an inducement he can recover it. This right would be explicable as based on duress if the creditor took the initiative in using his secession to apply pressure, but the right to restitution is not confined to that case. Again, therefore, it seems that the claim is recognised in order to protect a payor from a transaction in which his needs make him desperate and distort his judgement.[18]

The third of these examples concerns unconscionable bargains with heirs and other expectants. People who have expectations of wealth to come, as for example by inheritance or when a reversionary

---

[13] *Green* v. *Porstmouth Stadium Ltd*. [1953] 2 Q.B. 190.
[14] *Ibid.*, 196.
[15] *Mistry Armar Singh* v. *Kalubya* [1964] A.C. 142.
[16] *Hermann* v. *Charlesworth* [1905] 2 K.B. 123.
[17] Below, p. 301 f.
[18] *Smith* v. *Bromley* (1760) 2 Dougl K.B. 696; *Smith* v. *Cuff* (1817) 6 M. & S. 160.

interest has yet to fall in, easily succumb to the temptation to sell their hopes at an under-value in order to get access to money in the short term. This is a case in which the expectant heir can be said to be in the grip of his own immediate needs and desires. That in itself is a disability which is different only in degree from the effect of material desires on all consumers, but it happens in a context in which there is a special danger of exploitation. Equity, therefore, intervened to undo 'catching bargains' in which the heir could be shown to have received an inadequate consideration.[19] This early departure from the principle of free bargaining, and indeed the not easily predictable operation of the doctrine on which it was based, was no doubt made easier by the fact that while it served to protect vulnerable heirs it also conserved family fortunes from the effects of their prodigality.

(c) *Seeking Credit*

The last example is a particularly intense and specialised instance of a much more common weakness. Everyone who seeks credit, whether by borrowing money or obtaining benefits in kind on the faith of future payment, is vulnerable to exploitation by the creditor. This is especially true when he is driven to borrow in desperation; but, in societies whose economic welfare depends on encouragement of the consumer appetite, we can recognise that it is also true when the reason why credit is sought is not a pressing need to avoid disaster but only a desire for some material improvement. In either case the creditor is well placed to enrich himself because, in order to obtain the credit, the other is likely to agree harsh terms.

The control of the creditor's power in this type of transaction is a major concern of the law. It has a long and continuing history. The laws prohibiting usury and then controlling rates of interest are part of the history. More important in this context is the development of the equity of redemption, which is the foundation of the modern law of mortgages. From the standpoint of a society which prides itself on being a property-owning democracy, the equity of redemption might be said to be the product of the law's most important exercise in restitution. The story is well known.[20] The borrower conveyed away his land to the lender against a promise of reconveyance if the loan was repaid by a fixed date. Failure to repay by then meant that the lender was released from the duty of reconveyance and

---

[19] *Earl of Chesterfield* v. *Janssen* (1751) 2 Ves. Sen. 125; *O'Rorke* v. *Bolingbroke* (1877) 2 App. Cas. 814.

[20] Cheshire & Burn, *The Modern Law of Real Property*, 13th ed., London, 1982, 617 ff.

kept the land, typically worth far more than the sum advanced. Intervening at first in individual cases of hardship and abuse, equity would allow the borrower to redeem, and order the creditor to reconvey, where repayment was late by accident or illness or for some other good cause. From these individual interventions the relief was generalised, and its basis was shifted to the principle that the lending mortgagee could not enrich himself by taking beneficially an interest conferred on him by way of security: once a security, always a security. The mortgagor's right to redeem is a restitutionary right which thus became a permanent protection against one species of this kind of vulnerability, whereby in order to get credit a man would risk losing land of much greater value.

In more recent years an attempt had been made, in exactly the same spirit, to introduce equitable relief against forfeitures imposed on people seeking credit through hire purchase. The nature of the problem was expressed by Denning, L.J., in *Stockloser v. Johnson* in the form of a hypothetical case:[21]

Suppose a buyer has agreed to buy a necklace by instalments, and the contract provides that, on default in payment of any one instalment, the seller is entitled to rescind the contract and forfeit the instalments already paid. The buyer pays ninety per cent of the price but fails to pay the last instalment. He is not able to perform the contract because he simply cannot find the money. The seller thereupon rescinds the contract, retakes the necklace, and resells it at a higher price. Surely equity will relieve the buyer against forfeiture of the money on such terms as may be just.

In the case itself this suggestion neither fell to be applied nor secured unanimous acceptance. Somervell, L.J., thought a court would give relief if in all the circumstances the forfeiture was unconscionable, but Romer, L.J., thought bargains could not so easily be disturbed. In his view, in the absence of fraud or undue influence or other similar factor, the most the court would do was to give more time for the payment to be made which would redeem the forfeiture.[22] Later cases remained sceptical as to this jurisdiction,[23] but the initiative had now moved to the legislature. For under the *Consumer Credit Act, 1974*, the court is given a discretion, in relation to contracts of hire purchase with 'individual' hirers and below a credit maximum of £5000, to order the repayment of sums already

---

[21] *Stockloser v. Johnson* [1954] 1 Q.B. 476, 491.

[22] *Ibid.*, 495 ff.

[23] *Campbell Discount Co. Ltd.* v. *Bridge* [1961] 1 Q.B. 445 (reversed on other grounds [1962] A.C. 600); *Galbraith* v. *Mitchenall Estates Ltd.* [1965] 2 Q.B. 473.

paid when the contract is ended, and also to limit the amount to be paid where the contract makes sums payable on termination.[24]

The *Consumer Credit Act, 1974*, also contains a new and comprehensive discretion to open up and remake credit agreements where the court finds that the credit bargain behind the credit agreement was extortionate. An extortionate bargain is one in which the debtor or a relative of his has to make payments which are 'grossly exorbitant' or which 'contravene ordinary principles of fair dealing'.[25] The court must make a wide-ranging inquiry but must, in particular, have regard to the relationship between the parties, the relevant characteristics of the borrower (as age, experience and health), and the presence or absence of financial pressure on him.[26] The onus of proof is on the creditor to disprove the extortionate character of his bargain.[27] The remedial powers of the court are certainly not restricted to effecting restitution. The discretion allows the contract to be re-made to fit the court's notion of the justice of the case.[28]

(d) *Penalties and Forfeitures*

An expectant heir is easily exploited in a catching bargain. He suffers in an extreme degree from the same vulnerability to which all men are exposed when they seek credit. That is, they are too willing to sacrifice long-term prospects to short-term advantage. These are two degrees of special or abnormal temptation distorting the judgement and calling for protection. The 'abnormality' is much less in the second case, but uncertainty in the operation of relief is constrained within the confines of an identifiable species of exploitable transaction, namely seeking credit. We can take one step further. A still more general manifestation of the same weakening temptation is willingness to submit to dire consequences in the future—a pound of flesh, or eternal damnation—in exchange for some immediate benefit. Suppose that the penalty is demanded or, if it is already in the other's hands, is declared forfeit. Does the law offer any relief? We have already seen that there is a complex system of relief where money lending is involved. Hence the question now arises outside that field. Is there a general jurisdiction to relieve against the consequence of this temptation?

There is a preliminary point. If there is such a jurisdiction, it may

---

[24] *Consumer Credit Act, 1974* s. 132; s. 100.
[25] S. 138 (1).
[26] S. 138 (3).
[27] S. 171 (7).
[28] S. 139.

not fit well under the heading of 'inequality'. The reason is that this impulsive weakness is so widespread that it cannot be easily called abnormal or exceptional. We have already said that the uncertainty inherent in inequality must be contained by insisting on such additional aggravating characteristics, so that the circumstances giving rise to relief can be named and identified as exceptional. Hence it may be that, if there is such relief at all, it should be referred not to 'inequality' but to 'miscellaneous policy objectives'.[28a] Thus there might be an intelligible policy requiring the elimination of all penal sanctions form the law of contract (or from private law generally), and the relief could be related to that objective. However, being a rather low level policy that objective might be said to need its own higher justification. And that in turn might bring the argument back to the inequality which can be exploited when one person has a good to offer and the other will promise anything to get it.

There is a difference between promises of penalties and forfeitures. It has been established since the seventeenth century that the promise of a penalty payable on breach of contract, as opposed to a promise to pay a sum which is a genuine pre-estimate of the damages likely to flow from breach, cannot be enforced.[29] The plaintiff will be remitted to an action for compensatory damages. However, the position is less clear when the money or other wealth has already been paid or put into the power of the other so that the only question is whether it is irrevocably forfeit. A payment of this type falls into one of two main categories, as either a mere prepayment or as a sanctioning payment, as for example a deposit to bind the depositor to perform or a pre-payment expressed to be forfeit on breach. In all these cases denial of restitution in the event of the payor's breach may mean that the payee retains more money than he has suffered loss and, in particular, more than he would have recovered by action for breach of contract. It does not follow, however, that restitution ought to be made.

Mere pre-payments are recoverable even by a party in breach. They will be considered below.[30] The right of recovery is capable of being explained as based on failure of consideration, just as it would be if the other party were in breach or the contract were frustrated. The arguments for and against this will not be made here. Where the

---

[28a] Chapter IX, below.

[29] For the history, see A.W.B. Simpson, 'The Penal Bond with Conditional Defeasance' (1966) 82 *L.Q.R.* 392; for the definition of a penalty, see *Dunlop Pneumatic Tyre Co. Ltd. v. New Garage & Motor Co. Ltd.* [1951] A.C. 79.

[30] Below, p. 234 ff.

pre-payment is construed as a sanctioning payment there is no question of restitution if the amount is not penal according to the usual tests of the distinction between what is penal and what is a reasonable pre-estimation of damage. So the question is whether there is restitution of a penal forfeiture. The ground cannot be failure of consideration, since the consideration (to bind the payor or to sanction is breach) *ex hypothesi* has not failed. The traditionally orthodox answer is that there is no restitution.

The question takes the discussion back to *Stockloser* v. *Johnson*.[31] That case assumed that the special vulnerability in the pursuit of credit was not to be considered separately from this more general vulnerability in securing benefits by promising dire consequences. That unexamined assumption weakened its impact on the law relating specifically to the credit-seeking transaction of hire purchase. But the result is that, whatever effects the case can be said to have achieved, they have been achieved on the wider front. If the view of Somervell and Denning, L.J.J., ultimately prevails the courts have jurisdiction to effect restitution of these payments on terms. If Romer, L.J.'s view is right, extra time can be given, but without special facts no other relief is available to the payor.

The law is at a cross-roads. The Law Commission believes that the payments should be recoverable so far as penal.[32] And this seems right, since, in the law of restitution, it is always very difficult to justify a situation in which a payment is irrecoverable in circumstances in which a promise to pay it would be unenforceable or, vice versa, where a payment is recoverable in circumstances in which a promise to pay it would be actionable.[33] This argument leads towards the conclusion that, since a promised penalty cannot be claimed, a penalty which has already passed into the other's hands should be recoverable.

However, in recent cases there has been a marked hardening of judicial opinion and, undoubtedly to promote certainty, a refusal to generalise the jurisdiction to grant restitution in respect of forfeitures. Two points emerge. First, restitution will not be given if the indirect effect would be to deprive the defendant of his right to terminate the contract for repudiatory breach and thus to achieve a

---

[31] Above, n. 21.

[32] Working Paper No. 61 (1975). More than one regime is possible: see paragraphs 61 *et seq.*

[33] Cf. the situation which used to obtain in relation to *Stilk* v. *Myrick* and *Skeate* v. *Beale*, above p. 176.

covert specific performance.[33a] Secondly, there is certainly no secure restitutionary right outside the case in which the wealth which is forfeited is an interest in land.[33b]

(iii) *Personal Disadvantage*

We have been considering inequality arising from a relationship in which the plaintiff finds himself, or from a transaction in which he is specially vulnerable. The third species arises from personal circumstances. It may be that personal disadvantages should be divided between external and internal. External personal disadvantages would then be constituted by the examples of 'circumstantial compulsion' where the plaintiff is put under an acute anxiety. We saw earlier that that phenomenon is not entirely comfortable under the head of compulsion.[34] Internal personal disadvantages are those which relate to a person's capacity to understand the world and manage his affairs in it.

At this point the difficulty of drawing lines becomes acute. Not only is there in reality a sliding scale with no natural cut-off point between those who can manage very well and those who cannot manage at all, but also there is a semantic difficulty. 'Sub-normal capacity' will not do, since it lacks respect for people's dignity. Under whatever name, the concept in question is of a category of incapacity, extending beyond minority and mental illness, arising because the person in question is easily exploited by reason of lacking, to a marked degree, the social and intellectual advantages of the average citizen.

The common law identified only two main categories of protective incapacity among natural persons: those adults whose minds were disturbed and minors. Everyone else was presumed equal. Even within the two categories of incapacity not a great deal was done to allow for active claims after unwise transfers. The protection which was provided was mainly given by way of defence against actions by the other party. Thus minors were made liable for necessaries and, subject to the option of repudiation, for the claims arising out of durable

---

[33a] *Scandinavian Trading Tanker Co. A.B.* v. *Flota Petrolero Ecuatoriana, The Scaptrade* [1983] 2 A.C. 694.

[33b] *Sport International Bussum B.V.* v. *Inter-Footwear Ltd.* [1984] 1 All E.R. 376, limiting *Shiloh Spinners Ltd.* v. *Harding* [1973] A.C. 691. Notice however a greater willingness to confine a party to compensatory damages where he unreasonably *refuses* to accept a repudiation: *Clea Shipping Corp.* v. *Bulk Oil International Ltd., The Alaskan Trader* [1984] 1 All E.R. 129.

[34] Above, p. 203.

property; but otherwise they normally had a secure defence against adult claims.[35]

Suppose, however, that the minor sells his watch or exchanges his motor-cycle or buys and pays for a record-player. If these executed contracts turn out to be unfavourable to him, can he undo them? Unwise executed bargains are the very things one might have expected him to be protected against. But it seems at first sight that he has no rights that an adult does not have. Leaving fraud and misrepresentation aside, an adult who finds himself disappointed by such transactions has to find a breach of contract. If there is one he can sue for damages; alternatively, if the breach is repudiatory, he can recover any money given to the other provided that the consideration has failed totally. As regards goods transferred, they do not revest but, if there has been a total failure of consideration, the adult may recover their reasonable value in the same circumstances as, with money, he would have recovered the sum paid.[36] In *Pearce* v. *Brain*,[37] following *Valentini* v. *Canali*,[38] it was held that a minor's restitutionary rights were likewise dependent on a total failure of consideration. The minor had exchanged his motor-cycle for the defendant's car which turned out to be defective. He had had it a few days when it broke down. There had been no total failure of consideration. So there could be no restitution.   *12

On closer examination this severe position is nevertheless not necessarily identical to that of the adult. The adult's claim has two elements, (a) getting rid of the contract for repudiatory breach, and (b) showing that the consideration has totally failed, which means that he must have received nothing which he cannot give back. The minor can get rid of the contract on the ground of his minority[39] without pointing to any breach. Hence he only has to give back in full all benefits received in order to get restitution. This is perfectly compatible with *Valentini* v. *Canali* where the minor failed in his claim to recover money paid for furniture which he had used for four months. The obstacle was not that he could not get rid of the contract but only that he could not make counter-restitution. There is, therefore, room for the conclusion that there is such a thing as a restitutionary claim based on the inexperience of the minor but that it is easily lost. There may possibly be one other string to his bow,

---

[35] Below, p. 432 ff.
[36] Below, p. 226 ff.
[37] *Pearce* v. *Brain* [1929] 2 K.B. 310.
[38] *Valentini* v. *Canali* [1889] 24 Q.B.D. 166.
[39] Either under the *Infants Relief Act 1874* or at common law, so long as the contract is not for necessaries.

for in *Chaplin* v. *Leslie Frewin (Publishers) Ltd.*[40] Lord Denning, M.R., maintained, albeit in a minority of one, that a minor cannot make effective assignments, here of copyright, if the law requires a deed or writing.

Adults who are mentally ill so that they are unable to understand the transaction in question cannot be held to the terms of a contract by a party who knew of the want of understanding.[41] In such a case a reasonable price can be claimed for necessaries.[42] Once the patient's property is subject to the control of the court he cannot divest himself of it. Similar provisions apply to those who are temporarily unable to understand because of intoxication.   *13

Extending beyond these familar categories of disadvantage is a further group of easily exploited people. If there is evidence of exploitation in the form of an inadequate consideration given by the defendant the court will set aside a transfer made by someone who is poor or ill-educated or old if these attributes unfit him to manage the matter in question. In *Cresswell* v. *Potter*[43] a wife, who was a telephonist, released her interest in the matrimonial home after the breakdown of the marriage. She executed the document at the request of the enquiry agent who worked for her husband. All she received in return was an indemnity against her liability under the mortgage. Megarry, J., set the transaction aside. In the terms of the old cases she was 'poor and ignorant' in the sense of being a low income earner and not highly educated. These attributes had to be judged relative to the transaction in question, a conveyance. She had sold away her interest at an undervalue. And finally she had had no legal advice.

In situations in which it is doubtful whether a minor or a person of unsound mind has restitutionary rights emanating from his own particular disadvantage, his proper tactic will be to present himself in this larger category of personally disadvantaged people. Since the courts' jurisdiction to help the weak directly on account of their inability to manage the transaction in question is evidently not dead, it must be available to assist in these best known cases of incapacity no less than in the less easily defined instances of easily exploited disadvantage.

---

[40] *Chaplin* v. *Leslie Frewin (Publishers) Ltd.* [1966] Ch. 71.
[41] *Imperial Loan Co.* v. *Stone* [1892] 1 Q.B. 599.
[42] *Sale of Goods Act, 1979*, s. 2.
[43] *Cresswell* v. *Potter* [1978] 1 W.L.R. 255; cf. *Fry* v. *Lane*, (1888) 40 Ch. D. 312.

VII

NON-VOLUNTARY TRANSFER II: QUALIFICATION

IN the last chapter the reason for restitution lay in the fact that the plaintiff's judgment was vitiated. Either he did not even know that the defendant was being enriched at his expense or else he knew but was disabled by a mistake or by pressure or by inequality. In this chapter it is different. Here the plaintiff has exercised his judgment to the full. He has taken pains to qualify the transfer, making clear that, although he wanted the defendant to have the enrichment, his intent to that effect was not absolute but conditional. Now, as events have turned out, the condition has failed; and with its failure the transfer has become non-voluntary. In cases of 'vitiation' the plaintiff can say that at no time did he properly intend the defendant to be enriched. In cases of 'qualification' he asserts that he did form an unimpaired intent that the defendant should be enriched but only in events other than those which have happened.

The essence of the matter is that the plaintiff specified the basis of his giving. That is what distinguishes him from the risk-taking volunteer, who hopes that a particular state of affairs will eventuate but does not stipulate that the hoped for event must happen.[1] When it comes to the claim for restitution, that volunteer, no less than this plaintiff, can say that he never wanted to benefit the defendant except on the basis of events which have not happened. Thus, someone who cleans my windows while I am out, hoping for payment, can say that the benefit was intended to be conditional on his being paid. But this volunteer can be driven back to bear the risk which he ran when he chose to do the work without specifying the conditions on which it was done. By contrast the plaintiff in this chapter is immune to that objection. He took no risks. He specified the events in which his intent to give would become absolute.

The traditional terminology which the common law uses to describe this restitutionary event is 'total failure of consideration'. Suppose that I pay you £2000 as part of the price for work which you have agreed to do on my house. Perhaps it was a term of our contract that I should pay that sum in advance, or perhaps I paid in

---

[1] Above, p. 102.

advance merely for my convenience or for yours. Either way, if you now refuse to do the work I can terminate the contract on account of your repudiatory breach and, instead of claiming compensatory damages, I can claim restitution of the £2000. I shall recover the sum 'as money had and received to my use upon a total failure of consideration'.[2]

There is no question of arguing that this language should be abandoned. 'Money had and received' now serves no purpose which is not better expressed in the alternative vocabulary of restitution, but 'total failure of consideration' is, beyond argument, the phrase which the common law has chosen to describe the failure of the basis of a transfer. That restitution-yielding event has to have a name, and the common law gives it no other. None the less, it is a name which has some endemic difficulties, and the best way of introducing this restitutionary topic is to consider the four main ways in which the traditional terminology can be misleading.

Throughout the ensuing discussion it is desirable to bear in mind that 'failure of consideration' manifests itself most commonly when contracts are prematurely discharged, by frustration or in reaction to a repudiatory breach. The same event can, however, happen where there is no contract at all, as where a gift is made on a basis which fails to materialise or fails to be sustained. The theme of the discussion will be that for all these events a unified regime, similar to that which has been introduced for frustration by the *Law Reform (Frustrated Contracts) Act, 1943,* is within the range of interpretative development. In order to achieve that, two main steps would have to be taken. First, it would have to be accepted, as indeed it must be accepted, that all grounds for restitution which have been worked out in relation to money do apply equally to non-money benefits where those benefits qualify as enrichments. Secondly, the courts would have to isolate and solve the specially difficult problems which arise in relation to the 'enrichment' issue in those cases in which the non-money benefit consists in work incompletely performed under an entire contract. Sadly, the unity of the law of restitution in relation to failure of consideration, though within interpretative reach, is all too likely to be broken up by separate statutory regimes for the different manifestations of this single species of unjust enrichment. Legislative interventions in the common law scheme are considered at the end of the chapter.

---

[2] *Giles* v. *Edwards* (1797) 7 Term Reps., 181; *Rugg* v. *Minett* (1809) 11 East 210; *Devaux* v. *Connolly* (1849) 8 C.B. 640; *Ashpitel* v. *Sercombe* (1850) 5 Ex. 147. Cf. for Scots law: *Cantiere San Rocco S.A.* v. *Clyde Shipbuilding & Engineering Co.* [1924] A.C. 226.

One more preliminary point must be made. Where a failure of consideration arises from a failure of contractual reciprocation—as when I have paid you to build me a new kitchen and you have pocketed the money but not done the work—the plaintiff will often have a claim for compensatory damages based on the wrong of breach of contract. Such a claim will be available unless the failure arises from frustration or from some other excusable reason for non-performance. In this chapter we are not concerned with the question whether a plaintiff, basing himself on the wrong of breach of contract as such, can also obtain damages in the restitutionary rather than the more familiar compensatory measure. The question whether breach of contract can ever be a restitution-yielding wrong belongs in the chapter on 'restitution for wrongs'.[3]

Where a plaintiff seeks restitution for failure of consideration, he is not relying on the wrong of breach but on a distinct event identifiable by alternative analysis[4] alongside the wrong of breach (but often discoverable even where there is no breach). The two events give rise to different claims. Nevertheless it is possible as a matter of policy to make one predominate over the other. For example it would be possible to say, while admitting the existence in principle of the independent restitutionary cause of action, that where the plaintiff has a cause of action for breach of contract he shall not have recourse to the action in unjust enrichment. It is very important that a decision of that kind should be exposed as a question of policy: What do we want? rather than, What is logically available? Unwillingness to accept that there are two separate causative events, and, hence, that there are in principle two separate avenues of recourse, merely leads to confusion. It is neither confusing nor impossible to admit that there are two such avenues and then deliberately and openly to block up one of them.[5]

1. FOUR ERRORS

The word 'errors' is somewhat tendentious since, after the first, the others have as yet only the status of difficulties which can be said to arise from the traditional vocabulary. They are habits of thought which ought henceforth to be regarded as errors.

---

[3] Below, p. 334—6.
[4] Above, p. 44.
[5] Below, p. 244.

(i) *Contractual Consideration*

This point can be dealt with briefly since it involves an error which has been identified and eliminated. Before the *Fibrosa Case*[6] an argument had taken hold to the effect that, if there had once been consideration sufficient for the formation of a contract, you could never afterwards say that there had been a total failure of the consideration for any payment made under that contract, not even if the payor received nothing at all for his payment.[7] The argument theoretically admitted one exception, namely the case in which the contract could be rescinded *ab initio* so as to cut away the consideration relied on for its formation. But we can see that that exception conceded nothing at all. Breach, no less than frustration, is a ground for terminating a contract, not for rescinding it.[8] You agree to do work in my house for £5000; I pay you £2000; you refuse to come and do the work. I can terminate for the future but I cannot cut away the contract originally made between us, in which your promise to work was consideration for my promise to pay, and *vice versa*. So I cannot bring about a failure of consideration *ab initio*, notwithstanding the fact that I have received none of the work for which I paid. It does not matter. *Fibrosa* settled once and for all that the question whether the consideration for a payment has totally failed is quite different from the question which asks whether there was originally sufficient consideration to bind the contract under which the payment was made. Hence rescission *ab initio* is not a requirement for restitution on this ground. As Viscount Simon, L.C., said:

In English Law, an enforceable contract may be formed by the exchange of a promise for a promise, or by the exchange of a promise for an act—I am excluding contracts under seal—and thus, in the law relating to formation of contract, the promise to do a thing may often be the consideration, but when one is considering the law of failure of consideration and of the quasi-contractual right to recover money on that ground, it is, generally speaking, not the promise which is referred to as the consideration, but the performance of the promise. The money was paid to secure performance and, if performance fails, the inducement which brought about the contract is not fulfilled.[9]

The error of supposing that the contractual consideration had to be cut away entirely before there could be said to be a 'total failure

---

[6] *Fibrosa Case* [1943] A.C. 32.
[7] *Chandler* v. *Webster* [1904] 1 K.B. 493.
[8] *Johnson* v. *Agnew* [1980] A.C. 367.
[9] *Fibrosa Case* [1943] A.C. 32, 48; cf. p. 72, *per* Lord Wright.

of consideration' for the purposes of the law of restitution, was based on the assumption that both areas of law used the word 'consideration' in the same sense. The next error has the same root.

(ii) *Species and Genus*

The link between 'consideration' and contracts makes it easy to suppose that 'total failure of consideration' must always refer to a failure in contractual reciprocation, whereas in fact that is only the most common species of the genus so described. In the law of restitution the word 'consideration' should be given the meaning with which it first came into the common law. A 'consideration' was once no more than a 'matter considered', and the consideration for doing something was the matter considered in forming the decision to do it.[10] In short, the reason for the act, the state of affairs contemplated as its basis. Failure of the consideration for a payment should be understood in that sense. It means that the state of affairs contemplated as the basis or reason for the payment has failed to materialise or, if it did exist, has failed to sustain itself.[11]

By far the most common case is indeed the failure of a contractual reciprocation. The contract which I make with you for that work on my house makes clear the basis, first, that you are bound to do the work and, secondly, that in due time your obligation to do the work will become work done. You then refuse to do your part; I terminate the contract. At that moment the basis of my payment falls away; you cease to be bound and have not done the work. So the once extant basis fails to sustain itself and the state of affairs which was to be brought about fails to materialise. Nothing turns on the fact that in this example the termination of the contract came about in reaction to your breach. A frustrating event would have had the same effect, as in *Fibrosa* itself.[12] There the plaintiffs were a Polish company. They had bought machinery for later delivery in Poland and had paid £1000 in advance. The Nazi occupation of Poland frustrated the contract before delivery. The plaintiffs recovered their advance payment.

But the basis of a payment is not always specified in a contract or as a contractual reciprocation. Take the case in which I see a house which I want to buy. I immediately pay a small deposit, say £200.

---

[10] A. W. B. Simpson, *A History of the Common Law of Contract*, Oxford, 1975, 321.

[11] The language of the *Digest* for the same phenomenon is *causa data causa non secuta* (things given upon a consideration, that consideration having failed): D.12.4.

[12] *Fibrosa Case* [1943] A.C. 32.

My intention is merely to show *bona fides* and establish good will. The payment is made 'subject to contract'. A month later I call the whole thing off; no contract materialises. I can recover the £200.[13] There is no need to twist the facts into an implied contract under which you promise to repay in the event of the negotiations being aborted. That is one way to conclude for repayment, but the temptation to adopt that approach is a reflection of the old insecurity about all non-contractual analyses. It is quite sufficient to say that when my purchase goes off the consideration for the payment fails. There can be a consideration in this sense without there being a contract about the payment. The phrase 'subject to contract' means, as a matter of construction, that my payment was conditional on the successful conclusion of the contract. That is, the only consideration for the payment was the making of that contract. Without that contract, the consideration failed. It would have been different if the exercise of construction had shown that the payment was intended to operate as a sanction against my withdrawal. If that had been the basis of the payment, there would have been no failure of consideration when I did withdraw.[14]

Again, suppose that I am in dispute with you as to whether, as a matter of law, a certain payment which you claim is actually due to you. In the end I pay 'pending judicial determination of the doubtful question of law'. A court decides in my favour. Once more there is a temptation to spell out an agreement whereby, in consideration of my paying, you promised to repay if the point was found against you.[15] But there is no need. My words make plain that the basis on which I am willing for you to have the money is that the court should decide in your favour. When the court decides for me, that state of affairs fails to materialise. In other words, the consideration for the payment fails.

You are marrying X who is my niece. I write to you in these words: 'I am delighted to hear of this marriage. I hope you will both be very happy. The enclosed is to help you begin your married life together.' I enclose a cheque for £5000. Then the engagement is broken off. You must return the money.[16] I have made plain that the marriage is the basis of my gift: the money is for the marriage and in particular for setting up after it. You have not agreed to repay

---

[13] *Chillingworth* v. *Esche* [1924] 1 Ch. 97.

[14] Cf. *Howe* v. *Smith* (1884) 27 Ch.D. 89; *Mayson* v. *Clouet* (1924) A.C. 980.

[15] As in *Sebel Products Ltd.* v. *Commissioners for Customs & Excise* [1949] Ch. 409; cf. *Banque de l'Indo-Chine* v. *J.H. Rayner (Mincing Lane) Ltd.* [1983] 1 All E.R. 468.

[16] *Essery* v. *Cowlard* (1884) 26 Ch.D. 191; *Re Ames' Settlement* [1946] Ch. 217; cf. *Burgess* v. *Rawnsley* [1975] Ch. 429.

it. It would be quite artificial to discover a contract to repay. It is enough to say that the consideration for the payment fails. In the case of engagement presents between the couple themselves the same principle applies, but the exercise of construction has proved difficult.[17] In the case of rings statute now inverts the old common law presumption.[18] The starting point nowadays, therefore, is that an engagement ring is an out and out gift, not conditional upon the marriage taking place. But the donor can still expressly or impliedly specify the contrary. In the case of other gifts there is no presumption. There must be restitution if the gift was expressly or impliedly conditional.

A rather different qualification of the intent to give occurs where the donor specifies a purpose for which he wants the donee to use the money, as where I give you £5000 to suppress vivisection on monkeys, to educate your daughter, or to pay such and such a debt. *14 This is a very difficult subject. But the difficulties mostly arise in the exercise of construction which tries to answer the question whether I intended to benefit you absolutely (with a merely precatory exhortation super-added) or conditionally (only for the given purpose). That exercise is distorted outside the area of charity by the desire to avoid the conclusion that the donor has created a trust for the purpose, because non-charitable trusts of that kind are void unless the purpose is one whose execution redounds to the benefit of ascertainable human beneficiaries;[19] and even if they clear that hurdle they encounter other very considerable practical and theoretical difficulties.[20] So there is a strong pressure against the conclusion that the donor intended to specify the purpose as the basis of his giving.[21] Nevertheless, that unwanted conclusion can be reached. If and when it is reached, failure of that specified basis will mean failure of the gift. That is, if the purpose cannot be pursued whether for a factual or a legal reason, equity will turn the donee into a trustee for the donor, holding on resulting trust.[22] The same phenomenon is observable with loans for specified applications. I lend you £5000 for the payment of a particular debt. If you are prevented from paying

---

[17] *Jacobs* v. *Davis* [1917] 2 K.B. 532; *Cohen* v. *Sellar*, [1926] 1 K.B. 536.

[18] *Law Reform (Miscellaneous Provisions) Act, 1970.* 1–3 (2).

[19] *Re Denley's Trust Deed* [1969] 1 Ch. 373.

[20] Especially in the requirements against uncertainty, capriciousness and perpetuity: cf. *Re Astor's S.T.* [1952] Ch. 534; *Leahy* v. *A-G. for N.S.W.* [1959] A.C. 457.

[21] Cf. *Re Lipinski's W.T.* [1976] Ch. 235; *Re Osoba* [1979] 1 W.L.R. 247.

[22] *Re Astor's S.T.* above; *Re Shaw* [1957] 1 W.L.R. 729; *Re Abbot* [1900] 2 Ch. 326; *Re West Sussex Constabulary's Fund* [1971] Ch. 1.

that debt, so that the basis of my lending fails, you will hold on resulting trust for me.[23]

The object of these examples has been to show that payment for a contractual reciprocation, an agreed counter-performance by the payee, is only the most familiar example of something more general, namely qualified giving. In *Fibrosa*, which *was* a case of payment for a counter-performance, Lord Wright said: 'The payment was originally conditional. The condition of retaining it is eventual performance. Accordingly, when that condition fails, the right to retain the money must simultaneously fail.'[24] That captures the wider notion. The condition of retaining the money may be that an existing state of affairs should sustain itself into the future; or should be brought about by the payee; or should happen to be brought about, whether or not by the payee; or a combination of two or more of these. It is when the payee undertakes to make the condition happen that there occurs a coincidence between conditional giving and contractual reciprocation. And it is in that common case that there is a cross-over between the consideration for a payment and the consideration which suffices for contracts to be made.

(iii) *Exclusive Focus on Money*

The event 'total failure of consideration' was developed as a cause of action in relation to the count in *assumpsit* for money had and received. Consequently you do not often hear of restitution on this ground in respect of benefits in kind. It sounds almost wrong to speak of recovering the value of work done 'for total failure of consideration'; similarly with goods.[25] Suppose I give you a car under a contract of sale, expecting to receive a price of £5000 as we had agreed. You do not pay. Of course I have my action in the contract. But do I, even in theory, have an action for the value of the car on the ground of total failure of consideration? If the choice had fallen in favour of rescission *ab initio* as the consequence of repudiatory breach, I would re-vest the car in myself and then switch, if need be, to those remedial rights, restitutionary and otherwise, which would be triggered by your conversion of what would once again be my car. But, despite a recent flirtation with that approach in relation to land,[26] the choice has gone the other way: the effect of your

[23] *Barclays Bank Ltd., v. Quistclose Investments Ltd.* [1970] A.C. 567; cf. *National Bolivian Navigation Company v. Wilson* (1880) App. Cas. 176.

[24] *Fibrosa Case* [1943] A.C. 32, 65.

[25] But see *Pearce v. Brain* [1929] 2 K.B. 310, p. 315, *per* Swift, J.

[26] *Horsler* v. *Zorro* [1975] Ch. 302.

breach is, if I so choose, termination *de futuro*,[27] and that means that the car for which you have not paid remains yours. The path to restitution via rescission *ab initio* being blocked, there is a real and important question whether I can recover the value of the car as on a total failure of consideration. And the answer must be that in principle I can. The contrary view is an error derived largely, but, as we shall see, not entirely, from the historical linkage between 'total failure' and the action for money had and received.

The case in favour of the answer which is given here rests on the rational need for symmetry in the law applicable to both parties, whichever of them happens to make the first transfer. Thus, if I pay money for a car which I never get, I can recover that money as paid for a consideration which has failed. If, *vice versa,* I transfer a car for money which I do not get, I must in principle be able to recover the value of the car on the same ground, since otherwise different law would apply without there being any sufficient reason for the difference. For on the second hypothesis nothing changes except the nature of the benefit. If failure of consideration is a good ground for restitution in the one case, it must be equally effective in the other. It is exactly the same in the case of work done. Again there is a change in the nature of the benefit received but none in the ground for restitution (going not to 'enrichment' but to 'unjust'). You ask me to burn your rubbish for £100; I do it. You do not pay. I must be entitled to a *quantum meruit* on the ground of total failure of consideration.

These propositions—that a plaintiff can recover the value of goods or work for total failure of consideration—are so unfamiliar that we must carefully set down the reasons why they are still startling and why they must be handled with caution.

(a) *Why are these propositions unfamiliar?*

There is a historical reason and an analytical reason. Historically it is a fact that failure of consideration was introduced into the common law as part of the attempt to settle the scope of the action for money had and received. If, which seems likely, Lord Mansfield saw that action as the English equivalent of the Roman *condictio,* he must have meant 'a consideration which happens to fail'[28] to be the

---

[27] *Johnson* v. *Agnew* [1980] A.C. 367.

[28] *Moses* v. *Macfarlan*, above, p. 36–7. There are many indications of Roman influence on Lord Mansfield's judgment in this case, in particular the exclusion of restitution where payment is made under a *naturalis obligatio*; the enumeration of the grounds for bringing the action, which closely follows the typology which the *Digest* uses for the non-contractual application of the *condictio*; reliance on *aequum et bonum* to explain the grounds; and location of the grounds within the category of obligations *quasi ex contractu*.

English ground corresponding to the Roman '*causa data causa non secuta*'.[29] However, the English action, unlike the *condictio*, was tied, as its name shows, to money claims. A plaintiff who wished to claim the reasonable value of benefits in kind had to forsake 'money had and received' and was obliged to advance the form of words based upon the defendant's 'special instance and request'.[30] Under those forms there never was any development according to which the request and promise to pay would be 'implied' from the combination of the receipt of an enriching but non-money benefit, and the failure of the consideration for that receipt. In other words there was in this field no parallel to the development which we have noticed in relation to *Exall* v. *Partridge,* according to which the request and promise could be implied from the combination of enrichment and compulsion.[31] Hence the historical reason why we never speak of failure of consideration in relation to benefits in kind is that, in the *assumpsit* counts outside money had and received, that ground had neither an overt nor even a covert rôle.

The analytical reason is rooted in the fact that plaintiffs who seek restitution in respect of non-money benefits always face difficulties under the head of enrichment. They have to meet the argument from subjective devaluation.[32] The easiest and commonest way of doing so is for them to establish that the defendant freely accepted the benefit in question. However, since it happens that free acceptance not only settles the issue of enrichment but also is in itself a ground for restitution,[33] plaintiffs who are driven to prove a free acceptance for the former reason will almost inevitably rely on it also for the latter. Consequently no mention will be made of failure of consideration. In the case of the car which I have transferred to you but have not been paid for, it is thus likely that I would base any claim to its value solely on your free acceptance, without ever bothering to insist that I could equally advance an analysis according to which the ground for restitution, going to 'unjust', was total failure of consideration, while the free acceptance was relied upon only to settle the issue of enrichment. On the face of things there is no obvious reason why I should want to make that more complicated assertion. The consequence is that in practice the behaviour of plaintiffs still seems to vindicate the division made historically by the

---

[29] *Digest,* 12.4.
[30] Above, p. 111 ff.
[31] Above, p. 186–7.
[32] Above, p. 109 ff.
[33] Above, 104, 116; below, 266 ff.

different forms of action: when claiming the value of non-money benefits, they tend to rely on free acceptance.

To accept that pattern as theoretically necessary or correct is to overlook the fact that, as *Craven-Ellis v. Canons Ltd.* shows, [34] the issue of enrichment can sometimes, albeit rarely, be settled by tests other than free acceptance even when the defendant has received a benefit in kind and not in money. Those other tests do not have the same bi-polarity as free acceptance. They do not settle the issue of 'unjust' at the same time as the issue of enrichment. Craven-Ellis could show that his work was necessary for the company and was thus an enrichment to it within the 'no reasonable man' test, but he still had to identify his ground for restitution. In his case the ground was mistake; he could not rely on free acceptance. His case, therefore, had to be founded on the combination of a factor negativing voluntariness and an objective test of enrichment. The same tactic ought to be possible in relation to factors other than mistakes and hence in relation to failure of consideration.

Although this has not yet been explored, it should not be regarded as theoretically weak or doubtful. For, once a plaintiff has surmounted the enrichment issue, it would be absurd and irrational to suggest that he cannot draw on any ground for restitution which is documented in the cases, whether those cases concern money or non-money benefits. The grounds for restitution must be common to all enrichments. The contrary view derives from the failure to separate the issues of 'enrichment' and 'unjust'. It does easily seem as though there are less grounds for restitution available to plaintiffs who have conferred non-money benefits than to those who have transferred money, whereas the truth is that exactly the same grounds are available to all. The relative poverty of the law of restitution in relation to non-money benefits is entirely due to the fact that money plaintiffs encounter no difficulties in relation to the issue of enrichment. So long as this is accepted as correct, the unfamiliar proposition that a non-money plaintiff can recover on the ground of total failure of consideration will not seem wrong.

(b) *The need for caution*

However strong the theoretical force of the proposition in his favour, the plaintiff who has conferred a non-money benefit will not often be able to obtain restitution on this ground. The reason, true to what has been said in the preceding paragraphs, is that he

---

[34] Above, p. 118–9.

faces extra-ordinary difficulties on the issue of enrichment. A major shift in the law's approach to that issue may be necessary if his chances of restitution are to be improved. That change may be introduced by statute. For the case in which the consideration fails by reason of frustration it has already been so introduced.[35] For the moment we are concerned only with the position at common law, with a view to establishing the base on which legislative or other reform is or will be built.

This plaintiff's difficulties arise in relation to incomplete performances. In the preceding discussion we used the case of a car transferred by the plaintiff to the defendant and not paid for. In that example the plaintiff's performance is complete. It is the very performance which, under the contract, the defendant wanted. Because the performance is complete the plaintiff can successfully assert that the defendant freely accepted it; and then, as we said, he can either rely solely on free acceptance or he can rely on the combination of failure of consideration and free acceptance, using the latter only in its enrichment role. Much more commonly the matter in issue will be an incomplete performance. An incomplete performance is something which *ex hypothesi* the defendant never wanted. Hence an incomplete performance can never be said to have been freely accepted.[36] The common test of enrichment is therefore excluded. This can be illustrated by an inversion of the facts of *Fibrosa*.[37]

In *Fibrosa* the Polish plaintiffs had pre-paid money for machinery to be made and delivered to them. When the contract was frustrated before they had received any benefit, they recovered their money for total failure of consideration. The earlier case of *Appleby* v. *Myers*[38] is exactly the non-money version of this case. In *Appleby* v. *Myers* it was the makers of the machinery who, at the time of the frustration, had already made their transfer. The plaintiffs had agreed to erect certain machinery on the defendants' premises. The price was itemised part by part but nothing was to be paid until the whole mechanism had been installed. When the work was very far advanced, though before any one of the separately priced sections had been completed, there was a disastrous fire. Everything was burned down. At first instance the Common Pleas held that the plaintiffs could recover the value of the work which had been done, but the

---

[35] *Law Reform (Frustrated Contracts) Act, 1943*, below, p. 249 ff.
[36] Below, p. 286–9.
[37] *Fibrosa Case* [1943] A.C. 32.
[38] *Appleby* v. *Myers* (1867) L.R. 2 C.P. 651; cf. *Cutter* v. *Powell* (1795) 6 T.R. 320.

Exchequer Chamber then took the opposite view. The case is notable for very learned arguments, taking account of several Roman texts; but in the end it was decided very Englishly by looking for the right contract to 'imply' in order to meet the eventuality of destruction by fire. Since the express contract was entire, no contract could be implied against the defendants to the effect that they would pay for work done towards the complete performance.

If we now put the search for a contractual explanation aside and, still without reference to the 1943 Act, look instead for the plaintiffs' cause of action in autonomous unjust enrichment, we will find that their difficulty remains much the same as it was in 1867. *Fibrosa* tells us, with hindsight, that they had a good ground for restitution: total failure of consideration. The consideration for their work and materials had failed as obviously and comprehensively as had the consideration for the money pre-payment in Fibrosa. So the plaintiffs in *Appleby* encountered no difficulty under 'unjust'. Nor under 'at the expense of', since there had been a straight transfer of work and materials from them to the defendants. But they could not overcome the routine difficulties of plaintiffs who have to establish that a non-money benefit is an enrichment. The tests other than free acceptance are always hard to satisfy, and free acceptance was excluded by the fact that the plaintiffs had only done part of the work required under an entire contract. If the contract had been divisible, with payment fixed as so much per completed section or so much per unit of time worked, each several fraction would have been a complete and freely accepted performance. But since the contract was entire there could not be said to have been an acceptance of anything less than the whole performance. The defendants never indicated that they wanted anything less than the whole.

Appleby v. *Myers* was a case in which the contract came to an end, and the consideration failed, by reason of frustration. We will see in the next section that the same explanation applies where the discharge happens by reason of the plaintiff's breach, as in *Sumpter* v. *Hedges*[39] where the plaintiff builder had abandoned a building contract when he had already done a good deal of the work and was refused restitution in respect of the half-finished buildings which he left behind. However, where the discharge arises neither from the plaintiff's breach nor from frustration, but from the defendant's own breach, the opposite conclusion is reached. This is the one case in which there is actual, as opposed to merely theoretical, symmetry between the money and the non-money plaintiff.

---

[39] *Sumpter* v. *Hedges* [1898] 1 Q.B. 673.

In *Planché* v. *Colburn*[40] the plaintiff had been signed up to write a book for a series promoted by the defendant and called *The Juvenile Library*. When the plaintiff had done some of the work, the defendant decided to abandon the series and declined to pay the plaintiff. The plaintiff was allowed his *quantum meruit*. This is difficult to explain. The ground for restitution remains unchanged; but, so far as concerns the issue of enrichment, it is impossible to say that the defendant freely accepted the plaintiff's incomplete performance. The fact that he himself precipitated the discharge by his repudiatory breach cannot alter the conclusion that he did not freely accept anything less than the complete manuscript, which was never delivered to him. The best answer seems to be that on these facts, even although there is no free acceptance, there is a 'limited acceptance' sufficient to make it impossible for the defendant to advance the argument from subjective devaluation. That is to say, the defendant freely accepted the whole work and, therefore, in a limited sense also accepted that work which would be necessary in order to achieve the complete performance. It may be objected that a 'limited acceptance' of that kind is not peculiar to recipients who are themselves in breach of contract, for exactly the same could be said of a defendant who had received an incomplete performance under a contract brought to an end by frustration or as a result of the plaintiff's breach. However, it is reasonable to suggest that the courts may intuitively have resolved to take a more robust line with the defendant who is in breach. In short, 'limited acceptance' may be a test of enrichment which will work against a defendant whose resort to subjective devaluation appears unconscientious in the light of his own conduct in relation to the receipt of the benefit. Yet it is also true that the isolation of the *Planché* v. *Colburn* claim may be due to nothing more than that the efficacy and scope of limited acceptance as a test of enrichment have never been thoroughly examined. If the matter were squarely faced, 'limited acceptance' might turn out to be a sufficient test of enrichment even in the other situations.

The theme of these paragraphs has been that the non-money plaintiff can claim on the ground of total failure of consideration but, except against a defendant in breach of contract, is likely to encounter insuperable difficulties on the issue of enrichment. There is one further point which needs to be added to that theme. It is a negative one. The problem for the plaintiff in a situation such as

---

[40] *Planché* v. *Colburn* (1831) 8 Bing. 14; cf. *Clay* v. *Yates* (1856) 1 H. & N. 73.

Appleby v. *Myers* is not that the defendant is left with no end-product of work done, no marketable residuum. It is only that he cannot make out a free acceptance, in the absence of which it has never been decided whether the limited acceptance might suffice. The absence of a marketable residuum does not matter. Often there will be none even where the performance is complete. Suppose that I am to demolish a bridge. This is only one of countless services which by nature leave no end-product. Yet once they are complete nothing obstructs a claim made on the basis of a free acceptance. Indeed under the old pleading practice a claim made for a *quantum meruit* would invariably have backed up the claim made for the contract price.[41]

Just as the absence of an end-product will not hinder his claim if only he can establish a free acceptance, so the fact that an incomplete performance does leave such an end-product will not necessarily help the plaintiff over the issue of enrichment. In *Sumpter* v. *Hedges* the defendant benefited by retaining partly completed buildings, but it was still impossible for the plaintiff to demonstrate that the defendant had been enriched, because he was unable to establish a free acceptance.[42] Nevertheless, there are circumstances in which a plaintiff's hopes of restitution will be increased by the fact that he has not merely laboured for, but has in addition conferred a valuable end-product on, the defendant. It may, for example, be that the defendant realises the marketable residuum in money (as by selling an improved car or house)[43] or that the law will override subjective devaluation because the end-product is valuable according to the 'no reasonable man' test; also, as we shall see, an end-product can be important in considering the impact of legislative reforms on the common law regime.[44]

The summary of this section is this: it is wrong to suppose that total failure of consideration is a ground for restitution peculiar to money had and received; that ground is (like all grounds for restitution) common to all types of enrichment; however, plaintiffs claiming restitution in respect of non-money benefits have little chance of success unless either the defendant is in breach of contract or the performance conferred on the defendant is not an incomplete performance; the reason for this pessimism is that such plaintiffs can rarely satisfy any test which establishes that the defendant has been enriched; the task of satisfying such a test is sometimes, but not

---

[41] C. H. S. Fifoot, *History and Sources of the Common Law,* London, 1949, 363.
[42] Below, p. 239
[43] Above, p. 121.
[44] Below, p. 251–2.

often, easier where the non-money benefit does leave behind a valuable end-product.

(iv) *Exclusion of the Party in Breach*

The fourth error is the proposition that a party in breach of contract cannot himself claim restitution on this ground. We have already contrasted two different views of total failure of consideration. According to one view, total failure is always a matter of fundamental breach of contract, and the plaintiff who claims on this ground is always complaining of a complete failure of contractual reciprocation, which has brought the contract to an end and entitled him to seek restitution. According to the other view, failures of contractual reciprocation are merely the most common species of a larger genus, and the essence of the matter is 'failure of basis' or 'failure of condition'.[45] Anyone who subscribes to the contractual view is bound to find it impossible to see how a party who is himself in breach can ever claim on the ground of total failure, since it seems obvious that a party whose repudiatory breach has brought the contract to an end cannot himself maintain any claim which is in substance a complaint against that breach. However, the conditional view of total failure, which we preferrred, leads to a different conclusion. If the essence of the matter is that the money is recoverable because the condition for retaining it fails, it is hard to see how the failure or fulfilment of that condition can ever depend on the character of the remoter causes behind the happening or the failure to happen of the events contemplated. We have already seen that it makes no difference whether the consideration fails by reason of frustration or by reason of the defendant's breach. The same must in principle be true even where the remoter cause for the failure is the plaintiff's own breach. For the condition for retaining the enrichment either fails or it does not.

Suppose that I give you £1000 for work which you are to do on my house. A week later, before you have even begun, I decide to call the contract off. That is to say, I repudiate the whole transaction. You accept the repudiation and terminate the contract, but you do not give my £1000 back. There is no doubt that you can sue me for damages, but your loss is likely to be far less than the £1000 which you hold because of my pre-payment. If I can recover the £1000, the result will be that you will be confined to compensatory damages,

---

[45] Above, pp. 223—6.

and in effect what I will get back will be the balance between your loss and my pre-payment. If I cannot recover the £1000, you will make a windfall profit from the fact of my pre-payment. Can I recover? It is submitted that the law is that, despite my being in breach, I can have restitution; and, furthermore, that the ground of my recovery is as correctly described as total failure of consideration as in the other cases where the ultimate cause for the failure is either frustration or the defendant's breach. However, this is difficult. The cases do not clearly admit the notion of a plaintiff-precipitated failure of consideration.

(a) *Money claims*

It is crucial from the outset to distinguish between cases in which, on close inspection, the consideration has not failed, and those in which it has. We have already looked at deposits 'subject to contract' in which, because the condition of the payment is construed to be nothing but the successful finalization of the main contract, the plaintiff depositor can recover even if he himself precipitates the failure.[46] Contrast the deposit paid in circumstances in which it is construed to be a sanction against the payor's withdrawal.[47] Or where a deposit is paid to keep an offer open, so as to give the depositor an option. Suppose such a depositor does withdraw. He never gets the wealth which was the ultimate object of his interest. So in a sense it seems as though he ends up with nothing for his money. But that is wrong. The consideration has not failed. He bought the payee's reliance and the payee did rely, the payee's patience and the payee did wait. According to the construction of the circumstances and purposes of these deposits the 'condition for retaining them' does not fail on the payor's withdrawal or repudiation.

Again suppose that I have paid you half the price of a purchase already made, say £2500 for a £5000 car to be delivered by you next week. Then I write and tell you that I have changed my mind. I do not want the car and I certainly will not pay the balance. You refuse to accept the repudiation. At this stage the consideration has not failed. Even supposing that the pre-payment was not paid by way of a sanctioning deposit but was simply done for my own convenience or because of my passing enthusiasm for the car (to make myself, not you, more certain of completion free from hitches), the basis of the payment remains unaffected provided you remain bound and willing

---

[46] Above, p. 224.
[47] *Mayson* v. *Clouet* [1924] A.C. 980.

to deliver the car. And on these facts you do so remain, for it is given that you have declined to terminate the contract. An unwilling buyer is not in a position, as against a willing seller, to bring about a total failure of consideration.[48]

Suppose in the last case that the pre-payment of £2500 had indeed been taken as a sanctioning deposit. In that case you could decide to terminate the contract and still the consideration would not fail, for the reasons discussed in the preceding paragraph. My only hope would then be that, despite the payment's having become unconditional according to my original intent, I might yet bring myself within some doctrine relieving (for a reason quite other than failure of consideration) against burdensome payments in the nature of penalties and forfeitures.[49]

If we now exclude altogether the construction of the payment as a sanction, we can isolate the critical question. If you do accept the repudiation by terminating the contract, thus making yourself free to resell the vehicle elsewhere, what is then the position of my pre-paid £2500? Suppose that your bargain with me was a good one. I agreed to pay £5000 but on the market the car will fetch only £4500. Let it be that you actually sell it for that sum. As against me you have lost £500 (which you would have been able to recover as damages for my breach) but you have gained £2500 by reason of my pre-payment. So you are £2000 up. This can hardly be right, given the construction of the payment as non-sanctioning. It is a conclusion which is avoided if it is correct to say that your discharge, even when consequential on my breach, destroys the condition for your retaining my payment.

In *Dies* v. *British and International Mining and Finance Corporation*,[50] the plaintiff bought arms at a price of £135000, paying £100000 in advance. Unable to take delivery, the plaintiff then sought to recover the pre-payment. There was a clause in the contract relevant to the fate of that money, but it was held to cover only the case of frustration, whereas on the facts the buyers were in breach. Stable, J., construed the payment as non-sanctioning and allowed recovery. His reasoning falls into a familiar mould: the recovery is made to depend on construction of the contract itself.

---

[48] *Thomas* v. *Brown* (1876) 1 Q.B.D. 714; *Monnickendam* v. *Leanse* (1923) 39 T.L.R. 445, *Heyman* v. *Darwins Ltd.* [1942] A.C. 356. Note however, that the innocent party cannot keep the contract open unless he has a 'legitimate interest' in so doing: *Clea Shipping Corp.* v. *Bulk Oil International Ltd., The Alaskan Trader,* [1984] 1 All E.R. 85.

[49] Above, p. 213−6.

[50] *Dies* v. *British and International Mining and Finance Corporation* [1939] 1 K.B. 724.

The cause of action in unjust enrichment is not fully examined. Indeed Stable, J., goes so far as to say that the ground for recovery is not total failure of consideration. But the reason why he does so is clearly in order to circumvent the proposition that an unwilling buyer cannot impose a failure on a willing seller. So the question is never asked whether the sellers, BIMFC, did not accept the repudiation and thus, albeit reactively, themselves effect the discharge through which the consideration failed. Yet that is the safest explanation of the conclusion in favour of recovery. Only so long as BIMFC still retained the arms, and remained ready and willing to deliver, could it be said that the consideration had not failed.

In one respect *Dies* is a clear case. The buyer paid for guns and ammunition and got nothing. So, unless prevented from saying so by being himself the cause, he clearly did suffer a total failure of consideration. It can be different with contracts for work or work and materials. There the plaintiff may well have had some of the enjoyment for which he bargained. Suppose you want to have a cottage restored. You contract with me for the job to be done for £15000; you pay £5000 in advance. Then you suddenly repudiate when I have only taken off the old roof and begun clearing up the inside of the shell. Even if I accept your repudiation and thus discharge the contract, you will not be able to get back your £5000, because you have had the benefit of some of my work. The consideration has not totally failed.[51]

This point came up obliquely, in *Hyundai Heavy Industries Co. Ltd. v. Papadopoulos*.[52] There Hyundai were building a ship for a Liberian company under a contract which provided for payment by instalments as the building progressed. There was an article in the contract providing detailed machinery for cancellation in the event of late payment of an instalment. Papadopoulos was guarantor. An instalment was missed; Hyundai cancelled the contract and claimed the amount of the unpaid sum from the guarantor. The House of Lords, affirming the judgements below, held that the guarantor remained liable. Three of their Lordships also held that the Liberian company would itself have had to pay the instalment even though the whole contract had been discharged after it had fallen due. That is tantamount to saying that, had the money actually been paid, it would have been irrecoverable even though the company never got the ship. There is some tension between this and the conclusion in

---

[51] Below, p. 242 f.

[52] *Hyundai Heavy Industries Co. Ltd. v. Papadoulos* [1980] 2 All E.R. 29.

Dies.[53] But the distinction is that this was not simply a contract of sale. The company was to pay for the work of building as it was done, so that the instalments were not mere pre-payments of the price of a still to be completed ship but rather the rewards for units of work completed or in progress. In other words the case is like that of the cottage above, not like *Dies* itself. If the money had been paid, rather than merely payable, the reason for barring restitution would not have been the claimants' breach of contract but the fact that the consideration for the payments had not failed.

Even if this explanation is correct, there is in such cases still the possibility of a hidden windfall for the party who receives the pre-payment. The payor's claim to restitution is defeated because he has received something of what he paid for, but the amount of the irrecoverable pre-payment may be much greater than either the value of the partial performance or of the loss inflicted by the pre-payor's repudiatory breach. The recipient may thus retain in his hands a sum greater than he could have recovered by either his non-contractual claim to a *quantum meruit* or his contractual claim for compensatory damages. This windfall derives from the requirement of *total* failure of consideration, the reasons for which will be considered below.[54]

The position taken in these last paragraphs has been that a party in breach can recover money where the consideration for the payment has totally failed. It is always necessary to look carefully to see what the basis of the payment was. But once it does appear that the condition for retaining the money has failed the fact that it failed *15 in response to the payor's own breach does not matter.

(b) *Non-Money benefits*

What is the position of the party in breach when he has conferred a non-money benefit on the other? The technique for switching from money to benefits in kind need not be re-stated. The same law applies, subject to sensitive handling of the enrichment issue. The cases offer little hope of restitution as they stand. But it is impossible to say whether they have yet taken a final position, because the enrichment question has not been isolated or addressed. Since the plaintiff in this situation will, *ex hypothesi*, have thrown the contract over before completion, free acceptance will never be demonstrable except in relation to completed fractions of a divisible contract, or benefits still susceptible of fresh acceptance after the contract has

---

[53] See, in particular, p. 33, *per* Viscount Dilhorne; p. 40 *per* Lord Edmund Davies p. 44, *per* Lord Fraser.
[54] Below, p. 242–5.

been terminated. The cases do not explore other means by which the plaintiff in breach might confront subjective devaluation.

In *Sumpter* v. *Hedges*[55] a builder had abandoned half-completed houses on the defendant's land and also building materials lying loose. The Court of Appeal refused any *quantum meruit* for the buildings. The land-owner had no choice whether to accept or not. It was different with the materials. Being loose they could still be either rejected or accepted. *Munro* v. *Butt,*[56] forty years earlier, is almost exactly the same case. There Lord Campbell, C.J., negatived any acceptance saying: 'It may be essential to the owner to occupy the residence if it be only to pull down and replace all that has been done before. How then does mere possession raise any inference of waiver of conditions precedent of the special contract or of the entering into a new one?'[57] This approach assumes that free acceptance, and contractual free acceptance at that, is the plaintiff's only recourse. But we know, from the earlier discussion, that the plaintiff can in principle also base himself on the ground of failure of consideration combined with any viable test of enrichment.

The need to take this seriously becomes especially acute the more complete is the plaintiff's defective performance, up to the point at which he breaks the barrier of the doctrine of substantial performance.[58] Once he has 'substantially performed' he is able to bring his contractual action. So the negative result in *Sumpter* v. *Hedges* is most painful in the cases in which the performance is not quite 'substantial'. In the very centre of that group, the harshest case of all is that in which common sense would say that he has substantially performed, but, where as a matter of law, he has technically committed a repudiatory breach allowing the other to discharge the contract. It is also true that, on the crucial issue of enrichment, the gap between 'free' and 'limited' acceptance is then also very narrow.

An example of a repudiatory breach which may, none the less, be insubstantial is found in a carriage of goods by sea. If the ship deviates from the chartered voyage, the other party is entitled to end the contract, no matter how slight the deviation. Yet the goods may in the end arrive at the intended destination in good time. In *Hain Steamship Co.* v. *Tate & Lyle.,*[59] Lord Wright said:

---

[55] *Sumpter* v. *Hedges* [1898] 1 Q.B. 673; cf. *Forman & Co.* v. *S.S. Liddlesdale* [1900] A.C. 190.

[56] *Munro* v. *Butt* (1858) 8 E. & B. 738.

[57] At p. 753.

[58] *Hoenig* v. *Isaacs* [1952] 2 All E.R. 176; *Bolton* v. *Mahadeva* [1972] 1 W.L.R. 1009.

[59] *Hain Steamship Co.* v. *Tate & Lyle Ltd.* [1936] 2 All E.R. 597.

Let me put a quite possible case: A steamer carrying a cargo of frozen meat from Australia to England deviates by calling at a port outside the usual or permitted route: it is only a matter of a few hours extra steaming: no trouble ensues except the trifling delay. The cargo is duly delivered in England at the agreed port. The goods owner has had for all practical purposes the benefit of all that his contract required; he has had the advantages of the use of a valuable ship, her crew, fuel, refrigeration and appliances, canal dues, port charges, stevedoring. The shipowner may be technically a wrongdoer in the sense that he has once deviated, but otherwise over a long period he has been performing the exacting and costly duties of a carrier at sea.[60]

In that case itself the principal issue was general average contribution. A ship carrying sugar from Cuba had deviated because a message from the shipowners telling the master his next port of call failed to reach him. Contacted by radio, he doubled back. But then the ship ran aground and its cargo had to be transferred, such of it as could be saved, to another boat. Tate & Lyle were consignees. The shipowners only agreed to deliver, releasing their lien for general average, against a Lloyd's average bond and a substantial deposit in cash. The main question was whether Tate & Lyle were liable for the contribution covered by the bond, but there was also a claim for a small amount of unpaid freight. The House of Lords held that, on the facts nobody had at any stage intended that the consignees were to pay freight. It was to be paid by the charterers in New York. Because of this gratuitous intent *quoad* Tate & Lyle, the question raised by Lord Wright's example did not have to be finally decided. Had it arisen, could the shipowners, deprived of their contract by virtue of their deviation, have had a *quantum meruit* for the work done? The Court of Appeal had said that they could not. The House of Lords, *obiter,* inclined to the view that there could be no such inflexible rule but left the matter open.[61]

It is not easy to explain such a *quantum meruit.* On facts such as those advanced by Lord Wright in the hypothetical example about the Australian meat, there is no doubt that the consideration for the work fails, just as in a money case such as *Dies* v. *BIMFC.* The doubt once again relates to enrichment. If there is no free acceptance, on account of the fact that the plaintiff's breach makes the service different from that which the defendant wanted, the only explanation would seem to be that the House of Lords was willing to contemplate 'limited acceptance' as a sufficient test of enrichment

---

[60] At p. 612.
[61] At p. 603 (Lord Atkin); p. 604 (Lord Thankerton and Lord Macmillan, *conc.*); p. 612 f (Lord Wright); p. 616 (Lord Maugham).

even in a claim by a plaintiff in breach against the victim of that breach.[62] If that is right, it opens the question whether the same test should not be used even in all those cases where the performance is more than technically defective, as in *Sumpter v. Hedges.* The effect would be to soften considerably the impact of the doctrine which requires substantial performance of an entire contract before any claim can be made under that contract.[63]

There is some support for the *Hain quantum meruit* in *Societé Franco Tunisienne D'Armement* v. *Sidermar.*[64] A vessel chartered to carry a cargo of iron ore from Masulipatan in India to Genoa via Suez did the voyage via the Cape instead. The 1956 war had blocked the canal in the days immediately preceding the loading of the ship. Relying partly on the *dicta* in *Hain*, Pearson, J., allowed the ship-owners a *quantum meruit* for the much longer journey. But there are two important differences from *Hain*. First, the discharging event was frustration rather than the carriers' breach. Indeed the charterers were anxious to affirm the original contract and to pay freight for the shorter distance. Secondly, there may have been no need for any notion of limited acceptance. It seems that the charterers had full knowledge of all the facts and of the prospects for the canal from before the time when the ship was loaded and, at least from only one day after the ship sailed, knew that the shipowners were maintaining that the contract had been frustrated. In these circumstances it would probably have been possible to find a full free acceptance by the charterers. In which case the facts are taken out of the difficult category. Pearson, J.'s judgement was later overturned. But the *quantum meruit* received no further consideration. For the higher court concluded that the original contract had, after all, not been discharged.[65]

This concludes the first part of this chapter. Of its four sections the first recalled that, in the law of restitution, there can be a total failure of consideration even though the facts do reveal sufficient consideration to support the formation of a contract; the second argued that failure of contractual reciprocation is only a common species of failure of consideration, a genus which includes also the failure of non-contractual bases for the transfer of wealth; the third sought to show that, contrary to traditional usage, the ground called 'total failure of consideration' can be relied upon in relation to

---

[62] Cf. *Planché* v. *Colburn*, above, p. 232 (claim *against* the party in breach).
[63] Above, p. 220, 232.
[64] *Societé Franco Tunisienne D'Armenent* v. *Sidernar* [1961] 2 Q.B. 278.
[65] *Ocean Tramp Tankers Corporation* v. *V/O Sovfracht* [1964] 2 Q.B. 226.

enrichments other than money; the fourth aimed to establish that even a party in breach can seek restitution on the ground of total failure of consideration provided that the consideration has indeed failed and provided that he can, if he has conferred a non-money benefit, overcome the perennial difficulties surrounding the issue of *16 enrichment.

2. THE REQUIREMENT OF TOTAL FAILURE

This short section focuses on the word 'total'. There are two questions: Why must the failure be total? What counts as total failure?

(i) *Why must the failure be total?*

The easiest starting point is unexpected. Suppose that you are building me a house or installing a central heating system in my flat. Half way through, I throw you out without any justification. This gives you the right to claim a *quantum meruit* even if the contract was 'entire'. It is the one example in which a *quantum meruit* for incomplete performance is secure, being brought against a defendant who is himself in breach. We said that the best analysis is: total failure of consideration (the ground of restitution) and limited acceptance (the test of enrichment).[66] But now suppose that I had made a pre-payment. When I threw you out, you had done half the work and had received already 10 percent of the price. It has never been suggested that receipt of such a pre-payment would obstruct the *quantum meruit*; and it can be seen at once that it should not, because there is no difficulty whatever in allowing for it in the award of reasonable remuneration. This can be put in two ways. Either, simple arithmatic allows the pre-payment to be deducted from the award; or, the pre-payment can easily be given back as a condition of the full award. This shows that the requirement of *total* failure disappears when counter-restitution is easy. In other words, provided it can be said that the consideration for which the plaintiff stipulated has failed, the fact that he has received something of what he wanted will not defeat his claim to restitution so long as nothing prevents his off-setting or returning that benefit.

Suppose now that the parties are turned around. I have paid you the full price of the work. You have begun but have abandoned the project at the mid-point. Now I cannot recover my money, because

---

[66] Above, p. 232.

the consideration has not totally failed. Why? The reason is that, this way round, there are great difficulties in the way of counter-restitution; and they are the very same difficulties which are always encountered in relation to benefits in kind. The half-complete performance cannot easily be valued in money and cannot, therefore, be returned or set off so as to allow me to get back all or part of my pre-payment.

Nevertheless, it can be argued that, in this context, these difficulties of valuation should not be exaggerated and that the law should be able to reach a rule of restitution and counter-restitution even without legislative assistance. The context in which we have previously met the problem of subjective devaluation is the plaintiff's own claim to restitution for such benefits from a defendant who is unwilling to pay. It is the same when he claims money had and received and wants to off-set a benefit in kind, except in one crucial respect. That is, the general problem, of putting a value on a benefit which normally takes its value from the agreement of parties, remains the same, but the person whose subjective viewpoint is chiefly to be taken into account, namely the recipient of the benefit, is now plaintiff and is in danger of losing his pre-payment. With this effect: while still naturally anxious not to pay too much, he will not want to make a vigorous appeal to subjective devaluation, since he must make counter-restitution in order to recover any of his money. In short he is not in a position to object if the court's way out of its difficulties in the exercise of valuation is to lean heavily in favour of the defendant's view. Half a loaf is better than none.

This tactical disposition of the parties suggests that the valuation of non-money benefits should pose less of a problem in the context of counter-restitution, because a court cannot easily decline to enter on a difficulty against a litigant anxious to have all doubts resolved against him. But there is also another way of looking at the same issue. It can be analysed as involving two separate claims. I want my money; you want the value of your half-completed work. The argument of the previous section was that, even when you are in breach and have yourself precipitated the failure of consideration, the only obstacle to your using the *Planché* v. *Colburn* claim is the issue of enrichment and, in particular, the question whether, when the matter is explored, 'limited acceptance' will turn out to be a sufficient test of enrichment even against a party who has not committed a wrong. Suppose that this question were resolved in favour of your claim. There would then be nothing in the way or your success, for, as we have already seen, the *Planché* v. *Colburn* claim does not fail merely because you have received some part of your expected payment. If your claim would succeed, then necessarily mine must also do so, in respect of the difference between your *quantum meruit* and my pre-payment. A development along these lines, really going no further than a generalization of the *Planché* v. *Colburn* attitude to enrichment, would have a profound effect. It would take the whole law in this field down the path already beaten by the *Law Reform (Frustrated Contracts) Act, 1943.*[67]

This discussion has asserted that the requirement of *total* failure is an outwork of the courts' reluctance to enter on the valuation of non-money benefits. It can be objected that there is much more to it than that. Thus, there is a case for saying that one reason for exaggerating the requirements which must be satisfied before a restitutionary claim can be made on the ground of failure of consideration is to defend the notion that the normal remedy for breach of contract is compensatory damages: the more difficult it is to bring the action in unjust enrichment, the more people will regard damages for breach as the usual recourse, and the fewer will be the puzzles arising from apparently conflicting principles of recovery.

This is a dangerously blunt argument, since in many cases the claim based on failure of consideration does not compete with a claim for damages (as where the contract is discharged by frustration or where the condition for retaining the wealth is not expressed as a contractual reciprocation demanded by the transferor). Moreover, as a matter of logic the only point at which to exercise control is in answering the question whether the contract has been discharged. Until it has been discharged the only remedy can be damages for breach. For, where the consideration for a benefit is a contractual reciprocation, it cannot fail until the contract is discharged, the primary basis of the transfer being the other's obligation to perform. Once the obligation to perform is gone (unless by performance, for then the condition is fulfilled and the transfer is voluntary) it is logically too late to keep at bay either of the two principles of recovery which naturally become available to the plaintiff.

However, even if one does arrive at the stage of admitting the theoretical or logical availability to the plaintiff of two different actions, one for breach and the other for failure of consideration, one can for reasons of a non-logical kind inhibit one or other of the two. What would the policy grounds be for this artificial inhibition? The answer is that there is, superficially, a contradiction

---

[67] Below, p. 249 ff.

between the two measures of recovery growing from the two actions and that it is therefore attractive to confine the plaintiff to one or other measure, since this saves the courts from elaborate (but feasible) explanations of the duality.[67a] This possibility of artificially inhibiting one of the two actions leads us to conclude by suggesting that, quite apart from the desire to evade the difficult task of putting a money value on partial performances, one intuitive reason for the insistence on *total* failure of consideration may indeed have been that an extreme requirement of that kind cuts down the number of cases in which there can be a conflict between two measures. *'Total'* makes restitution for failure of consideration into a rarity, and a rarity, however contradictory, does not need much explanation.

(ii) *What constitutes total failure?*

Interpretative development along the lines indicated above, or legislative reform, may make this question less important; but at the moment it still has to be asked. The key to the answer is that the word 'total' is generally construed strictly and literally. But in one area artifice has entered in.

It is important to know first what was the condition upon which the defendant might retain his benefit. For it is perfectly compatible with the strict approach, which usually favours the defendant, that work done or expense incurred by him will not prevent there being a total failure of consideration unless they did constitute at least a partial fulfilment of that condition. *Fibrosa*[68] itself illustrates this. The Polish company had ordered textile machines and had paid £1000 in advance. After the frustration of the contract they asked for the money back. The English company resisted the claim on the ground, *inter alia*, that a great deal of work had already been done in making the machines ready for shipment. But the Polish company nevertheless recovered. It was a contract of sale, c.i.f. Gdynia. It was not a contract for work and materials. The work to be done to make the machines was thus merely preliminary. The basis of the payment was that the payor should receive the machines themselves.

But once the defendant has done something which is not preliminary to but part of the performance of the condition it can no longer be said that the consideration has wholly failed, unless the plaintiff can put him back into his original position. It is here that

---

[67a] Cf. Lord Mansfield's discussion of *Dutch* v. *Warren* in his judgement in *Moses* v. *Macferlan* (1760) 2 Burr. 1005, 1013.

[68] *Fibrosa Case* [1943] A.C. 32.

need arises for an expansion of pecuniary counter-restitution. For the courts' reluctance to value partial performances means that the possibility of any giving back, so as to re-establish total failure, is very limited. Services rendered cannot be given back. The enjoyment of corporeal things over time is in the same case. Even the corporeal things themselves will often have been consumed before the need for giving back becomes apparent. So once the condition begins to be performed there is not much chance of restitution.

In *Whincup* v. *Hughes*[69] the plaintiff apprenticed his son to a watchmaker. He paid a premium for an apprenticeship which was to last six years. After one year the watchmaker died. Nothing of the premium could be recovered because the consideration had not totally failed. What if the master had died after just one month or one week? The answer would have been the same. In *Hunt* v. *Silk*[70] the plaintiff contracted for a lease to be executed within ten days. The premises in question were also to be repaired by the landlord. The plaintiff paid £10 and was let into possession. The repairs were not done and at the end of the ten days the lease had not been executed. So after some further days of protest Hunt accepted the repudiation and left. But he could not recover his £10. The consideration had not totally failed. Arguments have been advanced to water down the strictness of the *Hunt* v. *Silk* approach and to explain the case as turning an affirmation, as though Hunt only failed because he did not throw the contract over soon enough. But, beyond a sensible application of the *de minimis* rule, that is not the best path forward. A diluted notion of total failure would be merely confusing. An expansion of counter-restitution in money would make such stratagems unnecessary.

Total failure does not coincide with discharge. The termination of a contract may remain possible when it is no longer open to claim that the consideration has totally failed. In *Yeoman Credit Ltd.* v. *Apps*[71] there was a hire purchase contract for a car which was unroadworthy when delivered. It suffered from a whole series of defects. It was only five years old but brakes, clutch, and steering were defective, and it took one and a half hours to get three or four miles. Apps struggled on, complaining and trying to get things put right. He paid three monthly instalments. Then he gave up and rejected the car. He was held to have been entitled to do so, but he could not say that the consideration had failed. There would have

---

[69] *Whincup* v. *Hughes* (1871) L.R. 6 C.P. 78.
[70] *Hunt* v. *Silk* (1804) 5 East 449.
[71] *Yeoman Credit Ltd.* v. *Apps* [1962] 2 Q.B. 508.

been a total failure if he had rejected the car at the beginning. But he had tried to keep on with the contract and had had the possession and use of the car, such as it was, for several months.

One series of cases seems to lean the other way, favouring the plaintiff and denaturing the notion of total failure. Starting with *Rowland* v. *Divall*[72] it has been held that where the object of the contract is to confer title on the payor, as under sale or hire purchase, the consideration totally fails if the property does not pass. In the leading case Rowland was a dealer in cars. He bought the car in question from Divall for £334 in May, 1922. At the end of July he sold it on to a Colonel Railsdon for £400. In September the police took it from Railsdon because it had been stolen before Divall had bought it. Rowland repaid Railsdon his £400 and re-bought the car from the insurance company which had paid the former owner's loss arising from the theft. This second purchase cost him £260. He then turned against his first seller, Divall, and claimed back the price of £334 on the ground that the consideration had totally failed. Bray, J., held that there had been no total failure, because Rowland and Railsdon had had the use of the vehicle for four months. But the Court of Appeal unanimously reversed him. Atkin, L.J., said:

In these circumstances can it make any difference that the buyer has received and has used the goods before he found out the there was a breach of condition? To my mind it makes no difference at all. The buyer accepted them upon the representation by the seller that he had the right to deal with the goods, but, inasmuch as the seller had no right and could convey to the buyer no right to use the goods at all, the seller cannot say. 'You have got a benefit under the contract which you have not become entitled to, and that must be taken into account.' It seems to me that in these circumstance the buyer has not received any part of that which he is entitled to receive. He has not received the goods, he has not received the right to possession of the goods, and in those circumstances there has been a complete failure of consideration.[73]

'He has not received the goods.' Physically he had received them, but he had not received the right to hold them; and that was enough. There have been more extreme cases since. In *Butterworth* v. *Kingsway Motors Ltd.*[74] the plaintiff won a similar claim. Nearly a year after buying his car from the defendants the plaintiff discovered that he had no title to it. It had previously been sold by a hirer under a hire purchase agreement, but, despite the sale, the hirer had

[72] *Rowland* v. *Divall* [1923] 2 K.B. 500; 129 L.T. 757.
[73] *Rowland* v. *Divall* (1923) 129 L.T. 757, 760. The same passage in the *Law Reports* is slightly less fully stated.
[74] *Butterworth* v. *Kingsway Motors Ltd.* [1954] 1. W.L.R. 1286.

continued paying the instalments. Very shortly after Butterworth lodged his claim against Kingsway Motors, the hirer paid the last instalment and thus fed all the titles dependent on his own. So if Butterworth had not moved quickly he would have had nothing to complain about. As it was he had a year's free motoring.

These cases could be understood as construing the condition for retaining the money as the receipt of title, as much as to say that the enjoyment which comes with title is as irrelevantly consequential as the work done in *Fibrosa* was irrelevantly preliminary. But a simpler way of putting it is to say that the buyer is relieved of the need to make counter-restitution because the benefit which he ought to give up is one which the seller had no right to confer: it was not the seller's to give; so he cannot expect it back.[75] Nevertheless, the Law Commission provisionally recommended that the buyer, when recovering the price on the ground of failure of consideration, should give credit for the non-money benefit consisting in his enjoyment of the car over the period of his possession. This provisional recommendation is to receive further consideration in relation to
★17   other problems arising in the context of goods supplied.[76]

It cannot be said the court's attitude to defects of title has been completely consistent. In *Linz* v. *Electric Wire Co. of Palestine*[77] the plaintiff bought shares which were nullities because issued without the necessary authority. It was held that she had not suffered a total failure of consideration. She had sold on to a third party (as had the plaintiff in *Rowland* v. *Divall*), but it is not easy to see why such a defective sale to another person should have any bearing on the question whether the consideration for payment under the first contract had or had not failed.

There is a hypothetical case at the extreme end of the spectrum. It has never been tested. Suppose you sell me food or drink which belongs to a third party, just as the car did in *Rowland* v. *Divall*. I eat the food and drink the wine. Can I still say that the consideration has failed? If I can it is a good case of having cake and eating it. But perhaps the maxim *consumptos suos facit* produces an opposite conclusion. The food and drink become mine by consumption; fortuitously I do at last become owner so that the condition is fulfilled though not by your act.

---

[75] Cf. *Goff and Jones,* 375 f. 'But it appears that he did not enjoy that benefit as the seller's expense; the seller had no right to any recompense for the intermediate use of the car because he had not been deprived of the use of a car to which he had title.'

[76] Working Paper No. 65 (1975), para. 79; see now Law Com, 121 (1983) para. 1.12; and below, p. 423 ff.

[77] *Linz* v. *Electric Wire Co. of Palestine* [1948] A.C. 371.

3. LEGISLATIVE REFORMS

Statute has modified the common law principles in some areas. Much the most important change has been made in relation to frustration.

(i) *The Law Reform (Frustrated Contracts) Act, 1943*

Hard upon *Fibrosa*, this Act made considerable changes not in the doctrine of frustration but in the regime of restitution after the discharge. It applies to most contracts, but not to all.[78] Until recently there had been no litigation to help in its interpretation, but now we have *B.P. Exploration Co. (Libya) Ltd. v. Hunt (No. 2)*,[79] happily set down at first instance for Robert Goff, J., as he then was. That great case chiefly concerns the statutory provisions for restitution in respect of non-money benefits.

The basic principle of the Act was to abandon the approach based on total failure of consideration and to adopt instead the notion of mutual restitution. If it is possible to draw a distinction between 'mutual restitution' and 'restitution with counter-restitution', the former may be the more accurate, because, for the situation in which one party has paid money and the other has conferred a benefit in kind, the dominant scheme of the Act really contemplates two separate claims. Chiefly because of *B.P. v. Hunt* it is convenient to consider non-money benefits first, though this inverts the order of the Act itself.

(a) *Non-money benefits: s. 1 (3)*

Where any party to the contract has, by reason of anything done by any other party thereto in, or for the purpose of, the performance of the contract, obtained a valuable benefit (other than a payment of money . . .) before the time of discharge, there shall be recoverable from him by the said other party such sum (if any), not exceeding the value of the said benefit to the party obtaining it, as the court considers just, having regard to all the circumstances of the case and, in particular,-

(a) the amount of any expenses incurred before the time of the discharge by the benefited party in, or for the purpose of, the performance of the contract, including any sums paid or payable by him to any other party in pursuance of

---

[78] Section 2 (5) exempts (a) some charterparties and all contracts for carriage of goods by sea, (b) contracts of insurance, and (c) contracts for the sale of specific goods which are frustrated by destruction of the goods before the risk passes to the buyer.

[79] *B.P. Exploration Co. (Libya) Ltd. v. Hunt (No. 2)* [1979] 1 W.L.R. 783. The judgment of Robert Goff, J., was affirmed in the Court of Appeal and in the House of Lords (where only narrow points were taken) but remains the leading exposition of the working of the Act. All three stages are reported together at [1982] 1 All E.R. 925.

the contract and retained or recoverable by that party under the last foregoing subsection, and

(b) the effect, in relation to the said benefit, of the circumstances giving rise to the frustration of the contract.

This sub-section says what is to be done about non-money benefits. The court has a discretion to award a just sum. There is a maximum above which the just sum cannot go. And there are matters which have to be taken into account. The main issues reduce to two questions: What is the maximum award? What is the just sum? Before examining these, it is convenient to give a brief account of the facts of *B.P. v. Hunt.*

In outline the facts of the case were these. Hunt obtained an oil concession from the Libyan government in 1957. It related to a given area of desert in which there might or might not be commercial quantitites of oil. Hunt did not have resources to exploit the concession himself. He made a contract with BP under which they undertook the exploration and, if they found viable quantities, the extraction. Hunt gave up to BP one half of his concession. In return BP were to do all the work of exploration and also, even before it was known whether anything would come of the venture, were to pay him money and oil (called 'farm-in' contributions). But then, if and when a field was found and came on stream, Hunt was to reimburse one half of BP's entire speculative investment by giving up three eighths of his half of the oil until by that means BP had recouped not merely 100 percent but 125 percent of its input referable to Hunt's half of the concession. So, having borne the enormous risk of there being no oil, BP were ultimately to be allowed to repay themselves from the fruits of successful production. In the event BP's investment was not in vain. They found a giant oilfield.

The agreement was made in 1960. The oil came on stream early in 1967. Late in 1971 the frustrating event happened. The Libyan Government expropriated BP's interest. Afterwards, in 1973, Hunt's interest was taken too. At the time of the discharge, in 1971, BP had been reimbursed with oil to the extent of about two-thirds of the total number of barrels due to them. Between 1971 and 1973 when Hunt himself was expropriated production was low but Hunt nevertheless received a substantial quantity of oil.

The maximum award   The maximum is the value of the non-money benefit obtained by the recipient before the time of discharge. Before the Act or without the Act, this would be a case in which it would have been difficult to persuade the court to put a money value on the benefit. The Act requires it to be valued. As a result of the statute the courts are therefore in a position which they might have reached interpretatively, either by developing the 'limited acceptance' test of enrichment or, more radically, by going over to an objective approach. At all events this is the first major change: the non-money benefit must be valued. The Act, and the leading case decided under it, have a great and general importance for the law of restitution in that they show what kind of questions arise and what kind of difficulties have to be faced when the courts do embark on the valuation of non-money benefits.

On the facts of *B.P.* v. *Hunt*, Goff, J., concluded that Hunt had received a non-money benefit which should be valued at $85 million. He arrived at this figure by holding that the benefit to be valued was not the day-to-day work done by B.P. in looking for and extracting oil, but was the end-product of that work, namely the enhancement of Hunt's concession, transformed from a mere hope into an asset of almost incalculable value. However, that enhanced asset had itself been curtailed by the frustrating event. Taking the event into account as required by s. 1 (3) (b), the asset to be valued was to be regarded not as the transformed concession itself but as the oil actually obtained by Hunt from the time when the field came on stream. It was then necessary to make an apportionment between the value attributable to BP's performance (as the subsection requires) and the value attributable to Hunt's ownership of the concession and his enterprise in obtaining and managing it. That apportionment was done roughly, on a fifty-fifty basis.[80] Hence Hunt's valuable benefit was half of all the oil he had obtained.

This part of Goff, J.s, judgment does not finally settle all the questions which can arise in relation to the maximum award. There are three cases which present problems: work which does have an end-product but one which is eccentric in the sense that, although wanted by the recipient, it would be valueless on the market; work which has no end-product; work whose valuable end-product is destroyed by the frustrating event.

Goff, J. indicates that an eccentric end-product should not be regarded as valueless for the purpose of the maximum award. The example used is the incomplete decoration of rooms to an expensive standard but in execrable taste.[81] The value of the property might

---

[80] With the assistance of a 'fair and probably generous' solution proposed by B.P. See *B.P.* v. *Hunt* [1979] 1 W.L.R. 783, 816.

[81] Ibid. 803.

even be reduced by such work. Nevertheless the decoration should be valued, using the contract price as a guide. This is not incompatible with the traditionally subjective orientation of the law towards enrichment, and is tantamount to the admission of 'limited acceptance' as a test of value even against an innocent recipient.[82] It also suggests that there can be no absolute requirement that, in order to qualify as a valuable non-money benefit, the plaintiff's work must have an end-product. For there is no purpose in insisting on an end-product if one which is eccentric and worthless will suffice. Whitened coal might be said to be the end-product of coal whitening, whereas book burning arguably leaves no product at all. It would be absurd to say that a maximum award can be calculated for whitened coal simply because a visible end-product can be identified when the work is done. It would lead to a ridiculous inventiveness in the identification of end-products. Are empty shelves the product of book burning? This kind of absurdity points to the conclusion that, in the case of work which leaves no end-product, the valuable benefit must be the labour itself.

Goff, J., does not clearly say that the labour itself can, or that it cannot, be valued for the purpose of establishing the maximum award. He certainly accepts that 'in an appropriate case'[83] the valuation should be made of the end-product and not the day-to-day work, and that is what he actually does in relation to Hunt. The words 'in an appropriate case' indicate that, in other circumstances, the labour itself would be valued, the waste-disposal, demolition, advice, market research, and so on. On the other hand there are some indications that Goff, J., took the view that the Act had regrettably failed to provide that the labour itself might be counted as the valuable benefit.[84] This doubt ought to be resolved in favour of allowing the labour to be valued even where it does not leave any end-product. That would not only be consistent with the judge's willingness to value eccentric end-products; it would also agree with the words of the Act itself, which requires that the recipient should have received the valuable benefit *before* the time of discharge, not that he should hold it at the time of discharge. If I am working on management advice for you, or if, week-by-week, I am disposing of your rubbish under an entire contract for an undivided period of time, my labour is a marketable commodity which I am conferring upon you. If the contract is then frustrated before my report is

---

[82] Above, p. 232.
[83] *B.P.* v. *Hunt* [1979] 1 W.L.R. 783, 801.
[84] Ibid., 802 E, F, 803 D.

written or my undivided period of time has run there should be no doubt that you have received a benefit *before* the time of discharge, even though you have nothing tangible or visible to show for it at the time of discharge. To reach any other conclusion would be to decide that the Act had taken an arbitrary distinction between manufacturing and non-manufacturing labour. A large part of the population markets its labour in non-manufacturing (i.e. service) industries. It would be perverse to maintain that such people are not conferring valuable benefits on those who enter into contracts with them. The fact that such people do obtain employment shows that their labour is, in the words of the Act, 'a valuable benefit other than the payment of money'.

The third difficult case is where there is some end-product but, as in *Appleby* v. *Myers*,[85] it is destroyed by the frustrating event. If it were right that the particular circumstances set out in paragraphs (a) and (b) must be taken into account only in relation to the maximum award,[86] which is the non-discretionary element in the calculation, and not in calculating the just sum, which does lie in the judge's discretion, then there would indeed be no hope for the plaintiff in the *Appleby* v. *Myers* situation. For, although he has, *before* the time of the discharge, both worked for the defendant and conferred an end-product upon him (he has built, and he has by building made half a house), yet the effect, under paragraph (b), of the circumstances giving rise to the frustration is absolutely to destroy the benefit. Hence the maximum award, on that assumption, must be zero. But if, as seems closer to the wording of the subsection itself, paragraph (b) can be taken at the discretionary phase, the effect of circumstances which deprive the defendant of an opportunity to enjoy the benefit conferred on him prior to the discharge need not be such as to reduce the award to nil. If I pay you money by mistake and, as you are walking home with it, you are mugged, your loss of the enrichment once received does not extinguish my claim. So here if you were enriched before the fire, the fact the the statute says that the effect of the fire on your enjoyment must be taken into consideration does not mean that the award must be nothing at all. Though the general principle of the Act is not to share losses, that idea could be used at this point as a basis for the exercise of discretion.

The just sum   The subsection says that, within the maximum, the

---

[85] Above, p. 230 f.
[86] So Goff, J., at *B.P.* v. *Hunt* [1979] 1 W.L.R. 783, 801, 803 f.

court may award the sum which it considers just. The Court of Appeal in *B.P.* v. *Hunt* attached great weight to the freedom of the judge's discretion.[87] While on the one hand this shows a disappointing lack of interest in settling the principles on which the discretion should be exercised, on the other it serves to confirm the unusual status of the judgement at first instance, which remains the only guide to the operation of this part of the Act. In exercising his discretion Goff, J., had to ask himself two main questions: What basic principle should be applied? What rôle, if any, should the terms of the original contract have?

As for the basic principle, he said that the aim to be pursued in fixing the just sum was the prevention of the unjust enrichment of one party at the expense of the other.[88] Hence what was required was that the party who had been enriched should give up so much of his enrichment as had been obtained at the expense of the other. The just sum would therefore be the value, up to the figure of the maximum award, of the other's input. In making this assertion Goff, J., succeeded in bringing the statute back into line with the obscured pattern of the common law. For the scheme which he recognises in the subsection is essentially an extension of the *quantum meruit* for an incomplete performance which *Planché* v. *Colburn*[89] allows after discharge for breach. What *Planché* allows after breach, the Act allows after frustration.

Between the *Planché* claim and the statutory scheme the one difference of apparent importance is the statute's insistence on a two-tier approach: first, a maximum award; then, a just sum. But this difference is only capable of becoming real and substantial if, contrary to the argument advanced above, the courts insist that the maximum award must be fixed by reference to the valuable end-product left with the plaintiff rather than by reference to the labour of creating it. Suppose the scheme of the subsection were applied to the facts of *Planché* v. *Colburn* itself. The plaintiff had done research and writing but had not given the defendant any manuscript. So, if only an end-product can be valued, the maximum award would be zero. On the other hand, if the daily labour done under the contract before the time of discharge can count as the benefit to be valued, the maximum award and the *quantum meruit* become one and the same sum. For the same labour which is the benefit to the defendant is also the input of the plaintiff, just as

---

[87] *B.P.* v. *Hunt* [1981] 2 W.L.R. 232, 242 f.
[88] *B.P.* v. *Hunt* [1979] 1 W.L.R. 783, 805.
[89] *Planché* v. *Colburn* (1831) 8 Bing. 14, L.J.C.P. 7.

though the plaintiff paid the defendant a sum of money. So, if labour can be counted as the valuable benefit, the two-tier approach adopted by the subsection turns out to be only a cautious way of ensuring that the issues of 'enrichment' and 'at the expense of' are separately addressed, as they always ought to be. The temptation might otherwise be to award the full value of the end-product (if any there be) without paying attention to the quantum of the plaintiff's input.

As for the rôle of the dead contract, Goff, J., held that it was an indispensable aid to fixing the value of the *quantum meruit* which the plaintiff ought to get.[90] The contractual reward was evidence of the reasonable value of the plaintiff's input. But terms of the contract which reflected other considerations than the value of the work should be rejected. In general, the idiosyncracies of the contract should be considered carefully in order to draw the right inference as to the proper non-contractual payment for the benefit. There were two aspects of the contract with Hunt which had to be rejected. The provision for 125 percent reimbursement was not a reflection of the value of the input but a provision for interest. It represented the fact that Hunt did not have to pay his contribution until years after the outlay made by B.P. Goff, J., held that the time value of money was a benefit too remote from that which he had to value. Hence he had to ignore the 125 percent and revert to a principle of flat reimbursement at 100 per cent.[91] Secondly, after the oil came on stream the parties had settled up the amount of Hunt's liability in a fixed number of barrels rather than a fixed sum of money. This meant that both parties took a speculative risk on the movement of the market in oil. In the event the price went up, so that, in money terms, Hunt's fixed debt in oil meant that he had to pay much more. But Goff, J., treated this varied provision as irrelevant to the calculation of BP's *quantum meruit.* It was explicable simply as a speculation. The safest course was to abandon the mode of payment envisaged by the contract and to concentrate on the sum to be reimbursed.

In the end, therefore, the 'just sum' which represented the reasonable value of BP's input was the same sum in money as Hunt would have had to make good in oil under the unvaried contract, shorn, however, of the obligation to make it good to the tune of 125 percent. What he had already paid in oil had to be deducted. Since different currencies applied to different items the final figure

---

[90] *B.P.* v. *Hunt* [1979] 1 W.L.R. 783, 805, 821 f.
[91] Ibid. 825 f.

was $15 823 plus £8 922 060, considerably less than the approxima-
tely $85 million at which the maximum award had been valued.

Much of the apparent complexity in this operation arises from the
details of the exercise of valuation. The principles enunciated are not
difficult. I am building a house for you. The contract is frustrated
when it is partly finished. I am entitled by way of 'just sum' to a
quantum meruit for my partial performance. The contract can be
used, with discrimination, as evidence for the value of my work. The
award must not in the end exceed the amount of the valuable benefit
received by you. Consideration must be given to all the
circumstances and in particular to the matters in paragraph (a), your
expenses, and (b), the effect on the benefit of the events causing the
frustration. There is still room for argument whether these matters
should be taken as bearing on the maximum or the just sum.

(b) *Money received: s. 1 (2)*

All sums paid or payable to any party in pursuance of the contract before the
time when the parties were discharged (in this Act referred to as 'the time of
discharge') shall, in the case of sums so paid, be recoverable from him as money
received by him for the use of the party by whom the sums were paid, and, in
the case of sums so payable, cease to be payable:

Provided that, if the party to whom the sums were so paid or payable
incurred expenses before the time of discharge in, or for the purpose of, the
performance of the contract, the court may, if it considers it just to do so
having regard to all the circumstances of the case, allow him to retain or, as the
case may be, recover the whole or any part of the sums so paid or payable, not
being an amount in excess of the expenses so incurred.

This is more straightforward. It does not have the two-tier structure
of s. 1 (3). Where money has been received, the enrichment of the
defendant payee is also the just sum to be returned. In *B.P.* v. *Hunt*,
the exploration and the development of the concession raised issues
under subsection (3), as we have seen. But one benefit conferred by
BP on Hunt was a payment of $2 000 000 (the farm-in money)
during the early stages, before the field was discovered. At first
instance that sum was not disentangled from all the non-money
benefits which enhanced the value of Hunt's concession. This point
was picked up by Bridge, L.J., in the Court of Appeal. Amendments
were allowed to correct what was described as a mere matter of
form. The claim to this sum as money received to BP's use was
transferred to s. 1 (2).[92]

---

[92] *B.P.* v. *Hunt* [1981] 1 W.L.R. 232, 240.

There are two important statutory departures from the common law position. First, there is no requirement of total failure of consideration. The money is recoverable even if the plaintiff has received half or three-quarters of the benefit for which he stipulated. It is left to the defendant who has conferred such a benefit to claim for it under the proviso to this subsection or independently under subsection (3). Secondly, there is the very existence of the proviso itself. This discretionary allowance for expenses is not easy to integrate into the framework of common law principle. So far as the expense incurred is capable of being understood, from the other side, as having conferred an enrichment on the plaintiff, the proviso allows counter-restitution. And to that extent its work can equally be done independently under subsection (3). But where the allowable expenses are not correspondingly enriching, on what basis are they recoverable?

In *B.P. v. Hunt*, Goff, J., said that the rationale of the allowance for expenses in s. 1 (3) (a) is to be found in the defence of change of position.[93] Presumably he would say the same of the proviso to s. 1 (2). The defendant is *prima facie* bound to make restitution of the whole enrichment received at the expense of the plaintiff but is allowed to show that in reliance on the receipt or the expectation of the receipt he incurred a loss to himself. This is a brilliant suggestion, and it is an important part of the reintegration of the Act into the common law. But it has some rough edges. The subsection envisages pre-payments, whether required by the contract or merely proffered by the payor. In the latter case, where the payor has chosen to pay in advance, it is difficult to say that expense by the other is made in reliance on the payment, especially if made before the payment was received. Without the element of reliance it is a question whether there is a sufficient nexus between enrichment and expenditure on which to base a defence of change of position.

Moreover, not all the allowable expenses appear to be explicable in terms of change of position. The expenses must have been incurred 'before the time of discharge' and 'in or for the purpose of' performance. The time requirement is uncontroversial; and 'in' performance is clear enough. But 'for the purpose of' performance is capable of being carried very far back. The equipment bought by a buisness might be said to be 'for the purpose of' performing all its contracts. Section 1 (4) says that 'overhead expenses' and 'work or services performed personally' are to be included under the head of expenses allowance within the proviso. In the light of this extended

[93] *B.P. v. Hunt* [1979] 1 W.L.R. 783, 804.

range evidently intended for the proviso, it would seem difficult to integrate it into the common law picture through the defence of change of position, and unsafe to say that the discretion should be settled on that narrower basis.

In the context of expenses, it is worth noting that, in a case in which the contract contains no provision for a pre-payment and in which none happens to be forthcoming, there is no avenue by which the party incurring the expenses can make a claim unless they happen to be expenses which confer a non-money enrichment on the other. That is, if he cannot bring himself within s. 1 (3), the party incurring such expenses cannot claim at all. This omission tends to confirm Goff, J.s, view that the principle underlying the Act is the recovery of unjust enrichment. Any independent claim to expenses of that kind would be unintelligible in terms of that principle.

(ii) *The Apportionment Act 1870*

This Act may offer assistance to some who remain unpaid after incomplete performance of an entire contract or of one portion of a divisible contract. For example, if a man is to do work at £500 per month and his contract is discharged after two weeks' work, the Act allows him, at the end of the month, to claim a daily rate *pro rata*. But its operation can be excluded. Section 7 says that it shall not apply to a case where it has been 'expressly stipulated than no apportionment shall take place'.

The character of the Act can be inferred from its preamble: 'Whereas rents and some other periodical payments are not at common law apportionable (like interest on money lent) in respect of time . . .'. Section 2 then says that certain payments 'shall, like interest on money lent, be considered as accruing from day-to-day, and shall be apportionable in respect of time accordingly'. The payments named are 'rents, annuities, dividends, and other periodical payments in the nature of income'. Section 5 expressly makes 'annuities' include salaries and pensions.

The scope of the Act has not been much explored. So far as it makes reference to premature discharge it speaks quite generally and neutrally of determination by re-entry, death, or otherwise. Hence there is no obvious justification for drawing a line between discharge by the claimant's breach and by other events.[94] It is not completely

---

[94] But see *Moriarty* v. *Regent's Garage & Engineering Co.* [1921] 1 K.B. 423, where Lush, J. inclines to the contrary position.

clear, quite apart from the danger of a restrictive *eiusdem generis* interpretation, what can amount to a periodical payment in the nature of income. Presumably it must be a payment made referable to a period of time, so that '*£x* for a year's carpentry' would count, '*£x* for making a wardrobe within one year' would not.

(iii) *Sale of Goods Act 1979, s. 30 (1)*

If the seller makes a short delivery, say of 75 instead of 100 bags of fertilizer, the buyer is entitled to reject the whole lot. If he accepts, then under s. 30 (1) he has to pay at the contract rate. Often this acceptance will amount to a free acceptance, with full knowledge of the facts. But, if for example the farmer applies the fertilizer to his fields and only realises afterwards that his full order for 100 is not being honoured, it is difficult to say that he has freely accepted.

(iv) *Proposals by the Law Commission*

Where benefits are transferred conditionally, the most common form which the condition takes is a stipulation for a contractual reciprocation. Where that reciprocation fails, then, so long as it fails totally, restitution follows. At common law this proposition is most secure where the defendant has received money and has, by his own breach, made himself responsible for the failure. But the earlier argument tried to show, (a) that the character of the benefit received by the defendant makes no other difference except that, where the benefit received is not money, the plaintiff finds it difficult to say that the defendant has been enriched and to express the measure of that enrichment in money, (b) that in principle the ground for restitution is not affected by the reason for the failure, whether breach by the defendant, frustration, or breach by the plaintiff, and (c) that insistence on *total* failure is an outwork of the reluctance to value non-money benefits which, that reluctance once overcome, could give way to either restitution with counter-restitution or, completely separating one claim from another, to mutual restitution. All this at common law. Then we saw that the statutory regime for restitution after discharge by frustration has been brought closely into line with the basic common law position by Goff, J's, judgement in *B.P. v. Hunt*.

Proposals first made by the Law Commission in 1975 can be seen in the same light. These proposals were made in the working paper called 'Pecuniary Restitution on Breach of Contract'.[95] The central concern of the working paper was the situation typified by *Sumpter* v. *Hedges*,[96] where the contract was terminated as a result of the plaintiff builder's breach. He was unable to recover anything for the incomplete houses taken over by the defendant. The main proposal was that such a plaintiff should be entitled to payment. The amount of the payment was to be calculated very much on the lines used by Goff, J., in the BP case. The contract was to be used, sensitively, to overcome the difficulties of valuation. And the judge was to have a discretion to disallow an award in favour of a cynical contract breaker who threw over the contract to seek profit elsewhere.[97]

The next proposal concerned the recovery of money received (called 'money paid' in the working paper, in defiance of history). Here the suggested reform was that a party in breach who had received a payment should have to make restitution even if he had gone some way to performing his part. Counter-restitution would be effected in his favour by allowing him to retain a sum representing the value of any benefit conferred by him on the payor by virtue of his incomplete performance. For example, a builder who had received payment for work abandoned at the mid-point would have to give back the money he had received, subject to an allowance for the value of the half-finished work. There would, in other words, be restitution of the money on the ground of failure of consideration, notwithstanding the fact that the failure was not total. Against that claim for money received for a consideration which had failed, the plaintiff would have to allow a *quantum meruit* for the non-money benefit conferred upon him.[98]

Changes of this kind are in line with the underlying structure of the common law and of the statutory scheme which now applies after frustration. However, it is very undesirable that slightly different schemes should be introduced for different species of discharge. There are three discharging events which have to be contemplated: plaintiff's breach, frustration, and defendant's breach. The regime controlling restitution after these events also has to extend to those other failures of consideration which are not failures of contractual reciprocation.[99] From the standpoint of the law of restitution only one species of causative event is in question in these

---

[95] The Law Commission, *Working Paper No. 65.*
[96] *Sumpter* v. *Hedges* [1898] 1 Q.B. 673; cf. *Bolton* v. *Mahadeva* [1972] 1 W.L.R. 1009.
[97] *Ibid.*, paras. 9–25, 39–47.
[98] *Ibid.*, paras. 48–56.
[99] Above, p. 223 ff.

superficially different manifestations. That single event can be called 'conditional enrichment' or 'qualified transfer'. It happens where one person transfers value to another and qualifies his intent that that other should be enriched by specifying what must be or become the case in order for his intent to become absolute. Then, if the specified basis of enrichment fails, restitution follows. So far as possible the unity of that single area of restitution must be maintained. If it is not, the structure of principle which makes for coherence and intelligibility will be lost in a mass of disparate detail.

This danger, that piecemeal statutory reform will detach the law from the principles implicit in the cases, is all the more likely to eventuate if the proposals to which the 1975 Working Paper has now given rise do succeed in reaching the statute book. In a 1983 Report[1] the Law Commission has heavily modified its provisional recommendations, especially in relation to the position of a party who has made an advance payment of money, with the effect that the proposals now contemplate an asymmetrical regime for plaintiffs claiming restitution in respect of money, and plaintiffs claiming in respect of non-money benefits.

We have seen that a plaintiff who has paid in advance for a non-money benefit can recover his payment at common law if the consideration fails *totally*; while, if he gets something of what he paid for, he is remitted to a claim for compensatory damages. The divergent measures are most noticeable in practice in the case in which the payor has made a bad bargain. Where the consideration totally fails he is saved. Where it does not fail totally, his being remitted solely to a claim for compensation will mean that he loses the element of overpayment.[2] The fundamental reason for insisting on *total* failure has been, we said, the difficulty of putting a value on the incomplete performance by the party who received the payment of money, which difficulty impedes the counter-restitution which the payor would have to make in order to obtain restitution of his money. Alongside this fundamental reason — fundamental in the sense that it is based on the logic of restitutionary principles — lies another reason for the same restrictive rule, namely the policy of making compensatory damages the normal consequence of breach of contract and of avoiding apparent conflicts between different measures of recovery (even where, by alternative analysis, different

---

[1] Law Com. No. 121, (July 1983): *Law of Contract: Pecuniary Restitution on Breach of Contract.* As usual, the report included a draft Bill for an Act to be called the *Law Reform (Lump Sum Contracts) Act, 1983.*

[2] Above, p. 246.

causative events are implicit in the same facts).[3] The Law
Commission now proposes that the common law position should be
maintained, the payor thus being entitled to restitution only where
the consideration fails totally.[4] The reason is not, or is not chiefly,
to do with valuation under the head of enrichment; it is the policy
reason just referred to, arising under the head of factors which
inhibit restitutionary claims which are in principle available.[5] What is
said is that the court should not be given the power to value the part-
performance in this situation, for the reason that the payor should be
held to his bargain.[6] Once this policy reason for excluding the
restitutionary claim is brought out into the open and accepted, it
becomes difficult to say why the payor should be allowed to recover
even when he has suffered a *total* failure of consideration. When the
matter is considered wholly separately from the valuation problem,
as is possible now that the valuation of partial performance is
regarded as being in principle a viable operation, the conflict between
different bases of recovery is no less where the payor has received
nothing than in the case in which he has received something for
which, if valuation were allowed, he could make counter-restitution.

So far as concerns the party who has conferred a non-money
benefit, the Report abides by the principal recommendation of the
Working Paper. Whether under an entire contract or within the
severable units of a contract which is not entire, the party who has
conferred a benefit on the other by an incomplete performance is to
be given a right to restitution in money.[7] Hence, a builder who leaves
behind half a house, or an incomplete central heating system, will be
able to claim the value of what he has done. The mode of valuing the
benefit is different from that proposed in the Working Paper. The
contract price is, in the first instance, to be put aside. 'It should be
made absolutely clear that what is being valued is the benefit
obtained by the innocent party: viz. the extent to which he had been
enriched. Since our purpose in providing a remedy is to reflect the
enrichment of the innocent party, it is this which is the relevant
measure of compensation and the value of the benefit should not be
based on the contract price.'[8] Where there is an end-product of work
done, it seems that the value of the end-product is to be taken, rather

---

[3] Above, p. 245.

[4] Law Com. 121, para. 3.11.

[5] Above, p. 221.

[6] Law Com. 121, para. 3.8.

[7] Paras., 2.33, 2.77; draft Bill, clauses 1 (1) (d) and 1 (5) The 'cynical' contract breaker
is no longer to be excluded: para., 2.60.

[8] Para., 2.52.

than the value of the services themselves,[9] so that, if the end-product is worth less than the work, that lesser sum alone will count as the value of the benefit conferred, but the Report lacks any theoretical discussion of this point. It is certainly not the case that services which produce no end-product are intended to be excluded altogether from the notion of a benefit capable of giving rise to the new restitutionary right. Once the exercise of valuation has been done, independently of the contract, a new mechanism is to be used to prevent the plaintiff from recovering more than the contract rate: the sum actually awarded must be reduced, if need be, so as not to exceed 'such proportion of the sum payable on completion as is equal to the proportion that what has been done under the contract bears to what was promised to be done'.[10] Obviously, it will often be very difficult to say what proportion of the work has been done, since input and output are not always evenly distributed over time. But, in the valuation of non-money benefits difficulties of that kind are endemic. The Commission's willingness to embrace those problems in the case of the non-money plaintiff serves to highlight the policy-motivated asymmetry of its proposal in respect of money plaintiffs. In order to get restitution of their payments, those plaintiffs want to make counter-restitution in money of non-money benefits received. The valuation problems are the same, but they are not to be allowed to tackle them in the counter-restitution context.

If one were asked to put a finger on the single reason why the law relating to 'failure of consideration' is so difficult, perhaps the best answer would be to point to the fact that the Law Commission's Report comes out under the main heading 'Law of Contract'. The tacit assumption is always, not only in the Report but deeply in the thinking of all common lawyers, that only one major causal event (contract) is in question. This is the silent damage done by centuries of 'implied contract' thinking.[11] There are two events involved, not only contract (or, more accurately here, breach of contract) but also unjust enrichment, in the particular sub-form called 'qualified transfer'. The beginning of the process of reaching secure conclusions must be to recognise the independence of these two events. Only when the legal consequences naturally arising from each have been

---

[9] Para., 2.52, *init.*

[10] Para., 2.53. Further reductions may be made thereafter by reason of the set-off allowed to the defendant recipient of the benefit in respect of loss arising from the plaintiff's breach of contract or in respect of 'irrecoverable loss' which would be recoverable as damages for breach were it not for an exemption of limitation clause protecting the plaintiff, paras. 2.63–65, draft Bill, clause 2.

[11] Above, p. 34 ff.

documented is it possible to draw on policy arguments whose effect may be to inhibit one so as to allow the other to become dominant and thus to eliminate the conflict between the different measures of recovery.

More seriously, the Law Commission's proposals reveal the disastrous effects on the common law of a habit of mind given over to piecemeal statutory improvement of the law in the cases. The fundamental structure of ideas in the cases no longer has to be discussed. What is already the case does not matter much when the law can so easily be changed to what it ought to be. But there is a strong argument for ecological conservation. It is rather like Bradbury's butterfly. If you step on one small organism, the whole pattern goes to pieces. In this area, so long as there is no legislation to break it up, there is a pattern common to all kinds of failure of consideration.

VIII

FREE ACCEPTANCE

IN the last two chapters we have been looking at factors which call for restitution because they negative the voluntary character of the transfer to the defendant. The reason for restitution has, therefore, been found on the side of the plaintiff, since he is the person shown to have the qualified or vitiated intent that the defendant should be enriched. At this point there is a major change of focus. Where a plaintiff relies on free acceptance, the reason for restitution is found on the side of the defendant, the person accepting the benefit. The elements of free acceptance will be looked at in more detail later. It is enough for the moment to say that the word 'free' is only intended to emphasise the requirement, arguably implicit in the notion of acceptance even without the addition of any adjective, that the defendant must have had a choice whether to accept or reject and must have had sufficient knowledge of the facts to make that choice a real one. A free acceptance occurs where a recipient knows that a benefit is being offered to him non-gratuitously and where he, having the opportunity to reject, elects to accept.

The actual mechanism of acceptance will vary from case to case. Sometimes there will have been an earlier request and sometimes not. Sometimes the acceptance will be active. For example, it is difficult to imagine the acceptance of inanimate chattels without an affirmative act. Sometimes it will be passive. One can accept work by merely standing by while it is done. Sometimes an active acceptance will amount even to tortious seizure of the value in question.[1] But such extreme cases are *a fortiori* from what is minimally necessary and sufficient.

It is convenient to start from a clear and simple example. Suppose that I see a window-cleaner beginning to clean the windows of my house. I know that he will expect to be paid. So I hang back unseen till he has finished the job; then I emerge and maintain that I will not pay for work which I never ordered. It is too late, I have freely accepted the service. I had my opportunity to send him away. I chose instead to let him go on. I must pay the reasonable value of his work.

---

[1] As in *Lightly* v. *Clouston* (1808) 1 Taunt. 112 and *Weatherby* v. *Banham*, below, p. 269.

1. REASONS FOR RELYING ON FREE ACCEPTANCE

There are two reasons why a plaintiff may want to rely on free acceptance of value rather than on non-voluntary transfer. Each may operate on its own, or both concurrently. The first is an 'unjust' reason. The second is an 'enrichment' reason.

Some would-be plaintiffs cannot point to any factor negativing the voluntary character of their transfer. Such volunteers fall into two groups. There are those who have obtained what they originally wanted, either nothing at all, if they were gift-givers, or else the very reciprocation which they specified. They ought to be satisfied and can never have restitution. If they made any claim it could only be on the basis of a change of mind after the original transfer. The second group of these volunteers comprises those who are disappointed risk-takers who hoped for a reciprocation but obtained none and, not having made any contract, now have to claim in restitution or not at all. Suppose that the window-cleaner did my windows merely in the hope that I, like my various neighbours, would want them done and would agree to pay. He could then point to no factor negativing voluntariness and, if I had been out, he would have had no basis on which to claim restitution. But because I stood by and tacitly accepted the work he can, as we shall see below, claim its reasonable value. This, therefore, is the essential point: volunteers who are disappointed risk-takers can get restitution on the basis of free acceptance.

The other reason for turning to free acceptance has to do with the establishment of 'enrichment'. A plaintiff who has conferred a non-money benefit on the defendant may encounter the argument which we called 'subjective devaluation'.[2] A defendant who has freely accepted the benefit cannot use that argument. The reason is that, if he has freely accepted, he has *ex hypothesi* chosen to receive it, and subjective devaluation is an argument whose premiss is that where something has *not* been chosen by its recipient it cannot normally be said to have been of value to him. This efficacy of free acceptance in relation to the issue of enrichment means that a plaintiff who has conferred a non-money benefit may be driven to rely on free acceptance even if he *can* point to a factor negativing voluntariness. If the window-cleaner did my windows by mistake, believing that I had placed an order for them to be cleaned,[3] he would be able to

---

[2] Above, p. 109 ff.

[3] Cf. mistaken or 'ignorant' suppliers of goods: *Boulton* v. *Jones* (1857) 2 H. & N. 564; *Greer* v. *Downs Supply Co.* [1927] 2 K.B. 28.

show that he had acted non-voluntarily; but he would still want to rely on my free acceptance because of the difficulty of establishing enrichment by other tests independent of the expression of my choice.[4]

In such a case the plaintiff can analyse his claim in either of two ways. He can say that the enrichment issue is satisfied by the defendant's free acceptance and that the factor calling for restitution and going to the word 'unjust' is his mistake. Alternatively, he can take advantage of the fact that free acceptance satisfies both issues at once, in which case he will give up all reliance on the mistake except perhaps for the purpose of showing that he did not act with the intention of conferring a gift.[5] Should he prefer to advance the former explanation his claim will appear to be 'mixed', partly relying on free acceptance and partly on a factor negativing voluntariness. It is important to notice that a plaintiff who has acted on the basis of a mistake of present or past fact can make this choice, but that a plaintiff whose only 'mistake' is a misprediction of the defendant's willingness to respond can only rely on free acceptance in respect of both issues. The window-cleaner who merely mispredicts my willingness to pay him can use that 'mistake' to indicate that he never intended a gift but not to negative voluntariness on his part.[6]

There are many cases of non-voluntary transfer in which it is possible, but completely unnecessary, to explain the plaintiff's claim in terms of free acceptance. If I pay you £100 by mistake, and you share my mistake, the only possible analysis is: non-voluntary transfer (mistaken) of unequivocal enrichment (money). On the other hand if you know that the money is not due to you, an additional explanation becomes possible: knowing the facts and with an opportunity to reject, you chose to accept a benefit which I was offering non-gratuitously. There is, however, no reason in relation either to the issue of enrichment or to the issue of 'unjust' why this less familiar analysis should be adopted. A claim which can be made out in all respects against a defendant, who is himself mistaken, absent, or mentally disabled, will not be impeded if it happens that the defendant was all along aware of what was occurring and willing that it should occur. Hence, on such facts, plaintiffs will not choose to turn to free acceptance.

[4] Above, p. 116 ff.
[5] Below, p. 278 f.
[6] Above, p. 147.

2. THE DEVELOPMENT OF FREE ACCEPTANCE

Until very recently it was formally maintained that free acceptance worked through contract. That is to say, the theory upon which the plaintiff obtained his right against a freely accepting defendant was, that on facts amounting to a free acceptance it was possible to infer that the defendant had promised to pay. This 'implied contract' was of a completely different order from the fictitious or deemed contract recited in the action for money had and received. It was considered to be a contract implied in fact, a genuine but tacit promise to pay.

(i) *The Contractual Explanation*

The best starting point for understanding the development of free acceptance is the doctrine which is familiarly associated with *Lampleigh* v. *Brathwait*, decided in 1616. In that case the defendant had requested the plaintiff to get him a royal pardon for a murder. After the plaintiff had obtained the pardon the defendant promised him £100 for the service, but did not pay it. The case established, or more accurately confirmed, that a promise given after a requested service was actionable and was not caught by the rule that a past consideration is no consideration:

First, it was agreed that a mere voluntary courtesy will not have a consideration to uphold an *assumpsit.* But if that courtesy were moved by a suit or request of the party that gives the *assumpsit,* it will bind; for the promise, though it follows, yet it is not naked, but couples itself with the suit before and the merits of the party procured by that suit, which is the difference.[7]

If the defendant did promise to pay a named sum for the requested benefit, the action could be brought for that named sum. If he did not, then an action could be maintained on an implied promise to pay the reasonable value, *quantum meruit* for work and *quantum valebat* for a chattel. Except for the fact that, when it came to the stage of substantiating allegations before a jury, this promise of reasonable recompense would be inferred from the request and not separately evidenced, the theory upon which the claim for reasonable recompense proceeded was the same as that described in *Lampleigh* v. *Brathwait*. The words of the proposition to be substantiated would, subject to some variation, be as follows:

---

[7] *Lampleigh* v. *Brathwait* (1616) Hobart, 105.

Whereas Martin afterwards at the special instance and request of Thomas had sold and delivered to Thomas other wines, the said Thomas in consideration thereof afterwards assumed upon himself and faithfully promised that he the said Thomas so much money as he the said Martin for the wine last mentioned should reasonably deserve would well and faithfully pay: nevertheless the said Thomas [has not paid].[8]

Moreover, where the plaintiff had not himself bestowed the benefit on the defendant but had laid out money so as to cause a third party to confer the benefit, the plaintiff's claim to reimbursement, maintained by the common count for money paid to the defendant's use, again worked on a substantially similar logic.[9]

If we pause there, we can see that the key to the plaintiff's claim was taken to be a tacit promise to pay, which was inferred from a genuine request. However, the business of inference was taken one stage further. The request itself could be inferred from a free acceptance. The plaintiff's right would then be based on a promise inferred from a request inferred from an acceptance. Two cases serve to illustrate this. In *Weatherby* v. *Banham*[10] the plaintiff always sent off *The Racing Calendar* to one Westbrook as soon as it came off the press. Westbrook died. Not knowing that this had happened the plaintiff went on sending the magazine. It came to the defendant, who had taken over Westbrook's house, and the defendant took it in and used it. He had never asked for it but he had clearly accepted it knowing that it was not intended for him as a gift. Lord Tenterden, C.J., allowed the plaintiff's claim. Again, in *Lamb* v. *Bunce*[11] the question was whether the plaintiff surgeon could claim a fee from the parish responsible for a pauper whom he had attended. The surgeon had been called in by someone other than the parish officer. Lord Ellenborough, C.J., held that, although the officer had not in reality requested the surgeon's intervention, yet by standing by knowing that he was attending he had done the same thing in effect: 'I consider that when the parish officer visited the pauper according to his duty, and knew that the plaintiff, who was generally employed for the poor, was in attendance upon him, and did not repudiate his attendance, he in effect commanded it.'[12]

The acceptability of this double inference meant that, in the

---

[8] This is an abbreviated version of the example from *Tomkins* v. *Roberts* (1701) given in Lilly's *Entries* and reproduced in C. H. S. Fifoot, *History and Sources of Common Law*, London, 1949, 379.

[9] See the example of 'money paid' at p. 112 above.

[10] *Weatherby* v. *Banham* (1832) 5 C. & P. 228.

[11] *Lamb* v. *Bunce* (1815) 4 M. & S. 275.

[12] Ibid., at p. 277.

pleadings, the plaintiff would recite that the defendant had requested the intervention (whether work, goods, or money paid to a third party) and that the defendant had promised to pay; but before a jury he would not have to prove more than that the defendant had freely accepted the benefit. In 1886 Bowen, L.J., summed this up in *Falcke* v. *Scottish Imperial Insurance Co.*[13] It will be recalled that the question was whether a claim could be made for reimbursement in respect of a payment made to save a life policy from lapsing. The claimant was the owner of the ultimate equity of redemption, the policy having been mortgaged more than once. He needed a lien for his expenditure. An unsecured claim would not have given him anything. But the court took the view that he could not begin to succeed unless he could establish a free acceptance on the part of the other people interested in the property. And on the facts there was no evidence of any such acceptance. Bowen, L.J., said:

> It is perfectly true that the inference of an understanding between the parties—which you may translate into other language by calling it an implied contract—is an inference which will unhesitatingly be drawn in cases where the circumstances plainly lead to the conclusion that the owner of the saved property knew that the other party was laying out his money in the expectation of being repaid. In other words you must have circumstances from which the proper inference is that there was a request to perform the service. It comes to the same thing, but I abstain from using the word 'request' more than is necessary, for fear of plunging myself into all the archaic embarrassments connected with the cases about requests.[14]

★2   (ii) *Abandonment of the Contractual Explanation*

In the quotation from Bowen, L.J., which has just been given, the only facts, as opposed to inferences, which are insisted on are 'that the owner of the saved property knew that the other party was laying out his money in the expectation of being repaid'. In the absence of good reasons to the contrary, a defendant's liability ought to be based on real facts, and not on secondary inferences from them designed to support some abstract theory as to why the real facts produce the consequence contended for. There was in retrospect an inevitability about the development which established that a free acceptance was sufficient in itself. Nevertheless, this did not happen till 1957. The delay was due chiefly to the superficially plausible nature of the double inference. We have already seen that, where the

---

[13] *Falcke* v. *Scottish Imperial Insurance Co.* (1886) 34 Ch.D. 234; above, p. 194 f.
[14] At p. 249; cf. p. 241, *per* Cotton, L.J.; p. 253, *per* Fry, L.J.

allegations of request and promise were deemed to be satisfied by non-voluntary transfer and incontrovertible enrichment[15] —facts which were incapable of supporting the allegations, except constructively—the contractual analysis was exposed as fictitious some twenty years earlier.[16] Where the promise to pay was an inference from a request or free acceptance it was much easier to turn a blind eye to the shortcomings of the traditional explanation. There were even some who thought the best way forward was to develop the contractual theory.[17]

That would have been to take the path of fiction. For there were serious difficulties just below the surface. The contractual inference was often drawn in defiance of realities. Even in a case such as *Weatherby* v. *Banham*,[18] where the defendant had to pay for his copies of *The Racing Calendar*, we know that what the defendant probably intended was to have the magazine for nothing. In other words, the inference of a promise to pay was drawn more on the basis of what good men ought to intend than by genuine interpretation of what this defendant did intend or what the generality of mankind would have intended. If the ideal man were a permissible standard by which to imply contracts there would be no need of a law of tort. For no doubt that man willingly undertakes to compensate for damage which he does. But the average negligent motorist does not. The same is true of the obligation to repay a mistaken payment. Restitutionary obligations have to be imposed by law, no less than tortious obligations, precisely because real people do not make all the promises which good men should. *Weatherby* v. *Banham* is much more satisfactorily explained as a case in which the defendant became liable because he freely accepted the magazines. As soon as we add, with the pleadings, that the free acceptance took its effect because it signified that he promised to pay, a note of artificiality creeps in.

Way v. *Latilla*[19] reveals the same tension. The plaintiff had obtained valuable mining concessions in Africa for the defendant. He had been given nothing for his labour. There had been strenuous negotiations about his having a share in such concessions as he obtained, and it appeared that the defendant did intend that he

---

[15] Above, pp. 118 f., 159 f.

[16] *Brook's Wharf and Bull Wharf Ltd.* v. *Goodman Bros.* [1937] 1 K.B. 534; *Craven-Ellis* v. *Canons Ltd.* [1936] 2 K.B. 403.

[17] A.T. Denning, 'Quantum Meruit: The Case of *Craven-Ellis* v. *Canons Ltd.*' (1939) 55 L.Q.R. 54.

[18] Above, p. 269.

[19] *Way* v. *Latilla* [1937] 3 All E.R. 759.

should be so repaid. But the negotiations never reached a sufficiently certain conclusion for the plaintiff to be able to allege a breach of a contract to grant a share in the concessions. Nevertheless, the House of Lords concluded that he was entitled to a *quantum meruit* on the basis of a second contract somehow discoverable behind the one which had failed to be finalized. The result was entirely satisfactory, but the discovery of a second contract was artificial. It looks like an implied contract discovered notwithstanding the fact that expressed intentions were travelling towards a flatly different arrangement. Without an elaborate and unrealistic hypothesis to the effect that the parties intended that, if negotiations for a share failed, then the defendant would pay the plaintiff in money, there is a repugnancy between the parties' actual intentions and the intentions which the court attributed to them in order to reach a satisfactory conclusion within the framework of the contractual theory. This repugnancy does not arise if the defendant's liability is attached directly to the free acceptance without any mediating inference.

In some cases the factual obstacles illustrated in the last two paragraphs were aggravated by a legal impediment to the routine contractual inference. For example, where corporations accepted goods the courts were reluctant to allow them to escape payment merely because they could contract only in writing under their seal.[20] Yet, if free acceptance had to work through contract, it was not easy to award a *quantum valebat*. No satisfactory escape from this dilemma was proposed, but claims by suppliers were, none the less, upheld.[21]

In 1957 Barry, J., following the pattern of what had been achieved by the Court of Appeal in *Craven-Ellis* v. *Canons Ltd.* on facts amounting to a non-voluntary transfer of incontrovertible enrichment but not disclosing a free acceptance,[22] escaped these unnecessary tensions by laying down that the inference of a promise to pay *quantum meruit* was mere surplusage. In *William Lacey (Hounslow) Ltd.* v. *Davis*[23] the plaintiffs had tendered to redevelop a war-damaged site owned by the defendant, who then demanded a whole series of revisions, some to meet conditions for licences and grants, some to meet his own requirements. They were told that they had tendered lowest and were given to understand that the contract

---

[20] A seal is not now required: *The Corporate Bodies' Contracts Acts, 1960*, s. 1; *Companies Act, 1948*, s. 32.

[21] Cf. *Lawford* v. *Billericay R.D.C.* (1903) 1 K.B. 772.

[22] Above, p. 118–9.

[23] *William Lacey (Hounslow) Ltd.* v. *Davis* [1957] 1 W.L.R. 932.

would be awarded to them. After they had done more work than could ever be reasonably expected of builders in pursuit of a lucrative contract, they were told, first, that the defendant intended to contract with another firm and, then, that he had decided not to redevelop the site himself but to sell it on to another developer. The defendant argued that the common expectation of the parties was that the plaintiffs would be remunerated, if at all, by the award of the development contract. He maintained that that affirmative intention excluded any implied contract for other remuneration. Barry, J., rejected that argument. It made too much of the notion that the obligation to pay *quantum meruit* rested on an implied contract. Barry, J., said:

In truth, I think that Mr Lawson's proposition is founded upon too narrow a view of the modern action for *quantum meruit*. In its early history it was no doubt a genuine action in contract, based on a real promise to pay, although that promise had not been expressed in words, and the amount of the payment had not been agreed. Subsequent developments have, however, considerably widened the scope of this form of action, and in many cases the action is now founded upon what is known as quasi-contract, similar in some ways to the action for money had and received. In these quasi-contractual cases the court will look at the true facts and ascertain from them whether or not a promise to pay should be implied irrespective of the actual views or intentions of the parties at the time when the work was done or the services rendered.[24]

This judgment was an important advance. There were, however, two matters in respect of which it left room for further explanation. First, while it is right to say that the court will look at the true facts (as opposed to the facts traditionally recited in the declaration), it is a needless perpetuation of the old ways to say that on those facts the courts will decide whether to 'imply a promise'. Barry, J., uses the word 'implied' in the sense of 'imposed'. A promise which is 'imposed irrespective of the actual view or intentions of the parties' is not a promise at all. An 'imposed promise' is a contradiction in terms. So, the implied promise which survives in his vocabulary should more aptly have been an 'imposed obligation'. Beneath the words actually used, that is undoubtedly what he meant. Secondly, the judgment does not take any distinction between the different bases of non-contractual claims for *quantum meruit*. It relies heavily on *Craven-Ellis* v. *Canons Ltd.*, but does not say that the 'true facts' in that case were analytically different from those in *William Lacey* itself: *Craven-Ellis* was a case of non-voluntary transfer to a company

---

[24] At p. 936.

unable to make a free acceptance, while *William Lacey* could not be explained except on the basis of free acceptance, since the only 'mistake' which the builders made was a misprediction of the developer's future behaviour. However, Barry, J., did not need to make this distinction since for his purposes the role of *Craven-Ellis* was only to establish that the old request-based pleadings had indeed succeeded in engendering non-contractual claims.

In the Commonwealth *William Lacey* was anticipated. In *Watson* v. *Watson* two brothers in New Zealand had joined in setting up a sawmill.[25] There was a loose understanding between them that, in the initial period, neither would expect anything out of the venture but that a contract of partnership would ultimately be settled between them. The defendant brother began to prevaricate, with the result that the plaintiff eventually gave up hope and began this action for *quantum meruit* instead. Allowing recovery, Gresson, J., affirmed the non-contractual nature of the claim. Similarly in *Deglman* v. *Guaranty Trust Co. of Canada and Constantineau* the Supreme Court of Canada held that a non-contractual *quantum meruit* lay where Constantineau had looked after his aunt for a number of years on the unwritten understanding that she would leave him her house by will.[26] There was no sufficient part performance to make good the absence of a Statute of Frauds writing, but there was, none the less, a restitutionary duty imposed on the aunt's estate. More recently Sheppard, J., in the Supreme Court of New South Wales has affirmed in a very careful judgment that the rational strength of the position taken by Barry, J., was such as to give it priority over 'weighty Australian authority' which appeared to insist on the contractual analysis. The case was *Sabemo Pty. Ltd.* v. *North Sydney Municipal Council.*[27] Its facts were strikingly similar to *William Lacey.* The Council had embarked upon a massive project for a civic centre. Sabemo had tendered successfully to do the work under a building lease. Acceptance of the tender did not constitute a contract but put the parties into a close planning relationship. Three years later, planning approval had been finally given, an immense amount of work had been done and the parties were negotiating in a firm but optimistically co-operative spirit to resolve important differences between them. Then the Council suffered a political change of heart. The ambitious scheme was

[25] *Watson* v. *Watson* [1953] N.Z.L.R. 266.

[26] *Deglman* v. *Guaranty Trust Co. of Canada and Constantineau* [1954] 3 D.L.R. 2d. 785; cf. *Preeper* v. *Preeper* (1978) 84 D.L.R. 3d. 74.

[27] *Sabemo Pty. Ltd.* v. *North Sidney Municipal Council* [1977] 2 N.S.W. 880.

dropped. Nevertheless Sabemo obtained reasonable payment for all the work which the Council had requested and accepted between and tender and the cancellation.

In New Zealand another similar claim was upheld by Jeffries, J., in *Van den Berg. v. Giles.*[28] When his work brought him to the Wellington area, the plaintiff became tenant of the defendant's weekend house. In the belief, as the defendant well knew, that she had agreed that she would sell him the property for $30 000 at a future date, the plaintiff laid out $22 500 on the improvement of the house and the addition of a garage, with the effect that he raised its value by $20 500. Although she had never requested the work the defendant had stood by while it was done and had failed to disabuse the plaintiff of his expectations. Jeffries, J., held that on the basis of this free acceptance she had incurred a liability to pay him so much of his outlay as had enhanced the value of her property, namely, $20 500.

These developments do not mean that free acceptance must always be non-contractual. It is still of course true that if someone sends me goods in circumstances amounting to an offer of sale my taking them in will constitute an acceptance of that offer;[29] and if I order a suit from a tailor without discussing the price I will similarly be found to have made a contract with him. The only cases in which it is necessary to insist upon the non-contractual efficacy of free acceptance are those in which the routine inference of a promise to pay is obstructed, usually by indications of a contrary intent. Nevertheless, it must also be true that, if the contractual inference is shown to be inessential by those cases in which it cannot be drawn, it must in strict logic be otiose in all cases. In other words, although some examples of free acceptance can be analysed in terms of genuine implied contract, all can be understood independently of contract, as examples of unjust enrichment. Only if the plaintiff seeks compensatory damages for breach must he be able to draw the inference of a contract.[29a]

Why exactly is it that a freely accepted enrichment is 'unjust' to retain? It would not have been possible to dispense with the contractual explanation if there were not a sound basis for imposing the restitutionary obligation. In an extreme case it is possible to say that the defendant's free acceptance amounts to dishonesty or at

---

[28] *Van den Berg* v. *Giles* [1979] 2 N.Z.L.R. 111.

[29] *Stevens* v. *Bromley & Son* [1919] 2 K.B. 722, esp. p. 728, *per* Atkin, L.J.

[29a] *British Steel Corporation* v. *Cleveland Bridge and Engineering Co. Ltd.* [1984] 1 All E.R. 504, 509–512, (Robert Goff, J.).

least a violation of all the rules of ordinary decency.[30] But it is unnecessary to go so far. The question presents itself in this way. The plaintiff has conferred a benefit on the defendant expecting some return for himself and not intending to confer a gift upon the defendant. Once the enrichment issue is out of the way, why should he not receive the value? The answer is that he ought not to be relieved of a risk which he took and which turned out to his disadvantage. His replication is then that that answer cannot cover every case. First, if he can show some factor negativing voluntariness, he will not have assumed a risk at all.[31] Secondly, if the defendant freely accepted the benefit, it is not true that he 'ought not to be relieved' of any risk which he did run. For the freely accepting defendant could have rejected, but, in deciding to accept, makes himself party to the risk. He has himself to blame for not coming forward to issue a warning. His failure to reject estops him from making the sweeping answer that the plaintiff ought to have looked before he leaped.

There is a related but secondary matter. A freely accepting defendant might say, even if in his particular case he has estopped himself from driving the plaintiff back to the risk which he ran, that nevertheless society has an interest in defeating the expectations of risk-taking interveners. He could say that busy-bodies must be discouraged generally, lest people be easily saddled with liabilities behind their backs.[32] But the answer to this is that, even if society does have a general interest in discouraging intermeddlers, that protection is never needed by individuals who are present at the time of the interevention and know what is being done, so that they could, if they chose, put an end to it. In short the social interest against intermeddling is sufficiently protected so long as risk-takers are given no claims against those who are absent at the time of the intervention, or who, though present, lack knowledge of the facts sufficient to alert them to the need to take steps to reject the intervention.

---

[30] Cf. *City Bank of Sydney* v. *McLaughlin* (1909) 9 C.L.R. 615, 625, *per* Griffith, C.J.

[31] *Greenwood* v. *Bennett* [1973] 1 Q.B. 195, 202, *per* Lord Denning, M.R.: 'We all remember the saying of Pollock C.B.: "One cleans another's shoes; what can the other do but put them on.": *Taylor* v. *Laird* (1856) 25 L.J. Ex. 329, 332. That is undoutedly the law when the person who does the work knows, or ought to know, that the property does not belong to him. He takes the risk of not being paid for his work on it. But it is very different when he honestly believes himself to be the owner of the property and does the work in that belief.'

[32] *Falcke* v. *Scottish Imperial Insurance Co.* (1886) 34 Ch.D. 234, 248, *per* Bowen, L.J.

(iii) *A Parallel Doctrine in Equity*

In equity the phenomenon of free acceptance is encountered most commonly in the context of improvements to land. One man has built on another's land and the question is whether he must lose, without redress, the work and materials which he has put in. The words 'free acceptance' do not occur. The cases refer to 'the doctrine in *Ramsden* v. *Dyson*' or to 'acquiescence'. The idea is the same. The question is whether the owner of the land stood back and let the improvement happen in such a way as to make himself answerable for it, disabling himself from the rebuff which he wants to give the improver: 'You should not have taken the risk of working on my land.' In *Ramsden* v. *Dyson*[33] itself, a case crammed with social history of the nineteenth century, a whole town had grown up on private land. Many of the people were tenants at will. They maintained that to the knowledge of the land-owner's agents they had built their houses on parcels of land allotted to them in the belief that, if they did so, they would be granted long leases. The House of Lords agreed that, if the landowner had allowed the building to go ahead knowing that it was done in that belief, the tenants at will were entitled to a remedy. That holding is the basis of the doctrine. On the facts it was found that the landowner had no reason to believe that the tenants relied on more than the *de facto* moment-to-moment security available under his benevolent regime. Hence, since he believed that their view of the matter was the same as his, nothing called for him to come forward with a warning.

The assertion that this equitable doctrine is one and the same as free acceptance is not uncontroversial. In particular, it encounters competition from the contention that the equitable doctrine turns on mistake and should, therefore, be considered not with free acceptance but rather with factors negativing voluntariness. Thus, in *Willmott* v. *Barber*,[34] Fry, J., said: 'The equitable doctrine of acquiescence is founded on there having been a mistake of fact.'[35] That was a remark made in the course of argument, but his judgment too made clear, as a first requirement, that the plaintiff 'must have made a mistake as to his legal rights'.[36] Goff and Jones also consider *Ramsden* v. *Dyson* under the general heading of 'services rendered under a mistake'.[37] This classification must therefore be tested.

---

[33] *Ramsden* v. *Dyson* (1866) L.R. 1 H.L. 83.
[34] *Wilmott* v. *Barber* (1880) 15 CH.D. 96.
[35] At p. 101.
[36] At p. 105.
[37] At p. 106 ff.

Suppose I believe Blackacre is mine and build a house on it. You know that Blackacre is yours and you secretly watch me completing the house, intending to take its value. In that story there is undoubtedly a mistake on my part. The question is, what is the rôle of the mistake in my claim against you? There are two possibilities. It might be either to negative voluntariness on my part or to establish a non-gratuitous intent, showing that I am not trying to change my mind after having initially intended to give you a gift. Which rôle does it have for the purpose of the doctrine in *Ramsden* v. *Dyson*? This can be tested easily. Suppose that the mistake which I make is not that Blackacre is already mine but that you will in future give it to me. That kind of mistake will never negative voluntariness. It is a mere misprediction as to the future, exactly the kind of 'mistake' which you make when you clean my car believing, wrongly, that I will pay.[38] A misprediction is nothing but the taking of a risk, an exercise of judgment which turns out badly rather than a judgment vitiated.[39] That is why the law requires mistakes to be of present or past fact. But both mispredictions and mistakes of present fact do serve to demonstrate a non-gratuitous intent. So, as we have just seen at common law, William Lacey Ltd. mispredicted Davis's willingness to give them the development contract. It was the same with Sabemo, *vis-à-vis* the North Sydney Municipal Council. And a trader who sends me goods which I have not asked for also has nothing to offer by way of negativing voluntariness; yet if I freely accept them I shall have to pay. Thus the question for *Ramsden* v. *Dyson* becomes this: if the mistake which is said to be necessary is in a given set of facts no more than a misprediction, does the doctrine still operate? If it does not, then it is correct to assert that the doctrine turns on mistake and belongs in the treatment of factors negativing voluntariness. If it does, then it has nothing to do with negativing voluntariness and belongs with, indeed is the same as, free acceptance.

The answer comes out of *Ramsden* v. *Dyson* itself. The 'mistake' which the tenants at will made, and which the House of Lords regarded as sufficient if the landowners had had knowledge of it, was no more than a misprediction: they believed that if they built they would be granted long leases; they knew they were all tenants at will for the present. This point was expressly considered by the Privy Council in *Plimmer* v. *Wellington Corporation*.[40] The opinion there expressed was that the House of Lords had not intended to limit the

---

[38] See above, pp. 273–4.

[39] Above, p. 147. And see esp. *Re Cleadon Trust Ltd*. [1939] Ch. 286.

[40] *Plimmer* v. *Wellington Corporation* (1884) 9 App. Cas. 699, 710 f.

doctrine to mistakes of present fact as opposed to mistaken expectations. That must be right, for, even if there were no authority whatever, it would be obvious that, if you stand by and watch me building on your land and say nothing, my claim is just as good when the explanation of my conduct is that I believe that you *will* pay me or *will* grant me an interest in the land as it is when I believe that I already have an interest. The reason is, that the ground for restitution here lies in your conduct, your standing by and letting me get into trouble. *Inwards* v. *Baker*[41] provides a modern example of a case in which equity responded even though the plaintiff merely mispredicted the future. A son had built a bungalow on his father's land. He knew the land was not his, but he believed, and his father had assured him, that he would be able to live in the bungalow for as long as he liked. So there was no mistake, not at least in the sense in which that word denotes a factor capable of negativing voluntariness.

The conclusion of this argument is that the doctrine in *Ramsden* v. *Dyson* is the equitable equivalent of free acceptance in the common law and does not depend on mistake. It remains true of course that, as in those cases at common law which are susceptible of analysis either in terms of free acceptance or in terms of a factor negativing voluntariness, a case in which the improver is labouring under the influence of a mistake of present or past fact, as opposed to a misprediction, can indeed be considered as turning on mistake, so long as the enrichment issue is then separately considered. If I build because I believe I already have an interest I certainly am not forced to rely on free acceptance in order to meet the inquiry under 'unjust'. The common law parallel is then *Greenwood* v. *Bennett*.[42] But, as in that case, the issue of enrichment will not be easy without recourse to the defendant's acceptance. There are the routine difficulties of 'subjective devaluation'.

This is not the end of the difficulties with *Ramsden* v. *Dyson*. There is another problem which will be touched on in the next section: the response of equity is not rigidly restricted to awarding restitution but extends also to the fulfilment of expectations, at least on some facts.

3. THE ELEMENTS OF FREE ACCEPTANCE

The detailed requirements for à free acceptance have not yet been fully worked out. Nor will they become completely clear until the

[41] *Inwards* v. *Baker* [1965] 2 Q.B. 29.
[42] *Cit.* n. 31 above.

influence of the contractual explanation has receded into the past. For, so long as the theory which had to be satisfied was that the free acceptance had supposedly to justify the inferences of request and promise, it was impossible to concentrate on the line between acceptances which do, and acceptances which do not, justify non-contractual claims to restitution. The facts of *Boulton* v. *Jones*[43] exemplify this problem. Jones had ordered goods from Brocklehurst, previous owner of Boulton's shop. Boulton treated the order as made to the business, not to Brocklehurst, and he therefore supplied the goods, which Jones consumed. To satisfy a contractual theory, it may be that Jones' acceptance of the goods was insufficient because it was vitiated by his ignorance as to the identify of the supplier. But it is not clear that that particular defect of knowledge should nullify the effect of non-contractual free acceptance. The question is: How 'free' must a non-contractual free acceptance be? On the equitable side it has not been contractual theory, but rather a wrong assertion that the doctrine in *Ramsden* v. *Dyson* turned on mistake, which has obstructed development of the detailed picture of free acceptance.

(i) *The Opportunity to Reject*

It is certain that the defendant cannot be said to have freely accepted if the benefit was irreversibly committed before he knew about it. This is merely a matter of timing. Once an unrequested benefit has been bestowed, even an express promise to pay for it will not be actionable.[44] In *Leigh* v. *Dickeson*[45] the question was whether one co-owner who had repaired and improved the property could claim to be reimbursed by another co-owner in proportion to the latter's share. The Court of Appeal held that, outside an action for partition and consequential adjustment, he could not do so unless the defendant co-owner had had a genuine option to adopt or to decline. Brett, M.R., said:

Voluntary payments may be divided into two classes. Sometimes money has been expended for the benefit of another person under such circumstances that an option is allowed to him to adopt or decline the benefit: in this case, if he exercises the option to adopt the benefit he will be liable to repay the money expended; but if he declines the benefit he will not be liable. But sometimes the

---

[43] *Boulton* v. *Jones* (1857) 1 H. & N. 564.

[44] Because the consideration will be past: *Re McArdle* [1951] Ch. 669; *Eastwood* v. *Kenyon* (1840) 11 A. & E. 438.

[45] *Leigh* v. *Dickeson* (1884) 15 Q.B.D. 60.

money is expended for the benefit of another person under such circumstances that he cannot help accepting the benefit, in fact that he is bound to accept it: in this case he has no opportunity of exercising any option, and he will come under no liability.[46]

This needs to be carefully qualified. When Brett, M.R., concludes that in the absence of the option to adopt or decline the recipient will come under no liability, he means that there will be no liability specifically on the basis of a free acceptance. We know that even a defendant benefited in his absence can be made liable on the basis of non-voluntary enrichment, so long as the plaintiff can indeed point to some factor negativing voluntariness and can demonstrate the enrichment by some test which does not rely on the defendant's having made his choice as to how to spend his money. However, once that qualification is built in, the sense of Brett, M.R.'s statement is apparent: a forced acceptance is no acceptance at all. If you improve my property in my absence I cannot be said to accept your work or expenditure merely because I begin to use and enjoy my property again.

This point was encapsulated by Pollock, C.B., in *Taylor* v. *Laird*: 'One cleans another's shoes. What can the other do but put them on?'[47] In *Sumpter* v. *Hedges*[48] a builder abandoned half-finished houses on the defendant's land. The defendant could not be made liable on the basis of free acceptance when he took over the incomplete structures. They were fixed to his land. He therefore had no choice whether to accept or to reject them. But it was different with loose materials left behind by the builder. He did have an option whether or not to use those. Choosing to do so, he became liable for their value.

(ii) *Knowledge of Non-Gratuitous Intent*

A non-gratuitous intent is an intent other than to give a gift. Such an intent can be found in the risk-taking volunteer, who expects some return but fails to stipulate for one. The builders in *William Lacey*[49] hoped and expected to be rewarded by winning the development contract. They did not intend to confer a gratuitous benefit on the developer. Similarly, a non-gratuitous intent can be found in a non-

---

[46] At p. 64.
[47] *Taylor* v. *Laird* (1956) 25 L.J. Ex. 329, 332.
[48] *Sumpter* v. *Hedges* [1898] 1 Q.B. 673.
[49] *William Lacey (Hounslow) Ltd.* v. *Davis* [1957] 1 W.L.R. 932.

volunteer such as a mistaken improver who believes the land on which he is working to be already his own. He does not intend to confer a gift on the actual owner, of whom he knows nothing. He intends the benefit to accrue to himself.

It is not enough that the plaintiff had a non-gratuitous intent. The defendant must also have known of that intent. Otherwise nothing calls the defendant to ask himself whether he should take steps to reject the benefit; for, as everyone knows, people do accept as gifts some benefits which they would certainly reject if they thought they were expected to pay. In the case of improvements to land made by someone who mistakenly believes the land is his, the actual owner looking on must, therefore, be shown to have known that the improver's view was mistaken.[50] If the owner shared the improver's view, he will not even have perceived himself as a donee. He will have regarded the improver as one bent on improving his own condition and will, therefore, have had no intimation whatever of any need to intervene or warn.[51]

Sometimes it will happen that the plaintiff does very clearly have a non-gratuitous intent but that the defendant will, none the less, be justified in perceiving it as gratuitous *quoad* himself. Thus in *Brown and Davis Ltd.* v. *Galbraith*[53] the plaintiff's garage had repaired the defendant's sports car. The defendant's insurance company failed. The garage therefore turned for payment against the defendant, as recipient of the benefit of their work. Their claim was rejected. The work had been on the credit of the insurance company only. The Court of Appeal's analysis is entirely contractual. An approach through non-contractual free acceptance would certainly not have produced a different result. So far as the defendant was concerned, the work being done on his car was reasonably perceived as gratuitous. He accordingly had no cause to ask himself whether it might be wiser to do without it. Nothing called for him to alert the garage to a danger of loss or disappointment.

In *Gilbert and Partners* v. *Knight*,[53] the plaintiff firm of surveyors agreed with Mrs Knight, the defendant, to supervise some building

---

[50] *Ramsden* v. *Dyson, Willmott* v. *Barber*, above, p. 277.

[51] In *Avondale Printers* v. *Haggie*, [1979] 2 N.Z.L.R. 124, the plaintiffs had worked on land while equitably entitled to it and had continued working on it after assigning their equitable interest to the defendant who had then warned them not to continue unless at their own risk. Mahon, J., rightly held that the defendants could not be held to have freely accepted the work done by the plaintiffs while they were beneficially entitled: at p. 143 f.

[52] *Brown and Davis Ltd.* v. *Galbraith* [1972] 3 All E.R. 31.

[53] *Gilbert and Partners* v. *Knight* [1968] 2 All E.R. 248.

work for her at a fee of £30. When the work came to be done her appetite for improvements increased, so that in the end they had supervised an operation whose size had multiplied four-fold since the original fee had been agreed. The claim for the reasonable value of their extra work failed. The reason was that, in the circumstances, they had not done enough to communicate to her mind the fact that the original fee had been exhausted. She perceived the extra work as gratuitously offered, in the sense that she thought that the one fee covered everything.

(iii) *Neglect of the Opportunity to Reject*

The defendant must have had his opportunity to reject and must have decided to accept. But in addition there must, in that decision, have been some element of neglect sufficient to draw him into responsibility for the transfer of value to him. We have already observed that the key to free acceptance is that it prevents the defendant from driving the plaintiff back to bear the risk which he took.[54] If this is right, it follows that the circumstances of the acceptance must be such as to make the plaintiff a party to that risk. The question must be: Does the acceptance, in the given circumstances, disable the defendant from that retort?

In *Brewer Street Investments Ltd.* v. *Barclays Woollen Co. Ltd.*[55] the defendants were anxious to take a lease of the plaintiff's premises and were confident that negotiations would succeed. There was one *★19 matter outstanding. It concerned the right to purchase the reversion. Believing that this issue would be settled, the defendants asked the plaintiffs to make extensive alterations in the premises. When the alterations had been partly done, negotiations broke down. The cause of the breakdown was precisely the issue of the reversion. The plaintiffs then paid off the subcontractors and sought to be reimbursed by the defendants, the disappointed would-be tenants. It was held that they were entitled to succeed. And it is tolerably clear that, if the parties had been the other way about, so that the defendants themselves had gone in and done the work and then had tried to claim its reasonable value, the court would have come to the same conclusion. That is, the claim of the would-be tenants would have been disallowed. Hence it can be said that, if the lease went off because of a failure to agree about the reversion, the would-be tenants were bound to lose the value of the work, whichever mechanism they

---

[54] Above, p. 276.
[55] *Brewer St. Investments Ltd.* v. *Barclays Woollen Co. Ltd.* [1954] 1 Q.B. 428.

had chosen for getting it done. Yet in a very similar case the Court of Appeal reached the opposite conclusion. In *Jennings and Chapman Ltd. v. Woodman, Matthews & Co.*[56] the would-be sub-tenants won. They too had ordered work to be done in anticipation of a sub-lease which ultimately failed to be granted. The reason why the sub-lease went off was that, unknown to them, there was a provision in the head lease allowing the head lessors to forbid a sub-lease to a would-be tenant who wished to conduct the type of business which was in question. The sub-lessors had not borne that danger in mind and had therefore failed to warn the sub-lessees.

The question which these cases raise for free acceptance is this: Since in such circumstances the landlord knows exactly what is being done and does not forbid it, why does it not follow automatically that he freely accepts the work which is done on his property and, therefore, that he must make restitution of its value? The answer would seem to be that on the facts of *Brewer Street* the *prima facie* free acceptance was, on closer inspection, not such as to make him party to the tenant's risk. It was perfectly clear that one doubtful matter remained outstanding—the issue of the reversion—so that the lessors were entitled to take the view that there was no need to issue any warning to the effect that if that particular stumbling-block was not removed the would-be tenants would lose the value of the work. The obviousness of the danger meant that the lessors were not afterwards subject to any embarrassment in asserting that the tenants should bear the risk which they had taken. By contrast in *Jennings* the danger which ultimately materialised was unknown to the would-be tenants. The sub-lessors could object that they too had had no real opportunity to warn since they themselves had been unaware of the obstacle in the sub-lessee's path. None the less, if the matter is approached from the standpoint of the question whether the sub-lessors could fairly say that the sub-lessees had taken a risk of which they ought not now to be relieved, it is clear that they could not do so, because they themselves should have known of the fact that the head lessors had the power to insist on the covenants in the head lease and thus make it impossible for the would-be sub-tenants to take the benefit of their work, and they also knew that the would-be sub-tenants were not contemplating that eventuality as one of the risks which they were running. So here the sub-lessors did make themselves party to the risk which the sub-tenants took in beginning to get work done before they had their lease.

---

[56] *Jennings and Chapman Ltd. v. Woodman, Matthews & Co.* [1952] 2 T.L.R. 409; cf. *Pulbrook v. Lawes* [1876] 1 Q.B.D. 284.

There is, however, no simple rule to the effect that a free acceptance is inoperative if a danger supervenes which was known to, and known to be known to, the plaintiff at the outset. In *Peter Lind* v. *Mersey Docks & Harbour Board*[57] the plaintiff builders also jumped the gun. Negotiations were proceeding for a large building contract. There was a crucial matter outstanding. The parties could not agree on a formula to express the price to be paid for the work. In the end negotiations failed to resolve that very issue. But in the meantime the plaintiffs did the work, worth more than a million pounds. There was no contract at any stage, just as in the last two examples there never was either a lease or a contract to grant a lease. Furthermore, as in *Brewer Street*, the reason why the contract failed to be made was the very obstacle centrally in view. Yet Peter Lind were granted their claim for a *quantum meruit*. What, therefore, was the crucial difference? The question has to be tested by asking whether the Harbour Board could fairly drive Peter Lind back to bear the risk which they had taken; they could not. If there was any question of their refusing to pay, they should have taken the opportunity, which they did have, to order that the work should stop or, at least, to make clear that if it went on it would not be paid for unless the negotiations reached a successful conclusion. In *Brewer Street* it was reasonable to suppose that the lessees were entirely reconciled to the danger of losing the value of the alterations if the lease failed on the issue of the reversion. In *Peter Lind* the Harbour Board could not say the same. Two particular facts contribute to that different conclusion. First, the scale and value of the work was much greater. Second, as between the two parties it was the Harbour Board, left in possession of the product of the work, which had initially wanted it to be done.[57a]

Again, in *Hussey* v. *Palmer*[58] a mother-in-law spent money on an extension of her son-in-law's house in the expectation of being able to live there indefinitely. He accepted the improvement on that basis. The arrangement broke down. She was allowed to recover her input.

---

[57] *Peter Lind* v. *Mersey Docks & Harbour Board* [1972] 2 Lloyds L.R. 234.

[57a] Very similar in facts and conclusion is *British Steel Corporation* v. *Cleveland Bridge and Engineering Co. Ltd.*, cit. n. 29a, above.

[58] *Hussey* v. *Palmer* [1972] 1 W.L.R. 1286. The case is explicable in terms of free acceptance but it many be that the factor going to 'unjust' is more aptly said to be 'inequality' of a species compounded from, (a) the nature of the relationship, and (b) the nature of the need which the plaintiff was endeavouring to satisfy. Both elements are expressed in the phrase 'family accommodation': she needed permanent accommodation, and she sought it within the structure of family relationships. It is also to be noted that (though she refused it) the court was willing to grant her a proportionate beneficial share in the house (see below, p. 292).

It could not be said that the son-in-law was to blame any more than the mother-in-law. A simple inquiry into fault will not explain the result. But if the question is asked whether the son-in-law could fairly keep her input by driving her back to the risk she had taken the answer must be that he could not. They had both taken the risk, he just as much as her. A breakdown of their arrangement was foreseeable, but there was no reason why the material consequences should be suffered only by her.

4. THREE DIFFICULT TOPICS

We have been trying to break down the constituent elements of free acceptance. When it comes to the practical application of the concept there are three areas of special difficulty. This chapter closes by noticing these problems.

(i) *Free Acceptance and Contracts*

So far we have only contemplated cases in which there is no contract. At most the plaintiff has hoped for some reciprocation or has expected that some contract would later materialize under which he would get some return for the value conferred. Suppose, however, that there is a contract between the parties. Can there, none the less, be a concurrent free acceptance sufficient to found a claim independent of contract? Where there is an entire contract, as for a house to be built or a book to be written, can there be said to be a free acceptance of the work as it proceeds?

This question has to be answered in two parts. First, there is the case of the incomplete performance. There is a contract for a complete house. Suddenly the end comes, and the client is left with only half a house. The cause may be breach by the builder, frustration, or breach by the client. For present purposes we need to contemplate only the third of these three possibilities. If there cannot be said to have been a free acceptance by the client when he himself repudiates, then there certainly cannot be such an acceptance in the other two cases.

We know that on these facts the builder is allowed his *quantum meruit*, for this is the claim upheld in *Planché* v. *Colburn*.[59] The only question is whether that claim can be rested on a free acceptance; it

---

[59] *Planché* v. *Colburn* (1831) 8 Bing. 14, above p. 232.

cannot. A client who decides to accept a complete house can never be said freely to accept either the half-completed structure itself or the work as it proceeds day-by-day and moment-by-moment. This can be explained in either of two ways. It can be said that he actually has no opportunity to reject, since, under the contract, he is legally bound to accept the particles which appear to be leading up to the complete performance which he ordered. Alternatively it could be said that though he does have from moment to moment an opportunity to reject the work, yet his failure to do so does not connote any element of neglect such as to draw him into a shared responsibility for the builder's subsequent plight. In the end, of course, his breach is the cause of the builder's difficulty, and it is that fact which makes it tempting to say, retrospectively, that he freely accepted the builder's work bit-by-bit. But free acceptance is a phenomenon which cannot be established retrospectively. It depends on the acceptor's state of mind at the time when the benefit in question is being committed. At the time when a part of an entire performance is being committed to him the recipient cannot be said freely to accept it. This does not mean that *Planché* v. *Colburn* is wrong but only that it has to be explained as an example of non-voluntary transfer, not as a case of free acceptance.

Secondly, however, the question must be repeated in relation to complete performances. Suppose the builder does complete the entire house and then the client refuses to pay. Can the builder choose to make a claim on the basis of a non-contractual free acceptance? The answer must be that he can. The contrary conclusion, in relation to an incomplete performance, turned on the fact that acceptance of the whole precluded separate acceptance of the parts which went to make up the whole. But here that problem is out of the way. The client did want the entire house, and now he has got it. His opportunity to reject extended up to the moment at which he placed the contract. He could have called the project off but he did not; and clearly he knew throughout that the builder was not working with gratuitous intent.

Deglman v. *Guaranty Trust Co. of Canada and Constantineau*[60] exemplifies the use of recourse to a non-contractual free acceptance in this situation. In this Canadian case the nephew agreed to do various services for his aunt and she for her part agreed to leave him her house. This was a contract, but it was unenforceable for want of a

---

[60] *Deglman* v. *Guarantee Trust Co. of Canada and Constantineau* [1954] 3 D.L.R. 2d. 785.

Statute of Frauds writing. He did his part but she never made the will is his favour. Unable to sue on the contract, the nephew nevertheless obtained a *quantum meruit* for his services. There is no obstacle to explaining this on the basis of a non-contractual free acceptance because there was no question of his recovering the value of some unwanted part-performance.

Even though there is a good theoretical basis for allowing claims of this kind the plaintiff does not have an unrestricted choice whether he will sue on the basis of the contract or the non-contractual free acceptance. That option would allow him to obtain the reasonable value even where he had been foolish enough to agree to perform at less than the market rate. So a free election between the routes would subvert bargains. Hence he must not bring the contractual claim unless and until the contract is discharged;[61] and, even then, it is probably right to say that he cannot do better from his non-contractual claim than he could have done in contract.[62]

★20

(ii) *Free Acceptance and the Discharge of Debts*

We have already noticed above[63] that the law relating to the particular benefit which consists in the discharge of another's obligation is made very complicated by the fact that the English rule is that, in general, the debt is not discharged by the payment unless, and until, the discharge is accepted by the debtor.

If the rule were that the debt itself was always discharged by the stranger's payment there would be no analytical difference, for the purposes of the law of restitution, between this species of non-money benefit and any other. There would be, however, the practical difference that, in relation to the issue of enrichment, the non-money benefit would very easily satisfy the 'no reasonable man' test of incontrovertible benefit. So the questions to be asked would arise in the normal way under the issue of 'unjust': could the stranger point to a factor negativing voluntariness and, if not, could he show that the defendant debtor had freely accepted the discharge? The inquiry into free acceptance would then be very simple and short-

---

[61] *Toussaint* v. *Martinnant* (1797) 2 T.R. 103; *The Olanda* (1917) [1919] 2 K.B. 729; *Stevens* v. *Bromley & Son* [1919] 2 K.B. 722; *Luxor (Eastbourne) Ltd.* v. *Cooper* [1939] 4 All E.R. 411; *Re Richmond Gate Property Ltd.*, [1964] 3 All E.R. 936.

[62] Cf. *B.P. Exploration Co. (Libya) Ltd.* v. *Hunt* [1982] 1 All E.R. 925, 942–3. The same reasoning applies to complete performances as to part performances interrupted by frustration, though the statutory peg is lacking.

[63] Above, p. 190.

term: did the defendant debtor know that the stranger was paying the creditor, and did he stand by when he could have stepped forward to prevent the payment.[64]

The effect of the rule that the debt is not discharged by the stranger's payment is to prolong the period during which the benefit remains open to rejection. It therefore prolongs the period during which a free acceptance is possible. The stranger who pays my debt, even though he actually puts the money into my creditor's hands without my knowledge and in my absence, is then analytically in the same position as a man who places a crate of whisky on my door-step.[65] If I believe that the proffered benefit is a gift I can safely take it up without incurring any liability. But if I know that it is offered with non-gratuitous intent I shall be found to have freely accepted. The practical consequence is that in most cases of debts 'physically paid' as opposed to 'technically discharged', the debtor's acceptance of the discharge should amount to a free acceptance sufficient to oblige him to make restitution to the stranger-payor. For when he puts himself the question whether he will accept the discharge, he will not, on many facts, be in a position to form the belief that he is being offered a gift. The natural interpretation is that if he elects to accept the discharge he does so knowing that it is offered non-gratuitously.

In *Re Cleadon Trust Ltd.*[66] a director paid off the obligations of the company under a guarantee. He was a risk-taking volunteer. He confidently expected that the company would accept the discharge later. But, with his vote disqualified on the ground of his personal interest, the board became inquorate. It could not, therefore, cause the company to adopt the discharge. The company then went into liquidation. The director's proof in respect of his payment was rejected by the liquidator. In the Court of Appeal that was said to be correct. Lord Greene, M.R., dissented. He may well have been right to favour restitution. It depends on when the liability was discharged. If this was a case in which the payment automatically and immediately discharged the company's obligation, then there was no room for any free acceptance. If it was not, then the liquidator's own decision to treat the obligation as extinguished would have amounted to a free acceptance of the still imperfect discharge. And, in that event, Lord Greene, M.R.'s position, reached by different reasoning,

---

[64] *Roberts* v. *Champion* (1826) 5 L.J. (O.S.) K.B. 44.
[65] *Stevens* v. *Bromley & Son*, above, n. 61.
[66] *Re Cleadon Trust Ltd.* [1939] Ch. 286.

would seem right. Unfortunately the case does not examine the crucial question, whether the debt was discharged by the payment or by the acceptance.

In *Reversion Fund and Insurance Company Ltd.* v. *Maison Cosway Ltd.*[67] the plaintiffs had lent money to a director of the defendant company and he had paid legal debts owing by the company. The plaintiffs knew that the director had no authority from his company to borrow. As in *Re Cleadon Trust Ltd.* the plan was to obtain authority later, but again the confident prediction that the company would accept and adopt what was done turned out to be wrong. Nevertheless, the Court of Appeal, Vaughan Williams, L.J., dissenting, held that the plaintiffs could recover to the extent that the director had used the loan to pay valid debts. Vaughan Williams, L.J., would have confined the right of recovery to the case in which the plaintiff could point to a factor negativing voluntariness, as for example a mistaken belief in the director's authority to borrow for the company.[68] Buckley and Kennedy, L.J.J., held that there was no such requirement. As their judgments stand it is impossible to identify any factor going to 'unjust' and calling for restitution. For the loan by the plaintiffs to the unauthorised director and his payment of the debts was, so far as the company was concerned, *res inter alios acta*. Their conjoint operation amounted to no more than if an out and out stranger had put his hand in his pocket and paid the company's debt. Yet the case is explicable in terms of free acceptance. The stranger's payment of the debts remained imperfect till the company accepted the discharge. Although the company had never formally adopted the transaction, it had also not repudiated the discharge of its liability. If there was a sufficient acceptance to perfect the discharge, it would have been difficult to argue that there was not also a free acceptance sufficient to give the volunteer stranger a right to restitution.

(iii) *Remedial Uncertainty in Equity*

The doctrine in *Ramsden* v. *Dyson* has a dimension to it which has nothing to do with restitution/unjust enrichment. On some facts the courts will respond in a way which gives the plaintiff far more than he would get if he could claim only the enrichment obtained by the defendant at his expense. The variety of response is at present

---

[67] *Reversion Fund and Insurance Company Ltd.* v. *Maison Cosway Ltd.* [1913] 1 K.B. 364.
[68] As in *Bannatyne* v. *MacIver* [1906] 1 K.B. 103.

treated as a matter of discretion, not as something controlled by identifiable differences between one class of fact-situation and another. This makes for deplorable uncertainty. It may later turn out to be possible to predict, with better accuracy, which facts will give only restitution and which will give more. If so, the exercise will be tantamount to a recognition that 'the doctrine in *Ramsden v. Dyson*' was really not one doctrine but two. And the dividing line which is most likely to be drawn is between a doctrine of free acceptance (or, acquiescence) and a doctrine of promissory estoppel.

The variety of responses was summed up a century ago in *Plimmer v. Wellington Corporation.*[69] The Judicial Committee there described the possibilities in this way:

In . . . *Ramsden* v. *Dyson*[70] the evidence . . . showed that the tenant expected a particular kind of lease, which Vice-Chancellor Stuart decreed to him though it does not appear what form of relief Lord Kingsdown himself would have given. In . . . *Duke of Beaufort* v. *Patrick*[71] nothing but perpetual retention of the land would satisfy the equity raised in favour of those who spent their money on it, and it was secured to them at a valuation. In . . . *Dillwyn* v. *Llewelyn*[72] nothing but a grant of the fee simple would satisfy the equity which the Lord Chancellor held to have been raised by the son's expenditure on the father's land. In . . . *Unity Bank* v. *King*,[73] the Master of the Rolls, holding that the father did not intend to part with his land to his sons, who built upon it, considered that their equity would be satisfied by recouping this expenditure to them. In fact the court must look at the circumstances in each case to decide in what way the equity can be satisfied.[74]

In this too great flexibility of response, the crucial division seems to lie along the line between these two questions: (a) Is the court going to repay the plaintiff in the coin of his actual expectations? (b) Is the court going to confine the plaintiff to restitution of his expenditure? The only justification for ever giving an affirmative answer to (a) is that the facts disclose that the defendant did something to induce those expectations. There is a difference between inducing and not undeceiving. In the case of that window-cleaner who begins to clean my windows without having been asked to do so, the difference is between the case in which I lurk in the kitchen so that he shall not see me (where my intention is to preserve my freedom to rush out afterwards and tell him that I did not want the

[69] *Plimmer* v. *Wellington Corporation* (1884) 9 App. Cas. 699.
[70] *Ramsden* v. *Dyson* (1886) L.R. 1 H.L. 129.
[71] *Duke of Beaufort* v. *Patrick* (1853) 17 Beav. 60.
[72] *Dillwyn* v. *Llewelyn* (1866) 4 De G. F. & J. 517.
[73] *Unity Bank* v. *King* (1858) 25 Beav. 72.
[74] *Plimmer* v. *Wellington Corporation* (1884) 9 App. Cas 699, 713.

work done) and another quite different case in which, in a different frame of mind, I wave to him to continue. In the second case I have created or induced in him the firm expectation that he will be paid. In the former case I have not. If it were said that by secretly remaining out of sight I encouraged his hope, that statement would only mean that I did so passively by failing to undeceive him. I certainly did not encourage him in the sense of creating or inducing or confirming his expectation. I could not, since the object of my stratagem was to prevent his discovering even that I knew he was there.

The fulfilment of expectations has nothing to do with restitution. It belongs to contract and, so far as the entity beneath the word is any different, to estoppel. A contract and an unjust enrichment based on free acceptance may exist concurrently; and so may an estoppel and an unjust enrichment. In *Inwards* v. *Baker*[75] the father assured the son that, if he built a bungalow on his, the father's, land he could live in it for as long as he pleased. The son did build. That was enough to create an equitable estoppel. When the trustees of the will wanted the son to leave, the Court of Appeal said he had an equitable interest for as long as he wanted to use the bungalow as his home. The expectation had been raised by the father and acted upon, the court fulfilled it. The son had no need to drop back to the unjust enrichment. The father had also freely accepted the building work, but it was more than his expenditure that the son was after. He wanted his expectations fulfilled. He therefore had to show facts going beyond mere free acceptance.

Crabb v. *Arun R.D.C.*[76] shows how clearly the estoppel is separable from the unjust enrichment. The Arun RDC had created an expectation in Crabb that he would get an easement of way over a strip of their land. They had orally agreed it and later continued to act as though the agreement stood. For example they had put up gates corresponding to the entrance at which Crabb was to have access to a road. He divided his land and sold part, leaving the rest cut off save for this not yet granted access. The court fulfilled the expectation. There was an estoppel, but there was no unjust enrichment at all. The Council gained nothing by Crabb's acting on his detriment. *Hussey* v. *Palmer*[77] on the other hand is more like *Inwards* v. *Baker*. A mother-in-law put £6000 into extending the house of her

---

[75] *Inwards* v. *Baker* [1965] 2 Q.B. 29; cf. *Dillwyn* v. *Llewelyn*, n. 72 above.

[76] *Crabb* v. *Arun R.D.C.* [1976] Ch. 179; cf. *Salvation Army Trustee Company* v. *West Yorkshire Metropolitan County Council* (1981) 41 P. & C.R. 179.

[77] *Hussey* v. *Palmer* [1972] 1 W.L.R. 1286, above, p. 285.

son-in-law. The arrangement was that she would move in. She did, but after a while there was a breakdown. The court was willing to fulfill her expectations by giving her an interest in the house where she had hoped to live for the rest of her life, but she was content to have back her expenditure. In other words, though the case does not put it explicitly in these terms, she was willing to fall back from the expectation-inducing estoppel to the unjust enrichment based on free acceptance.

This concession on the mother-in-law's part provides the model for what the courts themselves should insist on doing, namely distinguish between the cause of action based on promises and the cause of action based on free acceptance.[78] Where there is no promise or expectation-inducing conduct, only the cause of action in free acceptance should be recognised and only the restitutionary measure of recovery should be allowed. That is not to say, however, that there may not be other circumstances in which, despite the presence of some expectation-inducing conduct, the court may not be justified in confining the plaintiff to the restitutionary measure.

An objection may be taken to the view that this remedial uncertainty in equity is bad. Some lawyers nowadays believe that judicial discretion is good. In the past it has been more easily assumed that power should be contained by rules, an attitude which has two good effects. It promotes certainty so as to allow clients to avoid litigation. And it protects judges from political criticism. Belief in wide discretions can thus be seen as an abdication of law's traditional mission. However that may be, there are, in relation to this particular discretion, special intellectual difficulties for the organisation of Restitution, because at the moment it is impossible to say, till after the court has spoken, whether a restitutionary or a non-restitutionary response will be made.

---

[78] For evidence of this dividing line see *Amalgamated Investment* v. *Texas Commerce* [1981] 1 All E.R. 923, 935 *per* Robert Goff, J (aff'd. [1981] 3 All E.R. 577); cf. *Taylor Fashions* v. *Liverpool Victoria Trustees Co.* [1981] 1 All E.R. 897, 917-23 *per* Oliver, J.

IX

MISCELLANEOUS CASES:
POLICY-MOTIVATED RESTITUTION

IT is true that all restitution can be said in a broad sense to be 'policy-motivated'. Thus, even the mistaken payor's right to restitution rests ultimately on a policy or value-judgement to the effect that, even when account is taken of the social interest in the security of receipts, still relief ought to be given for mistakes. In short the right is the product of a decision which balances different goods and bads; and that is nothing if not policy. However, the phrase 'policy-motivated restitution' is used here to include only policies distinct from those which favour restitution for non-voluntariness or free acceptance. Another way of putting the same point is to say that the phrase indicates reasons for restitution which override the policy which dictates that, in general, a volunteer who cannot establish a free acceptance should not have restitution.

There is a certain danger that a heading of this kind may seem to be unruly and likely to draw the subject back into the mysteries of 'unjust'. Two disciplines are necessary in order to combat that danger. First, the policies said to call for restitution must be clearly spelled out. Nothing gives rise to so much uncertainty as arguments which are referred loosely to 'policy reasons' without ever saying what specific goals are supposed to be in view. Secondly, care must be taken to avoid coming too easily to the conclusion that a particular example of restitution should be explained under this miscellaneous heading rather than as a case of non-voluntariness or free acceptance. Provided that these restraints are observed, there is no reason why the number of cases of policy-motivated restitution should be regarded as closed or necessarily small. This chapter in fact discusses only five examples but it is certain that other cases could also be *21 included.

1. NO TAXATION WITHOUT PARLIAMENT

This policy is concerned with protecting the citizen from *ultra vires* demands by public authorities. The law is as yet unclear on the issue of restitution, but it seems likely that the courts will recognise that, at least on some facts, restitution ought to be awarded where, for example, a minister or an agency of local government has exacted payments without lawful authority. There is already no doubt whatever that in other respects the courts take a strict view of powers which are claimed to allow the imposition of anything in the nature of a levy or a tax. In construing provisions which are said to confer such a power the courts insist that only very clear words can have that effect,[1] and if the demand is found to be *ultra vires*, there will be no hesitation in declaring it void.[2] Such a declaration suffices in the case in which the demand is challenged before payment is made. Where the challenge is made after payment, the effect of a declaration that the demand was unlawful is sometimes to induce repayment on an *ex gratia* basis.[3] The crucial question is, however, whether there is ever restitution as a matter of right.

The dominant modern view appears to be that the citizen who pays an *ultra vires* demand must establish the same facts against the public authority as would entitle him to restitution from a private individual. This is assumed to mean that he must in practice show that he paid under a mistake of fact or under duress, or that he made a contract for repayment in the event that it should turn out that the money was not payable. On the other side of the line, those who pay by mistake of law, or even under no mistake at all but simply because they despair of making their view prevail against the position taken by the bureaucratic machine, must on this view be said to have no hope whatever of obtaining restitution.

If this is correct, the cases in which restitution is possible are those which fall under one of the heads considered in the earlier chapters, and there is no case in which restitution would require to be explained by the policy now under examination. On the other hand if the dominant orthodoxy is wrong, so that a right to restitution can be derived directly from the fact that the demand for payment was *ultra vires* the demanding authority, the conclusion must be that that right is recognised for the sake of this policy, namely to protect the citizen from unlawful impositions. The paragraphs which follow will first introduce the cases which support the orthodox position and will then show why they leave the position still unsettled.

In *Slater v. Burnley Corporation*[4] the defendants calculated the

---

[1] *A-G. v. Wilts United Dairies Ltd.* (1921) 37 T.L.R. 884 (C.A.); (1922) 127 L.T. 822 (H.L.); *Brocklebank v. R.*, [1925] 1 K.B. 52.

[2] *Daymond v. South West Water Authority* [1976] A.C. 609; *Congreve v. Home Office* [1976] Q.B. 629; *Bromley v. G.L.C.* [1982] 2 W.L.R. 62.

[3] Below, p. 298.

[4] *Slater v. Burnley Corporation* (1888) 59 L.T. 636.

water rate on the wrong basis. Slater 'raised a contention' but gave in. He was denied recovery. The Corporation had power to turn off his water but had not threatened to do so. There was, therefore, nothing in the nature of duress. The Divisional Court regarded this demand as indistinguishable from an honest claim made and settled between individuals. In *William Whitely Ltd.* v. *R.*,[5] the company had strenuously maintained that employees who served meals were not 'male servants' within the meaning of the *Revenue Act, 1869*, and did not therefore have to be licensed. They litigated the question and won. But Walton, J. rejected their petition of right to recover licence fees paid during the dispute. In *Twyford* v. *Manchester Corporation*[6] the plaintiff stonemason paid fees for access to local cemeteries in order to do work on headstones. He paid under protest, and it did turn out that the demands were not authorised under the *Burials Acts, 1852–1906*, but Romer, J., refused restitution. The judge found as a matter of fact that the plaintiff had not paid in the apprehension of being excluded if he should decline to do so. In the absence of that pressure the public dimension of the case added nothing: it was an ordinary settlement of an honest claim. Romer, J., clearly took the view that if the plaintiff could not establish duress he could not obtain restitution at all.

In *Mason* v. *New South Wales*[7] the High Court of Australia had to consider whether road hauliers could recover payments made for permits required under a licensing scheme which had been declared unconstitutional. It was held that they could. But the reason given was not that the scheme was *ultra vires* but rather that, as well as being *ultra vires*, it also contained an unlawful power to seize unlicensed lorries. The court was therefore able to conclude that the payments had been made under this threat of duress. Though the conclusion is different, the law is the same as in the cases which have just been set out. The court appeared to be satisfied that English authority did not support the existence of a special right of recovery where public authorities went beyond their powers. But Owen Dixon, C.J., said at one point that, had it been necessary, he would have been willing to open up that question for further examination.[8]

The question cannot be regarded as settled. The English cases have never received a re-examination worthy of modern administrative law, transformed beyond recognition in the last twenty-five years.

---

[5] *William Whitely Ltd*. v. *R*. (1909) 101 L.T. 741; cf. *National Pari-Mutuel Association* v. *R*., (1930) 47 T.L.R. 110, *Glasgow Corptn*. v. *Lord Advocate* 1959 S.C. 203.

[6] *Twyford* v. *Manchester Corporation* [1946] Ch. 236.

[7] *Mason* v. *New South Wales* (1959) 102 C.L.R. 108.

[8] Ibid, at 114.

They also do not take account of the constitutional principle against executive taxation.[9] Finally, they fail to tap a series of cases which seem to support a precisely contrary view, namely that, against public authorities, the ground for restitution is simply the want of authority to make the demand.

In *Hooper* v. *Exeter Corporation*[10] the plaintiff recovered harbour dues paid on the import of limestone. He had paid because he did not know there was a statutory exemption where, as in his case, the stone was brought in to be burned for the purpose of making lime. The Divisional Court seems to have based the right to restitution directly on the Corporation's want of authority. In *Queens of the River Steamship Co. Ltd.* v. *The Conservators of the River Thames*,[11] Phillimore, J., made the Thames Conservancy repay tolls overcharged for use of a pier. Again the ground appears to have been want of lawful authority. *South of Scotland Electricity Board* v. *British Oxygen Co. Ltd., (No. 2)*[12] assumes a similar doctrine in relation to charges for electricity in excess of the statutory tariff.[12a]

These cases involve facts in which there was a potentiality for pressure, as, for instance, by withholding goods, or refusing the use of a facility or the supply of a commodity. But, differently from *Slater* v. *Burnley Corporation* and *Twyford* v. *Manchester Corporation*, nothing turned on the question whether that pressure had actually been applied or apprehended. This point is clearly brought out by the facts of the old case of *Steele* v. *Williams*.[13] There the plaintiff recovered a sum wrongly demanded for the taking of extracts from a parish register. The *ultra vires* claim had been paid after the extracts had been taken. The case cannot be explained in terms of duress. Even although the parish clerk had the power to apply pressure by withholding the register until he was paid, on the facts he had not done so. He had allowed the extracts to be made and had then made the unauthorised demand and had been paid. The incompatibility between this case and *Twyford* is manifest.

Recent cases of *ultra vires* demands have caught the public eye. None more so than the Bromley opposition to the Greater London

---

[9] Enshrined in the *Bill of Rights* (1688) 1 W.m. 3 and M., Sess. 2, C.2; cf. *Newdigate* v. *Davy* (1693) 1 Ld. Ray. 742; *Campbell* v. *Hall* (1774) 1 Cowp. 204.

[10] *Hooper* v. *Exeter Corporation* (1887) 56 L.J.Q.B. 457.

[11] *Queens of the River Steamship Co. Ltd.* v. *The Conservators of the River Thames* (1899) 15 T.L.R. 474.

[12] *South of Scotland Electricity Board* v. *British Oxygen Co. Ltd. (No. 2)* [1959] 1 W.L.R. 587.

[12a] Cf. these Irish cases: *Dolan* v. *Neligan* [1967] I.R. 247; *Rogers* v. *Louth County Council* [1981] I.R. 265.

[13] *Steele* v. *Williams* (1853) 22 L.J. Ex. 225.

Council's policy of subsidising London transport rates.[14] But that case stopped short of asking the restitutionary question. It was the same in *Daymond* v. *South West Water Authority*[15] in relation to sewerage charges unlawfully imposed on homes not connected to the public system, and in *Congreve* v. *Home Office*[16] in relation to over-payments for television licences. There was a wide-spread assumption that these cases were about 'getting the money back', but technically only the lawfulness of the demands was in issue. Nevertheless prominent cases of this kind do show that the question of a public law right to restitution based on the doctrine of *ultra vires* is certain to be squarely raised in the near future.

The arguments do not, however, all run one way. In some cases there may be a massive disproportion between the amount at stake for particular individuals and the amount repayable from some public purse to all such individuals. Where there is a serious danger that public finances will be disrupted it may be necessary to limit or exclude a right to restitution.[17] This has been a consideration of some importance in jurisdictions where the existence of a written constitution contains the danger that general taxing statutes may be struck down. But, on the other hand, it is arguable that the resources of a modern state can bear such dangers in the interest of defending the rule of law. After the *Daymond* case an Act was passed precisely to enable the authority to repay the money obtained *ultra vires*.[18] So restitution was effected as a matter of legislative, and ultimately executive, grace. But this fact itself undermines the argument based on the fear of disrupting public finances. For if restitution can be conceded *ex gratia* without chaos, then clearly it could equally be ordered as a matter of right. The recognition of that right would be in tune with the developments in administrative law in the post *Ridge* v. *Baldwin*[19] era.

A final point in favour of this position is that it is required as a matter of reciprocity between citizen and government. For it may be that when the parties are the other way about, with the public agency seeking to recover money which it had no authority to pay out, the public body already has the benefit of a stringent right of recovery based directly on the want of authority. This has not been

---

[14] *Bromley London Borough Council* v. *G.L.C.* [1982] 2 W.L.R. 62.

[15] *Daymond* v. *South West Water Authority* [1976] A.C. 609.

[16] *Congreve* v. *Home Office* [1976] Q.B. 629; cf. *Air Canada* v. *Secretary of State for Trade* [1983] 2 W.L.R. 494.

[17] *Sargood Bros.* v. *The Commonwealth* (1910–11) 11 C.L.R. 258, 303, *per* Isaacs, J.

[18] *Water Charges Act*, 1976.

[19] *Ridge* v. *Baldwin* [1964] A.C. 40.

tested in England, but in *Commonwealth of Australia* v. *Burns*[20] it was said that the stringency of this claim went as far as to deprive the payee of any defence of estoppel based on what was said and done by civil servants actually making the payment: no individual could give the authority power to part with the money. This is a doctrine which is likely to be subject to limitations as yet unexplored. If it is correct, even in some modified form, its policy-motivation cannot be 'No taxation without Parliament' but something more like 'No abuse of public funds'. Both are of course no more than restatements, at a lower level, of the single policy of safeguarding the rule of law.

*22

2. DISCOURAGEMENT OF UNLAWFUL CONDUCT

The last heading was concerned with discouraging public bodies from unlawful behaviour. This one returns to the private domain. The question here is whether a restitutionary right is ever given directly in order to induce people to abstain from unlawful conduct. A distinction has to be taken at the outset between defences and claims, for there is no doubt that in the law of restitution this particular policy does find expression in the behaviour of defences. The treatment of defences belongs chiefly to Chapter XII; but it is convenient to begin this discussion by looking briefly at a defence which is explicable in terms of this policy.

If I pay you money for an unlawful purpose, as for instance to induce you to steal, your refusal to go through with the theft is something which the law must applaud and encourage. Suppose therefore that, after I have paid you £1000, you refuse to perform the theft and I claim restitution. I say that my intent that you should have the money was qualified and that the consideration for which I paid has totally failed. It is obvious that I must lose. If I did not, people in my position would have a lever to compel completion of of the illegal performance. Unable to sue in contract, they might nevertheless find a sufficient sanction in the threat to sue for restitution. So, I might say to you on finding you hesitant to steal: 'If you do not carry out the theft, I shall recover my £1000.' And that might serve to make you go through with it. Hence you are given a defence to my claim based on total failure of consideration, and that defence is easily and obviously explicable by reference to the policy of discouraging unlawful behaviour.

---

[20] *Commonwealth of Australia* v. *Burns* [1971] V.R. 825.

If we analyse the explanation of this defence more closely, we find that there are in fact three separable discouragements to unlawful behaviour which are achieved by it. First, the plaintiff is deprived of a weapon for compelling completion of the illegal plan. Second, the defendant is allowed to retain the money and, therefore, has an incentive for not performing the illegal act. Third, the plaintiff is made to understand that the courts never help those who flout the law: *ex turpi causa non oritur actio* (no action arises from an unworthy cause).

It might be suggested that the best complement to the defence of illegality which has just been considered would be an active claim which became available as soon as the illegal plan was performed. The rule would then be: no restitution before performance, automatic restitution after performance. That rule would seem to maximise the pressure for legality since the defendant would stand to gain by abstaining from the unlawful conduct but would lose if he failed to abstain. Such a claim, if it existed, would be explicable only in terms of this policy, because the plaintiff would necessarily be a volunteer who had obtained through his payment exactly the reciprocation which he intended to obtain. However, no active claim of that kind does exist. And again the reason is obvious. Though a claim after illegal performance does have excellent deterrent and incentive value, it conflicts with the last of the three policy goals identified in the previous paragraph because it would involve the court in assisting a disgraceful plaintiff. Thus, suppose that I pay you £1000 to steal, and you do steal; then I claim the money back and, in order to do it, I set out my own initial contempt for the law. It is clear that no court could hear me: *ex turpi causa non oritur actio*. Despite the effect that such a claim would have in encouraging lawful conduct and discouraging unlawful conduct, the disgraceful plaintiff cannot be made the instrument of that policy. His exclusion from the courts is itself part of that policy. Hence the policy is easily expressed through the defence but not through a complementary active claim.

There is, however, an exceptional set of cases. The deterrent claim after performance was said in the last paragraph to have positive value, which could not be used because of the bar against assisting disgraceful plaintiffs. If that is right, the claim ought to be upheld in cases in which the plaintiff is untainted by any turpitude. In short where the *causa* is not *turpis* the claim after an illegal performance should be welcomed for its deterrent and incentive effects. That is exactly what we find. When the plaintiff is mistaken as to the facts creating the illegality, or defrauded by the defendant into believing that the purpose is legal, or is unequal to the defendant in that he is compelled or exploited, or repents of the illegal purpose before it is even partly fulfilled, he is allowed to recover.[21] These are the cases in which the *causa* is not *turpis* or, in the language of the other maxim in this field—*in pari delicto potior est conditio defendentis* (where the guilt is shared the defendant's position is the stronger)—the *delictum* is not *par*. In all these cases, except the last in which the repentance must come before performance, restitution is allowed even after the illegal performance has been completed: the deterrent effect of the claim after performance can be used because the plaintiff is in every case a worthy instrument of that policy.

Yet, again for the moment leaving aside the claim based on penitence, none of these claims actually requires to be explained as the product of this policy. That is, they serve the policy of discouraging illegality but are not engendered by that policy. The reason is that each one is independently explicable as generated by vitiated voluntariness (mistake, compulsion, inequality and so on). The proper analysis seems to be that the defence of illegality—*in pari delicto potior est conditio defendentis*—does not apply to claims based on vitiated voluntariness. The claims themselves do not need to be explained by reference to illegality.

The case of penitence has to be treated differently. It does require to be explained as and solely as the creature of this policy. Under an ordinary lawful contract which you are willing to perform, I cannot unilaterally call the transaction off and recover whatever I may already have transferred to you.[22] But the cases acknowledge that a party to an illegal contract does have a time during which to change his mind—a *locus poenitentiae* (a space for repentance).[23] So long as he repents spontaneously before any of the illegal plan has been achieved he may have restitution.[24] His change of mind has two crucial effects. First, it brings the matter out into the open so that the unlawful plan is exposed and can go no further. Second, it clears away the taint of turpitude, putting the plaintiff outside the category of persons unworthy to invoke the court's assistance.

Spontaneity is essential on both these counts. Where the plaintiff has merely been foiled by the other's refusal to carry through the illegal performance, his case remains unworthy. Furthermore, if he

---

[21] See below, p. 425 ff.
[22] *Thomas* v. *Brown*, (1876) 1 Q.B.D. 714.
[23] *Taylor* v. *Bowers* (1876) 1 Q.B.D. 291.
[24] *Kearley* v. *Thomson* (1890) 24 Q.B.D. 742.

were allowed to recover when foiled, the effect would be to give him a lever with which to compel performance and, at the same time, would deprive the other party of his incentive to abstain from the illegality. Suppose, for example, that I give you money to place fraudulent bets on a particular horse. I want you to do it in such a way as to rig the odds by concealing the amount of money which is being put on this horse. You are sure my horse will lose anyhow. So you take the risk of putting my money straight into your own pocket. You never place any of the bets. No illegal purpose is ever achieved, since your dishonesty foils mine. Yet I cannot recover.[25] To allow restitution on the ground of 'repentance' would be nonsense. It would in effect be to allow the claim based directly on total failure of consideration; and we have seen that that contradicts all three elements in the policy against unlawful behaviour.[26] It follows that there must be both a change of mind and a change of heart.

Yet, on the whole, people who embark on illegal projects to not repent spontaneously. The *locus poenitentiae* therefore remains a not much patronised ground for restitution. *Taylor v. Bowers*,[27] which is usually regarded as the leading case supporting the possibility of a claim on the ground of penitence, may in fact support a variant of the doctrine, in which, in certain circumstances, a change of mind need not be accompanied by a change of heart.

The plaintiff returned from America to find his business in trouble. He tried to defraud his creditors by transferring a steam-engine and some other machinery to his nephew, but the nephew double-crossed him. He collusively arranged for the chattels to be made over to the defendant, who was one of the' creditors. This not only foiled the plaintiff's scheme but also compounded the fraud on the others. The plaintiff therefore brought detinue for the value of the machinery and the engine. He was allowed to recover. Yet clearly there was here no spontaneous change of heart. The point may be that, overlooking the *turpis causa*, the court will respond to a change of mind unaccompanied by a change of heart so long as both the illegal purpose has not been achieved and recovery can only prevent its being achieved. Here, if Taylor recovered, the creditors could only be the less defrauded. So recovery would merely tend to diminish the forces working for the illegal plan: it would kill it stone dead. The threat of restitution could not possibly be used as a lever to compel complete performance.

---

[25] *Harry Parker* v. *Mason* [1940] 2 K.B. 590; *Bigos* v. *Bousted* [1951] 1 All E.R. 92.
[26] Above, p. 300.
[27] *Cit.*, n. 23 above.

Whether or not the doctrine admits of this variation, there is a two-tiered problem in relation to its operation with regard to chattels. It is now clear, as it was not clear at the time of *Taylor* v. *Bowers* itself, that property does pass under an illegal contract.[28] Thus, under an illegal contract of sale the general property passes, since that is what is intended. And under an illegal bailment or lease a temporary property passes whose duration is defined by the terms of the contract itself. The first question which arises is what happens at the moment at which the plaintiff repents. Presumably, the effect of repentance is to extinguish the property which passed under the contract. It must, therefore, be a species of common law rescission analogous to rescission for fraud, so that during the *locus poenitentiae* the recipient has a voidable title. The second part of the problem is as to the nature of the relief which the penitent then gets. The rescission is itself restitutionary. The penitent revests the *res* in himself. But in *Taylor* v. *Bowers* the claim which the plaintiff maintained was then simply in tort, for detinue. Presumably, therefore, the correct analysis is that the plaintiff has a restitutionary right *in rem* which, once it has been exercised, puts him in a position to make all the usual claims in respect of tortious interference with chattels. That is, he may seek an order for delivery up or he may obtain damages in either the normal compensatory measure or the less familiar restitutionary measure. The range of possiblities will be discussed in the chapter on restitution for wrongs.[29]

The conclusion of this part is that the policy goal which consists in the discouragement of unlawful conduct is directly responsible only for the restitutionary claim based on penitence. For the rest, it is expressed chiefly in the behaviour of defences to restitutionary claims which themselves arise in the ordinary way from mistake, compulsion and inequality. The claim based on penitence thus has an important place in the theoretical structure of the law of restitution, though in practice it is never likely to be much used.

There is other matter capable of being considered under this head, but it lies on the other side of the division between restitution for unjust enrichment (by subtraction) and restitution for wrongs. 'Where a plaintiff is allowed restitution of a wrongdoer's profits' the reason is nearly always to be found in the need to discourage recourse to certain unlawful modes of enrichment. This will be discussed below.[30]

---

[28] *Singh* v. *Ali* [1960] A.G. 167; *Belvoir Finance Co.* v. *Stapleton* [1971] 1 Q.B. 210.
[29] Below, p. 321 ff.
[30] Below, p. 326 ff.

3. ENCOURAGEMENT OF RESCUE AT SEA

Where property is saved at sea the rescuers are entitled to a reasonable reward. In 1949 the *Queen Elizabeth* ran aground as she was coming into Southampton. Attempts were made to tow her off on the first high water after she grounded. After some of the cargo and fuel had been removed she was pulled free on the second high water. Wilmer, J., awarded £43 500 to be divided among eight of the tugs which had been engaged in the operation. The ship had been stuck fast for twenty-four hours. With her cargo she was worth more than £6 million, even in the money of that time.[31]

This right to maritime salvage awards is based on the practice of the Court of Admiralty. It was never infected by the explanation in terms of implied contract. It extended only to ships and their cargoes, though an allowance would be made for saving life so long as property was also saved. This parasitic approach to rewards for saving life has been given up by statute. The statutory right is available even where lives are saved and property is not.[32] Statute has also brought aircraft within the same principles.[33]

It may be thought that maritime salvage should have been considered earlier, as a case in which the plaintiff's claim rests on non-voluntariness and, in particular, on moral compulsion arising from the defendant's urgent need. *Goff and Jones* give it a chapter of its own but co-ordinate that chapter with another on non-maritime emergencies under the general heading '*Necessity. Restitution in Respect of Benefits conferred in an Emergency without Request.*'[34] That heading, in its turn, belongs in a series in which two previous members are 'Compulsion' and 'Mistake'. This suggests that the authors do believe that maritime salvage ought to be explained in terms of vitiated voluntariness, the rescuer being constrained to intervene by the moral compulsion emanating from the emergency. Nevertheless, the chapter itself abstains from any such assertion.

Many individual cases of salvage do certainly involve acts of heroism and self-sacrifice done under moral compulsion. But the law does not require a claimant to show that he did so act. He may have felt no call of duty whatever. He may have acted simply in the hope of winning a reward if successful in the attempt to save property. It is the policy of the law to encourage rescue from emergencies, but

---

[31] *The Queen Elizabeth* (1949) 82 Lloyds L.R. 803.
[32] *Merchant Shipping Act 1894*, s. 544 (1).
[33] *Civil Aviation Act* 1982, s. 87 (replacing *Civil Aviation Act* 1949, s. 51).
[34] At p. 280.

the encouragement is given by making the reward available to all who succeed.

There is no doubt about the underlying policy; it is often re-affirmed. In *The Telemachus*,[35] Wilmer, J., asked in argument: 'Is it not the underlying principle of salvage that seamen must be encouraged by awards of salvage to render assistance to property?' In his judgment he answered his own question by describing this as a 'root principle'.[36] In *The St. Blane*,[37] Brandon, J., speaking of the attitude taken by the courts to minor errors of judgment made by the salvor, affirmed the same overriding objective: 'This principle of the lenient approach to mistakes is an important one. It derives from the basic policy of the law relating to salvage services, which is always to encourage rather than discourage, the rendering of such services.'[38]

But, given this aim, it cannot be said that the law confines awards to those who have felt compelled to give the assistance. This is shown most vividly by awards given to salvors who have behaved shabbily, in such a way as to make perfectly clear that they did not feel duty-bound to intervene. The courts censure such claimants but do not refuse them payment. In *The Medina*,[39] a ship carrying more than 500 pilgrims from Sumatra to Jedda was wrecked on a rock in the Red Sea. The pilgrims had to abandon ship. There was barely room for them to stand on the rock, only just above the level of the sea. Another ship, the *Timor* came up; her master would not take the pilgrims aboard and into the port of Jedda unless he was promised £4000 by the master of the *Medina*. That was the full sum payable to the *Medina* for the whole trip from Sumatra. But the master of the *Medina* was not in a position to choose. He was faced with the very real possibility that the pilgrims would otherwise drown. Brett, J.A., said: 'The amount claimed by the *Timor* was exorbitant—not merely too large, but, for the services to be rendered, grossly exorbitant—and it was forced upon the captain of the *Medina* by practical compulsion.'[40] This, therefore, was an intervener who was so little moved by moral compulsion that he preferred to bargain with the victims of the disaster. 'Nevertheless,' said Sir Robert Philli-more at first instance, 'it was certainly a valuable salvage service according to the principles upon which such services have always

---

[35] *The Telemachus* [1957] P. 47.
[36] At p. 49.
[37] *The St. Blane* [1974] 1 Lloyds Rept. 557.
[38] At p. 560.
[39] *The Medina* (1876) 1 P.D. 272, affd. (1876) 2 P.D. 5.
[40] Ibid. 2 P.D. 5, 7.

been considered in this court . . . and I shall award £1800.'[41] And that was the award upheld in the Court of Appeal. Similarly, in *The Port Caledonia and The Anna*,[42] the master of a tug was severely criticised for exacting a promise of £1000 before offering the *Port Caledonia* a rope during a storm in Holyhead harbour; but he was awarded £200.

This same point is made by the attitude of the courts to professional salvors. If moral compulsion were the gist of the claim such people would be outside its range as having sought out the need by which they claimed to have been compelled. But the opposite view is taken. In *The Queen Elizabeth*, Wilmer, J., who also described the award as made to 'volunteers, who voluntarily performed the services', said

In the case of the *Bustler* and the *Metinda III* I have tried to give effect to the fact that they are, primarily and in the first instance, professional salvors. As Sir William McNair put it, salvage awards to such plaintiffs are bread and butter, whereas to the other plaintiffs claiming in this case they may more properly be described as jam. I need not refer to authority for the proposition . . . that salvors of this character are entitled to a special measure of generosity.[43]

Finally, in *Scaramanga* v. *Stamp*[44] the question arose whether a deviation which would otherwise be a breach of contract would be justified if done to save life or property. The *Olympias* had met the *Arion* in trouble and had tried to tow her into Texel. The *Olympias* herself went aground in the operation and lost her cargo. The plaintiff cargo owner's claim for breach of contract was upheld. The deviation was not justified by the attempts to save the *Arion*. The ship could, therefore, not rely on a clause in the contract exempting it from losses arising from perils of the sea. Cockburn, C.J., drew a distinction between the minimum deviation necessary to save life (then not subject to salvage) and further deviation to save property. It was unnecessary to relieve a ship from liability in the latter case, or to preserve its insurance, because there was no moral compulsion to save property and, even if there were arguments for recognising such a duty, 'the law has provided another and a very adequate motive for the saving of property, by securing to the salvor a liberal proportion of the property saved'.[45] Here it is clearly the hope of reward and not moral duty which is regarded as explaining the

[41] Ibid. 1 P.D. 272, 275.
[42] *The Port Caledonia and The Anna* [1903] P. 184.
[43] *The Queen Elizabeth* (1949) 82 Lloyds L.R. 803, 821.
[44] *Scaramanga* v. *Stamp* (1805) 5 C.P.D. 295.
[45] At p. 305.

salvor's intervention; and many cases in which an award has been given for bringing in some piece of wrecked ship or her cargo could not be otherwise explained.[46] There is no real possibility, therefore, of classifying this species of claim other than as policy-motivated. It exists to encourage rescue; it is not based on compulsion.

There is another difficult question about maritime salvage's place in the law of restitution. According to what was said at the beginning, nothing counts as restitution unless the measure of the defendant's liability is the enrichment received by him at the plaintiff's expense. The effect of laxity on that score is to turn the subject into an *omnium gatherum* for everything beyond contract and wrongs. We were careful to say that restitution/unjust enrichment only forms a coherent body of law if it is regarded as a category found within, and removed from, that larger miscellany. So, after restitution has been taken out, some cases still remain to be classified under 'Other Events', the residual miscellany which comes after the three nominate heads, namely Consent, Wrongs, and Unjust Enrichment.[47] Possibly maritime salvage belongs there.

This turns on the measure of the award. In order to qualify as restitutionary the measure would have to be the value of the salvor's work, plus his outlay. There would be some room for argument on details. In particular, there would be partisans of the view that the end product, here presumably the value of the property saved, would constitute the maximum within which the 'just sum' based on the salvor's input would be calculated. In short the manner of calculating the defendant's enrichment at the salvor's expense would be drawn into the difficulties explored in *B.P. Exploration (Libya) Ltd. v. Hunt.*[48]

However, the cases do not enter on these difficulties. The reason is that they contain no overt commitment to the restitutionary measure in the first place. The courts' task is to fix a fair and reasonable reward. They have to bear in mind the need to encourage similar efforts in the future, and they have to take into account the danger, the skill, and the value of whatever was saved. This might be thought to be conclusive against membership of the category called restitution. But the case remains on the borderline. Although the restitutionary measure is not overtly appealed to and may possibly not apply, it is not clear that the factors which are taken into account are not the very factors defining the value of the salvor's

---

[46] E.g. *The Boiler ex Elephant* (1891) 64 L.T. 543.
[47] Above, p. 32 and 54.
[48] Above, p. 250 ff.

services. Much depends on the theory of value which is ultimately applied in this field. Only when that is more clearly settled will it be possible to see whether maritime salvage can properly be regarded as an example to restitution.

When salvage is detached from moral compulsion and referred instead to a policy in favour of rescue, it can be recognised as a specialised case of *negotiorum gestio*. Civilian systems recognise the regime of *negotiorum gestio*, not to relieve plaintiffs who have intervened in another's affairs by reason of moral compulsion, but rather to promote the policy that the affairs of the absent should not be allowed to go to rack and ruin. The *gestor* (the intervener) does not have to prove either a factor negativing voluntariness on his side or a free acceptance on the defendant's side. As with salvors, there is room for argument whether the measure of recovery allowed to a *gestor* can be called restitutionary.

4. PROTECTION OF CREDITORS AND INVESTORS

There are a number of examples of restitution which can most realistically be said to serve this policy though some might possibly be explained in other ways. The most prominent case is the creditor's right to avoid a conveyance of property made with intent to defraud him.[49] Similar in principle is a spouse's right to have a disposition set aside if it was made with a view to defeating a claim to financial relief by making the other spouse seem poorer than he or she really is.[50]

In such cases it is tempting to say immediately that the right to restitution is based on wrongdoing. The alienor—that is, the debtor or the evasive spouse—undoubtedly does commit a wrong. But the person who is caused to give up the property is not the alienor but the alienee. As between the claimant and the alienee it is difficult to say that the right is born of a wrong. The alienee may have committed none. Though it is true that an alienee who is a *bona fide* purchaser for value without notice will have a defence, it is not possible to infer from that fact that only the *mala fide* alienee will be liable, for an entirely innocent donee will not have the defence, on the ground of having given no value. Such an alienee cannot be said to have committed any wrong even in the sense of 'breach of duty', according to which a wrong does not require moral culpability.

---

[49] *Law of Property Act, 1925*, s. 172.
[50] *Matrimonial Causes Act, 1973*, s. 37.

An alternative explanation might rest the right on 'ignorance':[51] the alienee takes wealth which would have accrued to the creditor if it had not been intercepted by the alienee (an interceptive subtraction), and the creditor does not assent to the enrichment (because ignorant of it). But that explanation is unsatisfactory because it relies on what might seem to be an overstretched notion of an interceptive subtraction.

Since both these explanations encounter difficulties, it is easiest to account for the creditor's right against the alienee by saying that it has been recognised directly in response to the need to protect creditors from this species of malpractice.

A different example comes from the field of company law and, in particular, from the operation of the doctrine of *ultra vires*. We are only concerned here with claims by the company as plaintiff.[52] Claims against the company can certainly not be explained as part of the machinery for protecting its creditors and investors. But the company's own right to recover an *ultra vires* payment can indeed be so explained, because the entire rationale of the doctrine of *ultra vires* was from the beginning to ensure that those who put up money for a company should be able to know that it would be used for the project described in the memorandum of association and would not be dissipated on entirely different purposes. The company's right to restitution of an *ultra vires* payment is thus an outwork of the need, in the interests of creditors and investors, to keep the fund committed to those purposes for which the company was formed. However, two considerable qualifications have to be placed on what is said in this paragraph.

First, recourse to the doctrine of *ultra vires* will now be very rare because statutory reforms have supervened whose effect is to allow the outsider to affirm, in almost all cases, that the company must be treated as having had the power to effect the transaction in question.[53] The principal statutory conditions which must be satisfied are that there must have been some transaction between the company and the outsider capable of being described as a 'dealing with the company', and the outsider must have been in good faith.

---

[51] Above, p. 141 ff.

[52] *Brougham* v. *Dwyer* (1913) 108 L.T. 504. But even at common law the company may be able to sue on the contract itself, since it is difficult for incapacity to be pleaded against the incapax: see the difference of opinion in *Bell Houses Ltd.* v. *City Wall Properties Ltd.* [1966] 1 Q.B. 207; [1966] 2 Q.B. 656.

[53] *European Communities Act, 1972*, s. 9 (1). This will be relevant chiefly in claims *against* the company but may also be relied upon by a defendant to a claim *by* the company in order to maintain the validity of the payment to him, as in *International Sales*, below, p. 310.

The reason why the protection of creditors and investors has now had to be so reduced is that careful drafting of very wide objects clauses in memoranda of association effectively destroyed the restrictive effect which the doctrine was intended to have and turned it instead into a trap for the occasional person who had the misfortune to encounter a company with a less than comprehensive range of purposes. The notion that memoranda were public documents, which every careful businessman would consult, clearly could not conceal the fact that the doctrine in practice damaged more people than it could protect.

Secondly, there are again two competing explanations of the company's right. It can be said that the company, acting through its organs, voluntarily parts with its money but is allowed restitution for the policy reason which is now under discussion. Or, alternatively, it can be said that the company is a helpless and mindless entity whose affairs have to be managed by trustee-like natural persons who ought not to give away the company's property for purposes outside its powers. On this second view there is no need to analyse the right as the creature of this protective policy since it can be explained as a subtractive enrichment obtained by the outsider without the company's knowledge. Recently, in *International Sales and Agencies Ltd.* v. *Marcus*[54] the plaintiff company recovered a payment which had been made out of its funds to the defendant by way of repaying a loan made by the defendant to a former director and majority shareholder. That is to say, company money was used to repay a personal debt. Lawson, J., rested the restitutionary right on two distinct bases. First, the payment was a misapplication by a fiduciary in breach of his duty. Secondly, the payment was *ultra vires*. These two bases correspond to the explanations which have just been advanced. On the first basis the director who paid the money was the channel through whom the company's money passed, subtractively, to the defendant, and the company was 'ignorant' of the transfer. On the second, the facts being such that the defendant could not satisfy the statutory conditions for forsaking the aims of the doctrine of *ultra vires*,[55] the company did pay the money but was, none the less, allowed recovery because creditors and investors still need and get protection against this kind of voluntary misapplication of the company's funds.

---

[54] *International Sales and Agencies Ltd.* v. *Marcus* [1982] 2 All E.R. 551.
[55] He could not show that, in accepting the payment in discharge of the personal debt, he had been 'dealing with the company' and dealing 'in good faith': ibid.

5. THE ELIMINATION OF ANOMALIES

Summum ius summa iniuria: the application of a logical framework of rules can sometimes produce an anomalous and outrageous result. If it does, the elimination of the anomaly may be more laudable than an extremely technical defence of the rules which allow it to happen. Moreover, the framework of those rules will remain substantially undamaged if the elimination of the anomaly is openly admitted to be a policy objective capable of overriding their logic in, and only in, an extreme case where they happen to interact unsatifactorily.

Owen v. *Tate*[56] is a case in which this kind of argument ought to have prevailed. We have already seen[57] that the plaintiff was a voluntary surety who had discharged the defendant's debt but who failed in his claim to restitution. If he had been a volunteer payor who paid the debt at once, instead of first promising to pay it and then paying, he would have been able to recover against the debtor on the basis of free acceptance (if the debtor had accepted his discharge) or against the creditor on the basis of total failure of consideration (if the debtor had repudiated the discharge). On the other hand, if the debtor had asked him to give the promise to pay, or if necessity had constrained him to do so, he would have been able to recover irrespective of the debtor's attitude to the payment itself, since in those circumstances a payment made under legal compulsion does discharge the debt and does entitle the payor to restitution. Again, if the plaintiff had taken an assignment of the debt he would have been able to sue the defendant. So there were four paths to restitution each of which was nearly but not quite available to the plaintiff.

These multiple paths to restitution nevertheless fall short of the conclusion that a volunteer payor should always have restitution against the debtor. There is a good reason for this, but it does not extend to the particular facts of *Owen* v. *Tate*. The good reason for the shortfall is this: even though the law of assignment means that the debtor may have a new creditor foisted on him against his will, creditors have an interest in knowing whether the person who pays off a debt does so with or without the intention of turning against the debtor.[58] For a creditor may be well-disposed to his debtor and may be willing to accept a discharge offered by a person to whom he would never assign the debt. Hence, from the creditor's and not

---

[56] *Owen* v. *Tate* [1976] 1 Q.B. 402.
[57] Above p. 189.
[58] *Norton* v. *Haggett* (1952) 85 A. 2d. 571.

from the debtor's point of view, it is necessary to prevent a would-be assignee from masquerading as a person who is anxious to pay off the debt as a kindness to the debtor. But in *Owen* v. *Tate* the plaintiff paid as a surety and there was no actual or hypothetical danger that the creditor would be surprised by his subsequently looking for reimbursement from the debtor since that is what all sureties do when they have to pay.

Hence, the plaintiff in *Owen* v. *Tate* was surrounded by different paths to restitution and was himself clear of the only serious mischief. Yet the logic of the rules would not let him recover. He ought to have been allowed restitution, on the ground that the development of the law in this area has left the volunteer surety in an indefensibly isolated position of disadvantage.

Another example in a different field is *Re Banque des Marchands de Moscou, Wilenkin* v. *The Liquidator.*[59] If I supply necessary goods to a minor or someone suffering under an incapacity I can sue for the reasonable value even in the absence of moral compulsion so long as I intended to charge. Such recipients lack contractual capacity but are, none the less, made liable. In this case, however, the recipient was not merely disabled but, temporarily, non-existent. The claimant conferred necessary and valuable services in preserving the Bank's property after the Bank itself had been dissolved by the Russian Government. His restitutionary claim failed. Vaisey, J., could not escape the logic of his finding that, between the dissolution and the subsequent appointment of the liquidator in England (which was the period of the claimant's activity), there was no entity capable of accepting or receiving the benefit of these services. If the services were necessary and thus passed the test of incontrovertible benefit, the technical objection that there was no entity to receive them might well have been overridden. It is certain that the liquidator, when he was finally appointed, did take the benefit of the work which had been done. Even supposing that the analogies of the minor and the mental patient do not naturally extend to an extinct company, the difference is nevertheless, so insubstantial as to be difficult to defend in such a way as to satisfy any litigant. While bearing in mind that this argument should be used sparingly and only in an extreme case, we can say that restitution ought to have been allowed for the sake of avoiding a conclusion which, despite being logically defensible, seems substantially anomalous and unnecessary.[60]

---

[59] *Re Banque des Marchauds de Moscou, Wilenkin* v. *The Liquidator* [1952] 1 All. E.R. 1269.

[60] Mr Wilenkin was in fact subsequently allowed a payment, when Vaisey, J., agreed that the court could sanction the making of an *ex gratia* allowance without waiting for the consent of other creditors: see *Re Banque des Marchands de Moscou, Wilenkin* v. *The Liquidator, (No. 2)* [1953] 1 W.L.R. 172.

X

RESTITUTION FOR WRONGS

AT this point we cross a major divide. Hitherto we have been concerned with plaintiffs whose *prima facie* claim to restitution is that they have lost what the defendant has gained. That is to say, they put themselves within the subtraction sense of 'at the expense of' and then, having shown that the defendant has been enriched at their expense in that sense, they go on to identify a factor which calls for restitution and thus shows that the enrichment is 'unjust'. We have seen that such plaintiffs never need to rely on the wrong as the factor calling for restitution.[1] They point instead to vitiated voluntariness, qualified voluntariness, free acceptance, or an identifiable policy favouring restitution in the given circumstances. By contrast in this chapter the plaintiff puts himself within the other sense of 'at the expense of'. His *prima facie* title to restitution rests on the statement that the defendant has enriched himself by committing a wrong against him. Having shown that that is so, he still has to establish that the wrong is one for which restitution is available, for it is incorrect to assert that the victim of every acquisitive wrong is entitled to claim the wrongdoer's gains. It will be recalled that this was one of the main reasons for dividing in two the generic conception of the restitutionary event and for criticising indiscriminate appeals to 'the principle against unjust enrichment'.

The word 'wrong' is used here in order to avoid restricting the scope of the discussion to torts actionable at common law. The word cannot be defined in terms of moral blame, since even some torts can be committed without fault. It is used to cover all conduct, acts or omissions, whose effect in creating legal consequences is attributable to its being characterised as a breach of duty. The term thus includes not only all torts but also breaches of equitable and statutory duties and breaches of contract.

It is important to notice that this notion of wrongs, as breaches of duty rather than blameworthy conduct, involves accepting not only that morally innocent conduct can be a wrong but also that culpable conduct may not be. For example, one who stands by while another confers value on him in circumstances amounting to a free acceptance

[1] Above, p. 99–106.

will often be morally culpable. Yet restitution on such facts does not depend on characterising free acceptance as a breach of duty owed to the intervener. On the contrary, the intervener gets restitution simply because the recipient, having passed up the opportunity to reject to proffered value, cannot reasonably say that the intervener ought to bear the risk. If he objects to having to pay, he has only himself to blame for not coming forward earlier. The same kind of comment can be made in relation to the recipient of a mistaken payment who knows that it is not due. He is morally culpable, but the payor's restitutionary right is not attributable to any characterisation of his conduct as a breach of duty.

The most important question in this chapter is this: Which wrongs do give rise to restitution? It is a question which cannot at present be given a firm and clear answer. One major reason for this is that, in the common law sector of the topic, the term 'waiver of tort' has encouraged and perpetuated ambiguities which have to be eliminated before the courts and can give a coherent answer to the question about restitution for wrongs *qua* wrongs. Hence the first task here is to address the meanings of 'waiver of tort'. The position which will

*23 be taken is that this phrase ought to be abandoned.

1. WAIVER OF TORT

If we speak for the moment, in an untechnical sense, of restitution 'after' as opposed to 'for' wrongs, there are three entirely different ways in which the victim of an acquisitive wrong may obtain restitution against the wrongdoer. The purpose of beginning from this use of 'after wrongs' is to allow us to include routes to restitution which do not rely on the facts in their character as a wrong, and it is only with that licence that we say that there are three ways of obtaining restitution from a wrongdoer. These three are as follows.

(i) *Alternative Analysis in Unjust Enrichment*

The victim of the wrong may be able to analyse the facts in such a way as to make out a claim to restitution on a basis which has nothing whatever to do with the wrong. That is to say, in the terms of the diagram which was set out and discussed earlier,[2] he may be able to ignore the wrong and to make out his cause of action in autonomous unjust enrichment. The simplest examples of this are

---

[2] Above, p. 43.

found under the heading of 'ignorance', one of the four main types of vitiated voluntariness.[3] For instance, in *Neate* v. *Harding*[4] the defendant had broken into the plaintiff's mother's house and had taken away money which belonged to the plaintiff. This is a case in which the claim for restitution maintained by the action for money had and received is explicable wholly without reference to the trespass. The defendant was enriched by subtraction from the plaintiff; and the plaintiff was ignorant of the taking and therefore did not consent to it. On facts like this, restitution happens on the same rationale as for mistaken payments; indeed *a fortiori*. For one who parts with money by mistake has a vitiated intent to give, while one from whom money is taken has no intent to give at all. Had the plaintiff been looking on, the case would have been the same, for then he would have been 'helpless' or 'compelled'. Many cases of pressure fall in the same category. If you falsely imprison me to make me pay you money,[5] that is both the tort of false imprisonment and, independently, the unjust enrichment which consists in a transfer made under compulsion. The fact that false imprisonment is an actionable wrong is not what establishes that my transfer was non-voluntary. It would be non-voluntary even if, *per impossible*, false imprisonment were removed from the list of torts.

(ii) *Extinctive Ratification*

The technique just described as 'alternative analysis' does not extinguish the wrong; it simply ignores it. However, there is a case in which, according to the ordinary rules of agency, the victim of a wrong can ratify the wrongdoer's act and thus make it lawful *ex post*.[6] Suppose that I sell your car without authority to do so but actually purporting to act as your agent. A self-styled agent's acts can be ratified. So you can, if you wish, adopt the wrongful sale. You are most likely to do this if you want to sue the buyer for the unpaid price, but one of the consequences of a genuine ratification will be that the agent will incur all the usual obligations of an agent, including the obligation to make over whatever he receives on his principal's account. So here, if I do receive the price of your car, wrongfully sold to a third party, one way for you to get restitution is by ratifying and thus turning me into your lawful agent. In

---

[3] Above, p. 140 f.

[4] *Neate* v. *Harding* (1851) 6 Exch. 349; cf. *Moffat* v. *Kazana* [1968] 3 All E.R. 271.

[5] *Duke de Cadaval* v. *Collins* (1836) 4 A. & E. 858.

[6] *Verschures Creameries Ltd.* v. *Hull and Netherlands Steamship Co.* [1921] 2 K.B. 608.

practice it is usually unnecessary for you to do this, since even without ratification you can have restitution under one of the other two heads. But from the point of view of theory and history, ratification is a possibility not to be forgotten.

(iii) *Restitution for the Wrong*

The third possibility is that the victim of the acquisitive wrong may get restitution without either ignoring the wrong or extinguishing it: he may show that it is a wrong of a kind which does give rise to restitution *qua* wrong. That is, he may show that from this one wrong there hang two remedial strings, one compensatory, the other restitutionary. Yet another way of saying the same thing is this: he may show that for this kind of wrong the money award of damages to which he is entitled can be calculated in the restitutionary, instead of the compensatory, measure. We know that this third route to restitution is available (even if we do not know precisely which wrongs do yield restitution as well as compensation) because the House of Lords has so held.

In *United Australia Ltd.* v. *Barclays Bank Ltd.*[7] the facts were as follows. A cheque came in for United Australia and was fraudulently endorsed over by their secretary in favour of a company, MFG, in which he was interested. Barclays Bank collected and paid the fraudulently endorsed cheque. United Australia began an action for restitution against MFG, expressed to be either for money had and received or for money lent. But before reaching judgment they dropped that claim and began this second action against Barclays. This time the claim was for the tort of conversion. Barclays maintained that it was too late for United Australia to complain of a conversion because by their earlier action against MFG, they had extinguished the tort in order to claim restitution. The House of Lords held that the claim for restitution had not extinguished the tort and would not have done so even as against the same defendant, MFG. The reason was that on these facts the tort was just as much the cause of action whether the damages sought were restitutionary or compensatory. In short, the one wrong gave rise to both remedial possibilities. It was false to suppose that a claim in the restitutionary measure entailed an extinctive ratification of the wrong.

As between these three routes to restitution after an acquisitive tort, the term 'waiver of tort' makes no clear discrimination. The

---

[7] *United Australia Ltd.* v. *Barclays Bank Ltd.* [1941] A.C. 1.

phrase has become a loose and anachronistic description of the decision by the victim of such a tort to seek restitution. *United Australia* shows that that option does not necessarily entail an extinctive ratification of the tort. Yet, according to the normal meaning of 'waiver', extinctive ratification is what is most readily brought to mind by the traditional terminology. This confusion is worse confounded by the fact that as a matter of history there is much to be said for the view that waiver of tort was originally conceived in terms of such ratification, albeit both fictitious (in that the victim never had any genuine desire to adopt the wrongdoer's act) and over-extended (in that the wrongdoer never purported to act as the victim's agent).

The leading case of *Lamine* v. *Dorrell*[8] illustrates this link between 'waiver' and extinctive ratification. The defendant had converted some Irish debentures by selling them. The plaintiff did not sue for the conversion but brought this action for money had and received for the price which the defendant had obtained. He succeeded in his claim. There were two areas of uneasiness which drove the court towards an analysis in terms of ratification. First, since the form of the action for money had and received included an allegation of a promise by the defendant to pay (an *assumpsit*) there was an uncomfortable repugnancy between the wrong done and that allegation. But that could be got over by a ratification. As Powell, J., said,[9] 'And when the act that is done is in its nature tortious, it is hard to turn it into a contract, and against the reason of *assumpsit.*' That constitutes the difficulty. So he went on to smooth it away: 'But the plaintiff may dispense with the wrong and suppose the sale made by his consent, and bring an action for the money they were sold for as money had and received to his use.'

The second uneasiness in *Lamine* v. *Dorrell* concerned the fear of double recovery. What if the plaintiff were later to sue for the conversion which the defendant had undoubtedly committed? An extinctive waiver would answer very well. So Holt, C.J., said:[10] 'This recovery may be given in evidence upon not guilty in the action of trover, because by this action the plaintiff makes and affirms the act of the defendant in the sale of the debentures to be lawful, and consequently the sale of them is no conversion.' This is history, not modern law. It does not survive *United Australia*, but it does show

---

[8] *Lamine* v. *Dorrell* (1701) 2 Ld. Ray. 1216.
[9] *Ibid.*, 1217.
[10] At p. 1217.

how the notion of waiver of tort began as a strained extension of extinctive ratification.[11]

In conclusion it may be said that, since, in the context of restitution from a wrongdoer, extinctive ratification is rare and unnecessary, the main complaint against the phrase 'waiver of tort' is that it fails to distinguish between (i), alternative analysis, and (iii), restitution for wrongs *qua* wrongs. This complaint is then aggravated by the fact that the phrase is, according both to its natural meaning and its history, most closely linked with neither (i) nor (iii) but rather with (ii), extinctive ratification. We will see below that these matters have serious practical consequences which cannot be handled unless the confusing terminology is given up.

The rest of this chapter will abstain so far as possible from the word 'waiver', and will not be concerned with extinctive ratification. It will distinguish between the other two routes to restitution using the terms 'alternative analysis' and 'restitution for wrongs'. Clearly the main focus must be on the latter, as the title of the chapter itself shows. All cases of the former ought already to have been accounted for in the earlier chapters of this book. But unfortunately a clean division is not yet possible, precisely because of the fact that the ambiguities of 'waiver' have prevented the courts from drawing the distinction between alternative analysis and restitution for wrongs.

2. RESTITUTION-YIELDING WRONGS

In this section the discussion addresses the question whether it is possible to say which wrongs do give rise to restitution. But in the first part of the section an attempt is made to show how difficult it is in the present state of authority to bring that question clearly to the surface.

(i) *Preliminary Difficulties*

Though there are many cases in which plaintiffs have obtained restitution from wrongdoers it is not often possible to say whether they succeeded on the basis of alternative analysis or restitution for wrongs. In particular there are very few cases which fall unequivocally into the latter category, which is the one in which we are chiefly

---

[11] And cf. *Re Hallett's Estate* (1880) 13 Ch.D. 696, 727 *per* Jessel, M.R.

interested. Normally we would expect to be told by the judges themselves whether they were giving restitution on the one basis or the other. However, since, as we have just seen, 'waiver' has elided all the theoretical possibilities, the judgments do not overtly take any distinction between alternative analysis and restitution for wrongs.

It is therefore necessary to proceed with great caution, for any case which is capable of being understood as an example of alter-' native analysis may tell us nothing about the question whether the wrong committed by the defendant does or does not yield restitutionary damages. Reverting to the example of false imprisonment, we can see that a plaintiff who recovers the ransom which he pays for his release cannot be said to have had restitution for the wrong *qua* wrong, since his restitutionary right is also explicable on the basis of alternative analysis as a non-voluntary transfer, independent of the characterization of the facts as a wrong. If the award of restitution attaches to the non-voluntary transfer no comment is made on the remedial rights engendered by the wrong; and it follows that, unless the judge makes clear the basis on which he is proceeding, a case of that kind is unsafe evidence for a class of restitution-yielding wrongs. It is equivocal between two of the three routes to restitution outlined above. The next paragraphs first seek to identify a class of case which does unequivocally exemplify restitution for wrongs and then turn back to the equivocal examples.

The unequivocal cases are those in which the plaintiff cannot connect himself to the enrichment which he wants to recover except by saying that the defendant obtained it by committing a wrong against him. Thus, if someone paid you £1000 for beating me up I could not establish even a *prima facie* claim to that money without showing that it was earned by the wrong done to me. Without the wrong to me, your earnings are no business of mine. If there were a case which said that I could have that £1000 as restitutionary damages, there would be no doubt that your battery would be an example of a restitution-yielding wrong. Alternative analysis is impossible on such facts.

Reading v. A.-G.[12] is a case of this kind. The sergeant, who took money to guide smugglers through army road-posts in Cairo, enriched himself by breach of duty to the Crown. But without the breach there would have been no connexion between the Crown and the money. It certainly was not money which would have accrued to the Crown if Reading had not taken it. Hence there was no interceptive subtraction. The Crown had to rely on the wrong. It was the

---

[12] *Reading* v. A.-G. [1951] A.C. 507.

same, despite the completely different moral quality of what was done, in *Boardman* v. *Phipps*.[13] There the solicitor appellant had obtained shares for himself in breach of his fiduciary duty to a trust. There was no question of holding that the trust would have got the shares if Boardman had not. The only ground upon which the beneficiaries under the trust could claim Boardman's profit was that he had obtained it, albeit in good faith and in order to promote the best interests of the trust, by means of a technical breach of his duty to abstain from making personal acquisitions from any position in which his interests might conflict with the interests of the trust.

The reason why these two cases are unequivocal examples of restitution for wrongs is that it is beyond argument that the only connexion between the plaintiff and the defendant's profit was a wrong. In the common law most instances of conversion by sale conform to the same analysis. We have already considered the case of the sale of a car.[14] We concluded that the plaintiff owner of the car cannot say that the wrongdoer received the price by an interceptive subtraction from him. To connect himself to the price he has to rely on the wrong. For it is not certain that he would himself have received that or any price; and the wrongdoer having perhaps paid another for the car may not seem to have been enriched at all once the focus is taken off the sum which he received by the wrong itself; and the victim may not be at all reduced in wealth, since the car is likely to remain his albeit in other hands. For all these reasons it is true that the owner can claim that the wrongdoer has obtained the price by a wrong committed against him but cannot make any other connexion between himself and that money. Yet that conclusion does not mean that every conversion which realises an asset must necessarily be treated in the same way. In particular there is room for a different conclusion in relation to cheques. In *United Australia*[15] the asset which was said to have been converted was a cheque payable to the plaintiffs. It is obvious that the plaintiffs could say that MFG, who presented the cheque for payment, had obtained the money by committing a wrong. But it is less certain that they could not equally have pointed to an enrichment by subtraction. It depends on the extent to which you are willing to look behind the theory and to see a cheque as nothing more than a vehicle for moving money around. On that view, the fraudulent secretary who forged the indorsement, and MFG who then cashed the cheque, merely intercepted money

---

[13] *Boardman* v. *Phipps* [1967] 2 A.C. 46.
[14] Above, p. 138.
[15] Above, n. 7.

which was *en route* to *United Australia*. That finding would open the way to explain the restitutionary claim against MFG as having been based on alternative analysis: an interceptive subtraction without the plaintiffs' knowledge, the same kind of claim, except for the interceptive nature of the subtraction, as is exemplified by *Neate* v. *Harding* or *Moffatt* v. *Kazana*.[16]

On the facts of *United Australia* there is, therefore, some doubt whether there can or cannot be said to be a subtraction as well as a wrong. In other cases there is no doubt whatever that the plaintiff can make both allegations. It is then that it becomes especially difficult, in the absence of judicial guidance, to say whether restitution was given for the wrong or for the independent unjust enrichment. Often it will not matter to the parties. But sometimes it will, as the next section of this chapter illustrates. In *United Australia* itself the question was whether a claim for restitution had the effect of extinguishing a cause of action in tort. It would have done so if it had been based on extinctive ratification. If the restitutionary claim was made out by alternative analysis, on the basis of non-voluntary subtractive enrichment, it would not have extinguished the tort, because it would have ignored the tort completely. On the other hand, if it was based on the wrong itself, being a claim for restitutionary damages for the tort, it would also not have extinguished it but for a different reason, because it would have actually relied on it. The House of Lords said that this was what had happened, but, strictly speaking, all that was necessary was that extinctive ratification should be ruled out. Thus, in relation to the particular issue, it happened that nothing turned on the difference between alternative analysis and restitution for wrongs. It is quite different when the measure of recovery is in issue, as we shall see. Equally important is the fact that, where there are a number of different possibilities latent in the same facts, arguments tend to cross over from one to another almost without noticing. Also, some points get missed out in whole or part. The nature of these problems will be considered first in the abstract and then in relation to the difficult case of *Phillips* v. *Homfray*.[17]

In the abstract, a plaintiff who has suffered an acquisitive wrong of a kind which does involve a subtraction of wealth from himself to the defendant, so that he can, in principle, connect himself to the enrichment either as something subtracted from him or as something earned by doing him wrong, ought to ask himself two main questions.

[16] Above, n. 4.
[17] *Phillips* v. *Homfray* (1883) 24 Ch.D. 439.

Does he want to seek his remedy in unjust enrichment independently of the wrong? Or, does he want to rely on the wrong itself? If the former, he must inquire into all the different grounds (non-voluntary transfer, free acceptance and so on) but he cannot expect any measure of recovery other than those which come within the notion of restitution. If the latter, he must contemplate a further choice between compensatory and restitutionary damages. That is to say, even on one single set of facts he may be able to seek restitution *either* by alternative analysis *or* by taking the restitution option between the different remedial rights available for the wrong. Hence even on one set of facts there should be a two-stage inquiry: (a) Is there an independent unjust enrichment giving rise to a restitutionary right without reliance on the wrong? (b) Is the wrong itself a member of the category of wrongs giving rise to restitutionary damages?

Phillips v. *Homfray*[18] shows how difficult it is to handle cases which have not kept all these issues distinct. It is chosen as a prominent example of the problem which recurs whenever a plaintiff has suffered both a subtraction and a wrong. Unless counsel and the court expressly say which route to restitution is being followed it is impossible to be sure which is primarily in mind when any reason is given why restitution should or should not be awarded. However, in *Phillips* v. *Homfray* itself we have the advantage of being able to say, with hindsight, that the plaintiffs could only succeed if they could establish a claim by alternative analysis. The reason is, that the defendant was the personal representative of the original wrongdoer, and any action based on the wrong itself was barred by the rule that actions in tort could not survive the tortfeasor: *actio personalis moritur cum persona.*[19]

The defendant's *de cuius* had drawn coal from the plaintiffs' land and had used passages running through the land for the purpose of transporting that and other coal mined from his own land. The plaintiffs had obtained a decree for an inquiry into the volume of the coal transported through the passages and, dependent on that, into the value of the wayleaves which the trespasser had avoided paying. This decree had been obtained in equity but on the basis that the cause of action was nothing other than the trespass itself. Before the decree could be acted upon, the trespasser died. The question then arose whether his personal representative was entitled to have the inquiry discharged on the basis of the *actio personalis*

---

[18] *Cit.* n. 17 above.
[19] Abolished by *Law Reform (Miscellaneous Provisions) Act, 1934.*

rule. The Court of Appeal, Baggallay, L.J., dissenting, held that the decree did have to be discharged. The question presented itself in this form: could the victim of a trespass to land waive the trespass and claim instead, by means of an action in the nature of *assumpsit*, the enrichment wrongly obtained by the trespasser? If he could waive the tort in that way, he could maintain the action against the personal representative.

One reason given by Bowen and Cotton, L.J.J., was that trespass to land was not a tort which could be waived at all.[20] This has had a lastingly inhibiting effect on restitutionary actions for that wrong.[21] Yet it cannot be understood as meaning that trespass is a tort for which, *qua* wrong, restitutionary damages cannot be awarded. For the remedial potential of the tort of trespass itself was not in issue in the case, for the very reason that, if the plaintiffs relied on the trespass, they could not outflank the *actio personalis* rule. They needed to put the trespass completely on one side. Hence, whatever *Phillips* v. *Homfray* stands for, it cannot be authority for the proposition that a plaintiff cannot claim restitutionary damages for trespass to land even in a case in which there is no reason why he cannot found on the wrong itself.

Another reason given by the majority of the Court of Appeal was that the deceased had not been enriched. He had obtained only a negative benefit by saving himself the expense of paying for permission to use the passages through the plaintiff's land.[22] It is certain that a decision that the defendant had been enriched is a necessary condition for all restitutionary claims, whether formulated by alternative analysis or on the basis of the wrong itself. But it cannot be right to say that a negative benefit, saving expenditure rather than adding a positive increment, can never be an enrichment. If this were so there could never be restitutionary claims in respect of services (unless they happened to leave some end-product) or in respect of debts discharged. Hence this reason, which, if right, would apply to all routes to restitution, must be discounted.

It is now possible to ask whether the facts did disclose any claim by alternative analysis, leaving aside the trespass. The deceased had used the underground passages without the knowledge of the plaintiffs. Hence they could say in the strongest possible way that whatever benefit he had received from them had passed to him non-

---

[20] *Phillips* v. *Homfray* (1883) 24 Ch.D. 439, 461, 463.
[21] *A.-G.* v. *De Keyser's Royal Hotel* (1920) A.C. 508; *Morris* v. *Tarrant* [1971] 2 Q.B. 143; but see, *Nissan* v. *A.-G.* [1968] 1 Q.B. 286.
[22] *Phillips* v. *Homfray* (1883) 24 Ch.D. 439, 454–5.

voluntarily. In short, it was a case of 'ignorance'. The user had also been subtracted from them: it was their land to control and dispose of as they pleased, and he had taken from them a particle of the potential enjoyment inherent in their ownership. The remaining issue is, once again, enrichment. If the user could have passed the 'no reasonable man' test of incontrovertible benefit, there would be no more to say.[23] The plaintiffs should then have succeeded on the basis of non-voluntary enrichment at their expense, exactly in the same way as a man recovers money paid by mistake. On the other hand, if the user did not pass the 'no reasonable man' test, the plaintiffs would have had to show that the benefit had been freely accepted by the deceased. If they had turned to free acceptance on the issue of enrichment, they would in all probability have relied on it also as the cause for restitution, since free acceptance is bivalent in the sense that it settles both issues at once.[24]

Could the plaintiffs have established a free acceptance? It seems likely that they could have done so. Earlier proceedings in the same case make it absolutely clear,[25] contrary to an assertion of my own elsewhere,[26] that the deceased and his associates did know that they were trespassing under the plaintiffs' land. Hence it is impossible to say that a free acceptance was obstructed by a mistake or other innocent belief. Consequently the case ought, as Baggallay, L.J., maintained, to have been decided in the same way as *Lightly* v. *Clouston*.[27] In that case the plaintiff was allowed a *quantuum meruit* in respect of the work and labour of his servant whom the defendant had tortiously seduced away. No rational distinction can be taken between knowingly usurping enjoyment of land and knowingly seducing the labour of someone else's articled servant. In both cases there is a free acceptance of a benefit in kind. If 'free acceptance' sounds at all odd in such a context it is only because it is too feeble a description of what the defendant does. Whatever is true of someone who stands by while a benefit is committed to him must be true *a fortiori* of one who goes out of his way to take that benefit without its owner's knowledge. This same conclusion was reached by Lord Mansfield in *Hambly* v. *Trott*[28] when he said that someone who rode a horse without its owner's permission would be liable, in *assumpsit*, to pay a reasonable hiring charge.

---

[23] Above, p. 116 ff.
[24] Above, p. 267.
[25] (1870) L.R. 6 Ch.Ap. 770.
[26] 'Restitution and Wrongs' [1982] C.L.P. 53, 60.
[27] *Lightly* v. *Clouston* (1808) 1 Taunt. 112. Cf. the opinion of *Goff and Jones*, p. 474 ff.
[28] *Hambly* v. *Trott* (1776) 1 Cowp. 371.

The proper approach to *Phillips* v. *Homfray* would have been to say, first, that the *actio personalis* rule could not be evaded by merely seeking a restitutionary rather than a compensatory measure of recovery and, hence, that any claim based directly on the trespass must fail; and, then, to identify the cause of action in independent unjust enrichment; and, finally, to ask whether the *actio personalis* rule should be applied, analogically and not logically, to that alternative cause of action. The stage in the law's development from the forms of action had not been reached at which that type of approach could be used. But, a century later, we should no longer be deterred from imposing it on cases which themselves could not use it.

Morris v. *Tarrant*[29] is a much more recent case in the line descending from *Phillips* v. *Homfray*. It arose out of a divorce. The husband defendant had stayed on in the matrimonial home after the decree absolute. It was clear that from that time he became a trespasser as against his ex-wife. One question was whether he could be made to pay her an occupation rent for his accommodation during that period. Lane, J., did hold that he had been incontrovertibly enriched, on the ground that he would have had to find the money for somewhere to live elsewhere if he had not stayed on in the house.[30] But was there any restitutionary cause of action independent of the tort? Lane, J., ruled out any such claim without analysing the different causes of action which constitute the several species of unjust enrichment. On the facts that conclusion was probably correct. The reason is that there was a relationship of grumbling negotiation between the parties. Such a relationship would seem to negative both 'ignorance' on the wife's part and compulsion on the husband's. So there was probably no factor negativing voluntariness. As for free acceptance it may be that he would have been held to have believed that he was entitled to stay on without payment. At all events these matters were not fully tested. Was there a restitutionary cause of action based on the tort itself? There is no consideration of that issue as a separate question. However, the wife did obtain an award of an occupation rent under the head of mesne profits for the trespass. This was regarded as part of her ordinary compensatory award, since what she had lost—her use of the property—was compensable by the award of a reasonable rent. So again the issue of restitution for the wrong, *qua* wrong, did not escape for independent consideration. It is a question which is difficult to isolate unless the plaintiff claims that the defendant was

---

[29] *Morris* v. *Tarrant* [1971] 2 Q.B. 143.
[30] At p. 162.

enriched by more than his own user. For the user itself usually is neutral between restitution and compensation.[31] If the defendant has made a further profit from his user, over and above enjoyment for a time, the restitutionary question is clearly raised, as where the defendant has run some business on property which is not his.[32]

The purpose of the discussion up to this point has been to argue that, because questions are raised in terms of 'waiver of tort', even cases in which restitutionary issues seem likely to be exposed and settled often end without satisfying the need for better explanations. The chief reason is that 'alternative analysis' and 'restitution for wrongs' are not separately considered. Whether admitting a restitutionary claim, as in *Lightly* v. *Clouston*, or rejecting one, as in *Phillips* v. *Homfray*, the cases do not say whether they are talking of one route to restitution, or the other, or both. Moreover, they do not keep separate the arguments and objections which properly apply to only one or other of these routes to restitution.

(ii) *Three Tests*

Notwithstanding the problems which have just been described, it is possible to suggest three tests which between them appear to account satisfactorily for the incidence of restitution as a response to wrongs as such.

(a) *Deliberate Exploitation of Wrongdoing*

Where a defendant has deliberately set out to enrich himself by committing a wrong against the plaintiff, he ought to be liable to make restitution of that profit. Suppose that you decide to sell a story about me knowing full well that it is untrue and defamatory and that you succeed in making a profit of £10 000 by doing so; or, again, suppose that you are paid to damage my shop or to beat me up. In such cases I should be able to recover your profit or reward, likely on many facts to be greater than the loss for which I could claim compensation. My claim could not be advanced except on the basis of the wrong itself since on these facts there is no subtractive connexion between me and your enrichment. The additional ground for restitution would then be that you had deliberately used that wrong as a means to enrich yourself.[33]

---

[31] See *Strand Electric and Engineering Co. Ltd.* v. *Brisford Entertainments Ltd.* below, p. 330.

[32] See *Edwards* v. *Lee's Administrators* below, p. 355.

[33] It is not enough to establish that you were enriched at my expense (by doing me wrong). The enrichment must in addition be shown to have been made in circumstances calling for restitution (*unjust* enrichment at my expense): see above, p. 105.

It is difficult to prove that this test is already accepted by the law. The strongest argument that it is comes from outside the area of restitution. In the law of civil wrongs penal damages are a rarity. When Lord Devlin reviewed their incidence in *Rookes* v. *Barnard*[34] one of the categories in which he thought that they should still be awarded was that in which the wrongdoer consciously and cynically committed the wrong in the belief that his profits were likely to outweigh anything he might have to pay by way of compensation. In *Cassell & Co. Ltd.* v. *Broome*,[35] in which a majority of the House of Lords followed the line taken by Lord Devlin in *Rookes* v. *Barnard*, Lord Diplock said that this was the category of punitive damages about which he had no doubts at all. He described it as 'a blunt instrument to prevent unjust enrichment by unlawful acts' and he justified its want of sensitivity by saying that the wrongdoer must have the cards stacked against him. He must have to contemplate the possibility of losing more than he might hope to gain.[36]

The need for punitive damages in this area is created by the danger, as Lord Diplock said, that the cynical wrongdoer may see that profits are likely to exceed any loss payable to the victim of the wrongs, so that the duty not to seek enrichment unlawfully can in that event seem to be only feebly sanctioned. The same rationale applies to the award of restitutionary damages. The difference is only that punitive damages are a blunt instrument, and restitutionary damages would be more sensitive. The insensitivity of punitive damages consists in the fact that they do not attempt to give the plaintiff the wrongdoer's actual gain. They run beyond that measure. The bluntness of the instrument necessarily leads to a requirement of a high degree of wickedness on the part of the defendant. Restitutionary damages, restricted to the defendant's actual gain, could be allowed in a slightly wider range of cases entailing a less extreme degree of wickedness.

There are some other indications that the law does respond to this test. As we shall see below the measure of recovery can be affected: the deliberate wrongdoer can be made to pay the value of benefits received which in the case of an innocent wrongdoer would be regarded as too remote.[37]

---

[34] *Rookes* v. *Barnard* [1964] A.C. 1129.
[35] *Cassell & Co. Ltd.* v. *Broome* [1972] A.C. 1027.
[36] At p. 1130.
[37] Below, p. 354–5.

(b) *Anti-Enrichment Wrongs*

The commonest example of a wrong which gives rise to restitution is conversion, and no suggestion is made that the right to restitution is limited to cases in which the defendant has deliberately exploited the plaintiff's property. By contrast it is usually considered that defamation is not a wrong which gives rise to restitution.[38] Although a particular instance might fall under the test of deliberate exploitation, if you innocently defame me and happen to sell more magazines because of the story, I will not be able to sue for your profit. Similarly a man may profit by a nuisance, in that he may earn his livelihood by means of the noxious activity conducted on his

★24 premises. Yet nobody has ever recovered the profits of a nuisance. The same can be said of negligence. I may save money by not keeping my machinery in good repair. I may make money by running machines or transport too fast or too long. But, when some disaster happens, compensation is always claimed and nobody has ever obtained the enrichment derived from the negligently conducted process.

Goff and Jones appear to take the view that there may be no theoretical bar to claims for restitution in respect of any acquisitive wrong. Thus they say:

> There can be no restitution unless the defendant is unjustly enriched. For this reason, certain torts cannot generally be waived: assault, battery, malicious prosecution and negligence do not ordinarly enrich the tortfeasor. On the other hand, conversion and deceit will frequently result in the defendant's enrichment, and, therefore, can be waived.[39]

This should be understood as meaning, and certainly the context confirms that it does mean, that the only torts for which restitution does not lie are those which, in the particular case, give the wrong-doer no gain. This must be too wide, as the examples of defamation, nuisance and negligence show.

The test proposed under this head supposes that some wrongs are, and some wrongs are not, recognised by the law for the purpose of preventing disapproved modes of enrichment. More accurately this means that the primary duties, of which the wrongs are breaches, either are or are not designed to prevent enrichment. If an anti-enrichment duty is broken, so that the preventitive mechanism has failed, the policy behind the duty can be redeemed by ordering restitution from the wrongdoer. On the other hand, if the duty which has been broken is not aimed against enrichment, restitution

---

[38] See e.g. *Hart* v. *E.P. Dutton Ltd.* (1949) N.Y.S. (2d.) 871.
[39] At p. 470.

cannot be congruently related to the policy behind it and should not be allowed. This is made more complicated by the fact that the duties behind wrongs often serve mixed policies. For example, the duty to respect confidences protects privacy and prevents unjust enrichment.[40] So the question has to be asked in relation to the particular facts: Was the prevention of the enrichment which the defendant has acquired a main purpose behind the wrong which he has committed? If it was, the wrong counts as an anti-enrichment wrong, and restitution follows.

It is certain that not every wrong will fall neatly on one side or other of the line. But it is equally plain that this test does sufficiently explain why restitutionary claims are not made for nuisance, negligence and defamation. These are anti-harm wrongs, not anti-enrichment wrongs. In relation to them it is impossible, even though they do sometimes lead to enrichment of the wrongdoer, to elevate the prevention of enrichment to the level of a main purpose.

By contrast it can be said to be one main purpose of the tort of conversion to prevent enrichment. That is not to say that it is not also aimed at preventing loss. The reason why I must not eat your cake, or sell your cake behind your back, is, indifferently, that you must not lose your wealth and I must not gain it. Both purposes have equal weight. That is why it is possible to say that conversion is an anti-enrichment wrong. It is the same with trespass to land. You must not suffer intrusions, but, equally, I must not enjoy and use your land. On the other hand, all manifestations of trespass to the person are manifestly designed to prevent harm to a victim, not gain to the wrongdoer. Suppose that A hits B and then, because both A and B were trying to win a lucrative contract, A gains because B is out of action with a broken jaw. There would be no question of B's getting A's gain, because battery is not an anti-enrichment wrong. It might be different if A could show that B's blow was a deliberate stratagem to get A out of the way on the crucial day, since that would fall to be considered under the first test.

The fact that a wrong does count as an anti-enrichment wrong does not mean that it must on every occasion be enriching. Suppose I eat your cake believing it to be mine. My mistake means that there is no free acceptance; and a cake is unlikely ever to be regarded as an incontrovertible benefit under the 'no reasonable man' test. Hence

---

[40] Privacy: as where people in the public eye seek to prevent disclosure of personal details, e.g. *Prince Albert* v. *Strange* (1849) 1 Mac. & G. 25; *Duchess of Argyll* v. *Duke of Argyll* (1967) Ch. 302; enrichment: as where trade secrets are exploited, e.g. *Peter Pan Mfg. Corp.* v. *Corsets Silhouette Ltd.* [1964] 1 W.L.R. 96.

a claim based on alternative analysis would be likely to fail on the enrichment issue. But would a claim based on the wrong itself succeed? It would depend on a question which we contemplated earlier, namely whether the enrichment issue would be handled more robustly against a wrongdoer.[41] If it would not, then even a restitutionary claim for the wrong itself would be defeated by the argument from subjective devaluation. This is not a wholly theoretical point. It would come to practical life if a statute barred claims to compensation in the given circumstances but allowed claims to restitution.

In *Strand Electric and Engineering Co. Ltd.* v. *Brisford Entertainments Ltd.*[42] the plaintiffs brought an action of detinue for theatre lighting equipment which they had first lent and then hired to the Bedford Theatre Co., which had been trying to buy the Bedford Theatre from the defendants. When the deal fell through the defendants insisted on keeping the lights in the theatre, which would otherwise not have been marketable because not in working order. The plaintiffs secured an order for delivery up of the equipment or payment of its value and also judgment for the full rate of hire for the forty-three weeks during which it had been detained. The Court of Appeal held that the defendant had to pay the full value of the user even though the loss to the plaintiffs was probably less in that they would very likely not have been able or willing to hire out the lights for the full period. This could have been explained in terms of alternative analysis on the basis of a free acceptance. In fact it was all done in calculating damages for the detinue. Denning, L.J., conceived himself to be awarding restitution, while Somervell and Romer, L.JJ., seem to have thought that the hire charge was within the notion of compensation. Denning, L.J.'s approach is preferable since it frees the court from artificial attempts to demonstrate that the award of a hire-charge does correspond to a loss suffered by the plaintiff.[43] Moreover, his approach is readily explicable by the fact that the detinue was[44] indisputably an anti-enrichment wrong.

We will see below that in this context the wrong which is committed when a fiduciary breaks his duty to avoid conflicts of interest raises special problems in some cases.[45] Outside that area of

---

[41] Above, p. 126.

[42] *Strand Electric and Engineering Co. Ltd.* v. *Brisford Entertainments Ltd.* [1952] 2 Q.B. 246.

[43] Nevertheless the compensatory analysis seems to be used by Parker, J., in *Hillesden Securities Ltd.* v. *Ryjack Ltd.* [1983] 2 All E.R. 184, 188.

[44] Detinue was abolished by s. 2 (1) of the *Torts (Interference with Goods) Act, 1977.*

[45] Below, p. 341–2.

difficulty there is no doubt that a main purpose of the duty is to prevent enrichment of the fiduciary at the expense of the person relying on him. The danger is always that the fiduciary will line his own pocket. A company director who takes a contract which might have been taken by his company,[46] and a trustee who accepts a secret commission for placing out trust business,[47] must make restitution of their profit. Many such cases can be explained as examples of restitution for the commission of an anti-enrichment wrong. They can, however, also be explained by the third test below. Extreme cases such as *Reading* v. *A.-G.*[48] can also be regarded as examples of the deliberate exploitation of unlawful means.

English v. *Dedham Vale Properties Ltd.*[49] is a case which, on its face, exemplifies restitution for breach of the fiduciary duty just mentioned, but it would have been more easily decided by drawing directly on the notion of an anti-enrichment wrong. The defendants were property developers; they wanted the plaintiffs' land. A price was agreed which reflected a view that planning permission for development was unlikely to be forthcoming. Before contracts were exchanged the defendants put in an application in the name of the plaintiffs for permission to build. Before completion the permission had been granted. The plaintiffs were never told. When they later discovered what had happened they successfully claimed the profit made as a result of the development of the site. Slade, J., held the defendants liable by means of an elaborate argument according to which, as self-styled agents to acquire the planning permission, they became fiduciaries. It is a very strained fiduciary relationship since vendor and purchaser typically seek to get the better of each other and, therefore, bargain at arm's length. But it is obvious that this is an instrumental finding. The fiduciary character of the relationship is really part of Slade, J.'s conclusion, derived from other facts. It is a conclusion whose misleading form is necessitated only by the judge's need to find an accepted explanation why the defendants had to make restitution: they had to refund because they were in breach of duty, and they were in breach of duty because they were fiduciaries. But they were fiduciaries because it was certain that they had to make restitution.

There was a less circular path. The *Town and Country Planning Act, 1962*, provided in s. 16 (1) that non-owners applying for

---

[46] *Industrial Development Consultants Ltd.* v. *Cooley* [1972] 1 W.L.R. 443.
[47] *Williams* v. *Barton* [1927] 2 Ch. 9.
[48] Above, n. 12.
[49] *English* v. *Dedham Vale Properties* [1978] 1 W.L.R. 93.

planning permission must certify that they had given notice to the owners. Inferentially, this put a duty on such applicants to notify the owners. The defendants had not done so; they had pretended to apply as owners. This effectively short-circuited all the machinery by which the plaintiffs should have learned of the application. What was the purpose of that machinery? One main purpose was precisely to prevent this mode of fishing for development profits. Failure to comply with s. 16 (1) was thus an anti-enrichment wrong. The award of restitution reinforced the policy of the statute when the anti-enrichment machinery failed to have the desired effect. This line of reasoning would have made it unnecessary to have recourse to what was essentially a constructive fiduciary relationship.

(c) *Prophylaxis*

Whether your ultimate purpose is to prevent enrichment or to prevent loss or other harm, it is possible to adopt a prophylactic approach. That is to say, instead of waiting for the mischief to supervene, you can take steps beforehand to guard against its coming about. One prophylactic technique is to impose a duty not to bring about a situation in which the mischief in question *might* happen. The sanction for such a duty cannot ever be compensatory damages, since, *ex hypothesi*, you are not waiting for the loss to supervene. For example, if you are anxious about damage from things falling off roofs, you can impose a duty not to place anything on a roof which might do damage if it did fall. Such a duty would have to be sanctioned by injunctions or fixed penalties or in some other way, but at all events not by compensatory damages: to wait for the loss to happen would simply be to abandon the prophylactic approach.

Equity adopts a prophylactic approach in relation to trustees and to others in a trustee-like position. A very rough guide to the category of trustee-like positions (only the clumsiness of that adjective provokes the Latinate usage 'fiduciary', from *fiducia*, 'a trust') is that they involve the management of other people's property or affairs, as does trusteeship, but without legal title to the property so managed. Company directors and the governing bodies of colleges are not trustees because they have no title to the property which they manage, so that there is no division of legal and equitable ownership as between these managers and the companies or colleges whose property is managed. However, the temptations of such managers are so similar to those of trustees that equity imposes on them the same disciplines as it imposes on trustees and calls them fiduciaries. It is convenient to be able to use the word 'beneficiary' to denote both the *cestui que trust* and the person who relies on a fiduciary agent other than a trustee; and also to use the word 'fiduciary' to include trustees.

A fiduciary will often see an opportunity for personal profit arising in relation to the beneficiary's affairs. The mischief which equity seeks to avoid is the sacrifice of the beneficiary's interests which is likely to happen if the fiduciary pursues such an opportunity. It does not wait for the beneficiary's interests to be sacrificed. It creates a duty in the fiduciary not to pursue his own interest if in doing so he might be tempted to sacrifice the interests of the beneficiary.[50] This is the duty to avoid conflicts of interest. Even an innocent fiduciary can commit a breach of the duty: if he makes an acquisition for himself in circumstances in which he might have been tempted to sacrifice the beneficiary's interest, he has to make over his profit to the beneficiary. The rule is very strict, and the strictness consists precisely in the hypothetical nature of the inquiry.[51]

The sanction for breach of the duty is restitutionary. It could not, compatibly with the prophylactic approach, be compensatory. That would involve waiting for actual harm to supervene. Even if the only aim was to prevent harm to the beneficiary as opposed to enrichment of the trustee (as, arguably, on some facts it is), the fact that a restitutionary award serves the prophylactic approach would be a sufficient explanation of that response to breaches of this duty. In fact, however, it is rarely necessary to rely on this explanation because except on some special facts, which will be considered below,[52] the duty to avoid conflicts of interest is directed against both harm to the beneficiary and, equally, enrichment of the fiduciary. Hence breaches of the duty are on most facts anti-enrichment wrongs under the previous head.

(iii) *Some Specific Wrongs*

It is impossible to review all or even a large number of the wrongs recognised by law and equity. This part, therefore, looks very briefly at some problematic examples, with the double purpose of noticing their difficulties and illustrating the operation of the tests which have just been proposed.

---

[50] *Parker* v. *McKenna* (1874) L.R. 10 Ch. 96, 124 f; *Bray* v. *Ford* (1896) A.C. 44, 51; *Wright* v. *Morgan* (1926) A.C. 788, 797; *Boardman* v. *Phipps* [1966] 3 W.L.R. 1009, 1066.
[51] This remains true even if the hypothetical possibility of conflict must be real and sensible rather than fanciful: see *Boardman* v. *Phipps*, above, p. 1067, *per* Lord Upjohn.
[52] Below, p. 341–2.

(a) *Breach of Contract*

We have already discussed the restitutionary rights which arise in respect of benefits conferred under contracts discharged after the defendant's breach, by frustration, or after the plaintiff's breach.[53] Those rights arise by alternative analysis, not from the wrong of breach but from the unjust enrichment which happens where the plaintiff transferor has a qualified intention to enrich the defendant transferee, and where, in the events which supervene, the condition for retaining the enrichment fails. At this point we are concerned with the different question, whether a breach of contract as such can be a restitution-yielding wrong.

Of the three tests proposed above, the third—prophylaxis—is out of the question. But the other two could in principle produce a positive result. *Goff and Jones* affirm that 'the innocent party cannot bring a restitutionary claim against the defendant for the profits which the defendant has made from his breach of contract', but they also observe that the principles applicable to torts might yet be held to apply.[54] They instance the Louisiana case of *City of New Orleans* v. *Fireman's Charitable Association*[55] in which the defendants, who were contractually bound to maintain a fire-fighting force at a given strength, turned out to have successfully run the risk of under-providing. They had not failed to put out any fires, but they had made a large profit by not laying out the money on men and equipment which their contract bound them to make. The plaintiffs recovered nothing; they had suffered no loss. *Goff and Jones* say that common law jurisdictions would have reached the same conclusion. But this is a type of case in which the test of 'deliberate exploitation' ought to be brought into play, so as to allow recovery of profits against an unscrupulous contract breaker.

Another important question will be whether a breach can ever be an anti-enrichment wrong and thus give rise to restitution independently of deliberate exploitation. The answer cannot be given for all breaches generally. It will be a matter of looking at the purpose of the particular term. One case in the Privy Council comes very close to showing that there can be restitution under this head. In *Reid-Newfoundland Co.* v. *Anglo-American Telegraph Co.*[56] the telegraph company had installed a telegraph wire along a railway line for the conduct of the railway's own affairs and had made it a term

---

[53] Above, pp. 219–64.
[54] At p. 370.
[55] *City of New Orleaus* v. *Fireman's Charitable Association* (1891) 9 So. 486.
[56] *Reid-Newfoundland Co.* v. *Anglo-American Telegraph Co.* [1912] A.C. 555.

of the contract that that wire should not be used by the railway as a means of making money from the business of transmitting telegraph messages: if any payments were received for such business they were to be held for the account of the Telegraph company. The railway company did use the wire commercially. The Judicial Committee's advice was that the telegraph company was entitled to an account of the profits so made. It can be argued that it was crucial that the contract included an express term obliging the railway to account for such profits, but it is difficult to accept that a bare promise not to use the wire commercially would not have led the Judicial Committee to the same conclusion. Such a term would have created a duty, a main purpose of which manifestly was to prevent the railway's enrichment by this particular mode.

In *Wrotham Park Estates Ltd.* v. *Parkside Homes Ltd.*[57] the defendants had built houses which infringed a restrictive covenant imposed for the benefit of the plaintiffs' land. Declining to issue a mandatory injunction for the houses to be pulled down, Brightman, J., awarded damages in lieu. The sum he gave was the amount for which the owner of the land benefited by the covenant might reasonably have agreed to relax it. This award was made notwithstanding the fact that that land had not suffered any loss of amenity or depreciation. A restrictive covenant is of course a right *in rem* but, in that it is born of contract and then given real effect, its breach is analogous to a breach of contract. One explanation of the nature of the award obtained by the plaintiffs in this case is that a main purpose of the duty undertaken by agreement when the covenant was entered was that the covenantors should not be enriched in this particular mode. If that conclusion can be reached where an agreement is given effect *in rem*, it ought equally to be reachable in the case of promises which, as is more usual, take effect only *in personam*.

In retrospect, *Moses* v. *Macferlan*[58] itself may have seemed to Lord Mansfield to be a case in which the plaintiff was seeking to recover the proceeds of a breach of contract, exactly as, in *Lamine* v. *Dorrell*, the plaintiff sought the proceeds of a conversion. Macferlan had promised not to sue Moses on the notes, but he had done, and Moses had paid. Lord Mansfield clearly thought an ordinary action for breach of contract remained open to Moses. The only

---

[57] *Wrotham Park Estates Ltd.* v. *Parkside Homes Ltd.* [1974] 1 W.L.R. 798.

[58] *Moses* v. *Macferlan* (1760) 2 Burr. 1005; and note Lord Mansfield's solution, in his discussion of *Dutch* v. *Warren* at 1011, to the problem of reconciling restitutionary and compensatory measures of recovery.

question, in modern terms, was whether he could have restitution instead. If one tries to analyse Moses' claim as based on some other ground, one is driven inexorably to say that it was a payment under compulsion of legal process and should therefore have been irrecoverable, since that species of compulsion, when applied by the defendant, does not give rise to restitution.[59]

★25

(b) *Interference with Contractual Relations*

It does appear at first sight that this is a wrong for which restitution lies. For the modern tort has its origin in the old action on the case for seduction *per quod servitium amisit*, by which damages were obtainable for the services lost when employees, or wives, were enticed away;[60] and it was early held that a *quantum meruit* would equally well lie against the seducer. That is *Lightly* v. *Clouston*, which has already been discussed.[61] However, that case cannot be fully relied on for this point because its facts allow the restitutionary claim to the explained as an example of alternative analysis, based on free acceptance. And, quite generally, whenever a defendant has so interfered in the plaintiff's contractual relations as to obtain for himself a benefit proceeding directly from the plaintiff, it will always be true that the plaintiff will be able to make out his claim independently of the wrong. So, in *Universe Tankships Inc. of Monrovia* v. *International Transport Workers Federation*, which will be discussed below,[62] the trade union (ITF) blacked the plaintiff-appellants' ship and, by thus preventing it from fulfilling its contracts, obtained a payment of money. The Union's liability to make restitution did not depend on the tort which it committed, for the facts also amounted to a non-voluntary transfer: the union was enriched by subtraction from the shipowners, and the factor going to 'unjust' was compulsion.

However, not every case of unlawful interference involves a subtractive enrichment. If I induce you to repudiate your contract with X and to contract instead with me for the same performance, the profit which I make can be said to have been made by my wrong committed against X and therefore at his expense in that sense. In the United States this species of the tort has been held to give rise to restitution. In *Federal Sugar Refining Company* v. *U.S. Sugar*

---

[59] *Marriott* v. *Hampton* (1797) 7 T.R. 269.
[60] *Lumley* v. *Gye* (1853) 2 E. & B. 216.
[61] Above, p. 324.
[62] *Universe Tankships Inc. of Monrovia* v. *International Transport Workers Federation* [1982] 2 W.L.R. 803, below, p. 349 f.

Equalisation Board,[63] the defendant Board had induced the Norwegian Food Commission to abandon its contract to buy sugar from the plaintiffs and to buy instead from themselves at a higher price. The plaintiffs claimed the profit made by the defendants. The defendants demurred. The claim was held to be good. The motive behind the restitutionary action clearly appears from the fact that the price at which the plaintiffs had agreed to supply the Norwegians was below the market rate, so that they would have made a loss if the Norwegians had not been induced to buy elsewhere and ordinary compensatory damages would therefore have given them nothing.

There is no necessary reason why the alternative analysis cases noted in the previous paragraph should lead an English court to follow the American view that this tort does itself give rise to restitutionary damages. It is difficult to assert that the duty not to interfere in other people's business relations has, as a main purpose, the prevention of a mode of enrichment. The duty would seem to be anti-harm rather than anti-enrichment. If that is right, the victim would be entitled to restitution only when the facts fell within the 'deliberate exploitation' test. The intentionality required for the tort would not automatically satisfy that test. In *Universe Tankships*, for example, the union undoubtedly believed that it was acting within its rights. That did not impede the claim based on compulsion, which does not require *mala fides*, but it would certainly have prevented any claim based on deliberate exploitation of wrongdoing as a means of enrichment.

One species of interference which must always fall within the deliberate exploitation test is bribery. Where a briber has corruptly bribed the plaintiff's agent, he is liable to make good the loss. At common law that compensatory liability is usually said to flow from the fact that the briber commits the tort of deceit against the agent's principal.[64] But it is rather easier to see the tort as being interference with contractual relations between agent and principal. In equity the briber's liability to make good the loss can be explained, in the case of fiduciary agents corrupted, as an example of the accessory liability incurred by anyone who knowingly participates in a dishonest breach of fiduciary duty.[65] The briber will usually himself receive an enrichment as a result of giving the bribe. In some

---

[63] *Federal Sugar Refining Company* v. *U.S. Sugar Equalisation Board* (1946) 26 Wash. (2d.) 282.

[64] *Salford Corporation* v. *Lever* [1891] 1 Q.B. 168; *Mahesan* v. *Malaysia Housing Society* [1978] 2 W.L.R. 444, 449.

[65] *Barnes* v. *Addy* (1874) 9 Ch.App. 244, 251.

cases he will not, as where he pays to get the agent to destroy a document or to refrain from revealing a fact.

Where the briber does receive an enrichment, the plaintiff has an alternative remedy by way of restitution rather than compensation. So, if a briber pays a buying agent a secret commission to induce the agent to buy from him, so that the briber receives a price of £1000 and gives the buying agent a secret commission of £100, the principal has a restitutionary claim against the briber for the £100.[66] This is not immediately easy to explain,[67] since the £100 is apparently not money received but money laid out. But the explanation would seem to be that the payment out to the agent provides the measure of the principal's overpayment to the briber, and it is that unintended overpayment which is recoverable. The restitutionary right can be explained on the basis of alternative analysis (a subtractive enrichment obtained by misrepresentation of the true price); but, since bribery is so clear a case of deliberate recourse to unlawful means of enrichment, it is equally explicable as an example of restitution for the wrong itself.

These claims for compensation and restitution which lie against the briber lie also against the bribee though, as we shall see, not necessarily on precisely the same theoretical basis.[68] However, contrary to what was once thought, the principal cannot cumulate his civil remedies. He can have either restitution or compensation; and whichever he chooses he cannot have it from both briber and bribee.[69]

(c) *Conflict of Interest*

Here we are concerned with the fiduciary's duty not to pursue his own interest where if he did so he might be tempted to sacrifice the interest of his beneficiary. Some cases involve fiduciaries who have succumbed to the temptation. Little more needs to be said about them. As we have just seen, their liability to make restitution is explicable on the test of deliberate exploitation. *Reading* v. *A.-G.* is a paradigm case;[70] *Mahesan* v. *Malaysia Government Housing*

---

[66] *Hovenden and Sons* v. *Millhoff* (1900) 83 L.T. 41.

[67] See *Mahesan*, above, at p. 451: 'This extension to the briber of liability to account to the principal for the amount of the bribe as money had and received, whatever conceptual difficulties it may raise, is now . . . too well established in English law to be questioned' *per* Lord Diplock.

[68] See below, p. 339.

[69] *Mahesan*, above, esp. p. 451.

[70] Above, n. 12.

Association[71] is another. There Mahesan, a director of the Housing Association, decided to buy land for the Association but came to an arrangement with a third party in exchange for a bribe, so that the third party bought the land at the asking price and sold it on the Association for twice the original amount. The Judicial Committee advised that the Association was entitled either to restitution or to compensation. There is an important difference between the restitutionary liability of these bribees and the restitutionary liability of an enriched briber which has just been discussed. In the case of the bribee there is no doubt whatever that his liability can rest directly on the wrong, but it is very doubtful that it can ever be explained by alternative analysis, since that would require the rare finding of fact to the effect that a receipt obtained from a third hand would certainly have accrued to the plaintiff if it had not been intercepted. In *Reading* that finding was unequivocally impossible.[72]

Then there are the cases in which the fiduciary has acted in good faith. All cases in which such fiduciaries have to make restitution of benefits acquired in breach of this duty can be explained by reference to the policy of prophylaxis. Equity does not wait to see whether the beneficiary has actually suffered and it cannot, therefore, sanction the duty by compelling the fiduciary to repair a loss. Instead the question is whether, in the given circumstances, the fiduciary *might have been* tempted to sacrifice the interests of the beneficiary. The only available sanction, once the fiduciary has actually made the acquisition in question, is therefore restitution.[73] Even where there is no loss to the beneficiary but only a hypothetical possibility that there might have been loss, the unfortunate fiduciary can still be made to disgorge his profit.

It is perfectly clear that in most cases restitution for breach of this duty is also explicable on the basis that a main purpose of the duty is to prevent enrichment. Those who manage the affairs of others must not seek opportunities to line their own pockets. In short, the particular harm to beneficiaries which equity chiefly fears is the harm which consists in the diversion of wealth into the fiduciary's pocket. It is above all to prevent that actual and non-hypothetical evil that equity adopts its anxious prophylactic approach. However, it is a question whether every breach of this duty to avoid conflicts of interest can be regarded as an anti-enrichment wrong. The better

---

[71] Above, n. 64, and cf. *Boston Deep Sea Fishing & Ice Company* v. *Ansell* (1888) 39 Ch.D. 339; *Lister* v. *Stubbs* (1890) 45 Ch.D. 1; *A.-G.* v. *Goddard* (1929) 45 T.L.R. 609.

[72] Above, p. 319.

[73] Above, p. 332.

answer is that some cannot. In those cases the only possible
explanation of restitution is prophylaxis against harms other than
enrichment of the fiduciary at the beneficiary's expense.

The important distinction is between facts on which the profit
could possibly have reached the beneficiary and cases in which it
could not have done so, whether because of a legal or a factual
impossibility. In *Industrial Development Consultants Ltd.* v.
Cooley[74] the defendant architect was managing director of the
plaintiff company. He took in his own name a contract which was
very unlikely to have been available to the company. Roskill, J., said
there was at most a 10 per cent chance that the company might get
it.[75] Even in such a case the defendant's liability can be said to be
based on an anti-enrichment wrong. The fiduciary must use all his
efforts for his beneficiary and must not turn aside to enrich himself
while there is the least possibility of enriching the beneficiary. But
there is a difference when there is no real possibility at all of the
beneficiary's obtaining the enrichment. There is then not the least
danger that the fiduciary will enrich himself by sacrificing the
acquisitive interests of the beneficiary, since there is *ex hypothesi*
no such acquisitive interest to protect. Hence, if his duty survives,
so that he remains under a prohibition from taking the particular
profit, the danger which equity perceives cannot be his enrichment as
such but rather some other harm.

The purpose of the duty to abstain from wealth which the
beneficiary could not take (as opposed to the content of the duty,
which is, undoubtedly, to abstain from enrichment) is the prevention
of loss, and the breach of the duty is not an anti-enrichment wrong
but an anti-harm wrong. Since *ex hypothesi* there is no question of
deliberate exploitation of unlawful means (because we are speaking
of honest fiduciaries) it follows that the only justification for restitution on such facts is the decision not to wait for the harm to
supervene, in other words the prophylactic policy itself. In short,
the law's concern is to stop loss to the beneficiary by bad management of funds, risk-taking, poor advice and so on. But prophy-
lactically. And, injunctions aside, the only prophylaxis which is
possible is, first, to impose a duty not to seek gains whose pursuit
might distract the fiduciary's attention or distort his judgment and,
then, to sanction that duty by effecting restitution of gains acquired
in breach of it. Without the prophylactic element, the deletion of
which would remove the inquiry from the hypothetical to the actual

---

[74] *Industrial Development Consultants Ltd.* v. *Cooley* [1972] 1 W.L.R. 443.
[75] At p. 454.

plane, it would be obvious that the mischief at issue in these cases is loss: the non-hypothetical, and therefore non-prophylactic, inquiry would be whether the beneficiary had suffered harm. Two cases illustrate this.

In *Boardman* v. *Phipps*[76] the appellant was the solicitor to a trust. The respondent was one of the beneficiaries. The appellant had been defendant below. The trust held a minority of the shares in a company which was not doing as well as it might. The trust did not want to, and without applying to the court had no power to, acquire the majority holding. By an extremely skilful operation, but also by using information which he had obtained in his fiduciary capacity and without a sufficiently complete revelation of his plan to the trustees to enable him to say that he had their consent, Boardman acquired the majority holding in the company, with profitable consequences both to himself and to the trust holding. Despite his honesty and his assiduous attention to the interests of the trust, he had to give up the profits which he made, subject to a liberal allowance for his skill and labour.

Since the trust could not take these shares there was no danger to it merely in the fact of his taking them. Hence, in order to defend the case's conclusion, it is necessary to identify some other danger needing to be guarded against. That other danger would seem to be that, in pursuing this plan, the hope of personal advantage might possibly have led him to close his eyes to the risks and to the need to warn the trustees to tell him to desist. Although in the event the operation was very successful, it might have gone wrong. It might have alienated the majority shareholders and made them hostile to the trust. In short there were risks of harm which had nothing to do with his intercepting trust opportunities. There was a real and sensible possibility (albeit hypothetical) that he might have been tempted to conceal dangers of loss. On this view the justification for ordering restitution was not that he committed an anti-enrichment wrong but that the duty which he broke survived as a prophylaxis against misleading and loss-causing advice.

In *Regal (Hastings) Ltd.* v. *Gulliver*,[77] Regal's directors wanted it to acquire two more cinemas to go with the one which it already had. They found that Regal could not afford to take the opportunity. They therefore put up money themselves. They formed a second company, and made Regal subscribe for 2000 shares while they themselves took 3000. The second company then acquired the two

---

[76] *Boardman* v. *Phipps* [1967] 2 A.C. 46.
[77] *Regal (Hastings) Ltd.* v. *Gulliver* [1942] 1 All E.R. 378.

extra cinemas; and the shares in both companies were thereafter sold at a considerable profit. But the new controllers of Regal struck back. They successfully caused the company to recover the profits made on the sale of the second company's shares, thus in effect recouping part of the price paid for the sale.

The House of Lords accepted that Regal could not have taken the opportunity. The directors were, none the less, in breach of their fiduciary duty. If the finding of fact that the company was itself too poor is accepted, the danger against which the duty was maintained cannot have been the directors' enrichment as such. But again it was true that, once they had decided to pursue their own profit, it was really and sensibly possible that they would not see or say what was truly best for the company. The prophylactic duty is intelligible as a protection against bad advice, not as an instrument against an enrichment dangerous in itself.

Regal (Hastings) Ltd. v. *Gulliver* is in one respect a much weaker case than *Boardman* v. *Phipps*. There was only a factual, not a legal, impossibility of the beneficiary's getting the enrichment which the fiduciary took. It is easy for a court to conclude that there is such a factual impossibility if that finding does not actually exonerate the defendant from his liability to make restitution.[78] If the finding of fact did exonerate the defendant, the onus of proving the impossibility would have to be placed on the fiduciary and would rarely be discharged.

The theme of this part has been that breaches of this duty lead to restitution in circumstances which illustrate all three tests for restitution-yielding wrongs. It may be thought that the difference between the last two categories is chimerical. The question can be examined by supposing a relaxation of the prophylactic approach. If equity decided not to impose liability till the mischief had actually supervened, what mischief precisely would it look for? The question would be: Did he actually sacrifice the beneficiary's interests? There are more ways of damaging those interests than by intercepting his gains. The beneficiary can also be caused loss by bad advice or even by the infliction of moral damage as in *Reading* v. *A.-G.* The prophylactic approach means that the court cannot wait to see that damage happen. It follows that, even in circumstances in which there is no danger of an anti-enrichment wrong, the duty to avoid conflicts of interest has to be equipped with a restitutionary sanction. In such circumstances the only explanation of the resti-

---

[78] The same story is indeed stated in a somewhat different light in *Luxor (Eastbourne) Ltd.* v. *Cooper* [1941] A.C. 108, 112, *per* Viscount Simon, L.C.

tution is the desire to guard against a wrong which, if committed, would be naturally remediable by an award of compensation.

(d) *Breach of Confidence*[79]

There are two main reasons why people expect the law to protect the secrecy of confidential information. One is simply to defend their own privacy, as where the personal details of some celebrity's life are about to be revealed[80] or governmental secrets are about to leak out.[81] The interest in privacy is best defended by means of injunctions. While the person seeking to make the revelation will often be trying to make money, the person who turns to the law to protect his privacy will usually not regard the information in question as wealth. However, the second reason for seeking the law's protection is precisely to defend wealth. Ideas for processes, products, books, and entertainments are as much the means of making money as are machines, labour, land, and other forms of property.

Within the context of fiduciary relations there is a certain reluctance to say that confidential information is a form of property.[82] The reason is that, as soon as you say that it is, you are driven inexorably and without further inquiry to the conclusion that a fiduciary who uses it must automatically be liable to make over any profit he makes from it, just as certainly as if he had used trust money. The remedy is not to eschew the property analogy but to remember that the information may, in some circumstances, be property which the fiduciary may use.

Outside the context of such relationships there is not the same inhibition. A money-making idea can be regarded as an item of wealth analogous, despite being intangible, to a car or a machine. The law was in effect committed to this view as soon as the duty to respect confidential information was severed from contract.[83] But, because the regime of protection has been developed in equity and, in particular, because equity has always found difficulty in awarding damages except in lieu of injunctions, it has taken some time for the remedial potential of breach of confidence to develop to the point at

---

[79] See Law. Com. 110 (1981): *Breach of Confidence.*

[80] *Prince Albert* v. *Strange* (1849) 2 De G. & Sm. 652; *Duchess of Argyll* v. *Duke of Argyll* [1967] Ch. 302.

[81] *Fraser* v. *Evans* [1968] 1 Q.B. 349; *A.-G.* v. *Jonathan Cape Ltd.* [1976] Q.B. 752 (the Crossman Diaries case).

[82] See *Boardman* v. *Phipps* [1967] 2 A.C. 46, 102, 127; *contra*, 107, 115. Cf. Law Com. No. 110 (1981) para. 2.10.

[83] *Saltman Engineering Co. Ltd.* v. *Campbell Engineering Co. Ltd.* (1948) [1936] 3 All E.R. 413.

which it can be said to be symmetrical with that available for tortious interference with chattels. Even now one hesitates to assert a perfect remedial symmetry. Though it is clear that development has been proceeding in that direction, history grates against the growth of an equitable tort.

The tort of conversion is conceived to prevent, equally, loss of wealth to the person rightly entitled, and wrongful increase of wealth to people not entitled. This double main purpose is reflected in the fact that the wrong gives rise to either compensation or restitution. In the case of abuse of confidential information, which is an anti-enrichment wrong notwithstanding the fact that it also protects privacy, the right to restitution became secure first, because equity had no hesitation about allowing an account of profits. So in *Peter Pan Manufacturing Corporation* v. *Corsets Silhouette Ltd.*,[84] the defendants had manufactured brassieres which, as they knew, incorporated manufacturing techniques which they had learned in confidence during the time when they had made some of the plaintiff's products under licence. Pennycuick, J., ordered an account of all the profits made using the confidential process:

It seems to me that . . . what a plaintiff who elects in favour of an account of profits is entitled to, is simply an account of profits in the sense which I have indicated, that is: What has the [defendant] expended on manufacturing these goods? What is the price which he has received on their sale? And the difference is profit. That is what Peter Pan claims . . .[85]

That is the restitutionary right. It is exactly analogous to the claim made by the owner of goods in respect of the price received by their conversion, as allowed by *Lamine* v. *Dorrell.*[86] The difference is that the proceeds of the wrong are received over a period, day by day as the confidential idea is repeatedly used.

The compensatory remedy had already begun to be established before the *Peter Pan* case, but only under the aegis of the injunction. In *Saltman Engineering Co. Ltd.* v. *Campbell Engineering Co. Ltd.*,[87] where the defendants had made and sold leather punches, using as their springboard a drawing put temporarily and confidentially into their keeping, the Court of Appeal intimated that, since under the *Chancery Amendment Act, 1858*, section 2, it could award damages to cover both past and future acts, in lieu of an injunction, it seemed undesirable to make an order which would involve the destruction of

---

[84] *Peter Pan Mfg. Corporation* v. *Corsets Silhouette Ltd.* [1964] 1 W.L.R. 96.
[85] At p. 108.
[86] *Lamine* v. *Dorrell* [1701] Ld. Ray. 1216.
[87] Above, n. 83.

the tools; and the form of relief would therefore be an order for delivering up of the confidential drawing and an inquiry what damages have been and might be suffered by Saltmans.[88]

Later, in *Seager* v. *Copydex*,[89] the plaintiff had revealed his idea for a pronged carpet-grip to the defendants but had failed to interest them in it. They for their part had subsequently used the idea without consciously remembering that they had got it from him. The Court of Appeal did not trouble to rehearse the justification in terms of the statutory powers of the chancery under Lord Cairns' Act and merely ordered 'reasonable compensation'.[90] Later the case came back to the Court to have that phrase explained.[91] It was then said that, on the analogy of damages for conversion, it meant the market value of the information. If it was information available from a consultant, the market vlaue would be a consultant's fee. If it was an original and inventive idea, it would be the price as between willing vendor and buyer, being a sum representing the capitalised value of the royalties for which inventive ideas were usually sold.

Seager v. *Copydex* would have introduced a more or less perfect symmetry between the regime for confidential ideas and for conversion of goods, had it not also done something else rather surprising. Even though the restitutionary right had been established earlier than, and had a more secure base than, the compensatory right, the Court of Appeal refused to allow the plaintiff to have an account of the profits which the defendant had made.[92] Thus the plaintiff was in effect allowed compensation but denied restitution. It is not said on what basis the restitutionary alternative was refused. The explanation must presumably be found in either the difficulty of taking the account or in the innocence of the defendants, who were 'unconscious plagiarists' whereas in *Peter Pan* the defendants had been conscious wrongdoers, or else in a combination of these two factors.[93]

The Law Commission, while recognising the great difficulty of taking an account in some cases, has nevertheless proposed that, at the discretion of the court, the restitutionary remedy should always be available, as an alternative to compensatory damages. But the Commission seems to envisage the discretion as operating to with-

---

[88] At p. 415; cf. *Nicrotherm Electrical Co. Ltd.* v. *Percy* [1957] R.P.C. 207.
[89] *Seager* v. *Copydex* [1967] 2 All E.R. 415. Cf. for an award of damages without any elaborate explanation: *Fraser* v. *Thames Television* [1983] 2 All E.R. 101.
[90] But see *English* v. *Dedham Vale Properties Ltd.* [1978] 1 W.L.R. 93, 111, *per* Slade, J.
[91] *Seager* v. *Copydex* [1969] 2 All E.R. 718.
[92] *Seager* v. *Copydex* [1967] 2 All E.R. 415, 419.
[93] Below, p. 355.

hold the account solely on the ground of difficulty in taking the account, not on the ground of the moral quality of the defendant's conduct.[94] Yet it has usually been a matter for the plaintiff himself whether he will or will not embrace the complexities of an account.[95]

The restitutionary claim to the profits, allowed in *Peter Pan* but refused in *Seager*, is indisputably an example of restitution for the wrong as such. There is no subtractive nexus between a plaintiff and the price received by a defendant who has sold his car. Similarly, to reach the profits the plaintiff has to rely on the 'wrong' sense of 'at the expense of'; he has to say that the profits have been received as a result of a breach of a duty of confidence owed to him. The explanation of that restitutionary right, generated by the wrong, is, it is submitted, that the abuse of confidential information is, like conversion of chattels, an anti-enrichment wrong.

It is another question whether, on the facts of *Seager*, there could also have been a restitutionary claim, based on alternative analysis, in respect of the user of the information as opposed to the profits of that user. The crucial difference between the user on the one hand and the profits of the user on the other is that the user itself is a subtractive benefit, while the profits are only obtained by the wrong. In respect of a subtractive benefit the plaintiff can, in principle, obtain restitution of the reasonable value if he can establish that the defendant was enriched and can point to a recognised factor calling for restitution. The plaintiff in *Seager* could not establish a free acceptance in order to settle those two issues, because the defendant did not know the full facts.[96] However, the defendant had used the information without the plaintiff's knowledge and had realized the value in money. Hence, on the basis that the defendant was enriched according to the 'realization test'[97] and that the 'ignorance' of the plaintiff showed that the enrichment was unjust,[98] there would have been a restitutionary claim independent of the defendant's wrong.

3. PRACTICAL CONSIDERATIONS

We have seen that a plaintiff who has suffered an acquisitive wrong may have to review these options: compensation for the wrong,

---

[94] Law Com. No. 110, paras. 4.86, 6.114; draft Bill, clauses 13 (1) (c) and 14 (2).
[95] Below, p. 354.
[96] *Cf. Boulton v. Jones* (1857) 2 H. & N. 564.
[97] Above, p. 121.
[98] Above, p. 324.

restitution for the wrong, and restitution for unjust enrichment by alternative analysis. In this section we are concerned with the practical implications of his choice. They are considered under two heads, the evasion of bars, and the measure of recovery.

(i) *The Evasion of Bars*

We have already seen in passing how one practical force in favour of waiving torts was exerted by the rule *actio personalis moritur cum persona*. If the victim's wrongdoer died his only hope was to find a claim which would not be caught by that bar. The *actio personalis* rule has passed into legal history, but the same type of tactical decision still arises in relation to other bars, such as the expiry of a period of limitation.

There is a fundamental principle which controls this type of tactical manoeuvre: a mere change of words cannot have any effective legal consequences unless it is accompanied by some change of substance and rationale.[99] This means that appeal to the phrase 'waiver of tort' cannot in itself take a plaintiff round an obstacle which he would encounter if he were maintaining an ordinary action for compensatory damages. It is necessary to ask exactly to what phenomenon the bar is expressed to apply. If it applies to the response (compensation), then a claim to restitution will not, as a matter of logic, be caught by it. On the other hand if it applies to the event (tort, or breach of duty, or named wrongs), then a claim to restitution which remains based on the wrong will be caught by it, while a claim to restitution based on an alternative analysis which ignores the wrong and identifies a different event (a non-voluntary transfer or a free acceptance) will as a matter of logic not encounter it.

There is a crucial rider which must be added to the statement in the last paragraph. As a matter of logic a claim based on alternative analysis cannot encounter a bar to claims based on wrongs, but logic is not in itself conclusive. It may be that the rationale behind the bar would be subverted if the plaintiff were allowed to slip past it, so that there would be a substantial nonsense even if not a logical nonsense. It follows that, before allowing the logical argument to prevail, a court must always ask whether the policy of the bar would be contradicted. If it would be, the court must extend the bar, for reasons of utility and not reasons of logic, to the claim in unjust

---

[99] Cf. *Beaman* v. *A.R.T.S. Ltd.* [1948] 2 All E.R. 89, 92, *per* Denning, J.; *Universe Tankships* v. *I.T.F.* [1982] 2 W.L.R. 803, 814, *per* Lord Diplock.

enrichment. Exactly the same considerations would apply to a bar against claims to compensation which was sought to be evaded by a plaintiff claiming restitution. This kind of exercise would not be necessary if restitution/unjust enrichment had always received its own independent consideration in matters of this kind. It would then simply have its own rules.

In *Chesworth* v. *Farrar*[1] the plaintiff, an antique dealer, sought to evade the limitation period laid down by s. 1 (3) of the *Law Reform (Miscellaneous Provisions) Act, 1934*, as amended by the *Law Reform (Limitation of Actions) Act, 1954*. The statutory bar was expressed in relation to the cause of action:

No proceedings shall be maintainable *in respect of a cause of action in tort* which by virtue of this section has survived against the estate of a deceased person, unless either (a) proceedings . . . were pending at the date of this death; or (b) . . . proceedings are taken . . . not later than six months after his personal representative took out representation.

The plaintiff had been the deceased's tenant but during long absences had failed to pay her rent. The deceased had obtained possession by order of court. The plaintiff now maintained against the deceased's personal representatives that the deceased had converted antiques left in the premises and had not handed over the proceeds of their sale. One question was whether a claim for money had and received on the model of *Lamine* v. *Dorrell*[2] was caught by the statutory bar: Did such a claim arise on 'a cause of action in tort'? Edmund Davies, J., held that the claim did not so arise. Citing Lord Wright in *Fibrosa*[3], he concluded that the action arose in 'quasi-contract or restitution', categories different from tort.[4]

It is not certain that this was right. The burden of this chapter has been that a claim to restitution after wrongdoing may or may not arise from the wrong. *United Australia*[5] itself, is authority for the proposition that a claim to restitution may indeed be based on a cause of action which is a tort. The logical properties of the term 'quasi-contract' are unstable, but it is certainly unsound as a matter of logic to assert an exclusive opposition between an event and a response. Hence, as an abstract proposition, the assertion that the plaintiff's claim arose 'in restitution' did not exclude its also arising

---

[1] Chesworth v. Farrar [1967] 1 Q.B. 407.
[2] *Lauine* v. *Dorrell* (1701) Ld. Ray. 1216, above p. 000.
[3] *Fibrosa* [1943] A.C. 32, 61.
[4] Chesworth v. Farrar [1967] 1 Q.B. 407, 417f.
[5] *United Australia Ltd.* v. *Barclays Bank Ltd.* [1941] A.C. 1.

'in tort'[6] Furthermore we have seen that where goods are converted and sold the owner cannot usually connect himself to the price received by the wrongdoer by means of the subtraction sense of 'at the expense of'. To establish a connexion he has to rely on the wrong.[7] It follows from this, subject to what will be said in the next paragraph, that on the facts of *Chesworth* v. *Farrar* the restitutionary claim did arise from and only from the tort.

It does not follow, however, that the conclusion was necessarily wrong. On closer inspection the facts might have turned out to be exceptional in one of two ways. It is possible that the deceased sold as purported agent for the plaintiff, in which case it would have been possible for the plaintiff to obtain restitution via an extinctive ratification.[8] The cause of action could not then have arisen in tort. Secondly, since the plaintiff was a dealer who would have sold the antiques in the course of her business, it might have been possible to argue that, contrary to the normal case, the receipt of the proceeds of sale did here amount to an interceptive subtraction, in which case the claim could be explained in terms of an alternative analysis based on non-voluntary transfer: the deceased was enriched by interceptive subtraction from the plaintiff and wholly without the plaintiff's knowledge.

Apart from these exceptional possibilities, *Chesworth* v. *Farrar* is a case in which the switch from compensation to restitution should not have evaded the bar which lay across all proceedings for the wrong. A *prima facie* converse example is provided by *Universe Tankships Inc. of Monrovia* v. *International Transport Workers Federation*.[9] In that case the obstacle which the plaintiff-appellants faced was the immunity of trade unions from actions in tort. More particularly, the *Trade Union and Labour Relations Act 1974*, as amended in 1976, provided that, where acts were done in furtherance of a trade dispute as defined in s. 29 (1), then a trade union such as the ITF was immune from liability for particular torts enumerated in s. 13.[10]

The union, in pursuit of a policy of improving the conditions of employment of seamen working on ships sailing under flags of convenience, 'blacked' the appellants' tanker, the *Universe Sentinel*.

---

[6] Above, p. 10.

[7] Above, p. 138.

[8] Above, p. 315.

[9] *Universe Tankships* v. *I.T.F.* [1982] 2 W.L.R. 803.

[10] The specific tortious liabilities exempted are those which arise from inducing or threatening to induce a breach of contract or other interferences in trade: *Trade Union and Labour Relations (Amendment) Act, 1976*, s. 3 (2).

This involved depriving the ship of the services of tugs, without which it was immobilised in port. Only when the owners had made agreements and paid money on terms dictated by the ITF was the ship allowed to go. The owners, once free, claimed their money back on various grounds. We are concerned here with the claim based on duress, which was upheld by a majority in the House of Lords. The union's conduct would have constituted the tort of interfering with contractual relations[11] if it was not within the immunity conferred by ss 29 and 13; and the majority held that it was not so covered because the acts done had not in fact been in furtherance of a trade dispute within s. 29. However, the interest of the case in the present context lies in the relationship between the claim for restitution based on duress and the immunity from actions in tort.

There was a concession by the appellants' counsel to the effect that, if the acts done fell within the immunity, the claim in duress would fail. But was that because the bar applied as a matter of logic to claims in duress? Or was it because it had to be extended to such claims as a matter of policy? According to the principal distinction taken in this chapter, this was a case in which alternative analysis was possible. The plaintiffs could put themselves within the subtraction sense of 'at the expense of' and could then rest their claim on vitiated voluntariness. Hence they could ignore the wrong and, as a matter of logic, escape the immunity. It follows that the bar could only apply to this restitutionary claim, based on independent unjust enrichment, because it was extended for policy reasons from the field of tort. And this is the position taken by both the majority and the minority.[12] Lord Diplock put it this way:

The use of economic duress to induce another person to part with property or money is not a tort *per se*; the form that the duress takes may, or may not, be tortious . . . but where the particular form taken by the economic duress used is itself a tort, the restitutional remedy for money had and received by the defendant to the plaintiff's use is one which the plaintiff is entitled to pursue as an alternative remedy to an action for damages in tort.

In extending into the field of industrial relations the common law concept of economic duress and the right to a restitutionary remedy for it . . . this House would not, in my view, be exercising the restraint that is appropriate to such a process if it were so to develop the concept that, by the simple expedient of 'waiving the tort', a restitutionary remedy for money had and received is made

---

[11] *Merkur Island Shipping Corporation* v. *Laughton* [1983] 2 All E.R. 189.

[12] Lord Diplock's views are given in the text, immediately below: Lord Russell agreed with Lord Diplock; Lord Cross made a similar observation: *Universe Tankships* v. *I.T.F.* [1982] 2 W.L.R. 803, 820. So also Lord Scarman, *diss.*, at p. 829; Lord Brandon, *diss.*, declined to go behind the concession made by the plaintiffs that the bar to tortious liability would be a bar to the claim in duress, at p. 833.

enforceable in cases in which Parliament has, over so long a period of years, manifested its preference for a public policy that a particular kind of tortious act should be legitimised in the sense that I am using that expression.

It is only in this indirect way that the provisions of the *Trade Union and Labour Relations Act, 1974*, are relevant to the duress point. The immunities from liability in tort provided by sections 13 and 14 are not directly applicable to the shipowners' cause of action for money had and received. Nevertheless, these sections, together with the definition of a trade dispute in section 29, afford an indication, which your Lordships should respect, of where public policy requires that the line should be drawn . . . .[13]

This passage provides a model for handling all attempts to evade an obstacle by seeking restitution rather than compensation after wrongdoing. The first step is always to see whether the evasion works as a matter of logic. The second is, if it does, to see whether, in the light of the policy behind the bar, the logical argument ought to be inhibited or displaced. The cause of action in unjust enrichment for duress is, by alternative analysis, logically distinct from the tort and the immunity from tort. Nevertheless, the bar is capable of being extended to it for policy reasons. The separation of these two steps is the key to clarity.

(ii) *The Measure of Recovery*

At this stage we are operating solely within the first measure of restitution: as much as the defendant received, without regard to the question whether he retains anything representing that original receipt. Even within that measure there is room for debate as to how much of the gain which he did receive ought to be counted. In actions for compensation an ever-extending cone of loss is cut off by rules of remoteness. So also in restitution there is a need, as yet unsatisfied, for rules of remoteness of gain. Suppose I steal your money and invest it very successfully on the stock market. Changing the portfolio every day, I raise the original £100 to £10 000 and then on one awful day I lose the lot. What principle explains why you cannot have restitution of the highest amount I ever received in the course of this story, here the £10 000?[14] It is convenient to notice at once that this inquiry has nothing to do with the exercise of tracing. The issue is not whether I have anything left which repre-

---

[13] *Universe Tankships* v. *I.T.F.* [1982] 2 W.L.R. 803, 814.

[14] Cf. *Heathcote* v. *Hulme* (1819) 1 Jac. & W. 122. But Sir Thomas Plumer, M.R., there seemed to think that in some circumstances a plaintiff might be able to make such a claim, as where there was a major discontinuity between the successful and the unsuccessful business.

sents the £100 originally received, but whether, without regard to that question, 'value received' can include receipts consequential upon the first receipt.

This problem can only arise in relation to restitution for wrongs as such. All claims based on autonomous unjust enrichment have their own in-built and very restrictive rule of remoteness. The reason is that in such claims the plaintiff always identifies himself as the person from whom wealth was subtracted. It follows that the only wealth to which he can establish any claim without relying on a wrong committed by the defendant is that wealth which was indeed subtracted from him. Thus in the example of the invested money in the last paragraph you can only identify £100, plus user over time represented by interest, as having been subtracted from you. In order to establish any connexion at all with the £10 000 you would have to say that I obtained it by virtue of my wrong. It follows from this that all restitutionary claims after wrongdoing which are based on alternative analysis must be restricted to this limited measure of recovery, because the key to all such claims is that the plaintiff relies solely on the subtraction sense of 'at the expense of'.

Where the plaintiff founds on the wrong there is no similar cut-off point. The wrong itself creates the nexus between the plaintiff and the enrichment. Anything which the wrongdoer receives can plausibly be said to have been obtained at the expense of the plaintiff, provided only that it can be described as having been obtained because of or through the wrong. If you deceive me into giving you money when you are hard-up, and then your luck turns and a business grows from that one injection of capital, I can plausibly say that all your prosperity was won by committing a wrong against me. This is the ever lengthening cone of gain into which a rule of remoteness has to be inserted. Yet no case has squarely faced the need to formulate a test. Behind the problem of remoteness there are also serious problems of quantification. In the example just given you will want to say that even your earliest gains were partly attributable to your own skill and labour and only partly to the capital wrongly obtained from me. So the problems of attribution and quantification set in even before the point is reached at which some principle must be invoked to cut off further gains on the ground of remoteness.

It is useful to approach these questions through the concept of 'the first non-subtractive receipt'. 'Non-subtractive' is used to denote a receipt in respect of which the only nexus between it and the plaintiff is that it was obtained by a wrong committed against him. If I wrongfully use your car for a month for my own purposes, the user is a subtractive receipt. You will be able to claim a reasonable rental. Suppose now that in the next month the way in which I use your car is that I hire it out to X for £400. That £400 is the first non-subtractive receipt. If I drove a hard bargain with X, you will want, in respect of the second month's user, not the reasonable rental attributable to the continuing subtractive receipt (for I did continue to use your car, albeit in this particular mode, that I used it by hiring it to X), but rather the £400 actually obtained by me by means of the wrong committed against you. If you claimed only the subtractive user you would get, say, £250 for each month. If you can get the first non-subtractive gain, you will get £250 plus £400.

Next, let it be added that, on receipt of the £400, I bought a share in a company which I later sold for £500 after taking a dividend of £50. The share, the dividend and the £500 are 'second or subsequent' non-subtractive receipts, receipts which are obtained by user of the first non-subtractive receipt, namely the £400. One further point needs to be made: there can be multiple 'first non-subtractive receipts'. Thus, whereas in the example I hired out your car for the whole of one month to one man, I might have chosen instead to hire it day-by-day to different men. Each daily charge would then be a first non-subtractive receipt. For 'first' is intended to take its meaning from the contrast with 'second or subsequent', which itself identifies those receipts which are obtained from the receipts acquired, directly but non-subtractively, from the wrong.

It would be unsafe to affirm categorically that second and subsequent non-subtractive receipts are always too remote, but in general it must be true that they are. For the question which emerges from the cases is whether it is even possible for plaintiffs invariably to get the first non-subtractive receipt or receipts. The basic rule is that they can, but there is an exception of doubtful size and strength.

The basic rule is established by three types of case. First, whenever a plaintiff obtains the price received by a defendant who has sold his goods and has thus committed the tort of conversion, the price so recovered is not a subtractive but, on the contrary, an example of a first non-subtractive receipt. Second, in equity, a fiduciary who has to pay over a commission or other profit made in breach of his duty to avoid conflicts of interest, is equally plainly compelled to give up a first non-subtractive receipt. *Boardman* v. *Phipps*[15] sufficiently illustrates this point and also underlines the fact that this liability does not apply only to conscious or dishonest wrongdoers. Third, trustees who apply trust funds or use trust property in their own business are liable, after an account has been

---

[15] *Boardman* v. *Phipps* [1967] 2 A.C. 46. Above, p. 341.

taken, to pay over the proportion of profits attributable to the trust capital. Again it is clear that this is a liability to pay non-subtractive receipts. It attaches to honest trustees.[16] And in *Docker* v. *Somes*[17] Lord Brougham, L.C., held that the practical difficulties of taking such an account, although they were a good reason for encouraging the plaintiff to take compound interest in lieu of actual profits, did not, except in a very extreme case, entitle the court to compel him to accept that more approximate option.

Despite the basic rule allowing restitution in respect of first non-subtractive receipts, it seems that outside the area of fiduciary relationships an innocent defendant may be able to resist a claim which runs beyond the subtractive receipt if it would involve the taking of a complex account. If this is right it presumably rests on the notion that only a fiduciary, with special responsibilities to bear, or a dishonest person who has deliberately had recourse to unlawful means of enrichment, ought to bear the hardship of answering to a complex accounting inquiry.

The evidence for this exception is not overwhelmingly strong. In *Re Simms,*[18] a receiver had converted a bankrupt's materials and had used them to complete building contracts, for which he had been paid. The Court of Appeal said that the bankrupt could not reach the profits so made. Yet such profits were first non-subtractive receipts, and the only difference between them and the proceeds of a tortious sale would seem to be the difficulty of quantifying the contributions of the bankrupt's materials and the receiver's own input. Yet, as *Goff and Jones* say,[19] the case is not conclusive. The Court's reasoning is very much controlled by the logic of the implied contract theory of restitutionary obligations and by a pre-*United Australia* analysis of waiver of tort, according to which the plaintiffs could not both describe their cause of action as conversion and at the same time seek restitution.

Despite the weakness of *Re Simms*, we have already seen in the context of confidential information above[20] that the Court of Appeal has asserted a discretion to refuse an account of profits against an innocent though careless defendant who used the plaintiff's idea in making and marketing a product. If the idea had been sold on to another manufacturer for a single, instantly identifiable

---

[16] *Re Davis* [1902] 2 Ch. 314; *Re Jarvis* [1958] 2 All E.R. 336.

[17] *Docker* v. *Somes* (1834) 2 My. & K. 655; cf. *Siddell* v. *Vickers* (1892) 9 R.P.C. 152, 163, *per* Lindley, L.J.

[18] *Re Simms* [1934] Ch. 1.

[19] At p. 480.

[20] *Seager* v. *Copydex* [1967] 1 All E.R. 419.

sum, it is inconceivable that the plaintiff would have been refused restitution of that non-subtractive receipt. Hence the only explanation would seem to be that a complex account is an undue burden for an innocent defendant.

In the United States a distinction is clearly taken between cases in which the defendant is 'consciously tortious' and cases in which he is 'no more at fault than the claimant'.[21] The former defendant is bound to give up any profit derived from dealing with property tortiously obtained, while the latter is not. In *Edwards* v. *Lee's Administrators*[22] the defendant discovered a scenic cave which he turned into a major tourist attraction. The entrance was on his land but one third of the cave and some of the best sights extended, as he well knew, under the plaintiff's land. The defendant maintained that he should only have to pay the reasonable rental value of the space under the plaintiff's land (i.e. the subtractive enrichment). But the court held that, as a wilful trespasser, he had to pay one-third of all the profits gained by the admission of tourists (the non-subtractive enrichment).

In English law that decision could be adequately explained, subject to *Re Simms*, by reference to the recovery of the proceeds of a tortious sale. No less than such proceeds, the money taken from the tourists was the first non-subtractive receipt from the wrong, with the difference that it was a receipt obtained from day-to-day over years rather than in one outright sale. The difficulty in English law would be to say why such recovery was only available against a wilful wrongdoer, since even innocent converters are liable to make restitution of their first non-subtractive receipts (i.e. the proceeds of the sale). But it may be right that the innocent should not be subjected to the hardship of a complex account covering a substantial period of time, though that does seem a flimsy ground for allowing the retention of enrichment obtained with the plaintiff's capital. The best solution is to allow recovery of the defendant's first non-subtractive gain in every case, subject to a liberal allowance for the defendant's input.[23]

4. A PROBLEM OF NOMENCLATURE

There has been a famous discussion of the question whether a breach of confidence is a tort and of what must theoretically be the case in

---

[21] *Restatement of Restitution*, sections 150–157, 202–205.
[22] *Edwards* v. *Lee's Administrators* (1936) 96 S.W.2d. 1028.
[23] See below, p. 419 ff.

order for that statement to become true.[24] There is another important and not dissimilar question: what is the appropriate name for legal wrongs (if any there be) which yield restitutionary damages but not compensatory damages? In *Brocklebank* v. *R*.[25] the petitioner wanted to recover money paid for a licence in circumstances in which the demand for payment was *ultra vires*. One weakness in his case seemed to be that an *ultra vires* demand was not a tort and, if it was not, could not give rise to the cause of action called 'waiver of tort'. In point of fact, since this was a case of enrichment by subtraction, the petitioner did not actually need to establish any wrong in order to make out a case for restitution. However, supposing he had needed to rely on the wrong, it would have been absurd to say that in order to obtain restitution he had to show first that the wrong was actionable for compensation, which is the tacit proposition behind the notion that you must identify a tort before you can waive one. Once the language of waiver is given up it becomes obvious that there may well be legal wrongs which are actionable only for restitution. In equity there are familiar examples, on account of chancery's recourse to the policy of prophylaxis. *Goff and Jones* contemplate the possibility of restitution of benefits obtained by some improper infringement of privacy which is not yet actionable for compensatory damages. They suggest that the ground can be called 'reprehensible means'.[26] The danger in that phrase is that it suggests the necessity of moral fault, whereas we earlier determined that a 'wrong' must be no more than a 'breach of duty'. The name itself is less important than that it should be remembered that 'restitution-yielding wrongs' form a category which is not coterminous with 'compensation-yielding wrongs': just as some compensatory wrongs do not give rise to restitution, so some restitutionary wrongs do not give rise to compensation. It should never be assumed that every wrong must give rise to restitutionary, compensatory and punitive damages or that every wrong must be confined to one of these responses. On the contrary each wrong may give rise to remedial rights in one or more of these different measures. That is the meaning of the diagram set out in the introductory section of this book.[27] What is needed is, not names which distinguish civil wrongs according to their remedial consequences,

---

[24] See esp. P.M. North, 'Breach of Confidence: Is there a New Tort?' (1972) 12 *J.S.P. T.L.* 149. Cf. Law Com. No. 110 (1981), para. 6.2.

[25] *Brocklebank* v. *R*. [1925] 1 K.B. 52.

[26] At p. 523.

[27] Above, p. 43.

but rather a steady resolve not to quadrate such wrongs with any one measure of response. In that way it is possible to avoid the danger of determining the answer as to a particular wrong's remedial potential even before the question has been put.

XI

THE SECOND MEASURE
OF RESTITUTION

The first and normal measure of restitution is 'value received', but sometimes a plaintiff will want to switch to the second measure, which is 'value surviving'. 'Value surviving' is what the defendant still retains in his hands when the claim is made. Suppose that the plaintiff originally paid the defendant £1000, which the defendant put into a building society account specially opened for the purpose. The defendant then drew out and spent £250. The plaintiff's claim in the first measure remains £1000, just as it would if the defendant had been robbed of the £1000 immediately after receiving it; but the claim in the second measure has now fallen to £750. At first sight it is not obvious why any plaintiff should find the second measure attractive, since on these simple facts it is less valuable. The tactical advantages of making such a claim will be considered in the second part of this chapter.

It is very important to make a clear distinction between two questions. The first is whether any of the enrichment originally received can be identified as surviving in the defendant's hands. The second is whether any kind of claim can be made to the enrichment which has been identified. It is in relation to that second question that it becomes important to know what tactical objective the plaintiff is trying to achieve. Some objectives can only be achieved at the cost of sacrificing or endangering the interests of third parties. When the plaintiff's claim does or may prejudice a third party it may become necessary to deny him restitution in the second measure. However, the question whether any of the original enrichment can still be identified in the defendant's hands can be answered without regard to the plaintiff's reasons for preferring this kind of claim, for a conclusion that the defendant does still hold some of what he received does not mean that the plaintiff is necessarily entitled to all or any of it.

1. IDENTIFYING THE SURVIVING ENRICHMENT

The exercise of identifying the surviving enrichment is called tracing. No problem arises if the defendant still visibly retains the very thing which he received, the cow or the car or the unopened bag of money. Equally unproblematical are the cases in which he has obviously destroyed or consumed what he originally received, as where he lost the money, or received wine which he then drank. In between these two extremes fall the cases in which he has something which might, on some views, be said to represent, or be the product of, what he originally received, as when he used the money to buy shares in a company and later sold the shares to buy a car. Both the common law and equity do accept that an enrichment can survive in some substituted form, but equity is more flexible and resourceful in dealing with mixed funds. The rules are artificial. They are also not complete. Claims in the second measure have not been very common.

(i) *The Basic Rules*

Since tracing is artificial, based on rules rather than nature, the inquiry can be influenced by the moral quality of the defendant. That is, the rules can be made to favour plaintiffs who have to deal with a defendant guilty of misconduct. The effect of misconduct will be considered in the next section. By 'basic rules' are here meant those rules which apply even as between innocent claimants, rules which do not depend on any re-inforcement derived from the misconduct of the person who effected the substitutions.

(a) *Common Law and Equity*

The common law will not trace through a mixed fund. If I pay you £100 and you mix that sum with £1 and then buy shares with the £101 it seems that that mixing puts an end to identifiability at common law.[1] In other words, at common law the question whether anything survives in your hands becomes a question whether there is anything which you hold as the result of one or more clean substitutions, without adding outside funds to those originally received. This limitation means that common law tracing is easily defeated.

Taylor v. Plumer[2] is the leading case. Plumer gave money to a broker to buy exchequer bonds; Walsh, the broker, decided to abscond to America. He used Plumer's money to buy American investments and some bullion. Plumer's attorney caught up with him before he could leave Falmouth. He took the investments and the bullion. On Walsh's bankruptcy, his assignee tried unsuccessfully to

---

[1] *Re Hallett's Estate* (1879) 13. Ch.D. 696, 717, *per* Jessel, M.R.
[2] *Taylor v. Plumer* (1815) 3 M. & S. 562.

recover what Plumer had seized. In order to be able to retain them Plumer had to establish that the investments and the gold were his by substitution for the money. On the issue of identification, Lord Ellenborough, C.J., said this:

'It makes no difference in reason or law into what other form, different from the original, the change may have been made, whether it be into that of promissory notes for the security of the money which was produced by the sale of the goods of the principal, as in *Scott* v. *Surman*,[3] or into other merchandise, as in *Whitecomb* v. *Jacob*,[4] for the product of or substitute for the original thing still follows the nature of the thing itself, as long as it can be ascertained to be such, and the right only ceases when the means of ascertainment fail, which is the case when the subject is turned into money, and mixed and confounded in a general mass of the same description. The difficulty which arises in such a case is a difficulty of fact and not of law, and the dictum that money has no ear-mark must be understood in the same way; i.e. as predicated only of an undivided and indistinguishable mass of current money. But money in a bag or otherwise kept apart from other money, guineas, or other coin marked, if the fact were so, for the purpose of being distinguished, are so far ear-marked as to fall within the rule on this subject, which applies to every other description of personal property whilst it remains (as the property in question did) in the hands of the factor or his general legal representatives.[5]

In fact tracing at common law is not very important. Just as the common law action of account was displaced by the equitable equivalent because Chancery had better machinery for taking the account, so here common law tracing is displaced by the equitable rules for identifying surviving enrichment, since equity can do all that the common law does in the case of clean substitutions but can also keep a marker on money as it passes into or through a mixed fund. If I pay you money which you place in an empty pocket, it is identifiable at common law; if you transfer it to another pocket in which you also have some money of your own, it ceases to be identifiable according to the rules of the common law but still remains identifiable in equity. In these circumstances it is obvious that the equitable rules can be seen as taking up at the moment in the story at which the common law rules begin to be defeated or as displacing the common law rules completely. All that matters is that, since in nearly all cases there will have been a mixing, in nearly all cases the surviving enrichment will be identifiable according to the equitable rules or not at all. This relationship between the legal and the equitable rules, such that the equitable rules simply displace or supplement the common law as

---

[3] *Scott* v. *Surman* (1742) Willes, 400.
[4] *Whitecomb* v. *Jacob* (1710) 2 Salk. 160.
[5] *Taylor* v. *Plumer* (1815) 3 M. & S. 562, 575.

and when needed, accords with the spirit of Jessel, M.R.'s account in *Re Hallett's Estate*[6] and was clearly accepted by the Court of Appeal in *Banque Belge pour l'Etranger* v. *Hambrouck*.[7]

In that case Hambrouck had been a clerk working for a M. Pelabon. He had forged cheques in his own favour purporting to be drawn by his employer. He had paid the cheques into his own account with Farrow's Bank, which had collected the money from Banque Belge, bankers to M. Pelabon. Hambrouck then drew cheques on his acccount with Farrow's in favour of his mistress Mlle Spanoghe, who in turn paid them into a deposit account with her bank, the London Joint City and Midland. At the time when Hambrouck's frauds were discovered there was a sum of £315 standing in Mlle Spanoghe's account. The question was whether Banque Belge was entitled to that £315. The London Joint City and Midland paid the sum into court. Hence the question arose in the form of a competition between Banque Belge and Mlle Spanoghe. Was the £315 the identifiable remnant of the money originally received by Hambrouck? The Court of Appeal held that it was. The objection on behalf of Mlle Spanoghe was that the money had passed into and through one bank account, with Farrow's, and then into a second bank account, her own deposit account with the London.

The Court of Appeal never made it completely clear whether any money at all had been mixed in either account with the money obtained through Hambrouck's frauds. Atkin, L.J., for example, says; 'In the present case less difficulty than usual is experienced in tracing the descent of the money, for substantially no other money has ever been mixed with the proceeds of the fraud.'[8] The reason why the court could avoid a clear holding on this issue of fact and could by contrast be satisfied with the less precise 'substantially' is that it considered that even in the context of a claim made at common law the issue of identifiability could be resolved by the more ingenious rules of equity. Thus, Scrutton, L.J., after observing that Mlle Spanoghe might have had an answer according to the strict common law rules, says:

But it is clear that the equitable extension of the doctrine as based on *Re Hallett's Estate*[9] and explained in *Sinclair* v. *Brougham*[10] enables money though

---

[6] In *Re Hallet's Estate* (1879) 13 Ch.D. 696, 717 f. Jessel, M.R., criticises Lord Ellenborough for not pointing out that Equity's arm could reach further: 'He did not know that Equity would have followed the money, even if put into a bag or into an indistinguishable mass, by taking out the same quantity.'

[7] *Banque Belge pour l'Etranger* v. *Hambrouck* [1921] 1 K.B. 321.

[8] At p. 336.

[9] Cit. n. 6 above.

[10] *Sinclair* v. *Brougham* [1914] A.C. 398.

changed in character to be recovered, if it can be traced. As Lord Parker says in the latter case,[11] on equitable principles, the original owner would be entitled 'to follow the money as long as it, or any property acquired by its means, could be identified'.[12]

Again Atkin, L.J., says:

The question always was, Had the means of ascertainment failed? But if in 1815 the common law halted outside the bankers' door, by 1879 equity had had the courage to lift the latch, walk in and examine the books: *Re Hallett's Estate*. I see no reason why the means of ascertainment so provided should not now be available both for common law and equity proceedings.[13]

The contrary position is unarguable. If anyone were to say that it is only on some special facts that the rules of equitable tracing can come into play (as, for example, only within the context of a fiduciary relationship), the answer would have to be, quite apart from the authority of *Banque Belge* itself, that the role of such special facts surrounding the original receipt must be to determine whether, if and when some surviving enrichment has been identified, equity will recognise any species of claim in respect of the matter thus put in view. The character of the circumstances surrounding the original receipt is decisive of the question whether the plaintiff has any restitutionary rights, whether legal or equitable, and whether in the first or in the second measure. But the character of those circumstances cannot, subject to one exception, have any bearing on the self-contained and mechanical question whether something which the defendant still retains is the identifiable remnant of the original receipt. The exercise of identification — what the cases call 'the means of ascertainment' — is neutral as to the entitlement to restitution and independent of the circumstances which determine that entitlement. The exception has been mentioned already.[14] Where the person responsible for intermixtures and substitutions has been guilty of misconduct the law not unreasonably adjusts the rules of identifiability. Otherwise such a person might too easily escape a liability for a reason unrelated to his misconduct, namely the fortuitous breakdown of the means of ascertainment.

---

[11] Ibid., 447.
[12] *Banque Belge pour l'Etranger* v. *Hambrouck* [1921] 1 K.B. 321, 330.
[13] Ibid., p. 335.
[14] Above, p. 359.

(b) *Mixed Funds*

(α) *The **pari passu** rule*   In the absence of misconduct on the part of the person who effects the mixture the basic rule is that equity regards the fund as declining *pari passu*. That is to say, the fund which is held by the defendant is regarded at the moment of the mixing as containing both the plaintiff's money and his own and then as depreciating in the same proportions as it was originally constituted. Thus, if we suppose that the defendant mixed £100 of the plaintiff's money with £300 of his own already in a deposit account, and then paid out £200, the reduction in the fund retained is to be borne in the proportions 25 : 75 by both, so that what remains is still attributable to each in the original proportions. This basic rule means that there is in general no question of applying a rule of 'first in, first out',[15] according to which the plaintiff's money would remain in the account until £300 had been paid out.

This starting point − the *pari passu* rule − was approved in *Re Diplock*.[16] There the defendants were charities who had mixed with their own money the sums which they had received as the result of a an error of law made by executors of a will. The plaintiffs were the next of kin of the deceased to whom the money ought properly to have been paid. So it was a case in which those who had mixed the money were themselves innocent. The same basic starting point was considered correct in *Sinclair* v. *Brougham*[17]. In that case the claim was made by depositors who had been the customers of an *ultra vires* banking business run by a building society. The mixing had been effected when the directors of the society allowed the *ultra vires* money to enter the general funds of the society. If this mixing done by or on behalf of the directors is regarded as a breach of duty by them, then *Sinclair* v. *Brougham* is authority for the proposition that the *pari passu* rule applies even where the mixing is done by someone guilty of misconduct, so long as the competition in question is between claimants who themselves have not been guilty of misconduct. So there the society itself had no power to accept or to mix the *ultra vires* money. Its directors had been guilty of misconduct, but the society itself had not been. As between the depositors and the society there was, therefore, nothing to displace the *pari passu* rule.

(β) *An exception: 'first in, first out'*   Even in the absence of misconduct, *Re Diplock* shows that there is one common species of

---

[15] 'The rule in *Clayton's Case*: *Devaynes* v. *Noble, Clayton's Case* (1816) 1 Mer. 572.

[16] *Re Diplock* [1948] Ch. 465, affd. *sub nom. Ministry of Health* v. *Simpson* [1951] A.C. 251.

[17] *Sinclair* v. *Brougham* [1914] A.C. 398.

mixed fund to which, exceptionally, the *pari passu* rule does not apply. Where money is mixed in an active current banking account the identification of payments turns on the rule 'first in, first out'. That is to say, a payment remains in the account until a sum has been paid out which in aggregate equals the amount which was already there at the time of the payment in. The Court of Appeal appeared to regard this exception as somewhat reluctantly to be accepted on the ground of convenience, although it is not clear that in fact there are any compelling reasons for adopting a rule which in practice produces more extreme and arbitrary results. The Court said:

It might be suggested that the corollary of treating two claimants on a mixed fund as interested rateably should be that withdrawals out of the fund ought to be attributed to the interests of both claimants. But in the case of an active banking account this would lead to the greatest difficulty and complication in practice and might in many cases raise questions incapable of solution. What then is to be done? In our opinion, the same rule as that applied in *Clayton's Case*[18] should be applied. This is really a rule of convenience based on so-called presumed intention. It has been applied in the case of two beneficiaries whose trust money has been paid into a mixed banking account from which drawings were subsequently made, and, so far as we know, its application has not been adversely criticised (see *per* Fry, J., in *Hallett's Case*,[19] and *per* North, J., *Re Stenning*[20]). In such a case both claimants are innocent, neither is in a fiduciary relation to the other, and if the mixed fund had not been drawn upon, they would be entitled to rateable charges upon it. Exactly the same occurs where the claimants are not two beneficiaries but one beneficiary and one volunteer, and we think, accordingly, that the same principle should be adopted.[21]

The exception thus preserved should be regarded as open to review. It rests on the undemonstrated strength of the reasons of convenience and so-called presumed intention. *Goff and Jones* also condemn it.[22]

(γ) *Replenishment of depleted funds*   Whether the mixed fund is one which attracts the general rule and thus reduces *pari passu* or is an active current account caught by the 'first in, first out' rule of *Clayton's Case*, it seems that a plaintiff whose money has once vanished from the fund cannot claim that it has been restored by reason of the defendant's choosing to replenish the fund with new money. Thus, if the plaintiff's money is represented in a mixed fund

---

[18] Cit., n. 15 above.
[19] At the first instance: *Hallett's Case* (1879) 13 Ch.D. 696, 699 *et seq*; and see Thesiger, L.J., *diss.* at 745. The majority of the Court of Appeal displaced *Clayton's Case* only against a defendant guilty of misconduct.
[20] *Re Stenning* [1895] 2 Ch. 433.
[21] *Re Diplock* [1948] 1 Ch. 465, 554.
[22] At p.59.

in a proportion of 25 per cent and the fund falls from £400 to £100, the plaintiff can only say that £25 of the £100 represents the enrichment received from him. If, next day, the defendant replenishes the depleted fund by adding £300 of his own, the plaintiff can, none the less, only identify £25 as the remnant of his payment. This has been held to be true even against a mixer guilty of misconduct. It must therefore be the case *a fortiori* against the innocent. In *James Roscoe (Bolton) Ltd.* v. *Winder*,[23] Sargant, J., held that, where Winder had paid his company's money into his own account and had spent it all except £25 18s and had then made payments in so that there was a balance of £358 5s 5d, the company could not identify more than £25 18s in the account. This seems absolutely correct since, however artificial the rules are, once the court reaches a point in the story at which it is bound to say that the enrichment has disappeared, it is impossible for it to affirm that it has subsequently reappeared. The position is different, however, if the defendant himself declares that the replenishment is for the plaintiff's account; for the defendant then holds, not the surviving remnant of his original enrichment, but something else which he himself has put in the place of the enrichment which has disappeared.[24]

(δ) *Assets bought from a mixed fund* The preceding paragraphs have been concerned with the question whether the defendant's original enrichment survives in the mixed fund itself. The same question can arise in relation to purchases out of the mixed fund. Suppose that the defendant has bought shares with £100 withdrawn from the mixed fund. Can the plaintiff identify the original enrichment in the shares so bought? The general answer is that, whatever he could assert in respect of the money at the moment when it was withdrawn, he can equally assert in relation to an asset acquired by the defendant with that money. Thus, in *Re Diplock*, one of the charities, Dr Barnado's Homes, paid its grant of £3000 into its current account. *Clayton's Case* therefore applied and, when the 'first in, first out' principle was worked through, it turned out that the Diplock £3000 had been used in part-payment of the price of £40000, 2¾ per cent Funding Loan. The plaintiff next of kin were therefore entitled to identify their £3000 in the Funding Loan.[25] If the money had come out of a mixed fund which was within the general rule for *pari passu* reduction, the claim would have had to be based on the

[23] *James Roscoe (Bolton) Ltd.* v. *Winder* [1915] 1 Ch. 62.
[24] Ibid., p. 69. Essentially, he thus declares hinself trustee of a new trust for the person entitled to the fund before depletion.
[25] *Re Diplock* [1948] 1 Ch. 465, 552ff.

assumption that that part of the price payed from the mixed fund came proportionately from the plaintiff and the defendant. If £1000 came from the mixed fund in which the plaintiff's proportion was 25 per cent his contribution to the asset would be £250.

(ε) *Appreciated assets*   When an asset is bought with, or partly with, money coming from the plaintiff, whether or not it comes from him through a mixed fund, there is always a problem if the asset changes in value. But a mixed asset is not in principle different from a mixed fund. Hence if its value decreases the general rule should apply, with the result that it depreciates *pari passu* for both contributors, though again the rule is different when the competition is between an innocent claimant and a defendant guilty of misconduct. Where the mixed asset appreciates in value there are in principle two ways of looking at the result. Suppose that the plaintiff's contribution is £1000 and the defendant's contribution is £3000, and the asset rises in value from £4000 to £8000. It could be said that what survives in the defendant's hands of the original enrichment is £1000, no more or less than the value he originally received. Alternatively, more favourably from the plaintiff's point of view and more symmetrically with the rule for *pari passu* reduction in the case of depreciation, it could be said that what survives is a proportionate (here 25 percent) share in the asset.

In *Re Hallett's Estate*, Jessel, M.R., appeared to take the view that even against a wrongdoer the second approach would not be permissible.[26] If that is right, it follows *a fortiori* that as against an innocent defendant the recipient can only say that there survives, in the appreciated asset, the full value of the enrichment originally received. However, in *Hallett* the opinion expressed by Jessel, M.R., was *obiter*, since no appreciated asset was in question. It also seems inconsistent with the view expressed in relation to purchases from an unmixed fund: where a trustee makes a clean substitution, buying some asset with, and only with, trust money, the beneficiary is allowed to take the asset itself and not just the sum which went into its acquisition.[27] Hence it would seem to follow that if the trustee uses money which comes partly from the trust and partly from himself the beneficiary should be able to claim a proportionate beneficial share. This seems now to be the preferred view, at least against a wrongdoer.[28] The argument from the *pari passu* rule for reductions in value suggests that the same conclusion should apply even as

[26] *Re Hallett's Estate* (1879) 13 Ch.D. 696, 709.
[27] Ibid.
[28] *Re Tilley's Will Trusts* [1967] Ch. 1179.

against an innocent defendant, for, if the main case for the *pari passu* rule in relation to reductions in value is that in the absence of wrong-doing neither claimant can point to any factor entitling him to priority over the other,[29] it is difficult to say the basic rule should not also apply to the case in which the asset increases in value. Nor is it irrelevant to observe that where resources are contributed by more than one person to the acquisition of an asset in the name of one, then, if the situation is one which readily attracts the doctrine of resulting trusts, the conclusion drawn by presumption is that the contributions are reflected in proportionate shares, so that the con-tributors do then take the benefit of any increase in the value if the asset.[30]

(ς) *Operation of intent*   These basic rules can sometimes turn out to have been modified by the intent manifested by the defendant or, possibly, by other interested parties. We have already noticed that a payment made to replenish a depleted mixed fund normally does not count as replacing the value received from the plaintiff but sub-sequently dissipated. Yet, if the defendant paid the new money in with the intent of replacing what had been lost, his intent will be given effect.[31] As for payments out of the mixed fund, the intent of the defendant can displace the effect of *Clayton's Case* or the rule imposing reduction *pari passu*. In *Re Diplock* the Court of Appeal held that if one of the recipient charities withdrew money from the mixed fund and placed it in a separate account with the intention of ear-marking it as the trust money, the next of kin could trace into that separate sum even though the normal rules would have identified the money in a different location. Lord Greene, M.R., said:

A volunteer who mixes what turns out to be trust money with his own, can surely himself 'unmix' it subsequently if he thinks fit to do so. And as the operation of equity is directed to preventing the volunteer doing what is un-conscionable, surely it would be unconscionable for the volunteer who, for his own purposes, has earmarked the trust money, to assert that what he has earmarked is not trust money but money which he is entitled to keep as his own.[32]

A more extreme and exceptional departure from the ordinary rules is indicated by *Re Tilley's Will Trusts*.[33] In that case a trustee had mixed a relatively small sum of trust money in her own account and

---

[29] *Re Diplock* [1948] 1 Ch. 465, 539.
[30] *Dyer* v. *Dyer* (1788) 2 Cox Eq. 92, 93 per Eyre, C.B. The doctrine has been distorted by innumerable matrimonial cases: see *Cowcher* v. *Cowcher* [1972] 1 W.L.R. 425.
[31] Above, p. 365.
[32] *Re Diplock* [1948] 1 Ch. 465, 552.
[33] *Re Tilley's Will Trusts* [1967] Ch. 1179.

had then made successful investments in property using money from the account. A mechanical application of the ordinary rules might have produced the conclusion that the beneficiaries under the trust were entitled to a proportionate share in the very profitable investments. However, Ungoed Thomas, J., found himself able to conclude that she had not in fact used trust money. This finding was based on a combination of two other facts. First, she had never intended to use the trust money for her own purposes but had put the money into her account merely as a convenient, albeit technically wrongful, way of keeping it; second, she always had adequate funds or overdraft facilities for her own business deals.[34] The conclusion of fact was, therefore, that the beneficiaries' money had never been paid out of the account but had at most served from time to time to reduce the trustee's recourse to her ample overdraft facilities. Lastly, there may be facts which show that a mixed fund is to be regarded in the same way as a normal joint account, so that a payment out which is made for the purpose of acquiring an asset can be regarded as an application for the benefit solely of the acquirer, free from the other party's claims.[35] Such a conclusion will necessarily be rare.

We have now briefly considered the rules of identification as they operate when a mixed fund reduces in value, when it is subsequently replenished, and when an asset is bought out of it. We have also noticed that the rules can be modified in some circumstances when contrary intentions are manifested and acted upon. The discussion so far has assumed that the competition in relation to the mixed asset has arisen between a claimant and an innocent defendant. It is now necessary to take into consideration the effect of misconduct on the part of the defendant.

(ii) *The Effect of Misconduct*

There is a maxim which says: *'Omnia praesumuntur contra spoliatorem* (Everything is presumed against a thief).' This is the spirit in which the exercise of identification has been conducted against those who have been guilty of wrongful misappropriation. Technically, the effect of such misconduct is to displace the basic rules for identifying the survival of an enrichment in and through a mixed fund. That is to say, a defendant guilty of misconduct cannot take advantage of the rule that a mixed fund reduces *pari passu* or that a current bank account is turned over on the principle 'first in, first out'. Instead the starting

---

[34] *Re Tilley's Will Trusts* [1967] Ch.D. 1179, 1192f.
[35] *Re Bishop* [1965] Ch. 450; cf. *Borden (U.K.) Ltd.* v. *Scottish Timber Products Ltd.* [1981] Ch. 25.

point is that he is not entitled to any part of the mixed fund unless and until he himself discharges the onus of proving that some part of it represents his own input.[36] Then, when it comes to discharging that onus, the wrongdoer is put into the position in which he cannot deny that he intended to preserve the claimant's contribution and to consume or dissipate his own. This means in effect that, if there is something left in the mixed fund, the claimant will be able to say that that remnant represents his contribution; and, if there is nothing left in the mixed fund but the trustee holds an asset bought out of an earlier withdrawal from the fund, the claimant will be able to identify his contribution in that asset.

Thus in *Re Hallett's Estate*,[37] a solicitor who acted for a Mrs Cotterill had wrongfully sold certain Russian bonds which she had deposited with him. He had paid the proceeds into his own bank account. He had also directed into the same account capital belonging to a trust in which he had a life interest. He then dissipated some of the money. The main question was whether the money left in the account represented his input or rather the contributions of the claimant whose funds he had misappropriated. The Court of Appeal held that it had to be presumed that he intended to act honestly and thus to spend his own funds, preserving the money which was not rightly his. Jessel, M.R. said:

> It seems to me perfectly plain that he cannot be heard to say that he took away the trust money when he had a right to take away his own money . . . . What difference does it make if, instead of putting the trust money into a bag, he deposits it with his banker, then pays in other money of his own, and then draws out some money for his own purposes? Could he say that he had actually drawn out anything but his own money? His money was there, and he had a right to draw it out, and why should the natural act of simply drawing out the money be attributed to anything except to his ownership of money which was at his bankers?.[38]

This approach seemed to mean that the court would regard the wrongdoer as invariably spending his own money first. However, that overlooked the possibility that the first slice of his spending might leave some durable asset while the next tranche might exhaust the fund without leaving any identifiable product. Suppose that, having mixed £1000 of the claimant's money with £1000 of his own, he spends half the money in buying shares and, subsequently, the second half on a luxury cruise. A mechanical application of *Hallett*

---

would produce the undesirable conclusion that the claimant's money had been used in paying for the holiday.

These facts arose in *Re Oatway*.[39] Here Oatway was a trustee who mixed £3000 of trust money in his own account. He then bought Oceana shares for £2137 at a time when there was enough money of his own in the account to cover that acquisition. Afterwards, he used up the balance of the account. The question was whether the shares represented the money taken from the trust. Joyce, J., held that they did. He rightly understood *Hallett* to be authority, not for a presumption that the wrongdoer withdrew his own money first, but rather for a presumption that he intended honestly to preserve the other's property. Consequently Joyce, J., held that the dissipation which had followed the purchase of the Oceana shares was a dissipation of the trustee's own contribution. On Joyce, J.'s reasoning the shares had been bought wholly with trust money. That ought to mean that, if (which was not the case) they had risen in value to £6000, the trust would have been entitled to the full sum. Another alternative would have been to say that the shares contained in their value the £2137 actually laid out in their purchase. In fact Joyce, J., followed an intermediate course the logic of which is not easy to reconstruct. He said that the trust was entitled, by means of a lien, to take from the shares the sum of £3000, that being the amount of trust money originally paid into the mixed fund. The point was, however, academic, since the shares were worth much less.

These hostile presumptions against the wrongdoer leave a number of questions unanswered. It is in particular not clear what rule of identification applies when the wrongdoer both invests the first tranche of his spending and retains the balance of the mixed fund in his hands. Can the claimant say, reverting to *Hallett*, that his money was withdrawn first and thus went into the successful investment? In *Re Tilley's Will Trusts*, Ungoed Thomas, J., certainly seemed to hold that, if the claimant could show that his money had been used, he would be able to identify it in the investment not merely as a fixed sum but as a proportionate share. If that is right the claimant certainly has a reason for arguing that he should trace into the investment rather than into the balance of the fund. But it is not clear on what principle it should be decided whether the defendant did use the plaintiff's money. The proper course in such a situation may be to revert to the normal rules of *pari passu* application from a mixed fund other than a current account, and 'first in, first out' from such an account.

*26

---

[39] *Re Oatway* [1903] 2 Ch. 356.

(iii) *Extinction of the Surviving Enrichment*

There are some very clear cases. The clearest of all is that in which what was originally received has been literally consumed or destroyed, as where a bottle of wine received has been drunk by the recipient. Subject to one hesitation or complication which will be mentioned below, the case is no less clear when the original receipt consists in a sum of money which is then spent in such a way as to leave no product (as, on a world trip) or to leave a product which is then consumed (as, on a bottle of wine which is then drunk). There are, however, two situations which do require some discussion. The first is where the end of the exercise of identification shows that the original enrichment was spent on improvements or alterations to an asset already held by the recipient. The second is where the tracing exercise shows that the enrichment received was spent in discharging debts.

Where the original receipt is spent on alterations, as for instance in building work done on land, *Re Diplock* holds that the money cannot any longer be traced.[40] However, the case does not make it completely clear whether what is meant is that in such circumstances the enrichment has been extinguished or that, even although some surviving enrichment is still identifiable in the product of the work, no claim can be allowed in respect of that enrichment. This second possibility has led to the suggestion that *Re Diplock* accepted, in substance even if not in name, that the defence of change of position does operate in relation to claims in the second measure of restitution. That will be considered below.[41] At this point it is only necessary to indicate that the first of the two explanations seems correct and sufficient in itself to account for the denial of any claim.

The reason lies under the head of enrichment. Even though some alterations in assets can be described as 'improvements', no non-money benefits can count as enrichments unless they have either been freely accepted or they pass some other test of enrichment compatible with the phenomenon of 'subjective devaluation'.[42] In practice this means that such benefits rarely count as enrichments if they have not been freely accepted, since the other tests have been little explored and are hard to satisfy. Where someone puts money into an alteration of existing asset in the erroneous belief that that money has become irrevocably his, it is difficult to say that he has freely chosen the end-product which survives in his hands as a

---

[40] *Re Diplock* [1948] 1 Ch. 465, 546 ff.
[41] Below, 411. cf. *Goff and Jones*, p. 59 and p. 547.
[42] Above, p. 109 ff.

result of the work. This is vividly apparent when the end-product is eccentric — as, for instance, a monstrous folly or a scheme of interior decoration done in appalling taste — but, so long as one remembers the subjective orientation of the law in relation to enrichment, it is equally true in relation to alterations which, objectively, do enhance the value of the asset. For except in areas in which the subjective theory of enrichment, according to which the value of non-money benefits depends primarily on an exercise of free choice by the recipient, is flatly overridden, no non-money benefit counts as an enrichment merely because there is a sufficient demand for it in society generally to endow it with a money value. Hence, according to this view, the reason why no claim can be made in respect of money traced into alterations is that the enrichment has been extinguished. The recipient who applies the money in that way is, in effect, in the same position as one who returns from abroad to find that some uninvited intervener has done the work for him. The corollary of that explanation is that if, exceptionally, the alteration does satisfy a test of enrichment compatible with the phenomenon of subjective devaluation, then it must follow that the tracing exercise will successfully identify some surviving enrichment still retained by the defendant. In such circumstances there will be no bar *in limine* to a claim in the second measure.

It may be objected that this argument to the effect that, within the context of a subjective approach to the value of non-money benefits, money expended on alterations leaves no surviving enrichment in the defendant's hands, can be applied to every case in which he expends the original enrichment on a non-money benefit, as for example even when he buys a car or shares in a company. But that is not correct. The reason is that where tracing shows that the original receipt survives, if at all, in some independent asset acquired after the receipt, a money judgment can be imposed on the defendant without offending or contradicting the notion of subjective devaluation. For if the defendant is minded to say that the car which he bought with the plaintiff's money was not freely chosen by him and was therefore not an enrichment, he thereby admits that he can have no objection to its being taken from him. It cannot matter to him that he must give up what he does not want. There is no infringement of his freedom of choice.

The other difficult question is whether the enrichment is extinguished when the original receipt is applied by the defendant in the discharge of a debt. Authority aside, it would be impossible to maintain that it is extinguished. Suppose that you pay off my creditors. Once the debt is technically discharged, which in some circumstances happens *ipso iure* and in others happens if and when I accept the discharge which you have arranged for me,[43] I receive the benefit of that burden removed. It is a non-money benefit, but we have seen that it passes the 'no reasonable man' test of incontrovertible enrichment.[44] And, so long as you can identify some factor going to 'unjust' and thus calling for the enrichment to be reversed, you will be entitled to restitution.[45] It follows that the discharge of a debt is capable of counting as an enrichment when the facts are such that the discharge is conferred directly. In such circumstances the discharge is the 'enrichment received' and will support a claim in the first measure. But 'enrichment received' will, if retained unchanged, always become 'enrichment surviving'. If I receive a car and retain it till you make your claim, the car is both what I originally received and what I still retain. A discharged debt is a species of enrichment which by nature is retained in the same form. It is an enrichment which endures at least so long as the creditor, had he not been paid off, would have been able to maintain his action. Hence one would have thought it beyond doubt that a discharged debt is not only an enrichment but also one which survives from day-to-day in such a way as to cause the two measures of restitution to coincide: the enrichment which survives is the same as the enrichment which was received.

If all this is true when the debt is discharged directly by the plaintiff's payment to the creditor it is difficult to deny that it must also be true when, in the simplest case, the plaintiff has paid money to the defendant and the defendant has used all or part of the original receipt to pay off his creditor. Suppose, therefore, that you pay me £1000 and I then lose or dissipate £500 but use the other £500 to pay a debt due to a third party. Here it would seem to be undeniable that the original enrichment which I received was £1000 and that my surviving enrichment, after paying the debt, is a debt of £500 discharged, valued in money as a benefit worth £500.

Nevertheless, it is held in *Re Diplock* that, where an original receipt is traced into the payment of a debt, no claim can be made in the second measure of restitution.[46] This conclusion must be regarded as open to review because it is contrary not only to the logic of the argument made in the last two paragraphs but also to the conclusion reached in many cases in which claims to an enrichment surviving in

---

[43] Above p. 190.
[44] Above p. 117 f.
[45] Above p. 191–2, 288–90.
[46] *Re Diplock* [1948] 1 Ch. 465, 548f.

the form of a debt discharged have been allowed.[47] Some of these cases will be further considered below.[48] The reason why they tend to escape attention in this context is that they express their conclusion in the language of subrogation, saying that the plaintiff is entitled to be subrogated to the claim discharged by the defendant with the money received from himself. For example, in *Baroness Wenlock* v. *River Dee Co.*[49] it was held that the lender to a company, whose loan was irrecoverable because *ultra vires*, could none the less recover such sums as the company had applied in the discharge of *intra vires* debts, and, further, that it did not matter whether those debts had been incurred before or after the *ultra vires* loan had been made. Nor did it matter that the money had not been applied directly by the company to the payment of debts but had, rather, been paid into the company's bank account. So long as the rules of tracing could be applied to show that the lender's money had in fact gone to the discharge of valid debts, the amount of the enrichment thus accruing to the company could be recovered.

This case is a precursor of *Sinclair* v. *Brougham*.[50] The *ultra vires* lender could not recover the amount of the enrichment originally received. To allow him to formulate a claim in unjust enrichment, instead of in contract, would have made nonsense of the policy of *ultra vires*, since the measure of recovery would have been exactly the same, but to allow a claim in the second measure, value surviving rather than value received, did not involve the same flat contradiction of the *ultra vires* rule, since the amount of the judgement would depend entirely on the amount of the enrichment still identifiably surviving in the defendant's hands. That much is common to both cases. The difference between them is that in *Sinclair* v. *Brougham* the surviving enrichment was identified as a proportion of a mixed fund of money. In *Wenlock* v. *River Dee Co.* the surviving enrichment consisted in debts discharged.

The reason why *Re Diplock* found it impossible to contemplate tracing into a discharged debt is that it assumed that, if any enrichment was successfully identified, any claim made in respect of it would have to take the form of a claim of ownership. That is, the plaintiff would have to say that he had an equitable proprietary

---

[47] *Re Cork & Youghal Rly.* (1869) L.R. Ch.App.; *Blackburn Benefit Building Society* v. *Cunliffe, Brooks & Co.* (1882) 22 Ch.D. 61; *Re Wrexham, Mold & Connah's Quay Rly.* (1899) 1 Ch. 440. Cf. *Bannatyne* v. *D. & C. MacIver* [1906] 1 K.B. 103; *B. Ligget (Liverpool) Ltd.* v. *Barclays Bank* [1928] 1 K.B. 48.

[48] Below, p. 397 f.

[49] *Baroness Wenlock* v. *River Dee Co.* (1887) 19 Q.B.D. 155.

[50] *Sinclair* v. *Brougham* [1914] A.C. 398.

interest in the matter identified. It is difficult to contemplate an assertion of ownership in relation to a debt which has been discharged. The metaphor of subrogation helps to avoid this difficulty, though it too encounters problems when the claim to which the plaintiff is supposed to be subrogated has been extinguished, so that there seems nothing for him to take over. But these are chiefly semantic difficulties. They disappear once it is accepted that the object of tracing is only to identify what enrichment, if any, still survives in the defendant's hands, and that the nature of the claim to be made can and does remain open till after the exercise of identification is complete. The claim need not be proprietary. This will be a matter for discussion in the next section.

If it is right that enrichment does survive in debts discharged, and that claims can in principle be measured by the enrichment identified in that form, one difficulty does have to be faced. Some cases of extinction which seem to be very clear cease to be so. If I receive £100 from you and spend £10 of it on a bottle of wine which I then drink the wine is undoubtedly gone. But, if you can indeed show that it was your £10 which paid the wine merchant's bill, the discharge of that debt still survives. It should therefore be possible for you to make a claim in the second measure of restitution for £10.[51] Such a claim will never be proprietary, but, as we shall see, there may yet be a circumstance in which you will find it to your advantage to make a claim *in personam* in respect of the surviving enrichment.

2. MAKING CLAIMS TO THE SURVIVING ENRICHMENT

A great deal depends on the objective which the plaintiff has in mind in turning from 'value received' to 'value surviving'. In particular a distinction must be drawn between two kinds of case. In the first the primary aim of the plaintiff is to assert that he has a beneficial or a security interest in the *res* which represents the original receipt or in which the original receipt is partly represented. That is to say, he wants to assert that he owns the surviving enrichment in whole or in part or that he has a lien over it. In such cases, if he succeeds in his assertion, the conclusion will be expressed differently according as his claim is made out with or without the help of rules which, historically, derive from the Chancery. Usually he will have had to rely on equitable rules in the exercise of identification itself, for the reason

---

[51] This possibility would not arise if, contrary to *Wenlock*, above, debts incurred after the receipt were excluded from the process of identification.

that the common law techniques of tracing are so easily defeated.[52] Hence, in most cases, if the plaintiff establishes that he is entitled to a beneficial interest in the *res*, the conclusion will be expressed by saying that the defendant holds on trust for him or for him and others in given proportions and if the plaintiff establishes that he has a security interest he will be said to have an equitable lien or charge. By contrast a plaintiff who establishes a beneficial interest without any help from rules of equity will simply be said to own the *res*, since the defendant will then have no interest whatever in it, not even the bare legal title. In all these cases, where the primary aim is to assert a right *in rem*, the reason why the plaintiff turns to the second measure of restitution is, not because he finds that measure intrinsically more attractive than the other, but that rights *in rem* yield priority in an insolvency over unsecured creditors and cannot be asserted in the first measure.[53] In order to be able to say that he owns or has a lien, he must be able to identify in the defendant's hands the asset in which he claims to have that right. Hence in these cases the plaintiff's desire for restitution in the second measure is consequential upon his desire to assert a right *in rem*.

In the other kind of case the plaintiff's primary objective is to recover in the second measure. That is to say, his situation is such that 'surviving enrichment' is, as he sees it, more attractive than 'enrichment received'. This may be because the claim in the first measure is barred and the claim in the second measure is not. In such a case the claim in the second measure is bound to seem more attractive even if what the defendant has left is very much less than what he received. On the other hand it may be that the plaintiff believes that he can show that what now represents the original receipt has a much higher value than the original enrichment itself. Assuming that the plaintiff does not also want some advantage attaching only to a right *in rem*, these cases concern nothing but the measure of recovery. That is, there is no reason why the plaintiff should be compelled to seek the second measure of restitution through the medium of a right *in rem*, even though it is true that a right *in rem* will give him that measure simply because such rights necessarily yield no other.

Suppose, for example, that the exercise of identification traces £5000 which you received from me last month into a diamond ring which you now wear on your finger. If I have a reason for claiming that surviving enrichment, and that reason consists solely in the fact that in my circumstances the claim in that measure is more attractive

---

[52] Above, p. 360–1.
[53] Above, p. 83–8.

than the claim for the £5000 originally received by you, it will not matter to me whether I succeed by saying: 'That ring is mine'; or 'You ought to give me that ring [*scilicet* that ring which is yours, not mine] or the value of the ring.' To put this in more technical language, it will not matter to me whether my claim is *in rem* or *in personam*, proprietary or personal. And if a court were to say that, on my facts, I could not have a proprietary claim, I would reply that I have no wish to assert such a claim.

(i) *The First Category: Proprietary Claims*

The restitutionary context in which a right *in rem* is most frequently revealed to be superior to a right *in personam* is where the defendant is insolvent. If I pay you money by mistake there is no doubt that I have a personal claim against you for the amount received by you. If you become bankrupt, however, I shall have to bring in my personal and unsecured claim with those of your other unsecured creditors, and my mistaken payment will go to swell the dividend, if any; which we all receive after the secured creditors have been paid off. If, however, I can establish that I have a charge over some identifiable asset in your hands or that you hold some asset on trust for me, I shall be able to realize my security or withdraw my asset before the general creditors get anything.

The same applies, though there are differences of detail, where a company is in liquidation and is insolvent. The facts of *Chase Manhattan Bank N.A.* v. *Israel-British Bank (London) Ltd.*[54] provide a vivid illustration. There the plaintiffs transferred a sum of more than $2 million to the defendants' account with the Mellon Bank International. Later the same day, apparently acting on different instructions, the plaintiffs made a second transfer of the same sum to the same account. But this second transfer was made by mistake. It arose from a clerical error, which was in fact picked up in time to stop the payment. Instructions were issued to prevent the transfer but were not acted upon quickly enough. Shortly after receiving the additional $2 million the defendant company was put into liquidation. It was insolvent, so that the plaintiffs could not hope to recover the full sum by means of dividends in the winding-up. Deciding the matter before the tracing exercise had been attempted, Goulding, J., held that the defendants would be trustees of any parts of the sum which could be identified in their hands, as also of any interest or income on it which could similarly be traced. So, if

---

[54] *Chase Manhattan Bank N.A.* v. *Israel-Bristib Bank (London) Ltd.* [1981] Ch. 105.

something could be identified still in the defendant's hands, the plaintiffs could take it out of the aggregate of assets available to the liquidator for distribution to the creditors.

It is obvious that the advantage which accrues to a plaintiff when he can assert a right *in rem* against an insolvent defendant is a danger and a detriment to the whole class of unsecured creditors. It follows from this that such rights must not be lightly conceded and ought to be known with certainty and precision. At the moment that is not the case. The facts on which a right *in rem* can be asserted in respect of surviving enrichment have never been clearly stated. Nor do *Goff and Jones* encourage the quest for certainty when they say:

> In our view the only relevant question should be this: is it just, in the circumstances of the particular case, to impose a trust or an equitable lien or to allow subrogation to a lien? In answering that question it should not be necessary to find that there is in existence a fiduciary relationship between the parties.[55]

The vagueness of the proposed question can only be understood as a reaction against the restrictive (but no less uncertain) requirement recited in the second part of the statement, the fiduciary relationship. It has indeed been asserted that equitable proprietary rights cannot be raised in relation to the surviving enrichment identified through the tracing exercise unless the original enrichment was received within the context of a fiduciary relationship. We will address that unsatisfactory assertion in the next paragraphs. But, whatever may be the defects of that way of approaching the question whether the plaintiff has or has not got a right *in rem*, those shortcomings cannot be cured by tackling the issue as though it were something to be decided from case to case on the basis of abstract reasonableness or justice.

(a) *The Proprietary Base*

The only satisfactory basis for raising a restitutionary proprietary right in the assets in which, by substitutions and intermixtures, the original enrichment now survives is as follows: the circumstances of the original receipt by the defendant must be such that, either at law or in equity, the plaintiff retained[56] or obtained the property in the matter received by the defendant, and then continued to retain it

---

[55] At p. 61.

[56] If when you receive a coin from me I both retain the property in it and am given a new right *in personam* (that you ought to return its value to me), the continuing right *in rem* is not restitutionary (see above, p. 50 f.) but the new right *in personam* is. If you substitute a ring for the coin, and the law gives me a right *in rem* in the ring, that new right, created to cause you to give up your enrichment, is restitutionary.

until the moment at which the substitution or intermixture took place. For example on facts such as those of *Chase Manhattan*: at the moment at which the defendant received the money paid to it by mistake, the plaintiff bank obtained a personal right to have the original enrichment (the $2 million) refunded; and, at the same time, the mistake being sufficiently fundamental to prevent the property passing, the plaintiff bank retained its ownership of the money till the moment of the intermixture in the defendant's account or, more accurately, would have retained the property in the money till that moment if there had been any interval between receipt and mixture. Another way of saying the same thing is that, if the defendant had kept the original enrichment separate, the plaintiff bank would have been able to say that the property had not passed.

In these circumstances, where the defendant receives an enrichment which, apart from substitutions and intermixtures, would have continued to belong to the plaintiff, the law can raise a new restitutionary right *in rem* in the different assets in which the original receipt is represented at the time of the claim. By contrast, if the mistake is insufficiently fundamental to prevent the property passing then, always supposing that it does, nevertheless, have the effect of giving the plaintiff a personal claim to the value received by the defendant, there can be no question of recognising a right *in rem* in any surviving enrichment since, apart from the neutral or contingent fact of intermixture or substitution, the facts are *ex hypothesi* such as to reduce the plaintiff to purely personal claim. The phrase 'proprietary base' is used to capture this idea: if he wishes to assert a right *in rem* in the surviving enrichment, the plaintiff must show that at the beginning of the story he had a proprietary right in the subject-matter, and that nothing other than substitutions or intermixtures happened to deprive him of that right *in rem*.

The reason for this difference is as follows: where, at the moment of the original receipt, the property passes to the recipient so that, at that moment, the plaintiff is already reduced to a claim *in personam*, which would have to rank with other unsecured personal claims, the law has already thereby decided that, on those facts, he shall not have the advantages of any right *in rem*. Consequently, the fact that the defendant later happens to intermix the matter received or to exchange it for other assets cannot serve to restore to him the priority of a claimant *in rem*. To maintain otherwise would be to endow the fortuitous acts of intermixture or substitution with legal effects incapable of being explained. If I receive £5000 which at law and in equity is mine but in circumstances in which I come under an obligation to repay you a like sum, it cannot be said that by paying the sum into my account or by buying a car with it, I thereby confer on you a right *in rem* in the car or a lien on my account. Not only are all these subsequent acts of mine intrinsically incapable of triggering such effects but, if they were, every unsecured lender in the country would acquire a good security as soon as the borrower applied or banked his loan. By contrast, where the facts are such that, at the moment of the receipt, the recipient does not obtain title, but on the contrary takes subject to the plaintiff's interest, then the subsequent intermixture or substitution, being absolutely neutral as to the issue of the plaintiff's priority, leaves room for the law to use what means it can to preserve his original status, which it can do by raising new rights *in rem* in the surviving product of those acts. The shortest summary of all this is that if the plaintiff wants to assert a right *in rem* in the surviving enrichment he must show, not only that the enrichment originally received does at least in part survive, but also that the story of the changes which have overtaken it began from matter belonging to him and passed through no events (other than the neutral events of intermixture and substitution) such as would by nature extinguish his title: to end with a right *in rem* he must start with a right *in rem* and nothing must happen to extinguish that right *in rem*, other than loss of identity.

There has never been any doubt that this proprietary starting point is what the common law requires in order to raise a restitutionary interest *in rem* in the surviving enrichment. But as we have seen the common law's means of identifying that residuum are easily defeated. In equity the matter has been put differently. It has been asserted that equitable proprietary interests can only be raised where the subject-matter has passed through the prism of a fiduciary relationship, so as to split the legal from the equitable entitlement. Thus in *Re Diplock* the Court of Appeal made a careful analysis of *Sinclair* v. *Brougham*, which will be considered below,[57] and concluded that the equitable right there recognised after tracing had been based on the fact that the depositors who had made *ultra vires* deposits with the Birkbeck bank had parted with their money within the context of a fiduciary relationship between themselves and the directors who received the money from them. Lord Greene, M.R., giving the court's judgment, said:

Lord Parker and Viscount Haldane both predicate the existence of a right of property recognised by equity which depends on there having existed at some stage a fiduciary relationship of some kind (though not necessarily a positive duty of trusteeship) sufficient to give rise to the equitable right of property.

[57] Below, p. 396 f.

Exactly what relationships are sufficient to bring such an equitable right into existence for the purposes of the rule which we are considering is a matter which has not been precisely laid down. Certain relationships are clearly included, e.g. trustee (actual or constructive)and *cestui que trust*, and 'fiduciary' relationships such as that of principal and agent. *Sinclair* v. *Brougham* itself affords another example. There a sufficient fiduciary relationship was found to exist between the depositors and the directors by reason of the fact that the purposes for which the depositors had handed their money to the directors were by law incapable of fulfilment.[58]

There are two reasons for this insistence on the 'fiduciary' relationship. The first is that, historically, the cases in which equity would raise a right *in rem* in relation to surviving enrichment extended from the case of the trustee who misapplied trust property. The word 'fiduciary' maintains the contact with that central and original case, since it means 'trustee-like': a fiduciary relationship is one which can be handled in the same way or in some of the same ways as the relationship between trustee and *cestui que trust*. The second reason is that it is in the context of fiduciary relationships that equity is prepared to affirm that, just as between *cestui que trust* and trustee, the beneficiary or principal obtains an equitable interest in the *res* which is the subject matter of the dispute. In other words, the affirmation that there was a fiduciary relationship between X and Y at the time when a *res* passed from X to Y is synonymous with and indeed is one way of expressing the conclusion that, in the eyes of equity, even if not in the eyes of law, X retained the property in the *res*.

Laying aside the historical rôle of the term, which can be described once and for all and then dismissed from the day-to-day vocabulary, we can say that the requirement of a fiduciary relationship is, in this context, one and the same as the requirement of an undestroyed proprietary base which has already been described: a plaintiff who wants to assert an equitable proprietary interest in the surviving enrichment must show facts such that the property in the original receipt did not pass at law *and* in equity to the recipient. If he can show such facts, so that, at least in equity, he retained the property in the *res*, he will, after identifying the surviving enrichment, be able to raise an equitable proprietary interest in those different assets. Where such facts are shown, the relationship between him and the recipient can, rightly, be described as 'fiduciary' in that it will resemble the relationship between *cestui que trust* and *trustee*. Indeed if the facts are such that legal title to the enrichment did pass to the defendant and equitable title sprang up and remained in the plaintiff, the relationship will not be 'like' that between *cestui que trust* and

[58] *Re Diplock* [1948] 1 Ch. 465, 540.

beneficiary but will be just such a relationship. It would be better always to ask whether the actual facts were such that, at least in equity, even if not in law, the plaintiff passively retained or actively obtained title at the moment of the original receipt. Once one can establish this equitable proprietary base — at the moment of the transfer the plaintiff did become or did remain equitable owner — the language of fiduciary relationship or of trust and trustee follows automatically, for it does no more than re-describe the proprietary base.

Even in the passage already cited from *Re Diplock* it is manifest that the requirement of a fiduciary relationship is used as part of the conclusion drawn from other facts and is not itself a reason for drawing a conclusion. Lord Greene, M.R., says of *Sinclair* v. *Brougham*: 'There, a sufficient fiduciary relationship was found to exist between the depositors *by reason of the fact that the purposes for which the depositors had handed their money to the directors were by law incapable of fulfilment.*'[59] It was not that there was a fiduciary relationship, before the event, between depositors generally and bankers generally — quite to the contrary, for the relationship between a bank and its customers is as between debtor and creditor — but rather that, because the purpose of the delivery could not be fulfilled, equity was willing to intervene and to recognise, at the moment of the original enrichment of the directors, a continuing proprietary interest. And once the depositors were recognised to have that interest, then necessarily the directors were fiduciaries. In *Sinclair* v. *Brougham* itself, Viscount Haldane, L.C., made it plain that the operative fact in his view was precisely this failure of the consideration. The society running the Birkbeck Bank was to have the money entirely at its own disposal in exchange for a valid banking contract creating the debtor-creditor relationship:

But it was none the less intended that in consideration of giving such an undertaking the society should be entitled to deal with it freely as its own. *The consideration failed* and the depositors had the right to follow the money so far as invalidly borrowed into the assets in which it had been invested. . .[60]

And in the speech of Lord Parker it is equally clear that what mattered to him was not that the relationship had special inherent characteristics which allowed it to be described as fiduciary but rather that the facts were such that they created the proprietary starting point from which it was possible to raise an equitable right *in rem* in the identified surviving enrichment, i.e. in matter which

---

[59] Ibid., italics added.
[60] *Sinclair* v. *Brougham* [1914] A.C. 398, 423.

merely represented the original subject of the right. Lord Parker believed that the depositors retained even their legal title in the interval between payment over and mixing,[61] and then he super-imposed on that legal proprietary base what he called the different approach of equity:

Equity, however, treated the matter from a different standpoint. It considered that the relationship between the directors or agents and the lender was a fiduciary relationship. and that the money in their hands was for all practical purposes trust money. Starting from a personal equity, based on a consideration that it would be unconscionable for anyone who could not plead purchase for value without notice to retain an advantage from the misapplication of trust money, it ended, as was so often the case, in creating what were in effect rights of property, though not recognised as such by the common law'.[62]

When this passsage is read in context it is tolerably clear that the need for this development of equitable proprietary rights arose, in Lord Parker's mind, from the very fact that the law itself took the view that property did not pass but was then also unable to keep track of the surviving enrichment representing the original receipt. It was for that reason that equity had to respond to the situation in the same way as it responded to the need to protect trust funds.

In *Chase Manhattan*, the facts of which have already been outlined, Goulding, J., had to address the argument that the plaintiffs, even if they could identify some surviving enrichment, could not raise any equitable interest in it because there was no fiduciary relationship between them and the defendant recipients of the mistaken payment. He very clearly took the view that the qualification of the relationship as fiduciary was a matter consequential upon the decision whether or not the plaintiff could point to a proprietary base at the moment of the original enrichment. If the plaintiff retained an equitable property when the *res* moved into the wrong hands, then, because of the proprietary base at that point of the story, the relationship was fiduciary for the purposes of raising a new right *in rem* in the surviving enrichment.

It was once thought that Lord Atkin had laid down that an administrative decision could only be open to judicial review if the person taking the decision not only had the power to affect the individual's rights but also had a duty to act judicially.[63] In *Ridge* v. *Baldwin*, Lord Reid demonstrated that Lord Atkin's meaning had been that the duty to act judicially was an inference to be drawn from the

[61] As to which, see below p. 387.
[62] *Sinclair* v. *Brougham* [1914] A.C. 398, 441.
[63] *R.* v. *Electricity Commissioners* [1924] 1 K.B. 171, 205.

decision affecting rights. The judical quality was not an independent requirement which had to be verified before any decision could be reviewed by the courts.[64] In *Chase Manhattan* Goulding, J., gives a similar explanation of the fiduciary relationship in relation to proprietary claims in respect of surviving enrichment. In this important passage he holds that the fiduciary character of the relationship is an inference from the equitable proprietary base:

This fourth point [*scilicet* of his summary of the *Re Diplock* judgement] shows that the fund to be traced need not (as was the case in *Re Diplock's Estate* itself) have been the subject of fiduciary obligations before it got into the wrong hands. It is enough that, as in *Sinclair* v. *Brougham*, the payment into wrong hands itself gave rise to a fiduciary relationship. The same point also throws considerable doubt on counsel's submission for the defendants that the necessary fiduciary relationship must originate in a consensual transaction. It was not the intention of the depositors or of the directors in *Sinclair* v. *Brougham* to create any relationship at all between the depositors and the directors as principals. Their object, which unfortunately disregarded the statutory limitations of the building society's powers, was to establish contractual relationships between the depositors and the directors as principals. In the circumstances, however, the depositors retained an equitable property in the funds they parted with, and fiduciary relationships arose between them and the directors. In the same way, I would suppose, a person who pays money to another under a factual mistake retains an equitable property in it, and the conscience of that other is subjected to a fiduciary duty to respect his proprietary rights.[65]

In summary, therefore, there are two different situations in which the law does raise an equitable right *in rem* in the surviving enrichment. One is where the recipient did receive legal title to the original enrichment but where the circumstances were such as to detach the equitable title and to vest it in the plaintiff, thus creating a trust-like relationship between them. The other is where the recipient obtained no title at all by virtue of the transfer to him, so that the plaintiff remained the legal owner until, the legal title being defeated by some intermixture, equitable rules had to be invoked in order to identify the assets in which the original value survived. In both cases the plaintiff has the necessary proprietary base, at the moment after the original enrichment of the defendant; on that base there can be raised a new equitable interest in those different assets in which the original enrichment is, by the process of tracing, identified as surviving.

By contrast there is a third situation, in which no proprietary right can be asserted in the surviving enrichment. This is where wealth

---

[64] *Ridge* v. *Baldwin* [1964] A.C. 40, 74ff.
[65] *Chase Manhattan Bank N.A.* v. *Israel-British Bank (London) Ltd.* [1981] Ch. 105, 119.

belonging to the plaintiff passes to the defendant in circumstances in which, though he may come under a restitutionary obligation to repay its value, he does, so far as concerns rights *in rem*, become fully entitled, legally and beneficially. This is the category of case to which the Court of Appeal must be understood to refer in *Re Diplock* when they say in regard to the speeches in *Sinclair* v. *Brougham*: 'It is to be observed that neither Lord Parker nor Viscount Haldane suggests that the equitable remedy extends to cover all cases where A becomes possessed of money belonging to B, a view which Lord Dunedin seemed inclined to accept if he did not actually do so.'[66] That is, they here refer to the case in which the money belonging to the plaintiff ceases to belong to him on the transfer to the defendant. On such facts the plaintiff loses his proprietary base.

Somewhat specialised examples of this third category occur where A sells and delivers good to B with a clause which reserves title to A until payment is made or until all debts owed by B to A are paid off. In such circumstances it may be that B is also given power to resell or to use the goods, notwithstanding the fact that they belong to A under the reservation clause. The question then arises whether the power in B is exercisable for his own interest or solely on A's account. If B re-sells for £1000 does that sum become his or can A assert a proprietary interest in such parts of that sum as he can trace? The starting point is that A does have the necessary proprietary base from which to make a claim *in rem* to the identifiable surviving enrichment, but his *prima facie* right depends on the construction of the power which he bestowed on B. If the intention was that B should be free to sell on his own account, then A must be remitted to such claims *in personam* as he may be able to make out;[67] but if the power was intended to be exercised for the account of A, then A will be able to make his proprietary claim and B will be characterised as a fiduciary for A.[68] However, it has to be borne in mind that the courts are hostile to this reservation of equitable title and will easily find that the attempt has not succeeded.[68a]

---

[66] *Sinclair* v. *Brougham* [1948] Ch. 465, 540; cf. at p. 543: 'Attractive though Lord Dunedin's view may be, we cannot regard it as agreeing with those of Lord Haldane, Lord Atkinson and Lord Atkin. Those noble and learned lords limited the right to recover to cases where there is what equity regards as a right of property. Lord Dunedin, on the other hand, treats the principle which he favours as applicable wherever the property of A has, without justification, got into the hands of B.'

[67] *Borden U.K. Ltd.* v. *Scottish Timber Products Ltd.* [1981] Ch. 25.

[68] *Aluminium Industrie Vaasen B.V.* v. *Romalpa Aluminium* [1976] 1 W.L.R. 676.

[68a] See, for example, *Re Peachdart Ltd.* [1983] 3 ALL E.R. 204. Cf. *Re Bond Worth Ltd.* [1979] 3 ALL E.R. 99.

(b) *Two Problems*

The central proposition of the preceding section has been that the plaintiff who wants to assert a right *in rem* in the surviving enrichment must show that he had and, apart from intermixtures and substitutions, would never have lost, a 'proprietary base'. References to fiduciary relationships distract attention from the inquiry into the proprietary base because they can be misunderstood as describing the condition necessary in equity to create such a base rather than the situation which exists when such a base has been created. Even if that is right, there remain two major problems both of which must be noticed here but both of which require an investigation on a scale which is beyond the scope of this book.

The first problem is this: what precisely are the circumstances in which a plaintiff who has a restitutionary claim *in personam* against the defendant does *not* have a sufficient proprietary base, at least in equity, to enable him to claim a beneficial or security interest in the surviving enrichment? We have hypothesised one case: where a transfer is made under a mistake sufficient to generate a personal restitutionary claim in the first measure (value received) but insufficiently fundamental to preserve the plaintiff's proprietary base. No concrete example can be given. We have given one other case: where a *prima facie* sufficient proprietary base is displaced by a contrary intent expressed by the plaintiff, to the effect that the defendant shall be absolutely entitled to the product of any substitution or intermixture.[69] Such cases are exceptional and, from the standpoint of the question whether a restitutionary plaintiff lacks a sufficient proprietary base, they are uninteresting, because the plaintiff does not lack that base but chooses to abandon it.

Two sets of facts, in particular, need close attention. First, where a plaintiff transfers value for a consideration which fails. Where the consideration which he specified as the basis of his payment was a contractual reciprocation from the payee, we know that the contract is not rescinded *ab initio* but is terminated *de futuro*. I give money for goods promised by you or, *vice versa*, you give goods for money promised by me; neither breach nor frustration cuts away the contract altogether.[70] This means that, at law, whichever of us is the first transferor, the property passes and (since termination has no retrospective effect) does not pass back. It follows that, at law, we can have only personal claims. We lose our proprietary base. Hence, even if I can show that you now hold a ring which represents the

[69] *Borden U.K. Ltd.* v. *Scottish Timber Products Ltd.*, above, n. 67.
[70] Above, p. 222, n. 8; p. 226, n. 26.

price which you received I cannot, by switching to the second measure or restitution, hope to promote myself from claimant *in personam* to claimant *in rem*.

This would seem to be a clear case. Nevertheless, it is brought into doubt by *Sinclair* v. *Brougham* itself, which seems to say that where a consideration fails the plaintiff does have a sufficient proprietary base.[71] Then even if that aspect of *Sinclair* v. *Brougham* may be wrong, as will be suggested in the next section, it remains true that equity does give effect to failures of consideration by means of resulting trust,[72] thus recognising that in such circumstances the plaintiff does have a sufficient proprietary base. It is difficult to see how a difference could be drawn between one failure of consideration and another. It would, for example, be impossible to argue that in some cases the proprietary base is preserved by reason of an especially clear or intense qualification of the transferor's intent to enrich the recipient. For the truth is that failure of consideration always depends on a clear manifestation of that qualified intent. If I give you £1000 merely expecting or hoping that you will give me a car next week, or that you will marry X next week, and then you do not give me the car or do not marry X, I will be in the weak position of a risk-taking volunteer if I did not clearly specify that the happening of these events constituted the basis of my giving. Hence, in the absence of a free acceptance on your part, the effect of their not happening will be to deprive me of all my rights to restitution, not merely of the proprietary base which would allow me to assert a right *in rem* in those assets in which at the time of my claim the original enrichment still survived.

The other case is where the original enrichment is received by the defendant from a third party in breach of a duty owed by the defendant to the plaintiff. This might be described as the *Lister* v. *Stubbs*[73] problem. Where the defendant's breach of duty to the plaintiff consists in a misapplication of his property there is no doubt that the plaintiff has a sufficient proprietary base. This is a simple and central case. You take my cow and exchange it for a horse, the horse for £1000, the £1000 for shares in a company. Here I can start from the cow, which in your hands remained mine. That gives me the proprietary base I need. So I can go on to claim a new right *in rem* in the shares which you now hold. It would be exactly the same if I were

---

[71] Above, p. 382 f.

[72] Above, p. 224 f.; esp. *Barclays Bank Ltd.* v. *Quistclose Investments Ltd.* [1968] 3 W.L.R. 1097; *Essery* v. *Cowlard*, (1884) 26 Ch.D. 191. Pursuit of this line leads towards a more sympathetic view of the heresy in *Horsler* v. *Zorro* [1975] Ch. 302.

[73] *Lister* v. *Stubbs* (1890) 45 Ch.D. 1.

cestui que trust with equitable title and you had legal title to the cow. There, my equitable interest would give me the necessary proprietary base. But where, by contrast, the defendant's breach of duty is not a misapplication of property, as for example in *Boardman* v. *Phipps*,[74] it is very doubtful that the plaintiff can assert a right *in rem* in the surviving enrichment. In *Boardman* v. *Phipps* itself, Boardman had enriched himself in breach of his duty to avoid conflicts of interest. He was described as a constructive trustee, but that term indicates no concrete conclusion whatever. All we actually know is that Boardman was under an equitable obligation to give up his profit; the beneficiaries under the trust had a correlative right *in personam* that he should do so. The vital fact is that he was not insolvent. It was not necessary, therefore, for the plaintiff to claim any right *in rem*. Also, they had no reason whatever to turn from the first measure of restitution to the second. 'Value received' was what they wanted.

According to what has been said above, the necessary condition for claiming a right *in rem* in the surviving enrichment is a proprietary base at the beginning of the story (i.e. at the moment of the original receipt). If this is right it would be necessary, on facts such as in *Boardman* v. *Phipps*, to say that acquisition in breach of the duty to avoid conflicts is an event which confers ownership on the victim of the breach. That is exactly what the Court of Appeal in *Lister* v. *Stubbs* would not say.

In that case Stubbs was foreman dyer to Lister & Co: he had the task of buying in whatever was needed in his employers' business. In placing contracts with a firm called Varley & Co he accepted a large commission for himself, which he invested. The question was whether Lister & Co. could take the investments. Stirling, J., held that they could not.[75] He drew a distinction between money paid to him by Lister & Co. for a particular application and money coming to him from outside. In the former case (where the plaintiffs would have had a sufficient proprietary base) it would have been possible for them to take the proceeds of a wrongful investment but in the latter case they never acquired any property in the money and could, therefore, have only a personal claim. In the Court of Appeal this judgment was upheld. Collins, L.J. said: 'In my opinion this is not

---

[74] *Boardman* v. *Phipps* [1967] 2 A.C. 46.

[75] Following *The Metropolitan Bank* v. *Heiron*, (1880) 5 Ex.D. 319, in which a distinction was taken between an equitable debt and an equitable proprietary right. 'The former case,' said Cotton, L.J., 'is very different from the case of *cestui que trust* seeking to recover money which was his own before any act wrongfully done by the trustee. The whole title depends on its being established by a decree of a competent court that the fraud of the trustee has given the *cestui que trust* a right to the money' (at p. 315).

the money of the plaintiffs, so as to make the defendant a trustee of if for them.'[76] They had only a right *in personam*: the bribe was due to them as a debt. Lindley, L.J., observed that to hold otherwise would mean that 'if Stubbs were to become bankrupt, this property acquired by him with the money paid to him by Messrs. Varley would be withdrawn from the mass of his creditors and be handed over bodily to Lister & Co.'.[77]

This seems to be right, though *Goff and Jones* regard it as wrong and describe it as a case in which injustice was done because the court failed to distinguish 'between the nature of a pure proprietary claim and that of a restitutionary proprietary claim'.[78] With respect there is no contrast between 'pure' and restitutionary' in this context. If the court was only prepared to say that the bribe, when received, was an equitable debt, there was no justification to be found, in the subsequent substitution of other investments in the place of the money, for promoting the plaintiffs from claimants *in personam* to claimants *in rem*. However, there remains a question which *Lister* v. *Stubbs* does not resolve. There was no doubt that, so far as concerned the exercise of identification, the investments represented the bribe. Lister's claim failed for want of a sufficient proprietary base to justify their being given a claim *in rem* in relation to the investments, but it is not clear what would have been said if they had asked only for a personal claim measured by the value of the investments. Such a claim would not have involved any promotion from *in personam* to *in rem* and would not have threatened creditors or other third parties. It cannot be that equity is incapable of recognising such a right without at the same time giving it effect *in rem*.[79] The judgements in *Lister* v. *Stubbs* contain nothing which would exclude a personal claim measured by the surviving enrichment.   *27

The second important problem is no less vexed, though it is confined within a narrower space. When the tracing exercise shows that the value originally received was ultimately applied to discharge a debt secured by a mortgage, is the plaintiff entitled to the security interest *in rem* discharged by the payment? This is a question distinct from one which will be further considered below, namely whether the plaintiff is entitled to a personal claim in the amount of the debt discharged.

---

[76] *Lister* v. *Stubbs* (1890) 45 Ch.D. 1, 12.
[77] At p. 15.
[78] At pp. 62-63.
[79] A counter-argument based on *Walsh* v. *Lonsdale*, (1882) 21 Ch.D. 9, could not be applied to the value of the *res* and would, even in relation to the *res* itself, be an ironic abuse of the maxim that equity regards as done that which ought to be done.

It is submitted that the answer to this question ought in principle to be as follows: if the plaintiff's circumstances were such that, had the money which was received from him been spent on some corporeal asset or been put into a mixed fund, he would have been entitled to a claim *in rem* in the enrichment identified as surviving at the time of the claim, then, if the money is instead traced into a discharged mortgage, he ought to be able to revive that security. In other words, a plaintiff with a sufficient proprietary base to justify a claim *in rem* should not be deprived of that advantage in a case in which the value originally received happens to be traced into the discharge of a mortgage. On the other hand a plaintiff with no proprietary base should not be promoted to the rank of a secured creditor merely because the rules of identification show that the money discharged a secured debt, no more than he would be so promoted if it should be shown that the money bought an asset such as a car or a house. This means that, if I lend money to you in circumstances in which the contract is wholly nullified (as for fundamental mistake of identity), and you buy a car with some of the money and discharge your mortgage with the rest, I will be entitled to claim ownership of the car and to revive the mortgage; nor will it matter whether I initially set out to be a secured or an unsecured lender. The crucial fact is that the money passed to you through an event in which my proprietary base was preserved. If the property in the money had passed to you I could not have asserted a right *in rem* in relation to the car and I could not have revived the mortgage. That would have been true even if, the facts being such that the property would have passed to you, I actually made the loan to you by sending cheques at your order directly to the garage which sold you the car and to the mortgagee whom you wished to pay off.

The situation in the last paragraph must be contrasted with a different set of circumstances, in which the plaintiff becomes entitled to the security by the operation of his own intent. There are two versions. In the first he deals directly with the mortgagee. He goes to the mortgagee and, for reasons of his own, pays off the defendant's mortgage. Here it seems that he is entitled to a presumption that he intended to preserve the mortgage for himself.[80] In the second version he puts the money into the hands of the defendant but attaches a string to it, making it a term of the agreement between them that the money is to be used solely to pay off the mortgage. Here too, by virtue of the string, the plaintiff is entitled to the mortgage which is paid off.[81] These are the two consensual routes to the security.

---

[80] *Ghana Commercial Bank* v. *Chandiram* [1960] A.C. 732, 745.
[81] *Wylie* v. *Carlyon* [1922] 1 Ch. 51.

In *Nottingham Permanent Building Society* v. *Thurstan*,[82] the Building Society lent money to Thurstan to buy land, intending to take a mortgage of that land. At her request they sent the price directly to the vendors. It later turned out that their loan and their mortgage were void because the borrower was an infant and the transaction was therefore caught by s. 1 of the *Infants' Relief Act, 1874*. The contract between the infant and the vendors, being a contract by which the infant acquired an interest in land, was not void but only voidable. Unless the infant had renounced the land the vendors would have been able to claim the price and, in addition, would have been entitled to an unpaid vendor's equitable lien. The vendors had, however, been paid off; they had received the price from the Building Society on the infant purchaser's instructions. The Building Society was held by the House of Lords to have been entitled to the security of the unpaid vendor's lien.

More recently, in *Orakpo* v. *Manson Investments Ltd.*,[83] the House of Lords has considered and explained *Thurstan's Case*. The basis on which it was said to have been right was that the transaction between the Building Society and the infant was absolutely void. The importance of that would seem to be that it allows the case to be contemplated as belonging in the second category discussed above. By entirely discounting the dealings between the Building Society and the infant the court was able to contemplate the case as one in which the Building Society had gone to the vendors and, dealing over the head of the purchaser, had made an arrangement to discharge the vendor's lien. In other words, the Building Society obtained the lien by the operation of their own intent, manifested, or presumed to have been manifested, in their dealing with the vendors.

This revised interpretation of *Thurstan's Case* is in fact the only one which is possible. If one looks at the non-consensual route and asks whether it could have been said that the Building Society was entitled to the lien because its money was traceable into the discharge of the lien, the answer should probably be negative. Under a contract made void by the *Infants' Relief Act, 1874*, such property as is intended to pass does pass.[84] Hence it could not be said, in relation to the money lent, that the Building Society retained any proprietary base. Though the money could, as a mere matter of identification, be traced into the discharge of the vendor's lien, there was, therefore, no justification for promoting the society to the status

[82] *Nottingham Permanent Benefit Building Society* v. *Thurstan* [1903] A.C. 6.
[83] *Orakpo* v. *Manson Investments Ltd.* [1978] A.C. 5.
[84] *Stocks* v. *Wilson* [1913] 2 K.B. 235; *Pearce* v. *Brain* [1929] 2 K.B. 310. Were this wrong, *semble* the minor could take advantage of *Rowland* v. *Divall* [1923] 2 K.B. 500, and, in addition, third parties would be jeopardized.

of the claimants *in rem*. It is nothing to the point to say that they intended initially to be secured claimants, because the security which they took was absolutely void.

In *Orakpo* v. *Manson Investments Ltd.*[85] the appellant had borrowed large sums of money from the respondent moneylenders. The loans were secured by mortgages. But the loans and the mortgages were unenforceable under s. 6 (1) of the *Moneylenders Act, 1927*, because the written memoranda of each contract were incomplete. The Court of Appeal held, following its own previous decision in *Congresbury Motors Ltd.* v. *Anglo-Belge Finance Ltd.*,[86] that the lenders were entitled, as in *Thurstan's Case*, to take over the vendors' liens, or other securities, which the loans had been used to discharge. That decision was reversed in the House of Lords, and *Congresbury* was overruled. There is no doubt that the lenders could not claim to have any proprietary base to justify their taking the discharged securities. Their contracts of loan were not void but only unenforceable. So it could not be argued that property in the money remained in them. It follows that they could revive the securities only on the consensual basis described in the second category above. On the facts they could only hope to succeed, therefore, if they had made it a term of their contract that the loans were to be used to discharge the earlier liens and charges. But a memorandum which did not include such a term would be defective, and a security dependent on such a term would be no more enforceable than the mortgages which the lenders had actually taken. Hence the lenders could not reach the securities via either the 'proprietary base' route or the consenual route.

The main difficulty in this field is the fact that, in denying the lenders the discharged securities via the consensual route and in explaining *Thurstan's Case*, the House of Lords in *Orakpo* did little to clarify or confirm the other kind of case, where the plaintiff cannot say that he contracted with either the mortgagor or the mortgagee to have the security, but has to rely solely on his proprietary base, saying essentially that his money discharged the mortgage. The result is that the very existence of that category may now be doubted. Nevertheless, there are cases which cannot be otherwise explained. In *Butler* v. *Rice*[87] the plaintiff lent specifically to discharge a mortgage, but the contract which he made was based on the mistaken suppo-

---

[85] Above, n. 83.

[86] *Congesbury Motors Ltd.* v. *Anglo-Belge Finance Ltd.* [1971] Ch. 81.

[87] *Butler* v. *Rice* [1910] 2 Ch. 277. It requires to be added that the matter would have been *res inter alios acta* if the wife, who did purport to repudiate her husband's agency, had not accepted the discharge.

sition that the borrower, Mr Rice, was the owner-mortgagor of the house in question, which in fact belonged to Mrs Rice. The contract between the plaintiff and Mr Rice was, so far as concerned Mrs Rice, *res inter alios acta*; it had nothing whatever to do with her. Nevertheless when Mr Rice did in fact pay off the mortgage the plaintiff was allowed to take the security. Again, in *Brocklesby* v. *Temperance Building Society*[88] the lenders were deceived into advancing money which was used, without the knowledge of the owner-mortgagor, to discharge a mortgage of his property; and, again, they were allowed to take the security. In both these cases, because of the mistake and the deceit, it is possible to say that, though there was no contract between the lender on the one hand and either the mortgagee or the mortgagor on the other, the lender retained a sufficient proprietary base to entitle him, after tracing, to finish as a claimant *in rem* and not merely *in personam*.

(c) *The Period of the Intermixtures or Substitutions*

This short section very briefly addresses the question as to the nature of the plaintiff's rights between the time of the receipt, which is the time at which it must be decided whether he has a sufficient proprietary base, and the time at which he claims his beneficial or security interest in the surviving enrichment. You receive £1000 as the result of a fundamental mistake made by the plaintiff. Let it be given that he does on these facts retain the property in the notes. You then mix the £1000 in your bank account. The application of *Clayton's Case* subsequently shows that the £1000 left your account when you wrote a cheque for £6000 in payment for shares which you later sold at £12 000 to provide the deposit on your house. The question is whether throughout this period the plaintiff has had rights *in rem* in your account, your shares, and now your house. The answer is that he has had no lien or proportionate interest in any of them but only a power to crystallise such a right.

This kind of question is difficult to answer because it only arises for decision in specialised contexts. In *Re J. Leslie Engineers Co. Ltd.*,[89] Oliver, J., had to consider the operation of s. 227 of the *Companies Act, 1948*, in relation to a mixed fund. Section 227 says:

In a winding up by the court, any disposition of the property of the company, including things in action, and any transfer of shares, or alteration in the status of members of the company, made after the commencement of the winding up, shall, unless the court otherwise orders, be void.

---

[88] *Brocklesbury* v. *Temperance Building Society* [1895] A.C. 173.
[89] *Re Leslie Engineers Co. Ltd.* [1976] 1 W.L.R. 292.

After the commencement of the winding up of this company, a director had withdrawn money from the company's account and had paid it into an account in the joint names of himself and his wife. He had then paid the sum out to a particular creditor who had done work for the company. The question was whether the payment out to that creditor was 'a disposition of the property of the company'. Oliver, J., held that while the money lay in the account it was not the property of the company. 'The property of the company' consisted not in the balance in the account but in the rights which had been created for the company by the events which had happened. Thus the company had a right *in personam* against its director to compel him to repay the sum originally taken, and it had a right to trace the money in equity.

The implications of the two holdings, namely that the company had 'a right to trace' but yet that the money in the account, or more accurately, the claim against the bank, was not 'the property of the company' is that, until the plaintiff makes his claim and conducts the exercise of identification, the plaintiff has no more than a power to crystallise a vested right *in rem*.[90] This analysis is useful because it explains why the right which the plaintiff finally asserts after all the intermixtures and substitutions can be different from that which he has at the moment after the original receipt by the defendant. That is, there is no need to understand what happens in terms of the survival of his original right of property. It also prevents a geometric multiplication of the plaintiff's property. If the director of a company took a company car and sold it to a *mala fide* purchaser for £1000, the company would on any other analysis, own both the car and the £1000.

(ii) *The Second Category: Personal Claims*

A personal claim to the surviving enrichment is one by which the plaintiff abstains from, or disclaims, any proprietary interest in the relevant assets identified by the process of tracing and asserts instead that the defendant is under an obligation to make over to him the value of the surviving enrichment. In the traditional language of equity the plaintiff does not say that the defendant holds the assets on trust for him or that he has any equity to revest them in himself but only that the defendant is personally accountable to him for their value. We noticed earlier that the language of 'account' should not be used loosely to mean 'pay'. Hence, what the plaintiff should

[90] Cf. the analysis of Slade, J., in *Re Bond Worth Ltd*. [1979] 2 All E.R. 919.

now say is that the defendant is under an obligation to pay him the value of the surviving enrichment. This kind of personal claim has the merit of obtaining no priority in an insolvency.

The reason why that characteristic can be regarded as a merit is that it means that a plaintiff who is seeking restitution in the second measure and who does not want the priority attaching to a claim *in rem* need not be sent away empty-handed merely because others in his position might be able to claim the priority which he himself neither needs nor wants. That is to say, a personal claim does not encounter the phenomenon of 'the highest common obstacle'. This can be illustrated by adapting the facts of *Boulton* v. *Jones*.[91] It will be recalled that Boulton supplied goods to Jones under the mistaken impression that Jones had ordered them and that Jones consumed the goods before he knew the full facts. We also said that the fact that Jones was ignorant of the true facts created a difficulty for any claim by Boulton on the basis of free acceptance. Even if Boulton had claimed on the basis of vitiated voluntariness (mistake), his claim in the first measure of restitution would have run into difficulties on the issue of enrichment. Suppose, however, that Jones still retained the original goods or their substitute-product. Let it be that he exchanged the original goods for a horse still held at the time of Boulton's claim. Unable to make a claim in the first measure by reason of the enrichment issue, why should not Boulton switch to the claim in the second measure and thus, on these facts, evade the possibility of subjective devaluation?[92] In short, why should he not claim the value of the horse? If surviving enrichment could only be claimed *in rem*, the answer would be that he would thus obtain an undeserved priority against other unpaid suppliers to Jones, and, if Jones were solvent, the answer would be that others in a like situation would get an undeserved priority against insolvent defendants. So Boulton's claim to the surviving enrichment would be frustrated by the highest obstacle which might be encountered by anyone who maintained a claim of the same kind. A claim *in personam* would not meet that obstacle. Unable to surmount the enrichment issue in a claim to 'value received', he would simply drop down to 'value surviving' because, on his particular facts, he could establish enrich-

---

[91] *Boulton* v. *Jones* (1857) 2 H. & N. 564

[92] Above, p. 128. Subjective devaluation is obstructed where the claim for restitution is made in respect of a specific *res* received or for its value, so long as the *res* is returnable to the claimant (since if it is returnable the defendant cannot object to returning it if valueless and cannot object to paying its value if he prefers not to return it despite describing it as valueless).

ment in that measure. In an insolvency he would take his place with the other unsecured creditors.

This hypothetical variation of *Boulton* v. *Jones* shows what kind of motivation can make a plaintiff want a personal claim in the second measure. In generic terms, it will happen in any situation in which a claim in the first measure encounters some obstruction which the claim in the second measure can avoid.

Sinclair v. *Brougham*[93] was just such a case. The *ultra vires* depositors could not claim in the first restitutionary measure, value received. The reason was that restitution in that measure would be effected by judgments exactly the same in content as those which would have been entered if the *ultra vires* contracts had been *intra vires*. In other words restitution in the first measure would have flatly contradicted the *ultra vires* rule. A claim in the second measure, what the Building Society still had left, did not contradict the rule because there was no necessary equivalency between what the society might be found to have left and the amounts which the depositors would have been able to recover if their contracts had been valid. The key to the whole case is that the House of Lords decided that a claim in the second measure was compatible with the letter and policy of the *ultra vires* doctrine. What was done for the depositors followed from that. As Lord Sumner said: 'What ought to be done I think is clear; the only difficulty is how to describe the principle and how to affili-ate it to other legal or equitable rules.'[94]

The assumption was that the depositors would have to claim *in rem* in order to be able to come down to the second measure. Viscount Haldane, L.C., said as much: 'Their claim cannot be *in personam* and must be *in rem*, a claim to follow and recover property with which, in equity at all events, they never really parted.'[95] Yet precisely what the depositors needed was a claim *in personam*, because the result of the case remains open to a criticism which attaches solely to the proprietary claim. The conclusion has to be drawn from the case, as it now stands, that *ultra vires* lenders must in principle have priority over unsecured creditors. This can be an acceptable conclusion, even though such lenders do not initially intend to become secured creditors, so long as it is really correct to say that, at least in equity, property does not pass in an *ultra vires* transaction. In other words it is acceptable so long as the *ultra vires* lenders really do retain their proprietary base. It is extremely doubt-ful that they do. In the analogous case of transactions made absolutely

---

[93] *Sinclair* v. *Brougham* [1914] A.C. 398.
[94] Ibid. p. 458.
[95] Ibid. p. 418.

void under the *Infants' Relief Act, 1874* it has been held that, despite the nullity of the contract, property does pass.[96] If it is true that *ultra vires* creditors can obtain priority over valid unsecured creditors there will be some facts on which it will be to their advantage not to take up the option, which statute now gives them,[97] of treating their loans as valid.

However, much the better view is that the House of Lords never intended to allow any such priority. On the particular facts of the case two circumstances made it possible not to focus too clearly on that problem. First, the unsecured creditors were paid off by agreement between the parties. Second, the nature of the mixed fund was such that, arguably, it would have been impossible for the depositors to identify the surviving remnant of their payments until the creditors had been paid. These two facts meant that the House of Lords was able to concede to the depositors a right which, on the particular facts, would behave as a claim *in personam*, without priority. If it were permissible to say that the law is what they did, not what they said, *Sinclair* v. *Brougham* would exemplify a personal unsecured claim in the second measure of restitution.

When the tracing exercise shows that an *ultra vires* loan went to discharge a valid liability, so that the company's enrichment survives in a debt discharged rather than in mixed fund or mixed asset, this same question arises in another form. If the debt which is discharged is itself secured, should an *ultra vires* lender have a secured claim? We argued above that, in the absence of a valid contract between himself and either the borrower or the secured creditor, he should never be allowed to become a secured creditor unless he can demonstrate that he retained a proprietary base.[98] This means that the right to the surviving enrichment recognised in *Baroness Wenlock* v. *River Dee Co.*[99] ought, in this context, to be confined to a personal claim if, as we have argued, an *ultra vires* lender does not retain the property in his loan at the moment after the payment over. In *Re Wrexham, Mold & Connah's Quay Railway Co.*,[1] that is exactly what the Court of Appeal did. It would be wrong to say that the court identified the question in the terms of this discussion — surviving enrichment and proprietary base — but it is certain that what they allowed was a

---

[96] Above, n. 84.

[97] The *European Communities Act, 1972*, s. 9 (1) provides in most circumstances for validity (see above, p. 309 f.) but only 'in favour of a person dealing with the company in good faith'. Presumably, this means that he has a choice.

[98] Above, p. 378 ff.

[99] *Baroness Wenlock* v. *River Dee Co.* (1887) 19 Q.B.D. 155.

[1] *Re Wrexham, Mold & Connah's Quay Railway Co.* [1899] 1 Ch. 440.

claim *in personam* measured by the surviving enrichment. *Ultra vires* lenders advanced money to the company which was used to pay secured creditors. The court regarded the lenders' claim to the priority of the discharged creditors as startling and quite unacceptable.[2] However, the rejection of the secured claim did not mean that the lenders had no claim at all. They had a personal claim in the amount validly spent.

Just as Lord Sumner found it difficult to classify what was done in *Sinclair* v. *Brougham*,[3] so the Court of Appeal in *Wrexham* also could see what ought to be done but not how it ought to be described. Lindley, M.R., said that it was not safe to explain the result in terms of 'subrogation'[4] since that might imply that the *ultra vires* lenders must stand in the shoes of the discharged creditors for all purposes or for none.[5] In another case Lord Selborne, L.C., said that the lender became a valid creditor: if the *ultra vires* loan was spent on *intra vires* debts there was in effect no increase in the company's liability as a whole, so that it was possible, consistently with the doctrine of *ultra vires*, to validate the lender's debt *pro tanto*.[6]

These pragmatic results are satisfactorily unified by the proposition that the Courts have accepted that claims in the second measure of restitution do not offend the doctrine of *ultra vires* and have been able to give effect to that perception by fashioning a claim *in personam*, so as not to give the *ultra vires* lender an undeserved priority over unsecured creditors.

A not dissimilar picture emerges in relation to loans to minors. These loans are void under the *Infants Relief Act, 1874*, as are contracts for the sale of goods other than necessaries. Nevertheless it is not offensive to common sense that, if it can be done without unfair advantage gained at the expense of other creditors, the minor should repay whatever he still has at the time of the adult's claim, at least unless he has changed the position in some other way. In short, there is once again a good case for a claim *in personam* measured by the surviving enrichment.

Where the minor has spent the void loan on necessaries or on any other liability binding on him — that is to say, in the situation parallel to that in *Wrexham* — there is no doubt that the adult is entitled to restitution *in personam*.[7] We have already seen that in *Thurstan's*

---

[2] Especially Romer, J., at first instance: [1898] 2 Ch. 663, 666.
[3] *Sinclair* v. *Brougham* [1914] A.C. 398, 458.
[4] *Re Wrexham, Mold & Connah's Quay Railway Co.* [1899] 1 Ch. 440, 447.
[5] Cf. Rigby, L.J., at p. 455.
[6] *Blackburn Benefit Building Society* v. *Cunliffe, Brooks & Co.* (1882) 22 Ch.D. 61, 71.
[7] *Marlow* v. *Pitfield* (1719) 1 P.Wms. 558; *Lewis* v. *Alleyne* (1888) 4 T.L.R. 650.

Case a void lender was also allowed a claim *in rem* when his money went to pay off the vendor of land.[8] We also saw that that aspect of *Thurstan's Case* requires a refined explanation. On the assumption that the lender retained no proprietary base, his acquisition of a lien can only be explained on the basis of an arrangement made between him and the vendor, the evidence being supplemented by a presumption. In *Thurstan* the lien is problematic, but the personal claim, which is a separate matter, is not. Just as in *Wrexham*, there is no need to speak of subrogation. If the invalid money is spent on a valid liability, the minor has surviving enrichment in his hands. When it takes this particular form there is no doubt that restitution in the second measure is allowed.

What if he retains the surviving enrichment in a bank account or in the form of some other asset? It might have been answered that, to maximise the protection, the minor should not be made liable even in the second measure. But the Court of Appeal in *R. Leslie Ltd.* v. *Sheill*[9] took the opposite view, at least in the case of a minor who had fraudulently misrepresented his age.[10] In that case the defendant minor had borrowed money. There was no possibility of tracing any surviving remnant of the loan. Hence no question could arise directly of any liability in the second measure. However, it was argued that a fraudulent minor could be compelled to make restitution even in the first measure, what he had received, not what he had left. The Court of Appeal flatly rejected that proposition. There could be no restitution which amounted to repayment, compelling the minor to find money which he no longer held. Restitution stopped where repayment began. However, it is perfectly clear that the Court of Appeal accepted that equity would compel restitution of the enrichment still in the minor's possession, so far as it could be identified. The whole gist of the judgments is that the right of restitution in the second measure must not exceed its proper bounds. It must not spill over into an order compelling the minor to repay or refund what he no longer held.

In the previous year in *Stocks* v. *Wilson*,[11] Lush, J., had indeed allowed the equity to run beyond its proper limit. The minor had bought furniture and a collection of swords and knives for £300, on credit. He later sold some for £30 and raised £100 as a loan by executing a bill of sale of the rest. Lush, J., entered judgement against

---

[8] Above, p. 391.
[9] *R. Leslie Ltd.* v. *Sheill* [1914] 3 K.B. 607.
[10] Whether common law fraud is necessary is a question. Equitable fraud, the desire to retain an unconscientious windfall, may suffice, as in *Clarke* v. *Cobley* (1789) 2 Cox 173.
[11] *Stocks* v. *Wilson* [1913] 2 K.B. 235.

him for £130, the amount of money realised by the minor from the goods. In *R. Leslie Ltd.* v. *Sheill*, Lord Sumner said: 'I think it is plain that Lush, J., conceived himself to be merely applying the equitable principle of restitution.'[12] However, he had applied it incorrectly because had not identified any of the £130 as still retained in some form by the minor. He had, so to say, stopped the process of tracing when only half done. Lush, J., himself had been uneasy about the judgment which he entered: 'Now if the defendant still had the furniture in his possession I should have felt no difficulty in holding that he must restore it.'[13]

These cases clearly recognise an equity to claim restitution in the second measure. They do not say that it should be expressed solely *in personam*, as an equitable debt. But, for the reasons already given in relation to *Sinclair* v. *Brougham*, it is in that form that it ought to be upheld. Formulated as a claim *in rem* it would encounter the obstacle of undeserved priority. There is no reason to say that the lender retains the property in the coins lent at the moment after their transfer, any more than he retains the property in a chattel sold under a contract made void by the *Infants Relief Act, 1874*. With no proprietary base, the invalid lender should, therefore, be confined to a personal claim in the second measure.

These cases, thus unified, would establish very little if they were confined to the context of incapacity, a subject of diminishing importance. Their importance is that they offer a model applicable to every case in which a claim which is *prima facie* available to the plaintiff in the first measure happens to encounter some obstacle. In the incapacity cases the obstacle is that restitution in the first measure would contradict the policy behind the incapacity. So the question is asked whether the claim in the second measure strikes the same rock. The same question ought always to be asked. We have already suggested that in some cases the claim in the second measure will escape difficulties under the head of enrichment. Again, in *Orakpo* v. *Manson Investments Ltd.*,[14] the question ought to have been asked[15] whether the words or policy of the rules rendering the money-lending contracts unenforceable precluded even a personal claim to the enrichment still retained by the borrower. The lenders in that case had not abused or sought to evade the statutory mechanisms of control. It may be that the claim could have been allowed at least for lenders of that kind. *Orakpo* is a case which makes no attempt to

---

[12] *R. Leslie Ltd.* v. *Sheill* [1914] 3 K.B. 607, 618.
[13] *Stocks* v. *Wilson* [1913] 2 K.B. 235, 244.
[14] *Orakpo* v. *Manson Investments Ltd.* [1978] A.C. 95.
[15] In the spirit of *Shaw* v. *Groom* [1970] 2 Q.B. 504.

establish any pattern of principle in the law of restitution. For the sake of consistency, intelligibility and predictability, that 'empirical' approach should be abandoned. One useful discipline is always to address the possibility of a claim in the second measure and always to make a distinct inquiry into the sub-question, whether that claim could succeed on a purely personal basis.

Finally, there is a difficult question for all cases in which it happens that 'enrichment surviving' is greater than 'enrichment received'. If a plaintiff's only motive for switching to the second measure is his desire to obtain a greater sum[16] (as where the defendant is solvent and has invested the money received so successfully that it has increased tenfold), can such a plaintiff claim in the second measure without showing any proprietary base? He must be able to do so. For if it is right that a plaintiff with no proprietary base can have a personal claim to the reduced remnant of the original receipt (provided the rules of tracing can identify it), it must equally be true that he can have a claim *in personam* to a remnant which happens to have increased. Nevertheless it is possible that, except against a defendant guilty of misconduct, a court might take the view that, as between the two bases on which enrichment can be said to survive, a personal claimant could use only 'fixed input' and not 'proportionate share'. The phenomenon of inflated recovery in the second measure would then cease to arise for that type of claimant. Even an asset bought wholly with his £1000 would be taken to contain only the fixed £1000.

Looking back over this chapter, there turn out to be three propositions which constitute the essential wood behind a cover of leaf more dense even than the chapter itself reveals. These are: (i) the exercise of identifying the defendant's surviving enrichment (i.e. tracing) must never be confounded by questions which go only to the nature of the plaintiff's claim, if any, in respect of such surviving enrichment as he does manage to identify; (ii) a plaintiff can only claim a proprietary right (i.e. a right *in rem*) in the surviving enrichment if he can demonstrate that he has a 'proprietary base', by which is meant that, at the first moment of the defendant's enrichment, he, the plaintiff, retained or obtained the property in the subject-matter and never lost that property unless by reason of the morally neutral facts of substitution and intermixture; (iii) where a plaintiff has no right *in rem* in the identified surviving enrichment, it does not follow that he has no claim at all in the second measure of restitution, because he may still have a claim *in personam* in that measure.

---

[16] As in *Re Tilley's Will Trusts* [1967] Ch. 1167.

XII

DEFENCES

This chapter considers six defences to restitutionary claims; Estoppel, Change of Position; Counter-Restitution Impossible; Illegality; Incapacity; *Bona Fide* Purchase. The list is not exhaustive, and there is room for argument whether illegality can be satisfactorily dealt with as a defence rather than as an independent ground of restitution. The phenomenon of repentance from illegal projects certainly is a distinct ground for restitution. I have included it in the mixed bag of policy-motivated restitutions discussed in Chapter IX. It may be demonstrable that more of the matter considered here should have found a place there. Another awkwardness is that the discussion of *bona fide* purchase provides the only context for consideration of the very difficult questions relating to third-party transferees. These would certainly need a chapter of their own in a longer book.

1. ESTOPPEL

The defence of estoppel depends first on the making of a representation. The particular kind of representation which is relevant in this context is a statement to the effect that the recipient of an enrichment may regard himself as secure in his receipt. The exact terms will of course vary from case to case. And there may be some qualification such as that the recipient may treat a payment as his own subject to allowing a reasonable time for checking procedures to operate. If a plaintiff has expressly or impliedly made such a representation and if the defendant has then acted to his detriment in reasonable reliance on it, the estoppel will operate and the restitutionary claim will be barred. As with all estoppels it is the detrimental reliance with makes it wrong for the other to go back on the representation. So here there must be such reliance, sufficient to stop the plaintiff disturbing the security and finality on which he led the defendant to rely.

(i) *Inherent Representations*

The representation on which the defendant seeks to rely may be inherent in the payment or other transfer or it may be collateral to it. A representation which is inherent is one which is inferred from the fact of the payment itself in the context in which it is made, while a collateral representation is one which is distinct from the inherent representation and which, if it is implied rather than expressed, is based on facts additional to the bare fact of payment. For example, if after payment to you I say to you that I have checked the reason for, and the amount of, the payment and can now confirm that the sum which I paid to you was in fact due to you, that separate and subsequent statement would be a clear case of a collateral representation. By contrast, it is not unreal to affirm that many payments are made in circumstances in which the payee can reasonably infer from the fact of the payment itself that the payor is saying: 'This money is for you. I want you to have it,' or 'This is money which I owe you.' An employer who sends money to an employee, or a customer who sends a sum to a trader, can be understood as making such a statement even if he encloses no letter in which he spells it out. Inherent representations of that kind do imply finality. They tell the recipient that he may treat the money as his own.

However, there is almost no hope of founding a defence of estoppel on the inherent misrepresentation. There are two reasons for this. First, if the law were otherwise in this respect, there would be an inexplicable contradiction between the admission of the defence of estoppel and the rejection of any general defence of change of position. The rejection of that defence, now a matter of more doubt than it formerly seemed to be, will be considered in the next section. However, it is certain that the defence of estoppel, based on the inherent representation, has so much in common with change of position that it would be impossible for the law to proceed with the former development without reviewing its position in relation to the latter. The second reason why the defence cannot be based on the inherent representation is that, at least in relation to mistaken liabilities, the recipient cannot usually claim any right to rely on such a representation, since he himself ought to know the state of his own affairs. Just as the payor ought to know the state of his affairs, so the recipient ought to be aware of sums owing to him. As between equals, therefore, the recipient cannot reasonably rely on the payor any more than the payor can reasonably insist that the recipient should have alerted him to the error; and, *vice versa,* if the payee claims to have relied, the payor can equally claim a right to have been notified of his mistake.

It is different where the parties are wholly unequal, as where the payor has all the information and expertise, and the payee has reasonably fallen into the habit of reliance. In such cases it is possible for the courts to recognise a duty of accuracy in the superior payor. An estoppel can then be founded on the inherent representation. In *Skyring* v. *Greenwood*,[1] the King's Bench held that army paymasters were bound by this type of estoppel. Abbott, C.J., said,

'The particular fact in this case on which my judgment proceeds is, that the defendants were informed in 1816 that the Board of Ordnance would not allow these payments to persons in the situation of Major Skyring, but they never communicated to him that fact until 1821, having in the meantime given him credit for these allowances. I think it was their duty to communicate to the deceased the information which they had received from the Board of Ordnance.'[2]

There was no other representation. They had simply failed to inform Major Skyring of his correct position, so that he relied on the payments made to him. That was enough to prevent their going back on the representation inherent in the payments.

A duty of accuracy is a very severe imposition. Where such a duty is found, the payor will have to act very quickly indeed in order to get restitution, since detrimental reliance on the fact of the payment itself will perfect the recipient's defence. Recently the Court of Appeal has suggested, in *Avon County Council* v. *Howlett*,[3] that a local government employer owes such a duty to an employee. However, that was a case in which the County Council had conceded that it had made collateral representations,[4] so that the matter of a duty of accuracy sufficient to activate the inherent representation cannot be said to have been squarely raised. It is possible that, in these cases of inequality, the superior payor should be understood to represent, not that the payment is correct and immediately final, but that such care has been and is being taken in making and checking the payment that any error will be brought to light in a reasonably short time.[5] That interpretation of the inherent representation corresponds with the expectations of ordinary people in dealing with employers, finance houses, department stores and so on and would create a less sudden and immediate bar to restitutionary claims made by such payors. On the basis of this more restrained version of the inherent representation, it might then be possible more actively to develop this defence as a protection for unequal payees.

---

[1] *Skyring* v. *Greenwood* (1825) 4 B. & C. 281.

[2] A p. 289.

[3] *Avon County Council* v. *Howlett* [1983] 1 W.L.R. 605, 621; cf. *Rogers* v. *Louth County Council* [1981] I. R. 265.

[4] [1981] I.R.L.R. 447, 449, *per* Sheldon, J.

[5] Below, p. 405.

(ii) *Collateral Representations*

Collateral representations — those, that is, which are not inferred solely from the transfer itself — offer the defendant more hope. For example, in *Holt* v. *Markham*,[6] the plaintiff bankers were agents of the Air Council to make payments to air force officers after the First World War. Two years after paying Colonel Markham's gratuity they wrote to say that he had received more than his due. The explanation they gave was itself wrong, and he corrected it by return of post. Two months passed before he heard again. They still claimed the overpayment but on different ground. But by that time he had lost the money in a failed business venture. Lush, J., held that the plaintiffs could not recover. The Court of Appeal upheld him. One ground was that the mistake was of law not fact. But, if it was a mistake of fact, then the plaintiffs were estopped. Scrutton, L.J., seems to have preferred an explanation in terms of the qualified inherent representation mentioned above, to the effect that any error would be notified within a reasonable time: 'The plaintiffs represented to the defendant that he was entitled to a certain sum of money and paid it, and after a lapse of time sufficient to enable any mistake to be rectified he acted upon that representation and spent the money.'[7] But Bankes and Warrington, L.JJ., thought there was a representation to be implied from their not answering his letter correcting their first mistake. By not answering they impliedly told him that the doubt had been resolved to their satisfaction and that he might now safely treat the money as his own.

Deutsche Bank v. *Beriro & Co.*[8] also turns on an estoppel by a collateral representation, though it might be said to have an alternative *ratio* according to which the plaintiffs were under a duty of accuracy entitling the defendants to rely on the inherent representation. The plaintiffs were indorsees of a bill from the defendants who were themselves indorsees from Benatar, a merchant in Morocco. The plaintiffs mistakenly told the defendants that the bill had been collected and paid the sum over. Relying not only on the payment but also on the separate representation that the bill had successfully been collected, the defendants paid out the money to Benatar. The Court of Appeal upheld Matthew, J.'s decision that on these facts the plaintiff's *prima facie* right to restitution was barred.

However, a collateral representation to the effect that a cheque has been collected cannot be relied upon for all purposes. In *National*

---

[6] *Holt* v. *Markham* [1923] 1 K.B.504.
[7] At p. 514.
[8] *Deutsche Bank* v. *Beriro & Co.* [1895] 73 L.T. 669.

Westminster Bank Ltd. v. *Barclays Bank International Ltd. and Another*,[9] Ismail, the second defendant, sent a cheque drawn on the plaintiffs to his own bank, the first defendants. He asked for the cheque to be specially collected and for him to be told as a matter of urgency whether it would be honoured. Barclays referred the cheque to the National Westminster. Since it appeared to be drawn by a trusted customer, they decided to clear it even though it put his account into substantial overdraft. They informed Barclays; Barclays informed Ismail. Ismail, who had bought the cheque at a premium in Nigerian currency in order to have sterling available in London, then paid off the person who had sold it to him. Two weeks later the National Westminster discovered that the cheque had been a skilful forgery. Kerr, J., held that they were not estopped. They were not strictly bound to know their customer's signature; and since the reference for special collection had not alerted them to any doubt about the cheque's being genuine, the representation could be relied on only in respect of matters routinely within the scope of such enquiries, namely, the sufficiency of the drawer's funds or credit.

More recently, in *Avon County Council* v. *Howlett*[10] the plaintiffs had overpaid a schoolteacher over a substantial time both in salary and in sickness benefit. At first instance Sheldon, J., found that the County Council was estopped. He would have barred the whole claim but for the fact that on the pleadings there had been detrimental reliance only in respect of part of the money overpaid. This, one of several points distorted by the parties' wish to use the case to test certain specific points, will be considered below. What was the representation relied upon? It does not clearly appear, because the Council conceded that there had been representations beyond the representation implicit in the payment. Sheldon, J., carefully distinguished between the duty cases and the others in which the payment is accompanied by additional circumstances amounting to an express or implicit representation of fact which led the recipient to believe that he was entitled to treat the money as his own. The Council's concession was not as to any duty of accuracy. So, at first instance, the case turned on a collateral representation which was never spelled out. As we have seen, the Court of Appeal later seemed to think that the Council had also been under a duty of accuracy.

It is essential, if the defence is to succeed, that the collateral representation on which the defendant acted to his detriment should

---

[9] *National Westminster Bank Ltd.* v. *Barclays Bank International Ltd. and Another* [1975] 1 Q.B. 654.
[10] *Cit.*, nn. 3 and 4 above.

have been made by the plaintiff. In *R. E. Jones Ltd.* v. *Waring &
Gillow Ltd.*[11] the defence of estoppel failed, seemingly because on
close inspection the representation did not emanate from the plaintiff.
The facts were unusual. A rogue, Bodenham, wanted to have a large
quantity of expensive furniture from Waring & Gillow on hire purchase. He deceived Jones into believing that Waring & Gillow were
backing the introduction of a new car. Jones agreed to take 500 of the
cars and were induced to draw two cheques, for £5000 in all, in
favour of Waring & Gillow. The money was intended to be a 10 per
cent deposit on the cars. Bodenham then used the cheques as though
they were for money available to his own order. When Waring &
Gillow received the cheques from him, they noticed a minor irregu-
larity in them. They contacted Jones who agreed to issue a new
cheque for £5000 to put matters right. This exchange between the
two victims failed to expose Bodenham's fraud. The new cheque was
issued, and Waring & Gillow acted to their detriment by putting
Bodenham in possession of the furniture. By a majority, the House
of Lords held that Jones was not estopped. So far as the inherent
representation is concerned — 'We owe you this money' — there was
no ground for saying that Jones was under a duty of accuracy: Waring
& Gillow ought to have known what was and what was not due to
them. As for any other representation, Waring & Gillow acted on the
belief that Bodenham commanded funds which he did not command,
but it was Bodenham and not Jones who made that representation.
The majority of their Lordships evidently found themselves unable
to saddle Jones with responsibility for Bodenham's representations.
To reach a different conclusion they would have had to hold that by
putting the cheques into his hands they had given him ostensible
authority to make on their behalf whatever explanation he chose.

(iii) *Detrimental Reliance*

Once there is a representation capable of being relied upon, the other
elements of the defence are that the defendant must actually have
relied on it and must have done so to his detriment.

The requirement of actual reliance does not mean that the belief
founded on the representation must have been the sole and overwhelming reason for the subsequent change of position. It is enough
that it was a reason operating on the defendant's mind. But if you do
not believe the representation you cannot afterwards pretend to have
relied upon it. In *United Overseas Bank* v. *Jiwani*[12] the defendant

---

[11] *R. E. Jones Ltd.* v. *Waring and Gillow* [1926] A.C. 696.
[12] *United Overseas Bank* v. *Jiwani* [1976] 1 W.L.R. 964.

was told that a credit had arrived for him. Owing to a clerk's mistake the credit was entered twice and he was informed again. He later cobbled together a story explaining how it was possible for him to have believed that a second identical credit had come in, but this was rejected by the court. The fact that he had not believed, and hence had not relied, would have been enough, without more, to destroy the defence of estoppel.

You cannot claim to have relied on the representaion if you yourself contributed to the other's mistake, or knew all along that he was mistaken, or made no move until you found out that he was, or if you had suspicions which you failed to communicate so that he could take them into account.[13] Your defence rests on the assertion that he led you into false security. It is obvious that you cannot succeed in it if you led him on or are snatching at a statement from which you could have saved him.[14]

Reliance is not enough. It must be detrimental reliance. What counts as sufficiently detrimental? There is a preliminary point. There is no reason to suppose that the acting for the worse must be done precisely with the items of wealth actually received: you do not have to show that you spent the particular coins on a meal or trip. In short there is no requirement of tracing. In *National Westminster Bank Ltd.* v. *Barclays Bank Ltd. and Another*,[15] the money paid out by the plaintiffs to the credit of Ismail's account had never been touched. Indeed the plaintiffs had obtained an injunction to freeze the account; but that did not exclude the defence. The question remained whether expenditure of other money in Nigeria in reliance on having this sterling in London could, in the circumstances, found an estoppel.[16]

It is easy to construct clear cases of detrimental reliance. Suppose you are a person of very ordinary means. You are suddenly paid a fortune as a legacy or a reward. It turns out to be a mistake, but by then you have treated yourself to a trip round the world. At the other extreme, suppose that you are paid £50 in cash; again it is a mistake. A week later you can show that, having that £50, you did not make your regular withdrawal from your bank. You spent the £50 on petrol for the car, your weekly groceries, and getting your suit back from the cleaners. You would have done all these things anyhow. So

---

[13] *Larner* v. *L.C.C.* [1949] 2 K.B. 683.

[14] This follows from the requirement that the representee must have been genuinely misled: see *United Overseas Bank* v. *Jiwani* [1976] 1 W.L.R. 964, 966, *per* Mackenna, J.

[15] *Cit.*, n. 9 above.

[16] *Ibid.*, 664f.

although it happens that it was this particular money which you have spent you have not acted to your detriment.

In *Avon County Council* v. *Howlett*,[17] the defendant schoolteacher and his wife lived on their income, adjusting their expenditure to the money available and occasionally putting something by in the way of savings. The overpayments of salary and benefit had been absorbed in that way, not by any major change in their style of life but by small improvements in its daily quality. Sheldon, J., held that that was enough. Adopting the words of Lynskey, J. in *Lloyds Bank Ltd.* v. *Brooks*,[18] he said that the defendant need only establish that he had altered his position to his detriment in that he was led to believe his income was greater than it was in fact and had spent more money than he otherwise would have done. In the Court of Appeal there was no dissent from that view.

By contrast in *United Overseas Bank* v. *Jiwani*,[19] where the defendant's account had mistakenly been credited twice over with $11 000, there was no reason for thinking that the defendant had done anything which he would not have done had he not received the extra credit. Even supposing that he had in fact relied on the representation, he would have lost on this separate ground. The extra $11 000 had only made it easier for him to buy a hotel, which he would have bought anyhow with money borrowed for the purpose. He had not only done nothing different in reliance on the mistaken credit; what he had done was also not in any way detrimental to him, since the purchase of the hotel had proved to be a good and continuing investment.

(iv) *Two Special Points*

There is a logical difficulty in the operation of the defence of estoppel which may turn out to cripple its development in this field. If the defendant can show a detrimental reliance the effect is that the plaintiff cannot deny the truth of his representation that the defendant might regard the money as his own. Hence it is arguable as a matter of logic that, even where the money received amounts to £50 000 and the detrimental reliance goes no further than £500, still the representation cannot be denied, with the effect that the partial reliance becomes a defence to the whole claim. The Court of Appeal in *Avon County Council* v. *Howlett* very reluctantly came to the conclusion, contrary to the view taken by Sheldon, J., at first instance, that the

---

[17] *Cit.*, nn. 3 and 4, above.
[18] *Lloyds Bank Ltd.* v. *Brooks* (1950) 6 Legal Decisions Affecting Banks, 161.
[19] *Cit.*, n. 14, above.

logical argument must prevail.[20] This extreme result is bound to favour the development of the defence considered in the next section, namely change of position. Nevertheless, it has to be said that the Court of Appeal left room for the point to be reconsidered in a stronger case. There may still be room to find that a partial detrimental reliance bars denial of the representation only pound-by-pound and not in respect of the entire sum. Certainly, if the sum was paid in separate amounts or instalments, albeit for one cause, the logic of the all-or-nothing estoppel would be less compelling.

There are special difficulties in the way of establishing the defence of the estoppel against a claim by a public authority which has acted beyond its powers. In *The Commonwealth of Australia* v. *Burns*,[21] a pension had been paid after the person entitled to it had died. The daughter of the pensioner tried without success to bring the mistake to the notice of the paying office. The case for an estoppel seemed *a fortiori* from *Holt* v. *Markham*.[22] But the Commonwealth was allowed resititution even after the defendant had finally spent the money. The conduct of its servants could not make good the want of authority to make these *ultra vires* payments. English decisions have not faced this issue specifically in relation to the right to restitution, though recently the courts appear to have hardened their position against the possibility of an estoppel on non-procedural matters.[23]

2. CHANGE OF POSITION

This defence is like estoppel with the requirement of a representation struck out. In other words the enriched defendant succeeds if he can show that he acted to his detriment on the faith of the receipt. Once again, it is not a question of tracing. That is, the defendant does not have to show what he did with the specific coins or property received or other property substituted for it. He only has to show that on the faith of his substance having increased he spent more than he would have done and so used up the increase. But it is necessary to proceed more carefully. For this is a defence admitted by American law but not yet recognised in England except in one or two special circumstances.

---

[20] *Avon County Council* v. *Howlett* [1983] 1 W.L.R. 605, esp. 624f., *per* Slade, L.J.
[21] *The Commonwealth of Australia* v. *Burns* [1971] V.R. 825.
[22] *Holt* v. *Markham* [1923] 1 K.B. 504.
[23] *Western Fish Products Ltd.* v. *Penwith District Council* [1981] 2 All E.R. 204; cf. *Maritime Electric Co.* v. *General Dairies Ltd.* [1937] A.C. 610; *Howell* v. *Falmouth Boat Construction Ltd.* [1951] A.C. 837. On the other side: *Robertson* v. *Minister of Pensions* [1949] 1 K.B. 227; *Lever Finance Ltd.* v. *Westminster Corpn.* [1971] 1 Q. B. 222.

(i) *Claims in the Second Measure*

Though change of position does not depend on tracing, yet in all claims which do so depend, and hence in all claims in the second measure of restitution, the defence is to a certain degree either unnecessary or built-in, depending on one's point of view. For the second measure of restitution is 'enrichment surviving'. If the defendant has consumed or dissipated what he received, to that extent it will not be identifiable in his hands and the claim will be diminished: you buy a cake with my money; slice by slice as it is eaten the claim in the second measure is reduced. But *Re Diplock*[24] shows that this in-built feature of such claims is cold comfort so long as the claim in the first measure remains unaffected.

Claims in the second measure thus have this in-built tendency to abate. But *Re Diplock* raised the further question whether, whatever may be the case with claims in the first measure, the English courts have not already accepted change of position as a defence capable of reducing claims in the second measure below the level of value identifiably surviving in the defendant's hands. That is to say, have they not grafted the ordinary defence on at the end, as a matter to be separately considered afer the tracing exercise has been completed?[25] For it was held that, even where the money had been traced into building operations done by the charities, and even where the facts were in principle right for the imposition of an equitable lien, still it might be inequitable for the lien to be attached; and, in particular, it would be inequitable if the improvements were so technically specialised or idiosyncratic as to add nothing to the market value.[26]

In order to assess this holding we need to recall the crucial role played by the issue of 'enrichment' in relation to benefits in kind such as improvements. When a stranger improves your land, you are not compelled to make restitution unless either you freely accepted the work or, more unusually, it was done non-voluntarily and passed some test of enrichment compatible with the law's acceptance of 'subjective devaluation'. The reason for this is that, even if the stranger can show some factor which usually calls for restitution, he cannot recover if you are not enriched. In discussing the exercise of tracing we suggested that the same pattern of thought applies when someone improves his own land using funds which he mistakenly believes to be at his disposal.[27] If this is right, it is true even of improvements

---

[24] *Re Diplock* [1948] 1 Ch. 465.
[25] Above, p. 371.
[26] *Re Diplock* [1948] 1 Ch. 465, 546 ff.
[27] Above, p. 371–2.

which, objectively, do increase the value of the recipient's land or other assets, up to the point at which they pass the 'no reasonable man' test of enrichment. It is, therefore, not necessary to say anything of alterations, such as follies or hideous redecorative schemes, which objectively add nothing to the value or detract from it. Unless an objective test of enrichment is used, and in the absence of a free acceptance, it is simply the case that when wealth is consumed in improvements, no value survives. The reason why you are not amenable to a claim in the second measure of restitution is, therefore, that you have no enrichment left. If you spend the money on objectively valueless improvements, the same reason applies *a fortiori*. It is not that circumstances make it inequitable for the claim to be maintained but that there is no claim because there is no surviving value. Hence *Re Diplock* does not, in the end, support the view that the defence of change of position has been recognised in relation to claims in the second measure. However, as we shall see, the same argument from subjective devaluation makes a powerful case in favour of the defence in relation to claims in the first measure.

(ii) *Claims in the First Measure*

The important question is whether there is or should be a defence of change of position against claims in the first measure. The short answer is that, the bias having been set by *Kelly* v. *Solari*,[28] the defence was ruled out very firmly in *Baylis* v. *Bishop of London*.[29] The rector of Greenford being bankrupt, the Bishop of his diocese became sequestrator of the income of the living. As sequestrator the Bishop was under a statutory duty to apply the money to meeting the spiritual needs of the parish, and then, after meeting certain specified charges, to pay the balance to the rector's trustee in bankruptcy. In respect of one parcel of land the plaintiff for many years paid a tithe commutation charge to the Bishop in his capacity as sequestrator. The Bishop applied it as his statutory duty required. It then appeared that the plaintiff had no interest in the land in question. He had mistakenly overlooked the expiry of a lease. The Court of Appeal upheld Neville, J.'s decision that the Bishop had no defence to the restitutionary claim based on mistake of fact. Although an agent who received for his principal could not be sued once he had paid the money over,[30] that was to be regarded as an isolated exception to

[28] *Kelly* v. *Solari* (1841) 9 M. & W. 54.
[29] *Baylis* v. *Bishop of London* [1913] 1 Ch. 127.
[30] *Sadler* v. *Evans* (1766) 4 Burr. 1984; *Buller* v. *Harrison* (1777) 2 Cowp. 565; *Kleinwort, Sons & Co.* v. *Dunlop Rubber Co.* (1907) 97 L.T.263; cf. *Gowers* v. *Lloyds and National Provincial Bank Ltd.* [1938] 1 All E.R. 766.

the general rule that payment out was no defence. The Bishop received as a principal, not as an agent, and therefore remained liable. ⋆28

In one respect *Baylis* is a specially strong and difficult obstacle in the path of any interpretative introduction of this defence into English law. The Bishop had used the money for purposes other than his own, and in the course of duty. The case therefore lay at a half-way mark between the agency cases (duty bound delivery to one's principal) and examples of self-regarding expenditure or consumption. Refusal to advance even to that stepping stone was, therefore, tantamount to saying that the rule in relation to agents had nothing to do with any kind of change of position but was merely a matter of selecting the right defendant so as to minimise litigation. In that light the agency cases are cut off from the possibility of further generalization. On the other hand, it can equally be argued that the case is weakened by the court's assumption that the defence could only succeed if the action was admitted to rest immediately on vague notions of justice and fairness.[31] That unnecessary prejudice had the effect that the merits of admitting the defence were never seriously examined.

At the level of general principle the best case for admitting the defence lies in the logic of subjective devaluation. If you mistakenly re-spray my car and tune it for high performance, I almost certainly will not have to pay the value of your work even if the market says that my car has gone up in value. My reason is that I can say I never asked for and do not want the work which you have done. Why should I sell the old car of which I was fond? On a larger scale, this is just the case of Pollock, C.B.'s *dictum*: 'One cleans another's shoes. What can the other do but put them on?'[32] But then, suppose instead that I did ask for this re-spray and tuning-up, but only because I relied on having at my disposal a large sum of money which the payor now seeks to recover from me. If the money led me to seek a benefit which I would not otherwise have chosen, repayment will be tantamount to forced payment for an unwanted service. So I may fairly argue that a system which allows subjective devaluation when a benefit in kind is directly conferred seems to behave illogically if it denies a defence of change of position when the same benefit has been sought in mistaken reliance on the enhanced material freedom arising from a supposed increase in wealth.

This argument works powerfully the other way about. If ever the law were to override the subjective argument altogether by imposing a market valuation on benefits in kind even after consumption, then

---

[31] *Baylis* v. *Bishop of London* [1913] 1 Ch. 127, 132, 137, 140.
[32] Above, p. 281.

it would become virtually impossible to support a defence of change of position. Thus if I had to pay for that work on my car despite not wanting it done, why should I not also make restitution of money which misled me into making choices I could not afford? For, either way, I have enjoyed a benefit for which the tastes of rich young men do create a market and hence a value. If the subjective approach to the issue if enrichment were overridden, the fact that my own tastes are such that I myself make no contribution to that value-creating demand could make no difference.

The future of this defence is uncertain. The importance of the issue should not be underestimated. Too much restitution unsettles security. The interest in stability is currently expressed by making restitution difficult, available only on rather extreme facts. If the defence were accepted, that interest could be differently expressed: restitution would be made more easily available, as for instance for less fundamental mistakes, but more quickly barred. At the same time, as *Goff and Jones* insist,[33] the ease with which a defendant might qualify to avail himself of the defence should not be exaggerated. In particular, the defence will always require detrimental reliance at least as great as is currently required by estoppel, and it will never be available to a defendant who is a wrongdoer or is otherwise at fault in purporting to rely on the apparent enhancement of his resources.

Four facts make it possible to predict that the uncertainty about the defence will be resolved in favour of admitting it. First, *Baylis v. Bishop of London*, although a clear and emphatic decision of the Court of Appeal, is weak in the manner already noticed: it wrongly assumes a necessary link between vague notions of fairness and the defence, such that to admit the defence would commit the law to general uncertainty. Second, *Goff and Jones* clearly favour the admission of the defence.[34] Third, judges who favour this defence have from time to time smuggled *dicta* into the cases in its support.[35] Fourth, the Court of Appeal has recently reduced the potential of the defence of estoppel in this field by holding that the defence bars the entire claim, even in a case in which the detrimental reliance to which the defendant can point shows that he has spent only part of

---

[33] At p. 546.

[34] At p. 545 ff.

[35] *Larner* v. *L.C.C.* [1949] 2 K.B. 683, 688: 'The defence of estoppel, as it is called — *or, more accurately, change of circumstances* — must, however, not be extended beyond its proper bounds', *per* Denning, L.J. (italics added); *Barclays Bank* v. *W. J. Simms Ltd.* [1980] 1 Q.B. 677, 690, 695 f., *per* Goff, J.; cf., in relation to the *Law Reform (Frustrated Contracts) Act, 1943*, the opinion of Goff, J., discussed above, at p. 257.

the enrichment which he received.[36] That decision means that the work of the defence of change of position can no longer be satisfactorily done by a liberal application of the defence of estoppel. If and when the matter next arises, the House of Lords is, therefore, likely to decide that the English exclusion of the defence was an error. If it does, it will commit the law to an entirely new strategy for balancing the instinct in favour of restitution against the interest which all recipients have in the security of their receipts. With the defence in place, we could expect to see a multiplication of the grounds on which restitution would *prima facie* be available.

3. COUNTER-RESTITUTION IMPOSSIBLE

The term 'counter-restitution' refers to the giving up which a plaintiff must do in order to qualify for restitution from the defendant. It is clear that in normal circumstances a plaintiff cannot expect both to get back something given to the defendant and at the same time to retain something received from him: if there is to be a taking back there must be a giving back too. Hence there is a defence to restitution where counter-restitution is impossible.

There are three kinds of case in which this defence is definitely inapplicable, (a) where the benefit received by the plaintiff is one which the defendant ought not to have conferred or ought to have conferred without exacting any charge or other recompense, (b) where the plaintiff received no benefit in exchange for the enrichment in respect of which he seeks restitution and will take no such benefit in the award of restitution, (c) where the plaintiff can and does make exact counter-restitution of any benefit received from the defendant. Cases of the first kind will be considered below.[37] Cases of the second kind raise no problems. The same is true of the third category, in which fall all cases where the plaintiff has received money. Precise counter-restitution is then always possible, not *in specie* but in exact equivalent.

It follows that the cases where the defence can arise are those in which the plaintiff has had a non-money benefit from the defendant and that benefit cannot be restored; as where he has paid the defendant for goods which he has used for a time. Or where the defendant did work for the plaintiff in order to earn the enrichment which the plaintiff now claims. The exact scope of the defence then turns on

---

[36] *Avon County Council* v. *Howlett*, above, p. 409–10.
[37] P. 423–4.

the degree to which the courts will insist on precise and perfect counter-restitution. There will be less room for it if approximate or 'substantial' restoration is enough, and, most importantly, there will be much less room for it if a substituted counter-restitution is permitted to be made in money. So, if I have paid you for work partly done, perfect counter-restitution is impossible since your work cannot be given back either *in specie* or in exact equivalent. But if the court will value your part performance and allow me to make my counter-restitution in money then my claim will not be barred. It is important to notice here that, far from embarking on the argument from subjective devaluation, I may well be willing to accept a valuation loaded against me. Suppose I paid you £5000 in advance for work which would ultimately cost me £50 000. You began; you did, say, one-hundredth of the whole project. You have received one-tenth of the price. Threatened by your defence I am unlikely to oppose a valuation at even £150 or £200, since otherwise I shall be driven to take my remedy in contract, which, if my bargain was a bad one, will suit me less well. So if it were objected that the difficulty of valuation made counter-restitution impossible, my answer would be that I will meet those difficulties by giving the defendant the benefit of every doubt. The crucial question is, therefore, whether the courts will allow pecuniary counter-restitution, to balance what cannot be returned *in specie*.

Before that question is directly addressed, there is one important preliminary point. Within the context of restitution *in specie* the fact that the benefit received from the defendant has declined in value will not be regarded as obstructing its return so long as the decline was not the plaintiff's fault. And there will be no requirement for a repayment of money to make good the depreciation. In *Adam* v. *Newbigging*,[38] the respondent, Major Newbigging, had been induced to enter a partnership in a spinning business by Adam's representations that the business was efficient and in small, but increasing, profit. These representations were false but not fraudulent. The accounts had been manipulated by another partner to conceal a slide into insolvency. By the time Major Newbigging discovered the truth and sought restitution the business was no longer a going concern. Its assets had been sold to pay creditors. Nevertheless the House of Lords held that he could rescind the contract by which he acquired his share, recover his capital in-put and be indemnified against partnership liabilities. In *Armstrong* v. *Jackson*,[39] a broker, mandated to buy shares

---

[38] *Adam* v. *Newbigging* (1888) 13 App. Cas. 308.
[39] *Armstrong* v. *Jackson* [1917] K.B. 822.

for the plaintiff, chose instead to sell the plaintiff shares of his own. He did not disclose this fact and thus broke his fiduciary duty. The shares fell from £3 to 5s. McCardie, J., nevertheless held that the plaintiff could recover his price on returning the depreciated shares. He observed that rescission would be a vain thing if deterioration of the subject-matter were sufficient in itself to make counter-restitution impossible. That conclusion would take the remedy away from those most in need of it.

These cases concern the situation in which subject-matter received by the plaintiff has deteriorated on account of its own inherent condition. That decline leaves counter-restitution *in specie* still possible. By contrast, when matters go further and the plaintiff has himself taken or consumed some benefit obtained from the defendant or from subject-matter got from him, counter-restitution is clearly impossible unless in money or some other substitute. Here the common law has traditionally ruled out approximate or substituted counter-restitutions of any kind. This means that it has given the maximum scope to the defence that counter-restitution has become impossible. This position has been expressed most obviously in the rule that, in order to get restitution for failure of consideration, you have to show that the failure has been 'total'. If you contracted to take an interest in land, and you paid before conveyance, you would not be able to recover your money on the other's refusal to convey, if you had enjoyed even a few days' possession.[40] Those days could not be given back. Similarly if you bought a car which was so seriously defective as to allow you to reject it you could lose your right to restitution of the price even before your contractual remedy of rejection. For if you had some use of the car for a time, even though not amounting to an affirmation of the contract, you would be barred from restitution.[41] Again that enjoyment over time could not be given back, so that the consideration could not be said to have failed totally. In cases where the failure was due to frustration the mistaken rule in *Chandler* v. *Webster*[42] carried the requirement of 'totality' to a further extreme. But *Fibrosa*[43] temporarily re-established symmetry between the restitutionary consequences of frustration and of repudiatory breach.

The position of the common law is seen most clearly in the cases on failure of consideration. But it is also a feature below the surface

---

[40] *Hunt* v. *Silk* (1804) 5 East 449; cf. *Giles* v. *Edwards* (1797) 7 T.R. 181; *Linz* v. *Electric wire Co. of Palestine Ltd.* [1948] A.C. 371.
[41] *Yeoman Credit Ltd.* v. *Apps* [1962] 2 Q.B. 508.
[42] *Chandler* v. *Webster* [1904] 1 K.B. 493. See above, p. 000.
[43] *Fibrosa Case* [1943] A.C. 32.

of cases on mistake. Insistence on liability mistake had the general advantage of stabilising this difficult subject. But why was it uncontroversial that mistakes of liability should give rise to restitution? Part of the answer is certainly that restricting restitution to this kind of mistake automatically recognised the most extreme version of this defence based on the impossibility of counter-restitution, since it excluded the possibility of restitution in every case in which counter-restitution might be called for. If I pay in order to discharge my liability and there is in fact no liability to discharge, *ex hypothesi* I will have received nothing in exchange for my payment and no questions need be asked about counter-restitution. *Bell* v. *Lever Brothers*[44] can be seen as the opposite case. Lever Brothers had not received nothing: they had induced Bell and Snelling to leave their posts without argument at a difficult time, and, from the other side, Bell and Snelling had in good faith given up their right to resist. So there was a problem of counter-restitution, evaded by withholding restitution on other grounds.

The traditional posture of the common law has served to avoid very considerable problems. In particular it has meant that no question has arisen in this context of trying to put a money value on those non-money benefits which take the form of fractional or incomplete performances. That in its turn has meant that the courts have not had to address a consequential difficulty encountered in such valuations: whether the objective market value of that incomplete performance should be governed in some way by the value of the whole as bargained for by the parties themselves. The common law approach has also had the related, but distinct merit, of fixing in a clear if arbitrary way, the relationship between a plaintiff's claims in autonomous unjust enrichment and his claims, if any, for breach of contract. Thus, as soon as you could no longer make exact counter-restitution (without the help of balancing payments in money), you had to take such remedy as you could find for breach of contract. Up to that time you could sue in unjust enrichment. It was desirable to cut down the period during which the plaintff might choose between alternative analyses. For the choice led into different measures of recovery. The claim in unjust enrichment could save a plaintiff from the consequences of a bad bargain. Logically defensible, this conflict was nevertheless best kept in a narrow compass.

Despite these advantages it is impossible to affirm that the common law position is, or will remain, the law; because equity and statute have preferred to allow counter-restitution in money; and this is not

---

[44] *Bell* v. *Lever Brothers* [1932] A.C. 161.

an area in which reason allows one to believe that different approaches are right for different situations. The choice in favour of allowing counter-restitution in money has been made in the following three contexts, (a) after frustration of contract, (b) after work done on, or to obtain, the matter in respect of which restitution is sought, and (c) in granting the remedy of rescission.

(a) *Frustration*

Outside the three excepted cases in s. 2 (5), the *Law Reform (Frustrated Contracts) Act, 1943*, in effect abolishes the requirement of total failure of consideration.[45] It allows a party who has paid money before the discharge to have restitution whether or not he has received a valuable non-money benefit. That is s. 1(2): all sums paid shall be recoverable, and all sums payable shall cease to be payable. If the plaintiff relying on this section has received a non-money benefit, the Act gives two possible paths to counter-restitution in money. First there is the proviso to s. 1 (2) itself: against the relief given by the section the court has a discretion to give the defendant an allowance for expenses incurred in or for performance of the contract. Secondly there is the independent claim given by s. 1 (3); the court has a discretion to award a just sum not greater than the value of the non-money benefit received before the discharge, regard being had to all the circumstances and, in particular, to expenses incurred and the effect of the frustrating event on the benefit.

The formidable difficulties from which the courts were protected by the old rule barring restitution as soon as perfect counter-restitution became impossible are now amply illustrated by *B.P. Exploration Co. (Libya) Ltd. v. Hunt.*[46] That case also demonstrates, however, that they are not insuperable. That being so, the fact that the will to overcome them was mustered only under statutory compulsion ought to make no difference so far as concerns rational inferences to be drawn in areas outside frustration: it is for example difficult, in view of what the Act regards as possible, to defend the requirement of total failure of consideration in any other context simply on the basis that counter-restitution in money would be impracticable.

(b) *Work on the Subject-Matter*

Suppose I claim restitution of property which you have laboured to

---

[45] See above, p. 249 ff., 256 ff.
[46] Above, p. 250–255.

acquire. There are three possibilities once it is decided that my claim is *prima facie* good: I can be denied success because counter-restitution of your input is impossible unless in money; I can be given the property and the value of your labour; or I can be given the property subject to counter-restitution in money. This third possibility is obviously most sensible. In *Boardman* v. *Phipps*[47] this was the path taken. The solicitor, Boardman, had acquired shares in breach of fiduciary duty owed to the plaintiff, but he had acted honestly and in the best interests of those whom it was his duty to advise. He had acted with great skill and patience. Though he had to make restitution of his profits he had counter-restitution in the form of liberal allowance for his work.

This species of counter-restitution has a long history in equity. In *Brown* v. *Litton*,[48] in 1711, the captain of a ship had taken with him a large sum of money to trade with; he died on the voyage. The mate took over the ship and employed the dead captain's money very successfully. He maintained that he should have to repay the captain's executors only the capital and interest. Lord Keeper Harcourt made him give up all his profits; but he added: 'To recompense the defendant for his care in trading with it, the Master should settle a proper salary for the pains and trouble he has been at in the management thereof.'[49] The same solution was applied in later cases,[50] and one strand in *Cooper* v. *Phibbs*[51] is similar. There an uncle had leased an Irish salmon fishery to his nephew together with other land; it turned out that the nephew had all along been tenant for life of the fishery. His bill for rescission was successful but one term was that the uncle should have a lien for improvements made during the time when he believed that he was owner. The uncle had died, so the lien accrued to the defendant who was trustee for the uncle's daughters.

At law a similar result is effected by s. 6 (1) of the *Torts (Interference with Goods) Act, 1977*, which provides that a mistaken, but honest, improver must be given an allowance against damages awarded for wrongful interference with goods. The judge has to reduce the award against him by the amount to which the value of the goods is attributable to the improvement. However, this is no more than an analogy. Formally it is not restitution and counter-restitution but simply the assessment of damages in tort. Outside that particular

---

[47] *Boardman* v. *Phipps* [1967] 2 A.C. 46.
[48] *Brown* v. *Litton* (1711) 2 P.Wms. 140.
[49] At p. 144.
[50] *Brown* v. *De Tastet* (1819) Jac. 284; *Wedderburn* v. *Wedderburn No. 4.* (1856) 22 Beav. 84.
[51] *Cooper* v. *Phibbs* (1867) L.R. 2 H.L. 149.

context the restitutionary rights of the improver depend not on this statute but in the correct interpretation of *Greenwood* v. *Bennett*.[52]

In this kind of case there is usually no question of the plaintiff's advancing the argument from subjective devaluation against counter-restitution in money. For one thing his interest lies the other way, lest the defendant be freed to argue that the impossibility of precise counter-restitution should defeat the claim. For another he is usually seeking restitution in money, and subjective devaluation is never possible once the benefit in kind has been realized in cash.[53] But this second reason would not apply in *Cooper* v. *Phibbs* in which, the lease once rescinded, the nephew held the land *in specie* together with improvements which he had not freely accepted.

(iii) *Rescission*

Equity does not insist on exact counter-restitution but is willing to make adjustments in money so long as results are achieved which are practical and just. In *Erlanger* v. *New Sombrero Phosphate Co.*,[54] the respondent company sought restitution from its promoters of the price it had paid them, partly in cash and partly in paid-up shares, for the phosphate island of Sombrero. The promoters had sold the island at twice the price they paid for it, without making sufficient disclosure of the facts. The company tried without success to exploit the phosphate deposits. After a while it discovered the full facts and sought rescission. The order made was for restitution to the company of the cash element of the price and the return of the shares or their proceeds where the shares themselves had been sold. By way of counter-restitution the company was to give up any profit made from the island. No allowance was ordered to cover deterioration, but in the House of Lords it was said that the court had power to order that kind of adjustment too. Lord Blackburn, looking back to the period of institutional separation, said the reason why the common law had to insist on perfect restoration, or none at all, was that it lacked the machinery to take account in money of benefits derived from the property and deterioration inflicted on it. 'And I think,' he said, 'the practice has always been for a Court of Equity to give relief whenever, by the use of its powers, it can do what is practically just, though it cannot restore the parties precisely to the state they were in before the contract.'[55]

[52] *Greenwood* v. *Bennett* [1973] 1 Q.B. 195.
[53] Above, p. 121 f.
[54] *Erlanger* v. *New Sombrero Phosphate Co.* (1878) 3 App. Cas. 1218.
[55] At p. 1278.

It is not easy to say how far the courts will go in exercising these powers to effect substantial if approximate counter-restitution. In contrast to the common law decisions mentioned earlier equity will certainly impose a term for payment to cover a period of enjoyment. That too was part of *Cooper* v. *Phibbs*. Part of the land had indeed belonged to the uncle. So the agreement was 'to be set aside, subject to the Appellant paying to the Respondents a proper occupation rent for the said excepted piece of land and cottage, and the buildings on the said land, to be ascertained by the Master in the usual manner . . . '.[56] It is also certain that the courts will go further in cases where the main claim is against a defendant guilty of misconduct. In *Lagunas Nitrate Co.* v. *Lagunas Syndicate*,[57] Lindley, M.R., drew a distinction according as the defendant was or was not guilty of 'fraud'. But this term should not be taken to mean *Derry* v. *Peek*[58] deceit. It has its equitable meaning of unconscionable conduct. Nevertheless, *Spence* v. *Crawford*,[59] which was indeed a case of fraud in the common law sense, best exemplifies the courts' reluctance to allow an unconscientious defendant to escape restitution on the ground that counter-restitution would be impossible.

In that case the respondent Crawford induced Spence to sell shares to him by misrepresenting the financial condition of the company. He arranged for accounts to show that the company was in a bad state. Several years later Spence sought restitution of the shares. There was no difficulty about counter-restitution of the cash element of the price. But Crawford contended that counter-restitution of other collateral benefits was impossible. In particular he had substituted himself in Spence's place as guarantor of the bank's overdraft and he had sold stock of his own in order, by advancing the proceeds as a loan, to maintain the company's liquidity. The House of Lords was prepared to discount the benefit of the guarantee. It could be ignored since it had in fact never been called on. As for the sale of stock, that difficulty was met by the appellant's willingness to pay the difference between the price obtained and that which would have been obtained after the market had later risen. In other words counter-restitution was allowed in money on the basis of a calculation unfavourable to the plaintiff but willingly accepted by him.

One aspect of equity's flexibility in this matter is willingness to ignore benefits of little or no weight. The guarantee was so treated in

---

[56] (1867) L.R. 2 H.L. 149, 173; cf *Lee Parker* v. *Izzet* [1971] 1 W.L.R. 1688.
[57] *Lagunas Nitrate Co.* v. *Lagunas Syndicate* [1899] 2 Ch. 392.
[58] *Derry* v. *Peek* (1887) 14 App. Cas. 337.
[59] *Spence* v. *Crawford* [1939] 3 All E.R. 271.

Spence v. *Crawford*. In *Hulton* v. *Hulton*,[60] a wife obtained rescission of a deed of separation induced by misrepresentation of her husband's means. The agreement obliged her, *inter alia*, to destroy her husband's letters. That was also something which, though irreversible, could be ignored. *Hulton* also illustrates the same flexibility in another way. Without making any adjustments in money the court was prepared to cancel out mutual non-money benefits. During the currency of the deed she had received benefits in kind under it, non-molestation and so on; but so had he. It was enough to set these off one against the other.

*29

When these three areas in which exact counter-restitution is not required so long as a satisfactory adjustment can be made in money or in some other way are aligned with the traditionally contrary rule of common law, the general condition of the defence based on the impossibility of counter-restitution becomes difficult to state. The best prediction is probably that the flexible approach will work into the common law claims even without further statutory interference. On that basis it may be safe to say that, though the impossibility of counter-restitution is always a defence (subject to the exceptions to be mentioned below), impossibility only supervenes when even pecuniary or other adjustment is obstructed by reasons which go beyond mere difficulty of valuation. Problems of valuation can be faced by methods similar to those now used the *Law Reform (Frustrated Contracts) Act, 1943.*

Unlawful or Void Considerations Sometimes there is no requirement of counter-restitution. Suppose I pay you money under duress of goods, as in *Astley* v. *Reynolds*,[61] because you will not give up my property otherwise. It would be absurd to say that I must give back the benefit I received before I can get back my money. You ought never to have withheld my goods. Or suppose you exact a premium from me when I am looking for accommodation. If there is legislation protecting me, the protection would be subverted if I could not keep the flat while at the same time recovering the sum paid to you. You ought to have let me in without this charge.[62] Again, in *Hulton* v. *Hulton*[63] the wife had received £500 a year for five years during the currency of the separation deed. She did not have to repay that money as a condition for getting rescission. For the husband would have had to pay at least that sum as maintenance pending divorce if

---

[60] *Hulton* v. *Hulton* [1917] 1 K.B. 813.
[61] *Astley* v. *Reynolds* (1731) 2 Str. 915.
[62] *Kiriri Cotton Co.* v. *Dewani* [1960] A.C. 192.
[63] *Hulton* v. *Hulton* [1917] 1 K.B. 813.

he had not fraudulently interposed the arrangements expressed in the separation deed. It was money which he ought not to have withheld against other advantages reserved for himself.

So the general rule is that there is no requirement of counter-restitution when the benefit received by the plaintiff is one for which the law would not, in the circumstances, have allowed the defendant to charge. With some hesitation *Rowland* v. *Divall*[64] and its successors,[65] may be put in this category. I sell you a car belonging to a third party and you use the car for some time before giving it up to its true owner. These cases show that that period of user does not prevent the consideration for your payment from failing totally at common law. In other words, you can have restitution of the price without making counter-restitution of the enjoyment. The reason may be that I have no right to charge for the use of someone else's property and cannot, therefore, expect any allowance for having done so. If this explanation is incorrect, it becomes, to all intents and purposes, impossible to account for the contrast between the willingness of the common law to dilute the notion of a total failure of consideration in these cases and its rigidly literal and absolute
*30 approach on other facts.

4. ILLEGALITY

When the defendant's acquisition involves unlawful behaviour he will, however undeservedly, often have a defence to a restitutionary claim. For the maxim is: *In pari delicto potior est conditio defendentis* (When both parties are alike guilty of wrongdoing, the position of the defendant is stronger). The maxim is only a guide, but it conveys two useful messages. Sometimes the defendant will end up with a windfall, and, the cases in which he will not are those in which the *delictum* is not *par*. Those, that is, in which, in some legally decisive manner or degree, the parties are not 'alike guilty' but, on the contrary, the plaintiff is relatively innocent and can be exonerated.

The cases show that the great difference is between those restitutionary causes of action which fall in the family called 'vitiated voluntariness' or are based directly on the defendant's wrongdoing and, on the other hand, those within 'qualification' or 'free acceptance'. The reason is that in the former category, but not in the latter, the nature of the causes of action is such that in establishing any one

---

[64] *Rowland* v. *Divall* [1923] 2 K.B. 500.
[65] Above, p. 246–8.

of them the plaintiff generally establishes that whatever illegality happened must have happened without his knowledge or against his will. If so, it follows that the *delictum* is not *par*. If we escape the words of the maxim, we can say that such a plaintiff may be taken to have wished that the illegality should not be committed, with the result that, (a) he is free from moral stigma, and (b) there is no need to fear that he, or others later in the same position, might use their right to restitution as a lever to compel performance.

The chapter on 'vitiation' includes many examples of claims in which an element of illegality was not fatal. In *Oom* v. *Bruce*[66] the plaintiff recovered insurance premiums which he had paid under what he supposed to be valid contract. He did not know that war had broken out with Russia, so that the cause of the contract's illegality was concealed from him by his mistake. In *Hughes* v. *Liverpool Legal Friendly Society*[67] the plaintiff recovered on the basis of a mistake of law induced by fraud. The defendant's agent had deliberately concealed the illegality of the type of policy taken out by the plaintiff. These are cases of mistake, spontaneous or induced. Not every mistake conceals the illegality. If it does not, then illegality will be a defence. For example the mistake may happen within the context of an illegal transaction; as where I promise to pay you £1000 if you murder X, and then I pay you, incorrectly believing that you have done the deed. In *Morgan* v. *Ashcroft*,[68] a bookmaker entered one credit twice in the defendant's account and so overpaid him. One reason for the Court of Appeal's conclusion against restitution was that no court could inquire into such a mistake 'without recognizing wagering transactions as producing legal obligations and therefore doing the very thing which the *Gaming Act, 1845* does not permit to be done'.[69] Finally, in the absence of fraud, one species of mistake which does conceal the illegality nevertheless does not constitute a cause of action: mistake of law.[70] A plaintiff, labouring under such a mistake, may be morally innocent but still unable to recover. He simply has no cause of action.

Then there are cases of oppression and inequality. In *Smith* v. *Cuff*[71] the defendant had stood out against a composition between the plaintiff and his creditors until he had received a promissory note for an extra payment to himself. After the plaintiff had paid the

---

[66] *Oom* v. *Bruce* (1810) 12 East 225.
[67] *Hughes* v. *Liverpool Legal Friendly Society* [1916] 2 K.B. 482.
[68] *Morgan* v. *Ashcroft* [1938] 1 K.B. 49.
[69] At pp. 66, 67.
[70] Above, p. 164–7.
[71] *Smith* v. *Cuff* (1817) 6 M. & S. 160.

amount of the note he recovered back the sum as money had and received. Lord Ellenborough, C.J., said: 'This is not a case of *par delictum*; it is oppression on one side, and submission on the other: it never can be predicated as *par delictum*, when one holds the rod, and the other bows to it.'[72] Many of the cases brought together under 'inequality' involve plaintiffs in vulnerable classes whose protection consists precisely in the statutory provisions infringed by the transfer for which they subsequently seek restitution. When accommodation is in short supply it may be necessary, if house hunters are to be protected, to prohibit the paying or taking of premiums. If an in-coming tenant pays and then seeks to recover such a premium it would clearly not be sensible to allow the landlord a defence of illegality. To do so would considerably weaken the protective scheme. In such cicumstances the defence is rightly excluded.[73]

The same conclusion is obviously necessary where the plaintiff has been the victim of a wrong and bases his claim to restitution on the defendant's having been enriched by conversion, intimidation, breach of fiduciary duty and so on. These cases differ from those in the last paragraph because in those the plaintiff is implicated in the illegality, albeit innocently, while in these he has no part whatever in it, save as victim. There can be no question of a defence based solely on the defendant's own misconduct.

In all these cases in which there is no defence of illegality the claim to restitution does not require there to be counter-restitution. In other words, there does not have to be a total failure of consideration. This has already been explained:[74] I cannot be expected to give back to you or make any allowance for a benefit which was unlawful and was therefore excluded from commercial exchange. But it is important to add here that this rule also has a role in the policy of discouraging unlawful behaviour. There is no point in committing the unlawful act if the remuneration or reward for it has to be given up anyway. If this policy were the only matter in issue the best rule would be: no restitution until performance, full restitution after performance. But it is not the only matter in issue, for it clashes with the policy against helping wrongdoers: *nemo suam turpitudinem allegans audiendus est* (nobody is to be heard who founds his case on his own turpitude). However, in the case of those plaintiffs discussed so far — the mistaken, deceived, oppressed, unequal or wronged —

---

[72] At p. 165.
[73] *Kiriri Cotton Co.* v. *Dewani* [1960] A.C. 192.
[74] Above, p. 423—4.

there is no question of hearing a disgraceful plaintiff and hence no obstacle to the policy of discouraging illegality.[75]

Where the plaintiff's judgment was not vitiated, so that, mistake of law apart, he knew what he was doing, he will usually be defeated by the defence of illegality. This often involves the unwanted consequence of leaving a rogue with a windfall but is explicable as, (a) an expression of the court's refusal to be invoked by disgraceful plaintiffs, and (b) an attempt to ensure that restitution is not made an instrument for compelling the completion of illegal projects. The commonest restitutionary cause of action arising for a plaintiff unable to point to any vitiating factor is failure of consideration, and a plaintiff who can recover for failure of consideration has an effective threat with which to try to ensure that the consideration does not fail. I give you £10 000 to kill X; you do not do it. I am a disgraceful plaintiff, and no court could hear me. But on top of that, the possibility of a suit to recover the £10 000 if the consideration failed would encourage performance, in this case murder. So you, a disgraceful defendant, have a defence: *potior est condition defendentis*.

In *Parkinson* v. *College of Ambulance*[76] the plaintiff had made a corrupt contract with Harrison, the secretary of the college, to the effect that, if he made a handsome donation to the college, arrangements could and would be made for him to get a knighthood: no knighthood came. The secretary had behaved fraudulently in the sense that he had represented that the college had a power to make such arrangements which in fact it did not have. But the fraud did not conceal the illegality. Parkinson still knew or ought to have known that attempts to buy honours were corrupt. So although the consideration for his payment failed, Lush, J., refused him restitution. And in *Berg* v. *Sadler and Moore*[77] the plaintiff tobacconist had been put on a stop-list by the Tobacco Trade Association. He had, therefore, been driven to try to get supplies by putting up another person to buy them with his money. After the money had been paid over but before the goods had been delivered, the defendant wholesalers realised what was happening. They declined either to deliver the goods or to return the money. Macnaghten, J., held that the defendants had foiled a criminal attempt to obtain goods by false pretences. The Court of Appeal upheld his refusal to allow restitution. Since the victim of deceit can be relied on never, once he knows the

---

[75] Above, p. 300–302.
[76] *Parkinson* v. *College of Ambulence* [1925] 2 K.B. 1.
[77] *Berg* v. *Saddler and Moore* [1937] 2 L.B. 158.

facts, to be levered into completing the illegal project, this case shows that the 'disgraceful plaintiff' principle can suffice on its own to justify the defence. Scott, L.J., said: 'If dishonest people pay money for a dishonest purpose, and then, by good fortune, the offence which they designed to commit is not committed, are they entitled in this court to come and ask for recovery of the money? In my opinion they are not.'[78]

The same principles apply in relation to non-money benefits. In *Bigos* v. *Bousted*[79] the issue arose on a counter-claim. Bousted had deposited a share certificate as security for a loan to be made in Italy. The purpose of the transaction was to defeat the exchange control regulations then in force, making Italian currency available to Bousted abroad, repayable in sterling at home. Mrs Bigos did not advance the Italian money. The condition for holding the certificate having failed, Bousted demanded it back. Pritchard J., held that he could not have it. Nothing was made of the fact that Bousted had been partly driven to the transaction by the serious illness of his daughter. It may be that, where the claim is based on total failure of consideration, such circumstances ought to be taken into account. Again, in *Chettiar* v. *Chettiar*,[80] a father had transferred land in Malaya to his son. His intention was that the son should hold the land for him. The relevant documents stated, falsely, that the son had paid a money price. The purpose was to defeat quota regulations applying to holdings of rubber-producing land larger than 100 acres. When the father decided to sell the land the son refused to co-operate in the transfer and claimed the land as his own. The father turned to the courts to recover his title and failed. The large ground on which the Judicial Committee rested its advice was that the courts will not aid disgraceful plaintiffs. More technically, the father's case had been put on the basis that the appropriate means for him to obtain restitution was through the doctrine of resulting trusts. He therefore needed both to show that the money consideration had never been exacted and then, with evidence of his actual intention, to rebut the presumption of advancement. The Judicial Committee held that he could not attack that presumption without disclosing his own turpitude and that the son should, therefore, retain the land.

In recent years the courts have shown themselves anxious that people should not needlessly be disqualified by illegality from enforcing private rights which they would otherwise have. This has

---

[78] At p. 168.
[79] *Bigos* v. *Bousted* [1951] 1 All E.R. 92.
[80] *Chettiar* v. *Chettiar* [1962] A.C. 294.

been especially true in relation to contractual rights endangered by illegalities committed during the performance of contracts *ex facie* legal at their inception and not intended from the start to be performed in an unlawful manner or for an unlawful purpose. The immediate reason for this more liberal approach was the modern proliferation of statutory controls often infringed without much moral turpitude. In the cases the ground was broken by Devlin, J., in *St. John Shipping Corporation* v. *Joseph Rank Ltd.*[81] and developed by the Court of Appeal in *Shaw* v. *Groom.*[82] Abandoning the technical distinctions which Devlin, J., could not avoid at the moment of innovation, *Shaw* v. *Groom* makes the fate of the plaintiff's contractual rights depend on whether the wording of the statute which has been infringed, or its policy, or the circumstances of the particular case, actually necessitate disqualification. In *Shaw* v. *Groom* itself, the Court of Appeal was able to conclude that a landlord who had failed to provide a properly informative rent-book of the kind statutorily prescribed did not have to be disqualified from his right to claim rent. And this conclusion was possible even though the policy behind the offence which he committed was to protect tenants by ensuring that they knew their rights. It was not necessary to reinforce that policy by adding disqualification from contractual rights to the penalties provided by the statute itself.

It is certain that, in any case in which a party's contractual rights survive the *Shaw* v. *Groom* inquiry, his restitutionary rights will also remain intact. For if there is no decisive objection to enforcing the contract there can, *a fortiori*, be no objection to the more oblique species of enforcement arising from restitution in the event of non-performance. So infringements which pass the *Shaw* v. *Groom* test are, both in contract and unjust enrichment, 'non-disqualifying illegalities'. But, while both kinds of right will usually stand or fall together, it is important that the possibility should be kept open that, even where contractual rights turn out to be barred, a second inquiry in the same style might still be able to conclude that the right to restitution for failure of consideration remained available. In other words disqualification from restitutionary rights should not be automatically inferred from disqualification from contractual rights. In conducting this inquiry it will be particularly important to ask the question in relation to both measures of restitution. Claims to 'what he has left' (surviving enrichment) may escape objections encountered by the claims to the full measure of 'enrichment received'. Also,

---

[81] *St. John Shipping Corporation* v. *Joesph Rank Ltd*. [1957] 1 Q.B. 267.
[82] *Shaw* v. *Groom* [1970] 2 Q.B. 504.

circumstances not themselves amounting to independent grounds for restitution, should in this inquiry be taken into account in order to determine whether a plaintiff might not be allowed to succeed in his claim where the consideration has failed. Such factors as mistake of law or pressure of circumstances might, in the absence of real moral turpitude, be allowed to override the defence of illegality where, even for reasons other than spontaneous repentance, the illegal purpose had not been achieved. An important question would be, whether the circumstances were likely to recur with such frequency that the availability of restitution would become a lever for compelling performance.

We have been concerned with grounds for restitution within 'vitiated voluntariness' and 'wrongs', where illegality is almost never a defence, and 'qualified voluntariness', where it nearly always is. Two other grounds need to be mentioned. First, free acceptance. Here from the standpoint of the plaintiff's implication in illegality everything said of failure of consideration must apply again. The plaintiff's eyes are equally open. Indeed many cases of failure of consideration can be turned round and, by alternative analysis, be expressed as examples of free acceptance; and that possibility ought not to alter the impact of a disqualifying illegality. Secondly, in cases within the miscellaneous group of policy-motivated restitutions,[83] the general principle must be that the particular policy in question must be weighed against the principles of not aiding disgraceful plaintiffs and encouraging lawful behaviour. Different policies will have different weights, and some will admit the defence of illegality while others will not. But one case which we have assigned to that category is dictated by those very policies and not by others in competition with it. The plaintiff who spontaneously repents before any of the illegal purpose has been achieved is allowed restitution because, (a) his moral standing is restored by his repentance, and (b) this reward offered to the penitent tends to encourage illegal projects to be aborted.

A special problem arises where the illegal transaction is intended to confer some temporary interest upon the defendant. As where illegality infects a contract of hire or pledge or where a lease is granted which is either *ex facie* illegal or is given for an illegal purpose or with some collateral aim of a corrupt kind. During the currency of such temporary interests the restitutionary issues are the same as those which arise under illegal transactions intended to transfer ownership, the interest which endures so long as the thing itself

---

[83] Above, p. 294–312.

exists. But after the temporary interest has ended, as ownership cannot end, a different question arises. Suppose that I hire you a car on illegal terms for one month. When the month is up, you refuse to give the vehicle up. Do I even now have a claim only if there was, in relation to the contract of hire, no *par delictum*? In other words, is illegality a defence unless I show that I was mistaken, deceived, oppressed and so on?

Delete for a moment all reference to the illegality. The car was mine before the hiring out. The immediate right to possession which I then had became eclipsed by the temporary interest granted to the hirer. That interest came to an end. Emerging from the period of eclipse my anterior right now survives in me. I can vindicate it by an action for tortious interference with my chattel. If the subject of the example had been land and lease, the same analysis would have given me the action for the recovery of land. Strictly speaking there is no restitution in this story, for the original right is merely preserved through its temporary eclipse.[84] Nevertheless it would be inconvenient not to ask the question: when the illegality of the hire or lease is added back into the facts, do these actions, based ultimately on the plaintiff's pre-existing title, fail unless he can show that he was not *in pari delicto*? The general answer seems to be that they do not.[85] The justification is that the remainder of time beyond the temporary interest itself never was brought into the illegal dealing. An illegal contract in relation to my car does not disqualify me from asserting rights in and to my house. In the same way an illegal contract in relation to one month's user of my car should not affect my rights save in relation to that one month, slices of time being no less distinct than separate physical entities.

This logic leads towards the conclusion that illegality should never be a defence to these 'anterior title' claims. That is not quite safe. Suppose I lend you a car for a week to help you rob a bank or kidnap a millionaire. You refuse to give it back. Such cases really call for forfeiture to the state, not a windfall to the defendant. But in the absence of such provisions a court has little choice but to depart from the logical position and to allow the windfall in cases in which the turpitude of the plaintiff is offensive.

One further question should be noticed, although a full discussion is out of range here. Temporary interests are defined in many ways. In particular they can, when lawful, be brought to an end on the happening of different events. I hire you my car for a month, the

---

[84] Above, p. 13–16.
[85] *Bowmakers Ltd. v. Barnet Instruments Ltd.* [1945] K.B. 65.

rental payable weekly in advance, the contract to be determined immediately in the event of your allowing any other person to drive. This hiring can end by effluxion of time, by a repudiatory breach accepted by me or by the happening of an event given automatically terminating effect. The previous paragraphs suppose the effluxion of time. Are the same arguments applicable where an illegal temporary interest ends in these other ways? The answer is in doubt; *Bowmakers Ltd.* v. *Barnet Instruments Ltd.*[86] suggests that the same answer is to be given however the temporary interest ends.

This interpretation has been encouraged as a means of cutting down the disqualifying effects of illegality. On the other hand just as restitutionary claims for failure of consideration can be seen as a lever for compelling performance, so the re-assertion of anterior title can have exactly the same effect in the case of illegal bailments and leases. This is especially true where the eclipse is ended by what, in a legal contract, would be a repudiatory breach accepted by the plaintiff. But it is also true of automatically terminating events, at least in the sense that careful drafting can use the effect of such events to build into the illegal contract a mechanism for its enforcement. Only when the temporary interest ends by effluxion of time is there no danger of oblique enforcement. For when the interest has expired then *ex hypothesi* the threat of action to reassert title cannot be used to induce performance, since for better or worse the whole business has receded into the past. But the argument for limiting this species of claim to cases in which time has expired meets a counter-argument in the case of temporary interests which have a substantial duration. There the bailor or, more likely, the lessor will suffer an acute and probably disproportionate penalty if he is disqualified from all his rights until the period of the interest has expired by the passage of time. The only satisfactory way out is to limit the class of disqualifying illegalities to those for which such consequences are not disproportionate.[87]

*31   5. INCAPACITY

There is as yet no coherent body of law about incapacity to bear liabilities arising from unjust enrichment. So the question presents itself chiefly in the form of an enquiry into the extent to which contractual incapacities of companies, minors and the mentally

---

[86] *Cit.*, n. 85, above.
[87] Above, p. 428–30.

disabled carry over into this different area; and the first proposition must always be that there is no logical reason why they should; that is to say, one who shows that the defendant would be immune from a claim in contract cannot automatically infer that the same protective disability applies in unjust enrichment. For contract and unjust enrichment are different events. It was a vice of the old implied contract theory of unjust enrichment that it concealed the fallacy in ostensibly logical arguments of this kind. Equity has not made the same mistake. A minor cannot be trustee by express appointment. But it is not said that he cannot be a constructive trustee.[88]

The warning against supposing that contractual incapacities necessarily apply to claims in unjust enrichment does not mean that there are not good reasons of a non-logical kind for extending some contractual defences to some unjust enrichments where on the facts to allow a claim in unjust enrichment would make nonsense of the contractual disability or would encounter the same need for a protective defence.

Where the *incapax* is identifiably still holding some part of the enrichment received there is no strong argument for allowing him to retain it unless in some collateral way he has changed his position. As where he still holds £90 of your £100 but in the meantime has spent £50 of his own on a treat which he would not have contemplated but for his reliance on having this payment from you. At least in the absence of such circumstances, a claim *in personam* in the second measure of restitution ought, therefore, always to succeed. The cases have falteringly struggled towards that conclusion. This was discussed in the last chapter.[89]

As for claims in the first measure, for the value received, it is convenient to consider the defence of incapacity separately in relation to money and to non-money benefits.

(i) *Benefits in kind*

The crucial question is whether the benefit in issue does or does not fall within the notion of 'necessaries'. If it does, incapacity will not be a defence. Necessaries are those things which the defendant, given his means and position, could be expected to acquire as a matter of course quite apart from his incapacity. From the standpoint of restitutionary claims what matters about necessaries is that they form a category of benefits in kind which cannot be subjectively devalued. You cannot say that a necessary good or service was valueless to you

---

[88] *Snell's Principles of Equity*, 28th ed., London 1982, 198.
[89] Above, p. 394 ff.

because not chosen by you, because if you had had the opportunity to choose you would have wanted to acquire it. Such things settle the difficult issue of enrichment by the test of 'incontrovertible benefit'. That test is objective. It does not depend on the actual wishes of the particular defendant. It can, therefore, be applied even where the defendant is incapacitated. So a defendant who has received necessaries has incontrovertibly been enriched at the supplier's expense.

Enrichment is not enough. There must also be a factor calling for restitution of the enrichment, going to the word 'unjust'; and even then those requirements do no more than explain why the plaintiff has a claim. They do not explain why that claim is immune to the defence of incapacity. Both points must be examined.

As for the factor calling for restitution, strictly speaking it calls for no discussion here, where the issue is only the availability of a defence and the premiss should be that a *prima facie* claim can be made out on one of the grounds discussed earlier in the book. But a precaution has to be taken against a confusion. There is no ground for restitution which stands in any peculiar relationship to the supply of necessaries. Thus, I might supply necessary food and lodging to you by mistake, at the point of a gun, out of compassion for your urgent need or on condition that you paid me £50 per week. Just as all these grounds can be associated with the supply of necessaries so they can all be associated with the supply of necessaries to an *incapax*. This range of possible grounds was not appreciated in *Re Rhodes*.[90] In that case a nephew who had paid to keep his aunt in a home for mental patients failed to get restitution because he had failed to produce affirmative evidence of an intent to recoup his payments from her. This supposes, tacitly, that the ground of his claim was failure of consideration. It is clear enough that you cannot succeed in a claim of that kind unless you can show that some counter-prestation was the condition of the giving. But it may be that the nephew's claim was intended to rest on moral compulsion. Those who rely on factors which vitiate voluntariness are never expected to show, in addition to their vitiated consent, independent evidence of non-gratuitous intent. A mistaken payor does not have to prove that he intended to get the money back. The victim of a gunman does not have to present a bill with the food which is taken. So *Re Rhodes*, which admits the claim for necessaries in principle, should not be taken as authority for the proposition that it lies only for those who show that they intend to charge.

---

[90] *Re Rhodes* (1890) 44 Ch.D. 94.

Supposing that there is an operative ground for restitution, why is the claim in respect of necessaries always immune from the defence of incapacity? This is the one case in which a claim to benefits in kind is stronger than a claim to money. For while it is true that *incapax* is equally enriched in both cases, yet money is more dangerous in that it confers a material freedom from which special protection may be required. A minor or mental patient who receives money may waste it and for that reason has to be relieved of liability to repay it. But a minor who receives necessaries in kind has, *ex hypothesi*, not wasted the enrichment. If we could be sure he would always spend his money on such things we would not need to protect him at all. Where it can be shown that he has — that is, where money received can be traced into necessaries acquired — we do not protect him.[91]

This reasoning applies no less to companies than to people who from youth or mental illness cannot be regarded as responsible. The doctrine of *ultra vires* has been whittled away to the point at which *bona fide* suppliers will hardly ever be driven by it from contract to unjust enrichment.[92] But the principle remains. If a company would have had need of coal or writing paper or accountancy on its *intra vires* business nothing should obstruct a restitutionary claim by an *ultra vires* supplier. For supplies necessary to the conduct of either business do not confer any special freedom to indulge in the one which is *ultra vires*. Before the statutory changes supervened, *Craven-Ellis* v. *Canons Ltd.*[93] pointed to the conclusion that a claim in respect of necessaries would lie, though strictly speaking it was a case of a contract made by impostor agents rather than on ordinary example of *ultra vires*. In *Re Jon Beauforte Ltd.*,[94] where coal was supplied to a company running an *ultra vires* business, the supplier was not allowed to make a claim for its value in the liquidation,[95] but no argument was advanced on the basis of *Craven-Ellis*. It might have been demonstrable that the company had been enriched on the 'no reasonable man' test, in that it had been saved expenditure on fuel which it would have had to have incurred anyway. As for 'unjust', the supplier might not have been able to argue that he had been mistaken, because he had constructive notice of the want of

[91] *Marlowe* v. *Pitfield* (1719) 1 P.Wms. 558; *Lewis* v. *Alleyne* (1888) 4 T.L.R. 650.
[92] Above, p. 309.
[93] Above, p. 118 f.
[94] *Re Jon Beauforte Ltd.* [1953] Ch. 131.
[95] At p. 135 Roxburgh, J., left open the possibility that the supplier might be able to make out a claim in the second measure on the model of *Sinclair* v. *Brougham*, above, p. 396 f.

capacity, but he could have shown that the consideration for his supplies had failed.

This discussion has assumed that a minor's liability to pay for necessaries, now statutory in the case of necessary goods,[96] is correctly analysed as a claim in unjust enrichment.[97] There is a competing or alternative analysis according to which it rests on the minor's vestigial contractual capacity. That is, the minor is not wholly unable to bear contractual obligations and can bear, among others, the obligation to pay for necessaries. This contractual analysis has difficulty with the fact that it is not his price but a reasonable price which must be paid. On the other hand, it has in its favour the fact that, in *Roberts* v. *Gray*,[98] the Court of Appeal decided that on a contract for necessary services the minor could be sued for compensatory damages. That species of judgment could not be explained by the unjust enrichment analysis. Moreover the contract was executory, the minor yet not having received his benefit. Hence there was no basis at all for a claim in unjust enrichment. This case was, however, decided at a time when the court was hostile to the notion that unjust enrichment existed as a basis of liability distinct from contract. Against that background it was easier to conclude that the liability for necessaries must be contractual.

Where the benefits received by *incapax* are not necessaries it will be very difficult for any claim in the first measure to succeed. The first reason is not, directly, that the defence of incapacity applies, but that, indirectly, the incapacity makes it impossible for the plaintiff to establish enrichment. For non-necessary benefits are open to subjective devaluation, and the obvious way round that obstacle is obstructed. Subjective devaluation usually drives a plaintiff to rely on free acceptance. But that probably cannot be done against someone under a contractual incapacity since, like contract, it too requires a conscious decision to have been made by the defendant.

In addition to that general objection there is a special objection to claims in respect of non-necessary benefits which arise from a failure in contractual reciprocation. Where a defendant relies on his contractual incapacity to refuse to pay for non-necessary goods or services, a claim in unjust enrichment for their reasonable value would stultify, or at best transform, the contractual protection. Thus, a minor who buys luxuries on credit is immune from any action on the contract.

---

[96] *Sale of Goods Act, 1979*, s. 2.
[97] *Nash* v. *Inman* [1908] 2 K.B. 1, 8, *per* Fletcher Moulton, L.J.; cf. *Pontypridd Union* v. *Drew* [1927] 1 K.B. 214, 220, *per* Scrutton, L.J.
[98] *Roberts* v. *Gray* [1913] 1 K.B. 520.

He is completely protected.[99] Superimposition of a rule to the effect that, on refusal to pay, he must incur a liability on the *Planché* v. *Colburn*[1] model would reduce his protection to no more than control of the price exigible from him.

(ii) *Money received.*

Where money is received by way of a loan, and *incapax* can rely on his incapacity to resist any action on the contract, the same argument applies as was made in the last paragraph. A non-contractual claim would make nonsense of the incapacity since its content would be identical to that arising under the loan and would lead to precisely the same judgement. *R. Leslie Ltd.* v. *Sheill*[2] and *Sinclair* v. *Brougham*[3] show that such claims must be defeated. They make the point in the language of implied contract. But that must be understood as no more than a rhetorical way of saying that the law cannot impose obligations whose effect would contradict the conclusions of the law of contract. In *R. Leslie Ltd.* v. *Sheill* the loan was void under s. 1 of the *Infants Relief Act, 1874,* and in *Sinclair* v. *Brougham* the same conclusion followed from the doctrine of *ultra vires* in respect of deposits with a bank, which for present purposes are not distinguishable from loans.

Where money is received under a contract for some performance other than the payment of money the position is less clear. There is no absolute contradiction between refusing actions on the contract and allowing restitution of the money, since here the two species of action will give different measures of recovery. Nevertheless, in *Cowern* v. *Nield*,[4] a claim of this kind failed against a minor. The plaintiff had paid for clover and hay. The defendant delivered no hay, and clover in such bad condition that it was rejected. The Court of Appeal allowed the minor to plead his contractual incapacity to the claim based on total failure of consideration. But a new trial was ordered since the court's opinion was that the action could succeed if the plaintiff could prove fraud: in that event the claim would be 'in substance *ex delicto*', in which case the contractual incapacity would not apply. The case again assumes that there are only two heads of liability to be considered.

In relation to the doctrine of *ultra vires* the contrary conclusion

---

[99] *Infants Relief Act, 1874*, s. 1; *Nash* v. *Inman*, cit., n. 97, above.
[1] Above, p. 232.
[2] *R. Leslie Ltd.* v. *Sheill* [1914] 3 K.B. 607.
[3] *Sinclair* v. *Brougham* [1914] A.C. 398.
[4] *Cowern* v. *Nield* [1912] 2 K.B. 419.

has been reached. In *Re Phoenix Life Assurance Co., Burges' and Stock's Case*[5] the company had accepted premiums for *ultra vires* policies of marine insurance. The claim to recover these for failure of consideration was upheld. In *Sinclair* v. *Brougham* there was some hesitation about this case,[6] but the difference between the law for companies and the law for minors can be defended on the ground that the minor though enriched by the receipt of the money needs to be protected against claims made after he has wasted it. At the moment his protection takes the form, in effect, of a presumption that he has changed his position after receiving the money, and this presumption can be rebutted only by tracing it into the purchase of necessaries or the discharge of other binding obligations.[7]

Where the ground for restitution is not failure of consideration the picture is less clear. In actions against companies their receipt of money by mistake, pressure and so on would probably never be *ultra vires* and the defence of incapacity would therefore not arise. *Cowern* v. *Nield* approaches the view that minority is no defence to a restitutionary claim based on a wrong. Lord Kenyon so held in 1794 in *Bristow* v. *Eastman*,[8] though the rule must be subject to the proviso that the claim must not be so implicated in a contract as to be no more than an attempt to circumvent the contractual protection. There are dicta in *R. Leslie Ltd.* v. *Sheill* to the effect that in all other cases infancy has always been an answer to any count in *indebitatus assumpsit*.[9] But these are thinly supported and vitiated by contract theory.

Bristow v. *Eastman* itself was a case of embezzlement where a young apprentice had been trusted by his employers to make payments out and had pretended to pay more than in reality he had paid. In retrospect it can be seen as a case in which the plaintiffs did not have to rely on the wrong.[10] It was simply money subtracted from them without their knowledge. On this analysis the case would point towards allowing liability even for mistake. A further argument towards the same conclusion is that the receipt of a mistaken payment is not a transaction requiring judgement of a kind which an inexperienced mind may lack. Hence if capacity is a defence it can only be explained by the bare hardship of repayment . The best

---

[5] *Re Phoenix Life Assurance Co.* (1862) 4 J. & H. 441.

[6] *Sinclair* v. *Brougham* [1914] A.C. 398, 414, 440.

[7] See n. 92 above and *Nottingham Permanent Benefit Building Society* v. *Thurstan* [1903] A.C. 6.

[8] *Bristow* v. *Eastman* (1794) 1 Peake 291; 1 especially 171.

[9] *R. Leslie Ltd.* v. *Sheill* [1914] 3 K.B. 607, 612, 621, 626.

[10] Above, p. 140 f.

solution would certainly be to allow restitution even in the first measure but subject to a liberal defence of change of position.

6. BONA FIDE PURCHASE

A restitutionary claim can, in some circumstances, be defeated by a defendant who shows that he acquired the subject-matter for value in good faith, without notice of the facts entitling the plaintiff to his claim. This defence arises, if at all, for recipients from the person against whom a restitutionary claim first comes into being. Suppose I pay you money by mistake and you hand it on to X. Here X, and people subsequently receiving from him, may somewhat loosely be described as 'third parties'. Such third parties may be able to use this defence. But clearly they will not need the defence unless they are first under a *prima facie* liability.

(i) *Who incurs a* prima facie *liability as a third party recipient?*

It is as well to say at once that we are not here concerned with another species of third party liability, namely that of the man who, by guilty participation, makes himself an accessory to a breach of equitable duty.[11] That accessory liability is based directly on the defendant's misconduct. It does not depend on the receipt of any enrichment and it cannot properly be described as restitutionary. We are only concerned with a recipient's liability *qua* recipient. But it is obvious that a recipient may also be an accessory; and that fact may become important in any case in which the liability *qua* recipient is barred or where proof of the greater moral improbity required for accessory liability will give a larger measure of recovery.[12]

The question whether a defendant did receive the enrichment cannot be determined impressionistically. Suppose my bank overpays me by £10 000 and next day, to celebrate my good luck, I give you my old car. Here it is true that indirectly you are the beneficiary of the bank's unintended generosity; but you incur no *prima facie* liab-

---

[11] *Barnes* v. *Addy* (1874) 9 Ch. App. 244, 251; cf. *Belmont Finance Corporation* v. *Williams Furniture Ltd. (No. 1)* [1979] 1 Ch. 250, 264 f, *(No. 2)* [1980] 1 All E.R. 393, 405, 412.

[12] Thus, a merely ministerial recipient may have a defence once he has paid the money received to, or on the instructions of, the beneficial recipient, but the ministerial recipient may, none the less, remain liable as a guilty accessory if sufficiently guilty knowledge is found in him: see below, p. 445.

ility whatever, because none of the bank's money can be traced to you. The rules of tracing have to be applied in order to identify the arrival in your hands of the money first received by me from the bank.

But tracing is not enough. It is also essential that, while the subject-matter was in the hands of the first recipient, the plaintiff should have had in relation to it a right *in rem*. Such a right will commonly be vested ownership, but can be something less, such as a power to revest after tracing or rescission. But if at that time the plaintiff had only a claim *in personam* against the first recipient, whether measured by the enrichment received or the enrichment surviving or both, then the second recipient will have received the subject-matter free of all claims. In short identifiability of the subject-matter in its passage to the defendant is not enough: the plaintiff must also have a proprietary interest in the matter so identified. An extreme example will serve to illustrate this. Suppose my bank lends me £10 000. I take the loan in £100 notes. Borrowed money belongs to the borrower. As I move from the counter and before I have in any other way disturbed the notes just received from the bank I give the top ten of them to you, a present of £1000. You take that money free of any claim from the bank. Identifiably the same notes, that £1000 was none the less mine to spend, and the bank must confine its attention to its personal claim against me. If it was wise it will have taken some real security too, though in subject-matter other than the notes lent.

This example of a loan has implications for payments by mistake and for other payments giving rise to restitution. Suppose the mistake is not sufficiently fundamental to prevent the property passing. The effect will be that a third party recipient will take the coins or notes free of any claim, just as with the loan just discussed. Similarly in the case of payment for a consideration which fails. If a plaintiff has paid me £5000 for work to be done and I have repudiated the contract and passed the very same £5000 on to you, that plaintiff's claim against you must fail. For the property in the money passed to me under the contract just as would the property in goods if goods had been transferred; and repudiatory breach does not give rise to rescission *ab initio* but only termination *de futuro*.[14] Hence the title cannot be revested when the breach is accepted. The money was, therefore, matter in which the plaintff had no interest. Even though it has been traced to you, the fact that it has identifiably arrived in your hands has no legal consequences.

---

[14] But see p. 387 above for doubts based on the equitable treatment of failures of consideration.

(ii) *What liability does the third party recipient incur?*

If there is subject-matter traced to the defendant and it is matter in which the plaintiff has a proprietary right, the defendant may, as a third party recipient, be liable in either of the two basic restitutionary measures: either for the value traced as arriving in his hands or for the value still surviving in his hands. The claim in the first measure will necessarily be *in personam* as are all claims which need to ask no questions about what the defendant still retains. The claim in the second measure can, in principle, be *in personam* or *in rem*. Since the plaintiff cannot reach the third party at all without showing that he had a right *in rem* while the *res* yet rested in the earlier recipient's hands, this is not a situation in which it is impossible for a court to recognise a claim *in rem* with its attendant priorities.

The last paragraph sets out the range of possible liabilities. Their actual incidence must depend primarily on the availability of the defence of *bona fide* purchase. Since the defence's primary requirement is the giving of value it can never avail a donee, sometimes called a 'mere volunteer'. ⋆32

(iii) *The Position of the Donee*

Unable to use this defence, the donee ought to be liable in both measures. Nor is there any doubt about the second measure: what the donee has left. In *Banque Belge pour L'Etranger* v. *Hambrouck*,[15] the defendant, Hambrouck, abstracted money from the plaintiffs without their knowledge. He paid it into his own bank account and then transferred it to the account his mistress had with Barclays. The Court of Appeal held that the plaintiffs were entitled to the balance of the mistress's account which had been paid into court by Barclays. If the plaintiffs' money lost its identity at law in passing through the account at Hambrouck's own bank, nevertheless, in equity it remained identifiable. Hence the plaintiffs had at least a right which courts of equity would have recognised at the moment at which the money arrived at the mistress's account. No other money had been paid in; so the plaintiffs were entitled to the balance. The case does not, however, say whether the mistress could have been made liable in the

---

[15] *Banque Belge pour l'Etranger* v. *Hambrouk* [1921] 1 K.B. 321.

first measure, for the value received. In *Re Diplock*[16] by contrast the wrongly paid charities were made liable in both measures. But the case is not strong authority for a general liability in donees to repay the full amount received. The reason is that the personal liability in that measure was evidently regarded as a peculiarity of the law relating to the administration of estates and further that it was made subject to the exhaustion of remedies against the personal representatives. This second limitation has been strongly and rightly doubted.[17]

Despite the weakness of *Re Diplock* in this regard the correct position is that even an innocent donee is personally liable in the first measure. If he were not, his position would be inexplicably different from that of an innocent first or immediate recipient of a mistaken payment. Like that recipient, the donee receives another's money without that other's free consent. Why then should the donee's liability be confined to the second measure while the innocent first payee must repay even after he has spent all the money? Another analogy points in the same direction. If my car is stolen and is sold down a chain of innocent buyers I can obtain damages for any one of these innocent conversions, and I can have restitution of the price obtained instead of compensation.[18] Nor is there any suggestion that my right to a restitution should depend on the innocent seller's retention of the price obtained or some part of it.

In *G. L. Baker Ltd.* v. *Medway Building and Supplies Ltd.*,[19] the auditor of the plaintiffs had been entrusted with a fund belonging to them and had fraudulently paid some of it to the defendants, a company of which he was a director. The question was whether the plaintiffs could recover that sum irrespective of its retention by the defendants. In other words, were the defendants personally liable for the amount received? The defendants proposed to fight on the ground of their innocence, thinking that their want of knowledge was sufficient to defeat the personal claim even when value had not been given. Danckwerts, J., refused to allow a last minute amendment which would have allowed them to switch from a defence of 'no notice' to the defence of *bona fide* purchase. On the basis that they were innocent donees, he found them liable, simply on the ground of having received money belonging to another. The Court of Appeal allowed the pleadings to be amended and ordered a new trial. The Court took the view that counsel for the defendants had reason-

---

[16] *Re Diplock* [1948] Ch. 465.
[17] *Goff and Jones*, pp. 452–3.
[18] Above, p. 246 f.
[19] *G.L. Baker Ltd* v. *Medway Building and Supplies Ltd.* [1958] 1 W.L.R. 1216.

ably believed that the plaintiff's claim was based on constructive trusteeship arising out of the knowledge on the defendants' part as to the provenance of the funds received by it. It clearly thought that a *Diplock* claim in the same measure, independent of knowledge, was sufficiently a novelty to allow counsel to escape blame for not anticipating it. Nevertheless it did not say that Danckwerts, J., had been wrong except in disallowing the amendment of the pleadings.

Hence we must affirm that a donee recipient from one who held wealth in which the plaintiff had a right *in rem* does incur a liability to make restitution to the plaintiff in this first measure. He cannot plead *bona fide* purchase because, *ex hypothesi*, he has not given value. The ground of recovery, going to unjust, will be 'ignorance', the receipt from the first recipient being from the plaintiff's point of view an example of receipt 'without knowledge' not substantially different from receipt by secret stealing or by chance finding.

(iv) *The position of recipients for value*

At common law the giving of value makes no difference in relation to property in goods even when it is given honestly and without notice. If I innocently buy your car and then sell it, my innocent giving of value will not help me. It is the same in equity if I myself obtain for value only an equitable interest as opposed to the legal estate. But at common law property in money behaves differently. For one thing, legal title to money quickly becomes inexigible because the law soon renounces all attempt to maintain its identifiability. For another, quite apart from the issue of identifiability, legal title is lost when the money is taken by someone who gives value in good faith. In equity, a *bona fide* purchaser of a legal estate for value without notice always takes free of equitable interests whether in money or other things.

If it is correct that a donee incurs a liability in both restitutionary measures, the same ought to be true of a recipient who has given value except in the cases just mentioned where the value has been given without notice. On general principles 'without notice' should be taken to mean that he lacked both actual and constructive notice or, adapting the words of s. 199 of the *Law of Property Act, 1925*, that the facts were not within his own knowledge and would not have come to his knowledge if such inquiries and inspections had been made as ought reasonably to have been made. In *Nelson* v. *Larholt*[20] the defendant had cashed cheques for an executor, drawn

---

[20] *Nelson* v. *Larholt* [1948] 1 K.B. 339.

on the estate's bank account. He thus obtained money from the estate in exchange for value given. Denning, J., none the less held him liable to make restitution of the full amount received. It was not said that he had been dishonest in the sense that he had actual knowledge that the executor was defrauding the estate, but the facts put him on inquiry. He ought to have gone more carefully into the matter. Very thin explanations had been offered by the executor as to why he wanted the cheques cashed by the defendant rather than by a bank in normal hours. The defendant pleaded *bona fide* purchase for value. Denning, J., simply said that good faith was not enough if the defendant had notice of the misapplication; and, as to notice, it was enough that he knew or ought to have known.

This needs to be glossed by the *ratio* of *Carl Zeiss Stiftung* v. *Herbert Smith & Co (No.2)*.[21] In that case the defendants were solicitors who had been paid money by their clients on account of fees and disbursements. When they received those sums they knew that the plaintiffs claimed to be entitled to all the property of their clients. So they had received funds for value in the knowledge that those funds were subject to an adverse claim, albeit one of complexity, which their clients strenuously contested. The Court of Appeal held that notice of a doubtful claim could not make them liable to pay back the money even in the event that the claim was ultimately successfully vindicated in court. Hence, differently from *Nelson* v. *Larbolt*, the recipients for value had no effective notice.

This is quite consistent with the position taken by Denning, J., in *Nelson* v. *Larbolt*, but there are *dicta* in *Carl Zeiss* to the effect that the liability to make restitution in the measure 'value received' depends on proof of something more than notice in the sense just set out. In other words it is suggested that that liability does not attach in every case in which the defence of *bona fide* purchase is excluded, but only in those in which there is in addition an element of dishonesty or moral improbity.[22] However, those observations must be taken to apply only to the accessory liability referred to at the beginning of this section. They cannot apply to the third party recipient's liability, which, where value has been given, requires only such knowledge as will defeat the defence of *bona fide* purchase. Thus, recently, in *International Sales and Agencies Ltd.* v. *Marcus*[23] Lawson, J., held that a recipient who received beneficially, as opposed to merely ministerially as or in the role of agent, would be liable to repay the full amount received if an ordinary reasonable man in

---

[21] *Carl Zeiss Stiftung* v. *Herbert Smith & Co. (No. 2)* [1969] 2 Ch. 276.
[22] At pp. 298, 301.
[23] [1982] 3 All E.R. 551; cf. *Belmont*, n. 11, above.

his position, and with his attributes, ought to have known of the relevant breach of fiduciary duty. So, constructive notice in the sense of s. 199 of the *Law of Property Act, 1925* was sufficient. In that case, Marcus, who had lent money to an individual who controlled the plaintiff company, received repayment after the borrower's death. The repayment was arranged by a friend and collaborator of the deceased. The friend, a director of the company, was able to divert the company's money to the repayment. Despite giving value in the form of discharge of the debt, Marcus was liable to make restitution to the company, and his liability required only constructive notice of the money's provenance. That is to say, it required only such knowledge as will defeat the defence of *bona fide* purchase.

It may be that when the third party recipient does receive ministerially and not beneficially he will not be liable in the first measure of restitution unless he displays the higher degree of wickedness called for *obiter* in *Carl Zeiss*. If so the correct explanation may be that his liability *qua* recipient is barred by a defence of change of position analogous to that which is available to an agent who has paid over his principal,[24] and that, with that liability barred, only accessory liability remains in play. Alternatively it might be said that a requirement of greater wickedness on the part of ministerial recipients is explicable on the ground that, even without reference to accessory liability, this particular manifestation of the defence of change of position is available to the merely careless, but not to the dishonest. Yet it is also possible that the ministerial recipient will not in fact be treated any differently from the beneficial recipient, so that his liability will after all turn, not on improbity, but only on constructive notice sufficient to defeat the defence of *bona fide* purchase. That harsher view was preferred by Ungoed-Thomas, J., in his very careful review if the cases in *Selangor United Rubber Estates, Ltd.* v. *Cradock (No. 3)*.[25]

(v) *Are third parties really third parties?*

In the midst of case-law which does not speak with one voice, the position taken in these last pages has been that, leaving on one side ministerial recipients and non-recipient accessories, the third party recipient incurs a liability in both restitutionary measures and that he does so irrespective of knowledge. That is, even an innocent recipient

---

[24] Above, p. 412–13. 'Ministerial receipt' is a form of words apt to describe, adjectivally, a receipt 'by an agent', and agents are the one category of recipient with an assured, though specialised, defence of change of position.

[25] *Selangor United Rubber Estates Ltd.* v. *Cradock (No. 3)* [1968] 1 W.L.R. 1555.

incurs not only the liability for what he has left but also the liability for what he received. The exception is that knowledge does become relevant where the defendant seeks to rely on the defence of *bona fide* purchase. If the circumstances are otherwise right for that defence, only the recipient with notice can be liable. One reason for holding that this picture is correct is the belief that, analytically, the 'third party' is not properly so described: his position is actually indistinguishable from that of the immediate recipient from whom he himself receives. If that is right he must bear the same liabilities.

As a matter of factual observation the 'third party' recipient can, obviously, be distinguished from the immediate recipient. I pay you £100 by mistake, and you pass the same £100 on to X. Clearly you are the first to incur a restitutionary obligation in respect of that £100, and X is, factually, a subsequent recipient from you. But, analytically, his liability depends on the existence of my right *in rem* in that money. It follows that he is in the position of one who intercepts wealth to which I am entitled, myself being ignorant of the transfer to him. This is so whether the right *in rem* exists by survival from before the events in question, in which case it is not itself a restitutionary right, or is newly created by those events, in which case it is restitutionary. Either way, the receipt by the subsequent recipient cannot be distinguished from receipt by the first recipient: both are enriched by subtraction from me, and the transfer in both cases alike is non-voluntary.

This appears even more clearly in relation to goods. Suppose that you take an ounce of caviar from me and eat it. If we blot out the possibility of any recourse to the law of tort, the question whether, as immediate recipient, you must make restitution, can be approached through non-voluntary transfer. That will encounter the routine difficulty: your benefit being in kind and not in money it is your right to say, contradicting the opinion of the market, that to you this was worth less than decent fish-paste. This argument on the issue of enrichment will shift the inquiry into free acceptance: did you sufficiently know what you were doing? If you did the conclusion that you must pay can be expressed wholly in terms of free acceptance or, equally, in terms of non-voluntary transfer *quoad* the issue of 'unjust' and of free acceptance *quoad* the issue of enrichment.[26] But suppose now that instead of eating my caviar you gave it as a present to your friend and he ate it. Factually, he is a third party. That is undeniable, but analytically the questions which arise against him are exactly the same as those which arose against you as first recipient. He too has received something by subtraction from me, my caviar. Again, there-

[26] Above, p. 267.

fore, we have to ask whether, on the facts, the caviar was to him an enrichment. If yes, was it received in circumstances calling for its reversal? (Was it 'unjust'?) Again, the answers turn on non-voluntariness and free acceptance. It follows that any inquiry into the liability of a 'third party' must start by recognising that the probability is that that liability will be the same in nature and extent as the liability of the first recipient, subject only to the possibility that subsequent recipients may sometimes be able to take advantage of the defence of *bona fide* purchase. When they have that defence, they extinguish my property in the *res* by and at the moment of their receipt. And the destruction of my interest in the thing carries away with it my restitutionary rights in both measures, since, obviously, the nature and purpose of the defence of *bona fide* purchase for value without notice is to allow the recipient who comes within the terms of the defence to take his enrichment free of all adverse claims. On the other hand, when recipients do not come within the terms of the defence, they must become liable in the same measures and degrees as anyone who, *invito domino*, takes or finds another's *res*. In the normal case, therefore, there is no question, once the defence is excluded, of having to establish the recipient's guilty knowledge or 'improbity' even in relation to liability in the first measure of restitution.

The same conclusion must apply where the subject-matter is money. For what can be clearly demonstrated in relation to goods cannot but hold good for money too. For throughout the law of restitution the only operative difference between the receipt of non-money benefits and the receipt of money is (if all other facts remain constant) that money is incontrovertibly enriching and other benefits almost invariably leave room for arguments on that issue. Hardly anything is more important for the future development of Restitution than that the cases should in future expose and analyse those arguments and make clear the law's position in relation to them.

ENDNOTES

1. p. 11: *misuse of 'restitution' and 'compensation'*

Just as 'restitution' is sometimes misused to mean 'compensation', so also, vice versa, 'compensation' is found in the sense of 'restitution', e.g. in the statutory regimes for tenants' improvements discussed in the note 21 to p. 294, below; also somewhat surprisingly in *Pavey and Matthews* v. *Paul* by Deane, J. ((1987) 69 A.L.R. 577, 604, lines 19–20; 605, line 17; and 607, lines 19, 25).

2. pp. 34–9, with 78, 112, and 270–6: *the emancipation of restitution from implied contract, the nature of quantum meruit and its place in the Limitation Act 1980*

This note provides an opportunity not only to introduce an important new case but also to redress a misjudgment. It is a weakness of the text at pp. 34–9, where the subject is the emancipation of restitution from false dependence on contract, that it fails to survey the difficulties, much greater than those of money had and received, which had to be surmounted by the 'request counts'—*quantum meruit, quantum valebat,* and money paid—before they could do non-contractual work in tandem with the count for money had and received. The reason for this omission lay in a mixture of fear of too great complexity and anxiety about re-inforcing the historical divisions according to the nature of the benefit received (text, p. 78). For, subject of course to the difficulty of establishing enrichment by a receipt in kind, the modern law of restitution must be, universally, about value received, not one law for money, one for goods, yet another for services, and so on. Nevertheless, maturer reflection suggests that the material at pp. 112 and 270–6, so far as it is concerned with the emancipation of the request counts from contract, ought to have been introduced at pp. 34–9 even if later to be partly repeated. To that material, with *William Lacey* and *Sabemo,* there must be added what is now the the most thorough judicial examination of the history (albeit in one respect flawed), namely *Pavey and Matthews Pty. Ltd.* v. *Paul* ((1987) 69 A.L.R. 577—High Court of Australia; (1985) 3 N.S.W.L.R. 114—N.S.W. Court of Appeal; brilliantly discussed by D. Ibbetson, 'Implied Contracts and Restitution: History in the High Court of Australia', (1988) 8 *Ox. J.L.S.* 312, and J. Beatson, 'Unjust Enrichment in the High Court of Australia', (1988) 104 *L.Q.R.* 12). *Pavey* was a case of building work completed under a contract which was unenforceable for want of writing under section 45 of the *N.S.W. Builders Licensing Act, 1971.* The client was entirely satisfied with the work but thought the price being asked was too high. This squarely raised the question whether, behind the unenforceable contract, there was a another non-contractual cause of action and, if so, whether the policy of the Act would allow recourse to that cause of action. Both questions were answered in favour of the builder, who was accordingly allowed his restitutionary *quantum meruit.* The judgments, especially that of Deane, J., are of first importance not only for the history of the emancipation of the request counts but also for the analysis of enrichment and the handling of restitutionary claims to limit the effects of failure of formal requirements, so far as permissible in the light of the policy of the Act in question.

   A related aspect of the nature of *quantum meruit* came up recently in *Amantilla Ltd.* v. *Telefusion p.l.c.* ((1987) 9 Constr. L.R. 139), a decision of Judge John Davies,

Q.C., the Official Referee. Was a duty to pay the reasonable value of work a debt? The plaintiff claimed *quantum meruit* for building and shopfitting more than six years after completion. The question was whether the claim was saved by a payment and an acknowledgment made by the defendants in the meantime, as it would be if this was an action for 'any debt or other pecuniary claim' within s. 29 (5) of the *Limitation Act, 1980*. It was held that it was, because, analytically, a *quantum meruit* was different in kind from claims in the opposite category, namely claims to unliquidated damages, and was sufficiently certain for the court to quantify it by calculation and circumstantial evidence, and because, historically, *quantum meruit* had been absorbed by *indebitatus assumpsit*, into which the action of debt had itself been emptied.

Given the absence from the *Limitation Act* of any perfectly suitable category, the analytical ground is a reasonable enough basis for a reasonable conclusion; but the history is more complicated. The judge followed Farwell, L.J., in *Lagos* v. *Grunwaldt* ([1910] 1 K.B. 41, 48), but Farwell, L.J., does not there commit himself to the view that *quantum meruit* was a species of debt, only that practice in relation to the *indebitatus* counts made the special count for *quantum meruit* obsolete. In fact claims to *quantum meruit* were not debts, not being for a fixed sum. But there have been several flirtations with the contrary view. (See D. Ibbetson, (1988) 8 *Ox. J. L.S.* 312, 316.) This was also the point that eluded the High Court in *Pavey* v. *Paul.*.

3. pp. 114–28: *enrichment, free acceptance as a test compatible with 'subjective devaluation, Beatson's challenge in the case of pure services received.*

Both for the tests of enrichment here propounded and in handling the enrichment issue in relation to the different grounds for restitution it will now be necessary for the reader to take a position on a thoughtful contribution by J. Beatson which is critical of the line taken in the text (J. Beatson, 'Benefit, Reliance and the Structure of Unjust Enrichment' (1987) 40 *C.L.P.* 71–92, cf. Beatson, [1988] 104 *L.Q.R.* 12, 16). In essence he says (a) that pure services cannot be counted as enrichments to their recipients unless they are incontrovertibly beneficial in the sense of saving necessary expenditure (in which case the enrichment consists not in the service but in the store of exchange-value not laid out); (b) that pure services which are not incontrovertibly beneficial but merely freely accepted therefore cannot be enrichments at all; and (c) that non-contractual claims in respect of such services in consequence ought not to be brought within the law of restitution/unjust enrichment by use of an over-inclusive, and fictitious, concept of enrichment but should be dealt with in a category of law concerned with making good reliance-losses.

These 'pure services' are, in his words, 'those with no marketable residuum in the hands of the recipient but an increase in his human capital (as where a teacher gives a lesson to an able pupil), and . . . those where there is neither a marketable residuum nor increase in human capital (as where an actor or musician performs his art or where the teacher's lesson falls on deaf ears)' (40 *C.L.P.* 71, 72). He regards *Planché* v. *Colburn* (text, pp. 126, 232, 241–4) as a paradigm example of a case inexplicable within restitution. His position is strengthened by the fact that Goff and Jones appear to have moved in the same direction (see their third edition, pp. 26, 466, 510; also G. H. Jones, 'Claims arising out of Anticipated Contracts which Do not Materialize', (1980) 18 *U.W. Ontario L.R.* 447).

This has to be met at two levels. First, and very important, there is the question of symmetry between restitutionary claims in respect of money and non-money. Historically there have been deep divisions (and compare the Scots law separation, since Stair, of restitution and recompense), but, now that pleading does not depend on forms of action, logic dictates that the law must be the same for all value received, whether that value is received in money (and would have yielded an action for money had and received) or in kind (and would have yielded a claim for *quantum meruit* or *valebat*). This theoretical symmetry could not be abandoned or brought into question even if it were demonstrated that in practice it would only be in a tiny number of cases that receipt of non-money would be counted as receipt of value. What is at stake is nothing less than the generalization of the action for money had and received to become the action for money or money's worth received, something that might have been achieved in 1770 if *Nightingal* v. *Devisme* (5 Wm.Bl. 684) had been allowed to go the other way. So the first point is this: Beatson's argument, though it might be read as an invitation to revert to the old divisions by subject-matter received, does not in fact impugn this theoretical symmetry, or universality, of the whole law of restitution for value received. This is proved by his acceptance that a service can be an incontrovertible benefit and as such valuable. His argument strikes only at a lower level: with pure services, the number of cases in which there can actually be a finding of value received is dramatically less than others have thought. Whence relief for the person who has performed such services must come, not in restitution, but in compensation for reliance-losses.

Less important, because not threatening to the logical structure of the subject, is the question whether he is indeed right in saying that a pure service freely accepted is never value received. There is a semantic preliminary, of which neither he nor I have been sufficiently wary: we should not get bogged down in the dictionary meanings of enrichment, wealth, value and so on but rather ask whether a pure service received can ever be the equivalent of money received—money's worth, though not money—because, if it can, it is that which gives practical content to the theoretical symmetry supported above, and it is that to which I would wish to give the name 'enrichment' for the purposes of this subject. So, in this sense, can a pure service freely accepted be value received or money's worth received or enrichment received (all synonyms)? This requires a sustained argument, but here can have only a more or less dogmatic response.

In my view Beatson both underestimates the implications of the subjectivity of value and overplays the usefulness, as an indication of enrichment, of 'exchange-value and transferability' (40 *C.L.P.76*). The latter alone threatens to exclude from the category of enrichments received all short-term consumables such as a drink in a glass or a meal on a plate; and even the discharge of a debt is only saved from exclusion by focusing on the stock of exchange-value saved (p. 77). The two together inexorably exclude virtually all cases where one person has the use of another's time but no marketable residuum when the work is done. Yet there must be something wrong, since this exclusion contradicts the facts of daily life: if we gauge money's worth by money spent, there is no denying that much of our money is spent precisely on people's time, and when command of that time leaves nothing behind, or nothing marketable, what we have bought is a pure service in Beatson's terms.

Suppose Mr. and Mrs. X, on their wedding anniversary, having both been in the morning to the hairdresser, take a taxi to the opera and, afterwards, another to a restaurant for dinner. For these treats they had saved £500, and with that money they commanded the time of hairdressers, taxi-drivers, musicians, cooks, and waiters. (The meal was not a *pure* service, but still it cannot be distinguished.) They might, if more eccentric, have paid the same sum to have people polish the leaves in their garden and paint their coal white. Their money would still have commanded the time of others; and, for them, by virtue of the use made of their freedom to choose, that useless work would then have been money's worth or, subjectively, value received (cf. (1985) 5 *L.S.* 67, 73–5).

Given, as this story illustrates, that contracts are largely about buying people's time for money, it is difficult to accept any theory of value received which denies that outside contract one person's time devoted to another cannot, unless it saves an inevitable outlay, be money's worth to that other, such that it can be said of him that he was as much enriched as if he had received a given sum of money. Hence, in the upshot, the right course seems to be to defend the view that the logical symmetry between restitution for money and for non-money can and does have a practical yield, even in the case of pure services, wherever the argument from subjective devaluation is obstructed, whether by an objective 'no reasonable man would deny' test or by a sufficiently free acceptance by the recipient.

Nevertheless, Beatson is entitled to invoke the old historical divisions in his support as having a wisdom which we challenge at our peril, with further support from the line between restitution and recompense in the Scots system. Further, Scots law does use another distinction which echoes his argument, namely that between *quantum meruit*, how much he (the worker) deserved, and *quantum lucratus*, how much the other was enriched (*Ramsay & Son* v. *Brand* (1898) 25 R. 1212; *Steel* v. *Young* 1907 S.C. 360; *Graham & Co* v. *United Turkey Red Co.* 1922 S.C. 533). Further, *B.P.* v. *Hunt* and the statutory regimes for tenants' improvements seem also to support him. Formidable weaponry, but in my view fighting a lost and backward-looking cause. As will appear below, free acceptance has come under a double attack. Here Beatson denies its utility in the proof of enrichment; Burrows, who also denies the usefulness of free acceptance as a test of enrichment, goes further and challenges its efficacy as an unjust factor, i.e. as a ground for restitution (see below, note **18** to pp. 265–80).

4. *p. 120: enrichment, the 'no reasonable man' test, the necessity of necessary expenditure*

In a case in which an invalidly appointed receiver and manager was allowed his expenses following *Craven-Ellis* v. *Canons Ltd.*, the penultimate paragraph of this page was approved: *Monks* v. *Poynice Pty. Ltd.* (1987) 11 A.C.L.R. 637, 640 (Supreme Court of N.S.W.).

5. *pp. 147–8: mispredictions, the choice between mistake and failure of consideration*

One kind of misprediction has recently been prominent, and it is necessary here to show that, so far as it does give rise to restitution, it does so for failure of consideration, not for mistake. A series of cases culminating in *Barder* v. *Caluori* ([1988] A.C. 20), all admittedly from a highly specialized context, vividly illustrate the kind of facts which cause the difficulties: in a divorce an order is made for transfer from one spouse to another of valuable property, typically the former matrimonial home; then circumstances change dramatically, so that the purpose of the transfer is subverted. In *Barder* itself, for instance, the wife killed the children and herself; the home in which they were to live, which the husband was being forced to give up for that purpose, would have accrued to the wife's next of kin. A way has in fact been found to undo some of these disasters: when the transfer is ordered by the court and the change of circumstances happens very soon and at all events before third-party rights have intervened, leave is given for an appeal out of time and the order itself is then reviewed in the light of the new evidence. Translated to normal transfers between parties, is this restitution for misprediction?

The text says that a claim for restitution cannot be founded on a misprediction (i.e. a misjudgment as to what will happen in the future). It should have been careful to keep emphasizing that no claim for restitution *for mistake* can be so founded, because of course if a transferor expressly specifies and communicates the future events on which a transfer is conditional, no longer merely predicting but requiring those events and qualifying his intent accordingly, he can claim, not for mistake, but for failure of consideration or basis (cf. text, p. 219). To recognize implied specification of the basis of a transfer is obviously dangerous, for, unless the implication be absolutely clear in content and strictly a genuine inference from conduct, it threatens to blur the line between restitution for mistake and restitution for failure of consideration. Nevertheless, some facts do call for treatment on those lines, and *Barder* provides a good example. But, so far as the result there can be translated into normal restitutionary terms so as to produce the same results after a similar transfer between parties, it must be firmly classified as restitution for failure of basis (i.e. of the basis impliedly specified), not restitution for mistake. Otherwise it would be difficult to explain to anyone why restitution should not always follow when any risk turns out badly.

The obvious danger of uncertainty in implied specification of basis cannot be met on the facts of *Barder* by the notion that the transfer was impliedly conditional on the recipient's surviving, or remaining single or alone or poor, for some given short period, say at least one year. That would be arbitrary and absurd. But it would not be intolerable to say that, since the implied basis was that the house should be the family home for an unspecified but substantial time, the transferor should be allowed restitution when essential expectations are falsified within a period that no reasonable man could describe as making good the basis of the transfer. Restitution on a ground similar to this has recently been illustrated in *Muschinski* v. *Dodds* (see below, note **14** to pp. 225–6).

6. pp. 149–59: *liability mistakes, fundamental mistakes and causative mistakes; mistakes and counter-restitution; economic analysis by Beatson and Bishop*

In *Australia and New Zealand Banking Group Ltd.* v. *Westpac Banking Corporation* (21 Apr. 1988, F.C. 88/014, as yet unreported) the facts resembled *Barclays Bank* v. *Simms* (text, pp. 151–2). An A.N.Z. customer authorized transfer of $14,158.00 to Westpac for the credit of Westpac's overdrawn customer, Jakes; A.N.Z. made a clerical error and transferred $114,158.20. The High Court of Australia affirmed, in line with a concession from Westpac, that 'the notion of "fundamental mistake" does not require either that the mistake be shared by the payee or that the mistake be as to a fact which, if it had existed, would have resulted in the payee being under a legal obligation to make the payment'. But, as for the crucial choice between fundamental and merely causative mistakes (text, pp. 156–7), the court showed itself sensitive to the importance of the question but, because of Westpac's concession of *prima facie* liability, found itself able to postpone an answer. Thus the passage just quoted continues: 'That having been said, it is preferable to leave for another day consideration of the question whether the requirement that the mistake be fundamental involves any more than that it appears that, without the mistake on the part of the payer, the payment would not have been made.' The case, apart from also containing a useful statement of the modern understanding of the nature of the claim, is especially important for its handling of Westpac's successful defence, which cut its liability to a mere $17,021.68 (see below, note **28** to pp. 410–15).

The observation in the text at p. 152 that a transfer of value under a liability mistake rarely entails any problem of counter-restitution remains true, but the rare case eventuated in *Films Rover International Ltd.* v. *Cannon Film Sales Ltd.* (reported at first instance at (1987) B.C.L.C. 540, but of much greater interest on appeal, as yet unreported). The project was that Rover would dub and distribute Thorn EMI films in Italy, first paying substantial sums in advance and then taking a share of the receipts. Thorn EMI was taken over by Cannon, who proceeded to look around for a pretext to break with Rover. Eventually they found two, a technical repudiatory breach by Rover in relation to the release of a film called *Highlander* and, more dramatically because rendering the contract void *ab initio*, the failure of Rover's promoters to incorporate the company until weeks after the contract purported to have been made. Cannon pushed home its advantage, aiming *inter alia* at 100 per cent of the receipts earned and to be earned from the Italian distributions made possible by Rover's work. Rover riposted with a claim to restitution of its advance payments and of the reasonable value of its work in doing the dubbing and arranging the distribution. There is an obvious structural similarity to *B.P.* v. *Hunt* (text, p. 249 f.), though this contract was void from the start and no help was available from the *Law Reform (Frustrated Contracts) Act, 1943*.

Rover's work and payments were transferred under a liability mistake (*cf. Craven Ellis* v. *Canons Ltd.*, text, p. 159): they believed they were acting under a valid contract. Nevertheless, it was undeniable that they had received some benefit, namely the use of the films to convert and distribute. Yet the claim succeeded, both on the ground of mistake and on the alternative ground of failure of consideration. The Court of Appeal was able to evade the counter-restitution problems by holding (*per* Kerr, L.J.) that the use of the films was not a relevant benefit, not a benefit bargained for but an incident of and means to the benefits which had been bargained for.

We shall return to this below in the context of failure of consideration. The case contributes to other major issues too, notably the question of a contractual ceiling to a non-contractual *quantum meruit*, the question of symmetry between grounds for restitution of money and benefits other than money, the availability of a defence of change of position, and, in an associated appeal by a company called Proper Films Ltd., the question whether a party in breach can recover pre-payments.

Notable among academic contributions on restitution for mistake is an important article by J. Beatson and W. Bishop, 'Mistaken Payments in the Law of Restitution' ((1986) 36 *U. of Toronto L.J.* 149–85), the first to review this area of law in the light of an economic premiss, namely that the rules should minimize the social cost of mistakes. This is shown to be a fruitful means of demonstrating insensitivities in

English law and allows the authors to argue for the necessity of, *inter alia*, acknowledging the relevance of fault—Scots law does this to a degree they would probably find too extreme: the mistake must be excusable (see *Taylor* v. *Wilson's Trustees* (1979) S.L.T. 105)—a new approach to mistakes of law, and a dynamic defence of change of position. Illuminating as this style of argument is shown to be, it is necessary to recall, especially in restitution which has had to defend itself against those who believed the phrase 'unjust enrichment' invited arguments from abstract principles of justice, that arguments from economics are of the same uncertain kind, not easily related to the greater complexities comprehended within the artificial structure of legal authority. Many lawyers will have some sympathy with the response of R. J. Sutton 'Mistaken Payments: An Inner Logic Infringed' ((1987) 37 *U. of Toronto L.J.* 389–412) which defends the place of traditional modes of legal scholarship.

7. pp. 160–1: *analysis of* Bell v. Lever Brothers; *discovery of a duty to disclose defaults*

The text depends heavily on a particular interpretation of *Bell* v. *Lever Brothers* which is not univerally accepted, a contrary view being that the mistake was so serious in Bell that the effect of the decision is in practice to warn that, except perhaps for instances of *res extincta*, contracts will never be void at law for common mistake. But in *Associated Japanese Bank International Ltd.* v. *Credit du Nord SA* ((1988) 138 N.L.J. Rep. 109) Steyn, J., did hold a contract void at law, and he followed an interpretation of *Bell* similar to the one relied on in the text, emphasizing the fact that Lever were bargaining for Bell and Snelling's co-operation at a sensitive juncture. There were no immediate restitutionary issues before Steyn, J. The void contract was a guarantee by the defendants of the obligations of one B under a sale and leaseback of machinery, under which B had obtained, by the sale to the bank, some £1m., to be repaid under the lease. In fact the bank had been defrauded; the machines did not exist. Hence the question whether the defendants' guarantee could be enforced and the conclusion that it was void.

This welcome rehabilitation of *Bell* v. *Lever Bros.* does not alter the fact that, however good a guide on matters of principle, the decision on its own facts has been undermined to a large extent by *Sybron* (text, p. 161), with which should also be read, for further comment on the very slight factual differences which would have put Bell and Snelling under a duty of disclosure, *Horcal Ltd.* v. *Gatland* ([1983] I.R.L.R. 459, affirmed [1984] I.R.L.R. 288 though without further discussion of this point).

8. pp. 184–5, with 204–8: *the distinction between actual and presumed undue influence, 'domination' in the latter; the requirement of ex facie disadvantage not explicable by ordinary motives; infection from pressure exerted by a third party*

The scheme of the text depends here on a division of undue influence between actual, treated as a species of compulsion, and presumed, treated as an example of relational inequality not connoting compulsion on the independent side so much as a dropping of the guard on the other. This division was threatened by language used in *National Westminster Bank p.l.c.* v. *Morgan* ([1985] A.C. 686) the early reports of which could just be noticed in the text: see pp. 206–8. In particular Lord Scarman drew on quotations which referred to 'domination of the will' ([1985] A.C. 586, 706–9). This language came home to roost in *Goldsworthy* v. *Brickell* ([1987] 1 Ch. 378), where Robert Pryor, Q.C., founded an argument for the defendant upon it: 'Following the decision in . . . *Morgan* the burden is now on the plaintiff to prove that, at the time of the tenancy agreement, he was under the domination of the first defendant so that the plaintiff did not enter the agreement of his own free choice . . . the judge expressly found that the relationship was well short of domination. Domination may be proved either directly by showing that the victim's will was in fact overborne . . . or indirectly by establishing that the relationship was such that it could properly be inferred that the victim was to be taken to be under such domination . . .' ([1987] 1 Ch. 378, 385). If this was right, all instances of undue influence would have to be analysed as forms of compulsion. But it was held to be wrong.

The plaintiff, fit in mind and body but already 85 in 1977 and on bad terms with his son, had become dependent on his neighbour, the defendant, for the running of his Oxfordshire farm. In the end he granted him a tenancy at a low rent and with an option to buy the freehold, such that he effectively halved the capital value of the farm in his hands. The Court of Appeal upheld Goulding, J.'s conclusion that this was voidable for undue influence because of the nature of the relationship between the parties, the crucial elements of which were the old man's dependence on Brickell, the power the latter had in the two things that chiefly mattered to his happiness, namely the farm and the problem with the son, and, finally, the failure to overcome the old man's reluctance to listen to legal advice. The Court of Appeal explained *Morgan* as not having intended to narrow the concept of undue influence to domination, something that could not have been done without expressly overruling several cases, the chief of which was *Tufton* v. *Sperni* ([1952] 2 T.L.R. 516). A petition to appeal to the House of Lords was refused.

Another factor given new prominence by *Morgan* and not brought out in the text is that the presumption of undue influence is not generated only by the quality of the relationship but requires also that the victim be shown to have acted to his disadvantage to a degree not immediately explicable by ordinary motives of friendship, charity, or so on. In *Goldsworthy*, Goulding, J., had not articulated this requirement, but, in the light of the fact that the tenancy agreement had reduced the plaintiff's wealth by some 50 per cent, the Court of Appeal had no difficulty in asserting that he must have treated it as selfevidently satisfied. But it was easy, before *Morgan*, to underemphasize this element.

In *Coldunell Ltd.* v. *Gallon* ([1986] 2. W.L.R. 429) a son in need of money had used actual undue influence on his very aged parents to compel his father to raise money on a mortgage of his home and to make his mother sign a form consenting to the charge. The plaintiffs were the mortgagees, aiming to exercise their power of sale after the son had let his parents down by paying only the first few instalments of interest. Were the mortgagees infected by the son's undue influence, so that their charge became voidable? They were not, because they had not made the son their agent to act for them, nor had they, in a looser sense, left matters in his hands. Further, the transaction (which was in other respects perfectly normal) was not extortionate within the meaning of ss. 137–8 of the *Consumer Credit Act, 1974*, because, even though s. 171 (7) of the Act reversed the onus of proof, once the mortgagees had shown that they had not used undue influence, which they showed by establishing that the son was not their agent, they had, given the *ex facie* normal terms of the transaction, discharged the onus of proving that it did not 'otherwise grossly contravene ordinary principles of fair dealing'.

It was the fact that the son had not been made the agent of the lender for the purpose of getting the parents to execute the charge that distinguished this case (cf. *Bank of Baroda* v. *Shah, The Independent*, 6 Apr. 1988) from two rather similar ones which were decided the other way, namely *Avon Finance Co. Ltd.* v. *Bridger* ((1979) [1985] 2 All E.R. 281 and *King's North Trust Ltd.* v. *Bell* ([1986] 1 W.L.R. 119).

9. pp. 194–202, with 304–8: *emergencies,interventions under moral compulsion and interventions for reward; salvage inland and the limits of admiralty jurisdiction*

The facts of *The Goring* ([1988] 2 W.L.R. 460 H.L., affirming [1987] Q.B. 687 C.A.) provided a rare and golden opportunity, if only the House of Lords had been inclined to take a wider view, to consider all the law relating to claims by people who intervene in emergencies and to review both the true meaning of *Falcke* v. *Scottish Imperial Insurance Co.* (text, p. 194 f.) and its relationship with the law of salvage in the admiralty jurisdiction and under statute.

The *Goring* is a large pleasure steamer used by Salters for trips on the Thames near Reading. Shortly before midnight on 14 September 1984 she came adrift and, unmanned, was in danger of colliding with other moored boats and ultimately of going over Reading weir. The plaintiffs, members of a club based on an island in the river at that point, managed to board her and secure her. They sought remuneration for salvage services. The owners applied to have the claim struck out, failed before Sheen, J., but succeeded in the Court of Appeal, the Master of the Rolls dissenting; the House of Lords then upheld· the Court of Appeal's decision, on the straightforward but not very satisfying ground that the salvage jurisdiction in admiralty did not extend beyond tidal waters. The absence of analysis of *Falcke*—there are routine citations of famous *dicta* in the Court of Appeal but no reference at all in the House of Lords—is explicable, even if disappointing. For, as Ralph Gibson, L.J., pointed out, albeit obliquely, this was not a case in which an action for restitution would have yielded anything, since the plaintiffs had suffered no expense, neither in money paid out nor in remunerative, but unremunerated, work.

The real disappointment is the lack of anything substantial to weigh against Sir John Donaldson, M.R.'s failure to find a reason behind the restriction: 'In the end I believe that I have to seek a rational basis of confining the cause of action to tidal waters and I can find none. It is, of course, a maritime remedy and the public policy considerations which support it are directed at commercial shipping and seagoing vesels. But that said, I can see no sense in a cause of action which will remunerate the salvors of an ocean-going vessel inward bound for Manchester up to the moment when the vessel enters the Manchester Ship Canal, but no further. Some of the perils facing the vessel in the canal may be different from those facing it at sea, but many, such as fire, will be the same. The need to encourage assistance otherwise than under contract may be greater at sea, but the skills required of the salvors will be the same or at least similar' ([1987] Q.B. 687, 706–7).

10. pp. 204–5: *inequality as a ground of liability and inequality as an organizing concept; the requirement of exceptional inequality and the superadded requirement of equitable fraud (unconscientious exploitation)*

National Westminster Bank p.l.c. v. *Morgan* ([1985] A.C. 686, 707) contains remarks by Lord Scarman against the formation of a general principle of relief for inequality. The observations are directed especially to the law of contract and made in reaction against Lord Denning's attempts at synthesis in *Lloyds Bank* v. *Bundy* ([1975] 1 Q.B. 326). It is as well to underline the fact that the present chapter does not seek to formulate, indeed opposes, such a 'general principle'; it only uses the concept of inequality as a super-category within which to assemble a number of more manageable heads, arranging them according to the source of the special inequality— relational, transactional, or personal—which impairs the weaker party's ability to judge the wisdom of his dispositions. I do not think this merely organizational use of the concept falls foul of the objections to generalization which were in Lord Scarman's mind. That is, it does not throw tolerably well-understood categories into a melting-pot in which limits can no longer be discerned. Nevertheless, it is not to be denied that even an organizing concept has its consequences, because, as an interpretation of known entities, it points in the direction in which others of the same kind may be found. In other words the categories organized cannot but become less closed. But that is neither threatening nor new: 'The classic example of an unconscionable bargain is where advantage has been taken of a young, inexperienced or ignorant person to introduce a term which no sensible well-advised person or party would have accepted. But I do not think the categories of unconscionable bargains are limited; the court could and should intervene where a bargain has been procured by unfair means' (*Multiservice Bookbinding Ltd.* v. *Marden* [1979] Ch. 84, 110, *per* Browne-Wilkinson, J.).

Alec Lobb (Garages) Ltd. v. *Total Oil (Great Britain) Ltd.* ([1985] 1 W.L.R. 173) involved a plea of inequality founded on facts which certainly did not arise under the first or third headings in the text (relational, p. 205, or personal, p. 216) but could be viewed either as seeking to extend the more open-ended second category (transactional, p. 208) or, illustrating the point made in the last paragraph, as pointing to innominate cases beyond these three heads. (*Quaere* whether some of these would not be best comprehended if 'circumstantial compulsion' were brought in here, from p. 203, as a fourth category of inequality.) The plaintiffs, already 'tied' to the defendants and falling into ever more desperate financial problems, negotiated a rescue operation the core of which was a fifty-one-year lease of their garage to the defendants for a £35,000 premium and at a peppercorn rent, with a twenty-one year leaseback at a rent of £2,500 and a tie for the whole term. This recapitalization was largely unsuccessful, but the package allowed the plaintiffs to limp on. After ten years they sought, unsuccessfully, to escape it, on the grounds that it was void for restraint of trade or voidable in equity under the head of inequality.

In the Court of Appeal it was held that any equitable relief for which they might have qualified had been lost by their laches. Their laches apart, would they have qualified? Their case, in the words of Dunn, L.J., was that they were under a compelling necessity to find financial help and that misconduct by the defendants was not a pre-requisite of their entitlement to relief: 'The fact of their impecuniosity, that they were already tied to the defendants by mortgages, that there was no other source of finance, that they could not sell the equities of redemption without giving up trading, coupled with the knowledge of the defendants of those facts, rendered the transaction unconscionable, and placed the onus upon the defendants to show that its terms were fair and reasonable' ([1985] 1 W.L.R. 173, 189). This argument failed for two distinct reasons.

First, supposing they succeeded *in limine* and were *prima facie* entitled to relief for inequality, still they had to show that the stronger party had 'used his strength unconscionably' ([1985] 1 W.L.R. 173, 183, *per* Dillon, L.J.). This is a theme to which we shall return in connexion with *Hart* v. *O'Connor* and personal disadvantage, below. Secondly, they had anyhow failed to cross the threshhold of exceptional inequality so as to trigger even a *prima facie* entitlement to redress. Dillon, L.J., pointed out that inequality was omnipresent and that the courts would only interfere in 'exceptional cases where as a matter of common fairness it was not right that the strong should be allowed to push the weak to the wall' (*ibid.* cf. text, p. 204). And Dunn, L.J., said more brusquely, 'Mere impecuniosity has never been held a ground for equitable relief' ([1985] 1 W.L.R. 173, 189). This reinforces the fact that routine inequalities will not do; the threshhold is not crossed until there is an inequality which is exceptional, identifiable and unacceptable to exploit.

11. pp.207–8: *the nature of relational undue influence: vulnerable relationships*

National Westminster Bank p.l.c. v. *Morgan* ([1985] A.C. 686) and *Goldsworthy* v. *Brickell* ([1987] 1 Ch. 378) have been discussed in the context of compulsion, where the question was whether even relational undue influence has to interpreted as grounded in compulsion or rather, as in the text, on inequality arising from vulnerability and dependence. *Goldsworthy* recalls the law from the beginnings of an attempt to insist on the element of compulsion through use of the word 'domination' (see above, notes to text pp. 184 ff).

12. pp. 216–17: *personal disadvantage: the Minors' Contracts Act, 1987*

The *Minors' Contracts Act, 1987* simplifies the law in a number of ways, chiefly by 'disapplying' the *Infants Relief Act, 1874* and thus eliminating the category of absolutely void contracts. But, though it has important effects on claims by the adult against the minor (see below note **31** to pp. 432–9), the Act does nothing to improve the minor's chance of obtaining restitution after executed transactions, as where from inexperience he sells at an undervalue. Here, if he can take nothing from *Chaplin* v. *Frewin* ([1966] Ch. 71), the minor's hope lies in equitable relief against unconscientious advantage taken of people who, to a marked degree, are not able to stand up for themselves (*cf. Fry* v. *Lane*, immediately below. It is convenient, though not felicitous, to discuss the *Fry* relief as being for 'inadequates').

13. p. 218: *personal disadvantage: mental incompetence, inadequacy*

The current policy favouring care in the community over institutionalization is likely to increase the incidence of dealing by people unable to protect their own interests. The Judicial Committee's recent reaffirmation of the traditional approach to mental incapacity assumes greater importance against this background. But the law cannot yet be said to be clear. Those who part with wealth when mentally incompetent have two relevant paths to restitution, the first specifically for their incapacity to understand the nature of their acts, and the second as members of the larger class of inadequate persons entitled to equitable relief under *Fry* v. *Lane* ((1888) 40 Ch.D. 312). So far as concerns the first, one might have expected the modern trend to run in favour of relief based directly on the inability to understand (which would be in harmony with the law's position in other contexts where consent is needed: see recently *Re K.* and *Re F.* [1988] 1 All E.R. 358, *R.* v. *Hall* (1988) 86 Cr. App. R. 159). Indeed, as we shall see, the New Zealand Court of Appeal made a move in that direction. But the earlier orthodoxy, which requires not only the inability of the one party to understand but also knowledge on the part of the other of that incapacity and exploitation of it, has been reasserted. So long as this is insisted on, it will be impossible to make sense of the wider *Fry* v. *Lane* relief without giving a new emphasis to a requirement there too of knowing, and therefore reprehensible, exploitation of the disadvantaged party. Otherwise relief for the severer disadvantage, outright inability to understand, will be more difficult to obtain than for the less severe, which we are calling 'inadequacy'.

It was in *Hart* v. *O'Connor* ([1985] A.C. 1000) that the J.C.P.C. rolled back a new approach by the courts of New Zealand. An old farmer suffering from senile dementia but still the sole trustee of the family settlement sold the family farm to Hart, who farmed other land in the neighbourhood, for a price which was on the low side though set by an independent valuer. There had been long anxiety, as the old man's condition worsened, about what was to be done, and the initiative for the sale came largely from the solicitors who acted for the O'Connors and also for Hart. There was no suggestion that Hart knew of the mental incompetence of the vendor. He dealt always with the solicitors. The N.Z. Court of Appeal took the view that the transaction of a mentally incompetent person could be set aside not only if the other party knew that the mentally incompetent party could not understand the nature of what he was doing—of this there was no question—but also if the contract was unfair. And under this second limb the N.Z. court allowed rescission. The J.C.P.C. held that that was wrong. If the sane party did not know of the mental incompetence of the other, there could be relief only for equitable fraud, i.e. for procedural unfairness by the sane party, not for contractual imbalance (= not for the fact that the mental incompetent had made a bad bargain). The J.C.P.C. clearly did envisage the possibility of circumstances in which the incompetent's transaction would be voidable even though the other did not know of his condition. Yet, apart from matters such as undue influence which have no particular application to mental incompetence, it is not immediately easy to construct examples in which, innocent of that crucial knowledge, the other would none the less be guilty of equitable fraud.

This can be tested by comparison with *Ayres* v. *Hazelgrove* (9 Feb. 1984, 1982/NJ/ 1003, unreported), which was decided by Russell, J., shortly before *Hart* v. *O'Connor*. There an old and disoriented lady, suffering from advanced senile dementia, was visited by the defendant twice when she was alone at home. The upshot of their conversations was that she parted with six oil paintings, together with other items, for £390, about one-hundredth of their later valuation. Russell, J., allowed rescission on the ground, first, that the defendant did know of the vendor's inability to understand the nature of what she was doing. Then, secondly— independently and precisely because the first finding of fact might have been assailable—he came to the same conclusion by looking at the matter as an unconscionable bargain within the equitable doctrine in *Fry* v. *Lane*, as restated by Megarry, J., in *Cresswell* v. *Potter* (text, p. 218; compare two cases from N. Ireland: *Conlon* v. *Murray* [1958] N.I. 6 (C.A.) and *Buckley* v. *Irwin* [1960] N.I. 98).

Crucial to Russell, J.'s conclusion under this head were the undervalue, the knowledge on the defendant's part that he was getting a good bargain, the fact that the old lady was visited when alone and without advice, the virtual certainty that she would have manifested signs of her condition (even if, on this hypothesis, not sufficiently to make the defendant aware of its seriousness). The facts were thus of a different colour from those in *Hart*, and it cannot be seriously maintained that the J.C.P.C. would have decided *Ayres* differently even on this second hypothesis of fact. Yet, so long as one adheres to this hypothesis (that the defendant did not know of the vendor's incompetence), the words of their Lordships' advice, requiring procedural malpractice, do not encompass Russell, J.'s result quite as easily as one might wish. Can it be procedurally unfair to drive home a good bargain with an adult thought to be of sound mind? To match the second ground of Ayres with Hart, we would have to affirm that there is procedural unfairness within the meaning of *Hart* v. *O'Connor* whenever the *Fry* v. *Lane* conditions are satisfied, that is, where someone deals with an inadequate and, having so dealt, cannot show—the onus being reversed—either that that person was independently advised or that the bargain was, as was said in *Fry*, 'fair, just and reasonable'. But the element of deeming which is evident in this only highlights the problem. In order to see the vice genuinely in terms of procedural malpractice as *Hart* v. *O'Connor* insists, we are therefore compelled to add a further requirement of facts calculated to alert the stronger party to the need to restrain the normal bargaining process or, put objectively, facts calculated to create a suspicion in a reasonable mind that the other party is, to a marked degree, unable to cope with the normal bargaining process. Only then can one make a genuine finding of procedural unfairness—exploitation of weakness as well as contractual imbalance—in behaviour that will otherwise look like no more than driving home a good bargain. In *Ayres* itself on the second hypothesis as to the facts, Russell, J.'s findings could certainly have supported such an inference of procedural unfairness, and the same is true of the two Northern Ireland cases mentioned above (*Conlon* and *Buckley*).

In summary, we have to say that, short of actual knowledge of the other's want of understanding, the mental incompetent's relief on the wider ground of inadequacy nevertheless always requires some indication of equitable fraud, which means 'an unconscientious use of power arising out of the circumstances and conditions' (*Earl of Aylesford* v. *Morris* (1973) L.R. 8 Ch. App. 484, 491, *per* Lord Selborne, L.C.). This extra requirement of procedural unfairness or equitable fraud, seemingly necessitated by *Hart*, is supported in related categories of inequality by *Morgan* and *Lobb*.

The alternative approach would be to assert that, even though the class of inadequates is larger than and necessarily includes the insane, yet the *Fry* equitable relief for inadequacy is different in kind from the law's relief for insanity and is based solely on the facts of the personal disadvantage and the undervalue. But this goes back, as it cannot now safely do, to the repudiated position of the New Zealand Court of Appeal. So far as any question mark may legitimately remain, it is partly because the old cases did regard it as possible to infer the equitable fraud from the weakness on one side and the under-value, without further evidence of unconscientiousness, and partly because that approach does yield a better measure of protection for those who, by reason of personal disadvantage, are, to a marked degree, inadequately equipped for the management of their affairs. (In *McCrystal* v. *O'Kane* (1986) 18 N.I.J.B. 1, decided after *Hart* v. *O'Connor*, Murray, J., though refusing on the evidence to accept the defendant's story of alcohol-induced mental incompetence, would evidently have been willing at least to refuse specific performance of his contract to convey his farm to his nephew if the price, which was indeed disadvantageous, had been so low as, in his view, to raise a presumption of fraud.)

14. pp. 225–6: *failure of consideration: transfers for the purposes, societies and movements, surplus and dissolution; mandates and joint ventures; implied specification of purpose.*

The text needs much more detail on transfers for purposes. For the moment it is only possible to add to the difficulties already compressed into these pages those which are implicit in *Conservative and Unionist Central Office* v. *Burrell* ([1982] 1 W.L.R. 522). A transfer to an unincorporated association can usually be explained on the model of *Re Recher's Will Trusts* ([1972] Ch. 526); but in *Burrell* it appears that, if someone subscribes to a movement or party which (a) is unincorporated, (b) happens not to have a membership bound together as an association, and (c) exists for abstract purposes, i.e. for purposes whose execution does not redound to the benefit of ascertained human beneficiaries and cannot therefore take advantage of *Re Denley's Will Trust* ([1969] 1 Ch. 373), that subscriber must be taken to give his money to the recipient officer of the movement personally, subject to a 'mandate', which here means no more than an authority coupled with a contractual duty, to apply it to the purposes of the movement. Brightman, L.J., saw 'no legal difficulty in the mandate theory' ([1972] 1 W.L.R. 522, 540). On the same page he says the subscriber's money cannot be demanded back once it has been mixed in the movement's fund (which fund is, of course, vested in the officer himself). But this must have been said on the assumption that the movement remains active and in being.

Suppose it collapses. Collapse of an unincorporated association holding on the *Recher* model means distribution to the members, since dissolution of the association is precisely the termination of the contract previously tying down property already vested in themselves and, the contract gone, nothing therefore stands between the members and their own: *In re Buckinghamshire Constabulary Widows' and Orphans' Friendly Society (No. 2)* ([1979] 1 W.L.R. 936). Does the collapse of a 'movement' mean the collecting officer takes all, free of the 'mandate'? A resulting trust for the subscriber is ruled out as incompatible with the manner of the officer's holding while the movement was yet in being: on the assumption of an abstract purpose as under (c) above, it would imply a trust void *ab initio*, precisely what the courts' ingenuity seeks to avoid. Hence restitution by resulting trust can be ruled out. But a claim for failure of consideration is not incompatible with the mandate theory of the original holding, so long as it can be shown that all or some of the subscriber's money remains unapplied. (*Quaere* whether this would be covered— semble, no—by Brightman, L.J.'s example at 529 d–f.)

Where the giving, whether or not in the context of a party or movement, is on the basis that the sum shall be committed to a purpose which is not abstract (that is, where its execution will redound to the benefit of ascertainable individuals so that there can be a valid trust), a choice has to be made, formally as a matter of construction, between on the one hand a trust absolutely for the benefit of those individuals subject only to an unenforceable wish that the purpose be pursued (*Re Lipinski's Will Trusts* [1976] Ch. 235; *Re Osoba* [1978] 1 W.L.R. 791), in which case the purpose ceases by construction of law to be the basis of the giving and its failure has no legal consequences at all, and, on the other hand, a trust for the class of beneficiaries restricted to the purpose specified (*Re Denley*, above), in which case failure of the purpose should produce a resulting trust for the donor. The Quistclose trust was one species of example (*Barclays Bank Ltd.* v. *Quistclose Investments Ltd.* [1970] A.C. 567).

Recently *Re EVTR* ([1987] B.C.L.C. 646, C.A.) produced an interesting variation on the Quistclose theme, though ultimately with the same result. The appellant, Barber, won a large prize with a premium bond and agreed to support a friend's ailing business, run through the company EVTR. He released £60,000 to the company 'for the sole purpose of buying new equipment'. The Court of Appeal was clear that at that stage, if that purpose had been frustrated, there would have been a Quistclose resulting trust. But in fact the money was paid out to the supplier, Quantel, and another company, Concord, which was going to help finance the deal through a leaseback arrangement. Then EVTR's bank put in a receiver, and the company ceased to trade. Quantel and Concord repaid about five-sixths of the money, retaining the rest for loss suffered through EVTR's withdrawal. Could the appellant claim that these repayments were held on trust for him? The Court of Appeal said yes. Dillon, L.J., identified two crucial factors. First, the purpose which was the basis of Barber's giving was the actual acquisition, not the ordering of, the equipment; secondly, having held the original £60,000 on trust, the company had to be subject to the same trusts in respect of its proceeds, which proceeds were now the sums repaid. That must be right. The judgments do, however, contain some more doubtful *dicta* on alternative factual hypotheses.

An Australian case on a purpose which failed makes a major contribution to this field and to the wide concept of failure of consideration the recognition of which is advocated in the text. *Muschinski* v. *Dodds* ((1986) 60 A.L.J.R. 55) was a case of resources transferred for the purpose of advancing a joint venture which had to be abandoned without fault on either side. The plaintiff and the defendant had entered on a joint project, both personal and commercial, to buy a piece of land, build a house for themselves on it, also to run a craft business there and, in order to raise extra capital, sell off some building plots carved out of it. Title was taken in equal shares in common, but the necessary money nearly all came from the plaintiff, Mrs. Muschinski. The idea was that Mr. Dodds's contribution would be made in the form of work, with, in addition, an expectation of some capital injection when his divorce was settled. The substratum of the venture collapsed when planning permission turned out to be unobtainable and, in reaction, the personal relationship began to deteriorate.

After the couple split up, the High Court held, Brennan and Dawson, JJ., *diss.*, that, the presumption of resulting trust in proportion to contributions having been rebutted, there would be a constructive trust under the terms of which, before sharing the surplus equally in accordance with their stated shares, they would first recover their contributions to the purchase. Deane, J., with whom Mason, J., agreed, saw the relevant doctrine as failure of basis: 'The circumstances giving rise to the operation of the principle were broadly identified by Lord Cairns, L.C., speaking for the Court of Appeal in Chancery, in *Atwood* v. *Maude* (1868) 3 Ch. App. 369, 375): where "the case is one in which, using the words of Lord Cottenham in *Hirst* v. *Tolson* ((1850) 2 Mac. & G. 134; 42 E.R. 52) a payment has been made by anticipation of something afterwards to be enjoyed [and] where . . . circumstances arise so that that future enjoyment is denied." Those circumstances can be more precisely defined by saying that the principle operates in a case where the substratum of a joint relationship or endeavour is removed without attributable blame and where the benefit of money or other property contributed by one party on the basis and for the purposes of the relationship or endeavour would otherwise be enjoyed by the other party in circumstances in which it was not specifically intended or specially provided that the other party should enjoy it. The content of the principle is that, in such a case, equity will not permit that other party to assert or retain the benefit of the relevant property to the extent that it would be unconscionable for him to do so' (60 A.L.J.R.55, 67).

This, as was suggested above, has direct bearing on the *Barder* pattern of facts discussed above (see note **5** to pp. 147–8), though not, of course, so long as the transfer is made by the order of a court. *Atwood* v. *Maude*, which is heavily relied upon, was a case in which the plaintiff had paid a premium to the defendant for a partnership of seven years. The relationship between them broke down, without fault. The court, showing itself determinedly flexible, allowed the plaintiff restitution of a part of the premium proportionate to the unexpired time.

15. pp. 236–42: *failure of consideration, rights of the party in breach to recover money*

The question whether a party in breach of contract can recover an advance payment was examined in *Films Rover International* (note **6** to pp. 149–59) in the Court of Appeal's judgment on the associated appeal of Proper Films Ltd. Proper had negotiated a licence to show films on Italian television. The contract required payment in advance, making punctual payment essential. The last instalment was late, and Cannon terminated the contract and claimed payment of the unpaid $900,000. Proper fought on the proposition that, had the money been paid, it would in the circumstances have been recoverable. The Court of Appeal held that it would have been and was therefore not due: *frustra petis quod mox es restituturus* (You claim in vain that which you will shortly be restoring). The payment had not been required by way of a sanctioning deposit and it was not referable to any consideration actually performed by Cannon. The advance was therefore covered by *Dies* rather than by *Hyundai* (see text, p. 237). In view of the rough handling of *Dies* in *Hyundai* it was highly desirable that it should be made clear that it is a question of construction in every case to determine which of the two, both right, governs the advance in question.

16. pp. 238–42: *failure of consideration, party in breach: non-money benefits; rights of such party when the other does not terminate the contract.*

In *Nye Saunders and Partners* v. *Bristow* ((1987) 37 Building L.R. 92) the plaintiff architects claimed some £15,000 on a *quantum meruit* for drawing up plans for the remodelling of the defendant's mansion. The defendant had made clear from the start that he had £250,000 to spend on the project; and, before being engaged, the plaintiffs had submitted a written estimate for £238,000. The defendant terminated the project and dismissed the plaintiffs when it appeared, some six months after they had been engaged, that the actual cost was likely to be nearly double the estimate. These events happened during the 1973–4 inflation, and the plaintiffs had failed to build in any allowance for escalation of cost during the contract period. They had also not told the defendant that the estimate included no allowance for inflation. The Court of Appeal confirmed the refusal of the *quantum meruit* below. In both courts it was regarded as conclusive that the estimate had been a clear case of negligence within *Hedley Byrne* v. *Heller* ([1964] A.C. 465). The plaintiffs could have been made liable for the loss thereby caused. Thus it appears that this too was a case of *frustra petis* (above), though this time the maxim operated against the party seeking restitution.

In *Nye* the court regarded the contract as having been quite properly terminated by Bristow. Whether it was terminated for breach (despite the fact that the default began non-contractually because there was no contract between the parties at the time the estimate was put in) or by the operation of a condition giving the defendant a right to withdraw if the price ceiling was broken, it must be a decisive answer to the *quantum meruit*, cross-claims for negligence apart, that the plaintiff's fault had deprived the defendant of the entire benefit intended to enure to him from their work, so that a finding that he had been enriched was, on any view of that contentious matter (see note 3 to pp. 114–28), impossible. A different conclusion might have been necessary if, subsequently, the defendant had reactivated the project and had used the plans prepared by the plaintiff, since there would then have been (*pace* Burrows, note 8 to pp. 265–80, below) a free acceptance on a par with that of the loose materials in *Sumpter* v. *Hedges* (text, p. 239).

Much more difficult are the *dicta* relevant to restitution in *Miles* v. *Wakefield Metropolitan District Council* ([1987] A.C. 539), where the party in breach had done work for which he had not been paid. It was a case in which superintendent registrars had been taking industrial action by refusing to perform marriages on Saturday mornings. The plaintiff continued to go in on Saturdays to do other work, even although the Council made clear to him that if he would not perform marriages then they did not wish him to come in at all. The Council stopped the 3/37ths of his salary referable to his Saturday hours. Applying the ordinary law of the contract of employment despite the special position of his office, the House of Lords rejected his claim for the unpaid salary. Lord Brightman and Lord Templeman thought that, if the Council had accepted the work offered, Miles could have had a *quantum meruit*; Lord Bridge thought not, and Lord Oliver and Lord Brandon left the question open.

That *quantum meruit* would be difficult to explain. In a note on the case Sales approves of the *quantum meruit* and says it would be based on a clear case of free acceptance (P. Sales, 'Contract and Restitution in the Employment Relationship', (1988) 8 Ox. J. L.S. 301, 307.) He adds that the contract of employment in the background provides no reason of principle why the free acceptance should not operate. But this ignores the well-established principle that restitution is not available so long as the relationship between the parties is governed by a valid and undischarged contract (text, p. 47, *Goff and Jones*, 3rd ed., 31–2). In this kind of situation the employer who does not dismiss is thereby keeping the original contract in being. Even if this principle did not obstruct, it would be a question whether, with one contracting party refusing full performance, the other could possibly be described as freely accepting the partial performance, which is the difficulty adverted to in the text, at p. 240. This is a case in which, if difficulties with sufficiency of consideration could be overcome, it might be better to work out a contractual rather than restitutionary explanation of the *quantum meruit*.

17. pp. 245–48, with 424: *failure of consideration, benefits compatible with 'total' failure.*

In *Films Rover International* (note **6** to pp. 149–59) Rover had received a benefit, the use of films for dubbing and distribution, which was held not to obstruct their claim to recover for work done and money paid on a total failure of consideration. Reliance was placed on *Chitty on Contracts* (25th ed., vol. 1, para. 1964) for the proposition that, because that use of the films was not the benefit bargained for but merely incidental to the intended benefit, its receipt did not prevent there being a total failure of consideration, and this was said to be the right explanation of the *Rowland* v. *Divall* line of cases too (see text, p. 248). But that explanation will not really do, because of the problem of counter-restitution. Even an incidental benefit should not be retained as a windfall by a plaintiff seeking restitution. The answer is not to bar the claim to restitution for want of counter-restitution but to allow for counter-restitution in money, very easily done on these particular facts by reducing the *quantum meruit*. *Rowland* is different: the defendant could be barred from counter-restitution because the benefit—use of a *res aliena*—was not one that he had any right to confer.

This interpretation of *Rowland* seems now to be accepted by the Law Commission, which has decided to recommend no change in the relevant law. Having been tempted to eliminate the claim to restitution of the price and allow only an action for damages, or in the alternative to allow the claim to the price subject to a deduction in money for the use of the chattel, the Commission now says that the problems cannot be solved by making the buyer pay the seller for his use of someone else's goods. 'What rightful claim', they quite correctly ask, 'does the seller have, therefore, to payment for the buyer's use and possession of the goods? We are now of the opinion that a requirement that the buyer should make some allowance in this respect to the seller, rather than constitute an improvement in the law, would simply confuse it further' (*Sale and Supply of Services*, Law. Com. No. 160, Cm. 137, 1987, para. 6.4; and see generally paras. 6.1 to 6.5).

18. pp. 265–80: *nature and development of free acceptance, law and equity*

It has been noted above (note **2** to pp. 34–9) that *Pavey and Matthews* v. *Paul* now provides an excellent account of the nature of the claim for reasonable remuneration (*quantum meruit*) and of its emancipation from contract. The case clearly belongs in the discussion in the text, from p. 270.

The operation of free acceptance has proved controversial. Beatson, as we have seen, criticizes its use as a test of enrichment (note **3** to pp. 114–28). In 'Free Acceptance and the Law of Restitution', shortly to be published in 104 *L.Q.R.* and read in an earlier version to the restitution group at the Cambridge S.P.T.L. (September 1987), Burrows, no less sceptical than Beatson in relation to the issue of enrichment, also doubts its efficacy as as an 'unjust' factor. Every case, he would say, involves a request or actual encouragement or else an independent 'unjust' factor from the field of non-voluntariness (such as the mistake in *Weatherby* v. *Banham*, text, p. 269); by contrast none bases recovery on a pure free acceptance and, certainly (as can be freely conceded), none uses the language of free acceptance. On this view the 'clear and simple example' on p. 265 is anything but: the window-cleaner even here should bear the risk he ran. But I am minded to adhere to the position in the text. The person who knows a benefit is being conferred on him and secretly lies by, apart from being squarely within the *dicta* in *Falcke* and *Leigh* v. *Dickeson* which sum up the effect of the older cases, is not satisfactorily distinguishable from one who accepts offered goods by taking them in (see *Stevens* v. *Bromley* and text, pp. 288–9). *Anchor Brewhouse Developments Ltd.* v. *Berkley House (Dockland Developments) Ltd.* might seem to suggest the contrary. There an owner who knew construction cranes were being erected and then were swinging over his land—the jibs have to be allowed to sail freely, like a weather vane, when the cranes are not in use—and who did not immediately complain and warn, was held not to have estopped himself from subsequently initiating an action for an injunction ((1987) 284 Est. Gaz. 626, 633, *per* Scott, J.). But that was not a case of someone lying by while a benefit was conferred on him, so that there was no element of benefit freely accepted.

The Burrows picture of restitution, shorn of free acceptance and with some hardening against subjective devaluation, is not unattractive. The symmetry between claims for money had and received and for other benefits received which was insisted upon above is promoted by the elimination of the very ground for restitution into which claims in respect of non-money benefits tend to be attracted; and analysis within the field of enrichment by subtraction (exclusively in terms of vitiation, qualification, and policy-motivations) acquires a new stability. Even if free acceptance ought not to be eliminated, some of these gains could be secured by a habit of mind, already long taken for granted in claims for money received, set against recourse to free acceptance unless and until the other grounds fail (i.e. never to use the 'weak' analysis unless the 'strong' analysis has been tried).

On the equity side cases of proprietary estoppel have continued to multiply, and a point has been reached at which it is clear that the artificial line between proprietary estoppel and promissory estoppel cannot be held (see for example *Salvation Army Ltd.* v. *West Yorks. Metropolitan C.C.* (1980) 41 P. & C. 179 distinguished in *A.-G. for Hong Kong* v. *Humphreys Estate Ltd.* [1987] 2 W.L.R. 343; *Re Basham* [1986] 1 W.L.R. 1498; *Walton's Stores (Interstate) Ltd.* v. *Maher* 19 Feb. 1988, F.C. 88/105, noted by A. Duthie, (1988) 104 L.Q.R. 362). Until the problem of the fusion of proprietary and promissory estoppel is resolved, and, if fusion happens, the subsequent amalgam is satisfactorily related to contract, it is unlikely that any real progress can be made on the issue which chiefly matters to the law of restitution, namely whether it may be possible to identify and hive off those facts (the text, pp. 292–3, suggests lying by without actual encouragement) in which the equity should be satisfied by restitution, not by making good the claimant's expectations. It should be noted that this issue cannot be separated from the problems raised by Burrows as to the effect of mere free acceptance at common law.

19. pp. 283–8: *abortive negotiations; the battle of the forms.*

It is a feature of the approach used in the text that there is no heading specifically for the recurrent fact situation in which transfers are made under contractual negotiations which are unexpectedly abortive. A contract's failure to materialize not being in itself a cause for restitution, the text's assumption is that restitutionary problems thus arising will be analysed according to the general principles of free acceptance or, where appropriate, other heads of restitutionary liability. In a notable example of modern restitutionary analysis, which is also careful not to claim too much, McKendrick has recently shown how the intractable problems of the battle of the forms, exemplified by *Butler Machine Tool Co. Ltd.* v. *Ex-Cell-O Corporation (England) Ltd.* ([1979] 1 W.L.R. 401), might be worked out. If the courts abandoned the attempt to discover a contract by rigidly applying, or distorting, the rules of offer and acceptance and instead concluded that there was no contract in the exchange of contradictory standard forms, transfers made under the abortive contract could indeed be handled through non-contractual (restitutionary) request and acceptance. (E. McKendrick, 'The Battle of the Forms and the Law of Restitution', (1988) 8 *Ox. J.L.S.* 197.)

20. p. 288: quantum meruit *and the contractual ceiling.*

An issue of general importance in *Films Rover International*, introduced above (note 6 to pp. 149–59), was whether Rover's *quantum meruit* for dubbing and distributing the films should be subject to the 'contractual ceiling', to a maximum, that is, set by the amount that they would have received if the contract had not been void *ab initio* by reason of the late incorporation of Rover. The text, p. 288, takes the position that 'it is probably right to say that he cannot do better from his non-contractual claim than he could have done in contract', but in fact the Court of Appeal went the other way. Although there are some indications that this was determined by the analytical independence from contract of the restitutionary claim—a strong but not decisive argument for the Court of Appeal's position—there were also special factors: first, Cannon was asking for a special type of contractual ceiling, the amount Rover would have earned if, had the contract been initially valid, Cannon had terminated it for the technical repudiatory breach committed by Rover in relation to the release of the film *Highlander*; and, secondly, it was evident that Cannon had done everything it could to discover a pretext to break with Rover, so that it was not well-placed to argue for a ceiling based on its own unnecessary termination. This second factor clearly influenced the court, though in later cases it may prove difficult to say what weight should be attached to the fact that the defendant could, if he had been reasonable, have abstained from relying on his technical right to terminate. The contractual ceiling point could not come up in *Pavey* v. *Paul* because the unenforceable contract was itself expressly for reasonable remuneration, while in *British Steel Corporation* v. *Cleveland Bridge and Engineering Ltd.* ([1984] 1 All E.R. 504) the contract rate had never been settled. Goff and Jones, after discussing different conclusions reached by different American states, conclude in favour of the contract ceiling (3rd edn., pp. 467–8).

Burrows, not without reason, alleges (*op. cit.*, note **18** to pp. 265–80) that this position in favour of the contractual ceiling is, so far as it rests on the need to avoid undermining bargains, inconsistent with others taken by Goff and Jones and by myself, in particular with support for restitution of money paid for a (contractual) consideration which fails, even where such a claim saves the restitutionary plaintiff from a bad bargain. It may be that the rationale for the contractual ceiling is to be found, not in respect for bargains, but in the need, consistently with the subjective approach to enrichment, to accept so far as possible the parties' own valuation of non-money benefits bestowed.

21. p. 294: *policy-motivated restitution: omitted cases, the public interest in the improvement of real property*

One species of policy-motivated restitution which ought not to have been omitted is the statutory right which some tenants have on quitting to claim 'compensation' for improvements. Thus, business tenants within s. 17 of the *Landlord and Tenant Act,*

1927 can claim for an improvement which 'adds to the letting value of the holding' under s. 1, which also provides that the sum must not exceed either the net addition to the value of the holding or the reasonable cost of effecting the improvement at the termination of the tenancy, minus a deduction for whatever might be necessary to put the improvement into a good state of repair. Then, the landlord's freedom of choice is taken into account in this way, that in calculating the increase in the value of the holding regard must be had to the effect on the improvement of any change of use or even demolition which he intends (s. 1 (2)). For agricultural tenancies a not dissimilar regime is provided by ss. 64–78 of the *Agricultural Holdings Act, 1986.*

The Law Commission is currently considering this subject, though leaving aside agricultural tenancies. A recent working paper (*Landlord and Tenant: Compensation for Tenants' Improvements*, W.P. No. 102, 1987) provisionally rejects radical reform. In particular, the W.P. comes down, admitting the arguments to be finely balanced, against introducing a similar regime for residential tenancies, the case against being chiefly the need to leave landlords in control of the necessary resources—in the public sector to prevent preemption of dispositions of public money, and in the private sector to avoid adding a further disincentive to renting out (paras. 3.4–5).

The measure of recovery under the existing regime for business tenancies is examined critically but ultimately left alone. One criticism highlights the imperfectly restitutionary nature of current awards: 'The measure . . . may also be criticised because it bears no relation either to the tenant's expenditure or the loss he suffers. The present measure . . . is designed only to prevent the landlord from benefiting at the tenant's expense' (para. 4.4). But the last phrase is inept, since one distinct criticism is that 'at the tenant's expense' is not sufficiently attended to, as for instance when the tenant's claim in respect of the added value is allowed even though he has effected it with a grant from public funds (paras. 3.9 and 6.41). With agricultural tenancies that is taken into account under s. 66 (5) of the *Agricultural Holdings Act, 1986.*

The working paper brings out the policy-motivated character of these statutory rights. The common law took the view that the tenant improved with his own benefit in mind and knowing the length of his term—a typical example of the volunteer who gets the return he wants and needs no warning even from a landlord looking on. But there is a countervailing policy: '. . . it is in the general interest that properties be improved. Standards rise, and whether the improvements go to make industry more efficient and competitive, or residential premises more comfortable, it is desirable that these advances should be encouraged, or at least not discouraged' (para. 1.2).

22. pp. 297–9, with pp. 166–7: *payment of ultra vires demands*

The recent Justice/All Souls Report on Administrative Law, chaired by Patrick Neill, Q.C., has come down in favour of a general right to restitution of payments made in response to *ultra vires* demands: 'Cases can arise where in consequence of an invalid regulation a trader has made payments to a statutory body. In principle, he should be able to recover these together with interest. But the law says that some payments are "voluntary" or made under a "mistake of law" and so are not recoverable: see, for instance, *Twyford* v. *Manchester Corporation* [1946] Ch. 236. We intend that the legislation we are proposing should provide a general right to recover payments made in such circumstances' (*Administrative Justice: Some Necessary Reforms* (Oxford,

1988), 363, cf. 365). It is to be hoped that this may in due course receive legislative confirmation.

Meanwhile, the common law position remains uncertain. In *Reg.* v. *Tower Hamlets London Borough Council, ex p. Chetnik Developments* ([1988] 2 W.L.R. 654) the applicants for judicial review under Order 53 had paid rates on empty warehouses without realizing that they could have resisted the claim because they were in the circumstances prohibited from going into occupation of them. The Council considered the matter under s. 9 (1) of the *General Rate Act, 1967* and refused a refund on the ground, *inter alia*, that payment had been made by mistake of law. The House of Lords upheld the Court of Appeal's decision to quash and direct the Council to reconsider. The case is notable for two reasons. First, accepting that s. 9 (1) conferred a discretion, not a duty, to repay, the House of Lords nevertheless left the Council with virtually no room to refuse restitution in the absence of exceptional facts. Secondly, although the words of the section confer this discretion in respect of rates which could properly be refunded and are 'not recoverable apart from this s.', there was an assumption *ab initio* that these were indeed payments not recoverable as of right or, in other words, that a public authority, no less than a private individual, could resist a demand for restitution of a payment made by mistake of law. But this is the very question which modern administrative law still has to settle.

The procedural context of *Chetnik* draws attention to a serious deficiency in the text. In the light of the exclusivity of Order 53 procedure proclaimed by *O'Reilly* v. *Mackman* ([1983] 2 A.C. 237), how and within what time limit should restitution be claimed from a public authority? This was touched upon in *Wandsworth London Borough Council* v. *Winder* ([1985] A.C. 461), and it seems reasonable to make some predictions, as being compatible with *dicta* in that case and with the general lines of the development by which—with Dicey groaning in his grave—a separate corpus of English public law is emerging: claims based on grounds for restitution against a public body which would avail against a private individual, as for instance those based on duress or mistake of fact, will be maintainable by writ as before, but claims which have to be rested on the public character of the defendant will have to find some home within the Order 53 procedure.

But huge difficulties may be anticipated, both in relation to asymmetry between the active claim of the citizen who pays and seeks restitution and the passive defence of the citizen who refuses to pay and is sued, and also in relation to the classification as public or private of, for instance, the old *colore officii* cases or indeed of claims based on want of capacity, since company law, and *Sinclair* v. *Brougham* ([1914] A.C. 398) and *Brougham* v. *Dwyer* ((1913) 108 L.T. 504) in particular, provides ammunition to contest even the characterization as public of a restitutionary right based directly on *ultra vires*. Nobody would wish to have to open up these questions, but the procedural separation of public and private law may render them inescapable. There is some slight hope, however, that this separation may be undone, for the Justice/All Souls review cited above was critical of *O'Reilly* v. *Mackman*, as also of the very short limitation period placed on Order 53 proceedings: see *Justice/ All Souls Report*, pp. 149–56, 166–7.

It is possible that uncertainties in this area will be cleared up if there are further stages in *R.* v. *Inland Revenue Commissioners, ex p. Woolwich Equitable Building Society* ([1987] S.T.C. 654). In that case it was held by Nolan, J., that certain taxing regulations under which the Building Society paid many millions of pounds were *ultra vires*. In accordance with the practice described in the text at p. 298, the money was repaid, but a further issue arose on the question of interest, which raised the question whether there was a restitutionary claim as of right, since the court's discretion to award interest depends on the claim being a debt within s. 35a of the *Supreme Court Act, 1981*. At first instance Nolan, J., decided there was no restitutionary claim as of right in respect of the payments: *The Times*, 26 July 1988. If there is an appeal, the scene is set for a leading case which could hardly be more appropriate to the year of the 300th anniversary of the Bill of Rights.

Another case which might raise the same issues, and in which leave to appeal to the House of Lords has been given, is *Customs and Excise Commissioners* v. *Fine Art Developments* ([1988] S.T.C. 178), in which, after the *European Court in Direct Cosmetics Ltd.* v. *Customs and Excise Commissioners* ([1985] S.T.C. 479) had declared the Commissioners wrong in the basis of their demands for value-added tax, the Court of Appeal held (*contra* Simon Brown, J., in *Betterware Products Ltd.* v. *Customs and Excise Commissioners (No.2)* [1988] S.T.C. 6) that the legislation regrettably provided no machinery to allow a taxpayer who had overpaid V.A.T. to deduct the overpayment from future payments, leaving the taxpayer no option but to sue the Commissioners for restitution. Once again there had been an ostensibly *ex gratia* repayment; the dispute arose because (which raises a nice point of general importance) the Commissioners had declined to repay overpayments referable to a period in which, as the Commissioners maintained, the excess had in substance been met by the taxpayer's customers, who would not get the benefit of restitution to the taxpayer (on this argument, cf. B. Rudden and W. Bishop, 'Gritz and Quellmehl: Pass it On', (1981) 6 *E.L.R.* 243, concluding, on balance, against it).

23. pp. 313–14: *restitution for wrongs, general considerations, social concern and events in the public eye*

Social concern about profitable wrongdoing has become prominent in recent years. In this climate of opinion it has become both easier and more urgent to challenge the precarious hegemony in civil law of the compensatory principle. Among symptoms of anxiety on this score may be numbered: (i) on the criminal side, the report of the Hodgson Committee (*The Profits of Crime and their Recovery* (London, 1984)), some of whose proposals for criminal disgorgement, especially in relation to drugs trafficking, have already been implemented; (ii) the debate about regulation of the stock market and, in particular, the control of takeover procedures and, generally, of insider dealing; (iii) the case of Peter Wright and his book, *Spycatcher*, which has served in turn to draw attention to *Snepp* v. *United States* (100 S.Ct. 763 (1980)), in which the Supreme Court, using what the minority described as a novel blend of the law of trusts and the law of contract, allowed the U.S. government to recover the profits earned by Snepp, a former agent of then C.I.A., through the publication of a book based on his inside knowledge of the C.I.A. operation in Vietnam. Whatever one's position on what might be called the public-interest aspect of such cases, they undoubtedly draw attention to the weakness and artificiality of the orthodox doctrine as to contractual damages which, on the one hand, denies the possibility of any monetary remedy except to make good a loss and, on the other, allows that morally unsatisfactory dogma to be subverted by a mere shift of language, as by the instrumental invocation of fiduciary relations and accounts of profits.

On all the matter of this chapter the reader will now find invaluable further assistance in A. S. Burrows, *Remedies for Contract and Tort* (London, 1987), ch. 6.

24. p. 328: *restitutionary damages for nuisance*

Nuisance is here taken as a paradigmatic example of a wrong which is anti-harm, not anti-enrichment: 'nobody ever recovered the profits of a nuisance.' This is confounded, or begins to be, by *Carr-Saunders* v. *Dick McNeil Associates Ltd.* ([1986] 1 W.L.R.922) in which Millett, J., was prepared to award damages for infringement of light on a *Wrotham Park* basis (see text, p. 335). Giving the damages in lieu of a mandatory injunction to take down the offending building and 'not merely in compensation for the loss of the actual legal right', Millett, J., awarded £8,000, reflecting the price which a willing seller might have charged for the infringement usurped by the defendant. The judge had no evidence before him of the actual profits expected by the defendants but said that, if he had, he would have taken it into account.

25. pp. 334–6, 343–6: *restitutionary damages for breach of contract, instrumental fiduciary relations, profits in conflict of interest*

In the note to the introduction of this chapter (n. **23** to pp. 313–14) mention was made of *Snepp* and the practice of invoking confidence and fiduciary relations in order to reach what is in essence an award of restitutionary damages for a breach of contract or other wrong. In *Hospital Products Ltd.* v. *U.S. Surgical Corporation* ((1984) 156 C.L.R. 41; 58 A.J.L.R. 587; 55 A.L.R. 417), where profits had been made through flagrant breach of contract, the majority of the High Court of Australia thought that without the fiduciary label, which in point of substance they rightly withheld, profits could not be awarded. But in a pioneering dissenting judgment Deane, J., would have made the defendants disgorge, and he demonstrated the need to relate restitutionary awards to the real facts without the artificial mediation of the language of fiduciary relationships.

Further evidence of movement on this front is the decision of the Supreme Court of Israel in *Adras Ltd.* v. *Harlow & Jones GmbH* ((1988) 42 (1) P.D., noted by D. Friedmann, 'Restitution of Profits Gained by Party in Breach of Contract' (1988) 104 *L.Q.R.* 383) to allow a buyer, who had failed to establish that he had suffered a loss, to obtain restitutionary damages against the seller of goods who had sold to a third party at a profit.

The same sense of orthodoxy under reappraisal is apparent in the journals, in particular in G. H. Jones, 'The Recovery of Benefits Gained from Breach of Contract', (1983) 99 *L.Q.R.* 442; E. A. Farnsworth, 'Your Loss or My Gain? The Dilemma of the Disgorgement Principle in Breach of Contract', (1985) 94 *Yale L.J.* 1339; P. Birks, 'Restitutionary Damages for Breach of Contract: *Snepp* and the Fusion of Law and Equity', [1987] *L.M.C.L.Q.* 421.

Recent cases clarifying the nature of the money remedy in respect of profits arising from breach of fiduciary duty, as opposed to cases of profits arising from the use of the principal's property, show that awards measured by profits need have no unwanted consequences on the proprietary level. Developments need not therefore be inhibited by fear of overkill. These cases are considered below, in connection with *Lister* v. *Stubbs* (see n. **27** to pp. 387–9).

26. pp.368–70: *tracing: mixing by a wrongdoer; defining the mixed fund*

Where a wrongdoer mixes someone's money or fungibles with his own—as my wine with his—the cards in the exercise of identification are, as the text says, stacked against him. The text fails to bring out the fact that some statements of this leaning against the wrongdoer leave room for an extreme interpretation, calculated in practice to deprive him of the entire mass. Lord Eldon, L.C., makes several such statements in *Lupton* v. *White* ((1808) 15 Ves. 432, text, p. 369), as for instance when, at 436, he speaks of 'the great principle, familiar both at law and equity, that, if a man, having undertaken to keep the property of another distinct, mixes it with his own, the whole amount must, both at law and in equity, be taken to be the property of the other, until the former puts the subject under such circumstances, that it may be distinguished as satisfactorily, as it might have been before the unauthorised mixture upon his part'. The extreme interpretation would make this mean that the wrongdoer must be able to identify the very molecules that were his, a virtual impossibility. The text shrinks, somewhat evasively, from any such draconian position.

However, in *Indian Oil Corporation* v. *Greenstone Shipping S.A.* ([1987] 3 W.L.R. 869) Staughton, J., was pressed with its full rigour. Slightly simplified, the story was this. The defendant shipownwers had delivered to the plaintiffs a consignment of approximately half a million barrels of crude oil. It turned out that their tanker had taken on the plaintiffs' oil on top of the dregs of the previous cargo, about ten thousand pumpable barrels. The plaintiffs said the wrongful mixing made the whole mass theirs, and they claimed some $400,000 damages for failure to deliver those last ten thousand barrels. Staughton, J., agreed that *Lupton* v. *White* and its successors meant that doubts had to be resolved against the wrongful mixer, but he did not feel driven to accept the overkill contended for. Where, as here, the quantities of the inputs were known, the plaintiff was entitled to his full quantity before the defendant took anything, but he could not have more just because the defendant could not prove, teaspoon by teaspoon, which part of the mass had been his. That must be the right approach. It is worth noting, since Staughton, J., appears to limit the plaintiff strictly to his input, that it was not a case in which the plaintiff had any incentive to seek an interest proportionate to his input, rather than the quantity of the input itself. Though some of his words might seem to do so, Staughton, J.'s holding does not in fact exclude attempts to formulate such a claim where it would be advantageous. His aim was to ensure that the plaintiffs' argument did not give them the entire mass.

Another form of potential overkill was identified by Professor Goode in *dicta* of Lord Templeman in *Space Investments Ltd.* v. *Canadian Imperial Bank of Commerce Trust Co. (Bahamas) Ltd.* ([1987] 1 W.L.R. 1072 (P.C.)). When the bank was in liquidation a question arose, at the instance of the plaintiff unsecured creditor, whether funds of which the bank had been trustee and which it had deposited with itself were still impressed with a trust, giving the beneficiaries priority. The decision was that they were not, because the bank had power to make the deposits under the trust deeds. In the result the beneficiaries had only personal claims, the same as any customer with a deposit account. But Lord Templeman said, *obiter*, that, had the bank made the deposits in breach of trust, the beneficiaries would have had priority. He seemed to contemplate a situation in which, it being impossible to trace trust money into any asset since all deposits would immediately have been destined to the general purposes of the bank, the beneficiaries would nevertheless have a charge on the entire pool of assets, being relieved, by the *Lupton* v. *White* reversal of onus, of the burden a rigorous tracing exercise. This stops short of saying the beneficiaries would own everything until the bank proved otherwise, but it does give a proprietary right over even buildings and land, everything in fact in the pool of assets. As Professor Goode says, 'The implication in Lord Templeman's speech seems to be that *all* the assets of the bank constitute one enormous fund, so that the infusion of any part of the trust property into those assets impresses the totality of the assets with a charge in favour of the beneficiaries' (R. M. Goode, 'Ownership and Obligation in Commercial Transactions', (1987) 103 *L.Q.R.* 433, 447.

Professor Goode rightly says that the relevant fund must be, at the largest, the fund of the bank's money, not its general assets. He must also be right that the claimant has to be able to affirm, according to the rules of identification, that his money is in the relevant fund whatever it may be; if the rules show that the money has been dissipated from the relevant fund, a charge over the free assets would be inexplicable. On the other hand, it is difficult to see how, as Goode clearly wants him to be, the beneficiary in this situation could be compelled into a positive tracing exercise against a wrongdoing mixer. That would emasculate *Lupton* v. *White* altogether. Once the limits of the relevant fund are established, he is entitled to the presumption that it contains his money, even if not to a presumption that the entire pool is his. Against a bank, unless the relevant fund can be further narrowed, this still leaves him with an assured priority.

27. pp. 387–89: *conflict of interests, secret profits, personal nature of money remedy*
Despite having rather few friends, *Lister* v. *Stubbs* has received further support in the English courts. It stands above all for the proposition that the restitutionary liability of a fiduciary to surrender the profits of a mere breach of duty, as opposed to profits made by taking or exploiting the principal's property, is purely personal, not proprietary. This is defended in the text and has important consequences in the field of restitution for wrongs, since it frees this type of liability from the danger of being restricted from fear of overkill. So long as the liability remains personal, it looks and behaves like a liability to pay restitutionary damages; if it is given proprietary consequences it creates the danger of undeserved priorities in any insolvency. The undeserved nature of these priorities was examined and attacked by Professor Goode in his Mary Oliver Memorial Lecture (R. M. Goode, 'Ownership and Obligation in Commercial Transactions', (1987) 103 *L.Q.R.* 433, 441–5), and recent cases have favoured the purely personal interpretation of the liability.

In a criminal case the Court of Appeal was asked whether the manager of a tied house could be charged with theft from his employer of the money he received from selling beer bought in from elsewhere in breach of duty. The question was put explicitly in terms which raised the issue whether, by virtue of a constructive trust, the employer owned the proceeds of the illicit sales. Having examined and approved the reasoning in *Lister* v. *Stubbs*, the Court of Appeal answered negatively (*A.G.'s Reference (No. 1 of 1985)* [1986] 2 W.L.R. 735). Then, in *Islamic Republic of Iran Shipping Lines* v. *Denby* ([1987] 1 Lloyds Rep. 367, noted [1988] L.M.C.L.Q. 128), where a solicitor had accepted a commission from his clients' opponent and subsequently invested it in land, Leggatt, J., declined to be drawn into departing from *Lister*. He held that the solicitor's clients were confined by *Lister* to a personal claim. In reaching this conclusion it is evident that Leggatt, J., felt some difficulty with *Boardman* v. *Phipps*, which he assumed to be a case in which the claimants could have insisted on a proprietary claim. In fact (text, p. 388) that inference cannot be supported from anything said or done in the case itself. There is now some support for the personal interpretation of *Boardman* itself in *Guinness p.l.c.* v. *Saunders* ((1988) 138 N.L.J. Rep. 142 (20 May 1988)) where *Boardman* is distinguished as not having been a case in which the plaintiff was claiming property belonging to him. That would seem to be right, but a difficult question still remains as to the line between cases with and without proprietary consequences. *Semble* the plaintiff will only be able to claim *in rem* when the subject-matter was already his at the start of the story, was intercepted when certainly proceeding to him, or, thirdly, though this case is more problematical, represents profits made from some *res* which was either his at the start of the story or certainly proceeding to him.

28. pp. 410–15: *change of position; special defence of ministerial recipient.*

In *A.N.Z.* v. *Westpac* (note **6** to pp. 149–59) Westpac, having received a mistaken payment of $100,000, were finally obliged to repay only $17,021. The reason was that, as ministerial recipients, they could take advantage of the special defence available to an agent who has passed on the money to or for the benefit of his principal before having notice of the mistake. One interesting question was lost among the concessions made by Westpac: Does not a bank which immediately applies payments to the credit of its customers instantly and automatically obtain the benefit of that defence? Instead, the application of the money to the benefit of the customer was determined by a combination of *Clayton's Case* and concessions by Westpac.

But another important question was explored. Was it necessary for the intermediary to have acted *to his detriment*? An argument was advanced to the effect that, even if Westpac had passed on the money to Jakes, it would not be in any worse position by being made to repay A.N.Z. because Jakes's indebtedness to A.N.Z. would then end up the same as if the money had never been passed on. The court declined to examine this argument, saying that, supposing it right on the facts, it could not help A.N.Z. because the agent recipient's defence either did not require detriment or irrebuttably presumed it from the payment over. This is important. If it is right, it proves that this special defence is not a particular manifestation of and cannot be generalized to the defence of change of position, which certainly requires proof of actual detriment. The gist of the agent's defence is thus shown to be, not change of position, but identification of the proper defendant.

Even though driving a wedge between the agent's defence and change of position, the judgment of the High Court does contain a mildly favourable *dictum* in support of the more general defence. There is another such *dictum* in *ex p. Chetnik, per* Lord Goff ([1988] 2 W.L.R. 654, 670); and we have already noticed (above, note **6** to pp. 149–59) that Beatson and Bishop have argued that the development of the defence of change of position is in the nature of an imperative. Nevertheless, in *Rover* (above, note **6** to pp. 149–59) Dillon, L.J., said that it was not open to the Court of Appeal, in the existing state of the authorities, to contemplate recognizing the defence. Kerr, L.J., took a slightly different line, saying only that on the facts Cannon could not establish any detrimental reliance. Nicholls, L.J., agreed with both judgments.

29. pp. 415–23, esp. 420–23: *flexible counter-restitution; the allowance for work and skill.*

In *O'Sullivan* v. *Management Agency and Music Ltd.* ([1985] Q.B. 428) the Court of Appeal took a considerable step away from insistence on literal and exact counter-restitution. The plaintiff had been raised from an obscure life as a postal worker to international stardom as a pop-musician and composer. This he owed at least in part to his association with his manager, Mills, and the companies through which Mills worked. But his early dependence on Mills had put the latter, and his companies, into anfiduciary relationship with him, and Mills had abused his position of trust and confidence. The contract Mills imposed on O'Sullivan was held to be unenforceable as being in restraint of trade; and, further, the contractual arrangements and assignments of copyright by O'Sullivan were, saving the rights of *bona fide* purchasers, voidable for undue influence. It was strenuously argued against this conclusion that, after years of cooperation and work on both sides, rescission was barred by the impossibility of counterrestitution (*restitutio in interegrum*), but the court found itself able to do what was 'practically just between the parties' (text, p. 421), which it did by ordering rescission while at the same time conceding the defendants a *Boardman* v. *Phipps* allowance for their work, the allowance to include some participation in the profits of the venture although less than they would have had by fair negotiation from the start. A question was raised whether a fiduciary who had behaved badly should not forfeit any *prima facie* right to counter-restitution on the *Boardman* model. To which the answer was that there is no absolute rule to that effect, though dishonesty would be a factor to take into account in deciding whether, and at what level, the allowance for work should be granted: see especially p. 468, *per* Fox, L.J. Not unrelated is the question whether this flexibility in relation to counter-restitution is still tied to the defendant's bad behaviour. It clearly remains easier to be flexible when the defendant has behaved badly—this is an obvious theme of the judgment of Dunn, L.J.—but it is difficult to believe that in future this flexible approach will not be invoked whenever it achieves what is 'practically just between the parties'.

In *Hill* v. *Langley* (*The Times*, 28 Jan. 1988) a brother acting as his father's executor and trustee had taken an assignment of his sister's interest under the will without giving full information as to the value of the estate, or not to the standard required by his fiduciary duty. The estate had subsequently been sold for a good price. Did the assignment remain voidable? Once again displaying a flexible attitude to counter-restitution, the Court of Appeal affirmed the decision below that it did. The interest of the sister had merely crystallized in a fixed sum of money. There was no difficulty in requiring her to give credit, by way of counter-restitution, for the consideration she had received; further, the brother, had he claimed, could have had a *Boardman* allowance for his exceptional efforts in selling well.

Guinness p.l.c. v. *Saunders* (above, note **27** to pp. 387–9) reveals one situation in which restitution will be allowed without insistence on counter-restitution. In connexion with the ill-starred takeover of Distillers, Ward, a director of Guinness, was paid upwards of £5m. by the company under a contract in respect of which he had failed to disclose his interest to a full meeting of the board, as required by s. 317 of the *Companies Act, 1985*. He argued, first, that it was too late to rescind because he had done the work due under the contract and the company could not restore it to him. The Court of Appeal brushed that defence aside, on the ground that a fiduciary who, in breach of duty, received the property of his principal never received any title to that property such as could be set up against the principal.

Ward's second argument was that he should have, by way of·equitable set-off, a *Boardman* v. *Phipps* allowance for the work done. This was refused, not on the ground that he might not be entitled to remuneration, but because he would have to try a separate action to establish his claim and could not insist on counter-restitution by way of set-off. Ward's cross-claim could not be said directly to impeach Guinness's claim to recover property which had belonged to it from the start and could not be said to 'arise from the same transaction'. In this respect *Boardman* v. *Phipps*, and *O'Sullivan* v. *Management Agency and Music Ltd.* were different: they were not claims to recover property belonging to the plaintiff but claims to profits arising through the skill and labour of the defendant. It is important, finally, to avoid jumping to the conclusion that Ward's claims to counter-restitution were obstructed by fraud or dishonesty of any kind, of which no evidence was offered.

30 p. 424: *counter-restitution: benefits which do not have to be returned*

In *Films Rover International* (above, note 6 to pp. 149–59) it was held that Rover could recover its advances to Cannon, whether on the basis of mistake or failure of consideration, notwithstanding its receipt of a non-returnable benefit, namely the use of the films, and that was explained by saying that that benefit was not a bargained-for benefit but a means to the benefits which had been bargained for; and the *Rowland* v. *Divall* series of cases (text, pp. 246–8 and 424) was interpreted in a similar vein. This is not satisfactory, since it entails the risk of allowing plaintiffs to have restitution while still retaining valuable benefits, just because those benefits were peripheral to the bargain. The *Rowland* species of case, where a buyer of a car from a non-owner recovers the price without counter-restitution of the value of the use of the vehicle, is better explained as on the basis that the defendant had no right to confer that benefit; in *Rover* itself it would have been easy to say that the value of the use of the films should have been taken into account in calculating Rover's *quantum meruit*. (For further discussion: note 17 to pp. 245–8.)

31. pp. 432–9: *minors: claims against the party under the incapacity, a new statutory discretion*

The *Minors' Contracts Act, 1987,* which as was said above in relation to inequality arising from personal disadvantage does nothing to add to a minor's claims to restitution, does improve the position of the adult who cannot enforce his contractual rights. It has long been a criticism of the law that it allowed a minor to use his protection as an instrument of unjust enrichment, as by hanging on to non-necessary goods and not paying for them. Now the minor's defence is cut back: where an adult cannot sue on the contract, s. 3 of the new Act, while saving any other remedy which the he might have, gives the court a discretion to require the minor to transfer any property acquired under the contract or any property representing that property. So far as this appears to contemplate restitution of property still held by the minor, it reflects, albeit on a discretionary basis, Lord Sumner's principle, borrowed from Kindersley, V.-C., that restitution must stop where repayment begins (*R. Leslie Ltd.* v. *Sheill* [1914] 3 K.B. 607, 618).

32. pp. 439–47 (linking with pp. 140–6): *third party recipients, the personal liability becomes fault-based, contradictions with other restitutionary liabilities*

In what is probably the most important recent development, and one which goes directly against the position taken in the text, the personal liability of third party recipients has become strongly fault-based. The text argues that the recipient's personal liability, though commonly called a liability for 'knowing receipt', is in principle entirely independent of knowledge that the money was not due to him and that knowledge becomes relevant only so far as may be necessary to defeat a defence of *bona fide* purchase for value without notice. The text concludes therefore that the personal liability of a volunteer recipient in the first measure of restitution (value received, whether or not retained) is strict, while the liability of a recipient who has given consideration and has a *prima facie* defence of *bona fide* purchase must depend only on constructive notice since that is sufficient to destroy his defence. The underlying thought is that, though the recipient's restitutionary liability is in principle strict, it would be ridiculous for it to hold good against anyone who against a claim *in rem* would have the defence of *bona fide* purchase, since the availability of the personal claim would then subvert the defence altogether.

However, in *In re Montagu's Settlement Trusts* ([1987] 2 W.L.R. 1192) Sir Robert Megarry, V.-C., took the view that this link between the recipient's personal liability and the defence of *bona fide* purchase was misconceived and that, even in the case of a volunteer recipient against whom a claim *in rem* would lie while he retained the original receipt or its traceable proceeds, the claim *in personam* required a high degree of fault.

In that case the tenth Duke of Manchester had received and disposed of certain chattels from the trustees of a family trust, the trustees being in breach of trust. The plaintiff, the eleventh Duke, now maintained that the tenth Duke, and hence now his estate, had incurred a personal liability as a constructive trustee to make restitution. Shorn of nuance, the conclusion was that he had not incurred that liability, because he had honestly believed himself entitled to the chattels. Using as a guide the typology of knowledge attempted by Peter Gibson, J., in *Baden, Delvaux and Lecuit v. Société Générale pour Favoriser le Développement du Commerce et de l'Industrie en France S.A.* ([1983] B.C.L.C. 325 at 407), Sir Robert Megarry, V.-C., concluded that it would have been sufficient to show that the Duke had actually known that the delivery to him had been in breach of trust or that he would have had actual knowledge if he had not wilfully shut his eyes to the obvious or that he had wilfully and recklessly failed to make such inquiries as a reasonable and honest man would make (i.e. knowledge of the first three *Baden Delvaux* types); he inclined to the view that it would not have been enough to show that the Duke had knowledge of circumstances which would have indicated the facts to an honest or reasonable man or circumstances which would have put a reasonable man on inquiry, because these last two *Baden Delvaux* categories of knowledge connoted only carelessness, which in its turn did not amount to a want of probity ([1987] 2 W.L.R. 1192, 1211).

It follows that the recipient's personal liability is not only fault-based but actually requires a very high degree of fault, nothing less than the want of probity required by the liability of an accessory to a breach of trust. 'Knowing receipt' is thus becoming assimilated to 'knowing assistance', a development presaged in *Carl Zeiss Stiftung* v. *Herbert Smith & Co. (No. 2)* ([1969] 2 Ch. 276), in which for the first time the line between the two was blurred, and now given further impetus by Alliott, J.'s adoption of Sir Robert Megarry, V.-C.'s approach in *Lipkin Gorman* v. *Karpnale* ([1987] 1 W.L.R. 987), more recently cited with approval by Hirst, J. in *Allied Arab Bank Ltd.* v. *Hajjar* (*The Times* 11 Mar. 1988; *The Independent*, 8 Apr. 1988).

With this development the law of restitution finds itself saddled with a double contradiction. First, there is an obvious tension between the fault-based liability in *Montagu* and the strict personal liability of the recipients in *Diplock* (text, p. 442). The Duke of Manchester received from his trustees, the charities in *Diplock* received from the executors of Caleb Diplock's will; the charities, honest and innocent, had to repay the next of kin; the tenth Duke, also honest, owed his successor nothing. This contradiction cannot be satisfactorily explained by relying on the peculiarities of legal history relating to the administration of estates. Then, secondly and worse, there is a tension between the requirement of fault in *Montagu* and the fact that personal liability to repay mistaken payments is undoubtedly strict. Thus, *Kelly* v. *Solari*, the leading case (1841) 9 M.& W. 54, shows that a carelessly mistaken payor can recover against a wholly innocent payee, who does not normally have the benefit even of a defence of change of position, as appears vividly in *Baylis* v. *Bishop of London* [1913] 1 Ch. 127. This carries over *a fortiori* to one who receives not merely through the plaintiff's mistake but absolutely without his knowledge, as by finding (text, pp. 140–6). Nor is it irrelevant to recall in this connexion that, in tort, a totally innocent third party no longer in possession is liable to pay damages for conversion, and that conversion is a tort which can be 'waived', in the sense that the money award can be restitutionary instead of compensatory.

If it be true, at common law, that a defendant who receives a plaintiff's money by reason of the latter's mistake or absolutely without his knowledge is personally liable to repay without reference to the moral quality of his receipt, it is difficult to see how, in equity, there can be room for a requirement of fault, and *Diplock* says there is not. In *Montagu* it is no less true than in *Diplock* that, in circumstances excluding the defence of *bona fide* purchase, the recipient received without the consent of the person entitled. So there is a subtraction from the plaintiff and an 'unjust' factor (vitiation: ignorance) is present. Whence it should follow, if the requirement of enrichment is satisfied and there is no countervailing policy consideration, that the defendant should be personally liable in the first measure. The fact that there is suddenly an insistence on a fault-based liability (the fault having nothing whatever to do with deflecting the defence of *bona fide* purchase) can only be explained as an inconsistent policy choice, one which appeared to be open because the law of restitution is still very difficult to see as a whole and because the issue therefore presented itself, cloaked in the obscurity of characteristically impenetrable language, as a local problem of and in the fringes of the law of trusts.

Had *Montagu* been seen as a problem in restitution as it ought to have been, one intriguing point might have told in the tenth Duke's favour, a *Boulton* v. *Jones* point: himself mistaken, he had received a benefit in kind and not in money. Had he been enriched? Because of his own mistaken belief, he could not be said freely to have accepted. It follows that his obligation to make restitution would have depended on a finding that he had been incontrovertibly enriched according to the 'no reasonable man' test, either from the nature of the chattels originally received or by virtue of the realization of those chattels in money. This, of course, was not explored.

It is interesting to contrast with the English trend towards a recipient's liability based on a high degree of fault the approach of the New Zealand Court of Appeal in

Westpac Banking Corporation v. *Savin* [1985] 2 N.Z.L.R. 41, where it is said that the recipient's liability depends only on constructive notice (which, where the defendant is a recipient for value, is compatible with the approach taken in the text). The N.Z. Court of Appeal also took the distinction (text, p. 445) between ministerial and beneficial receipt, as to which see also the discussion of *A.N.Z. Bank* v. *Westpac* above (note **28** to pp. 410–15).

The references to some articles and cases which were unreported or unpublished when these endnotes were completed have subsequently become available. It has been possible to incorporate them in the case-list at the beginning or the bibliography at the end. The reader should also note the appearance of *Re Berkeley Applegate (Investment Consultants) Ltd.* [1988] 3 W.L.R. 95, a decision of major importance in relation to uninvited intervention in the affairs of another (*cf.* endnote 9, p. 456) and one in which the intervener's claim succeeded; also of *Stoke-on-Trent City Council* v. *W. & J. Wass Ltd.*, [1988] 1 W.L.R. 1406, [1988] 3 All E.R. 394, in which the Court of Appeal refused to extend *Wrotham Park* damages to the infringement of a franchise market (*cf.* endnote 24, p. 471). Further, Alliott, J.'s decision in the important case of *Lipkin Gorman* v. *Karpnate* is known to have been substantially varied in the Court of Appeal, though the judgement is not yet available (*cf.* endnote 32, pp. 477–8). The House of Lords has also finally disposed of the *Spycatcher* affair, holding *inter alia* that, had not Wright put himself beyond the jurisdiction, he would indeed have had to make restitution to the Crown of all the profits of his breach of duty: *Attorney-General* v. *Guardian Newspapers Ltd. (No. 2)*, [1988] 3 W.L.R. 776, [1988] 3 All E.R. 545 (*cf.* endnotes 23 and 25, pp. 470–1).

SELECT BIBLIOGRAPHY

Atiyah, P.S., *The Rise and Fall of Freedom of Contract* (Oxford, 1979).
Atiyah, P.S., *Essays on Contract* (Oxford, 1986).
Burrows, A.S., *Remedies for Torts and Breach of Contract* (London, 1987).
Chitty, J., *Law of Contracts*, 25th ed. (London, 1983), esp. vol. i, chap, 29 (Beatson).
Dawson, J.P. and Palmer, G.E., *Cases on Restitution*, 2nd ed. (Indianapolis, Kansas City, New York, 1969).
Finn, P.D., *Fiduciary Obligations* (Sydney, 1977).
Finn, P.D. (ed.), *Essays in Equity* (Sydney, 1985).
Fridman, G.H.L. and McLeod, J.G., *Restitution* (Toronto, 1982).
Goff, Lord, of Chievely and Jones, G. *The Law of Restitution*, 3rd ed. (London, 1986).
Gurry, F., *Breach of Confidence* (Oxford, 1984).
Jackson, R.M., *The History of Quasi-Contract in English Law* (Cambridge, 1936).
Munkman, J.H., *The Law of Quasi-Contracts* (London, 1950).
Klippert, G.B., *Unjust Enrichment* (Toronto, 1983).
Keener, W.A., *A Treatise on the Law of Quasi-Contracts* (New York, 1893).
Oakley, A.J., *Constructive Trusts*, 2nd ed. (London, 1987).
Palmer, G.E., *The Law of Restitution* (four vols., Boston, 1978).
Shepherd, J.C., *The Law of Fiduciaries* (Toronto, 1981).
Stoljar, S.J., *The Law of Quasi-Contract* (Sydney, 1964).
Waters, D.W.M., *The Constructive Trust* (London, 1962).
Winfield, Sir P.H., *The Law of Quasi-Contracts* (London, 1952).
Woodward, F.C., *The Law of Quasi-Contracts* (Boston, 1913).
Wright, of Durley, Lord, *Legal Essays and Addresses* (Cambridge, 1939).
Zweigert, K. and Kötz, H., *An Introduction to Comparative Law* (tr. T. Weir), 2nd ed. (Oxford, 1987).

ARTICLES

Atiyah, P.S., 'Contracts, Promises and the Law of Obligations', in *Essays* (above), 10.
Austin, R.P., 'Constructive Trusts', in *Essays*, ed. Finn (above), 196.
Ball, S.N., 'Work Carried out in Pursuance of Letters of Intent—Contract or Restitution', (1983) 99 *L.Q.R.* 572.
Barton, J., 'Contract and *Quantum Meruit*: The Antecedents of *Cutter* v. *Powell*', (1987) 8 *J. Leg. Hist.* 48.
Barton, J., 'The Enforcement of Hard Bargains', (1987) 103 *L.Q.R.* 118.

Beale, H., 'Inequality of Bargaining Power' (1986) 6 *Ox. J.L.S.* 123.

Beatson, J., 'The Nature of Waiver of Tort', (1979) 17 *Univ. of Ontario L.R.* 1.

Beatson, J., 'Duress as a Vitiating Factor in Contract', (1974) 33 *C.L.J.* 97.

Beatson, J., 'Discharge for Breach: The Position of Instalments, Deposits and Other Payments Due Before Completion', (1981) 98 *L.Q.R.* 389.

Beatson, J. (with Birks), 'Unrequested Payment of Another's Debt' (1976) 92 *L.Q.R.* 188.

Beatson, J., 'Benefit, Reliance and the Structure of Unjust Enrichment', (1987) 40 *C.L.P.* 71.

Beatson, J. and Bishop, W., 'Mistaken Payments and the Law of Restitution', (1986) 36 *U. Toronto L.J.* 149.

Burrows, A.S., 'Contract, Tort and Restitution – A Satisfactory Division or Not?, (1983) 99 *L.Q.R.* 217.

Burrows, A.S., 'Free Acceptance and the Law of Restitution', (1988) 104 *L.Q.R.* 576.

Corbin, A.L., 'Waiver of Tort and Suit in *Assumpsit*', (1910) 19 *Yale L.J.* 221.

David, R., 'The Doctrine of Unjustified Enrichment', (1935) 5 *C.L.J.* 204.

Davies, J.D., '*Shamia* v. *Joory*: A Forgotten Chapter in Quasi-Contract', (1959) 75 *L.Q.R.* 220.

Dawson, J.P., '*Negotiorum Gestio*: The Altruistic Intermeddler', (1960) 74 *Havard L.R.* 817.

Dawson, J.P., 'The Self-Serving Intermeddler', (1974) *Havard L.R.* 1409.

Dawson, J.P., 'Restitution or Damages?', (1959) 20 *Ohio State L.J.* 175.

Denning, Rt. Hon. Lord, 'The Recovery of Money', (1949) 65 *L.Q.R.* 37.

Denning, Rt. Hon. Lord, '*Quantum Meruit* and the Statute of Frauds', (1925) 41 *L.Q.R.* 79.

Denning, Rt. Hon. Lord, '*Quantum Meruit*: The Case of *Craven-Ellis* v. *Canons Ltd.*' (1939) 55 *L.Q.R.* 54.

Farnsworth, E.A., 'Your Loss or My Gain? The Dilemma of the Disgorgement Principle in Breach of Contract', (1985) 94 *Yale L.J.* 1339.

Finn, P.D., 'Equitable Estoppel', in *Essays*, ed. Finn (above), 59.

Fridman, G.H.L., 'Waiver of Tort', (1955) 18 *M.L.R.* 1.

Friedman, D., 'Restitution of Benefits Obtained through the Appropriation of Property or the Commission of a Wrong', (1980) 99 *L.Q.R.* 534.

Fuller, L.L. and Perdue, W.R., 'The Reliance Interest in Contract Damages', (1939) 46 *Yale L.J.* 52, 373.

Goode, R.M. 'The Right to Trace and its Impact on Commercial Transactions', 92 *L.Q.R.* 360 and 528.

Goode, R.M., 'Ownership and Obligation in Commercial Transactions', (1987) 103 *L.Q.R.* 433.

Grodecki, J.K., '*In pari delicto potior est conditio defendentis*', (1955) 71 *L.Q.R.* 254.

Hardingham, I.J., 'Unconscionable Dealing', in *Essays*, ed. Finn (above), 1.

Harpum, C., 'The Stranger as Constructive Trustee' (1986) 102 *L.Q.R.* 114 (Part I), 267 (Part II).

Harpum, C., 'Liability for Intermeddling with Trusts' (1987) 50 *M.L.R.* 217.

Haycroft, A.M. and Waksman, D.M., 'Frustration and Restitution', [1984] *J.B.L.* 207.

Hedley, S., 'The Myth of Waiver of Tort', (1984) 100 *L.Q.R.* 653.

Hedley, S., 'Unjust Enrichment as the Basis of Restitution – An Overworked Concept', (1985) 5 *L.S.* 56.

Ibbetson, D., 'Sixteenth Century Contract Law: *Slade's Case* in Context', (1984) 4 *Ox. J.L.S.* 295.

Ibbetson, D., 'Implied Contracts and Restitution: History in the High Court of Australia', (1988) 8 *Ox. J.L.S.* 312.

Jones, G.H. 'The Recovery of Benefits Gained from a Breach of Contract', (1983) 99 *L.Q.R.* 443.

Jones, G.H., 'Restitutionary Claims for Services Rendered', (1977) 93 *L.Q.R.* 273.

Jones, G.H., 'Change of Circumstances in Quasi-Contract', (1957) 73 *L.Q.R.* 48.

Jones, G.H., 'Unjust Enrichment and the Fiduciary's Duty of Loyalty', (1968) 84 *L.Q.R.* 472.

Jones, G.H., 'Restitution of Benefits Obtained in Breach of Another's Confidence', (1970) 86 *L.Q.R.* 463.

Jones, G.H. 'Claims Arising out of Anticipated Contracts which Do not Materialise', (1980) 18 *U.W. Ontario L.R.* 447.

Klippert, G.B., 'Restitutionary Claims for the Appropriation of Property', (1981) 26 *McGill L.J.* 506.

Lanham, D.J., 'Duress and Void Contracts', (1966) 29 *M.L.R.* 615.

Matthews, P., 'Proprietary Claims at Common Law for Mixed and Improved Goods' (1981) 34 *C.L.P.* 159.

McCamus, J.D., 'Restitutionary Recovery of Moneys Paid to a Public Authority under a Mistake of Law: *Ignorantia Iuris* in the Supreme Court of Canada', (1983) 17 *U.B.C.L.R.* 233.

McKendrick, E., 'The Battle of the Forms and the Law of Restitution', (1988) 8 *Ox. J.L.S.* 197.

McLeod, G. (with Birks), 'The Implied Contract Theory of Quasi-Contract: Civilian Opinion Current in the Century before Blackstone', (1986) 6 *Ox. J.L.S.* 46.

Mather, H., 'Restitution as a Remedy for Breach of Contract: The Case of the Partially Performing Seller', (1982) 92 *Yale L.J.* 14.

Matthews, P., 'Freedom, Unrequested Improvements and Lord Denning', (1981) 40 *C.L.J.* 340.

Matthews, P., 'Proprietary Claims at Common Law for Mixed and Improved Goods' (1981) 34 *C.L.P.* 159.

Maudsley, R.H., 'Proprietary Remedies for the Recovery of Money', (1959) 75 *L.Q.R.* 234.

Merkin, R.M., 'Restitution by Withdrawal from Executory Illegal Contracts', (1981) 97 *L.Q.R.* 420.

Millett, P.J., 'The Quistclose Trust: Who Can Enforce it?', (1985) 101 *L.Q.R.* 269.

Needham, C., 'Mistaken Payments: A New Look at an Old Theme', [1978] *Univ. of British Columbia L.R.* 159.

Needham, C., 'Recovering the Profits of Bribery', (1979) 95 *L.Q.R.* 536.

Nicholas, B., 'Unjustified Enrichment in Civil Law and Louisiana Law', (1962) 36 *Tulane L.R.* 605; 37 *Tulane L.R.* 49.

Oakley, A.J., 'Has the Constructive Trust become a General Equitable Remedy?', (1973) 26 *C.L.P.* 17.

Palmer, G.E., 'The Contract price as a Limit on Restitution for Defendant's Breach', (1959) 20 *Ohio State L.J.* 264.

Pearce, R., 'A Tracing Paper', (1976) 40 *Conveyancer* 277.

Rose, F.D., 'The Effects of Repudiatory Breach of Contract', (1981) 34 *C.L.P.* 235.

Scott, M., 'Tracing at Common Law', (1965–6) 7 *Western Australia L.R.* 463.

Scott, A.W., 'Constructive Trusts', (1955) 71 *L.Q.R.* 43.

Seavey, W.A. and Scott, A.W., 'Restitution', (1938) 54 *L.Q.R.* 29.

Sharpe, R.S., and Waddams, S.M., 'Damages for Lost Opportunity to Bargain' (1982) *Ox. J.L.S.* 290.

Shepherd, J.C., 'Towards a Unified Concept of Fiduciary Relationships', (1981) 97 *L.Q.R.* 51.

Stoljar, S.J., 'The Doctrine of Failure of Consideration', (1959) 75 *L.Q.R.* 53.

Stoljar, S.J., 'The Transformations of Account', (1964) 80 *L.Q.R.* 203.

Stoljar, S.J., 'Re-Examining *Sinclair* v. *Brougham*', (1959) 22 *M.L.R.* 21.

Stoljar, S.J., 'The Great Case of *Cutter* v. *Powell*', (1956) 34 *Canadian B.R.* 228.

Stoljar, S.J., 'Unjust Enrichment and Unjust Sacrifice', (1987) 50 *M.L.R.* 603.

Thal, S.N., 'The Inequality of Bargaining Power Doctrine: The Problem of Defining Contractual Unfairness', (1988) 8 *Ox. J.L.S.* 17.

Waddams, S.M., 'Restitution for the Part Performer', *Studies in Contract Law*, edd. B.J. Reiter and J. Swan, (Toronto, 1980) 151.

Winder, W.H.D., 'Undue Influence and Coercion', (1940) 3 *M.L.R.* 97.

Winfield, P.H., 'The American Restatement of the Law of Restitution', (1938) 54 *L.Q.R.* 529.

Winfield, P.H., 'Quasi-Contract Arising from Compulsion', (1944) 60 *L.Q.R.* 341.
Winfield, P.H., 'Quasi-Contract for Work Done', (1947) 63 *L.Q.R.* 35.
Wright, of Durley, Lord, '*Sinclair* v. *Brougham*', (1936–8) 6 *C.L.J.* 305.
Wright, of Durley, Lord, '*United Australia Ltd*, v. *Barclays Bank*', (1946) 62 *L.Q.R.* 40.

INDEX